February 22–24, 2015
Monterey, California, USA

**Association for
Computing Machinery**

*Advancing Computing as a Science & Profession*

# FPGA'15

## The 2015 ACM/SIGDA International Symposium on
## Field-Programmable Gate Arrays

*Sponsored by:*
ACM SIGDA

*Corporate Patrons:*
Altera, Inc., Lattice, Microsemi, Microsoft Research & Xilinx, Inc.

*Supported by:*
Algo-Logic, Atomic Rules & BEEcube

*With logistical support from:*
The Trimberger Family Foundation

**Association for
Computing Machinery**

*Advancing Computing as a Science & Profession*

**The Association for Computing Machinery**
2 Penn Plaza, Suite 701
New York, New York 10121-0701

**ISBN:** 978-1-4503-3315-3

Additional copies may be ordered prepaid from:

**ACM Order Department**
PO Box 30777
New York, NY 10087-0777, USA

Phone: 1-800-342-6626 (USA and Canada)
+1-212-626-0500 (Global)
Fax: +1-212-944-1318
E-mail: acmhelp@acm.org
Hours of Operation: 8:30 am – 4:30 pm ET

**ACM Order Number:** 480150

Printed in the USA

# FPGA 2015 Chairs' Welcome

It is our great pleasure to welcome you to the *2015 ACM International Symposium on FPGAs (FPGA 2015)*. This year's symposium continues the tradition of being a premier forum for the presentation of FPGA-related research across a wide variety of topics: new FPGA architectures and circuit designs, Computer-Aided Design (CAD) and high level synthesis algorithms and flows, applications well-suited to FPGAs, and design studies. In addition to facilitating the sharing of research results through the paper and poster presentations, FPGA provides an excellent opportunity for researchers from around the world to mingle and discuss research results and ideas.

This year we received 102 submissions from 22 different countries. The program committee accepted 20 full (ten pages) and 7 short (four pages) research papers as well as 8 design/tutorial papers (four pages), each of which is published in the proceedings. The acceptance rate for research papers is 26%. Full papers each have a 25-minute oral presentation, while short papers will have a 5-minute oral presentation, followed by a poster presentation at which attendees can further discuss the work with the authors. In addition, we will have four poster sessions in which a total of 46 additional research projects will be displayed on posters, and at which you may ask detailed questions of the authors.

This year, the program begins with a new full-day event called Designer's Day, which will provide tutorials and design experiences on known-interesting topics for FPGA describing effective design techniques, design flows, methods, and new tool features. It features 8 oral presentations on various FPGA design/tutorial topics and a Keynote Speech to be given by the BEEcube CEO Chen Cheng. The symposium also includes an evening panel on the topic of Building a Healthy FPGA Ecosystem — bring your questions for our panel of experts, and enjoy a lively discussion on how developers and vendors can bring killer applications, tools, and programmable logic devices to the market to accelerate datacenters for cloud computing.

We hope that you will find this program interesting and thought-provoking and that the symposium will provide you with a valuable opportunity to share ideas with other researchers and practitioners from institutions around the world.

**Deming Chen**  
*Program Chair*  
*FPGA 2015*

**George Constantinides**  
*General Chair*  
*FPGA 2015*

# Table of Contents

## Technical Session 2: Configuration and Processing
Session Chair: Steve Trimberger *(Xilinx, Inc.)*

## Technical Session 3: Architecture 1
Session Chair: Jonathan Rose *(University of Toronto)*

## Technical Session 4: Architecture 2: Memory Systems
Session Chair: Carl Ebeling *(Altera, Inc.)*

## Evening Panel
Session Chair: John Lockwood *(Algo-Logic Systems, Inc.)*

## Technical Session 5: Processors and Accelerators
Session Chair: Zhiru Zhang *(Cornell University)*

## Technical Session 6: High-level and System-level Synthesis
Session Chair: Brad Hutchings *(Brigham Young University)*

## Technical Session 7: Circuit Design
Session Chair: Vaughn Betz *(University of Toronto)*

## Technical Session 8: Applications
Session Chair: Kia Bazargan *(University of Minnesota)*

## Poster Session 1

## Poster Session 2

## Poster Session 4

# FPGA 2015 Organization

| | |
|---|---|
| **General Chair:** | George A. Constantinides, Imperial College |
| **Program Chair:** | Deming Chen, University of Illinois at Urbana-Champaign |
| **Finance Chair:** | Vaughn Betz, University of Toronto |
| **Publicity Chair:** | Mingjie Lin, University of Central Florida |
| **Social Chair:** | Mike Hutton, Altera, Inc. |
| **Designer's Track Chair:** | Steve Neuendorffer, Xilinx, Inc. |

## Program Committee:

Jason Anderson, University of Toronto, Canada

Trevor Bauer, Xilinx, USA

Kia Bazargan, University of Minnesota, USA

Vaughn Betz, University of Toronto, Canada

Philip Brisk, University of California at Riverside, USA

Stephen Brown, University of Toronto, Canada

Mike Butts, Synopsys, USA

Deming Chen, University of Illinois at Urbana-Champaign, USA

Peter Cheung, Imperial College, UK

Ray Cheung, City University of Hong Kong, Hong Kong

Derek Chiou, University of Texas at Austin, USA

Paul Chow, University of Toronto, Canada

Jason Cong, University of California at Los Angeles, USA

George Constantinides, Imperial College London, UK

Carl Ebeling, Altera, USA

Haohuan Fu, Tsinghua University, China

Jonathan Greene, Microsemi, USA

Yajun Ha, Institute for Infocomm Research, Singapore

James Hoe, Carnegie-Mellon University, USA

Mike Hutton, Altera, USA

Brad Hutchings, Brigham Young University, USA

Ryan Kastner, University of California at San Diego, USA

Martin Langhammer, Altera, UK

Miriam Leeser, Northeastern University, USA

Guy Lemieux, University of British Columbia, Canada

Philip Leong, University of Sydney, Australia

David Lewis, Altera, Canada

Mingjie Lin, University of Central Florida, USA

John Lockwood, Algo-Logic Systems, USA

Wayne Luk, Imperial College London, UK

Patrick Lysaght, Xilinx, USA

Stephen Neuendorffer, Xilinx, USA

Jonathan Rose, University of Toronto, Canada

Kyle Rupnow, Nanyang Technological University, Singapore

David Rutledge, Lattice Semiconductor, USA

Graham Schelle, Xilinx, USA

Herman Schmit, Altera, USA

Lesley Shannon, Simon Fraser University, Canada

Juergen Teich, University of Erlangen, Germany

Russell Tessier, University of Massachusetts at Amherst, USA

Steve Trimberger, Xilinx, USA

John Wawrzynek, University of California at Berkeley, USA

Yu Wang, Tsinghua University, China

Steve Wilton, University of British Columbia, Canada

Michael Wirthlin, Brigham Young University, USA

Zhiru Zhang, Cornell University, USA

# FPGA 2015 Sponsors & Supporters

**Sponsors:**

**Corporate Patrons:**

**Supporters:**

**Logistics support:**

# Physical Design Space Exploration

Ephrem Wu and Inkeun Cho
Xilinx, Inc.
2100 Logic Dr.
San Jose, CA 95124

## ABSTRACT

A polynomial accelerator implemented with a custom high-dynamic-range number representation operates up to 534MHz in the slowest speed grade on a 28nm FPGA, a clock rate that a typical FPGA tool flow cannot achieve. This design tutorial shows how to achieve a physically scalable and high-speed numerical design by partitioning it into a cascade of identical stages, and balancing the LUT-to-DSP ratio within each stage to match the available resources on the FPGA.

## Categories and Subject Descriptors

B.7.1 [**Integrated Circuits**]: Types and Design Styles – *algorithms implemented in hardware, gate arrays, VLSI.*

## General Terms

Algorithms, Performance, Design, Experimentation

## Keywords

Field-programmable gate arrays; FPGAs; hardware accelerators; placement; polynomials; synthesis; floating point; digital signal processing

## 1. INTRODUCTION

A $K^{th}$-degree polynomial $h_K[n] = \sum_{k=1}^{K} a_k u[n]^{k-1}$ can be evaluated with Horner's method [1] as a cascade of $K-1$ multiply-add stages shown in Figure 1. The authors of [2] show that this recursion is bounded given bounded coefficients and $|u[n]| < 1$.

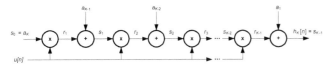

Figure 1    A Polynomial in $K$-1 Stages

For this design tutorial, each input sample $u[n]$ can change every clock cycle and is represented by an 18-bit fixed-point number in the range $[-(1 - 2^{-17}), 1 - 2^{-17}]$. The coefficients $a_k$'s are known ahead of time, have up to 17 significant bits, and are in the range $[-(1 - 2^{-17}) \times 2^7, (1 - 2^{-17}) \times 2^7]$. Mapping the Horner structure efficiently to Xilinx FPGA resources is the subject of this design tutorial.

Four design aspects are considered.

1.  Even though the input can be represented as an 18-bit fixed-point quantity, the dynamic range of the coefficients $a_k$'s and the intermediate values $r_k$'s and $s_k$'s can exceed this range. A number representation in Section 2 facilitates efficient implementation of addition and multiplication of high-dynamic range numbers.

2.  The Xilinx DSP48E1 slice [3] consists of a $25 \times 18$ two's complement multiplier followed by a 48-bit adder. The multiplier products ($r_k$'s in Figure 1) are not directly accessible for scaling. A method to pre-scale the coefficients to prevent overflow in the multiply-add unit is developed in Section 3.

3.  To achieve maximum clock frequency and to ease scaling, each stage in Figure 1 is physically mapped to the FPGA to pitch-match the regular layout of the resources, a subject of Section 4.

4.  Once one stage is mapped, multiple stages are cascaded to implement the structure in Figure 1. Section 5 presents the placement options beyond those provided by the standard tool flow.

## 2. NUMBER REPRESENTATION

### 2.1 Overview

Evaluating a polynomial requires a high dynamic range. A custom number representation called XDR is outlined here for efficient use of two's-complement hardware for high-dynamic-range operations. An $XDR(N, M)$ number is represented by the function $f_{N,M}(d, \varepsilon)$, such that $f_{N,M}(d, \varepsilon) = d \times 2^\varepsilon$, where $d$ is an $N$-bit two's-complement significand excluding the most negative number $-2^{N-1}$, i.e. $|d| < 2^{N-1}$, and $\varepsilon$ is an $M$-bit sign-magnitude integer exponent. Although normalization is optional in XDR and thus multiple representations of the same number are possible [4], the exponent is chosen so that the significand can be placed directly on the wires in two's complement arithmetic hardware. For instance, an $XDR(9,7)$ number $f_{9,7}(68, -63)$ represents $68 \times 2^{-63} \approx 7.37 \times 10^{-18}$. The significand 68 is placed on some input port of at least 9 bits wide of a two's complement arithmetic circuit, and the 7-bit sign-magnitude exponent -63 is kept track of elsewhere. One can also write the same number as $f_{9,7}(136, -64)$, effectively normalizing the significand. Note that by excluding the most negative $N$-bit two's complement number, the zero significand is represented uniquely and there are as many negative significands as positive ones. This property results in the absolute value of any $N$-bit XDR significand still fitting within $N$ bits, useful for normalization.

### 2.2 Specific to This Design Tutorial

Because the input sample $u[n]$ is an 18-bit fixed-point number and $|u[n]| < 1$, it can be written as $f_{18,5}(u[n] \times 2^{17}, -17)$. This value will be written as $f_{18,5}(x, \varepsilon_x)$ or sometimes just $(x, \varepsilon_x)$, where the significand $x = u[n] \times 2^{17}$ and the exponent is a constant $\varepsilon_x = -17$. The significand $x$ is meant to be placed directly on the wires of an 18-bit port of a two's complement multiplier.

## 3. A REPEATING STRUCTURE

### 3.1 DSP48E1 as a Multiply-Add Unit

Horner's method evaluates a polynomial as a series of multiply-add operations. Each multiply-add unit maps to one Xilinx DSP48E1 slice (Figure 2) and forms the compute core of a

*FPGA'15*, February 22–24, 2015, Monterey, CA, USA.
ACM 978-1-4503-3315-3/15/02.
http://dx.doi.org/10.1145/2684746.2689080

repeating structure. The multiply-add unit implements $P = A \times B + C$ as two's complement integers. Specifically, the internal product $Q = AB$ is added to $C$ to produce $P$. The bit widths of $A$, $B$, $C$, $Q$, and $P$ are $N_A = 25$, $N_B = 18$, $N_C = 48$, $N_Q = N_A + N_B = 43$, and $N_P = 48$ respectively.

Note that the XDR(18,5) significand of the input sample $u[n]$ is placed on the wires of the $B$ port of the DSP48E1 slice.

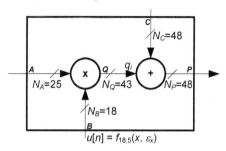

Figure 2    Multiply-Add Unit in One Stage of the Horner Chain

## 3.2  Input Pre-processing

The DSP48E1 slice is an integer multiply-add unit with neither its own leading-one detector nor arithmetic shifters. To minimize the area of the polynomial accelerator, pre-scaling inputs is necessary to fuse XDR multiplication and addition within one DSP48E1. Figure 3 shows a repeating structure that pre-processes the inputs to the multiply-add unit to avoid overflow while retaining as many significant digits as possible. A cascade of $K - 1$ stages of this structure implements a $K^{\text{th}}$–degree polynomial. The stages are labeled according to the indices of the polynomial coefficients attached to the adders. As a result, the leftmost stage in Figure 1 is stage $K - 1$, the stage immediately to its right is stage $K - 2$, and so on until the rightmost stage, which is stage 1.

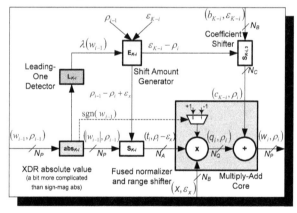

Figure 3    Repeating Structure for Place-and-Route

Stage $K - i$ performs the XDR recurrence multiply-add operation
$f_{N_P,M}(w_i, \rho_i) =$
$f_{N_P,M}(w_{i-1}, \rho_{i-1}) \times f_{N_B,M}(x, \varepsilon_x) + f_{N_B,M}(b_{K-i}, \varepsilon_{K-i})$ , where $M = 7$ is the common exponent width in this design. A common exponent $\rho_i$ is needed for the addition. Let $f_{N_P,M}(w_i, \rho_i) = f_{N_Q,M}(q_i, \rho_i) + f_{N_C,M}(c_{K-i}, \rho_i)$ as shown at the post adder in the DSP48E1 slice in Figure 3.

1.  The first addend $f_{N_Q,M}(q_i, \rho_i)$ is the product of the input $f_{18,5}(x, \varepsilon_x)$ and some version of the previous-stage input $f_{N_P,M}(w_{i-1}, \rho_{i-1})$. This version of the previous-stage input

must have the exponent $\rho_i - \varepsilon_x$ or else the product with $f_{18,5}(x, \varepsilon_x)$ would not result in the exponent $\rho_i$. This version of the previous-stage input turns out to be $f_{N_A,M}\big((-1)^{\text{sgn}(w_{i-1})} t_i, \rho_i - \varepsilon_x\big)$ , where the unsigned significand $t_i$ is a shifted version of $|w_{i-1}|$, and fits into the $A$ port of the DSP48E1 multiplier[1]. The shift amount to go from $|w_{i-1}|$ to $t_i$ is chosen to minimize loss of significant digits, and is coordinated with the shift amount for the coefficient. The bit-loss minimization algorithm that solves a recurrence formula across all stages is beyond the scope of this paper. It suffices to say that the shift amount generator $E_{K-i}$ in Figure 3 instructs the significand of the previous-stage input to shift by the appropriate amount.

2.  The second addend is some version of the coefficient, and again is shifted by the same shift amount generator that shifts the previous-stage input.

Now the DSP48E1 slice performs $w_i = (-1)^{\text{sgn}(W_{i-1})} t_i x + c_{K-i}$ with two's complement operands, blissfully unaware of all the exponent bookkeeping happening around it.

Unfortunately, the exponent bookkeeping uses many LUTs and creates a high LUT-to-DSP utilization ratio. Having too many LUTs per DSP slows down the maximum clock frequency and blocks many DSPs from being used (Figure 4). A ratio of about 300 LUTs to one DSP48E2 per stage achieves a good balance (Figure 5).

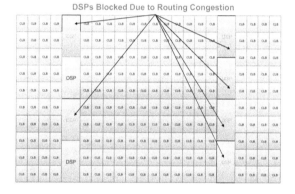

Figure 4    High LUT-to-DSP Ratio Per Stage

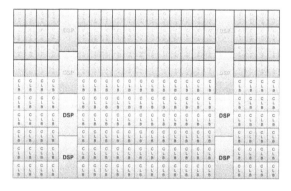

Figure 5    Balanced LUT-to-DSP Ratio

---

[1] An unsigned significand is used purely for implementation reasons and not for mathematical reasons.

# 4. REDUCING THE LUT COUNT

Converting some LUTs to DSPs results in a lower LUT-to-DSP ratio and is beneficial for pitch-matching each stage in the Horner form to rows of DSP48E1 slices. The absolute value block ($\text{abs}_{K-i}$) is a good candidate to map to a DSP48E1 slice. Taking the absolute value of an XDR significand is a bit more work than taking that of a sign-magnitude value, and even that of a two's complement value. This is because the most negative two's complement value is not allowed; its absolute value is saturated to the most positive value. For instance, a four-bit significand ranges from -7 to 7 but -8 is possible to be placed on the four wires by two's complement arithmetic units. The absolute value of -8 in this case is saturated to 7.

Let $d$ be an $N$-bit XDR significand. The absolute value of $d$ is

$$\text{abs}(d) = \begin{cases} d, & d \geq 0 \\ \neg d, & d = -2^{N-1} \\ \neg d + 1, & -2^{N-1} < d < 0. \end{cases}$$

The DSP48E1 slice can be configured to implement the XDR absolute function by setting CARRYIN to be $\text{sgn}(d)$ & $(-2^{N-1} < d < 0)$ and ALUMODE[0] to be $\text{sgn}(d)$.

# 5. MULTI-STAGE PLACEMENT

## 5.1 The Intuition

Now that there are two DSP48E1 slices per stage, a floorplan like that in Figure 5 can be achieved. For instance, the absolute value block occupies the DSP48E1 slice in the left column while the multiply-add block occupies the DSP48E1 slice in the right column. Since the LUTs to the left and the right of the two DSP48E1 slices may not be sufficient, not all DSP48E1 slices may be utilized in the DSP48E1 columns, resulting in a floorplan similar to that in Figure 6, in which a 5th-degree polynomial requires seven DSP48E1 slots across two rows.

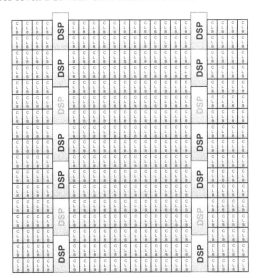

Figure 6    Floorplan for Two DSP48E1 Slice Per Stage

A 5th-degree polynomial has been implemented on a -1I grade (the slowest grade) on a mid-range Xilinx Kintex™-7 XC7K410T FPGA in the Vivado™ 2013.1 environment. A 5th-degree polynomial is chosen because it is the most common polynomial degree for digital predistortion. The maximum operating frequency is 519MHz and has sufficient margin above 491.52MHz for wireless base station applications. Table 1 summarizes the resource usage.

**Table 1 Implementation Results of a 5th-Degree Polynomial**

| | Total Used | Used Per Polynomial Degree | Available | Utilization % |
|---|---|---|---|---|
| FF | 2726 | 545.2 | 508400 | 0.54 |
| LUT | 2500 | 500 | 254200 | 0.98 |
| Memory LUT | 388 | 77.6 | 90600 | 0.43 |
| DSP48 | 10 | 2 | 1540 | 0.65 |
| Maximum Frequency at -1I | 515MHz | | | |

The per-degree results in Table 1 show fewer resources and a higher speed compared to the single-precision fused multiply-add unit in [5], which consumes 4 DSP48E1s, 802 LUTs, and 1233 FFs with a maximum frequency of 488MHz. Obviously, the two designs are not functionally equivalent, with the polynomial accelerator presented here especially created for a hybrid fixed-point and high-dynamic-range application. These resource usage and frequency values nonetheless show it is worth the effort analyzing a high-dynamic-range design with XDR and architecting the Horner polynomial chain with only one normalizer and two shifters.

## 5.2 Expanding the Placement Search Space

Given a rectangular region in Figure 6 with two columns of seven DSP48E1 slices each, how good is the DSP48E1 placement in Section 5.1 for a 5th-degree polynomial?

Across the two DSP48E1 columns, there are 14 DSP48E1 slices available, from which 10 are used to implement the polynomial. Thus there are $\binom{14}{10}10! = \frac{14!}{4!}$ different DSP placements. Assuming 10 minutes per place-and-route run, this would take over 69,110 years of run time.

Because there are two DSP48E1 slices per stage, this large search place can be pruned so that exactly five DSP48E1 slices are used in each of the two DSP columns. This pruning generates only $\binom{7}{5}^2 = 441$ placements. Along the dataflow of the polynomial, the absolute-value DSP and the multiply-add DSP are visited alternately, resulting in three reasonable orderings of these DSPs across the two columns: ping-pong, U-shaped, and S-shaped.

All placements are done stage-by-stage, starting with stage 5 of the 5th-degree polynomial.

1. The ping-pong placement has all the absolute-value DSPs in one column and the multiply-add DSPs in the other (Figure 7a).
2. The U-shaped placement requires one column of DSPs to be placed first before using the other DSP column (Figure 7b). For instance, the absolute-value blocks and the multiply-add units of stages 5 and 4 plus the absolute-value block of stage 3 occupy one DSP column, leaving the other column to the multiply-add unit of stage 3 and all of stages 2 and 1.
3. Like the ping-pong placement, the S-shaped placement places the absolute-value block and the multiply-add unit DSPs in the same stage in different DSP columns but the absolute-value DSP of one stage and the multiply-add DSP of its adjacent stage must be in the same DSP column (Figure 7c).

3

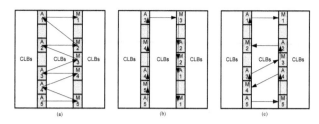

(a)                  (b)                  (c)

Figure 7    Three Placement Strategies. The green boxes prefixed 'A' are DSP48E1s used as absolute value evaluators. The pink boxes prefixed 'M' are DSP48E1s used as multiply-add units. Each box is suffixed with the stage number. Unlabeled grey boxes are unmapped DSP48E1s. (a) Ping-Pong Placement (b) U-Shaped Placement (c) S-Shaped Placement

# 6.  RESULTS

The distributions of the three placements are plotted in Figure 6. The ping-pong placement generally yields faster designs than the other two placement strategies.

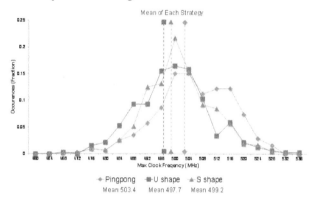

Figure 8    Placement Results

All final place-and-routed results are plotted in a histogram in Figure 9. 46.5% of the results exceed the 500MHz requirement and are represented by the green bars. With only a rectangular region constraint from Figure 6 specifying where all cells of the netlist should be placed, and without specifying which 10 of the 14 DSP48E1 slots should be used, Vivado™ 2013.1 produced a design at 473MHz on the Xilinx Kintex™-7 XC7K410T device. The fastest design achieved 534MHz, and this last 13% of speed improvement was not straightforward to obtain. The initial manual placement from Section 5.1 achieved a respectable performance at 519MHz.

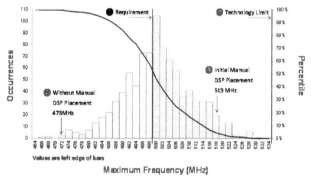

Figure 9    Placement Design Space

# 7.  CONCLUSIONS

A polynomial accelerator has been shown to operate up to 534MHz at the slowest speed grade on a 28nm FPGA. It accepts an 18-bit fixed-point input and high-dynamic-range coefficients. The FPGA polynomial accelerator has been architected with a custom number representation known as XDR. Because the two's complement significand of an XDR number models bits that are put directly on the wires of two's complement integer arithmetic circuits, XDR is useful for analyzing high-dynamic-range designs using two's complement integer arithmetic operators.

The polynomial accelerator is implemented with Horner's method and is physically partitioned into a cascade of identical stages. To balance LUTs and DSP48E1 usage, two DSP48E1s are used in each stage. One DSP48E1 slice serves as the XDR absolute value evaluator and the other DSP48E1 slices is the multiply-add unit. Place-and-route experiments of a 5th-degree polynomial including three DSP48E1 placement strategies reveal a design space with a range of maximum clock frequencies from 460MHz to 534MHz using Vivado 2013.1 on a -1I (slowest) grade of the Xilinx Kintex™-7 XC7K410T device . These experiments provide space for placing 10 DSP48E1s into 14 DSP48E1 slots, which are partitioned into two 7-slot DSP48E1 columns. An intuitive placement (the ping-pong placement) with unused DSP48E1 slots in strategic locations to give more room for LUTs proves to be effective since it yields a maximum frequency of 519MHz, 13% above what automatic placement can achieve and very close to the high end of the 460MHz-to-534MHz design space.

# 8.  REFERENCES

[1]  W. G. Horner, "A new method of solving numerical equations of all orders, by continuous approximation," *Phil. Trans. R. Soc. Lond.*, Part II, vol. 109, pp. 308–335, July, 1819.

[2]  C. S. Burrus, J. W. Fox, G. A. Sitton, and S. Treitel, "Horner's method for evaluating and deflating polynomials," DSP Software Notes, Rice University, Nov. 26, 2003, http://www.ece.rice.edu/dsp/software/FVHDP/horner2.pdf

[3]  7 Series DSP48E1 Slice User Guide (UG479), version 1.8, Nov. 10, 2014.

[4]  S. Boldo and M. Daumas, "Properties of two's complement floating point notations," *Int. J. Softw. Tools Technol. Transfer*, vol. 5, no. 2, pp. 237–246, Mar. 2004.

[5]  Xilinx LogiCORE IP Floating-Point Operator v6.2 Product Guide, PG060, Dec. 2012.

# Using Source-Level Transformations to Improve High-Level Synthesis Debug and Validation on FPGAs

Joshua Monson
Brigham Young University
459 Clyde Building
Provo, UT 84602
jsmonson@gmail.com

Brad Hutchings
Brigham Young University
459 Clyde Building
Provo, UT 84602
brad_hutchings@byu.edu

## ABSTRACT

This paper proposes a method for extending source-level visibility into the RTL of an HLS-generated design using automated source-level transformations. Using our method, source-level visibility can be extended into co-simulation, in-system simulation, and hardware execution of any HLS tool that provides the ability to infer top-level ports. Experimental results show the feasibility of our method in situations where visibility needs to be added without modifying the timing, latency, or throughput of the design.

## Categories and Subject Descriptors

B.m [**Hardware**]: Miscellaneous

## Keywords

FPGA, High-Level Synthesis, HLS, Debugging, Simulation

## 1. INTRODUCTION

One of the many reasons HLS tools increase productivity is that developers are able to quickly test and verify the functionality of their designs in software. While software-based verification and debugging is indispensable for HLS, it cannot simulate the errors that can occur due to concurrent behavior. Diagnosing such errors in RTL simulation is difficult because the developer is generally unfamiliar with the structure of the generated RTL. While some HLS tools support source-level debug during RTL simulation, some do not. No current commercial HLS tools of which we are aware support in-system debugging. In this paper, we propose an automated method for extending source-level visibility into HLS generated cores during simulation and in-system execution. Since our method is based on source-level transformations, it could, with tool-specific implementations, support almost any HLS tool. For tools that do not already support source-level debug this removes much of the manual effort required to instrument these designs for debug. But even

more importantly, we show how our techniques can be used to debug real problems in simulation.

## 2. PREVIOUS WORK

There have been several academic efforts to add support for source-level debugging of HLS generated cores. The earliest academic effort was Hemmert's source-level debugger for the JHDL-based Sea Cucumber Synthesizing Compiler [6]. Hemmert's source-level debugger could be used both in simulation and during hardware execution. Hemmert's in-system debugger leveraged JHDL's support for clock-controlled inspection of hardware registers. Calagar's Inspect Debugger [2] mirrors Hemmert's debugger in many respects. However, Inspect targets the Legup HLS tool and supports automated discrepency detection. Goeder's work also targeted Legup [4]. However, Goeder's worked focused on efficiently capturing a hardware trace during in-system execution. The research of Curreri et. al. [3] and Hammouda et. al. [1] has focused on the automatic generation of assertion checkers from source-level C-based assertions.

There have also been commercial efforts to support debugging. The most notable of these effort is the source-level debugger provided by CyberWorkBench [10]. CyberWorkBench is a full system development platform and supports source-level debugging all the way down to RTL system-wide simulation. Impulse C also has RTL simulation-based source-level debugging support [7].

**Listing 1: EOP Examples**

```
1   //original
2   int mult(int a, int b){
3           return (a * b);
4   }
5   //eop from pointer
6   int mult(int a, int b, int * eop0){
7           return *eop0 = (a * b);
8   }
9   //eop from global
10  int eop0;
11  int mult(int a, int b){
12          #pragma HLS interface port=eop
13          return eop0 = (a * b);
14  }
```

## 3. EVENT OBSERVABILITY PORTS

In their work, Monson and Hutchings [9] propose the use of Event Observability Ports (EOP) to provide a structure for source-to-hardware correspondence which could be added to either the RTL code (for simulation) or synthesis netlist (for in-system debugging). In practice, an EOP is a top-level RTL port that corresponds to the output of a specific expression or statement in the original source. The EOP contains two signals, an event signal and a data signal. The event signal is asserted when the source-level expression to which the EOP corresponds is evaluated within the generated HLS design. When the event signal is asserted, the data signal holds the result of the expression. EOPs provide the developer with a simple construct that can be connected-to and monitored that has a guaranteed source-level meaning. Because EOPs have a guaranteed source-level meaning, they relieve the developer of the task of becoming familiar with the structure of the generated hardware.

## 4. EOP INSERTION METHODS

Listing 1 demonstrates two approaches showing how a target expression ((a * b); line 3) can be instrumented with an EOP. Instrumenting the source code with an EOP requires that we add a new top-level port and then perform a write to it. Our first example (Listing 1, lines 5-8) uses the insertion of a pointer parameter on the function declaration to add the top-level port (line 6). The type of this pointer should match the return value of the target expression (in this case *int*). The write to the EOP is added by inserting an assignment statement that assigns the value of the target expression to the dereferenced EOP pointer (line 7).

The second example (Listing 1, lines 10-14) uses a global variable and Vivado HLS pragma to create the top-level port representing the EOP. The assignment operator is added in the same manner as before to initiate the write to the port. In both examples, Vivado HLS synthesizes a top-level port for the EOP. This port contains a 32-bit signal for the data (value of the target expression) and a 1-bit valid signal. The 32-bit data signal on this port corresponds exactly to the data signal needed for the EOP. The valid signal is only nearly analogous to the event signal of the EOP. Technically, the event signal should be asserted during the same clock cycle that the target expression completes its execution. In general, this should be the case, but it is possible that the HLS tool could schedule the write during a later clock cycle.

There are drawbacks of increasing inner-HLS-core visibility by adding EOPs to the source code. First of all, manually modifying source-code can be an error prone and time consuming. Second, modifying the source can alter the way that the HLS tool schedules and optimizes the circuit. The next two sections will discuss our solution to these problems.

## 5. SOURCE-LEVEL TRANSFORMATIONS

The current generation of HLS tools struggles with its ability to efficiently synthesize arbitrary C code. Often, this requires developers to make substantial modifications to their code before it will synthesize at all. This becomes a tedious process as the developer must determine how to modify his code without changing the behavior. Source-level transformations are a common solution to this problem [11]. The goal of source-level transformations is to increase the usefulness and productivity of HLS tools by removing the need for the programmer to make the necessary changes manually. Additionally, the source-level transformation allows the user to keep their original source code intact.

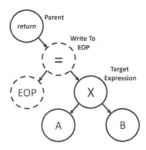

**Figure 1: Demonstration of EOP write insertion into Abstract Syntax Tree. Inserted nodes are represented with dotted lines.**

In this paper, we utilized the Rose compiler infrastructure [8]. Rose uses a standard compiler frontend to transform the source code into an Abstract Syntax Tree (AST). Rose provides an API that allows the user to both analyze and modify the AST. When the transformations have been completed, the AST undergoes an "unparsing" process in which the modified AST is written out again as source code.

The use of a source-to-source compiler framework allows us to leverage the AST to demonstrate that we can automatically insert EOPs without affecting the original behavior of the circuit. Figure 1 shows how we modified the AST to insert the EOP write. The tree nodes with solid outlines are nodes from the original subtree in the first example (Listing 1). The assignment operator and EOP variable reference node (dashed outlines) are the nodes that were inserted to implement the EOP write. In general, the syntax of the AST is that a sub-tree is resolved before its parent node is resolved. In Figure 1, this would mean that the multiply operation would be resolved before the return operation. Therefore, as long as the the value of the target expression is passed to the parent node, we can insert an EOP write without modifying the original behavior of the program. This is indeed accomplished since the assignment operator returns the value of its right-hand-side (RHS) operand.

## 6. DEBUGGING WITH EOPS

There are three points at which we may wish to use EOPs to accelerate our debugging efforts. They are co-simulation, in-system simulation, and in-system hardware execution. In co-simulation, the HLS tool generates an RTL test bench that matches the software test bench. The primary use of co-simulation is to prove that the generated RTL has the same functional behavior as the original C. Generally, the problems found during co-simulation are expected software/simulation mismatches which are explained in the HLS tool's user guide. On occasion, bugs in HLS tools are discovered as well. Since we are not concerned with interface timing, EOPs can be used liberally during co-simulation to provide software-like visibility to the developer.

Next, in-system simulation is used to ensure that the HLS core interacts properly with the other cores in the system. During in-system simulation (and hardware execution), bugs may be sensitive to the timing, through-put, or latency of the core. Therefore any transformation made should avoid modifying these characteristics of the core. The best way to accomplish this is to add EOPs to expressions that are not likely to be "optimized away".

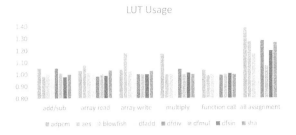

Figure 2: Lut usage compared to baseline uninstrumented design.

Figure 3: Minimum clock period compared to uninstrumented design.

Debugging is most difficult during in-system hardware execution. Since hardware execution operates much faster than software or simulation it may encounter bugs that occur less frequently. Additionally, the core may encounter input or other situations the developer did not expect. We believe that carefully targeted EOP insertion can minimize hardware overhead and provide useful visibility.

## 7. EXPERIMENT AND RESULTS

One potential approach to instrument the circuit without affecting the timing, latency or through-put is to target source code structures that are mapped to the HLS core in predictable ways. To test the feasibility of this approach we used our source-to-source translator to instrument expressions whose results were likely to survive HLS optimization. In particular, we instrumented several benchmarks from the assignment operations whose final result was an array read or write, add/subtract, multiply, or function call. Additionally, as a first order evaluation of the effect on latency, we co-simulated each instrumented design using Vivado HLS's co-simulation. Then we executed the implementation process using Vivado HLS's export functionality. Several benchmarks from the CHStone HLS [5] benchmarking suite were evaluated against a baseline design. The benchmarks were modified just enough to get the benchmark to synthesize and pass co-simulation in Vivado HLS. No directives were added to unroll or pipeline loops. To provide some additional context, we also ran an experiment that instrumented all of the assignment operations in the circuit. The one exception was assignments to pointers, since Vivado HLS does not support writing pointer values to output ports. We used Vivado HLS (2014.1) to generate the instrumented RTL.

The table in Figure 5 shows the number of EOPs that were inserted in each experiment. In the majority of the experi-

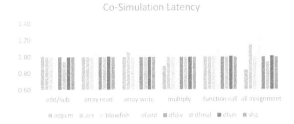

Figure 4: Co-simulation latency compared to uninstrumented design.

| Benchmark | add/sub | array read | array write | multiply | function call | all assignment |
|-----------|---------|-----------|-------------|----------|---------------|----------------|
| adpcm | 25 | 7 | 22 | 17 | 26 | 174 |
| aes | 1 | 176 | 226 | 0 | 3 | 324 |
| blowfish | 0 | 29 | 16 | 0 | 0 | 99 |
| dfadd | 7 | 1 | 0 | 0 | 15 | 73 |
| dfdiv | 8 | 1 | 0 | 4 | 12 | 77 |
| dfmul | 4 | 1 | 0 | 4 | 11 | 65 |
| dfsin | 17 | 1 | 0 | 4 | 33 | 138 |
| sha | 0 | 7 | 15 | 0 | 0 | 70 |

Figure 5: This table shows the number of EOPs added in each experiment.

ments, there were less than 30 opportunities to add EOPs. As shown in Figures 2, 3, and 4, these were the experiments that had almost no effect on simulation latency, LUT usage, or minimum clock period. This provides some evidence to show that if a small amount of EOPs are carefully selected we can instrument the design (at the source-level) with EOPs with little or no effect. In general, in-system debugging during hardware execution is just that; a trace of a small number of carefully selected signals.

It is important to note that there is some possible overlap between the array write experiment and the other experiments (see Figure 5). This is because array writes are left-hand-values while the operations targeted in the other experiments are right-hand-values. Therefore, anytime an array element is assigned a value there may be overlap. This occurs frequently in the AES benchmark.

We also note the significant drop in co-simulation latency for the *adpcm* benchmark in the "all assignment" and "multiply" experiments. These same experiments also exhibited a drop in DSP usage. Upon further investigation we found that the insertion of EOPs had prevented a few functions from being inlined. This change appears to have allowed Vivado HLS's scheduler to find a lower latency schedule.

## 8. CASE STUDIES

In this section, we provide examples using EOPs to solve real debug problems in RTL simulation and in-system simulation. Both examples, in Vivado HLS (2014.1), will execute correctly during normal execution and incorrectly during simulation. Vivado HLS does not provide any automated debugging support for either simulation or in-system execution. Therefore, our EOPs are important debug tools during co-simulation and in-system simulation.

Our first example, shown in listing 2, is an HLS core that accepts and accumulates a variable length data stream. In this core, the length of the stream is determined by reading the first word (line 3). Let us assume that the system this core has been placed in is off by one cycle and *length* is assigned the wrong value. At this point, two results are possible: 1) *length* is assigned a value that is less than the number of entries in the stream or 2) *length* is assigned a value that is higher than the remaining entries in the stream. In the first case, the read of *stream[i]* (line 5) will consume the part of the stream that was specified by *length* and then return the erroneous sum. The early return of the HLS core may cause the system to lock while it waits for the HLS core to consume the remainder of the stream. In the second case, it is likely that the HLS core would stall as it waits for streaming values that might never come.

In this case, a source-to-source transformation could be employed to add an EOP to capture the value of length (line 3). This would allow the developer to check whether the expected value for length was actually assigned to length and adjust the control of his streaming interface accordingly.

**Listing 2: Example of misaligned streaming Header read.**

```
1  int misaligned(int stream[1000]){
2     #pragma HLS INTERFACE ap_fifo ...
3     int length = stream[0], i, sum=0;
4     for(i=1;i<=length;i++)
5        sum += stream[i];
6     return sum;
7  }
```

Our second example is a product of our efforts to get the *blowfish* benchmark to pass co-simulation in Viavado HLS. During co-simulation, Vivado HLS transforms a self-checking C test-bench into a self-checking SystemC simulation model. After executing the software testbench correctly, we found that the benchmark did not pass co-simulation. The difficulty here is that Vivado HLS does not provide any kind of debugging support for co-simulation.

To help us locate the problem we ran our source-to-source transformation on the *blowfish* source code. We configured our source-to-source transformation to add EOPs to all of the assignment operations. In all, over 167 EOPs were added to the design. The instrumented source code was then synthesized by Vivado HLS. After synthesis, co-simulation failed again in the same manner. Using the source-level software debugger and EOPs together we identified discrepancies between the simulation and software execution. We found that a specific call to the main encryption function always returned an incorrect value. This was surpising because earlier calls to the same function were working properly. This led us to investigate the generated VHDL. The source of the problem was that some global arrays had been instantiated deep down one branch of the VHDL module hierarchy. Functions that were instanced below the instaniations of the global variables were properly wired to these memories. However, functions instanced in different call hierarchies were not wired and could not interact with these memories. To fix the problem, the C code was modified to change the global variables to local variables of the top-level function. This forced us to further modify the code so that each array was passed down through both function call hierarchies. After making these changes, co-simulation completed successfully.

## 9. CONCLUSION

In this paper, we have shown the feasibility of using source-to-source transformations to increase the source-level visibility of an HLS design during simulation. We have shown that, for several CHStone benchmarks, if the target expressions are carefully selected we can instrument between 0 and 30 expressions at the source level all while having little or no effect on the timing, throughput, latency, or resource usage of the design. We have also shown that in co-simulation all the assignment operations can be instrumented to provide software-like visibility for HLS tools that do not provide source-level debugger for simulation. We have shown how these techniques can be used to find real bugs during simulation. In the future we plan to demonstrate these instrumentation techniques in executing hardware.

## 10. ACKNOWLEDGMENTS

This work was supported by the I/UCRC Program of the National Science Foundation under Grant No. 1265957.

## 11. REFERENCES

[1] M. Ben Hammouda, P. Coussy, and L. Lagadec. A design approach to automatically synthesize ansi-c assertions during high-level synthesis of hardware accelerators. In *Circuits and Systems (ISCAS), 2014 IEEE International Symposium on*, pages 165–168, 2014.

[2] N. Calagar, S. Brown, and J. Anderson. Source-level debugging for fpga high-level synthesis. In *International Conference on Field-Programmable Logic and Applications*, 2014.

[3] J. Curreri, G. Stitt, and A. D. George. High-level synthesis techniques for in-circuit assertion-based verification. In *Parallel & Distributed Processing, Workshops and Phd Forum (IPDPSW), 2010 IEEE International Symposium on*, pages 1–8, 2010.

[4] J. Goeders and S. Wilton. Effective fpga debug for high-level synthesis generated circuits, September 2014 2014.

[5] Y. Hara, H. Tomiyama, S. Honda, H. Takada, and K. Ishii. Chstone: A benchmark program suite for practical c-based high-level synthesis. In *Circuits and Systems, 2008. ISCAS 2008. IEEE International Symposium on*, pages 1192–1195.

[6] K. S. Hemmert. Source level debugging of circuits synthesized from high level language descriptions. 2004.

[7] Impulse Accelerated Technologies. *CoDeveloper Version 3.70*, 2014.

[8] L. L. N. laboratory. Rose compiler infrastructure.

[9] J. Monson and B. Hutchings. New approaches for in-system debug of behaviorally-synthesized fpga circuits, 2014.

[10] K. Wakabayashi. Cyberworkbench: integrated design environment based on c-based behavior synthesis and verification. In *VLSI Design, Automation and Test, 2005. (VLSI-TSA-DAT). 2005 IEEE VLSI-TSA International Symposium on*, pages 173–176.

[11] F. Winterstein, S. Bayliss, and G. Constantinides. Separation logic-assisted code transformations for efficient high-level synthesis. 2014.

# High-Level Design Tools for Floating Point FPGAs

Deshanand P. Singh
Altera Corporation
150 Bloor Street West, Suite 400
Toronto, Ontario, Canada
dsingh@altera.com

Bogdan Pasca
Altera Corporation
Westwood, High Wycombe,
Buckinghamshire HP12 4PU,
United Kingdom
bpasca@altera.com

Tomasz S. Czajkowski
Altera Corporation
150 Bloor Street West, Suite 400
Toronto, Ontario, Canada
tczajkow@altera.com

## ABSTRACT

This tutorial describes tools for efficiently implementing floating point applications on FPGAs. We present both the SDK for OpenCL and DSP Builder Advanced Blockset and show that they can be effectively used to implement many floating point applications. The methods for optimizing application performance are also described.

In this tutorial we focus on a few applications, including Fast Fourier transform, matrix multiplication, finite impulse response filter and a Cholesky decomposition. In all cases we show what the tools are capable of achieving, and more importantly how a user can take advantage of the various floating-point centric features that are made available. We also discuss how these tools can automatically use FPGA architectural features such as hardened floating-point DSP available on Altera Arria 10 family.

## Categories and Subject Descriptors

C.1.3 [**Computer System Organization**]: Other Architecture Styles, Data-flow architectures.

## General Terms

Design

## Keywords

Floating Point; Optimization; FPGAs

## 1. INTRODUCTION

Many applications in a variety of different domains are first simulated or modeled using floating-point data processing. This is done using either programming languages such as C/C++ or tools such as Matlab. The final implementation on platforms such as FPGAs has usually been performed using fixed-point arithmetic because of area considerations. To do this successfully, the algorithms are carefully mapped into a limited dynamic range, and scaled through each function in the datapath.

Over the last 10 years FPGAs have grown sufficiently large to facilitate native floating point based applications. However, there has been a lack of support for floating point functions, which meant that designers were left on their own to ensure that the floating point implementation of a given function satisfies their application's criteria. This meant most designers chose not to use floating point operations simply because there was no convenient way to do so.

To truly enable floating point application development, it is imperative to provide both FPGAs and tools to program them. To that end, in this tutorial we introduce two tools that can enable users to take advantage of floating point capabilities on FPGA devices. These tools are: SDK for OpenCL and DSP Builder Advanced Blockset. We will also discuss how these tools can take advantage of architectural features of modern FPGAs, and specifically focus on Arria 10 device family as an example of how hardened FP DSP blocks can benefit designs in many application domains.

SDK for OpenCL [1] enables users to describe an application using a C-like description, as described by the OpenCL Standard [4]. One of the key advantages this standard brings to FPGAs is a front-end support for floating-point operations, enabling end users to seamlessly use floating point data types that they are used to when programing a wide variety of applications, while not having to worry too much about the low-level implementation details of floating point functions. DSP Builder Advanced Blockset [2] is a tool that uses Matlab's Simulink as a front end to describe an application, both fixed and floating point, to enable the user to abstract away low-level details of hardware implementation. In this tutorial, we will demonstrate how these two tools can be used to implement efficient floating-point benchmarks.

The remainder of this paper is organized as follows: Section 2 discusses the floating point formats and the key challenges floating point application designers face. In Sections 3 and 4, we discuss how many of the challenges of such design are alleviated by tools such as Altera's SDK for OpenCL [1] and DSP Builder Advanced Blockset [2]. We discuss these tools using a case study of several applications to illustrate the novelty and productivity the tools bring to end users. Finally, we summarize the paper in section 5 with concluding remarks and future work.

## 2. BACKGROUND

Traditionally FPGAs have been used for non-floating-point applications due to the fact that floating point operations can take considerable area when implemented using Lookup Tables (LUTs). The reason for this is the representation of floating point numbers as specified in IEEE754 standard [3]. Each floating point number consists of a single bit sign, an exponent and a mantissa. The exponent specifies the order of magnitude for a given number, whereas the mantissa specifies the value with more precision. Table 1 shows a variety of mantissa and exponent sizes commonly used by many applications.

*FPGA'14*, February 22–24, 2015, Monterey, California, USA.
Copyright © 2015 ACM 978-1-4503-3315-3/15/02...$15.00.
http://dx.doi.org/10.1145/2684746.2689079

**Table 1. Commonly used floating point formats**

| Precision | Exponent Bits | Mantissa Bits |
|---|---|---|
| Half | 5 | 10 |
| Single | 8 | 23 |
| Double | 11 | 52 |

In addition to supporting computation in normal range, thre are two special values: infinity and not-a-number (NaN). Infinity is used by floating point operations to signify that the result of an operation is outside of the range representable by a given floating point format. A NaN on the other hand signifies an operation that does not provide a valid result. For example, adding +Infinity to – Infinity does not produce a valid result.

One of the many opportunities afforded by using FPGAs is the optimization of floating point operations for a given application. Both Altera SDK for OpenCL [1] and Altera DSP Builder Advanced Blockset [2] enable users to take advantage of floating-point compiler mode [7]. The floating point compiler mode enables the user to reduce the area of floating point operations by removing support for infinity and NaN special values if the user can guarantee that their application will never make use of them.

In the following sections we will discuss various methods that can be used by FPGA system designers to take advantage of the floating point support offered by Altera OpenCL SDK and Altera DSP Builder Advanced Blockset flows as well as device families they can target.

## 3. SDK for OpenCL

Altera OpenCL SDK is a complete suite to facilitate the use of OpenCL Standard [4] for designing applications on FPGAs. An OpenCL application comprises a kernel and a host program. In SDK for OpenCL, the kernel is implemented using an automatically generated datapath on an FPGA, while the host program is executed on a processor that communicates with the kernel on an FPGA board via mechanisms such as PCIe. We demonstrate the utility of this tool for the implementation of an FFT and a general matrix-matrix multiplication.

## 3.1 FFT

The Fast Fourier transform is a classic application used in digital signal processing applications. Its regular structure yields itself nicely to an efficient hardware implementation. While many FFT architectures have been described in literature, as an example we implemented a particular one described in [5] for 4K-point FFT on an Altera Stratix V FPGA.

Floating point optimizations are especially important for algorithms such as FFT, where floating point operations comprise almost all of the required resources. Aside from minimal control and data movement logic, the complete data pipeline is effectively a sequence of floating point operators comprising addition, subtraction and multiplication.

The optimizations stem partly from proprietary optimizations known as the Floating Point Compiler (FPC) [7]. The FFT data path benefits from three such optimizations: removal of NaN and Inf support, changing rounding mode to round-to-zero, and fusing addition and subtraction into a single operation.

In algorithms such as FFT, support for non-finite results is typically superfluous when the input data ranges are known and bounded. The area required for adders and multipliers can therefore be reduced by not supporting these exceptions. Round-to-zero operations are simply truncations; consequently they require no hardware resources to implement. Further optimization is possible by fusing addition and subtraction operators when both inputs are the same (a+b, a-b). It is a well-known technique [6] that does not require reordering of operations and is thus safe to perform at any time. This transform is beneficial because most of the logic in a single adder module can be reused within the subtractor, avoiding logic duplication.

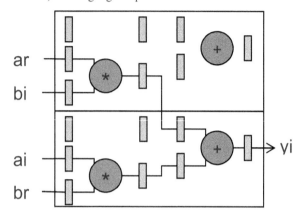

**Figure 1. Imaginary part of complex FP multiplication implemented using FP DSP Blocks.**

The implementation of an FFT becomes even more optimized on an Arria 10 device, where hardened floating point DSP blocks are available [8]. In particular, for FFT applications we can take advantage of the DSP blocks to perform complex multiplication compactly, as shown in Figure 1. In the figure, we show an abstract representation of two adjacent DSP blocks configured in a floating-point mode. Each DSP block comprises two operations, addition (or subtraction) and multiplication. The operators are connected by programmable paths that may take advantage of pipelining registers to connect to one another or to an adjacent DSP block. In this case we show the computation of the imaginary part of complex multiplication. To do this we use two DSP blocks, taking advantage of two multipliers and an adder, while one adder is left unused. If it is the case that complex multiplication is followed by complex addition the unused adder may be selected to perform the addition of the imaginary parts of the complex multiplication result and another complex number. A similar implementation is used for the real part of the computation. Table 2 summarizes the area for each optimization.

**Table 2. FFT Optimization Results**

| Optimization | ALMs | DSPs |
|---|---|---|
| IEEE754 Conformant | 62126 | 60 |
| FPC | 39662 | 60 |
| FPC+Fused add/sub | 34102 | 60 |
| Arria 10 (Hardened FP) | 6208 | 98 |

## 3.2 Matrix-Matrix Multiplication

In the matrix-matrix multiplication algorithm, shown in Figure 2, the multiplication is performed using blocks of data, where on each iteration of a loop a block of size BLOCKxBLOCK of each of the input matrices is read in, a dot product is computed and added to the sum until the entire column is processed for each element. To speed up the computation, an attribute *num_simd_work_items* is used to vectorize the application, thus increasing the throughput by a factor of V.

The key to an efficient design from a floating-point perspective is in how lines 19-20 are implemented in hardware. Due to the *#pragma* statement, the loop of multiplication and addition is unrolled into a chain of multiply and add operations. Usually, a balanced tree of adders works better than a chain as it reduces the area of the circuit. In SDK for OpenCL the users are not required to rewrite the application to do this; it is sufficient to supply a flag *--fp-relaxed* to the compiler. This flag signifies that the user is aware that reordering floating point operations may change the output, but it is acceptable for this application. The compiler will then examine the sequence of floating point operations and rearrange them to produce a more efficient implementation.

```
__attribute((reqd_work_group_size(BLOCK,BLOCK,1)))
__attribute((num_simd_work_items(V)))
__kernel void matmult(global float *A,
            global float *B, global float *C) {
  int w = get_global_size(0);
  int x = get_local_id(0); int y = get_local_id(1);
  int bx = get_group_id(0); int by = get_group_id(1);
  local float lA[BLOCK*BLOCK], lb[BLOCK*BLOCK];
  float sum = 0.0f;
  for(int i=0; i< w; i+=BLOCK) {
    lA[x+BLOCK*y] = A[i+x+(y+by)*w];
    lB[x+BLOCK*y] = B[bx+x+(i+y)*w];
    barrier();
    #pragma unroll
    for(int k=0; k < BLOCK; k++)
      sum += lA[k+y*BLOCK]*lB[k*BLOCK+x];
    barrier();
  }
  C[get_global_id(0)+get_global_id(1)*w] =  sum;
}
```

**Figure 2. Matrix-Matrix Multiplication pseudo code.**

Similarly to the example of the FFT, we can take advantage of the FPC flow using the *--fpc* flag as an argument to the compiler. In this case, the compiler will optimize the tree of adders to minimize their area. Doing this allows us to more than double the throughput of the application.

Finally, we can take this design to the next level by implementing it on an Altera Arria 10 device and take advantage of hardened floating point adder and multiplier blocks to reduce the area of the design. This particular optimization occurs automatically, when a user choses to target an Arria 10 device.

The results of synthesizing, placing and routing this design are shown in Table 3. This shows the use of hardened FP (HFP) on Arria 10 to achieve extreme area savings.

**Table 3. Matrix-Matrix multiplication area results**

| Configuration | ALMs | DSPs |
|---|---|---|
| BLOCK=128, V=8, FPC | 315061 | 1034 |
| BLOCK=128, V=8, HFP | 61293 | 1034 |

# 4. DSP Builder Advanced Blockset

The DSP Builder Advanced Blockset (DSPBA) is a high-level design tool with a model-based design entry which integrates with Matlab's Simulink Frontend. With DSPBA, users functionally verify and debug their designs at the Simulink level using scopes and variables. This allows for considerably faster algorithm iterations as opposed to traditional FPGA development using RTL languages and simulators. Once the desired functionality is achieved, DSPBA efficiently maps the implementation to a user-defined FPGA target and automatically pipelines the design to achieve a target clock frequency.

DSPBA offers users full flexibility when implementing datapaths allowing for a mixture of fixed or floating-point types. Moreover, both fixed and floating-point types are parametrizable: total width, fraction width and sign are used for fixed-point types and exponent and fraction width are used for floating-point types. For floating-point datapaths users may choose from implementing parts using the floating-point compiler technology [7] or IEEE-754 conformant implementation to trade-off resources for numerical conformance. The provided floating-point library of components uses state-of-the-art techniques [9] to efficiently map to modern DSP-enabled FPGAs.

In the following we exemplify the use case for DSPBA on two designs: a floating-point FIR filter and linear system solver based on the Cholesky decomposition.

## 4.1 FIR Filter

The Finite Impulse Response (FIR) filter is expressed using the following equation for a filter of order $N$:

$$y[n] = \sum_{i=0}^{N} c_i x[n-i]$$

DSPBA provides users a full library of efficient FIR filter implementations including decimating, interpolating, single-rate and fractional-rate. However, if users desire to manually create a simple FIR example they may do so using the scalar product block which receives on one input the twiddle coefficients and on the second input the input $x$ and its delayed versions using the $z^{-1}$ block. Figure 2 shows how such a filter would be used for N=4.

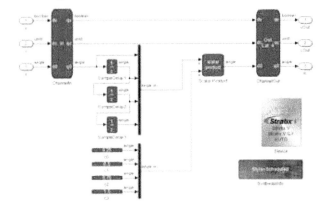

**Figure 2. FIR Filter Design in DSPBA**

One must note that DSPBA provides specialized blocks for the tapped delay line, which allow for a more compact description of the delay line. The scalar product block receives the two vectors of 4 elements and outputs the filter result to the channel out. The data types used for this example is floating-point single precision. This can be easily updated to other floating or fixed-point data types by updating the type of the input and allowing the default data type propagation. Table 4 shows the implementation results for this benchmark on Stratix V using soft logic and Arria 10 using FP DSP Blocks.

**Table 4. FIR Filter area results**

| Configuration | ALMs | DSPs |
| --- | --- | --- |
| Stratix V, 128-tap | 60881 | 128 |
| Arria 10, 128-tap, HFP | 1676 | 131 |

## 4.2 Cholesky Decomposition

DSPBA allows users to generate larger circuits which perform more complex tasks, such as solving linear systems of equations, $Ax=b$, using the Cholesky decomposition. The Cholesky decomposition relies on decomposing the matrix A into a lower triangular matrix L such that $A = L L^*$ where $L^*$ is the transpose conjugate (if A is a complex matrix). The system $Ax=b$ now becomes $L(L^* x) = b$ and using the variable change $L^* x=y$ we obtain $L y = b$. Solving this system for $y$ can be achieved using forward substitution. Having obtained $y$ the next system $L^* x=y$ can be solved for $x$ using backward substitution. Hence, solving the linear system is composed of 3 steps: decomposition, forward substitution followed by backward substitution.

There are multiple possible DSPBA implementations for this problem each trading latency and throughput for area. One possible implementation performs the decomposition and forward substitution in one module and the backward substitution in another. To maximize performance it is desirable to balance the latency of the two modules. Therefore, the first module would use extended vector-products whereas the second module would use fewer resources and perform the process iteratively. The two modules are depicted in Figure 3.

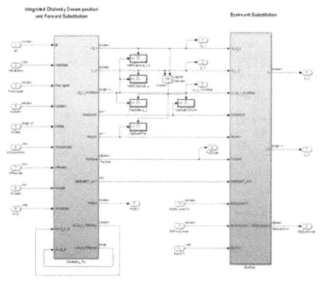

**Figure 3. Cholesky Decomposition in DSPBA**

The main computing kernel in the decomposition and forward substitution is the scalar-product. It is used in both stages using configurable multiplexers to feed the desired input data. The forward substitution stage overlaps with the decomposition stage.

Table 5 shows the implementation results for this benchmark on Stratix V using mostly soft logic and Arria 10 using hardened FP DSP Blocks.

**Table 5. Cholesky Filter area results**

| Configuration | ALMs | DSPs |
| --- | --- | --- |
| Stratix V | 109914 | 260 |
| Arria 10, HFP | 12716 | 270 |

## 5. CONCLUSION

In this paper we have briefly presented a two high-level design tools and described how they can be used to optimize floating point benchmarks. The key advantage for the end user is the ability to quickly create a fully functioning circuit that can be programmed onto an FPGA. The tools themselves contain many floating-point specific optimizations that significantly reduce the amount of time the user is required to consider low-level implementation details.

Finally, we showed the impact of FPGA architectural features such as HFP to enable extreme area reductions. Both presented tools take advantage of HFP seamlessly, enabling the implementation of ever more advanced applications on FPGAs.

## 6. ACKNOWLEDGMENTS

The authors would like to thank Simon Finn, Michael Kinsner, Martin Langhammer in providing benchmarking data and advice throughout this work.

## 7. REFERENCES

[1] Altera Corporation, Altera SDK for OpenCL, http://www.altera.com/products/software/opencl

[2] Altera Corporation, Altera DSP Builder Advanced Blockset, http://www.altera.com/technology/dsp/advanced-blockset

[3] IEEE standard for binary floating-point arithmetic. ANSI/IEEE Std. 754-1985, pages 1-58, 2008.

[4] Khronos OpenCL Working Group. The OpenCL Specification, version 1.1.48, June 2009.

[5] M. Garrido, J. Grajal, M. Sanchez, and O. Gustafsson. "Pipelined radix-2k feedforward FFT architectures", Very Large Scale Integration (VLSI) Systems, IEEE Transactions on, 21(1):23-32, 2013.

[6] E. Swartzlander and H. Saleh, " FFT implementation with fused floating-point operations", IEEE Transactions on Computers, 61(2):284-288, 2012.

[7] M. Langhammer, "Floating Point Datapath Synthesis for FPGAs", International Conference on Field Programmable Logic and Applications, pp. 355-360, 2008.

[8] B. Pasca, and M. Langhammer, "Floating Point DSP Block Architecture for FPGAs", ACM/SIGDA International Symposium on FPGAs, Monterey California, Feb, 2015.

[9] de Dinechin, F.; Joldes, M.; Pasca, B., "Automatic generation of polynomial-based hardware architectures for function evaluation," Application-specific Systems Architectures and Processors (ASAP), 21st IEEE International Conference on , pp.216-222, 7-9 July 2010

# Software-Driven Hardware Development

Myron King, Jamey Hicks, John Ankcorn
Quanta Research Cambridge
{myron.king,jamey.hicks,john.ankcorn}@qrclab.com

## ABSTRACT

The cost and complexity of hardware-centric systems can often be reduced by using software to perform tasks which don't appear on the critical path. Alternately, the performance of software can sometimes be improved by using special purpose hardware to implement tasks which *do* appear on the critical path. Whatever the motivation, most modern systems are composed of both hardware and software components.

Given the importance of the connection between hardware and software in these systems, it is surprising how little automated and machine-checkable support there is for co-design space exploration. This paper presents the Connectal framework, which enables the development of hardware accelerators for software applications by generating hardware/software interface implementations from abstract Interface Design Language (IDL) specifications.

Connectal generates stubs to support asynchronous remote method invocation from software to software, hardware to software, software to hardware, and hardware to hardware. For high-bandwidth communication, the Connectal framework provides comprehensive support for shared memory between hardware and software components, removing the repetitive work of processor bus interfacing from project tasks.

This framework is released as open software under an MIT license, making it available for use in any projects.

## Categories and Subject Descriptors

B.4.3 [**INPUT/OUTPUT AND DATA COMMUNICATIONS**]: Interconnections (subsystems)—*Interfaces; Asynchronous/synchronous operation*

## Keywords

Connectal; Design Exploration; Software

## 1. INTRODUCTION

Because they are so small and inexpensive, processors are now included in all but the smallest hardware designs. This grants flexibility to hardware designers because the non-performance-critical components can be implemented in software and the performance-critical components can be implemented in hardware. Using software for parts of the design can decrease the effort required to implement configuration and orchestration logic (for example). It can also offer hardware developers greater adaptability in meeting new project requirements or supporting additional applications.

As a system evolves through design exploration, the boundary between the software and hardware pieces can change substantially. The old paradigm of "separate hardware and software designs before the project starts" is no longer sustainable, and hardware teams are increasingly responsible for delivering significant software components.

Despite this trend, hardware engineers find themselves with surprisingly poor support for the development of the software that is so integral to their project's success. They are often required to manually develop the necessary software and hardware to connect the two environments. In the software world, this is equivalent to manually re-creating header files from the prose description of an interface implemented by a library. Such ad hoc solutions are tedious, fragile, and difficult to maintain. Without a consistent framework and toolchain for jointly managing the components of the hardware/software boundary, designers are prone to make simple errors which can be expensive to debug.

The goal of our work is to support the flexible and consistent partitioning of designs across hardware and software components. We have identified the following four goals as central to this endeavor:

- Connect software and hardware by compiling interface declarations.

- Enable concurrent access to hardware accelerators from software.

- Enable high-bandwidth sharing of system memory with hardware accelerators.

- Provide portability across platforms (CPU, OS, bus types, FPGAs).

In this paper, we present a software-driven hardware development framework called **Connectal**. Connectal consists of a fully-scripted tool-chain and a collection of libraries which can be used to develop production quality applications comprised of software components running on CPUs communicating with hardware components implemented in FPGA or ASIC.

When designing Connectal, our primary goal was to create a collection of components which are easy to use for simple implementations and which can be configured or tuned for high performance in more complicated applications. To this end, we adopted a decidedly minimalist approach, attempting to provide the smallest viable programming interface which can guarantee consistent access to shared resources in a wide range of software and hardware execution environments. Because our framework targets the implementation of performance-critical systems rather than their simulation, we have worked hard to remove any performance penalty associated with its use.

We wrote the hardware components of the Connectal libraries in Bluespec SystemVerilog[1, 2, 3] (BSV) because it enables a higher level of abstraction than the alternatives and supports parameterized types. The software components are implemented in C/C++. We chose Bluespec interfaces as the interface definition language (IDL) for Connectal's interface compiler.

This paper describes the Connectal framework, and how it can be used to flexibly move between a variety of software environments and communication models when mapping applications to platforms with connected FPGAs and CPUs.

**Paper Organization:** In Section 2, we present the running example in a number of different execution environments. In Section 3, we give an overview of the Connectal framework and its design goals. In Section 4 we discuss the details of Connectal and how it can be used to implement the example. Section 5 describes the implementation of Connectal, supported platforms, and the tool chain used to coordinate the various parts of the framework. The paper concludes with a discussion of performance metrics and related work.

## 2. ACCELERATING STRING SEARCH

The structure of a hardware/software (HW/SW) system can evolve quite dramatically to reflect changing requirements, or during design exploration. In this section, we consider several different implementations of a simple string search application [4]. Each variation represents a step in the iterative refinement process, intended to enhance performance or enable a different software execution environment.

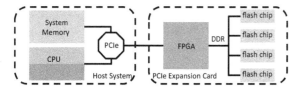

**Figure 1: Target platform for string search application**

Figure 1 shows the target platform for our example. The pertinent components of the host system are the multi-core CPU, system memory, and PCI Express (PCIe) bus. The software components of our application will be run on the CPU in a Linux environment. Connected to the host is a PCIe expansion card containing (among other things) a high-performance FPGA chip and a large array of flash memory. The FPGA board was designed as a platform to accelerate "big data" analytics by moving more processing power closer to the storage device.

## 2.1 Initial Implementation

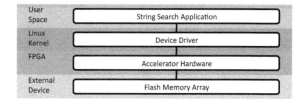

**Figure 2: Logical components of the string search system**

The design process really begins with a pure software implementation of the algorithm, but the first attempt we consider is the initial inclusion of HW acceleration shown in Figure 2. The search functionality is executed by software running in user-space which communicates with the hardware accelerator through a device driver running in the Linux kernel. The hardware accelerator, implemented in the FPGA fabric, executes searches over data stored in the flash array as directed by the software.

The FPGA has direct access to the massive flash memory array, so if we implement the search kernel in hardware, we can avoid bringing data into the CPU cache (an important consideration if we intend to run other programs simultaneously). By exploiting the high parallelism of the execution fabric as well as application aware caching of data, an FPGA implementation can outperform the same search executed on the CPU.

## 2.2 Multithreading the Software

The efficient use of flash memory requires a relatively sophisticated management strategy. Our first refinement is based on the observation that there are four distinct tasks which the application software executes (mostly) independently:

- Send search command to the hardware.

- Receive search results from the hardware.

- Send commands to the hardware to manage the flash arrays

- Receive responses from the flash management hardware

To exploit the task-level parallelism in our application, we can assign one thread to each of the four enumerated tasks. To further improve efficiency, the two threads receiving data from the hardware put themselves to sleep by calling **poll** and are woken up only when a message has been received.

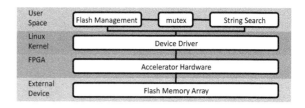

**Figure 3: Using a mutex to coordinate user-level access to hardware accelerator**

With the introduction of multithreading, we will need a synchronization mechanism to enforce coherent access to the hardware resources. Because the tasks which need coordinating are all being executed as user-space threads, the access control must be implemented in software as well. As shown in Figure 3, a mutex is used to coordinate access to the shared hardware resource between user-level processes.

## 2.3 Refining the Interfaces

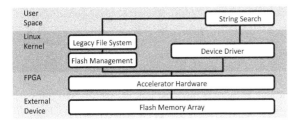

**Figure 4: Movement of functionality from user to kernel space. Software-based coordination between kernel and user processes are prohibitively expensive.**

Figure 4 shows a further refinement to our system in which we have reimplemented the Flash Management functionality as a block-device driver. Instead of directly operating on physical addresses, the string search now takes a file descriptor as input and uses a Linux system-call to retrieve the file block addresses through the file system. This refinement permits other developers to write applications which can take advantage of the accelerator without any knowledge of the internal details of the underlying storage device. It also enables support for different file systems as we now use a POSIX interface to generate physical block lists for the the storage device hardware. The problem with this refinement is that we no longer have an efficient SW mechanism to synchronize the block device driver running in kernel space with the application running in user space.

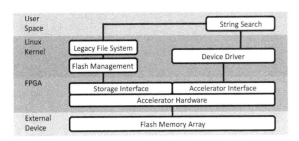

**Figure 5: Correct interface design removes the need for coordination between user and kernel threads.**

To solve to this problem (shown in Figure 5), we can remove the need for explicit SW coordination altogether by giving each thread uncontested access to its own dedicated HW resources mapped into disjoint address regions. (There will of course be implicit synchronization through the file system.)

## 2.4 Shared Access to Host Memory

In the previous implementations, all communication between hardware and software takes place through memory mapped register IO. Suppose that instead of searching for single strings, we want to search for large numbers of (potentially lengthy) strings stored in the flash array. Attempting to transfer these strings to the hardware accelerator using programmed register transfers introduces a performance bottleneck. In our final refinement, the program will allocate memory on the host system, populate it with the search strings, and pass a reference to this memory to the hardware accelerator which can then read the search strings directly from the host memory.

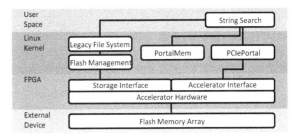

**Figure 6: Connectal support for DMA.**

Efficient high-bandwidth communication in this style requires the ability to share allocated memory regions between hardware and software processes without copying. Normally, a programmer would simply call application space **malloc**, but this does not provide a buffer that can be shared with hardware or other software processes. As shown in Figure 6, a special-purpose memory allocator has been implemented in Linux, using dmabuf[5] to provide reference counted sharing of memory buffers across user processes and hardware.

To conclude, we consider how the HW/SW interface changed to accommodate each step in the refinement process: The hardware interface required by the design in Figure 2 is relatively simple. Command/response queues in the hardware accelerator are exposed using a register interface with accompanying "empty"/"full" signals. To support the use of **poll** by the refinement in Figure 3, interrupt signals must be added to the hardware interface and connected to the Linux kernel. Partitioning the address space as required by the refinement in Figure 5 necessitates a consistent remapping of registers in both hardware and software.

## 3. THE CONNECTAL FRAMEWORK

In and of themselves, none of the HW/SW interfaces considered in Section 2 are particularly complex. On the other hand, implementing the complete set and maintaining correctness as the application evolves is a considerable amount of care, requiring deep understanding of both the application and the platform. The Connectal framework is a collection of tools and library components which was designed to address these challenges with the following features:

- Easy declaration and invocation of remote methods between application components running on the host or in the FPGA.

- Direct user-mode access to hardware accelerators from software.

- High performance read and write bus master access to system memory from the FPGA

- Infrastructure for sharing full speed memory port access between an arbitrary number of clients in the FPGA fabric

- Portability across platforms using different CPUs, buses, operating systems, and FPGAs

- Fully integrated tool-chain support for dependency builds and device configuration.

In this section, we introduce the Connectal framework through a discussion of its prominent features.

## 3.1 Portals

Connectal implements remote method invocation between application components using asynchronous messaging. The message and channel types are application specific, requiring the user to define the HW/SW interface using BSV interfaces as the interface definition language (IDL). These interfaces declare logical groups of unidirectional "send" methods, each of which is implemented as a FIFO channel by the Connectal interface compiler; all channels corresponding to a single BSV interface are grouped together into a single **portal**.

From the interface specification, the Connectal interface compiler generates code for marshalling the arguments of a method into a message to be sent and unmarshaling values from a received message. It generates a *proxy* to be invoked on the sending side and a *wrapper* that invokes the appropriate method on the receiving side. Platform specific libraries are used to connect the proxies and wrappers to the communication fabric.

In the hardware, each portal is assigned a disjoint address range. On the host, Connectal assigns each portal a unique Linux device (/dev/portal⟨n⟩) which is accessed by the application software using the generated wrappers and proxies. An application can partition methods across several portals, to control access to the interfaces by specific hardware or software modules. To support bi-directional communication, at least two portals are required: one which allows software to "invoke" hardware, and another for hardware to "invoke" software. Each portal may be accessed by different threads, processes, or directly from the kernel.

## 3.2 Direct user-mode access to hardware

We designed Connectal to provide direct access to accelerators from user-mode programs in order to eliminate the need for device-drivers specific to each accelerator. We have implemented a kernel module for both X86 and ARM architectures with a minimal set of functionality: the driver implements **mmap** to map hardware registers into user space and **poll** to enable applications to suspend a thread waiting for interrupts originating from the hardware accelerators. These two pieces of functionality have been defined to be completely generic; no modification is required to kernel drivers as the HW/SW interface evolves. All knowledge of the interface register semantics (and corresponding changes) is encoded by the interface compiler in the generated proxies and wrappers which are compiled as part of the application and executed in user-mode.

This approach is known as user-space device drivers [6, 7] and has a number of distinct advantages over traditional kernel modules. To begin with, it reduces the number of components that need to be modified if the HW/SW interface changes, and eliminates the need for device-driver development expertise in many cases. Secondly, after the hardware registers have been mapped into user address space, the need for software to switch between user and kernel mode is all but eliminated since all "driver" functionality is being executed in user-space.

## 3.3 Shared Access to Host Memory

Connectal generates a hardware FIFO corresponding to each method in the portal interface, and the software reads and writes these FIFOs under certain conditions. To improve throughput, Connectal libraries also support credit-based flow-control. Though credit-based flow-control with interrupts is more efficient than polling status registers from software, there is often the need for much higher bandwidth communication between the hardware and software.

Hardware accelerators often communicate with the application through direct access to shared memory. An important feature of Connectal is a flexible, high performance API for allocating and sharing such memory, and support for reading and writing this memory from hardware and software. The Connectal framework implements this through the combination of a Linux kernel driver, C++ libraries, and BSV modules for the FPGA. We implemented a custom kernel memory allocator for Connectal, **portalmem**, using the kernel dmabuf support. Any solution which allocates and shares memory between hardware and software must meet two high-level requirements:

- Allocated buffers must have reference counts to prevent memory leaks.

- Efficient mechanisms must be provided to share the location of allocated regions.

Using the portalmem driver, programs can allocate regions of system memory (DRAM) and map it into their own virtual address space. Reference-counted access to shared memory regions allocated using portalmem can be granted to other SW processes by transmitting the file descriptor for the allocated region. Reference counting has been implemented in the driver so that once an allocated memory region has been dereferenced by all SW and HW processes, it will be deallocated and returned to the kernel free memory pool.

Simple hardware accelerators often require contiguous physical addresses. Unfortunately, when allocating memory from a shared pool in a running system, obtaining large areas of contiguous memory is often problematic, limiting the size of the region that can be allocated. To support indexed access to non-contiguous memory aggregates, Connectal provides address translation support to hardware accelerators in the FPGA, similar to the MMU functionality on the CPU side.

## 3.4 Distributed Access to Memory Ports

When building accelerators for an algorithm, multiple parameters are often accessed directly from system memory using DMA. As the hardware implementation is parallelized, multiple accesses to each parameter may be required. In these cases, the number of memory clients in the application hardware usually exceeds the number of host memory ports. Sharing these ports requires substantial effort, and scaling up a memory interconnect while maximizing throughput and clock speed is extremely challenging.

To support this common design pattern, the Connectal framework provides provides a portable, scalable, high performance library that applications can use to to facilitate the efficient sharing of host memory ports. This library is implemented as parameterized Bluespec modules which allow the user to easily configure high-performance memory access trees, supporting both reading and writing.

## 3.5 Platform Portability

We structured Connectal to improve the portability of applications across CPU types, operating systems, FPGAs, and how the CPU and FPGA are connected. The software and hardware libraries are largely platform independent. As a result, applications implemented in the framework can be compiled to run on the range of different platforms.

Supported platforms are shown in Figure 7. Application software can be executed on x86 and ARM CPUs running either Ubuntu or Android operating systems. A range of different Xilinx FPGAs can be connected to the CPU and system memory via PCI Express or AXI. The BSV simulator (Bluesim) can be used in place of actual FPGA hardware for debugging purposes.

When the target application needs to interact with other Linux kernel resources (for example, a block device or a network interface), the application may run in kernel mode with the logic run either in an FPGA or in Bluesim.

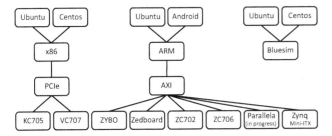

**Figure 7: Platforms supported by Connectal**

## 4. IMPLEMENTING STRING SEARCH

Having covered the features of the Connectal at a high level, we now explain more specifically how the framework can be applied to implement the refinements outlined in Section 2.

### 4.1 Initial Implementation

The FPGA is connected to the host system with a PCIe bus, and to the memory array with wires. In addition to implementing a search kernel, the hardware accelerator must communicate with the software components and with the flash chips. Communication with the software takes place through portals, whose interface declaration is given below:

```
interface StrstrRequest;
    method Action setupNeedle(Bit#(8) needleChars);
    method Action search(Bit#(32) haystackPtr,
                         Bit#(32) haystackLen);
endinterface
interface StrstrIndication;
    method Action searchResult(Int#(32) v);
    method Action setupComplete();
endinterface
```

The hardware implements the StrstrRequest interface, which the software invokes (remotely) to specify the search string and the location in flash memory to search. The software implements the StrstrIndication interface, which the hardware invokes (remotely) to notify the software of configuration completion or search results. The interface compiler generates a separate portal for each of these interfaces. Within each portal, a dedicated unidirectional FIFO is assigned to each logical interface method.

In our initial implementation the accelerator does not access system memory directly, so the search string is transmitted to the accelerator one character at a time via the `setupNeedle` method. We will see in Section 4.3 how to use a pointer to system memory instead.

### 4.1.1 Invoking Hardware from Software

Because the StrStrRequest functionality is implemented in hardware, the Connectal interface compiler generates a C++ **proxy** with the following interface to be invoked by the application software:

```
class StrStrRequestProxy : public Portal {
public:
    void setupNeedle(uint32_t needleChars);
    void search(uint32_t haystackPtr,
                uint32_t haystackLen);
};
```

The implementation of StrStrRequestProxy marshals the arguments of each method and en-queues them directly into their dedicated hardware FIFOs. To execute searches in the FPGA fabric over data stored in flash memory, the software developer simply instantiates **StrStrRequestProxy** and invokes its methods:

```
StrStrRequestProxy *proxy =
            new StrStrRequestProxy(...);
proxy->search(haystackPtr, haystackLen);
```

On the FPGA, the user implements the application logic as a BSV module with the StrStrRequest interface. A **wrapper** is generated by the interface compiler to connect this module to the hardware FIFOs. The wrapper unmarshals messages that it receives and then invokes the appropriate method in the StrStrRequest interface. Here is the BSV code that instantiates the generated wrapper and connects it to the user's `mkStrStr` module.

```
StrStrRequest strStr <- mkStrStr(...);
StrStrRequestWrapper wrapper <-
        mkStrStrRequestWrapper(strStr);
```

Figure 8 shows how all the pieces of an application implemented using Connectal work together when hardware functionality is invoked remotely from software. Direct access to the memory mapped hardware FIFOs by the generated proxy running in user-mode is key to the efficiency of our implementation strategy.

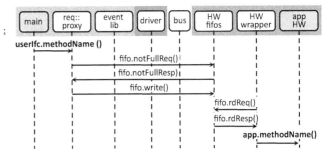

**Figure 8: SW invokes HW: 'main' and 'app HW' are implemented by the user.**

### 4.1.2 Invoking Software from Hardware

Invoking software from hardware takes a slightly different form, due primarily to the fact that "main" is still owned by software. Since the direction of the remote invocation is reversed, the proxy on this path will be instantiated on the FPGA and the wrapper instantiated on host side. The user implements the StrStrResponse interface in software and connects it to the generated wrapper using C++ subclasses:

```
class StrStrResponse:
  public StrStrResponseWrapper {
    ...
    void searchResult(int32_t v) {...}
}
```

The StrStrResponseWrapper constructor registers a pointer to the object with the event library which keeps track of all instantiated software wrappers. The wrapper implementation unmarshals messages sent through the hardware FIFOs and invokes the appropriate subclass interface method. To activate this path, main simply instantiates the response implementation and invokes the library event handler:

```
StrStrResponse *response =
  new StrStrResponse(...);
while(1)
  portalExec_event();
```

On the invocation side, the interface compiler generates a proxy which the application logic instantiates and invokes directly:

```
StrStrResponseProxy proxy <-
    mkStrStrRequestProxy();
StrStrRequest strStr <-
    mkStrStr(... proxy.ifc ...);
```

Figure 9 shows how all the pieces of an application collaborate when software functionality is being invoked from hardware.

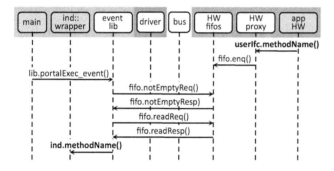

**Figure 9: HW invokes SW: 'main', 'ind::wrapper', and 'app HW' are implemented by the user.**

The simplest software execution environment for the string search accelerator is to have a single thread making requests and waiting for responses as follows:

```
void search(char *str){
  StrStrRequestProxy *req =
    new StrStrRequestProxy(...);
  StrStrResponse *resp =
    new StrStrResponse(...);
  while (char c = *str++)
    req->setupNeedle(c);
  // start search
  req->search(...);
```

```
  // handle responses from the HW
  while(1)
    portalExec_event();
}
```

The call to portalExec_event() checks for a response from HW. If there is a pending response, it invokes the method corresponding to that FIFO in the wrapper class. This generated method reads out a complete message from the FIFO and unmarshals it before invoking the user-defined call-back function, which in this case would be **StrStrResponse::searchResult**.

### 4.1.3 Connecting To Flash

On our target platform, the flash memory array is connected directly to the FPGA chip, and DDR signals are used to read/write/erase flash memory cells. The RTL required to communicate with the memory requires some commonly used functionality, such as *SerDes* and DDR controllers, both of which are included in the BSV libraries distributed as part of the Connectal framework.

## 4.2 Multithreading The Software

In many cases, we would like to avoid a hardware-to-software path which requires the software to poll a hardware register on the other side of a bus for relatively infrequent events. To accommodate this, the Connectal framework generates interrupts which are raised when hardware invokes software interface methods. The generic Connectal driver connects these signals to the Linux kernel and the software wrappers can exploit then by calling poll. Connectal applications often use a separate thread to execute hardware-to-software asynchronous invocations, since dedicated thread can put itself to sleep until the hardware raises an interrupt. The "main" thread is free to do other work and can communicate with the "indication" thread using a semaphore as shown below:

```
class StrStrResponse:
    public StrStrResponseWrapper {
  sem_t sem;
  int v;
  void searchResult(int32_t v) {
    this->response = v;
    sem_post(&sem);
  }
  void waitResponse(){sem_wait(&sem);}
};
StrStrResponse *resp;
StrStrRequestProxy *req;
int search(char *str){
  while (char c = *str++)
    req->setupNeedle(c);
  // start search
  req->search(...);
  // wait for response
  resp->waitResponse();
  // return result
  return resp->v;
}
```

The polling thread is started by a call to **portalExec_start()**, which ultimately invokes the **portalExec_poll()** function implemented in the Connectal event library. **portalExec_poll()** invokes the system call **poll** on the FDs corresponding to all the indication or response portals, putting itself to sleep. When an interface method is invoked in the hardware proxy, an interrupt is raised, waking the indication thread. A register is read which indicates which method is being called and the corresponding wrapper method is invoked to read-/marshal the arguments and invoke the actual user-defined methods. Figure 10 shows this process.

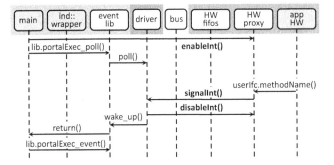

**Figure 10: HW invokes SW using interrupts**

Multithreading often leads to simultaneous access to shared hardware resources. If a software solution to protect these resources (such as mutex) is not available, the hardware interface can be refactored into separate portals, one for each control thread.

Each interface will generate a separate Portal which is assigned its own address space and Linux device. Using Linux devices in this way enables access control restrictions to be specified individually for each portal. This feature can be used to grant different users or processes exclusive access and prevent unauthorized access to specific pieces of hardware functionality.

## 4.3 Shared Access to Host Memory

In the first three refinements presented in Section 2, all communication between hardware and software takes place through register-mapped IO. The final refinement in Section 2.4 is to grant hardware and software shared access to host memory. The interface to the search accelerator shown below has been updated to use direct access to system memory for the search strings:

```
interface StrstrRequest;
  method Action setup(Bit#(32) needlePtr,
                      Bit#(32) mpNextPtr,
                      Bit#(32) needleLen);
  method Action search(Bit#(32) haystackPtr,
                       Bit#(32) haystackLen,
                       Bit#(32) iterCount);
endinterface
interface StrstrIndication;
  method Action searchResult(Int#(32) v);
  method Action setupComplete();
endinterface
```

In order to share memory with hardware accelerators, it needs to be allocated using `portalAlloc`. Here is the search function updated accordingly:

```
int search(char *str){
  int size = strlen(str)+1;
  int fd = portalAlloc(size);
  char *sharedStr = portalMmap(fd, size);
  strcpy(sharedStr, str);
  // send a DMA reference to the search pattern
  req->needle(dma->reference(fd), size);
  // start search
  req->search(...);
  resp->waitResponse();
  ... unmap and free the string
  return resp->v;
}
```

The application allocates shared memory via `portalAlloc`, which returns a file descriptor, and then passes that file descriptor to `mmap`, which maps the physical pages into the application's address space. The file descriptor corresponds to a dmabuf[5], which is a standard Linux kernel mechanism.

To share that memory with the accelerator, the application calls `reference`, which sends a logical to physical address mapping to the hardware's address translator. The call to `reference` returns a handle, which the application sends to the accelerator. Connectal's BSV libraries for DMA enable the accelerator to read or write from offsets to these handles, taking care of address translation transparently.

To fully exploit the data parallelism, `mkStrStr` partitions the search space into $p$ partitions. It instantiates two memory read trees from the Connectal library (`MemreadEngineV`, discussed in Section 3.4), each with $p$ read servers. One set is used by the search kernels to read the configuration data from the host memory, while the other is used to read the "haystack" from flash.

On supported platforms such as Zynq which provide multiple physical master connections to system memory, Connectal interleaves DMA requests over the parallel links. It does this on a per-read-client basis, rather than a per-request basis.

## 4.4 Alternate Portal Implementations

Connectal separates the generation of code for marshalling and unmarshaling method arguments from the transport mechanism used to transmit the messages. This separation enables "swappable" application-specific transport libraries. In light of this, a large number of transport mechanism can be considered. Switching between mechanism requires a simple directive in the project Makefile (more details are given in Section 5).

By default, each portal is mapped to a region of address space and a memory-mapped FIFO channel is generated for each method. Though software access to all FIFO channels in a design may occur through single bus slave interface, Connectal libraries implement their multiplexing to ensure that each FIFO is independent, allowing concurrent access to different methods from multiple threads or processes.

The default portal library implements the method FIFOs in the hardware accelerator. This provides the lowest latency path between hardware and software, taking about 1 microsecond to send a message. If higher bandwidth or transaction rates are needed, FIFOs implemented as a ring buffer in DRAM can be used instead. This requires more instructions per message send and receive, but may achieve higher throughput between the CPU and hardware.

During the design exploration process, a component originally implemented on the FPGA may migrate to software running on the host processor. Remote invocations which were originally from software to hardware must be recast as software to software. Without changing the IDL specification, the transport mechanism assigned to a portal can be re-specified to implement communication between software components running either on the same host or across a network.

Connectal uses UNIX sockets or shared memory to transport messages between the application software components or the hardware simulator. In other situations, TCP or UDP can be used to transport the messages to hardware running on another machine. Viable connections to the FPGA board range from low-speed interconnects such as JTAG, SPI, to higher-speed interconnects such as USB or Aurora over multi-gigabit per second transceivers.

## 5. WORKFLOW USING CONNECTAL

In this section, we give an overview of the Connectal workflow and toolchain. The complete toolchain, libraries, and many running examples may be obtained at *www.connectal.org* or by emailing *connectal@googlegroups.com.*

### 5.1 Top level structure of Connectal applications

The simplest Connectal application consists of 4 files:

**Makefile** The top-level Makefile defines parameters for the entire application build process. In its simplest form, it specifies which Bluespec interfaces to use as portals, the hardware and software source files, and the libraries to use for the hardware and software compilation.

**Application Hardware** Connectal applications typically have at least one BSV file containing declarations of the interfaces being exposed as portals, along with the implementation of the application hardware itself.

**Top.bsv** In this file, the developer instantiates the application hardware modules, connecting them to the generated wrappers and proxies for the portals exported to software. To connect to the host processor bus, a parameterized standard interface is used, making it easy to synthesize the application for different CPUs or for simulation. If CPU specific interface signals are needed by the design (for example, extra clocks that are generated by the PCIe core), then an optional CPU-specific interface can also be used.

If the design uses multiple clock domains or additional pins on the FPGA, those connections are also made here by exporting a 'Pins' interface. The Bluespec compiler generates a Verilog module from the top level BSV module, in which the methods of exposed interfaces are implemented as Verilog ports. Those ports are associated to physical pins on the FPGA using a physical constraints file.

**Application CPP** The software portion of a Connectal application generally consists of at least one C++ file, which instantiates the generated software portal wrapper and proxies. The application software is also responsible for implementing main.

### 5.2 Development cycle

After creating or editing the source code for the application, the development cycle consists of four steps: generating makefiles, compiling the interface, building the application, and running the application.

**Generating Makefiles** Given the parameters specified in the application Makefile and a platform target specified at the command line, Connectal generates a target-specific Makefile to control the build process. This Makefile contains the complete dependency information for the generation of wrappers/proxies, the use of these wrappers/proxies in compiling both the software and hardware, and the collection of build artifacts into

a package that can be either run locally or over a network to a remote 'device under test' machine.

**Compiling the Interface** The Connectal interface compiler generates the C++ and BSV files to implement wrappers and proxies for all interfaces specified in the application Makefile. Human readable **JSON** is used as an intermediate representation of portal interfaces, exposing a useful debugging window as well as a path for future support of additional languages and IDLs.

**Building the Application** A target in the generated Makefile invokes GCC to compiler the software components of the application. The Bluespec compiler (bsc) is then invoked to compiler the hardware components to Verilog. A parameterized Tcl scripts is used to drive Vivado to build the Xilinx FPGA configuration bitstream for the design.

A Connectal utility called *fpgamake* supports specification of which Bluespec and Verilog modules should be compiled to separate netlists and to enable separate place and route of those netlists given a floor plan. Separate synthesis and floor planning in this manner can reduce build times, and to make it easier to meet timing constraints.

Another Connectal utility called *buildcache* speeds recompilation by caching previous compilation results and detecting cases where input files have not changed. Although similar to the better-known utility *ccache*, this program has no specific knowledge of the tools being executed, allowing it to be integrated into any workflow and any tool set. This utility uses the system call **strace** to track which files are read and written by each build step, computing an 'input signature' of the MD5 checksum for each of these files. When the input signature matches, the output files are just refreshed from the cache, avoiding the long synthesis times for the unchanged portions of the project.

**Running the Application** As part of our goal to have a fully scripted design flow, the generated Makefile includes a **run** target that will program the FPGA and launch the specified application or test bench. In order to support shared target hardware resources, the developer can direct the run to a particular machines, which can be accessed over the network. For Ubuntu target machines, ssh is used to copy/run the application. For Android target machines, 'adb' is used.

### 5.3 Continuous Integration and Debug Support

Connectal provides a fully scripted flow in order to make it easy to automate the building and running of applications for continuous integration. Our development team builds and runs large collections of tests whenever the source code repository is updated.

Connectal also provides trace ring buffers in hardware and analysis software to trace and display the last transactions on the PCIe or AXI memory bus. This trace is useful when debugging performance or correctness problems, answering questions of the form:

- What were the last memory requests and responses?

- What was the timing of the last memory request and responses?

| | KC705 | VC707 | ZYBO | Zedboard | ZC702 | ZC706 | Parallel | Mini-ITX |
|---|---|---|---|---|---|---|---|---|
| HW → SW | 3 | 3 | X | 0.80 | 0.80 | 0.65 | X | 0.65 |
| SW → HW | 5 | 5 | X | 1.50 | 1.50 | 1.10 | X | 1.10 |

Figure 11: Latency ($\mu$s) of communication through portals on supported platforms

- What were the last hardware method invocations or indications?

# 6. PERFORMANCE OF GENERATED SYSTEMS

A framework is only useful if it reduces the effort required by developers to achieve the desired performance objective. Trying to gauge the relative effort is difficult since the authors implemented both the framework and the running example. On PCIE-based platforms we were able to reduce the time required to search for a fixed set of strings in a large corpus by an order of magnitude after integrating hardware acceleration using Connectal. Performance improvements on the Zynq-based platforms was even greater due to the relative processing power of the ARM CPU and scaled with the number of bus master interfaced used for DMA. In the Connectal framework, developing these applications took very little time.

## 6.1 Performance of Portals

The current implementation of HW/SW **portal** transfers 32 bits per FPGA clock cycle. Our example designs run at 100MHz to 250MHz, depending on the complexity of the design and the speed grade of the FPGA used. Due to their intended use, the important performance metric of Portals is latency. These values are given in Figure 11.

The Xilinx KC705 and VC707 boards connect to x86 CPUs and system memory via PCIe gen1. The default FPGA clock for those boards is 125MHz. The other platforms use AXI to connect the programmable logic to the quad-core ARM Cortex A9 and system memory. The ZYBO, Zedboard and ZC702 use a slower speed grade part on which our designs run at 100MHz. The ZC706 and Mini-ITX use a faster part on which many of our designs run at 200MHz. The lower latency measured on the ZC706 reflects the higher clock speed of the latency performance test.

## 6.2 Performance of Reads/Writes of System Memory

For high bandwidth transfers, we assume the developer will have the application hardware read or write system memory directly. Direct access to memory enables transfers with longer bursts, reducing memory bus protocol overhead. The framework supports transfer widths of 32 to 128 bits per cycle, depending on the interconnect used.

Our goal in the design of the library components used to read and write system memory is to ensure that a developer's application can use all bandwidth available to the FPGA when accessing system memory. DMA Bandwidth on supported platforms is listed in Figure12.

On PCIe systems, Connectal currently supports 8 lane PCIe gen1. We've measured 1.4 gigabytes per second for both reads and writes. Maximum throughput of 8 lane PCIe

| | KC705 | VC707 | ZYBO | Zedboard | ZC702 | ZC706 | Parallel | Mini-ITX |
|---|---|---|---|---|---|---|---|---|
| Read | 1.4 | 1.4 | X | 0.8 | 0.8 | 1.6 | X | 1.6 |
| Write | 1.4 | 1.4 | X | 0.8 | 0.8 | 1.6 | X | 1.6 |

Figure 12: Maximum bandwidth (GB/s) between FPGA and host memory using Connectal RTL libraries on supported platforms

gen1 is 1.8GB/s, taking into account 1 header transaction per 8 data transactions, where 8 is the maximum number of data transactions per request supported by our server's chipset. The current version of the test needs some more tuning in order to reach the full bandwidth available. In addition, we are in the process of updating to 8 lane PCIe gen2 using newer Xilinx cores.

Zynq systems have four "high performance" ports for accessing system memory. Connectal enables an accelerator to use all four. In our experiments, we have been able to achieve 3.6x higher bandwidth using 4 ports than using 1 port.

# 7. RELATED WORK

A number of research projects, such as Lime [8], BCL [9], HThreads [10], and CatapaultC [11] (to name just a few) bridge the software/hardware development gap by providing a single language for developing both the software and hardware components of the design. In addition, Altera and Xilinx have both implemented OpenCL [12] on FPGAs [13, 14] in an attempt to attract GPU programmers.

The computation model of software differs significantly from that of hardware, and so far none of the unified language approaches deliver the same performance as languages designed specifically for hardware or software. Connectal is intended to be used for the design of performance-critical systems. In this context we think that designers prefer a mix of languages specifically designed for their respective implementation contexts.

Infrastructures such as LEAP [15], Rainbow [16], and OmpSs [17] (to name just a few) use resource abstraction to enable FPGA development. We found that in their intended context, these tools were easy to use but that performance tuning in applications not foreseen by the infrastructure developers was problematic.

Some projects such as TMD-MPI [18], VFORCE/ VSIPL++ [19], and GASNet/GAScore [20] target only the hardware software interface. These tools provide message passing capabilities, but rely on purely operational semantics to describe the HW/SW interface. Apart from the implementation details, Connectal distinguishes itself by using an IDL to enforce denotational interface semantics.

UIO [7] is a user-space device driver framework for Linux. It is very similar to the Connectal's portal device driver, but it does not provide a solution to multiple device nodes per hardware device. The portal driver provides this so that different interfaces of a design may be accessed independently, providing process boundary protection, thread safety, and the ability for user processes and the kernel both to access the hardware device.

## 8.  CONCLUSION

Connectal bridges the gap between software and hardware development, enabling developers to create integrated solutions rapidly. With Connectal, we take a pragmatic approach to software and hardware development in which we try to avoid any dependence on proposed solutions to open research problems.

Use of Connectal's interface compiler ensures that software and hardware remain consistent and make it easy to update the hardware/software boundary as needed in a variety of execution contexts. The generated portals permit concurrent and low-latency access to the accelerator and enable different processes or the kernel to have safe isolated access through dedicated interfaces. Support for sharing memory between software and hardware makes it easy to achieve high transfer speeds between the two environments.

Connectal supports Linux and Android operating systems running on x86 and ARM CPUs. It currently supports Xilinx FPGAs and runs on the full range of Xilinx Series 7 devices. Our fully-scripted development process enables the use of continuous integration of software and hardware development. Integrating software development early makes it easier to ensure that the complete solution actually meets design targets and customer requirements.

## 9.  REFERENCES

[1] Bluespec Inc., http://www.bluespec.com.

[2] J. C. Hoe, "Operation-Centric Hardware Description and Synthesis," Ph.D. dissertation, MIT, Cambridge, MA, 2000.

[3] J. C. Hoe and Arvind, "Operation-Centric Hardware Description and Synthesis," *IEEE TRANSACTIONS on Computer-Aided Design of Integrated Circuits and Systems*, vol. 23, no. 9, September 2004.

[4] Z. G. Alberto Apostolico, *Pattern Matching Algorithms*, 1997, ch. 1, pp. 7–11, mp algorithm.

[5] S. Semwal, "DMA Buffer Sharing API Guide," https://www.kernel.org/doc/Documentation/dma-buf-sharing.txt.

[6] Y. A. Khalidi and M. N. Thadani, "An Efficient Zero-Copy I/O Framework for UNIX," Mountain View, CA, USA, Tech. Rep., 1995.

[7] "The Userspace I/O HOWTO," https://www.kernel.org/doc/htmldocs/uio-howto/index.html.

[8] S. S. Huang, A. Hormati, D. F. Bacon, and R. Rabbah, "Liquid metal: Object-oriented programming across the hardware/software boundary," in *ECOOP '08: Proceedings of the 22nd European conference on Object-Oriented Programming*, Berlin, Heidelberg, 2008.

[9] M. King, N. Dave, and Arvind, "Automatic generation of hardware/software interfaces," in *Proceedings of the Seventeenth International Conference on Architectural Support for Programming Languages and Operating Systems*, ser. ASPLOS XVII.  New York, NY, USA: ACM, 2012, pp. 325–336. [Online]. Available: http://doi.acm.org/10.1145/2150976.2151011

[10] W. Peck, E. K. Anderson, J. Agron, J. Stevens, F. Baijot, and D. L. Andrews, "Hthreads: A computational model for reconfigurable devices," in *Proceedings of the 2006 International Conference on Field Programmable Logic and Applications (FPL)*, *Madrid, Spain, August 28-30, 2006*, 2006, pp. 1–4. [Online]. Available: http://doi.ieeecomputersociety.org/10.1109/FPL.2006.311336

[11] Mentor Graphics, "Catapult-C," http://www.mentor.com/products/esl/.

[12] The Kronos Group, https://www.khronos.org/registry/cl/.

[13] Altera Inc., http://www.altera.com/products/software/opencl/opencl-index.html.

[14] Xilinx Inc., http://www.xilinx.com.

[15] K. Fleming, H. Yang, M. Adler, and J. S. Emer, "The LEAP FPGA operating system," in *24th International Conference on Field Programmable Logic and Applications, FPL 2014, Munich, Germany, 2-4 September, 2014*, 2014, pp. 1–8. [Online]. Available: http://dx.doi.org/10.1109/FPL.2014.6927488

[16] K. Jozwik, S. Honda, M. Edahiro, H. Tomiyama, and H. Takada, "Rainbow: An operating system for software-hardware multitasking on dynamically partially reconfigurable fpgas," *Int. J. Reconfig. Comp.*, vol. 2013, 2013. [Online]. Available: http://dx.doi.org/10.1155/2013/789134

[17] A. Filgueras, E. Gil, D. Jiménez-González, C. Alvarez, X. Martorell, J. Langer, J. Noguera, and K. A. Vissers, "Ompss@zynq all-programmable soc ecosystem," in *The 2014 ACM/SIGDA International Symposium on Field-Programmable Gate Arrays, FPGA '14, Monterey, CA, USA - February 26 - 28, 2014*, 2014, pp. 137–146. [Online]. Available: http://doi.acm.org/10.1145/2554688.2554777

[18] M. Saldaña, A. Patel, C. A. Madill, D. Nunes, D. Wang, P. Chow, R. Wittig, H. Styles, and A. Putnam, "MPI as a programming model for high-performance reconfigurable computers," *TRETS*, vol. 3, no. 4, p. 22, 2010. [Online]. Available: http://doi.acm.org/10.1145/1862648.1862652

[19] N. Moore, M. Leeser, and L. A. S. King, "Vforce: An environment for portable applications on high performance systems with accelerators," *J. Parallel Distrib. Comput.*, vol. 72, no. 9, pp. 1144–1156, 2012. [Online]. Available: http://dx.doi.org/10.1016/j.jpdc.2011.07.014

[20] R. Willenberg and P. Chow, "A remote memory access infrastructure for global address space programming models in fpgas," in *The 2013 ACM/SIGDA International Symposium on Field Programmable Gate Arrays, FPGA '13, Monterey, CA, USA, February 11-13, 2013*, 2013, pp. 211–220. [Online]. Available: http://doi.acm.org/10.1145/2435264.2435301

# InTime: A Machine Learning Approach for Efficient Selection of FPGA CAD Tool Parameters

Nachiket Kapre
Nanyang Technological University
Singapore
nachiket@ieee.org

Harnhua Ng, Kirvy Teo, Jaco Naude
Plunify Inc.
Singapore
harnhua@plunify.com

## ABSTRACT

FPGA CAD tool parameters controlling synthesis optimizations, place and route effort, mapping criteria along with user-supplied physical constraints can affect timing results of the circuit by as much as 70% without any change in original source code. A correct selection of these parameters across a diverse set of benchmarks with varying characteristics and design goals is challenging. The sheer number of parameters and option values that can be selected is large (thousands of combinations for modern CAD tools) with often conflicting interactions. In this paper, we present InTime, a machine-learning approach supported by a cloud-based (or cluster-based) compilation infrastructure for automating the selection of these parameters effectively to minimize timing costs. InTime builds a database of results from a series of preliminary runs based on canned configurations of CAD options. It then learns from these runs to predict the next series of CAD tool options to improve timing results. Towards the end, we rely on a limited degree of statistical sampling of certain options like placer and synthesis seeds to further tighten results. Using our approach, we show 70% reduction in final timing results across industrial benchmark problems for the Altera CAD flow. This is 30% better than vendor-supplied design space exploration tools that attempts a similar optimization using canned heuristics.

## Categories and Subject Descriptors

B.5.2 [**Design Aids**]: [Automatic Synthesis]; I.2.6 [**Learning**]: [Parameter Learning]

## General Terms

FPGA CAD, Machine Learning, Tools

## 1. INTRODUCTION

Modern FPGA backend CAD tools compile behavioral and structural descriptions of circuits in Verilog/VHDL down

to executable FPGA bitstreams. However, they are hard to configure correctly to satisfy intended design constraints. These CAD tools implement heuristics that tend to generally produce usable results, but often require careful configuration and setup to give you the desired QoR (quality of result). Designers today rely on ad-hoc tuning techniques based on intuition that is derived from years of experience. Intelligent tools like vendor-supplied design space exploration scripts attempt to guide the CAD process using vendor knowledge of the architecture-CAD interaction but fail to capture the full range of possibilities. Using the InTime framework, we hope to uncover the fundamental principles behind the selection of CAD tool options (called parameters in this paper) and deliver high-speed FPGA designs reliably across different circuit characteristics.

It is generally accepted that transformations at synthesis stage (high-level synthesis or RTL-level) have the maximum impact on circuit properties such as speed and area. However, verified RTL designs are often considered off-limits for optimization, particularly at late stages of the design process, to minimize risks of inserting functional errors in the design. This leaves us with the backend CAD flow as the only alternative for tuning and optimization. The control of the CAD flow is dictated to some extent by hard constraints such as pin location constraints, timing targets, and clock network choices, among others that are fixed. Beyond these fixed parameters, the correct setup and configuration of CAD tool parameters still requires managing a large space of possible option choices. Typically, designers will attempt to generate better QoR by varying placement and synthesis seeds. This is a scatter-shot approach that ignores the interactions with many other CAD tool parameters. Additionally, designers manage the CAD tool parameter selection complexity by heuristically making choices based on experience or intuition. CAD tools are often fussy and behave unpredictably when parameters are chosen incorrectly leading to wastage of designer effort. In most cases, the parameter choices are a tradeoff that can have unpredictable effects on an overall figure of merit. The correct selection of these parameters can give us freedom required to deliver better result quality without modifying RTL.

The key challenge in managing the fruitful operation of the FPGA backend CAD tools is addressing the magnitude of **parameter** choice combinations and automation of the search. Considering these effects, we may be tempted to consider a Monte-Carlo sampling based exploration of possible parameter combinations as a mechanism for achieving a high quality answer. We know this is not feasible due to

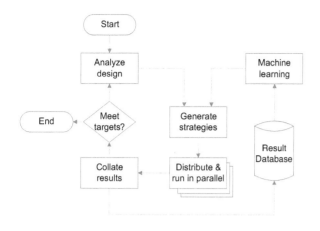

Figure 1: InTime Flow Diagram

long design times even for a single design instance which can take hours to days for large FPGAs. In this paper, we introduce a smarter, machine learning and cloud computing based approach for performing a series of CAD tool runs to determine an ideal combination of parameters to consider. This avoids the need for large-scale exploration while allowing us to reach close to the ideal answer with as few runs as possible.

The key contributions of this paper are:

- Development and design of machine learning and cloud computing infrastructure for FPGA CAD to deliver timing closure for industrial designs.

- Measuring and quantifying the quality and time gap between InTime and vendor-supplied design space exploration tools.

- Development and quantification of the benefits of a machine learning algorithm that identifies correlations between CAD tool parameters and solution quality.

## 2. THE INTIME FLOW

The problem of compiling circuits to FPGAs is a challenging problem that is managed by decomposing the compilation process into a series of sequential CAD stages *e.g.* synthesis, technology mapping, placement, routing. Each stage is typically an NP-complete problem and is associated with a *tunable heuristic*. Decisions made at each stage affect the quality of the solution by restricting/enhancing choice in the downstream stages. Furthermore, some of these heuristics use randomness that can add non-determinism in the solution if the user is careless with seeds. Circuit designers often spend weeks of design effort optimizing their circuit and to meet timing. If the correct set of compiler options are known in advance or discovered quickly, this tedious process can be eliminated and source code can stay unchanged. In this section we introduce InTime and discuss how it operates.

**What is InTime?**: To an FPGA developer, InTime is a plugin to the FPGA CAD flow that selects and tunes CAD tool parameters on behalf of the designer. After RTL verification, designers will often manually run their projects through different compiler parameters to see if performance

can be optimized. Sometimes this struggle to meet timing requires weeks of expensive designer time which can be better spent elsewhere in the design stack. While RTL redesign may be necessary for critical timing failures, in many cases, with experienced developers, the RTL design is sufficiently well-pipelined and organized. Simply relying on placement and synthesis SEEDs for exploring the design space only yields 5–10% variation in the timing results. However, EFFORT_LEVEL also introduces non-trivial randomness into the results, particularly for the Arria devices. In these instances, InTime takes over the tedious role of grinding the design through the CAD tools under various configurations. Additionally, InTime learns from the results to generate new strategies that help the design meet timing. While the FPGA vendors often supply tools that do these tasks, they are primitive in nature. InTime offers the following three advantages over vendor-supplied design space exploration products:

- **Multiple High-Quality Settings**: InTime analyzes and generates a broad range of synthesis and place-and-route settings based on pre-programmed recipes. In this configuration, InTime behaves similar to a vendor-provided design space exploration tools. However, a key difference, is that the goal of this initial exploration is to generate sufficient knowledge for use with our machine learning engine. Additionally, our exploration tools generate significantly more configurations for consideration.

- **Machine-Learning**: InTime's biggest asset is its machine-learning capacity. It learns from past results and subsequently adjusts the settings that it generates to go beyond the results produced from canned recipes. We use the Naive Bayesian approach for predicting good strategies while relying on Principal Component Analysis to isolate and focus on influential parameters.

- **Parallel Builds**: InTime is capable of operating sequentially on a single build machine, or more naturally in parallel on private cloud infrastructure (internal build clusters), or public clouds (Amazon EC2, Google Compute Engine) to parallelize builds and accelerate the search process. The use of cheap, affordable parallelism against expensive developer tinkering with the tools, allows InTime to be simultaneously faster and better in reducing implementation costs.

**How does InTime work?**: InTime uses a combination of machine learning, search-space pruning, and limited random exploration to guide and drive the optimization process. We show an operational diagram of InTime in Figure 1. The InTime flow starts by analyzing the characteristics and existing results of the design under test. We derived mathematical models that related design characteristics like target device family and logic structure; compiler settings like synthesis and place-and-route options; to the design performance metrics like timing, area and power estimates. These models are used to determine the statistical relevance of the CAD settings as a function of design characteristics. Such properties are then applied to answer questions like, which of the 70-plus compiler settings have the most influence on timing? Which compiler setting values are the most influential ones for a particular device family? We use device and toolchain specific initial machine learning estimates to guide the strategy generation engine. After each strategy is applied to the underlying FPGA toolchain, the strategies are distributed and evaluated on the selected run target. The InTime framework abstracts the IT infrastructure from the user and automatically analyzes and collates the generated results before they are incorporated into InTime's runs database. An iterative approach allows repeating the flow a configurable number of times. Each new round will use previously stored results to generate machine learning outcomes which guide the strategy generation engine to produce smarter strategies as the amount of training data increases. We use statistics to analyze the correlations between the design, the tool settings and the synthesis/implementation results. We discovered that as long as the median Timing Score improves from build to build, there is a good chance of improvement until Timing Closure is achieved. These correlations are saved so that knowledge of what works well is accumulated and more quickly applied onto subsequent designs

## 3. EVALUATION

For our experiments, we are interested in minimizing timing scores (*i.e.* critical path delay) at the end of the FPGA CAD process. Timing score is the sum of timing slacks of all paths that fail to meet timing. Timing score is a better, more insightful measure of which portions of the design need attention. A timing score of 0 indicates that the design meets timing, while a larger score indicates failing nets. We use a combination of open-source and industrial benchmarks that occupy between 50-90% of the FPGA capacity. We pick these benchmarks to cover various application domains and characteristics while also ensuring they stress the limits of the CAD tools through high occupancies.

*How well does InTime perform when compared to vendor-supplied design space exploration tools?* In Figure 2, we measure the final timing scores across our benchmark circuits when using InTime as well as the vendor tools. For this experiment, we collect benchmarks from open-source and industrial sources that are mapped across a variety of Altera devices taking up between 50–100% (average 73%) of the FPGA area. As you can see, the raw, original design generally has high timing scores. When using vendor-supplied exploration tools, we notice a reduction in these scores as expected but InTime consistently delivers routed designs with the lowest timing scores across our benchmark set.

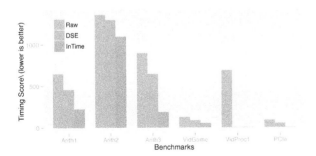

Figure 2: Comparing InTime with vendor design space exploration tool

*How does machine-learning affect the quality of InTime's results?* Machine-learning allows us to discover the best settings for CAD parameters with consistently better timing scores. In Figure 3, we show a distribution of timing scores obtained from 100 CAD compilation trials with and without InTime. After statistical analysis of the results, we can see that a large majority of InTime runs results in lower timing scores. This is despite starting with a higher timing score at the beginning (raw column in Figure 3). It is worth noting that for this benchmark, machine learning is not strictly necessary to meet timing, but very useful to reduce the CAD iterations and CAD runtime required to achieve timing closure.

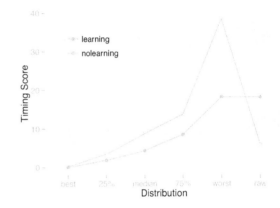

Figure 3: Understanding the impact of machine learning in InTime execution

*How does InTime affect CAD parameter choices?* The various CAD tool parameters explored by InTime eventually converge to steady-state values after a sufficient number of CAD trials. We show a representative sample set of 15 important CAD parameters in Figure 4 across 23 iterations of CAD jobs. The initial stages are seeded with strategies from our existing knowledge-base, but subsequent CAD jobs will try parameter values that are increasingly closer to their ideal results. The machine-learning algorithms help refine and revise the choices in a manner that helps us descend to the final solution.

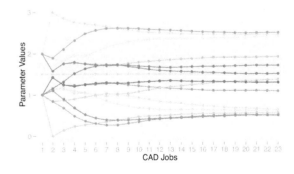

Figure 4: InTime exploring various CAD tool parameters over lifetime of one design run

*Which CAD tool parameters are most influential in calculation of resulting timing score?* In Figure 5, we show

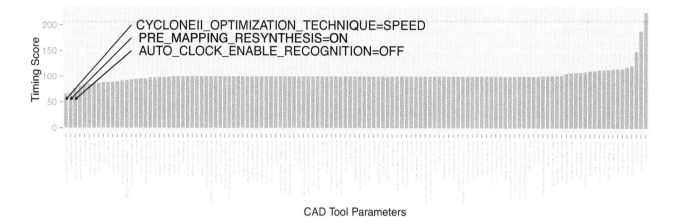

Figure 5: Sensitivity Analysis of CAD Parameter Settings

the impact of varying each individual CAD parameter (90 settings) while keeping the rest in their default settings for one benchmark. This allows us to do a limited sensitivity analysis to help isolate the parameters that matter. We use Principal Component Analysis on dataset produced in this fashion across various benchmarks to help build a pruned model of CAD tool behavior. While the exact settings vary with benchmark, the top-3 influential settings in this case were `CYCLONEII_OPTIMIZATION_TECHNIQUE=SPEED`, `PRE_MAPPING_RESYNTHESIS=ON`, and `AUTO_CLOCK_ENABLE_RECOGNITION=OFF`

## 4. RELATED WORK

Several academic studies have attempted to understand the impact of exploring multiple implementation parameters of the design space to better understand opportunity and potential.

For FPGA academic CAD tools in [3], the authors quantify the variation in solution quality when using VPR 5.0.2 under different timing targets and input net ordering. They report a critical path delay gap in the range of 17-110% when compared to nominal behavior. InTime moves beyond a trivial brute-force exploration of targets to employ machine-learning strategies to converge to the best answer sooner. In [4], the authors develop a strategy inspired by Design of Experiments (DoE) to customize the parameters of the soft processor design space. They do this by carefully selecting a subset of the parameters and their associated ranges for experimentation. Unlike DOE-techniques, we introduce learning-based techniques to allow tuning and customization of CAD runs particular to each design requirement. In [2], the authors consider the impact of ordering of LLVM passes on the quality of hardware solution for high-level synthesis. They observe a variation in excess of 10% by composing various compiler *passes* in different ways. InTime tackles the FPGA backend CAD flow choices rather than HLS flows and is aimed at developers who do not want to modify verified RTL code (or minimize the need for such modifications). In [1], for logic-synthesis, an area quality gap of between 70× was observed for industrial circuits when relying on the CAD tool heuristics to discover and exploit patterns in the input.

## 5. CONCLUSIONS

The correct choice of FPGA CAD tool parameters requires intelligence and learning for different combinations of FPGA platforms and applications. While human designers are capable of developing this intuition through years of practice, InTime complements this wisdom through an automated machine-learning based approach. When FPGA architectures and CAD tools evolve along with the characteristics of circuits that are mapped to FPGAs, the intuition is subject to continuing refinement and improvement that are better handled through automated tools like InTime. For modern Altera FPGAs and industrial circuit benchmarks, we are able to improve timing quality by as much as 70% for designs that often occupy most of the FPGA. More broadly, when coupled with the compute prowess of cloud-based technologies, the process of letting thousands of machines discover the best answer for CAD problems appears less wacky.

## 6. REFERENCES

[1] J. Cong and K. Minkovich. Optimality study of logic synthesis for lut-based fpgas. *Computer-Aided Design of Integrated Circuits and Systems, IEEE Transactions on*, 26(2):230–239, Feb 2007.

[2] Q. Huang, R. Lian, A. Canis, J. Choi, R. Xi, S. Brown, and J. Anderson. The Effect of Compiler Optimizations on High-Level Synthesis for FPGAs. *Field-Programmable Custom Computing Machines (FCCM), 2013 IEEE 21st Annual International Symposium on*, pages 89–96, 2013.

[3] R. Y. Rubin and A. M. DeHon. Timing-driven pathfinder pathology and remediation: quantifying and reducing delay noise in VPR-pathfinder. In *FPGA '11: Proceedings of the 19th ACM/SIGDA international symposium on Field programmable gate arrays*. ACM Request Permissions, Feb. 2011.

[4] D. Sheldon, F. Vahid, and S. Lonardi. Soft-core Processor Customization using the Design of Experiments Paradigm. In *Design, Automation & Test in Europe Conference & Exhibition, 2007. DATE '07*, pages 1–6, 2007.

# Unlocking FPGAs Using High Level Synthesis Compiler Technologies

Fernando Martinez Vallina and Henry Styles

Xilinx

## Abstract

FPGA devices have long been the standard for massively parallel computing fabrics with a low power footprint. Unfortunately, the complexity associated with an FPGA design has limited the rate of adoption by software application programmers. Recent advances in compiler and FPGA fabric capabilities are reversing this trend and there is a growing adoption of FPGAs for algorithmic workloads such as data analytics, feature detection in images, adaptive beam forming, etc. One of the pillars of this shift is the Vivado HLS compiler, which enables the compilation of algorithms captured in C and C++into efficient FPGA implementations. This talk focuses on how the HLS compiler creates algorithm specific compute architectures and how these elements are then used in an OpenCL based system level design abstraction. The evolution of these hardware design abstractions into software centric specifications enable application developers to leverage the flexibility of the FPGA fabric without the constraints typically found in fixed parallel architectures such as multi-core CPUs/GPUs.

**Categories and Subject Descriptors:** C.3 [Computer Systems Organization]: Special-Purpose and Application-Based System - Real-time and embedded systems; B.0 [Hardware]: General

**Keywords:** FPGA; opencl; accelerator; HLS; compiler

FPGA'14, February 22–24, 2015, Monterey, California, USA.
Copyright © 2015 ACM 978-1-4503-3315-3/15/02...$15.00.
http://dx.doi.org/10.1145/2684746.2721403

# Enhancing Hardware Design Flows with MyHDL

Keerthan Jaic, Melissa C. Smith
Holcombe Department of of Electrical and Computer Engineering
Clemson University, Clemson, South Carolina, USA
{kjaic, smithmc}@clemson.edu

## ABSTRACT

MyHDL is a Python based HDL that harnesses the power and versatility of Python for hardware development. MyHDL has excellent simulation capabilities and also allows for conversion to Verilog and VHDL, so developers can enter a conventional design flow as desired. Verilog and VHDL are used extensively, particularly because most synthesis tools only support these two languages. However, they are simply outdated; poor parameterization limits high level design and modern abstraction features such as classes are missing.

On the other hand, MyHDL has great support for parameterization. However, MyHDL did not have support for converting code that used attributes, so abstraction was limited. We extended MyHDL support to include attribute conversion. We explored methods for abstracting interfaces between components and hardware-software interfaces. The result is increased code reuse, simplified module declaration, and reduced boilerplate. These extensions result in streamlining between design, simulation, and a final synthesizable hardware, thus reducing limitations on high level development and making MyHDL an even more powerful design environment for rapid hardware prototyping.

## Categories and Subject Descriptors

B.6.3 [**Logic Design**]: Design Aids—*hardware description languages*

## General Terms

Hardware, Design

## Keywords

Hardware Description Language; Python; Interfaces;

## 1. INTRODUCTION

Technological advances over the last few decades have enabled us to build extremely powerful digital systems. However, Verilog and VHDL, which were developed in the 1980's,

are still the dominant HDLs. These languages only have basic parameterization features. Since chips are getting bigger and FPGAs are becoming more commonly used, many projects need to resort to ad-hoc methods such as shell scripts to work around the parameterization limitations. Additionally, Verilog and VHDL lack modern abstraction features such as classes. This causes code bases to contain large amounts of repeated information, which reduces developer productivity and makes the code harder to maintain.

SystemVerilog[1] solves some of these issues by providing a better type system, parameterization facilities and advanced verification features. However, it has not been widely adopted for hardware design because of non-uniform tool support and uncertainty about which features are synthesizable.

Academic endeavors have examined this issue recently, following one of two basic approaches to the problem. Some projects use the functional units of existing language to call on lower level HDL constructs. Included in this category are JHDL, built on Java, Genesis2, built on Perl, and SysPy, built on Python. JHDL[5] emerged as one of the early attempts in this field to serve hardware developers, striving to combine ease of use and functionality. Genesis2[9] extends SystemVerilog capabilities for connecting HDL to hardware simulation. SysPy is a relatively new Python based HDL undertaking[7].

Other projects choose instead to build a new language for describing hardware. Most notably is the tool Chisel[4], developed out of the University of California, Berkeley[4]. Chisel is built off Scala, though it does not keep the existing design language, instead opting to introduce a new hardware construction language. Chisel has the benefits of data type inference and high parameterization. The predecessor to this, out of the Massachusetts Institute of Technology, is Bluespec[8]. Bluespec adds to the basic functional units by offering flexible parameterization and is also keen to the need for dynamic modification in hardware generation.

MyHDL[6] is another hardware development environment based in Python. Python is a widely used high-level dynamic programming language with a design philosophy that emphasizes concise and readable code. Additionally, Python has a large standard library. These factors make Python a popular choice for creating quick prototypes of algorithms and applications. MyHDL serves several functions within hardware development: modeling, simulation, and verification. We explored methods for abstracting interfaces between components and hardware-software interfaces.

In our model interfaces, we have developed a framework for logically grouping data in models and sharing data structures between hardware and software. Our interface abstraction revolves around newly introduced attribute support that allows for increased code reuse and a reduction in development time. By adding these modifications to MyHDL, rapid prototyping of FPGA applications using MyHDL is facilitated.

## 2. MYHDL

MyHDL is an open-source package for using Python as a hardware description and verification language. Under the hood, MyHDL uses generators to model concurrency. In Python, a generator is a function that returns an iterator. Generators look like normal functions except for the fact that they use `yield` statements instead of `return`. When a function uses `yield`, it is suspended. When it is resumed, it picks up where it left off. Generators allow MyHDL to efficiently model hardware in Python itself.

Additionally, MyHDL provides decorators to facilitate hardware description. Decorators are syntactic sugar that allow one to easily modify a callable object such as a function, method or a class. For example, this:

```
@decorator
def function():
    ...
```

is equivalent to:

```
function = decorator(function)
```

This allows MyHDL to cleanly isolate procedural code from event driven code. MyHDL provides a simulation framework to run multiple generators simultaneously, which can be used for simulating hardware or high level models.

### 2.1 Designing hardware

MyHDL supports RTL (Register Transfer Level) modeling by providing two decorators called `@always_comb` and `@always_seq`. The following code blocks, taken from the MyHDL documentation[2] show how one can design hardware using MyHDL. Listing 1 shows the definition of a combinational multiplexer. Note that the direction and width of the ports are not defined. Since Python is duck-typed, they are automatically inferred during elaboration.

```
def mux(z, a, b, sel):
    @always_comb
    def logic():
        if sel == 1:
            z.next = a
        else:
            z.next = b

    return logic
```

Listing 1: Combinational multiplexer

As shown in Listing 2, A design's behavior can be observed quickly by simulating an instance of it with a stimulus.

```
z, a, b, sel = [Signal(0) for i in range(4)]
mux_1 = Mux(z, a, b, sel)


def stimulus():
    print "z a b sel"
    for i in range(8):
        a.next = randrage(8)
        b.next = randrage(8)
        sel.next = randrage(2)
        yield delay(10)
        print "%s %s %s %s" % (z, a, b, sel)

stim = stimulus()
sim = Simulation(mux_1, stim)
sim.run()
```

Listing 2: Running a simulation

The second argument of the `@always_seq` decorator accepts an instance of a specialized subclass called `ResetSignal` It can be initialized as follows:

```
ResetSignal(1, active=0, async=True)
```

The `@always_seq` decorater automatically infers the reset structure based on the `ResetSignal` and the initial values of the signals inside the block.

```
def inc(count, enable, clock, reset):
    @always_seq(clock.posedge, reset=reset)
    def logic():
        if enable:
            count.next = (count + 1)

    return logic
```

Listing 3: Sequential incrementer with enable signal

### 2.2 Conversion and Cosimulation

MyHDL can convert designs to Verilog or VHDL using the `toVerilog` or `toVHDL` functions respectively. The first argument of the conversion function is the module to be converted, followed by the arguments to instantiate the module.

```
count = Signal(intbv(0)[8:])
enable = Signal(bool(0))
clock  = Signal(bool(0))
reset = ResetSignal(0, active=0, async=True)

toVerilog(Inc, count, enable, clock, reset)
```

Listing 4: Converting a design to Verilog

The conversion function creates a testbench that can be used to cosimulate the design with an external simulator such as iverilog or modelsim through the VPI interface. This involves compiling the converted file, testbench through the eternal simulator and using the Cosimulation class.

## 3. EXTENDING MYHDL

The aim of this work is to simplify the hardware design process by enabling higher abstractions, and reducing boilerplate code. In modern programming languages, classes are used to logically group data and algorithms. This allows programmers to use powerful features such as class inheritance to facilitate code reuse. Current HDLs lack such abstraction capabilites.

MyHDL is a very powerful tool for concisely designing and testing hardware. However, it did not have support for converting code that used attributes. Therefore, it was not possible to use class instances to group together signals. Since this problem prevented using interfaces in any convertible code, we set out to fix it.

## 3.1 Attribute Conversion

When MyHDL receives a design to convert, it lets the Python interpreter handle the elaboration while using the Python profiler to infer design structure and name specs. It then extracts all relevant generators and their symbol dictionaries for further analysis and compilation. The converter analyzes the Abstract Syntax Trees (AST) of all these generators and builds the resulting HDL source code. We analyzed MyHDL's source code and discovered that the AST parsing logic assumed that all objects were either signals or integer bit-vectors. This made adding arbitrary attribute access support tricky. In order to prevent increasing the complexity of the conversion logic and introducing new bugs, we decided to apply a general transformation to the input code and leave the subsequent machinery untouched. We created an AST transformation function that smartly flattens attribute references and modified the MyHDL conversion source code to make all generators pass through our transformation function before proceeding to the main AST Parser. Additionally, we modified the hierarchy extraction code to find all generators that used attribute references and update the symbol dictionaries accordingly. Finally, the signal names are explanded by replacing '.' with '_' and ensuring that there are no name collisions. Name conflicts are automatically resolved by padding the expanded name with additional underscores. We also modified the conversion code to detect attribute accesses and create necessary ports in module declarations and instantiations.

This feature is similar to VHDL records and SystemVerilog interfaces. However, VHDL records are limited since all the signals in a record need to be of the same direction, and System Verilog interfaces are not uniformly supported by various synthesis tools. MyHDL conversion expands attribute accesses to plain names in the target HDL and maps them to the underlying signal. Therefore, classes can be used to create powerful abstractions without worrying about synthesis restrictions.

## 3.2 Utility Library

We have also developed a library to simplify using MyHDL for hardware design[1]. MyHDL's Cosimulation class is cumbersome to use because it requires you to supply the vpi file and map every signal to an object manually. Our library provides a uniform conversion and simulation API, which allows you to transparently use any simulation backend, including MyHDL itself. Additionally, it also provides a command line utility that automatically finds installed simulators downloads and compiles the corresponding Cosimulation VPIs. This is particularly useful for automated tests. The library also contains helper functions to simplify common tasks like clock generation.

---

[1]https://github.com/jck/uhdl

## 3.3 Interfaces

FPGA applications typically use highly parametrized interfaces to wire components together. This is especially true in the early stages of project development, when the requirements are less clear. One such example is the Avalon Streaming[3] (Avalon-ST) interface, which is widely used on Altera FPGAs. Avalon-ST is a low latency and high throughput bus designed for various use cases such as multiplexed streams, packets, and DSP data.

Adding attribute conversion support to MyHDL opens up a lot of opportunities for raising the abstraction level. Python classes can be used to create parametrized interfaces. Listing 5 demonstrates a parametrized interface with run time correctness checks and dynamic portwidths.

```python
class AvalonST(object):
  def __init__(self, symbolwidth=8, symbolsPerBeat=1):
    if symbolwidth not in range(1, 513):
      raise ValueError("symbolwidth must be between 1-512")

    if symbols_per_beat not in range(1,33):
      raise ValueError("symbolsPerBeat must be between 1-32")

    self.valid = Sig(False)
    self.ready = Sig(False)
    self.data = Sig(symbolwidth*symbols_per_beat)
```

Listing 5: Simple parametrization example

Advanced features, such as class inheritance, can be used to create complex interfaces while reusing code, particularly since elaboration is pure Python. Listing 6 demonstrats how class inheritance can be used to extend existing interfaces and provide additional features.

```python
class AvalonSTPkts(AvalonST):
  def __init__(self, symbolwidth=8, symbolsPerBeat=1):
    super(AvalonSTPkts, self).__init__(width, symbolwidth)
    self.startofpacket = Sig(False)
    self.endofpacket = Sig(False0)

    if symbols_per_beat > 1:
      self.empty = Sig(max=symbolsPerBeat)
```

Listing 6: Advanced parametrization using inheritance

Interfaces can be used as ports in MyHDL. This greatly reduces the amount of boilerplate required to declare a module.

```python
def some_module(clk, rst, asi, aso, amm):
  ..
  @always_seq(clk, rst)
  def logic():
    ..
    aso.data.next = asi.data
  ..
```

Listing 7: Module declarations using interfaces

Similarly, instantiation of modules is also simplified. This is very useful when writing testbenches. Interface classes can also define test bench methods to simplify common tasks such as sending or receiving data from buses.

```
   ..
   ..
asi = AvalonST()
aso = AvalonST()
amm = AvalonMM()
some_inst = some_module(clk, rst, asi, aso
                                     , amm)
```

Listing 8: Module instantiation using interfaces

As shown in listings 7 and 8, interface abstractions greatly reduce the amount of redundant information spread across various hardware modules and testbenches.

## 3.4 Models

HW/SW applications for FPGAs typically need to share data structures across hardware and software code. For example, register and bit field definitions need to be duplicated in the RTL models, driver and testbench code.

To facilitate sharing of data structures across hardware and software, we developed the Models system that uses Python Metaclasses to represent any structured data. Metaclasses are classes whose instances are classes. Our Models system was inspired by the Django web framework that provides a similar system to uniformly access database fields irrespective of the backend.

```
class SomeModel(Model):
    a = bits(4)
    b = bits(4)
```

Listing 9: Defining a Model

Listing 9 shows the definition Model named SomeModel with fields a and b. Models remember the order which that fields were defined in. This information is used by factory functions to transform the Model. Examples of useful factory functions include bitfields and ctypes. Bitfields can be used by logic to parse structured data from memory. Models converted to ctypes are useful in HW/SW systems, such as an FPGA connected to a host via PCIe, and there is a C api to communicate with the FPGA device. In such cases, the Host software could monitor status registers on the FPGA and write to the control registers. Additionally, the Model API can also be used to allow software programs to seamlessly interact with RTL simulations.

## 4. CONCLUSIONS

MyHDL is already a powerful language for hardware development. However, since MyHDL could not handle attribute conversion, the extent of abstraction was limited. We added attribute conversion and then explored the use of class inheritance and metaclasses for abstraction. We demonstrated that classes can be used to create reusable IP cores, and Models can be used to share data structures across hardware and software. These advanced abstraction features allow developers to write concise, maintainable code while reducing the development time.

## 5. ACKNOWLEDGEMENTS

We would like to thank Jan Decaluwe and Christopher Felton for providing valuable feedback and guidance during development, and the MyHDL community for testing and submitting bug reports.

## 6. REFERENCES

[1] Ieee standard for systemverilog–unified hardware design, specification, and verification language. *IEEE Std 1800-2012 (Revision of IEEE Std 1800-2009)*, pages 1–1315, Feb 2013.

[2] The MyHDL Manual. http://docs.myhdl.org/en/latest/manual/index.html, 2014.

[3] Altera. Avalon interface specifications. http://www.altera.com/literature/manual/mnl_avalon_spec.pdf, 2014.

[4] J. Bachrach, H. Vo, B. Richards, Y. Lee, A. Waterman, R. Avižienis, J. Wawrzynek, and K. Asanović. Chisel: constructing hardware in a Scala embedded language. In *Proceedings of the 49th Annual Design Automation Conference on - DAC '12*, DAC '12, page 1216, New York, New York, USA, 2012. ACM Press.

[5] P. Bellows and B. Hutchings. JHDL-an HDL for reconfigurable systems. In *Proceedings. IEEE Symposium on FPGAs for Custom Computing Machines (Cat. No.98TB100251)*, pages 175–184. IEEE Comput. Soc, Apr. 1998.

[6] J. Decaluwe. MyHDL: A Python-based Hardware Description Language. *Linux journal*, 2004(127):5, Nov. 2004.

[7] E. Logaras and E. S. Manolakos. SysPy: using Python for processor-centric SoC design. In *2010 17th IEEE International Conference on Electronics, Circuits and Systems*, pages 762–765. IEEE, Dec. 2010.

[8] R. Nikhil. Bluespec System Verilog: efficient, correct RTL from high level specifications. In *Proceedings. Second ACM and IEEE International Conference on Formal Methods and Models for Co-Design, 2004. MEMOCODE '04.*, pages 69–70. IEEE, June 2004.

[9] O. Shacham, S. Richardson, S. Galal, S. Sankaranarayanan, M. Wachs, J. Brunhaver, A. Vassiliev, M. Horowitz, A. Danowitz, and W. Qadeer. Avoiding game over. In *Proceedings of the 49th Annual Design Automation Conference on - DAC '12*, DAC '12, page 623, New York, New York, USA, 2012. ACM Press.

# Rapid Prototyping of Wireless Physical Layer Modules Using Flexible Software/Hardware Design Flow

James Chacko, Cem Sahin, Douglas Pfiel, Nagarajan Kandasamy, Kapil Dandekar

ECE Department, Drexel University, Philadelphia, PA 19104

{jjc652,cs486,dsp36,nk78,krd26}@drexel.edu

## ABSTRACT

This paper describes a step by step approach in designing wireless physical layer modules starting from a software implementation in MATLAB to a hardware implementation using Xilinx SysGen and ModelSim. The described design flow promotes baseband physical layer research by providing high flexibility and speed to the process of module creation verification and deployment. The novelty introduced into our system lies within the flexible components created using this design flow, which enables on-the-fly modification of multiple parameters to suit various wireless protocols.

## Categories and Subject Descriptors

B.6.3 [**Hardware**]: Logic Design - Design Aid—*Automatic synthesis; Verification; Simulation*

## Keywords

digital baseband, design flow, MATLAB, Xilinx SysGen, ModelSim

## 1. INTRODUCTION

Wireless protocols are often implemented in custom hardware in order to satisfy heavy computational requirements within tight time constraints. Hardware implementations can be cumbersome to design and verify and therefore require longer development times. A programmable software implementation of the physical layer, also called Software Defined Radio (SDR), is therefore very advantageous in terms of supporting multiple protocols, faster time-to-market, higher chip volumes and easy modifications. Though convenient, SDR relies on the researcher to choose between the wide array of solutions available that are different in their design language, implementation constraints and flexibility.

Apart from flexible characteristics inherent to SDR's, another factor that takes prominence on the choice of SDR would be the design flow involved, which can vary significantly in the flavor of software/hardware design languages

used. For instance, based on the chosen SDR platform designing can be either done with high level languages like MATLAB, Python, C, etc that may or may not translate automatically into hardware. It can involve writing codes in HDL languages such as Verilog and VHDL. Through this paper, we'll discuss the requirements we faced designing wireless physical layer modules and tools that were selected for implementation. This design tutorial is organized as follows: Section 2 discusses some of the major design tools wile Section 3 discusses the requirements in choosing the right one. Section 4 describes our proposed design flow in detail and we will finally conclude with Section 5.

## 2. DESIGN TOOLS

Developing any part of the wireless physical layer is easiest when first implemented in software, and MATLAB is the most extensively used tool in this area. MATLAB provides a high level interactive environment for numerical computation and programming. It is a powerful tool in developing wireless applications especially with its built in math functions and application specific toolboxes [1]. As an add-on to its coding environment, MATLAB also provides Simulink which is a graphical programming language tool for modeling dynamic systems, such as wireless systems, that require a wide range of signal processing capabilities. A similar piece of software to Simulink would be LabVIEW with its graphical communication toolsets [2] and its graphical object oriented approach in developing wireless models. LabVIEW is a newer addition to wireless design development tools with provisions to run m-code within its environment to translate models previously written in MATLAB script. Off the shelf SDRs such as WARPLab [3], GNUradio [4] and SORA [14] allow the user to program the baseband/physical layer in MATLAB, Python and C, respectively, and use modular radio front ends for transmission and reception. These SDRs are relevant for conducting wireless baseband level research in software but they do not provide the runtime advantage of having a hardware implementation to generate faster results.

Wireless hardware system development is often implemented through HDL coding languages like Verilog and VHDL at the basic level with common development environments being ModelSim, Altera Quartus and Xilinx ISE [5–9]. ModelSim is more simulation focused, while the latter two are more focused on targeting and running HDL code on hardware. Both Xilinx ISE and Altera Quartus have communication design toolboxes that ease the development of wireless modules. The availability of automatic script or graphical software design translations to hardware makes hardware development easier for the development of wireless physical layer designs. Examples of such designing platforms would be MATLAB Simulink/SysGen and Parallel Application from Rapid Simulation (PARS) which both translates designs directly to hardware [10, 11]. While PARS requires Sundance hardware, MATLAB Simulink/SysGen can target a wide variety of FPGA boards. In both cases, automatic translation depends largely on the complexity and availability of the hardware libraries to compile hardware equivalent designs. In certain research areas, such as wireless physical layer design, it can be difficult to know which libraries will be required, thought this might be evident later based on how a project matures and branches. In such cases the challenge then is drawn to programming within the constraints of the chosen tool. Switching design flows can be a cumbersome task in any project and therefore choosing the appropriate design environment and tool that can scale in the future is extremely important. Wireless research as described in [12, 13] develops a flexible software-hardware implementation that can be leveraged to research various current and future OFDM based wireless protocols.

No matter which design flow is chosen, there are certain essential requirements in a design environment which can also be relevant and specific to the kind of project being undertaken. In this paper, we are particularly interested in the design and research involving the baseband layer of wireless standards that benefit from the flexibility that is typical of a software implementation as well as real time performance which is typical of a hardware implementation. In the next section we will go over the requirements we saw essential in choosing an appropriate design tool.

## 3. DESIGN TOOL REQUIREMENTS

***Flexible Designing Environment:*** This is the most significant attribute in choosing a design language and environment. The programming method for building the design can either be script based or GUI based, but must provide granularity and flexibility in the aspect of building complex designs based on functions and libraries that are built-in to the programming language. In the case of designing the wireless baseband/physical layers, programs with built in communication libraries and functions are beneficial and would give the programmer an edge in implementing designs at a much faster rate than otherwise would have taken longer if implemented from scratch. The language should also be flexible enough to have user defined functions/modules integrate well with built in functions/modules, which requires well documented descriptions for ease in integration.

For instance, in order to build a quadrature amplitude modulation (QAM) module, that maps bits into waves, the presence of built in QAM functions and libraries would ease implementation but these libraries may not be available for more complex modules comprising the wireless baseband. QAM itself can vary in its scale setting which decides on how many bits to map at a time: BPSK, 4QAM and 16QAM that maps 1, 2 and 4 bits, respectively. Varying data rates through modules especially in a pipeline are much easier to implement in software than on hardware where implementation relies on data to be predictive. Thus, the need arises for flexibility in the use of available functions/libraries and the programming environment itself.

***Debugging and Verification Environment:*** The debugging and verification environment associated with a programming language is nearly as important as designing the system itself. The debugging environment becomes particularly relevant in complex designs that cannot can not be built in a tier system that are otherwise inherent in smaller designs. Complex system designs involving feedback and control loops, as in wireless baseband/physical layer designs, are far more complex to debug and verify.

The channel estimation block is an appropriate example of a complex module within the wireless baseband layer that provides channel data to rectify the received signal. The complexity in this block is due to the processing speed and data alignment with which it provides feedback. An error within would be harder to locate and often forces the programmer into tracing errors from scratch if not aided with higher level debugging tools like signal captures and waveforms. The effort of debugging and verification also changes based on if the design resides in software or on hardware and it is best to choose an environment that has strengths in debugging in both areas.

***Result Capture and Processing:*** Based on where the design resides, software or hardware, the process of gathering results for processing can be a challenge of its own. A fully software based implementation benefits from being able to capture data from across the entire design easily, whereas significant work needs to be done to capture the same for a hardware based implementation. In the area of wireless research, where designs may reside on software, hardware or consist of a complex integration of both software and hardware cores, the availability of capturing and processing data flexibly is a significant attribute of the right design tool.

For instance, in the case of implementing the QAM module discussed earlier, data going into and out of the module are totally different in it's characteristics, one being bits and the other fixed point decimal values on hardware or floating point in software. Research in this area depends on visualizing channel mapping results and the ability to capture data around the QAM module is necessary irrespective of whether its on software or hardware.

## 4. DESIGN FLOW

In this section of the paper, we are going to have a detailed discussion of our design flow that starts from utilizing the flexibility provided with a full software implementation to utilizing the speeds provided with a full hardware implementation. We use this design flow in implementing the baseband/physical layer modules targeted for wireless research.

### 4.1 MATLAB Script Implementation

As the first step towards implementing a module, we write MATLAB m-code that will also be used as a blueprint to build further upon the model if required. We chose MATLAB because of the high level interactive environment for numerical computation and availability of pre-built communication toolboxes and function libraries. At this stage, there are a few relevant points to be kept in mind while writing MATLAB scripts. The first would be to have the option of changing function variables and parameters from outside the function call itself for comparative flexibility which will get more clearer in the next few sections. The second would be to have a structured data source and data

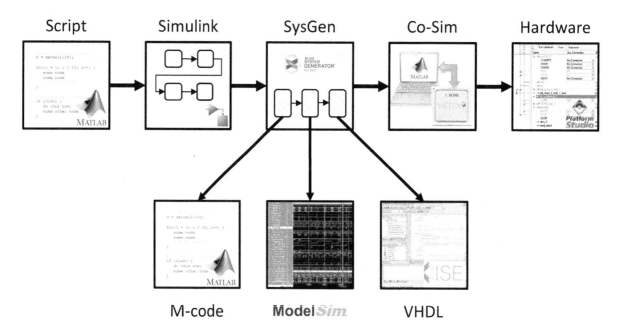

Figure 1: Proposed design flow for projects implementing baseband/physical layer modules for wireless research.

sink plotting/processing output data for quick script level verification of functionality and correctness.

## 4.2 MATLAB Simulink Implementation

As the next step, we use MATLAB's Simulink graphical design tool and create the functional equivalent of the script that was previously developed. The Communication Systems Toolbox available in Simulink provides a wide array of built-in wireless modules that helps the creation of wireless physical layer modules, but its library implementation may vary with the one in script. To continue, have the results from both the script and Simulink designs compared against each other to ensure script and Simulink design level coherence to the same set of input and output data that can be captured easily within MATLAB's workspace. For those modules that do not have built-in equivalents for the functions to be implemented, it can be put together with the logic level functions/modules Simulink provides.

## 4.3 SysGen Implementation

In this section, we are going to use Xilinx System Generator (SysGen) Toolkit that is present as an add-on within the Simulink library in MATLAB to create the SysGen functional equivalent of the Simulink design that was created in the previous step. By using building blocks provided in the SysGen library, we will be able to build custom hardware IPs and directly export them to hardware using SysGen's export tools. The implementation change from floating point arithmetic to fixed point arithmetic has to be kept in mind while designing blocks in SysGen. After completing the design it must be crosschecked for errors against its Simulink implementation by having the data to the SysGen modules sourced directly from the Simulink data source and results captured and processed within the MATLAB workspace. This will ensure functional correctness and show the range of error from conversion to fixed point implementation.

## 4.4 ModelSim Implementation

Complex Verilog/VHDL functions and controls can be created through ModelSim and imported into MATLAB's Simulink environment using the BlackBox SysGen module. This allows building of complex functions much quicker than otherwise would have taken for piecing together SysGen library blocks. Once created and imported into the design, the models can be further studied against the inputs from the Simulink/SysGen design by invoking ModelSim to scope the signal and control flow through waveforms for ease in debugging.

## 4.5 Software/Hardware Co-Simulation

Wireless communication research benefits greatly from hardware support in the form of accelerators and radio front ends. Since a full baseband implementation in hardware is difficult to implement from scratch, having the ability for software/hardware co-simulation enables software flexibility, hardware speeds and access to the wireless channel.

### 4.5.1 PC Driven Interface

At this stage, our hardware designed through SysGen will be verified for their correct functionality on an FPGA, a ML605 board in our project, using real data before moving forward. Our Simulink-based design provides capabilities to fulfill this need. Leveraging the features available through the Simulink software, we set up a software-hardware Ethernet co-simulation platform. In this scenario, the experiment master is set up as the host PC, which orchestrates the full experiment.

### 4.5.2 Data Input/Output

For our co-simulation experiment, we initialize the data using the MATLAB workspace, where each data vector is created and prepared for transmission through our FPGA design. The co-simulation feature feeds data into these entry points at the beginning of the experiment via the Ethernet connection onto the ML605, allowing them to flow through our FPGA design, and captures the data as the experiment is progressing. The captured data is finally saved back into the MATLAB workspace, where a final script checks the received data against the expected results for correctness. It should be noted that even though the ML605 is the one processing the data, this scenario allows us to tap into the data's flowpath at any point with the use of Simulink scopes and identify the problematic stages on the hardware if there are any error flags.

## 4.6 Hardware Implementation

Although the time and effort needed to set up a software-hardware Ethernet co-simulation experiment is short, the runtime for each experiment is extremely long. The performance of our custom FPGA design is diminished significantly due to the host PC being the experiment master. The co-simulation framework does prove to be a valid method to verify our hardware design rapidly for smaller data sets. Since it cannot provide results quickly for larger data sets within a reasonable time, we will discuss a faster method that will unleash the full performance of our hardware implementation.

### 4.6.1 Microblaze Driven Interface

Close-to-real-time measurements are ideal when trying to determine the characteristics of hardware designs. A fully embedded design achieves this goal with few additional design requirements. For a data sourced development process, we complemented our hardware design with an on-board data generator, which also has the capability to keep track of error rates. The control of the experiment has now been moved from the host PC to the on-board processor, MicroBlaze, available on the ML605. In addition to implementing and integrating the on-board data generator, the code loaded on the MicroBlaze initializes the board and starts and controls the experiment throughout its runtime. This design was developed by exporting the MATLAB Simulink/SysGen design directly to Xilinx Embedded Development Kit (EDK) and then using Xilinx Software Development Kit (SDK) that allows to communicate with the FPGA through C code running on the on-board MicroBlaze processor.

### 4.6.2 Data Input/Output

As introduced above, the data is fed into our design using our custom on-board data generator. This hardware block simply accepts a seed and outputs randomly generated data. Using carefully calculated delays, the same data (using the same seed) is generated at the receive end of the design as well for cross checking. Once the MicroBlaze sends the signal to start the design flow, the data is sent through all the stages of our design serially and looped-back to the receive path. The pre-generated data is then compared against what was captured from the receive path. The total bit count, and the bit error rates are updated in real-time within the data generation block registers, which are accessible from the MicroBlaze at any time for verification. Upon full completion of the experiment (i.e. the total bit count reached the user-preset count set for the experiment), the total bits sent/received, total number of errors, and the bit error rate (BER) data are also printed to the COM port for user analysis.

## 5. CONCLUSION

This paper throughly describes the requirements we found essential in choosing design tools for designing the base-band/physical layer for wireless research in software and then realizing it in hardware in a step-by-step process for assembling a novel research tool. The described design flow benefits from the flexibility provided with software implementation and hardware runtime speeds. We also described tool techniques that are relevant in SDR research that we used for debugging and verifying complex designs comprising of both software and hardware modules with ease.

## Acknowledgment

This project is supported by the National Science Foundation through grants CNS-0854946 and CNS-0923003.

## 6. REFERENCES

[1] Matlab Communications System Toolbox. http://www.mathworks.com/products/communications/.
[2] LabView Tools: IP for Software Designed Instruments. https://decibel.ni.com/content/docs/DOC-29613.
[3] "Rice University WARP - Wireless Open-Access Research Platform (WARP)." http://warp.rice.edu.
[4] GNU Radio Overview. http://gnuradio.org/redmine/projects/gnuradio.
[5] Xilinx Comprehensive Baseband Solutions. http://www.xilinx.com/applications/wireless-communications/baseband/index.htm.
[6] Xilinx Wireless IP, Reference Designs. http://www.xilinx.com/esp/wireless/.
[7] Altera Software Defined Radio. http://www.altera.com/end-markets/wireless/advanced-dsp/sdr/wir-sdr.html.
[8] ModelSim-Altera Edition Software. http://www.altera.com/products/software/quartus-ii/modelsim/qts-modelsim-index.html.
[9] ModelSim: ASIC and FPGA design. http://www.mentor.com/products/fv/modelsim/.
[10] Matlab HDL Verifier. http://www.mathworks.com/products/hdl-verifier/.
[11] Parallel Application from Rapid Simulation. http://www.sundancedsp.com/development-tools/pars.
[12] J. Chacko, C. Sahin, D. Nguyen, D. Pfeil, N. Kandasamy, and K. Dandekar. Fpga-based latency-insensitive ofdm pipeline for wireless research. In *High Performance Extreme Computing Conference (HPEC '14). 19th Annual HPEC Conference*, Sept 2014.
[13] B. Shishkin, D. Pfeil, D. Nguyen, K. Wanuga, J. Chacko, J. Johnson, N. Kandasamy, T. Kurzweg, and K. Dandekar. Sdc testbed: Software defined communications testbed for wireless radio and optical networking. In *Modeling and Optimization in Mobile, Ad Hoc and Wireless Networks (WiOpt), 2011 International Symposium on*, pages 300 –306, May 2011.
[14] K. Tan et al. Sora: high performance software radio using general purpose multi-core processors. In *Proc. USENIX Symp. Networked Systems Design & Implementation (NSDI)*, pages 75–90, 2009.

# The BEEcube Story—Lessons Learned from Running a FPGA Startup for the Past 7 Years

Chen Chang
BEEcube Inc.
Fremont, CA, USA

## Abstract

After running BEEcube Inc for the past 7 years, I learned many lessons the hard way as an entrepreneur fresh out of engineer school. Behind the glory of being the #9 fastest growing private company in Silicon Valley in 2013, there were many untold stories about our FPGA technology based startup company. A startup company is where dreams start by smart people, and also where harsh reality squashes them. This is not one of those "unicorn" billion-dollar-valuation-in-18-month stories, but rather a bootstrap startup managed to find its own pot of gold under the rainbow.

**Categories and Subject Descriptors:** B.7.2 [**Integrated Circuits**]: Design Aids

**Keywords:** FPGA startup

## Bio

Dr. Chen Chang is the Chief Executive Officer at BEEcube Inc. Previously he served as Chief Technology Officer at BEEcube where he led the development of the BEE3 product. Dr. Chang was the Chief Architect of the Berkeley Emulation Engine (BEE) project at the University of California in Berkeley, leading the design and implementation of three generations of FPGA-based emulation and computing systems, as well as unified FPGA/ASIC design environment using high-level descriptions from Mathworks Simulink environment. His research interests include large-scale FPGA-based real-time computer systems; digital systems design automation and hardware emulation; and wideband antenna array signal processing systems. Dr. Chang is a young entrepreneur who co-founded BEEcube in 2006 with professors from the University of California, Berkeley. He also participates actively in assisting many of the world's universities in FPGA-related research projects and academic exchanges. Dr. Chang holds B.Sc., M.Sc. and Ph.D. degrees in Electrical Engineering and Computer Sciences from the University of California, Berkeley.

*FPGA'15*, February 22–24, 2015, Monterey, California, USA.
ACM 978-1-4503-3315-3/15/02.
http://dx.doi.org/10.1145/2684746.2721405

# Application of Specific Delay Window Routing for Timing Optimization in FPGA Designs

Evan Wegley, Qinhai Zhang

Lattice Semiconductor Corporation · 2115 O'Nel Drive · San Jose, California 95131

{evan.wegley, qinhai.zhang}@latticesemi.com

## ABSTRACT

In addition to optimizing for timing performance and routability, commercial FPGA routing engines must also support various timing constraints enabling the designer to fine tune aspects of their design. The many intricacies of commercial FPGA architectures add difficulty to the problem of supporting such constraints.

In this paper, we show how the method of specific delay window routing can be applied to optimize for these various timing constraints constituting both long- and short-path requirements. Additionally, we enhance existing methods of routing according to specified delay by using dual wave expansion instead of single wave expansion with target delay estimation in order to improve accuracy and support sparser, more varied interconnect structures. Our results show that specific delay window routing is well-suited for optimization targeting a variety of timing constraints, and that using dual wave expansion to eliminate the estimation part of the router's delay cost function enables the router to support tighter timing constraints. For a suite of designs with known hold timing violations, we found that the dual wave approach can correct all such violations, whereas the single wave approach failed to correct the hold timing violations for several designs. Furthermore, for a suite of designs with maximum skew constraints of 250 ps on certain nets and buses, the dual wave approach met the constraints for all designs, whereas the single wave approach failed to meet the constraints for a majority of the designs.

## Categories and Subject Descriptors

B.7.2 [**Integrated Circuits**]: Design Aids—*Placement and routing*

## Keywords

FPGA; Routing; Timing Constraints

*FPGA '15*, February 22–24, 2015, Monterey, California, USA.
Copyright © ACM 978-1-4503-3315-3/15/02 ...$15.00.
http://dx.doi.org/10.1145/2684746.2689059.

## 1. INTRODUCTION

An effective FPGA router must balance its effort on the competing goals of routability and timing performance. If too much emphasis is given to either of these goals, the routing quality will be poor. This is the main premise behind the PathFinder algorithm [1], which is the basis of many modern academic and commercial FPGA routers. For a routed design to be fully functional, the routing result must be free of any timing violations, which includes both short- and long-path (i.e. hold and setup) timing violations. The most common forms of long- and short-path timing violations come from requirements on data paths between registers, input-setup requirements, and clock-to-output requirements. The problem of solving long-path timing violations has received the vast majority of attention in past research [2]. However, in industry we must also solve the problem of short-path timing violations to guarantee functionality of routed designs. Furthermore, there are a variety of timing constraints that give way to these long- and short-path timing requirements. One such constraint is to define a maximum skew value on a net or a bus. Optimization strategies for these constraints have received little attention in past research on FPGA routing. It is important to note that these optimizations are primarily left to the routing stage of the FPGA design flow due to the detailed timing information available in this stage as well as the relative flexibility of routing resources.

Routing nets according to each of these timing constraints can be reformulated into the more general problem of routing connections into a specific delay window. We define this specific delay window routing as follows. First we define a *connection* as the logical connection between the driver and one load of a net. For each load of a net, there exists one connection. We then define *specific delay window routing* of a connection to be the process of routing the connection given both upper and lower bounds on the delay of the routing result. These bounds, which we denote as a *window*, guide the router in selecting an appropriate path for the connection.

In [2], a method is proposed to simultaneously solve long- and short-path timing issues using specific delay window routing. This approach uses the technique of slack allocation proposed in [3][4][5] to calculate appropriate delay window bounds on each connection such that the connection will be free of long- and short-path violations. This delay window is factored into the cost formulae of a PathFinder-based router. As with most routing algorithms, searching for a path from a source node to a target node is accomplished using a wave-like search, using costs associated with routing resources to determine an optimal path. For a single wave search, as is implemented in [2], the delay cost function is based on the known delay from the source node to the current wave node, plus the estimated delay from the current wave node to the target node.

When using this technique to route connections using specific delay window routing, we found that the estimation term in the delay cost function was a source of inaccuracy that occasionally resulted in the failure to correct timing violations. The estimation of delay from the current wave node to the target node is both difficult and inaccurate in our experience due to certain characteristics of our FPGA architectures. First, the switchboxes in our interconnect structures do not have full crossbar, hence, if we estimate the delay based on the Manhattan distance that the connection spans, we may estimate a solution that is not possible due to the architecture. For example, suppose an architecture features wiring between either one or two switchboxes in the cardinal directions.

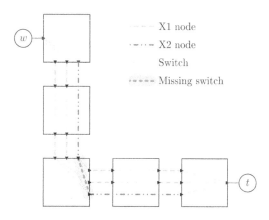

**Figure 1: Simple architecture excerpt to illustrate drawbacks of delay estimation**

Suppose we wish to estimate the delay from the current wave node $w$ to the target node $t$ with a Manhattan distance of four, as depicted in Figure 1. A common delay estimation scheme is to select a minimum set of wiring resources – in this case, X1 and X2 nodes that span one and two switchboxes, respectively – to cover the distance. With this delay estimation scheme, we will estimate a delay that corresponds to two X2 nodes. However, in this example, the corner switchbox is missing the switch that would connect these X2 nodes together, so that solution is infeasible. In reality, there are two possibilities for this path: one X2 and two X1 nodes, or four X1 nodes. Note that, in general, delays associated with these routing resources are not linear in the distance they cover, meaning that the delay cost of one X2 and two X1 nodes is not equal to that of four X1 nodes. If this area of the design is congested, we also may not be able to guarantee the likely less costly path using the X2 node; this fact also contributes to the difficulty of estimation. We have found that this issue arises in various architectures with different span lengths. Another architectural issue that hinders accurate estimation is the ability to swap the pins of lookup table (LUT) inputs. Since LUT inputs are logically equivalent, we are free to swap them so long as the variables of the logic equation the LUT is configured to realize are updated. The motivation for swapping the LUT pin inputs is

the fact that certain pins have lesser delay and more critical connections will be prioritized to use them. However, this makes estimation difficult when the target is a LUT input, as we don't know the actual pin (and thus, delay) that the target will take until the end of the routing process.

We have found that the inaccuracy of this estimation method can be intolerable for specific delay window routing due to the need to support multiple speed grades for setup- and hold-timing correction and also small skew constraint values; both of which result in narrow delay windows. As the width of the delay window decreases, the effect of poor estimation on the routing increases. To this end, the approach described in this paper uses dual wave expansion from both the source and target nodes, which allows us to replace the estimation term of the delay cost function with a known value. Though previous use of dual wave expansion has largely been for runtime reduction [6], we utilize the technique for accuracy improvement in delay measurement.

## 2. APPLICATIONS OF SPECIFIC DELAY WINDOW ROUTING

In this section, we illustrate how some timing constraints can be converted into a problem of specific delay window routing. Note that these optimizations occur after an initial routing phase, where all connections are routed with a focus on long-path timing and congestion avoidance. Using specific delay window routing, we correct timing violations resulting from the initial routing phase.

### 2.1 Maximum Skew Constraint

The maximum skew constraint sets a limit on the range of delays within a group of connections. The group of connections can belong to a single net or to a group of nets, which we call a bus. Typically each net of a defined bus has only one load, but this is not a requirement. Due to the fact that this constraint supports both single nets and buses, our solution must consider connections of multiple nets at the same time.

```
MAXSKEW NET "tx_data_out" 0.5 NS;
```

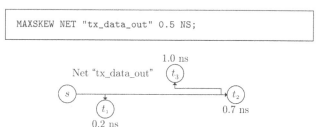

**Figure 2: Example maximum skew constraint on a net**

In Figure 2, we show the maximum skew constraint applied to a single net. For this example, we have constrained the delays on the three connections of net "tx_data_out" to be within a range of 0.5 ns. The diagram depicting the initial routing result shows that the net is in violation of this constraint since the skew is $1.0 - 0.2 = 0.8$ ns. The general strategy to correct connections that fall outside of the skew limit specified by the constraint is to add delay to the connections that have the smallest delay until the resulting range of delays satisfies the constraint. This is based on the assumption that the connection with the longest delay cannot be rerouted to have a lower delay value due to the fact that the initial routing stage already optimizes for long-path timing. Hence, the path to load $t_1$ should be rerouted in this example to correct the maximum skew violation. We use specific delay window routing to reroute the connection $(s, t_1)$ using a calculated delay window to ensure that the connection satisfies the constraint. The upper bound is taken from the maximum delay value of the net, $T_{t_3} = 1.0$ ns. The width of the window is the constraint value, so we set the lower bound to $1.0 - 0.5 = 0.5$ ns, giving us a specific delay window of $[0.5, 1.0]$, as shown in Figure 3.

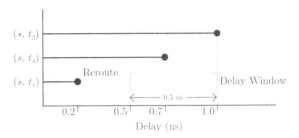

**Figure 3: Setting the delay window for a maximum skew constraint**

When the maximum skew constraint is used on a bus, we group the connections of all the nets comprising the bus. The maximum delay value of this group is then used as the upper bound for the delay window. Using the constraint value as the width of the delay window, we find the corresponding lower bound. Each connection within the group that was initially routed outside of this window is rerouted using specific delay window routing similar to the case of maximum skew on a single net. For example, Figure 4 shows a bus "clk_bus" consisting of two nets, "clk1" and "clk2". From the constraint, the delay window is calculated as $[0.85, 0.95]$. We can see that the initial delay value of "clk1" is out of this window, so we must reroute it accordingly.

```
DEFINE BUS "clk_bus" NET "clk1" NET "clk2";
MAXSKEW BUS "clk_bus" 0.1 NS;
```

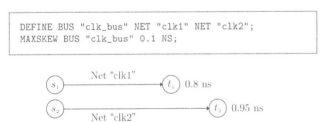

**Figure 4: Maximum skew constraint on a bus**

## 2.2  Hold Timing Correction

Hold timing requirements are an intrinsic part of any design with sequential logic elements. For data paths between registers completely internal to the FPGA device, CAD tools can automatically constrain for hold timing requirements based on the delays of the data path, the reference clock path, and the internal timing characteristics of the register. However, when only a portion of the data path lies within the FPGA device, the designer can constrain the setup and hold requirements from the data input pad to the register (input-setup) and from the register to the data output pad

(clock-to-output). An example of such a constraint is shown in Figure 5, where we constrain the setup and hold requirements of data paths driven by an input pad to 2.0 ns and 0.4 ns, respectively. The constraint gives us that the path from data port "data_in" to register A, minus the injection delay of the clock, should be greater than the specified hold time of 0.4 ns. However, the initial routing result yields a hold time of only $(1.0 + 0.3) - 1.2 = 0.1$ ns. Note that here we ignore logic delays of the input pad and the LUT to simplify this explanation.

```
INPUT_SETUP PORT "data_in" 2.0 NS HOLD 0.4 NS
CLKPORT "clk_in";
```

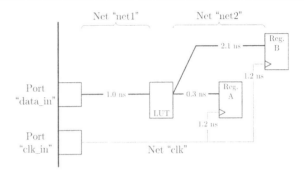

**Figure 5: Input-setup constraint on an input port to demonstrate hold timing correction**

To correct a hold timing violation, there are two options: add delay to the data path, or reduce delay on the clock path. Typically the delay of the clock path is difficult to reduce from the initial routing result since clocks are normally hardwired with global routing resources; hence, our strategy is to add delay to the data path. Therefore, to correct the hold timing violation in our example, we must add 0.3 ns of delay across the two connections spanning between "data_in" and register A. However, when we add delay to a connection, we must also consider both the setup and hold requirements of other paths that use the connection. For instance, the path from "data_in" to register B has a setup requirement of 2.0 ns specified in the constraint. The initial routing meets this requirement with 0.1 ns of positive slack since the delay difference between the data path and the clock path $(1.0 + 2.1) - 1.2 = 1.9$ ns is less than 2.0 ns by 0.1 ns. Note that the connection labeled "net1" is shared by both data paths driving registers A and B, so if we attempt to add more than 0.1 ns to "net1" in order to fix the hold timing violation at register A, we will cause a setup timing violation at register B.

We further note that data paths and clock paths often consist of multiple nets. Hence, there are several connections to which we can add delay to solve hold timing violations. As we observed in the preceding example, distributing too much delay to the wrong connection can result in further timing violations. In general, selecting the appropriate distribution of delay to add to the various connections comprising the path is a nontrivial problem. In order to solve the problem of distributing the delay across connections without causing any additional timing violations, we use the slack allocation technique introduced in [3][4] and further refined with adaptation for FPGA architectures in [5].

## 2.3 Slack Allocation

In this section, we give an overview of slack allocation and describe how it is used to compute specific delay windows on connections in order to correct hold timing violations. Slack allocation is the process of iteratively distributing positive and negative slack to all connections in a circuit until the cumulative slack reaches zero. Slack is distributed to the connections using weights, with various weighting schemes presented in [5]. The method of slack allocation was developed to solve the following problem. Given an initial set of delays on the connections of a circuit, we aim to calculate the corresponding set of delays such that each connection is free of timing violations and the cumulative slack is zero. Note that this process does not physically change the routing of any connection, but simply calculates potential delay values for each connection after distributing slack. The algorithm implementing slack allocation has two metrics of quality: first, the ability to converge to a solution with zero cumulative slack, and second, algorithmic complexity in the number of connections. In [5], slack allocation algorithms were proven to converge to a solution with zero cumulative slack given reasonable limits on the weighting scheme for slack distribution. Furthermore, many adaptations of the algorithm have been proposed to improve the algorithmic complexity, including Minimax-PERT in [4] and the Limit-Bumping Algorithm in [5] which is used in this work.

Using slack allocation, we compute a maximum tolerable delay for each connection; that is, the maximum delay that will satisfy the setup timing requirements of all paths that the connection occupies. These maximum delay values, obtained through slack allocation on setup timing, serve as the upper bounds to our delay windows. In [2], the same slack allocation technique is used to compute the minimum tolerable delay for each connection in order to satisfy all hold timing requirements. Likewise, these minimum delay values, obtained through slack allocation on hold timing, serve as the lower bounds of our delay windows. If any connections in the initial routing fall outside of the delay windows calculated via slack allocation, we reroute them using specific delay window routing.

### 2.3.1 Consideration of Multiple Speed Grades

In performing slack allocation for both setup and hold timing, the need for multi-corner timing analysis arises when targeting FPGA devices with varying speed grades. For setup timing, a design speed grade $K$ is selected from the available device speed grades and the design is optimized for all speed grades faster than $K$. This is due to the fact that delay values are lesser in these faster speed grades and thus, we can theoretically meet setup timing in these faster speed grades by targeting $K$ for setup timing optimization. Contrarily, for hold timing, we optimize for an artificial speed grade $M$ defined to be the fastest speed grade of a particular FPGA device. This is done in order to meet hold timing in any speed grade since the lesser delay values in speed grade $M$ present the worst case for hold timing optimization. Therefore, when we perform slack allocation on setup timing, we use delay values from the design speed grade $K$, but when we perform slack allocation on hold timing, we switch our timing model to use delay values from speed grade $M$. The consideration of both speed grades then affects the calculation of our delay window.

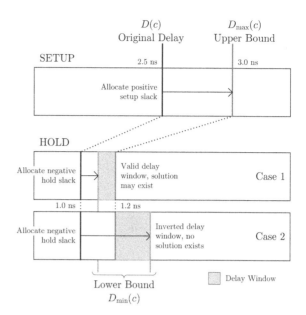

**Figure 6: Illustration of the narrowing delay window with consideration of the hold speed grade**

In Figure 6, we illustrate slack allocation being performed for a connection $c$ on both setup and hold timing. For this example, suppose that the original connection has a delay of $D(c) = 2.5$ ns and has positive setup slack. By distributing its positive slack, we arrive at an upper bound of $D_{\max}(c) = 3.0$ ns on the setup side for the delay window. Now, to find the lower bound for the delay window, we must switch to the hold speed grade. Assume, for the sake of example, that delay is uniformly 2.5 times less in the hold speed grade, and that the connection $c$ has negative hold slack. In this case, we distribute its negative slack by adding more delay to the lower bound and pushing it closer to the upper bound. This type of scenario, in combination with the consideration of multiple speed grades, can result in a narrow delay window. In the first case shown in Figure 6, we arrive at a narrow but valid delay window. Here we note that the lower bound $D_{\min}(c)$ can actually exceed the upper bound from the setup side, as is shown in second case of Figure 6. This occurrence indicates that there is no possible solution to satisfy both the setup and hold timing constraints for this particular connection. When we encounter such a connection, we either accept the hold timing violation as is, or we fix it with some penalty to the setup timing. In our commercial hold timing correction engine, we define an effort level parameter to control this decision. For each connection $c$, we let $D_{\max}(c)|_{\text{setup}}$ be the maximum delay value calculated by slack allocation for the selected setup timing speed grade $K$, and let $D_{\max}(c)|_{\text{hold}}$ be the same maximum delay value converted to the hold timing speed grade $M$. At the lowest effort level, we cap the upper bound delay value at $D_{\max}(c)|_{\text{hold}}$. At the intermediate level, we cap the upper bound delay value at $1.25 \times D_{\max}(c)|_{\text{hold}}$, effectively imposing a potential maximum 25 percent penalty on the setup performance in order to fix hold timing violations. Finally, at the highest effort level, there is no cap on the upper bound delay value, meaning that we fix hold timing violations without regard to setup timing performance.

# 3. METHOD OF SPECIFIC DELAY WINDOW ROUTING

In this section, we give an overview of routing algorithms used in our work and previous related works. These algorithms underlie the method of specific delay window routing. The basic paradigm behind a vast majority of FPGA routers is the maze search method, which uses wave propagation to traverse a graph of routing resources [7]. Costs on routing resources are universally used to direct the search to yield a favorable path and the use of A* search with a priority queue to order the nodes at the wave edge is common. Traditionally, methods of rip-up and retry were used to resolve conflicts on routing resources among multiple nets. In [1], the concept of negotiation-based conflict resolution was proposed in the PathFinder algorithm. This methodology has since been commonly adopted in academic and commercial FPGA routers. The PathFinder algorithm uses routing resource costs based on the weighted sum of a delay penalty $d_w$ and a congestion penalty $c_w$ on node $w$, where the weight is based on the overall criticality $\alpha$ of the connection $(s, t)$ containing the node $w$ within the circuit, as shown in (1)[1].

$$\text{Cost}_w = \alpha \cdot d_w + (1 - \alpha) \cdot c_w \qquad (1)$$

$$d_w = f\left(T_{(s,t)}\right) \qquad (2)$$

Essentially, the more critical a connection is, the more weight the delay penalty will carry in the cost function. Conversely, the less critical a connection is, the more weight the congestion penalty will carry. In competition for routing resources, this scheme encourages less critical connections to find a less costly alternative path. As shown in (2), the delay penalty term of the cost function is a function of the total delay of the connection from source to target. For this work, we use the PathFinder algorithm as described above to route connections into a specific delay window. In the following sections we describe how we target these specific delay windows with both single and dual wave expansion, highlighting the issues with the former approach.

## 3.1 Limitations of Single Wave Expansion

Using single wave expansion, we search for an optimal path from a source node $s$ to a target node $t$ by traversing the routing resource graph starting at source $s$ and expanding towards $t$. Since our cost function depends on the total delay of the connection $(s, t)$, we must use an estimation from the current wave node $w_j$ to the target node $t$, as depicted in Figure 7 and formulated in (3).

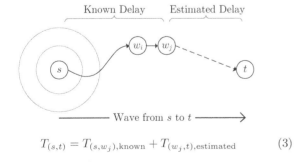

$$T_{(s,t)} = T_{(s,w_j),\text{known}} + T_{(w_j,t),\text{estimated}} \qquad (3)$$

**Figure 7: Illustration of single wave expansion with target delay estimation**

In order to direct the search to find a solution within the specific delay window, we test the estimated total delay (3) as we expand from each node in the wave edge against our delay window. If we find that the estimated total delay is outside this window, we add an additional cost to the node which lowers its priority in the queue so that other paths more likely to meet the specific delay window are prioritized. Note that we do not permanently block nodes that do not meet the specific delay window by estimation.

In [2], single wave expansion with target delay estimation is similarly used to route connections into a specific delay window. This is done by an adjustment to the cost function which factors in the delay window bounds. In the PathFinder cost function (1), the delay penalty $d_w$ is taken to be the total delay of the connection. The Routing Cost Valley (RCV) algorithm proposed in [2] adjusts this delay penalty term by increasing the penalty linearly as the delay value of the connection moves away from the center of the delay window towards the bounds of the delay window, and quadratically if the delay value of the connection surpasses those bounds. Though the inclusion of the routing cost valley in the delay penalty is effective in steering the wave search to yield a result within the specified delay window, the estimation term within the total connection delay still factors into this delay penalty. Due to architecture characteristics, the estimation term required for the single wave search can be a source of inaccuracy that yields suboptimal results, including missed opportunities to correct timing violations. As depicted in Figure 1, switchboxes without full crossbar can cause estimation to be inaccurate. Additionally, the varying lengths of interconnect spanning switchboxes contributes to the difficulty of delay estimation since, in general, the delay of a wire between switchboxes is not linear in the distance it spans. Finally, delay estimation can be difficult and inaccurate when the target is a LUT input pin since the logical equivalence of LUT input pins allows us to swap them for local delay optimization.

## 3.2 Enhancement with Dual Wave Expansion

Using dual wave expansion, we simultaneously expand downstream from source node $s$ towards target node $t$ and upstream from target node $t$ to source node $s$. We then check the intersection points of the two waves to find paths for the connection $(s, t)$. Since we expand from both sides, the actual delay cost is known from the source to the target through the intersection, as shown in Figure 8. With this actual delay value, we replace the estimation term from (3), as shown in (4). This adjustment yields more accurate delay measurement and thus, better routing quality for connections with specified delay windows.

In our dual wave approach, the two waves are individually implemented in the same fashion as the single wave approach, only without the introduction of extra penalties on nodes estimated to fall outside of the delay window. We replace that mechanism of adding additional cost with the selection of an intersection point between the two waves. As we expand both waves, we check if the new wave edge nodes form an intersection. If the resulting delay meets the requirement of the delay window, we accept the path through the intersection point as the solution; otherwise we compare the resulting delay against the best historical solution and keep the new path if its delay is closer to the window. In addition to the accuracy improvement, another advantage

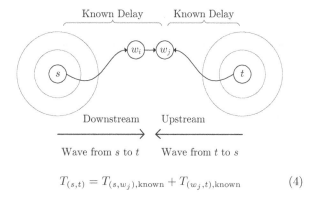

$$T_{(s,t)} = T_{(s,w_j),\text{known}} + T_{(w_j,t),\text{known}} \qquad (4)$$

**Figure 8: Illustration of dual wave expansion to replace target delay estimation**

of this technique is the size of the solution space, which is much larger than that of the single wave search. This yields many intersection points from which we may select one corresponding to a path that fits within our specific delay window. Additionally, if no such solution exists for the given delay window – that is, none of the intersection points of the two waves yield connections within the delay window – then we can select from the many path choices one that is closest to the delay window.

## 3.3 Overall Routing Flow

In this section, we describe our overall routing flow to show where timing optimization fits in our entire routing strategy. Before we begin optimization for timing constraints, we undergo an initial routing phase consisting of two stages: global routing and detailed routing. In the global routing stage, we route clocks and other architecture-specific dedicated connections with global routing resources. Clocks that are designated to use these global routing resources are hardwired to a low-skew clock tree network. Other dedicated connections are routed in this stage if there is only one expected path in the device for that connection. Connections that are routed in the global routing stage are locked down, meaning that they are not eligible for rip-up in further stages.

Our detailed routing stage is based on the PathFinder algorithm [1] and focuses only on long-path timing in the initial routing stage. This is where our approach differs from [2], where short-path timing is considered alongside long-path timing during the detailed routing phase by applying specific delay windows to the router's delay cost function via the routing cost valley model. We have elected to consider short-path timing – and thus engage in specific delay window routing – in the timing optimization phase rather than the initial routing phase in order to save runtime. The runtime cost of performing specific delay window routing for all connections in the initial routing phase is primarily due to the runtime of slack allocation for hold timing correction, which is particularly high due to the need to support multiple speed grades and complex timing constraints.

After the initial routing phase, we begin the timing optimization phase. By default, this phase will be skipped if the design still has setup timing violations resulting from the initial routing stage, unless those violations are related to the maximum skew constraint. During the timing optimization phase, we consider only the connections of the circuit

that are in violation of timing constraints. However, during the rerouting process, we may require other connections that were satisfied by the initial routing to be rerouted if their paths come in conflict with the new routing of the violating connections. Furthermore, we only use dual wave expansion on such connections with delay windows – that is, connections that were in violation of constraints from the initial routing – but not on other connections that may need to be rerouted as a consequence of rerouting the violating connections. In our flow, we first optimize for constraints that require only setup timing analysis, for instance, the maximum skew constraint. After all constraints related to setup timing are optimized, we start hold timing correction. Optimization for hold timing constraints requires both setup and hold timing analysis in order to compute the specific delay windows for each involved connection.

## 4. EXPERIMENTAL RESULTS

In our experiment, we tested two different methods of specific delay window routing: one using single wave expansion with target delay estimation and the other using dual wave expansion for the timing optimization phase. For both of the applications covered in Section 2 – maximum skew and hold timing correction – we selected ten designs each to be run by both methods. We then compared the resulting timing numbers from both runs to see the difference in accuracy and ability to find a solution to the timing issue.

## 4.1 Methodology

The two methods of specific delay window routing which we aim to compare belong to different generations of our commercial routing engine. With regard to specific delay window routing, these routing engines differ in two areas. First, the older one uses single wave expansion to route a connection into a specific delay window, whereas the second one uses dual wave expansion as described in Section 3. It is this major difference which we claim results in a difference in accuracy and runtime for the application of specific delay window routing. The second difference in the engines is the method of delay budgeting used to calculate the delay windows for hold timing correction. For the single wave approach, a heuristic method is used to calculate delay budgets for only the connections being considered for hold timing correction. For the dual wave approach, the slack allocation technique described in Section 2.3 is used, which gives a more global picture of the delay in the circuit. While this difference can have an impact on the delay windows calculated for hold timing correction, the difference is small and the phenomenon of narrow delay windows which motivates the need for dual wave expansion persists in both cases.

To test the performance of specific delay window routing targeting the maximum skew constraint, we selected five designs constraining maximum skew on nets and another five constraining maximum skew on buses. The maximum skew constraint (as described in Figure 2) was applied to the clock, clock enable, and local set-reset pins of individual nets that were prevented from using global routing resources such as low-skew clock trees. For buses, we selected input and output buses, as well as buses that are completely internal to the FPGA device. In our experiment, part of our aim was to show that as the maximum skew constraint value becomes more strict, the solution using single wave expansion would fail to meet the constraint sooner than the solution

Table 1: Design statistics

| Design | Device Family | LUT4s | Utilization |
|---|---|---|---|
| N0 | MachXO2 | 4K | 70% |
| N1 | LatticeECP3 | 150K | 11% |
| N2 | LatticeECP2 | 20K | 45% |
| N3 | LatticeECP3 | 150K | 66% |
| N4 | ECP5 | 85K | 67% |
| B0 | MachXO2 | 2K | 67% |
| B1 | LatticeECP2 | 20K | 74% |
| B2 | LatticeECP3 | 70K | 41% |
| B3 | LatticeECP3 | 150K | 28% |
| B4 | ECP5 | 45K | 23% |
| H0 | LatticeEC | 33K | 9% |
| H1 | LatticeEC | 33K | 9% |
| H2 | MachXO | 2K | 85% |
| H3 | MachXO | 2K | 85% |
| H4 | LatticeECP3 | 150K | 83% |
| H5 | LatticeECP3 | 150K | 14% |
| H6 | LatticeECP3 | 150K | 82% |
| H7 | LatticeECP3 | 150K | 87% |
| H8 | LatticeECP3 | 150K | 76% |
| H9 | LatticeECP3 | 150K | 84% |

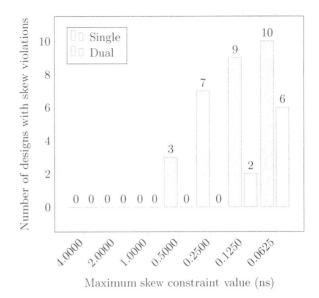

Figure 9: Number of designs with maximum skew violations by constraint value

using dual wave expansion. To this end, we used sweeping values for the maximum skew constraint, from 4 ns (relaxed) to 0.0625 ns (very strict) and recorded the resulting slack (constraint value minus achieved skew) from both methods for each constraint value.

To test the performance of specific delay window routing targeting hold timing correction, we selected ten customer designs known to have hold timing violations. After running each design with the two methods, we recorded the worst hold timing slack. The aim of this part of the experiment was to show that the solution using dual wave expansion could solve some hold timing violations that the solution with single wave expansion could not. In Table 1 we give various statistics on the designs selected for our experiments, which show a variety of different device densities and utilization percentages.

## 4.2 Results

The results of our experiments show that, overall, specific delay window routing with dual wave expansion is able to optimize for stricter constraints (or, more narrow delay windows) than the same process using single wave expansion with target delay estimation. In Table 2, we show the slack results of the experiment on the maximum skew constraint with sweeping constraint values. With a constraint value of 0.5 ns, three designs failed to meet the constraint with the single wave approach. Furthermore, when we reduced the constraint value to 0.25 ns, seven designs failed to meet the constraint with the single wave approach. In comparison, the dual wave approach was able to find a solution for all designs with constraint values at or above 0.25 ns. As we lowered the maximum skew constraint values even further to 0.125 ns and 0.0625 ns, the dual wave approach continued to outperform the single wave approach. Figure 9 shows the number of designs that failed for both single and dual wave approaches with decreasing maximum skew values.

The runtime of the dual wave approach, shown in Tables 3 and 4, is on par with the single wave approach for relaxed skew constraints and is even significantly reduced as the skew constraint becomes more strict. This downward trend in the ratio of dual wave runtime to single wave run-

time subsides as we reach the most strict constraints since the single wave approach may finish earlier without a solution. This is particularly apparent in the results for designs B0 and B3, where several more iterations of rerouting to correct skew violations were performed in the dual wave approach compared to the single wave approach. The main reason behind the satisfactory runtime performance for the dual wave approach is the increased solution space it yields, which allows us to more quickly select a path that meets the specific delay window. With the single wave search directed by a delay cost function which contains an estimation term, we can potentially waste time with suboptimal paths if the priority queue of path costs is incorrectly prioritized based on poor estimation. Essentially, since the search is directed in part by the estimation term, a bad estimation can result in the search being directed poorly. When a misguided wave search nears the target, the estimation (and thus, true cost) becomes more clear and we may have to retry other paths in the queue if the current path will not meet the specified delay window.

In Table 5, we show the results of the experiment on hold timing correction using specific delay window routing. In order to compare the hold timing correction results, the hold timing optimization is forced since most of these designs have setup timing violations after the initial routing phase. The worst slack and total negative slack columns for hold timing show that five designs had hold timing violations with the single wave approach, whereas all ten designs passed all hold timing requirements with the dual wave approach. The penalty to the setup timing of these designs can be seen in the corresponding setup timing columns. Note that, though the dual wave approach was able to add necessary delay to connections to fix hold timing violations, the setup timing was not significantly impacted for most designs.

In contrast to the maximum skew experiment, the runtime results of the dual wave approach for the hold timing correction experiment given in Table 6 shows a slight increase compared to the single wave approach. While the reasons

**Table 2: Slack results (ns) from varying maximum skew constraint values**

| | Constraint Value (ns) | | | | | | | | | | | | | |
| | 4.0000 | | 2.0000 | | 1.0000 | | 0.5000 | | 0.2500 | | 0.1250 | | 0.0625 | |
| Design | Single | Dual | Single | Dual | Single | Dual | Single | Dual | Single | Dual | Single | Dual | Single | Dual |
|---|---|---|---|---|---|---|---|---|---|---|---|---|---|---|
| N0 | 2.216 | 2.910 | 0.928 | 0.885 | 0.722 | 0.221 | -0.719 | 0.121 | -0.064 | 0.091 | -0.055 | 0.009 | -0.255 | -0.046 |
| N1 | 3.377 | 3.539 | 1.377 | 1.539 | 0.377 | 0.539 | 0.056 | 0.137 | -0.283 | 0.124 | -0.144 | 0.014 | -0.231 | -0.059 |
| N2 | 3.245 | 3.409 | 1.245 | 1.409 | 0.542 | 0.409 | 0.042 | 0.105 | -1.424 | 0.011 | -0.057 | 0.055 | -0.145 | 0.020 |
| N3 | 3.375 | 3.365 | 1.356 | 1.365 | 0.351 | 0.365 | -0.975 | 0.100 | -2.748 | 0.144 | -2.510 | 0.009 | -1.409 | -0.094 |
| N4 | 3.216 | 3.156 | 1.216 | 1.156 | 0.190 | 0.156 | 0.114 | 0.065 | -0.587 | 0.023 | -0.487 | 0.030 | -1.156 | -0.017 |
| B0 | 2.820 | 3.208 | 1.208 | 1.208 | 0.208 | 0.208 | 0.009 | 0.126 | 0.076 | 0.097 | -0.072 | -0.643 | -0.120 | -0.123 |
| B1 | 2.114 | 2.282 | 0.399 | 0.303 | 0.813 | 0.102 | 0.315 | 0.010 | 0.060 | 0.001 | -0.072 | -0.004 | -0.159 | 0.001 |
| B2 | 3.148 | 3.156 | 1.148 | 1.156 | 0.148 | 0.156 | 0.001 | 0.112 | 0.050 | 0.083 | 0.000 | 0.052 | -0.123 | 0.009 |
| B3 | 3.493 | 3.493 | 1.493 | 1.493 | 0.493 | 0.493 | 0.014 | 0.179 | -0.257 | 0.117 | -0.382 | 0.073 | -0.533 | -0.064 |
| B4 | 3.203 | 3.246 | 1.203 | 1.246 | 0.203 | 0.246 | -0.297 | 0.100 | -0.547 | 0.133 | -0.683 | 0.065 | -0.746 | 0.033 |

**Table 3: Total routing runtime (seconds) for designs testing maximum skew constraint**

| | Constraint Value (ns) | | | | | | | | | | | | | |
| | 4.0000 | | 2.0000 | | 1.0000 | | 0.5000 | | 0.2500 | | 0.1250 | | 0.0625 | |
| Design | Single | Dual | Single | Dual | Single | Dual | Single | Dual | Single | Dual | Single | Dual | Single | Dual |
|---|---|---|---|---|---|---|---|---|---|---|---|---|---|---|
| N0 | 7 | 8 | 7 | 8 | 32 | 8 | 19 | 8 | 20 | 8 | 19 | 9 | 25 | 12 |
| N1 | 185 | 107 | 184 | 106 | 186 | 106 | 186 | 106 | 203 | 105 | 205 | 105 | 205 | 103 |
| N2 | 41 | 30 | 41 | 30 | 41 | 30 | 41 | 30 | 63 | 30 | 62 | 30 | 63 | 30 |
| N3 | 737 | 595 | 726 | 595 | 725 | 596 | 1005 | 601 | 1015 | 601 | 1021 | 601 | 1019 | 572 |
| N4 | 189 | 225 | 186 | 225 | 186 | 225 | 491 | 226 | 764 | 230 | 773 | 228 | 844 | 327 |
| B0 | 4 | 5 | 4 | 6 | 4 | 5 | 8 | 5 | 12 | 5 | 11 | 497 | 12 | 70 |
| B1 | 112 | 107 | 112 | 106 | 233 | 110 | 200 | 139 | 199 | 183 | 258 | 227 | 375 | 173 |
| B2 | 147 | 167 | 143 | 167 | 149 | 168 | 195 | 173 | 202 | 180 | 221 | 182 | 251 | 207 |
| B3 | 284 | 290 | 330 | 295 | 334 | 308 | 412 | 310 | 452 | 307 | 453 | 310 | 464 | 1134 |
| B4 | 38 | 51 | 36 | 50 | 35 | 57 | 46 | 58 | 46 | 58 | 52 | 56 | 53 | 53 |

**Table 4: Runtime ratio (dual wave / single wave) for designs testing maximum skew constraint**

| | Constraint Value (ns) | | | | | | |
| Design | 4.0000 | 2.0000 | 1.0000 | 0.5000 | 0.2500 | 0.1250 | 0.0625 |
|---|---|---|---|---|---|---|---|
| N0 | 1.155 | 1.169 | 0.255 | 0.442 | 0.428 | 0.460 | 0.460 |
| N1 | 0.579 | 0.576 | 0.571 | 0.568 | 0.519 | 0.515 | 0.505 |
| N2 | 0.719 | 0.719 | 0.726 | 0.724 | 0.475 | 0.491 | 0.479 |
| N3 | 0.808 | 0.820 | 0.822 | 0.598 | 0.592 | 0.588 | 0.561 |
| N4 | 1.189 | 1.213 | 1.212 | 0.460 | 0.301 | 0.295 | 0.388 |
| B0 | 1.327 | 1.352 | 1.301 | 0.717 | 0.392 | 46.04 | 5.762 |
| B1 | 0.959 | 0.952 | 0.473 | 0.697 | 0.920 | 0.879 | 0.460 |
| B2 | 1.138 | 1.166 | 1.124 | 0.890 | 0.890 | 0.823 | 0.823 |
| B3 | 1.021 | 0.894 | 0.923 | 0.751 | 0.679 | 0.685 | 2.446 |
| B4 | 1.337 | 1.405 | 1.617 | 1.255 | 1.252 | 1.061 | 0.996 |
| Mean | 1.023 | 1.027 | 0.902 | 0.710 | 0.645 | 5.184 | 1.288 |

Table 5: Slack results (ns) for designs testing hold timing correction

| | Setup | | | | Hold | | | |
|---|---|---|---|---|---|---|---|---|
| | Worst Slack (ns) | | TNS† (ns) | | Worst Slack (ns) | | TNS† (ns) | |
| Design | Single | Dual | Single | Dual | Single | Dual | Single | Dual |
| H0 | -1.041 | -1.995 | 17.15 | 97.32 | -0.290 | 0.006 | 25.22 | 0.000 |
| H1 | -1.455 | -1.457 | 15.37 | 70.69 | -0.295 | 0.006 | 27.29 | 0.000 |
| H2 | -5.027 | -5.042 | 399.7 | 396.3 | -0.627 | 0.010 | 0.627 | 0.000 |
| H3 | -4.022 | -4.579 | 73.71 | 76.47 | -0.291 | 0.005 | 0.291 | 0.000 |
| H4 | -2.609 | -2.609 | 67.83 | 49.11 | 0.000 | 0.005 | 0.000 | 0.000 |
| H5 | 0.320 | 0.320 | 0.000 | 0.000 | 0.001 | 0.006 | 0.000 | 0.000 |
| H6 | -1.539 | -2.672 | 5.132 | 8.244 | 0.000 | 0.005 | 0.000 | 0.000 |
| H7 | 0.023 | -0.331 | 0.000 | 0.817 | 0.000 | 0.005 | 0.000 | 0.000 |
| H8 | -0.964 | -1.101 | 9.850 | 12.23 | -0.093 | 0.005 | 0.441 | 0.000 |
| H9 | -0.576 | -0.576 | 15.79 | 15.80 | 0.000 | 0.005 | 0.000 | 0.000 |

† – Total Negative Slack

Table 6: Total routing runtime (seconds) for designs testing hold timing correction

| Design | Single | Dual | Ratio |
|---|---|---|---|
| H0 | 184 | 206 | 1.120 |
| H1 | 173 | 213 | 1.231 |
| H2 | 94 | 119 | 1.266 |
| H3 | 50 | 75 | 1.500 |
| H4 | 2236 | 2553 | 1.142 |
| H5 | 236 | 414 | 1.754 |
| H6 | 5970 | 7289 | 1.221 |
| H7 | 6227 | 6575 | 1.056 |
| H8 | 2139 | 2527 | 1.181 |
| H9 | 4308 | 4837 | 1.123 |
| Mean | | | 1.259 |

for runtime improvement for the dual wave approach described in the discussion on the maximum skew experiment still apply to this case, the previously mentioned difference in routing engines results in the reverse trend for hold timing correction. Specifically, the heuristic method of delay budgeting used in the single wave approach is much faster than the slack allocation technique used in the dual wave approach. This is due to the nature of slack allocation, which requires us to perform several runtime-intensive iterations of timing updates between setup and hold analysis. For this reason, the runtime results of our dual wave approach are slightly higher than that of the single wave approach for this experiment.

## 5. CONCLUSION

Based on our experimental results, we conclude that, for specific delay window routing, dual wave expansion as a replacement for single wave expansion with target delay estimation increases the accuracy, and thus ability to find a solution for timing optimization. Furthermore, we've shown that specific delay window routing is a capable method for optimization targeting various timing constraints, including but certainly not limited to, maximum skew and hold timing correction.

## 5.1 Future Work

Specific delay window routing is already used in our commercial FPGA routing engine to optimize for constraints on maximum skew, maximum and minimum path delay, and hold timing correction. In the future, we aim to extend this method to enhance optimization for the clock-to-output constraint and "cycle stealing" feature. In supporting the clock-to-output constraint, a same clock path may be involved in several such constraints. Also, a data output path may have several connections. A method similar to slack allocation should be used not only on the data path, but also on the output clock path. The "cycle stealing" feature is used to add additional delay to clock paths (if allowed) to correct setup violations on data paths.

## 6. REFERENCES

[1] Larry McMurchie and Carl Ebeling. Pathfinder: A negotiation-based performance-driven router for fpgas. In *Proceedings of the 1995 ACM Third International Symposium on Field-programmable Gate Arrays*, FPGA '95, pages 111–117, New York, NY, USA, 1995. ACM.

[2] R. Fung, V. Betz, and W. Chow. Slack allocation and routing to improve fpga timing while repairing short-path violations. *Trans. Comp.-Aided Des. Integ. Cir. Sys.*, 27(4):686–697, April 2008.

[3] Peter S Hauge, Ravi Nair, and Ellen J Yoffa. *Circuit placement for predictable performance.* IBM Thomas J. Watson Research Center, 1987.

[4] H. Youssef and E. Shragowitz. Timing constraints for correct performance. In *Computer-Aided Design, 1990. ICCAD-90. Digest of Technical Papers., 1990 IEEE International Conference on*, pages 24–27, Nov 1990.

[5] J. Frankle. Iterative and adaptive slack allocation for performance-driven layout and fpga routing. In *Proceedings of the 29th ACM/IEEE Design Automation Conference*, DAC '92, pages 536–542, Los Alamitos, CA, USA, 1992. IEEE Computer Society Press.

[6] Frank Rubin. The lee path connection algorithm. *Computers, IEEE Transactions on*, C-23(9):907–914, Sept 1974.

[7] C. Y. Lee. An algorithm for path connections and its applications. *Electronic Computers, IRE Transactions on*, EC-10(3):346–365, Sept 1961.

# Fine-Grained Interconnect Synthesis

Alex Rodionov, David Biancolin, and Jonathan Rose
The Edward S. Rogers Sr. Department of Electrical & Computer Engineering
University of Toronto
{arod, Jonathan.Rose}@ece.utoronto.ca, biancolin@eecs.berkeley.edu

## ABSTRACT

One of the key challenges for the FPGA industry going forward is to make the task of designing hardware easier. A significant portion of that design task is the creation of the interconnect pathways between functional structures. We present a synthesis tool that automates this process and focuses on the interconnect needs in the *fine-grained* (sub-IP-block) design space. Here there are several issues that prior research and tools do not address well: the need to have fixed, deterministic latency between communicating units (to enable high-performance local communication without the area overheads of latency-insensitivity), and the ability to avoid generating un-necessary arbitration hardware when the application design can avoid it. Using a design example, our tool generates interconnect that requires 72% fewer lines of specification code than a hand-written Verilog implementation, which is a 33% overall reduction for the entire application. The resulting system, while requiring 4% more total functional and interconnect area, achieves the same performance. We also show a quantitative and qualitative advantages against an existing commercial interconnect synthesis tool, over which we achieve a 25% performance advantage and 17%/57% logic/memory area savings.

## Categories and Subject Descriptors

B.5.2 [**Register-Transfer-Level Implementation**]: Design Aids—*automatic synthesis*

## Keywords

FPGA, interconnect, automated synthesis

## 1. INTRODUCTION

An important and time-consuming aspect of hardware design is creating the interconnect that allows computation, storage, and control logic to communicate. This interconnect is often non-trivial, since any need for arbitration, routing, or pipelining precludes the use of wires alone.

Furthermore, an application's communication requirements may evolve throughout its development lifecycle, requiring effort and time to change the interconnect.

Interconnect synthesis tools have already been developed to automate the generation and parameterization of different kinds of interconnect, increasing designer productivity by avoiding the tedious and error-prone process of manually (re-)writing an RTL description[1, 15, 9, 12, 8]. Additionally, some of these tools also perform *system integration* and instantiate and parameterize the designer's functional modules as well as connecting them together using the automatically-generated interconnect, further reducing designer effort.

In the FPGA sphere, these existing tools are primarily focused on system-level design, connecting processors with peripherals, hardware accelerators, and other large chunks of IP. A key element of this design paradigm is *latency-insensitivity*[3], in which some form of "valid" and "ready" handshaking signals are used by the interface between the designer's modules and the interconnect to allow variable latency and backpressure. This decouples the interconnect's interface from its implementation, enabling IP re-use and drop-in replacement of interconnect (switching from a crossbar to an on-chip network, for example). Owing to their processor-centric roots, other common features of these interface protocols include memory-mapped addressing and support for read and write transactions.

However, with the increasing complexity of FPGA applications, IP blocks are starting to contain their own internal hierarchy and interconnect, which existing tools are not well equipped to generate. This *fine-grained* design environment is qualitatively characterized by the relatively small size of the blocks being connected, as well as an increased sensitivity to communication latency. Together, these factors make the area and performance overheads of coarse-grained interconnect prohibitive. For example, a pipelined network-on-chip router with virtual channels and a complex routing algorithm would be excessive for connecting together a handful of modules that are smaller than the router itself.

Additionally, coarse-grained interface paradigms such as latency-insensitivity, memory-mapping, and read/write transactions can incur secondary performance and area penalties if conforming to such interfaces forces the designer to insert extraneous logic. For example, supporting variable latency and backpressure requires pipelined datapaths to contain FIFOs or staging registers (two registers and a mux) instead of chains of ordinary registers, in order to avoid data loss upon deassertion of a Ready signal.

In this paper, we present a new interconnect synthesis and system integration tool called GENIE (GENeric Interconnect Engine). Our long-term goal is to automate and optimize interconnect for *all* levels of design granularity, but in this paper we will focus on its ability to generate fine-grained interconnect. We will show that the generated interconnect is comparable in area and performance to hand-crafted RTL, and requires less effort on behalf of the designer to specify.

GENIE's interconnect protocol lies between existing streaming and memory-mapped protocols in its level of abstraction. It defines signal roles for data, flow control, backpressure, and multicast-capable addressing, with most roles being optional. This allows for simple and minimal interfacing on the part of the designer. The tool's generated interconnect network is made of cascading Split and Merge primitives, which have been shown [8] to exhibit high performance and low area usage in FPGA applications.

To address the need for deterministic latency, GENIE allows the designer to query the latency of generated interconnect and pass it as a Verilog parameter to instantiated compute modules. Combined with GENIE's ability to pipeline interconnect, this aids in design space exploration and the hunt for timing closure, without the need for the designer to manually re-parameterize their non-interconnect datapaths. Additionally, GENIE generates smaller and faster versions of its interconnect by completely removing arbitration logic when the designer can guarantee the absence of competition on shared, many-to-one connections. Other features of GENIE, which are helpful and not limited to fine-grained use, include the support for configurable network topologies and optimized automatic clock domain crossing.

The structure of this paper is as follows: Section 2 provides relevant background on existing interconnect synthesis tools and paradigms. Section 3 describes the GENIE tool, its features, and interconnect microarchitecture. Section 4 describes the fine-grained design example that we will use to evaluate the capabilities of the tool - a compute unit in a parallel LU matrix decomposition[16] engine.

In Section 5, we generate interconnect for this design example using GENIE, Altera Qsys[1], and hand-optimized Verilog, and compare their area usage and achieved clock frequencies. We also attempt to quantify the productivity gains GENIE offers by comparing the amount of source code required to generate each of the three versions. Finally, we conclude our findings in Section 6.

## 2. BACKGROUND

In this section, we provide an overview of existing interconnect synthesis tools and methodologies. When studying existing tools, it is important to consider two aspects when considering applicability for fine-grained synthesis: the designer-facing protocol(s) afforded by the tool, and the architecture of the generated interconnect.

Altera and Xilinx include system integration tools with their FPGA design suites. Xilinx's Vivado IP Integrator[15] and Altera's Qsys[1] both provide two classes of interconnect protocols: memory-mapped and streaming.

Memory-mapped protocols, such as AMBA AXI[2] and Altera's Avalon-MM, are intended for connecting processors to peripherals and custom accelerators – what we consider to be a coarse-grained design space. Communications must be expressed as byte- or word-addressable reads and writes, between masters (initiators) and slaves (responders). Con-

forming to this high level of abstraction grants a designer a high degree of interconnect automation, with automatic insertion of data width converters, clock domain crossers, and the routing and arbitration logic necessary for decoding addresses and sharing a slave between multiple masters, respectively. The latter two functions of routing and sharing/arbitration are implemented with a shallow fixed-topology network such as a crossbar or a shared bus.

Meanwhile, streaming protocols such as AXI-Stream[2] and Avalon-ST are on the low end of the automation spectrum, with the intent mainly to provide a consistent IP interface rather than enable automated synthesis. Streaming protocols allow specification of only point-to-point connections, which consist of nothing more than data and flow control (Valid and Ready) signals, in typical use. The interconnect is implemented as point-to-point wiring, and the designer must explicitly insert any IP cores for routing and arbitration to communicate with multiple endpoints. This allows great control over implementation, at the cost of increased design effort.

Recent academic work in interconnect synthesis for FP-GAs has focused on automatic generation of on-chip networks. CONNECT[12] is an interconnect architecture specifically designed for the FPGA fabric, operating faster and with less area than direct ports of ASIC-targeted architectures. An online, web-based generator allows users to create custom networks with arbitrary topologies and architectural features such as number of virtual channels. However, CONNECT does not perform system integration, and the designer is responsible for instantiating the interconnect and connecting it to their functional modules.

The interconnect architecture presented in this paper is based on Split/Merge[8], another existing FPGA Network-on-Chip design. Instead of traditional monolithic routers, simple Split and Merge primitives are used to implement one-to-many and many-to-one communications respectively. These can be chained together to form arbitrary topologies, giving a designer more implementation control than the crossbar-based memory mapped interconnect provided by FPGA vendor tools.

Algorithms have been developed to synthesize application-specific network topologies from a high-level specification consisting of connectivity and bandwidth/latency/energy requirements[10, 11, 14]. In particular, the approach[6] used by Cong et al. removes complexity from the generated network if it is known a priori that certain communication traces will never occur simultaneously. We perform a similar optimization during our network generation flow.

## 3. GENIE

In this section we describe GENIE, our new system integration and interconnect synthesis tool. Its input is a logical specification of a system's desired communication links and its output is a synthesizable Verilog implementation of the system which instantiates and parameterizes the designer's functional modules as well as connecting them with an automatically-generated interconnect fabric. We begin with the detail of GENIE's designer-facing interface protocol, and then move on to the microarchitecture of the generated interconnect, and finally describe other features which ease designer burden in fine-granularity hardware contexts.

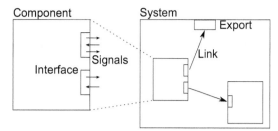

**Figure 1: GENIE Specification**

## 3.1 Input Specification

To use GENIE, the designer describes the functional modules to be instantiated and the logical communication links between them. This specification follows the component-based design paradigm used by most other system integration tools [1, 15, 9] which is essentially a higher-level representation of structural hardware design. The designer defines one or more *Systems*, each containing instances of *Components* which represent Verilog modules.

Each Component has one or more *Interfaces*, which have a direction of data flow and a type, and contain one or more Verilog input/output signals. Each signal within an Interface is assigned a communication-related role, such as transmitting data, providing an address, or synchronization. Interfaces allow Components to communicate with other Components and with hardware outside the System. An Interface's type specifies its communication protocol, and GENIE defines the following types of Interfaces:

- **Clock, Reset:** Delivers clock (or reset) signals to the Component.

- **Routed Streaming:** Serves as an endpoint for GENIE's Routed Streaming communications protocol, and can include a mix of data, handshaking, addressing, and packetization signals, further explained in Section 3.2. An associated Clock Interface determines the clock domain.

- **Conduit:** A catch-all for signals that wish to bypass GENIE's interconnect synthesis flow, such as those connecting to off-chip memory controllers. Connecting together two Conduits connects together their constituent signals with simple wires.

After instantiating Components within a System, the designer defines *Links* between their Interfaces. These are logical connections representing desired communication paths, and are made between Interfaces of the same type and opposite data flow direction. A System also contains one or more *Exports*, which enable communication into and out of the System. Exports are connected to Interfaces via Links, and the Export automatically takes on the same type and opposite polarity of its connected counterpart. Figure 1 provides an overview of the objects in GENIE's system specification.

GENIE also offers an addressing scheme that sits on top of the Interface abstraction, that allows an Interface to choose a subset of outgoing Links to transmit data, or allows a receiving Interface be notified of which Link is currently sending it data. This is achieved through abstractions called Linkpoints. Each Routed Streaming Interface, which is a physical collection of signals, may have one or more named Linkpoints defined inside of it, which are virtual connection

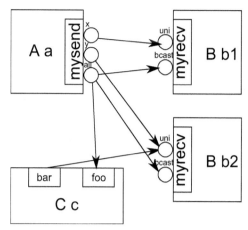

**Figure 2: Example System**

points associated with the physical Interface. A Linkpoint is simply a name and an associated binary encoding (a Linkpoint ID) chosen by the designer, used to refer to the Linkpoint by the Component's logic. At the System level, Links are normally made between two Interfaces to indicate logical connectivity. When an Interface has Linkpoints, a Link must terminate at one of the Linkpoints instead. During circuit operation, a Component drives (or receives) a Linkpoint ID to differentiate amongst multiple remote destinations.

| Component | Interface | LP Name | LP ID |
|-----------|-----------|---------|-------|
| A | mysend | x | 2'b00 |
| | | y | 2'b01 |
| | | all | 2'b10 |
| B | myrecv | uni | 1'b0 |
| | | bcast | 1'b1 |
| C | foo | - | - |
| | bar | - | - |

**Table 1: Linkpoint definitions**

The example System illustrated in Figure 2 shows a GENIE input specification, and the usage of Linkpoints. In this example, components A, B, C are Verilog modules created separately by the designer. In the system specification, modules A and C are instantiated once (named as instances a and c) and B is instantiated twice as instances b1 and b2. Components A, B, and C, each have Routed Streaming Interfaces, named in the rectangular labels within A, B and C, and are listed in the second column of Table 1. Associated Clock and Reset Interfaces are omitted for clarity. Components A and B use Interfaces that include also Linkpoints (shown as external circles in Figure 2) while C does not need to differentiate amongst destinations and thus does not use the Linkpoint addressing scheme. The third column of Table 1 gives the Linkpoint names, with their associated Linkpoint IDs (in Verilog notation) given in the fourth column.

The result is that instance a can send data to either b1, b2 (using the x→uni or y→uni connections) or broadcast to b1 and b2 and c simultaneously (using its all outgoing linkpoint). Module instances b1 and b2 can differentiate between received unicast and broadcast traffic, and take take appropriate action if they wish.

Note that Linkpoint IDs are defined during Component definition, effectively creating a local rather than global address space, thus removing the need for the designer to write additional address encoding/decoding logic. The ability to broadcast/multicast can have imporant application in coarse-granularity designs, but we have also found a natural use case for it in our fine-granularity design example described below in Section 4. There it is used to selectively fill several block RAMs simultaneously.

All of these specifications are written by the designer programatically, in the form of an executable script written in Lua[13]. The script makes API calls to our underlying interconnect synthesis engine that create Interface, Component, System, Link, Export, and Linkpoint definitions. In a future version of the tool, Interface definitions and signal roles will be extracted directly from Verilog signal definitions of each Component's source code, removing the current need by GENIE to replicate this information.

## 3.2 Communication Protocol

An important decision in creating a useful interconnect automation tool is the choice of the level of abstraction for the designer-facing interface protocol, which is dependent on the intended use of the tool. If there is insufficient abstraction and automation, then the designer must implement some interconnect functionality explicitly - for example, streaming protocols are extremely lightweight, but any arbitration or routing logic must be inserted manually, since the protocol has no concept of an address.

On the other hand, a protocol can be too *heavyweight* - for example, tools which synthesize memory-mapped interconnect allow masters to address different slaves and automatically insert the logic to route traffic accordingly. This includes enabling sharing and arbitration from competing masters. The price of this automation is that it requires the designer to express all communications as byte-addressable reads and writes, even in situations where it is unnatural to do so.

In the fine-granularity design space, which is the focus of this paper, we wish to elevate the level of automation above that of bare RTL and streaming protocols, but avoid the overhead of memory-mapped interconnect. We landed on using a streaming protocol, but augmenting it with the optional ability to reach different destinations using the Linkpoint addressing scheme described above. The tool automatically inserts lightweight logic to perform the requisite routing and arbitration. We call this a *Routed Streaming* protocol.

The Routed Streaming protocol defines several roles for the signals that constitute a Routed Streaming Interface:

- **Data**: The data to transmit, of arbitrary designer-specified width. There can be several independent Data signals within the Interface, for example, to carry Red, Green, and Blue color data separately if one is transmitting pixel data. This saves the designer from having to manually pack and unpack data fields in their Component logic. Multiple data signals must be differentiated with a designer-provided tag.

- **Valid**: Indicates whether all other signals carry valid values during the current clock cycle.

- **Ready**: Backwards-traveling backpressure signal that indicates if the interconnect, or designer logic, is able to accept data during a clock cycle.

- **EOP**: End-of-Packet. Used for transmitting a large block of data over multiple cycles, and is asserted on the last cycle. The interconnect uses this signal for arbitration purposes.

- **LPID**: The Linkpoint ID, if any Linkpoints are defined for this Interface

The direction of each signal matches the direction of the Interface, except for Ready signals which travel in the opposite direction. Most signals are optional, and GENIE avoids the generation of unnecessary logic when signals are left unused. The minimal possible Interface consists of either only a Data signal, or only a Valid signal. The latter case is useful for implementing data-less messages such as *go* or *done* commands issued by control logic. When a Valid, Ready, or EOP signal is ommitted, the Interface behaves as if there is a constant high value driving that signal.

## 3.3 Interconnect Micro-Architecture

In addition to a lightweight interface protocol, it is important that the generated interconnect have low area overhead and introduce minimal latency, especially in fine-granularity systems. GENIE's interconnect is based on two switching primitives called Split and Merge [8]. They perform all routing and arbitration functionality and can be cascaded to form arbitrary topologies.

The ability to control topology is an important feature when designing networks. GENIE allows the designer to specify topology on a per-System level as a parameter when declaring a System in the input script. There exist several built-in topologies such as crossbar, ring, and shared bus. These are topology-generating functions, which create the correct number of split and merge nodes depending on the System specification, and the designer can write their own generator function in Lua to implement custom topologies.

GENIE's interconnect employs static, table-based routing, which is generated based on the logical Links defined by the designer in the input specification. Internally, GENIE assigns a global Flow ID to each end-to-end Link that was specified by the designer. Table-based converters are inserted in front of Routed Streaming Interfaces of Components in order to convert between designer-defined Linkpoint IDs and global Flow IDs.

The conversion is expressed as a logic function, and we found that it optimizes to wires and one or two FPGA logic elements during back-end synthesis.

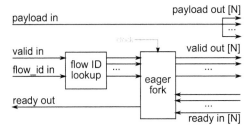

**Figure 3: Split Node architecture**

Routing is performed by Split nodes (as illustrated in Figure 3), which have a single input and multiple outputs. The data payload is broadcast to all destinations, and includes Routed Streaming signals such as Data and EOP that the Split node does not need to extract/examine. A split node contain a table, parameterized by GENIE, which looks up a one-hot vector of Valid outputs for each Flow ID. These Valid signals pass through an Eager Fork[4] stage. The Eager Fork is a sub-structure that is part of the Split Node, and is responsible for throttling Valid signals and managing state when only a subset of currently-targeted outputs are ready to receive the broadcasted payload. It also breaks combinational loops when Split nodes are cascaded with Merge nodes[4].

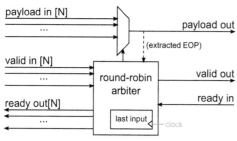

**Figure 4: Merge Node architecture**

Merge nodes (shown in Figure 4) allow multiple input streams to compete for one common output. A round-robin arbiter selects which input gets forwarded to the output. If multi-cycle packets are being sent, and the EOP signal is being used, then the Merge Node will wait until the entire packet is sent, and the EOP received, before switching inputs. This eliminates the need for the designer's logic to track multiple overlapping transmissions and the resulting complexity involved. If the inputs can be guaranteed to never simultaneously access the output, the round-robin arbiter can be removed (Section 3.5).

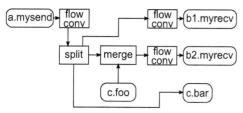

**Figure 5: Example System with Interconnect**

Figure 5 shows a GENIE implementation of the example system specification from Figure 2. Interfaces are shown with rounded boxes, and the regular boxes are GENIE interconnect (Flow ID converters, Split nodes, and Merge nodes). Clock and Reset connections are omitted for clarity.

## 3.4 Latency Introspection

In the context of high-performance functional element design (which we have labelled the "fine-grained" context) the latency of communication paths must often be short and of deterministic length. For example, it is common to have highly pipelined datapaths performing some computation. While the interconnect between individual pipeline stages is currently outside the scope of our synthesis flow, the communication between the pipeline's exterior with control logic or with a pipelined block RAM does fit into the fine-granularity realm we wish to target.

In the latter case, where data signals temporarily leave the pipeline to access a block RAM for reading, the read data must be reunited with associated data that stay within the pipeline - and those signals must be delayed by the correct amount. That amount depends on the RAM read latency plus the delay of the interconnect. If a traditional, latency-insensitive interface is used, the designer's pipeline must be able to tolerate backpressure, which introduces additional complexity and possibly even FIFOs, thus incurring area, performance, and design time overheads.

Instead, we'd like the interconnect, just like the block RAM being accessed, to have a deterministic and fixed latency, but one that can still be trivially modified later to ease timing closure. GENIE solves this problem with its *Latency Introspection* feature, which allows the actual interconnect latency to be queried and reported back to Components' Verilog code as parameter values. Queries are made during System definition in the Lua script, and values are propagated during Component instantiation.

## 3.5 Mutually-Exclusive Sharing

In general many-to-one communication, there must exist some method for the interconnect to allow two or more inputs to share a common destination. When there is competition, arbitration logic must choose the winner and stall the other inputs with backpressure. This necessitates support for backpressure on all competing links and their upstream sources. In GENIE, sharing and arbitration are accomplished with the Merge node.

However, if the application is deliberately designed such that no two inputs will ever simultaneously access their shared destination, arbitration is no longer necessary. Such mutually-exclusive access patterns can arise, for example, when each competing source has explicitly-scheduled access to the destination. When a designer creates a GENIE system specification, they can also specify a constraint indicating that all Links terminating at a shared destination will never compete during application runtime.

This generates a simplified Merge node with the round-robin logic in Figure 4 removed. In its place, the select input of the multiplexer is driven directly (in a one-hot fashion) by the incoming Valid signals, which are also ORed together to generate the outgoing Valid signal. The Ready signal is broadcast to all the inputs.

## 3.6 Automatic Clock Domain Crossing

Multiple clock domains are often used to decouple computation and communication circuitry if they have unbalanced demands. GENIE transparently supports multiple clock domains, and inserts crossing logic automatically in the form of dual-clock FIFOs.

When a design contains multiple clock domains, there is an interesting optimization problem that arises when crossing between any two domains: where in the generated interconnect network should the transition occur? GENIE intelligently chooses the point at which the minimum total number of signals undergo the crossing, because each signal incurs a non-trivial cost. For example, consider that building the crossing before the input to a Split node is cheaper than inserting multiple crossings after each output of the Split node. When the network contains a complex topology of Split and Merge nodes, the optimal choice may not be obvious.

The crossing-point selection algorithm represents the System as a graph, with vertices representing Routed Streaming Interfaces belonging to both designer-specified functional modules and those of internally-generated interconnect modules. Vertices are labeled with their clock domain (which is fixed for designer-specified Interfaces and initially unknown for interconnect), and edges are weighted by their total payload widths. A greedy multi-way cut[7] algorithm is run on this graph to cut it into partitions representing clock domains, minimizing the total cut weight. Once the cut points are identified, clock converter FIFOs are inserted.

This feature of GENIE contributes to rapid design exploration. In addition to evaluating different topologies, a designer can also experiment with assigning functional modules to different clock domains to try to optimize application performance, all without modifying the application's RTL source code.

# 4. DESIGN EXAMPLE

In this section, we present a hardware design example that, in Section 5, will be used to evaluate and compare GENIE's fine-grained interconnect synthesis versus manual design and a commercial interconnect synthesis tool. With this example, we also hope to better illustrate the nature of fine-grained interconnect and the challenges related to automatically synthesis.

Our application is a parallel LU Decomposition engine [16]. LU Decomposition is an important linear algebraic operation and is often used as the first step in efficiently solving systems of linear equations or calculating matrix inverses. It decomposes a square matrix $A$ into lower-triangular and upper-triangular matrices $L$ and $U$ such that $L \times U = A$. The application stores the matrix in off-chip memory so that very large matrices can be decomposed. It is arranged in blocked fashion (64x64) to support blocked computation, and partitioned across $M$ memory controllers. An array of $N$ Compute Elements (CEs), coordinated by a central Control Node, work in parallel to process the matrix and write back a transformed version in-place. A diagram of the full system is given in Figure 6.

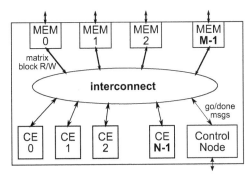

**Figure 6: LU Decomposition Engine**

The CEs, Memory Nodes, and Control Node are large (using between 1000 to 10,000 logic elements) and must tolerate variable communication latency, in part due to the nature of external memory. It is at this level that traditional coarse-grained interconnect synthesis is typically employed. The long-term goals of the GENIE project are to both generate at this level and the fine-grained level we have described so far, *and* to optimize across all those levels. However, in this paper we focus on the fine-grained system design within a *single* CE.

## 4.1 Compute Element Design

Here we describe the structure, functionality, and internal communication requirements of the CE, which is normally instantiated many times within the larger LU Decomposition application, but is examined in isolation as our design example.

The CE processes a specific column of blocks from the matrix by reading the blocks from external memory and writing back transformed data in their place. A simplified block diagram of the CE is shown in Figure 7, and contains four major components:

- A Control unit to orchestrate the fetching, processing, and writing back of blocks within the assigned column.

- Caches, implemented as FPGA block RAMs, to store the matrix blocks being operated on, locally within the CE.

- A computation Pipeline, which reads from and writes to the caches to produce the processed results.

- A data Marshaller to transfer matrix blocks to and from the caches and external memory outside the CE.

There are five, independent, dual-ported cache blocks in total: Top, Left0, Left1, Current0, and Current1. They are named after the types of blocks they store during processing, and relate to the spatial relationships between the cached blocks within the larger matrix. The Left and Current blocks are also double-buffered for increased performance, with the numerical suffix indicating which buffer it belongs to. While the caches of one buffer are being processed by the Pipeline, the other buffer is being filled from, or written back to, main memory by the Marshaller. The Top block is rarely written to, and does not need a second buffer.

The CE has two clock domains in order to decouple the performance requirements of the two tasks of processing matrix blocks and transferring them to and from memory. Processing a block takes much longer since each element in the matrix must be accessed more than once, on average. The Pipeline and Caches operate using "Clock A" and the rest of the design uses "Clock B", including the coarse-grained interconnect linking the CE with the greater LU Decomposition system.

There are two kinds of communications present within the CE shown in Figure 7: low-throughput control messages (shown as dashed arrows), and high-throughput matrix block read requests, read replies, and writes (shown as solid arrows). The former, while being point-to-point and not performance-demanding, can still benefit from automated interconnect synthesis rather than being implemented by hand, either because of the need to cross clock domains (Control to Pipeline), or the potential need to pipeline the links to close timing later in the design cycle.

In contrast, the high-throughput communications links require high-performance and non-trivial interconnect. They send data words (or requests for data words) every cycle, and originate or terminate at the read or write port of one of the five Caches – the actual connectivity between the Marshaller/Pipeline and the Caches is annotated in the figure, rather than being expanded out, for better readability. For all but two links (Pipeline to Top Cache reads), some mix of one-to-many or many-to-one communications is needed,

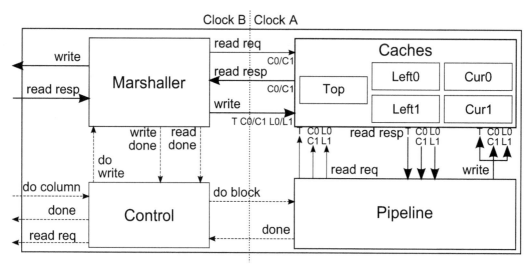

Figure 7: Compute Element Architecture

requiring distribution or arbitration hardware within the interconnect. Writes from the Pipeline also require broadcasting to multiple Caches during some modes of operation.

Read requests are 12 bits wide, and specify an address within a cache. Read replies are 256 bits wide, and carry multiple words of data to feed the Pipeline's SIMD datapath. Writes contain both an address and data and are 268 bits wide. It is important to mention the relatively large width of these connections, since it makes the interconnect's area usage that much more sensitive to its architecture.

## 4.2    Three CE Implementations

To illustrate the power, flexibility and quality of results of our new approach, we created three different implementation of the system and its interconnect: one generated by our tool GENIE, a manually-written and optimized reference design, and one generated by Altera's Qsys[1] system integration tool. This allows us to compare GENIE against the best possible hardware (at the expense of design time) and against an existing automated synthesis tool (at the expense of performance).

Each variant is a different realization of the CE system shown in Figure 7. In the Qsys variant, two different communication protocols are used: Avalon-MM (memory-mapped), and Avalon-ST (streaming). Connections to the Caches map naturally to random-access reads and writes, so we implement those using Avalon-MM, using an extra address bit to select between buffers of double-buffered Caches. The remaining connections, which are point-to-point and have no memory-like semantics, are implemented using Avalon-ST.

In the GENIE variant, all connections in Figure 7 are implemented as Links defined between Interfaces using the Routed Streaming protocol. Interfaces with multiple fanout, such as those to and from the Caches, have Linkpoints defined for each possible combination of destinations. The address is part of the data payload, rather than being an official part of the designer-facing interface as with Avalon-MM, so the purpose of Linkpoints is simply to direct traffic to the correct cache and buffer.

The manual variant uses no synthesis tool, and contains application-specific interconnect, designed by hand, to implement functionality such as connection sharing or clock

crossing. Pipeline registers were also manually added to improve timing on specific paths.

## 4.3    Tool-Related Issues

In this section, we highlight some important differences between the interconnect implementations of each variant in order to give some context to the results in Section 5. The goal of automation is to improve designer productivity while generating hardware with acceptable area and performance. To that end, we also hope to provide a qualitative picture of the design effort required to create each variant.

To avoid a detailed and exhaustive comparison, we focus on how each variant handles the following aspects of the CE design, since they required the greatest interconnect complexity:

- Clock domain crossing
- Marshaller to Cache read path
- Pipeline to Cache read paths

### 4.3.1    Clock Domain Crossing

Both the Marshaller to Cache connections and the Control to Pipeline connections cross clock domain boundaries, which is handled differently among the three variants.

In the manual variant, there exist two clock-crossing FIFOs for the whole design: one for connections travelling from Clock A to Clock B and one in the other direction. Each FIFO handles multiple links that travel in the same direction. This is the most efficient implementation, and is specifically tailored for the application.

Qsys performs automatic clock crossing for Avalon-MM connections, inserting dual-clock FIFOs when a master and slave are on different clock domains. However, it inserts FIFOs *after* routing traffic to multiple destinations, causing each destination path to have its own FIFO, including 9 FIFOs which must accommodate the cache read/write data width (256+ bits). Finally, no automatic clock crossing is performed on the Avalon-ST connections for the low-bandwidth control messages, requiring manual instantiation of clock crossing adapters from the Qsys component library.

The GENIE implementation has one clock-crossing FIFO for each connection (for a total of five), rather than the two used in the manual variant. All Marshaller to Cache write paths share a single FIFO, which GENIE inserts *before* a split node that broadcasts to up to five caches. The total number of FIFO memory bits is thus identical to the manual variant, but there is extra logic overhead since each FIFO requires its own read/write pointer and metastability protection registers. The upside is that all Routed Streaming connections receive automated clock crossing, with no designer intervention needed.

### 4.3.2 Marshaller to Cache Reads

Cache reads from the Marshaller need to be able to stall if the system outside the CE is unable to accept the outgoing data during any given clock cycle.

The manual variant's Caches have an explicit 'stall' signal as an input, which is generated by the Marshaller directly rather than being locally derived from any kind of backpressure conditions.

In the GENIE variant, the Caches have flow control and backpressure (Valid and Ready) signals on both read request and read response ports, and are able to stall the block RAM's internal pipeline if the read data is not accepted by the Marshaller.

The Avalon-MM protocol has backpressure for read requests in the form of the `waitrequest` signal role, allowing slaves (the Cache read ports) to stall the Master (the Marshaller). There exists no signal that allows the Marshaller to stall read data returning from the Caches. Our solution was to add a FIFO to the Marshaller to buffer this data until it can be sent outside the CE, and reserving space in this FIFO before sending any read requests to the Caches. Note that this missing functionality in Qsys requires extra effort for the designer to mitigate, while also costing area. This is not a general limitation of memory-mapped protocols, as, for example, AMBA AXI[2] has backpressure support for request and reply paths, but is cumbersome to use since many signals are mandatory.

### 4.3.3 Pipeline to Cache Reads

Read and write access to (some) of the cache blocks are shared between the Pipeline and Marshaller. However, due to double-buffering of the Caches, and careful orchestration by the Control logic, the design of the CE guarantees no competition between the Pipeline and Marshaller for the same buffer. This is ideal, because in theory it allows the Pipeline to operate as if it has sole point-to-point access to the Caches with the benefit of deterministic latency, simplifying the design.

This is the case in the hand-made variant. Sharing of the Cache ports is done with muxes controlled directly by the Control logic, which guarantees that the Marshaller and Pipeline never access the same Cache buffers at the same time. At the read data output of the Caches, a simple mux chooses the correct buffer's read response stream to send back to the Pipeline.

The GENIE variant handles the read path just as efficiently as the manual implementation, by virtue of allowing the system specification to declare that the Marshaller and Pipeline never compete for the same Cache ports. This generates Merge nodes that are nearly identical to the manual implementations, containing a mux which is controlled by the incoming Valid signals.

The Qsys interconnect has an arbiter block which is designed for the general worst case in which inputs compete for the output. However, even when there is no competition, we witnessed the generation of backpressure during the first cycle of a multi-cycle train of read requests. This required modifying the Pipeline by a FIFO in front of the read request port for the Current Cache, and another FIFO (wide, containing write data) in front of the write ports.

## 5. RESULTS

In this section, we quantitatively compare the three Compute Element variants presented in Section 4 in order to judge the efficacy (and ease of use) of GENIE in generating fine-grained interconnect.

Automation should increase productivity and make life easier for the designer. The implementation issues discussed in Section 4.3 give a qualitative view of the designer effort required. In this section we measure the amount of source code (and tool specification code) line counts as a first-order quantitative approximation of the difficulty of creating each CE variant.

At the same time, automation should strive to produce a high-quality interconnect implementation. We obtain the area and $F_{max}$ of each variant after being synthesized, placed, and routed on a modern FPGA.

### 5.1 Source Code Line Count

First, we measure the number of lines of source code (including scripting input lines for the tools) required to create both the functional modules and interconnect for each variant. For the interconnect part, we are interested in the size of the specification directly written by the designer. For the Qsys and GENIE variants, this would be the size of the TCL and Lua scripts, respectively, that are given as input to the tools to describe the system's communicating components and logical connectivity. The manual variant's interconnect is written in Verilog, as are the functional modules in all three variants.

| Variant | Interconnect + TOP Lines | Δ | FUNC Lines | Δ | TOTAL Lines | Δ |
|---------|---|---|---|---|---|---|
| Manual | 1029 | 0 | 1323 | 0 | 2352 | 0 |
| GENIE | 290 | -72% | 1289 | -3% | 1579 | -33% |
| Qsys | 440 | -57% | 1411 | +7% | 1851 | -21% |

**Table 2: Code Line Counts - Designer Effort**

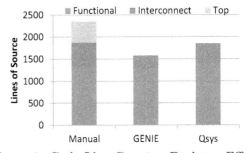

**Figure 8: Code Line Counts - Designer Effort**

Line counts were obtained using the CLOC[5] tool, which ignores comments and blank lines. Table 2 and Figure 8 give the results, with the table showing both absolute and relative (to the manual variant) line counts.

Note that the manual variant's 1029 lines of interconnect source code include 440 lines solely dedicated to the top-level Verilog module which instantiates all the other modules; this is referred to as 'TOP' in the table and figure. This glue code does not specify any true functionality, yet comprises a large portion of the source code base. Figure 8 gives it its own category to provide a better comparison of 'real' interconnect specification size. Nevertheless, using either system integration tool spares the designer from having to write the top-level instantiation code, so we include it in the "Interconnect + Top" code savings of 72% and 57% that GENIE and Qsys achieve, respectively.

The design of the functional modules is also affected by the choice of interconnect synthesis tool, in order to be compatible with protocols or mitigate lack of features, as described in Section 4.3. The Qsys variant required 7% more source code to make the changes described in Section 4.3. Meanwhile, the changes to the GENIE variant yielded a small savings, requiring no major architectural changes.

In the end, if a designer were to create the Compute Element with GENIE in mind from the very beginning, they would need to write 33% less source code than writing with no automation at all, with an even greater reduction if we focus on just the interconnect. It is a crude, but quantifiable, measurement of savings in design effort.

## 5.2 Area and Clock Frequency

Synthesis of each variant was performed using Altera Quartus II version 14.0, targeting a large Stratix V 5SGX-MBBR-1H43-C2 device, with the expectation of low congestion and device utilization. All external signals terminate at Virtual IOs rather than real device pins. Both clock domains in the design were over-constrained to 1 GHz, and results were geometrically averaged over 6 random seeds.

**Table 3: Clock Frequencies**

| Variant | Clock A | Clock B |
|---|---|---|
| Manual (MHz) | 406 | 461 |
| GENIE (MHz) | 400 | 500 |
| Qsys (MHz) | 320 | 394 |
| GENIE vs. Manual | -1% | +9% |
| GENIE vs. Qsys | +25% | +27% |

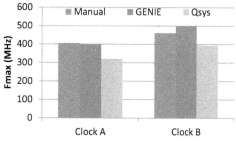

**Figure 9: Clock Frequencies**

Table 3 and Figure 9 show the achieved frequency for both clock domains for each variant, and a relative comparison of GENIE against the other two variants.

GENIE's interconnect achieves a Clock A frequency only 1% slower than the manual variant's. In the Clock B domain, GENIE achieves a 9% frequency advantage, but at the cost of extra registers. Since our Stratix V device's frequency is limited to 450 MHz anyway, a design choice was made in the manual variant to use fewer register stages – a detailed level of control we hope to include in a later revision of GENIE.

Like the hand-made interconnect, GENIE is able to take advantage of the application-level optimization that allows zero competition for caches, and thus generates very similar connection-sharing hardware. The simplified Merge nodes are one reason why, against Qsys, GENIE performs 25% better on average.

**Table 4: Area Usage**

| Variant | ALM | M20K |
|---|---|---|
| Manual | 6739 | 40 |
| GENIE | 6987 | 40 |
| Qsys | 8383 | 92 |
| GENIE vs. Manual | +4% | +0% |
| GENIE vs. Qsys | -17% | -57% |

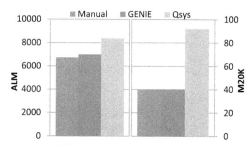

**Figure 10: Area Usage**

Table 4 and Figure 10 provide the area usage of the three variants, in terms of Stratix V Adaptive Logic Modules (representing logic, registers, and distributed memory) and M20K memory blocks. All variants also use 8 DSP (hard multiplier) blocks in addition to what is shown.

The GENIE-generated system is only 4% larger than the manually-created one, and occupies 17% fewer ALMs than the Qsys-generated system.

The Qsys interconnect contains an over-abundance of clock-crossing FIFOs (as discussed in Section 4.3), as well as additional FIFOs used to buffer cache read data. The increased number of FIFOs, and the fact that the GENIE and manual variants use distributed memory instead of M20Ks for their FIFOs, explains the high observed M20K usage.

Using M20Ks instead of distributed memory for FIFOs increases ALM usage, making the area gap between Qsys and manual/GENIE narrower than it otherwise might have been. Distributed memory uses ALMs itself, and can't pack as many downstream pipeline registers as M20Ks can. These registers then go on to use additional ALMs.

## Software Release

GENIE is open source software and is available for download at http://www.eecg.utoronto.ca/~jayar/software/GENIE/, complete with documentation and design examples, including Lua input specification scripts.

# 6. CONCLUSION

We have presented a new interconnect synthesis and system integration tool and showed its applicability in a fine-granularity design space that has been neglected by existing tools. We showed how to express interconnect requirements used this tool to synthesize the interconnect for a realistic fine-grained design example. This was compared with a hand-implemented version as well as one made with comercial interconnect synthesis tool.

Qualitatively, we found that the new tool, GENIE, reduced design effort by automating aspects of design such as clock crossing, as well as the generation of the switching fabric that allows the functional modules to communicate. All this was done without significant changes to the functional modules to support GENIE's protocol. This is in contrast with Qsys, which required changes to the functional modules to use, mitigating a lack of features in the signal protocol.

Quantitatively, using GENIE resulted in a 33% reduction in total source code line count compared to the hand-made implementation, and a significant 72% reduction if one only considers the code required to specify the interconnect. The cost for this productivity gain was a modest 1% decrease in achieved clock frequency (in one of the two clock domains) and a 4% increase in area. This demonstrates that the automation and ease of use provided by the tool, our primary goal, does not detract from the interconnect's performance in a frugal fine-granularity design context.

Against Qsys, GENIE achieved clock frequency gains of 25% and 27% in the Compute Element's two clock domains, and a 17% reduction in logic and register usage. The RAM block count reduction was more significant, at 57%. These gains demonstrate the efficacy of GENIE's automatic clock crossing insertion algorithm and lightweight Split/Merge interconnect microarchitecture in a fine-granularity design.

Although this paper focused on its fine-granularity use, we envision GENIE as a contender for interconnect synthesis at all levels of design, including the creation of the packet-switched networks and memory-mapped interconnect from the efficient Split/Merge primitives already in use. By having a single tool responsible for generating interconnect at all levels, it will be possible to explore new techniques such as optimizing interconnect across hierarchy boundaries.

# 7. REFERENCES

[1] Altera Corporation. QSys - Altera's System Integration Tool. http://www.altera.com/products/software/quartus-ii/subscription-edition/qsys/qts-qsys.html.

[2] ARM Ltd. AMBA Open Specifications. http://www.arm.com/products/system-ip/amba/amba-open-specifications.php.

[3] L. Carloni, K. McMillan, and A. Sangiovanni-Vincentelli. Theory of Latency-insensitive Design. *Computer-Aided Design of Integrated Circuits and Systems, IEEE Transactions on*, 20(9):1059–1076, Sep 2001.

[4] J. Carmona, J. Cortadella, M. Kishinevsky, and A. Taubin. Elastic Circuits. *Computer-Aided Design of Integrated Circuits and Systems, IEEE Transactions on*, 28(10):1437–1455, Oct 2009.

[5] CLOC. CLOC – Count Lines of Code. http://cloc.sourceforge.net/.

[6] J. Cong, Y. Huang, and B. Yuan. Atree-based topology synthesis for on-chip network. In *Proceedings of the 2011 IEEE/ACM International Conference on Computer-Aided Design*, ICCAD '11, pages 651–658, Washington, DC, USA, 2011. IEEE Computer Society.

[7] E. Dahlhaus, D. S. Johnson, C. H. Papadimitriou, P. D. Seymour, and M. Yannakakis. The Complexity of Multiway Cuts (Extended Abstract). In *Proceedings of the Twenty-fourth Annual ACM Symposium on Theory of Computing*, STOC '92, pages 241–251, New York, NY, USA, 1992. ACM.

[8] Y. Huan and A. DeHon. FPGA Optimized Packet-Switched NoC using Split and Merge Primitives. In *Field-Programmable Technology (FPT), 2012 International Conference on*, pages 47–52, Dec 2012.

[9] Lattice Semiconductor. LatticeMico System Development Tools. http://www.latticesemi.com/en/Products/DesignSoftwareAndIP/EmbeddedDesignSoftware/LatticeMicoSystem.aspx.

[10] A. P. Luca, L. P. Carloni, and A. L. Sangiovanni-vincentelli. Efficient Synthesis of Networks On Chip. In *in Proc. ICCD, 2003*, pages 146–150, 2003.

[11] U. Ogras and R. Marculescu. Energy- and performance-driven NoC communication architecture synthesis using a decomposition approach. In *Design, Automation and Test in Europe, 2005. Proceedings*, pages 352–357 Vol. 1, March 2005.

[12] M. K. Papamichael and J. C. Hoe. CONNECT: Re-examining Conventional Wisdom for Designing Nocs in the Context of FPGAs. In *Proceedings of the ACM/SIGDA International Symposium on Field Programmable Gate Arrays*, FPGA '12, pages 37–46, New York, NY, USA, 2012. ACM.

[13] PUC-Rio. The Programming Language Lua. http://www.lua.org/.

[14] V. Todorov, D. Mueller-Gritschneder, H. Reinig, and U. Schlichtmann. Deterministic Synthesis of Hybrid Application-Specific Network-on-Chip Topologies. *Computer-Aided Design of Integrated Circuits and Systems, IEEE Transactions on*, 33(10):1503–1516, Oct 2014.

[15] Xilinx Corporation. Accelerating Integration. http://www.xilinx.com/products/design-tools/vivado/integration/.

[16] W. Zhang, V. Betz, and J. Rose. Portable and Scalable FPGA-based Acceleration of a Direct Linear System Solver. *ACM Trans. Reconfigurable Technol. Syst.*, 5(1):6:1–6:26, Mar. 2012.

# Delay-Bounded Routing for Shadow Registers

Eddie Hung[*][†]
e.hung@imperial.ac.uk

Joshua M. Levine[*]
josh.levine@imperial.ac.uk

Edward Stott[*]
ed.stott@imperial.ac.uk

George A. Constantinides[*]
[*]Department of Electrical &
Electronic Engineering
Imperial College London, England
g.constantinides@imperial.ac.uk

Wayne Luk[†]
[†]Department of Computing

Imperial College London, England
w.luk@imperial.ac.uk

## ABSTRACT

The on-chip timing behaviour of synchronous circuits can be quantified at run-time by adding shadow registers, which allow designers to sample the most critical paths of a circuit at a different point in time than the user register would normally. In order to sample these paths precisely, the path skew between the user and the shadow register must be tightly controlled and consistent across all paths that are shadowed. Unlike a custom IC, FPGAs contain prefabricated resources from which composing an arbitrary routing delay is not trivial. This paper presents a method for inserting shadow registers with a minimum skew bound, whilst also reducing the maximum skew. To preserve circuit timing, we apply this to FPGA circuits post place-and-route, using only the spare resources left behind. We find that our techniques can achieve an average STA reported delay bound of ±200ps on a Xilinx device despite incomplete timing information, and achieve <1ps accuracy against our own delay model.

## Categories and Subject Descriptors

B.8.2 [**Hardware**]: Performance Analysis and Design Aids

## Keywords

Shadow Register; FPGA; Constrained Routing; Timing Measurement

## 1. INTRODUCTION

Aggressive process scaling has been the cornerstone behind the digital revolution that we live and breathe today. However, as the size of transistors shrink further and further into the nanometre spectrum, the ability to control any process variation has declined. This variation has required vendors to provision for the worse case, for example, by guaranteeing the performance of all of their devices only to the lowest common denominator.

By recouping some of this lost opportunity at runtime through per-device adaptation, ideally, we would expect

reduced power consumption, increased throughput, and extended device lifetime. One method for enabling this, that has been gaining popularity, is to augment a design with shadow registers [2, 4, 6]. Conceptually, shadow registers exploit temporal redundancy inside a synchronous digital circuit in order to infer live, on-chip, timing information that can be used to 'personalise' each circuit to its host device, for example, by reducing its supply voltage, or by increasing its clock frequency. In particular, the reconfigurable and prefabricated nature of field-programmable gate arrays (FPGAs) offer a compelling platform for pursuing this goal.

To ensure accurate timing measurements, shadow registers must be located at a precise delay away from the register it duplicates. However, whilst in custom layout silicon it is possible for arbitrary delays to be added to the data or clock signals of a shadow register, this same flexibility does not exist in an FPGA, where circuits must be constructed out of a predetermined set of resources. In this paper, we present a method for inserting shadow registers, that: *i*) can attach to the most critical paths of a circuit with a bounded routing delay; *ii*) only operates post place-and-route, using just the spare and unused resources on an FPGA such that the original timing behaviour of the circuit remains unaffected.

Our paper is organised as follows: Section 2 provides a background on shadow registers and related work, and Section 3 provides the motivation the pursuit of post place-and-route shadowing, and the necessity of delay-bounded routing. Section 4 describes how we modify Dijkstra's algorithm with a rollback feature to enable minimum delay bounds, Section 5 describes our experimental application. We present and analyse our approach in Section 6, before describing our future work and conclusion in Sections 7 and 8.

## 2. BACKGROUND AND RELATED WORK

The idea of on chip timing measurement and shadow registers is not new, having already been presented by [2, 4, 6].

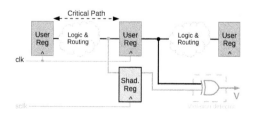

Figure 1: Illustration of a shadow register fed by a different clock, along with a violation detector circuit.

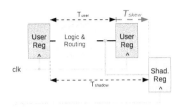

(a) Concept of path skew ($T_{skew}$)

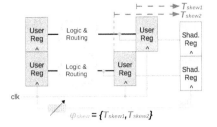

(b) Variance of $T_{skew}$ between user paths requires phase compensation ($\phi_{skew}$).

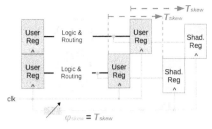

(c) Bounded $T_{skew}$ requires single $\phi_{skew}$ value.

Figure 3: Utility of bounding the skew between user path and shadow path.

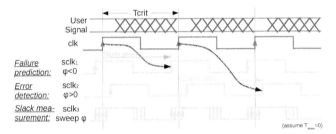

Figure 2: Timing diagram showing the three modes of operation for shadow registers.

The concept of shadow registers is shown in Figure 1. In particular, both the input and output of the user register must be accessible; the input is fed into a shadow register, and the outputs of both the user and the shadow register are compared using an XOR gate. Should the two latched values be different, the signal V would go high, thus indicating that (depending on the mode of operation) either the user or the shadow register experienced a timing violation in the previous clock cycle. The most challenging part of this method lies with inserting these shadow registers, which act as the (asynchronous) interface between the user circuit and any subsequent detection (XOR) or recovery logic — essentially, shadow registers decouple the latter from the former. For this reason, in this paper we focus only on the placement and routing of these register, and not on any downstream logic.

Three main modes of operating shadow registers exist, depending on the phase offset $\phi_{offset}$ between the user and shadow clock. Take for example Fig. 1, and let us assume that the critical net arrives at both the user and shadow register simultaneously. A negative $\phi_{offset}$ indicates a shadow clock that leads the user clock, thus the critical net is sampled into the shadow register earlier than being sampled by the user circuit, effectively shortening the circuit's clock period. This mode is commonly used for failure prediction, such as detecting when a device has aged sufficiently that the safety guard-band is breached. Bounding the skew of all shadow registers in this mode allows this guard-band to be positioned, and adjusted, more accurately and consistently across all registers.

A positive $\phi_{offset}$ corresponds to a lagging shadow clock, and effectively provides a longer clock period for the user circuit to return the correct result. This is the key technique for achieving Razor [6], a method that speculatively overclocks a circuit (most commonly, CPUs) beyond its rated limits, with the provision that any timing errors are infrequent, detectable, and recoverable. The final mode is when $\phi_{offset}$ is swept through a range of values in order to perform

on-chip slack measurement by determining the exact point at which each shadowed path starts to fail, and has been used for device characterisation [13]. Bounding the skew for these modes would allow more precise Razor detection, as well as reduce calibration effort during slack measurement. All three modes are illustrated in Figure 2.

## 2.1 Negating Path Skew

In reality, it is unlikely that a critical net will arrive at the user register at the same time as to its shadow register. Thus, for accurate timing measurement using shadow registers, we must also consider their path skew.

The data skew of a single shadow path is the difference in routing delay between a signal arriving at the user register ($T_{user}$) and the shadow register ($T_{shadow}$) where $T_{skew} = T_{shadow} - T_{user}$. Although it may be expected that $T_{shadow} > T_{user}$, this is not always the case given that it is possible to shadow a net into a register located closer to its source than the user register. For registers driven by the same global clock buffer and balanced clock tree, let us first assume that the clock skew is zero (though in practice, as seen later, vendor tools report that even registers that are located relatively close to each other can have clock skews up to several hundreds of picoseconds). This is illustrated in Figure 3a.

In order for the signal to be latched into a shadow register at the same time as it is latched into the user register (i.e. for $\phi_{offset}=0$) the shadow clock must lag the user clock by the absolute offset $\phi_{skew}=T_{skew}$. Conveniently, on FPGAs, dedicated clock resources exist to accurately tailor the total phase offset, $\phi_{skew} + \phi_{offset}$ (by deriving a phase-shifted version of the user clock) at run-time. This contrasts with data signals, which must use general-purpose routing resources that must be determined during compilation (thus establishing $T_{skew}$) and which remains fixed whilst the device is operating. When shadowing multiple paths in the circuit, however, it is likely that the data skew of each path will be different, and hence, the phase offset requirements of each shadow register will also be different. Unfortunately, limited clock resources on FPGAs means that it is infeasible to supply individually shifted clocks for more than a handful of paths (as an example, the device used in this work supports a maximum of 32 global clock nets).

This situation, where two shadow registers share one phase-adjustable global clock net, is illustrated in Fig. 3b. Here, either one of the two shadow registers can be clocked with respect to its user register, but not both simultaneously; thus, when it may not be possible to customise $\phi_{skew}$ for each path, it would be valuable to control $T_{skew}$ instead. Bounding the routing delay, and hence the data skew, to be identical across multiple shadow registers would allow them all to be shadowed simultaneously from the same clock net, as shown in Figure 3c.

## 2.2 Delay-Bounded Routing

Given that FPGA routing tools are required to find routes that meet both hold (minimum delay bound) and setup (maximum) time constraints, in some ways, existings tools already perform an element of delay-bounded routing. Thus, the allowed arrival window of all routed paths should be greater than $T_{hold}$ (in the order of 50–300ps) and less than $T_{crit} - T_{setup}$ (where $T_{setup}$ is in the order of 0–700ps). For $T_{crit}$=10ns (100MHz), this gives an arrival window of 9ns. In this work, we seek to make this window as small as possible.

The research community has primarily focused on improving circuit performance by minimising $T_{crit}$, the worse case delay of all paths through the circuit; algorithms like PathFinder [15] have been employed for this task. However, less attention has been paid to methods for elongating the best-case delay of paths in order to meet any minimum delay constraints; as an example, even the venerable VPR CAD suite [16] does not support hold time constraints.

Whilst the Altera routing tool supports both minimum delay (MINDELAY) and maximum delay (MAXDELAY) constraints for all nets, the Xilinx ISE router only supports minimum delay (OFFSET) constraints for nets that terminate at an I/O interface, to meet external hold requirements. In both tools, different worse case timing models are used — fast corner for MINDELAY (hold) and slow corner for MAXDELAY (setup) analysis — which makes precise routing difficult. For shadow registers, we care about the critical-path at the slow corner only. Fung et al. [7] describe a slack reallocation method to optimise both short paths (MINDELAY) and long paths (MAXDELAY) simultaneously on a regular routing algorithm, in order to meet hold and setup time constraints — this is the method reportedly used by Altera tools.

On the more general graph routing problem, $K$-shortest path algorithms exist (e.g. Yen's algorithm [18]) to find not just the shortest path from a single source to a single sink, but the set of $K$-1 next-shortest paths. By finding a sufficiently large value for $K$, it would be possible to find the shortest path which fulfils the minimum cost bound. Similar to Yen's, our algorithm removes edges from the graph to find longer paths, but unlike Yen's, we give up the ability to search the graph optimally (and exhaustively) for improved runtime by removing edges permanently, and not restarting Dijkstra on each removal.

Prior work on shadow registers [13] relies on standard incremental compilation techniques to insert shadow registers. MINDELAY and MAXDELAY constraints can be applied to (coarsely) bound $T_{skew}$ across all nets, though this can be difficult when each constraint is applied to a different timing corner. For certain applications though (e.g. timing slack measurement) variations in $T_{skew}$ can be calibrated out during post-processing.

## 2.3 Post P&R Instrumentation

Inserting timing instruments only after placing and routing the user circuit, and using only those resources left over, is a key part of being able to shadow critical registers without disrupting their timing characteristics. This statement is supported by the results of the following section, but prior research [12, 10] have also taken this approach for adding debug instrumentation.

Whilst, on the surface, it would appear that constraining the insertion process to use only spare resources that were left behind may be overly restrictive, significant flexibility is recouped from exploiting the convenient property that debugging signals can be connected to any trace-buffer input for it to be observable. Thus, unlike the user circuit, where nets need to be routed exactly from a single source pin to a predetermined set of sink pins, debug nets need only be routed from any point along the existing user net to *any* one of the many trace-buffer sinks that are available.

A keen similarity exists between shadow registers and trace-buffers, given that when shadowing a user net, tools will also have the freedom to connect to any one of the many spare register resources available; if anything, there are likely to be even more spare registers than trace-buffer inputs.

## 3. MOTIVATION

In this section, we present both a case for why shadow registers should be inserted post place-and-route, as well as a case for why delay-bounded routing is important for shadow register insertion. The delay-bounded experiments that follow targets shadow register insertion that minimises $T_{skew}$ subject to $T_{skew} \geq$+1ns after the user register.

### 3.1 Case for Post P&R Shadowing

Table 1 presents a comparison between inserting shadow registers before, and after, the place-and-route procedure (defined to be the map and par tools in ISE) of three benchmarks. On each, three experiments are performed: the 'Base' column represents the baseline compilation run of this benchmark (without shadow registers). In order to allow for shadow registers to be inserted prior to place-and-route, this baseline is generated over two stages. The first stage involves synthesising (but not placing or routing) the benchmark as normal, using ISE's xst tool. The second stage converts this synthesis result into a flattened, technology-mapped Verilog file using ISE's netgen tool, creating a functionally-equivalent structural description that is typically used for verification in a simulator. This Verilog file is then compiled again from scratch, as before.

By first flattening the benchmark, we preserve the exact logical structure of the circuit (prior to packing, placement or routing) given that it explicitly instantiates all LUT, FF, *etc.* primitives of the design, to allow for shadow register insertion. This allows us to maintain the one-to-one mapping between a critical register (only identifiable after place-and-route) with a reg in the original source code. For this same reason, we were unable to perform any pre-synthesis shadowing experiments. This flattening step would not be necessary if it was possible to directly modify the post-synthesis netlist; a more elegant approach that we would like to adopt in future work would be to directly instrument a synthesised EDIF netlist.

The 'Source' and 'Post P&R' columns show the results for inserting shadow registers at the source-level (by appending to the structural Verilog description) and after the place-and-route procedure. A number of statistics are shown: the first three rows list the logic utilisation figures for each of the experiments, whilst the fourth row shows the critical-path delay. The following row shows the number of unique endpoints (defined as register, IOB or RAM input pins) that are within the most critical percentile of the critical-path delay, as reported by the Xilinx STA tool. For the LEON3, we are interested in all critical-paths that are within 10% of its critical-path delay (at 13.33ns, this results in 1436 paths with a slack less than or equal to 1.333ns), and for the AES x3 and JPEG-x2 benchmarks, we extend this margin to 40%. The next two rows indicate the proportion of these endpoints

Table 1: Comparison between inserting shadow registers at the source, and post place-and-route, with the latter preserving significantly more critical nets. ('Source' recompiles the entire circuit which can unpredictably lead to better, or worse, results).

| | | Shadow Method | | | | Shadow Method | | | | Shadow Method | |
| | Base | Source | Post P&R (this work) | Base | Source | Post P&R (this work) | Base | Source | Post P&R (this work) |
|---|---|---|---|---|---|---|---|---|---|
| Slice util. | 93.5% | 88.9% | **94.5%** | 87.0% | 86.9% | **89.8%** | 86.8% | 88.8% | **90.1%** |
| LUT util. | 63.5% | 56.6% | **64.0%** | 71.4% | 71.7% | **72.7%** | 60.9% | 61.3% | **61.8%** |
| Register util. | 20.1% | 20.6% | **20.6%** | 10.6% | 12.4% | **12.3%** | 41.7% | 42.7% | **42.6%** |
| Tcrit (ns) | 13.329 | 13.331 | **13.333** | 6.055 | 5.865 | **6.055** | 13.936 | 15.611 | **13.939** |
| Num. critical nets | 1436 | 1222 | **1436** | 5362 | 7400 | **5362** | 3290 | 3335 | **3295** |
| Common to Base | 100% | 41.0% | **100%** | 100% | 53.1% | **100%** | 100% | 46.7% | **99.8%** |
| Shad. coverage | - | 41.0% | **98.7%** | - | 53.1% | **94.2%** | - | 46.7% | **84.0%** |
| Pack & Place time (s) | 1875 | 1974 | - | 1014 | 1408 | - | 871 | 911 | - |
| Routing runtime (s) | 1281 | 1241 | **183** | 479 | 486 | **224** | 748 | 3658 | **276** |

(a) LEON3 (all critical nets within 10% of Tcrit)   (b) AES-x3 (within 40% of Tcrit)   (c) JPEG-x2 (within 40% of Tcrit)

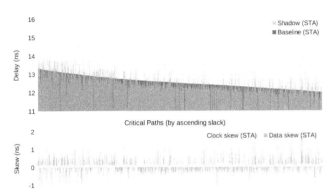

Figure 4: Unbounded — shadowing LEON3 critical endpoints into closest register, using Xilinx `par` (runtime: 810s).

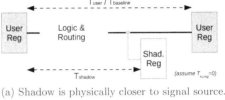

(a) Shadow is physically closer to signal source.

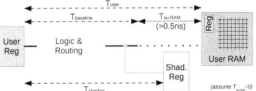

(b) Shadow path occurs within setup window of endpoint.

Figure 5: Two possible scenarios for negative data skew.

that are identical to the baseline experiment, and the number that were shadowed successfully, and the additional runtime required to do so.

Our experiments here show that, when inserting shadow registers at the source-level, the paths that were worse case originally do not remain so — in fact, approximately 50% of all worse case endpoints from the baseline remained critical after recompilation. In contrast, inserting shadow registers post place-and-route resulted in exactly the same endpoints remaining critical, of which over 80–90% of them were successfully shadowed. We analyse why not all endpoints can be shadowed in a following section.

Unsurprisingly, inserting shadow registers post place-and-route can still have a small effect on critical-path delay of a circuit due to the extra loading induced by adding an extra fanout to the critical net. For LEON3 and JPEG-x2, this amounts to 3–4ps, whilst no effect was observed on the AES-x3 circuit because this extra fanout occurred inside the logic slice. In contrast, inserting at source-level can be quite chaotic: for LEON3, utilisation of slice and LUT resources was less than the baseline circuit, and for AES-x3, inserting shadow registers turned out to improve its $T_{crit}$.

### 3.2 Case for Delay-Bounded Shadowing

Figure 4 compares the total path delay (from state element to state element) in the baseline LEON3 circuit, and the new path to the shadow register, when inserted post place-and-route, but without any delay bounding. We achieve this by placing a register at the closest possible site to the end of each critical net (mimicking an incremental placement algorithm that seeks to minimise net wirelength), and then

invoking Xilinx `par` to route to this new sink. We constrain all paths from the original circuit to this new set of shadow registers as being a multi-cycle path with a maximum delay of +1ns greater than the clock period, but no support exists for minimum delay constraints.

The result is that some shadow paths have a delay that is shorter than the baseline path, whilst in some other cases, this shadow path is longer, as shown in the upper graph. Highlighting this more clearly is the lower graph showing the path skew between the shadow and the baseline registers. A negative skew may exist because it has been possible to place and route a new shadow register: a) physically closer to the signal source than in the original baseline circuit; b) within the setup time window of the endpoint, which for RAM inputs as an example, can exceed 0.5ns. These scenarios are illustrated in Fig. 5.

Clearly, such a large range of data skews is undesirable as it requires an equal number of skewed clocks if all shadow registers are to be operated simultaneously.

## 4. DIJKSTRA WITH ROLLBACK

The FPGA routing problem can be described using a directed graph $G(V, E)$, where $V$ is the set of vertices in the graph, and $E$ describes the set of directed edges between two vertices. Each routing wire in the FPGA can be represented using a vertex, and each edge represents a programmable connection between two wires. A cost is associated with every edge, representing the routing delay of this wiring connection.

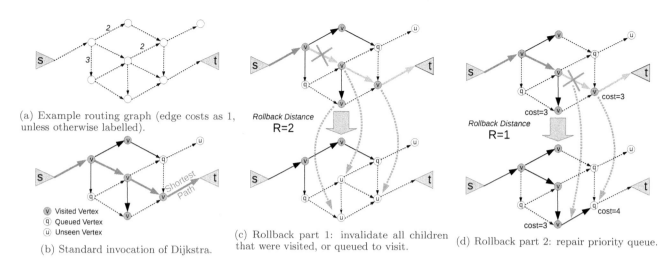

(a) Example routing graph (edge costs as 1, unless otherwise labelled).

(b) Standard invocation of Dijkstra.

Rollback Distance
R=2

(c) Rollback part 1: invalidate all children that were visited, or queued to visit.

Rollback Distance
R=1

cost=3
cost=3
cost=3
cost=4

(d) Rollback part 2: repair priority queue.

Figure 6: Illustration of Dijkstra with rollback.

During FPGA routing, the primary concern is typically to maximise performance, and that involves minimising the critical-path delay, which is equivalent to minimising the worse case cost of a path from some source vertex $s$ to a sink vertex $t$. Once all setup constraints have been met (or as many as possible), then the tool can return to fix any short paths that violate hold time constraints by adding additional delays. Based on its output messages, we hypothesise this is how the Xilinx `par` router operates.

Finding the shortest path through $G$ is a well-studied problem, with Dijkstra's algorithm being the de-facto choice for solving this optimally. This algorithm operates as a breadth-first search, and at a very high level, it works as follows: expand outward from $s$, explore the next closest unvisited vertex, expand outward from this vertex and repeat, until $t$ is reached. Guaranteeing that every vertex is visited using the shortest path is accomplished using a priority queue, which sorts all unvisited vertices by ascending cost, so that at each step, the lowest cost vertex is always processed next.

While it is possible to find the shortest path between $s$ and $t$ in this way, it is not trivial to find paths with any other constraints, such as a path with cost exactly equal (or as close as possible) to $T$. The reason for this is that Dijkstra's algorithm only records the shortest path to every vertex in the graph, rather than *all* possible paths, the number of which can be expected to grow exponentially with $|E|$.

In many ways, this is a problem that bears many similarities with the subset sum problem, which is NP-complete. Within the context of this work, we seek to solve the problem: given a set of wire delays, how can we compose a target delay $T_{skew}$ (exactly, or as close as possible)? Further constraints also exist on selecting wire delays since each wire may only connect to an adjacent wire, and multiple, non-overlapping, solutions are sought across all critical nets.

## 4.1 Differences from Regular FPGA Routing

Unlike regular FPGA routing, there are a number of key differences that set our problem apart: *i*) in order to preserve circuit timing, we are restricted to using only the leftover resources in the FPGA; *ii*) in order to allow the shadow register path to share as much of the original user path as possible, we branch from the original routing as close to the user register as possible; *iii*) we wish to keep the arrival window of all shadow registers as small as possible, by finding

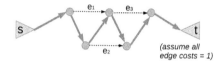

Figure 7: Example of a path with cost=6 that would never be found unless $e_1$, $e_2$ and $e_3$ were eliminated.

the shortest path that is at least our skew target; and *iv*) each critical net can reclaim any spare register in the FPGA as a shadow register.

Regarding that last point, unlike regular FPGA routing where each net must be routed to all of its sinks exactly, a critical net is free to connect to any spare register. This element of freedom was exploited in prior work [11], which applied a single-commodity minimum-cost flow algorithm to route signals into pipelining registers. However, a key limitation of the minimum-cost flow algorithm is that it is only capable of minimising for the total delay of all nets (equivalently, their average case delay), and is not capable of optimising for the worse case net delay (MAXDELAY), nor the best-case (MINDELAY). For this reason, a direct application of the minimum cost flow algorithm is unsuitable for inserting shadow registers.

## 4.2 Rollback

Rather than terminating when the shortest path to $t$ is found, we propose that the graph search continues in the hope of finding a longer path to the sink $t$. However, because $t$ has already been visited, it will never be visited by the algorithm ever again. To rectify this, we rollback the state of the algorithm as if a previous edge to on the shortest path had not existed.

Consider the graph shown in Figure 6a, and an unmodified invocation of Dijkstra as in Fig. 6b. Rollback consists of two parts, with a free choice of how many vertices to undo; let us define the number of vertices to rollback as $R$ and the last vertex to rollback as $v_R$. Part one is, if $R>0$, to eliminate all vertices on the heap that have already been visited, or in the priority queue, that are downstream from $v_R$. This is illustrated in Fig. 6c, where $R=2$. We perform this task by recursively checking the fanout vertices of $v_R$ and removing

```
# Place a shadow register for each net at its closest
    spare location
net2closest = placeClosest(criticalNets,allRegs)
foreach net in criticalNets:
    closestReg = net2closest[net]
    # Find the closest spare register from this net
    path = searchShortestPath(net,closestReg)
    # Keep searching for (longer) paths to only that
        chosen register until length meets target
    while not path.empty and path.length < Tskew:
        rollbackSearch(path, R)
        path = continueSearch(closestReg)
    # Remove path from future graph searches
    markAsUsed(path)
    # Reset Dijkstra state (i.e. priority queue)
    resetDijkstra()
```

Listing 1: One-Closest Algorithm

```
foreach net in criticalNets:
    # Find the closest spare register from this net
    path = searchShortestPath(net,allRegs)
    # Keep searching for (longer) paths to any spare
        register until length meets target
    while not path.empty and path.length < Tskew:
        rollbackSearch(path, R)
        path = continueSearch(allRegs)
    # Remove path from future graph searches
    markAsUsed(path)
    # Reset Dijkstra state (i.e. priority queue)
    resetDijkstra()
```

Listing 2: One-All Algorithm

```
do:
    # Find the closest spare register from any net
    path = searchShortestPath(criticalNets,allRegs)
    # Keep searching for (longer) paths from any net to
        any spare register until length meets target
    while not path.empty and path.length < Tskew:
        rollbackSearch(path, R)
        path = continueSearch(allRegs)
    # Remove path from future graph searches
    markAsUsed(path)
    # Reset Dijkstra state (i.e. priority queue)
    resetDijkstra()
while not path.empty
```

Listing 3: All-All Algorithm

any item with a predecessor (shortest path) edge that leads back to it.

Part two is to revisit all of the fan-ins of $v_R$ to consider if any of the previously visited vertices would have inserted it into the priority queue at the smallest cost that is higher (but not equal) to the previous smallest. This repair procedure is illustrated in Fig. 6d, for $R=1$.

A larger value for $R$ would result in backtracking further in the current shortest path, and to restrict the algorithm to finding a higher cost path from before that last vertex. Given that the number of vertices reachable can be expected to increase exponentially with distance from the $s$, larger $R$ values can also be expected to prune a greater number of paths from the solution space.

Performing rollback in this manner does not guarantee that we will find the shortest path no less than an arbitrary delay $T$, should one exist. Consider the example set out in Fig. 7, where unless all three edges $e_{1...3}$ were eliminated during rollback, it is impossible to find a path which is cost$\geq 6$, for any fixed value of $R$. Incidentally, the longest path through this graph is 6, and finding the longest path through a cyclic graph (such as those in FPGAs) is known to be an NP-hard problem.

## 4.3 Proposed Algorithms

We propose three different heuristic algorithms for finding the shortest-path, subject to a MINDELAY constraint, between a set of critical nets and a set of shadow registers. *One-Closest:* is intended to emulate a standard incremental compilation flow. First, it places a shadow register onto all critical nets, at the closest spare location, before attempting to find the shortest path to this register that is greater than or equal to the target $T_{skew}$ value. After each net is routed, the Dijkstra algorithm state is reset for the next search. This is shown in Listing 1.

*One-All:* improves on One-Closest by exploiting the freedom that each critical net may connect to any spare register, rather than a specific one chosen ahead of time. The pseudocode for this algorithm is shown in Listing 2.

*All-All:* goes further and considers routing all nets to any spare register simultaneously, as shown in Listing 3. In each iteration, this algorithm finds the shortest path (that is greater than or equal to the target $T_{skew}$) between any critical net and any spare register, and marks that path as being used. This approach is very similar to the successive shortest paths algorithm that is used to find the minimum-cost flow, with the difference that we employ rollback to ensure that each path meets a minimum delay requirement. Given that our rollback method does not preserve optimality, the All-All algorithm is also not guaranteed to find the minimum-cost solution in which all paths meet the $T_{skew}$ target.

A point of note is that all three algorithms are greedy; for the One-Closest and One-All approaches, each net is operated on in turn (as in PathFinder [15]) and for each the first path found that meets the minimum $T_{skew}$ target is claimed. Similarly, for the All-All algorithm, all nets are considered simultaneously, but for each iteration the first solution that meets the target is also claimed. Unlike PathFinder, however, no negotiated congestion is performed. As we see in the following sections, our proposed approach, combined with the sheer flexibility of the FPGA fabric, produces acceptable results even without negotiation.

## 5. EXPERIMENTAL APPLICATION

Although we believe that our techniques are valid for any FPGA vendor, we evaluate our techniques on the Xilinx platform, due to the fine-grained access that is available through the Xilinx design language (XDL) format. The XDL format is a text-based representation that allows designers to read and write to all aspects of the Xilinx netlists, and can be used to change LUT contents, how they are packed, where they are placed, and how they are routed. This level of access is sufficient to construct an entire CAD toolchain as evidenced by the VTR-to-Bitstream project [9]. The only information that is missing from this format is the delay of each individual wire on the FPGA. For this reason, we use wire delay and setup time values estimated (to picosecond accuracy, ranging from 10ps to 707ps) using a linear regression model.

In this work, we use Xilinx ISE 13.3 to place-and-route our benchmarks, and target the xc6vlx240t Virtex6 FPGA found on the ML605 evaluation board. We also use Torc [17] for manipulating the XDL format (such as extracting the set of all spare register and routing resources, including LUT route-throughs) and LEMON [5] for graph search operations. Experiments were performed on an Intel Core i7-3770 CPU workstation, with 16GB RAM, running Xubuntu 14.04. Runtime was measured using the /usr/bin/time utility.

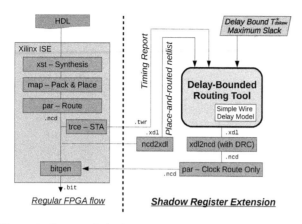

Figure 8: Proposed shadow register extension to design flow.

Table 2: Benchmark summary.

|  | LEON3 | AES-x3 | JPEG-x2 | xc6vlx240t capacity |
|---|---|---|---|---|
| Slices | 35217 | 32809 | 32733 | 37680 |
| LUTs | 95766 | 107685 | 91741 | 150720 |
| Registers | 60562 | 32025 | 125642 | 301440 |
| RAMs | 688 | – | 124 | 832 |
| DSPs | 32 | – | 172 | 768 |
| Tcrit (ns) | 13.329 | 6.055 | 13.936 | – |
| Wirelength | 2.1M | 1.1M | 1.6M | 6.3M |

## 5.1 Proposed Flow

Our proposed extension to the regular FPGA design flow is shown in Figure 8. On the left is a typical Xilinx flow: the HDL user circuit is first synthesised into FPGA resources, and then packed and placed onto physical locations on the target FPGA. The `par` tool is then called to find a viable routing configuration that connects all the necessary resources. Static timing analysis (STA) can then be performed using the `trce` tool, before generating a bitstream that can be programmed onto the device.

On the right is our proposed extension to this flow for inserting shadow registers. The inputs from the regular flow are a verbose STA report which details the exact resources that make up all critical and near-critical paths, as well as the place and routed netlist, which is converted from the binary format (`.ncd`) to the text-based `.xdl` format. On top of this, the user specifies the minimum $T_{skew}$ (e.g. +1ns from user register) as well as the maximum slack for paths to be shadowed.

The output of our delay-bounded shadowing tool is a modified XDL netlist with as many of the most-critical endpoints requested as possible routed to newly-placed shadow registers, using only the leftover resources on the FPGA. This XDL format is converted back into an `.ncd` (which includes passing the Xilinx design rule check, DRC) for use in downstream Xilinx tools, necessary for routing the newly-inserted shadow register clock, before returning into the regular flow for bitstream generation.

## 5.2 Benchmark Analysis

We evaluate our proposed techniques on three benchmarks: the LEON3 system-on-chip, an AES encoder/decoder chain, and a JPEG decompression circuit. The LEON3 [1] is a functioning, open-source, multi-core SPARC SoC that can boot Linux; we configure it with 8 cores, each with 64kB of instruction and data cache, as well as a DDR3 memory controller,

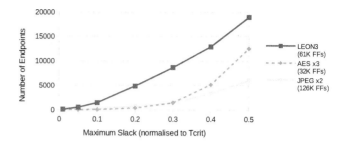

Figure 9: Number of endpoints at various slack values (normalised against Tcrit).

and Ethernet, CompactFlash and other peripherals. The arrangement of the DDR3 and other SoC components requires that the main CPU clock be constrained to 75MHz (13.33ns). We also constructed an AES encoder/decoder based on [3] consisting of three 128-bit AES encoders followed by three decoders. The encoder plaintext, and cipher-key, inputs are fed by LFSRs which are subsequently checked against the decoded output.

Our third benchmark is made up of two parallel instances of a C-based JPEG decoder [8], synthesised into Verilog using Vivado HLS 2013.4 with an aggressive timing constraint of 1ns in order to encourage pipelining and higher register utilisation. For the latter two benchmarks, no timing constraints are explicitly given for implementation and so we operate ISE in its performance evaluation mode, which aims to minimise the clock period. Table 2 summarises their resource utilisation and critical-path delays; we estimate the wirelength of each circuit by counting all occupied length 1, 2, 4 and 16 wires in the XDL netlist, and divide this by the total wirelength derived from the XDLRC device database.

Figure 9 plots the number of endpoints that have a slack value less than or equal to a fraction of the critical-path delay. This is an important metric as it shows how many paths must be shadowed in order to achieve a certain amount of timing coverage. For example, shadowing all endpoints within a normalised slack of 0.1 would allow, ideally, the circuit to be safely overclocked by up to 10% and still be able to detect all timing errors. Of the three benchmarks, LEON3 has the highest proportion of registers that are near-critical — we believe that this is due to it being the only one of the three benchmarks that has a timing constraint. With a timing constraint, the CAD tool will only attempt to optimise the circuit just enough to meet requirements.

## 6. RESULTS

Figure 10 shows a comparison of the path delay and skew values, as reported by the Xilinx STA tool, for the three proposed bounded routing methods. The data is presented similarly to Fig. 4, where the total path delay to the baseline critical endpoint and the shadow registers is shown on the upper graph, and the skew between these two registers shown on the lower graph, broken down into data skew and clock skew elements.

The effectiveness of the One-Closest approach — shadowing each signal into its closest register — with rollback distance R=4 is shown by Fig 10a. Although it is clear that applying a minimum delay bound does have an effect, not all signals were shadowed successfully (as indicated by a missing delay and skew value), and the skew variation is large, where the shortest path that was greater than $T_{skew}$ turned out to be much larger.

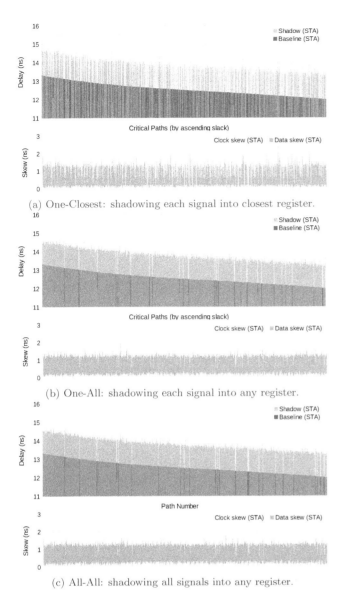

(a) One-Closest: shadowing each signal into closest register.

(b) One-All: shadowing each signal into any register.

(c) All-All: shadowing all signals into any register.

Figure 10: Delay and skew comparisons (as reported by Xilinx trce STA) between the proposed delay-bounded routing methods, on LEON3, for $T_{skew} \geq +1$ns.

The One-All approach is shown in Fig. 10b, and the All-All approach in Fig. 10c, both with $R=0$. Both show an improvement in the delay variation, as well as the number of signals that were successfully shadowed. Rather interestingly, the results show that the One-All algorithm performs almost as well as the more complex All-All algorithm, which considers all signals simultaneously.

The results for Figure 10 show that, despite targeting a shadow skew of +1ns, the final timing results by the Xilinx STA reveals that deviations from this value exist. These errors are captured in Table 3, which shows the maximum and mean absolute error, and the standard deviation and range of the error from the desired +1ns value. The range is a key metric which measures the phase offset over which an engineer must align in order to detect violations; ideally, a value of zero means that only one phase offset exists, and that all shadow registers can perform detection simultaneously.

Table 3: Summary of delay-bounded error for nets shadowed, on LEON3, with 1436 critical nets and $T_{skew} \geq +1$ns.

| (ns) | Unbounded | Delay-bounded | | |
| --- | --- | --- | --- | --- |
| | One-Closest | One-Closest | One-All | All-All |
| Nets shad. | 1424 | 1051 | 1417 | 1418 |
| Max. \|Err\| | 1.942 | 1.779 | 1.002 | 0.928 |
| Mean \|Err\| | 0.867 | 0.329 | 0.223 | 0.249 |
| StdDev Err | 0.367 | 0.187 | 0.111 | 0.107 |
| Range Err | 2.771 | 1.744 | 1.075 | 0.956 |

(a) From Xilinx trce STA.

| (ns) | Unbounded | Delay-bounded | | |
| --- | --- | --- | --- | --- |
| | One-Closest | One-Closest | One-All | All-All |
| Max. \|Err\| | 2.011 | 1.586 | 0.788 | 0.704 |
| Mean \|Err\| | 1.012 | 0.201 | 0.114 | 0.114 |
| StdDev Err | 0.431 | 0.183 | 0.090 | 0.092 |
| Range Err | 2.763 | 1.754 | 0.948 | 0.860 |

(b) From Xilinx trce STA, with clock skew omitted.

| (ns) | Unbounded | Delay-bounded | | |
| --- | --- | --- | --- | --- |
| | One-Closest | One-Closest | One-All | All-All |
| Max. \|Err\| | - | 1.636 | 0.114 | 0.114 |
| Mean \|Err\| | - | 0.089 | <0.001 | 0.001 |
| StdDev Err | - | 0.165 | 0.004 | 0.004 |
| Range Err | - | 1.636 | 0.114 | 0.114 |

(c) From our delay model, omitting clock skew.

Results are divided into 3 categories, corresponding to each of the three subtables (a)–(c), which presents results as reported by the Xilinx STA, results from Xilinx STA but with the effects of clock skew omitted, and results as viewed from our proposed router when using a simplified delay model, respectively. The first column shows the results corresponding to the One-Closest experiment from Fig. 4, which uses the Xilinx par router. Given that the Xilinx router does not support MINDELAY constraints, it seeks to optimise for MAXDELAY only and reports the highest mean error.

The remaining three columns show the results of our delay-bounded approach. The second 'One-Closest' column corresponds to routing each critical net, one at a time to its closest spare register, as shown in Fig. 10a. The third column 'One-All' considers each critical net to the closest of all registers (Fig. 10b) and fourth column 'All-All' considers all nets to all registers (Fig. 10c).

Table 3c shows the lowest mean error given that our tool optimises for and analyses against a simplified wire delay model (also without considering clock skew) as opposed to the accurate delay database to which the Xilinx STA tool has access to. When measured against our own model, we find a significant reduction in the mean and standard deviation of the bound error. Regardless, we find that the One-All algorithm performs just as well as the more complex All-All algorithm.

We believe that there are two main sources of error: *i*) neglecting the effects of clock skew; and *ii*) mismatch between our wire delay model and Xilinx's timing database. However, to reduce these errors would require proprietary Xilinx device information.

## 6.1 Effect of Rollback Distance

The choice of rollback distance $R$ can have an effect on the performance of the algorithm. Table 4 shows the effect of varying $R$ for each of the three algorithms, on the LEON3 benchmark. A value of $R=0$ represents that only the last edge into the target is rolled backed, which is sufficient for the

Table 4: Varying rollback distance $R$ for LEON3 ($T_{skew} \geq +1$ns); default in bold.

| $R \rightarrow$ | 0 | 1 | 2 | 3 | 4 |
|---|---|---|---|---|---|
| Nets shadowed | 13 | 323 | 533 | 824 | **1051** |
| Model $|Error|$: | | | | | |
| Mean (ps) | 79 | 38 | 44 | 81 | **89** |
| Max (ps) | 292 | 1252 | 1656 | 2373 | **1636** |
| Runtime (s) | 1705 | 1299 | 1067 | 757 | **509** |

(a) One-Closest

| $R \rightarrow$ | **0** | 1 | 2 | 3 | 4 |
|---|---|---|---|---|---|
| Nets shadowed | **1417** | 1415 | 1386 | 1090 | 318 |
| Model $|Error|$: | | | | | |
| Mean (ps) | **<1** | <1 | <1 | 4 | 61 |
| Max (ps) | **114** | 171 | 829 | 262 | 549 |
| Runtime (s) | **183** | 188 | 214 | 180 | 130 |

(b) One-All

| $R \rightarrow$ | **0** | 1 | 2 | 3 | 4 |
|---|---|---|---|---|---|
| Nets shadowed | **1418** | 1417 | 1398 | 993 | 139 |
| Model $|Error|$: | | | | | |
| Mean (ps) | **<1** | <1 | <1 | <1 | 11 |
| Max (ps) | **114** | 171 | 34 | 184 | 140 |
| Runtime (s) | **1281** | 1456 | 2358 | 2708 | 262 |

(c) All-All

Table 5: Varying $T_{skew}$ target for LEON3, using One-All algorithm; default in bold.

| $T_{skew}$ target$\rightarrow$ | +0.0ns | 0.5ns | **+1ns** | +1.5ns | +2.0ns |
|---|---|---|---|---|---|
| Nets shadowed | 1417 | 1419 | **1417** | 1416 | 1418 |
| Model $|Error|$: | | | | | |
| Mean (ps) | 110 | 3 | **<1** | <1 | <1 |
| Max. (ps) | 914 | 281 | **114** | 59 | 19 |
| Runtime (s) | 122 | 137 | **183** | 263 | 389 |

One-All and All-All algorithms, given that it can always route to another shadow register (that is further away). However, this is not the case for the One-Closest algorithm, which has no such freedom, and thus requires $R > 0$ in order to route more than a small fraction of all signals. In the latter case, the larger the value of $R$, the fewer paths to that same register are eliminated and hence the greater the number of nets that can be shadowed (with greater error).

Increasing $R$ appears to be detrimental for the One-All and All-All algorithms, matching intuition, as it eliminates that register from consideration to target another that is further away. The runtime of each of the three algorithms is also reported in Table 4, showing that One-All is faster than the more complex All-All algorithm (which considers all signals simultaneously) with comparable quality. The One-Closest algorithm is the slowest as it has the most failing nets, with each failing net requiring the entire routing graph to be exhausted before a signal is deemed unroutable.

## 6.2 Effect of Tskew Target Size

Table 5 shows the effect of varying the target $T_{skew}$ size, when applying the One-All algorithm. A smaller minimum $T_{skew}$ target allows more signals to be routed, but increases error given that not all signals can be routed to a shadow register within this delay budget. On the other hand, a larger target value provides more routing flexibility to assemble a net with a delay of at least $T_{skew}$, As can be expected, the runtime can also be seen to increase as the minimum target increases.

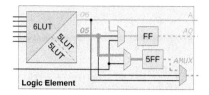

Figure 11: Virtex6 logic element where LUT output signal "O5" cannot reach any output pin.

Table 6: Reason for signals failing to shadow (for $T_{skew} \geq +1$ns using One-All algorithm)

| | LEON3 | AES-x3 | JPEG-x2 |
|---|---|---|---|
| Num. critical nets | 1436 | 5362 | 3290 |
| Nets shadowed | 1417 | 5049 | 2769 |
| i) Blocked in LE | 10 | 313 | 468 |
| ii) Blocked out LE | 4 | - | 23 |
| iii) Path search failed | 5 | - | 30 |

## 6.3 Unroutable Signals

Three possible reasons exist for why user signals fail to be routed to a shadow register, either: *i)* it was not possible to connect the critical net to an output pin; *ii)* it was not possible to connect the critical net to any shadow register, even without a delay bound; or *iii)* a path meeting the minimum $T_{skew}$ delay could not be found.

In the first scenario, the signal to be shadowed — i.e. the input signal of the user register — may be blocked from accessing the global routing network. Figure 11 shows the structure of a Virtex6 logic element, which contains 7 input pins, 6 of which feed a 6-input lookup table (which can be fractured into two 5-input tables) and a bypass input, as well as 3 outputs pins, fed by two registers. For scenario *i)*, consider when both fractured LUTs are used in this logic element, and the output of the second LUT (labelled "O5") is latched into the "5FF" register. In this case, it becomes impossible to connect the combinational signal to a free output pin so that it can be shadowed without modifying the user circuit.

For scenario *ii)*, where critical nets can already access the global network, we find that a small number of signals can never be connected to any shadow register, even without any delay bounds. We find this result by computing a maximum flow between all net sources and all net sinks. Scenario *iii)* represents the case when a signal that is equal or greater than the $T_{skew}$ target could not be found. Either this could be because such a path doesn't exist under any situation, or because our heuristic rollback mechanism we employ was unable to find one of the paths that do.

The frequency of each of these four scenarios in our experiments is shown in Table 6. Across all benchmarks, the majority of failing signals came from the first scenario, where signals could not be extracted from inside of their logic element, whilst scenario *iii)* represents only a small fraction of all signals. In future, this could be alleviated by modifying the FPGA architecture so that such signals can always be accessed, by modifying the baseline CAD tools to prevent such dense packing for critical nets, or by allowing the post place-and-route circuit to be modified during shadow register insertion. The latter solutions could also be used to combat the three remaining scenarios *i)* and *ii)* by ripping up and yielding non-critical resources to our delay-bounded shadow nets.

# 7. FUTURE WORK

As part of future work, we would like to reduce the number of critical nets that fail to shadow, possibly by relaxing the self-imposed constraint that we must preserve all aspects of the existing circuit; instead of using just leftover resources, it may be possible to move/duplicate some non-critical parts of the design in order to free up shadowing resources. Furthermore, this approach may also be necessary to enable access to both the input and output signals of each critical-path endpoint for detecting errors, which is particularly challenging for RAM and DSP hard-blocks, for example.

Another area that we would like to pursue is to explore ways to effectively insert the violation detector (XOR) logic which compares the value in the user register with the shadow register. In particular, this detection logic (and any downstream infrastructure) has the freedom to be placed anywhere on the device, as long as it does not extend $T_{crit}$; however, because this operation is a pairwise reduction (i.e. each user/shadow register pair must converge into the same XOR) a new approach will be necessary. Eventually, our target is to achieve 100% shadow register coverage, and be able to detect/measure all timing errors occurring on a live device.

Recently, Altera has introduced a number of architectural features into their FPGAs that we would like to explore for this shadow register application. For example, Altera provides logic clusters that support multiple clocks (whereas Xilinx only supports one per cluster) as well as fine-grained time borrowing for flip-flops [14]. Lastly, we would like to investigate how to apply negotiated congestion into our routing algorithms. Although our results show that a greedy approach works well for the vast majority of critical nets, routing negotiation may enable those last few signals to be shadowed. An open question, however, is whether incorporating congestion into edge weights would disrupt the ability for Dijkstra to find paths of monotonically increasing delay.

# 8. CONCLUSIONS

Shadow registers are an essential tool for detecting, measuring, and reacting to physical imperfections in silicon technology. In this work, we have presented a method for precisely inserting shadow registers into FPGA circuits. Given that FPGAs contain a prefabricated set of configurable resources, we focus on the challenge of how to attach shadow registers onto existing critical and near-critical paths at a fixed delay skew away from their original endpoint. The main contributions of this work are:

- A proposal for inserting shadow registers into an FPGA circuit post place-and-route, using only spare, leftover, resources in order to preserve circuit timing.
- A modification to the Dijkstra algorithm to achieve minimum delay bounds when routing to one, or many, potential shadow registers.
- Experimental evaluation of our techniques on a commercial Xilinx architecture.

Results show that the flexibility of the FPGA fabric, even when using leftover resources only, supports the majority of shadow registers to within ±200ps of the target skew bound, as measured using the Xilinx static timing analyser. The source of this error was found to be the lack of accurate wire delay and clock skew information; when measured against our own delay model, we find that the average error is <1ps.

# 9. ACKNOWLEDGMENTS

The authors would like to thank Jason Anderson for his timely suggestions, and Wenwei Zha for sharing his insight on how to model wire delays. This work was supported in part by Xilinx, the U.K. EPSRC (Grants EP/I020357/1 and EP/I012036/1), Imagination Technologies, the Royal Academy of Engineering, the European Union Seventh Framework Programme under Grant Agreements 287804 and 318521, and the HiPEAC NoE.

# 10. REFERENCES

[1] Aeroflex Gaisler. GRLIB IP Core User's Manual. http://www.gaisler.com/products/grlib/grip.pdf, Jan. 2013.

[2] M. Agarwal, V. Balakrishnan, A. Bhuyan, B. Paul, and S. Mitra. Optimized Circuit Failure Prediction for Aging: Practicality and Promise. In *2008 IEEE International Test Conference*, pages 1–10. IEEE, Oct. 2008.

[3] Altera. Advanced Synthesis Cookbook. http://www.altera.co.uk/literature/manual/stx_cookbook.pdf, July 2011.

[4] A. Amouri and M. Tahoori. A Low-Cost Sensor for Aging and Late Transitions Detection in Modern FPGAs. In *2011 21st International Conference on Field Programmable Logic and Applications*, pages 329–335. IEEE, Sept. 2011.

[5] B. Dezs, A. Jüttner, and P. Kovács. LEMON - an Open Source C++ Graph Template Library. *Electron. Notes Theor. Comput. Sci.*, 264(5):23–45, July 2011.

[6] D. Ernst, S. Das, S. Pant, R. Rao, C. Ziesler, D. Blaauw, T. Austin, K. Flautner, and T. Mudge. Razor: a low-power pipeline based on circuit-level timing speculation. In *22nd Digital Avionics Systems Conference. Proceedings (Cat. No.03CH37449)*, pages 7–18. IEEE Comput. Soc, 2003.

[7] R. Fung, V. Betz, and W. Chow. Slack Allocation and Routing to Improve FPGA Timing While Repairing Short-Path Violations. *Computer-Aided Design of Integrated Circuits and Systems, IEEE Transactions on*, 27(4):686–697, April 2008.

[8] Y. Hara, H. Tomiyama, S. Honda, and H. Takada. Proposal and quantitative analysis of the CHStone benchmark program suite for practical C-based high-level synthesis. *Journal of Information Processing*, 17:242–254, 2009.

[9] E. Hung, F. Eslami, and S. J. E. Wilton. Escaping the Academic Sandbox: Realizing VPR Circuits on Xilinx Devices. In *Proceedings of the 21st IEEE International Symposium on Field-Programmable Custom Computing Machines*, pages 45–52, April 2013.

[10] E. Hung, A.-S. Jamal, and S. J. E. Wilton. Maximum Flow Algorithms for Maximum Observability during FPGA Debug. In *2013 International Conference on Field-Programmable Technology (FPT)*, pages 20–27, Dec 2013.

[11] E. Hung, T. Todman, and W. Luk. Transparent Insertion of Latency-Oblivious Logic onto FPGAs. In *FPL 2014, International Conference on Field-Programmable Logic and Applications*, Sept. 2014.

[12] E. Hung and S. J. E. Wilton. Towards Simulator-like Observability for FPGAs: A Virtual Overlay Network for Trace-Buffers. In *Proceedings of the 21st ACM/SIGDA International Symposium on Field-Programmable Gate Arrays*, pages 19–28, February 2013.

[13] J. Levine, E. Stott, G. Constantinides, and P. Cheung. SMI: Slack Measurement Insertion for Online Timing Monitoring in FPGAs. In *Field Programmable Logic and Applications (FPL), 2013 23rd Int'l Conference on*, pages 1–4, Sept 2013.

[14] D. Lewis, D. Cashman, M. Chan, J. Chromczak, G. Lai, A. Lee, T. Vanderhoek, and H. Yu. Architectural Enhancements in Stratix V™. In *Proceedings of the ACM/SIGDA International Symposium on Field Programmable Gate Arrays*, FPGA '13, pages 147–156, 2013.

[15] L. McMurchie and C. Ebeling. PathFinder: A Negotiation-Based Performance-Driven Router for FPGAs. In *Field-Programmable Gate Arrays, 1995. Proceedings of the Third International ACM Symposium on*, pages 111–117, 1995.

[16] J. Rose, J. Luu, C. W. Yu, O. Densmore, J. Goeders, A. Somerville, K. B. Kent, P. Jamieson, and J. Anderson. The VTR Project: Architecture and CAD for FPGAs from Verilog to Routing. In *Proceedings of the 20th ACM/SIGDA International Symposium on Field-Programmable Gate Arrays*, pages 77–86, February 2012.

[17] N. Steiner, A. Wood, H. Shojaei, J. Couch, P. Athanas, and M. French. Torc: Towards an Open-Source Tool Flow. In *Proceedings of the 19th ACM/SIGDA International Symposium on Field-Programmable Gate Arrays*, FPGA'11, pages 41–44, February 2011.

[18] J. Y. Yen. Finding the K Shortest Loopless Paths in a Network. *Management Science*, 17(11):712–716, 1971.

# RapidSmith 2: A Framework for BEL-level CAD Exploration on Xilinx FPGAs

Travis Haroldsen, Brent Nelson and Brad Hutchings
NSF Center for High-Performance Reconfigurable Computing (CHREC)
Department of Electrical and Computer Engineering
Brigham Young University, Provo, UT 84602
travisdh@byu.edu, nelson@ee.byu.edu, brad_hutchings@byu.edu

## ABSTRACT

RapidSmith is an open-source framework that allows for the exploration of novel approaches to the FPGA CAD flow for Xilinx devices. However, RapidSmith has poor support for manipulating designs below the slice level. In this paper, we highlight many of the projects RapidSmith enables and present extensions incorporated into "RapidSmith 2" that expose LUTs and flip-flops for direct manipulation in custom-built CAD tools. To demonstrate the utility of RapidSmith 2 we present the results of work to identify BELs in a design which must be clustered together and a tool that does pre-packing clustering accordingly.

## Categories and Subject Descriptors

B.7.2 [**INTEGRATED CIRCUITS**]: Design Aids—*Placement and routing*

## Keywords

FPGA; Xilinx; RapidSmith; RapidSmith 2; CAD Framework; Xilinx Design Language

## 1. INTRODUCTION

Open source frameworks are an important tool in facilitating exploration of new algorithms for and approaches to the FPGA CAD flow. Frameworks such as RapidSmith [9] and TORC [17], have been released that enable researchers to directly experiment with physical CAD tools for Xilinx devices. RapidSmith, in particular, allows researchers to create floor-planners, placers, routers, and explore other novel CAD tools and flows for commercial Xilinx devices. Using the Xilinx Design Language, RapidSmith imports the routing graph, fabric primitives, and other physical details of Xilinx devices into an easy-to-manipulate graph structure implemented in Java. Researchers manipulate this graph structure to place and route designs onto the Xilinx fabric.

RapidSmith designs can be imported back into the commercial Xilinx CAD flow at various stages of completion so

that researchers can focus on the problems of interest and leave other aspects of design completion to the Xilinx tools. The Xilinx flow is used to generate bitstreams, compute clock-rate estimates, etc. Combining RapidSmith with the commercial Xilinx flow provides the flexibility of a research tool with the rigor, detail and accuracy of a commercial tool.

A current limitation of RapidSmith is that its device representation ends at the "slice" level; it essentially hides the slice internals and makes experimenting with tools and strategies for slice internals difficult. RapidSmith 2 is a backwards-compatible update that provides a transparent representation of the internal architecture of the slice. By exposing the details of the slice, RapidSmith 2 enables further exploration of CAD approaches that manipulate internal slice routing and clustering - something that is not possible with the current version of RapidSmith.

As an example, we demonstrate this new capability by exploring clustering possibilities prior to packing. This is done by identifying clusters of cells which *must* be packed into particular arrangements based on the internal slice structure revealed by RapidSmith 2. Our first experiments show that this type of clustered logic makes up a non-negligible portion of an ISE-mapped test design.

This paper is organized as follows:

1. Review of RapidSmith and various projects it enables.
2. Updates comprising RapidSmith 2.
3. Report of experiments done with RapidSmith 2.
4. Conclusion and future work.

## 2. BACKGROUND

### 2.1 Projects Using RapidSmith

RapidSmith has enabled research in a wide variety topics. Below we describe a number of ways that other researchers have made use of RapidSmith.

RapidSmith serves as the foundation of several new CAD flows. [11] uses it to implement the relocatable and dynamically reconfigurable modules of their Dreams framework. [12] implements a bidirectional mapping framework, StML, between RTL and FPGA primitives with it. HMFlow (the project that RapidSmith came out of) uses it to create hard macros and then place and route them into complete designs as part of its rapid prototyping tool flow [8] [4].

In [3], researchers use RapidSmith to extract hard macros from a netlist as part of their dynamic and partial reconfiguration framework. [5] uses it in realizing a Xilinx bitstream of a VPR-placed [14] design. [6] embeds logic analyzers into placed and routed circuits with it.

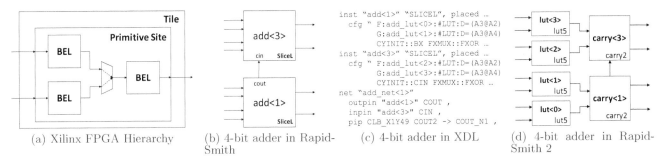

| (a) Xilinx FPGA Hierarchy | (b) 4-bit adder in Rapid-Smith | (c) 4-bit adder in XDL | (d) 4-bit adder in Rapid-Smith 2 |

**Figure 1: Xilinx Chip Hierarchy and Design Representations**

In the area of FPGA reliability, [2] uses RapidSmith to modify LUT equations and re-purpose carry chains to mask faults. [1] uses it to create hard macros of test configuration circuits for an online integrity test of the FPGA's components. In [18], the authors develop a fault-tolerant placement algorithm with it. [13] uses it to correlate bitstream frame addresses to the reconfigurable module located at that frame for use in their fault tolerant soft-core processer system. In [15], it serves as the basis of a soft-error vulnerability analysis framework for Virtex 5 FPGAs including a visualization tool for identifying vulnerable areas.

Finally, in the area of FPGA security, RapidSmith is used by [16] to insert a denial of service trojan post synthesis into an FPGA. [7] uses it to create a digital to analog converter on the FPGA's power rails.

## 2.2 RapidSmith 1

To permit CAD exploration, the RapidSmith framework provides both a logical netlist to represent designs and a physical description of the FPGA chip's resources. These are obtained from and closely based on Xilinx's XDL and XDLRC file formats.

Xilinx uses a three level hierarchy to represent their architectures consisting of tiles (CLBs, switch boxes), primitive sites (slices), and basic elements of logic or BELs (LUTs, flip-flops) (see Figure 1a). Interestingly, XDL and XDLRC directly represent only the top two levels of this hierarchy, obscuring the BEL-level details. Thus, the XDLRC file represents an FPGA device as an array of tiles, each of which contains zero or more primitive sites and a set of wires and connections between them. RapidSmith processes XDLRC files and provides an API into that information through its *Device* package for use in writing CAD tools such as placement and routing algorithms.

XDL presents a netlist structure of a mapped user design and is a human-readable representation of the Xilinx native circuit description (NCD). It represents designs as a set of *instances* interconnected by *nets*. These instances represent the configured slices, IOB's, and DSP48's making up the user design. For example, Figure 1b shows a simple XDL netlist of a 4-bit adder — containing two instances (slices) connected by a carry chain.

In XDL and in RapidSmith, instances may be unplaced or may be placed onto primitive sites by specifying a location string. Nets may be logical (contain only pins) or physical (also contain a list of PIPs). The configuration of an instance describes its BELs and muxes and is manipulated via text attributes. For example, the CYINIT attributes in Figure 1c specify the source of the initial carry-in signal to the carry logic BEL in that slice (the BX and CIN inputs, respectively in the figure). Modifying these attribute strings to properly configure an instance requires detailed knowledge of the structure of the underlying primitive site. RapidSmith provides an API for manipulating this netlist structure through its *Design* package.

## 3. RAPIDSMITH 2

As previously mentioned, RapidSmith, due to its relationship with XDL, only provides visibility down to the primitive site level. It does not describe the BELs or the inter-BEL routing that makes up the primitive site structure. While the instances do contain the information stored as attributes, we have found manipulating these attributes in any significant way to be tedious. Further, the lack of a graph structure at this level hinders any exploration of tools and algorithms attempting automated manipulations of the BEL-level netlist.

XDLRC does provide some visibility of the subsite structure through a section called the *primitive defs* section but is not always clear what each *element* in the section is describing. Through careful analysis, the meaning of each element can be discerned and a graph structure of the primitive site built. Additionally, further work is required to add and correct some seemingly mislabeled information. We use this information to add BEL-level support to RapidSmith 2 — its primitive sites now allow querying BELs and inter-BEL routing information, facilitating the creation of CAD tools that operate at the BEL-level.

To represent user designs at the BEL-level, RapidSmith 2 uses a new netlist structure (the old site-based netlist is preserved for backwards compatibility). Cells serve as the basis of this netlist. A cell is a logical element that can be placed on a BEL. Each cell contains a type (e.g. lut5 or carry2) that defines its pins and compatible placement locations (see Figure 1d). RapidSmith 2 supports custom cell libraries which could be useful for customized synthesis tools.

Correspondence between the logical netlist and the physical placement and routing is similar to the original RapidSmith. Each cell can be placed on a BEL. Nets can contain a set of programmable interconnect points (PIPs) specifying the route. With RapidSmith 2, some of these PIPs represent muxes inside the primitive site and are designated *site PIPs*.

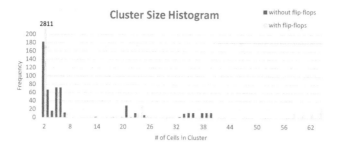

**Figure 2: Cluster Size Histogram, With and Without Flip Flops**

## 3.1 The Role of XDL in RapidSmith 2

One of the most useful features of RapidSmith is its ability to accept designs out of Xilinx's standard flow and return new or modified designs back into the flow through the use of XDL. This has allowed exploration using RapidSmith to focus on a particular portion of the FPGA CAD flow and defer to Xilinx's tools for the other parts. This also allows users to ultimately create bitstreams of their designs and execute them on physical FPGA devices.

We feel this is an important feature to preserve in Rapid-Smith 2. In RapidSmith, conversion to/from XDL was trivial as its design representation mirrored the format of an XDL design. However, RapidSmith 2's netlist no longer mirrors XDL. Packing and unpacking methods are thus required to go between RapidSmith 2's netlist and XDL.

To unpack an XDL instance into its equivalent Rapid-Smith 2 netlist the values associated with the attribute strings on the instance are interpreted and the corresponding netlist fragment created. Instance attributes defining the BELs are converted to cells (the cell type based off the type of BEL), mux attributes are converted to PIPs, and configuration attributes are paired with the appropriate cells (which can be a one-to-one or one-to-many pairing). XDL unpacking is automated with the support of XML files provided by the RapidSmith 2 system which identifies the cell type for each BEL type (SLICEL/A6LUT, SLICEM/CFF) in a given device.

Going the other direction, XDL packing converts the cells and site PIPs found in RapidSmith 2 netlists to instances with string attributes. Because XDL is represented as packed instances (attributes must reside in an instance), logical RapidSmith 2 netlists without sufficient placement information to be packed cannot be converted to XDL.

## 4. CLUSTERING EXPERIMENT

To demonstrate the possible uses and the capabilities of RapidSmith 2, we present the results of work looking at the flexibility of cells during the packing process. Specifically, we have identified groups of cells that are connected in ways such that the placement of one cell also determines the location of all other cells in the group. We refer to these groups of cells as *tightly-coupled cells*, and they are interesting in that they can be clustered together early with no ill effects since they ultimately must be placed next to one another. RapidSmith 2 enabled us to XDL-unpack a synthesized design from the standard Xilinx tool flow into a cell-level netlist (as described in a previous section). It also allowed us to analyze the primitive sites in Virtex 6 devices to identify cases where the physical wiring of the FPGA limits the flexibility

of the design's cells relative to one another, implying the existence of tightly-coupled cells.

We performed this experiment using a stereo vision benchmark from the Titan23 benchmark suite [10]. It was synthesized, mapped and placed by Xilinx ISE onto a Virtex 6 device. Using RapidSmith 2, we identified and grouped the tightly-coupled cells into clusters. We found that some of these tightly-coupled cells must be spread across different tiles such as in the case of carry chains. The tightly-coupled cells we found fall mainly into one of a few patterns including:

- cascaded carry chains with their source LUTs (XDLRC treats all carry-related logic as a single CARRY4 BEL)
- F7 and/or F8 muxes with their source LUTs
- cascaded BRAM/FIFOs or DSP48 blocks
- cells making up IOB primitive sites

Perhaps surprisingly absent from this list are any connections between LUTs and flip-flops. Though we tend to picture these two elements as always being grouped together and most clustering algorithms will typically pair them together, they are not required to be packed into the same site as each flip-flop can be driven directly from the general routing fabric.

The stereo vision benchmark we analyzed contained 18414 cells of which 28% are absorbed into tightly-coupled clusters. Most clusters contained only 2 cells but a number of clusters contained as many as 40 cells (see Figure 2). Of these clusters, 78% utilize only a single primitive site (and many allow for additional logic to be packed into that primitive site) while the remaining clusters require as many as 8 primitive sites (such as cascaded carry chains).

Next, we evaluated clustering when we allow absorbing flip-flops into clusters (such as with LUT/FF pairs) when the flip-flop is the only sink of its source. In this case we saw a 5x increase in the number of clusters, the majority of which are LUT/FF pairs. The clusters now encompassed 62% of the cells in the design with 86% of clusters containing 2 cells and the largest clusters growing to 64 cells. These experiments show that a significant portion of the cells in a design already must be combined into specific clusters and suggest that a sizeable portion of the FPGA packing process is deterministic. This offers opportunities for alternative approaches to packing.

## 5. CONCLUSION AND FUTURE WORK

In this paper we reviewed RapidSmith and showed a variety of projects that RapidSmith enables. We then presented extensions to RapidSmith that permit BEL-level manipulations of designs and demonstrated the utility of this by creating tightly-connected clusters from cells of a design extracted from the standard Xilinx flow. Future work will include exploring new packing and placement algorithms for Xilinx FPGAs and adding RapidSmith 2 support for Vivado devices and designs.

# 6. ACKNOWLEDGMENTS

This work was supported in part by the I/UCRC Program of the National Science Foundation within the NSF Center for High-Performance Reconfigurable Computing (CHREC), Grant No. 1265957.

# 7. REFERENCES

[1] M. Abdelfattah, L. Bauer, C. Braun, M. Imhof, M. Kochte, H. Zhang, J. Henkel, and H. Wunderlich. Transparent Structural Online Test for Reconfigurable Systems. In *On-Line Testing Symposium (IOLTS), 2012 IEEE 18th International*, pages 37–42, June 2012.

[2] A. Das, S. Venkataraman, and A. Kumar. Improving Autonomous Soft-error Tolerance of FPGA through LUT Configuration Bit Manipulation. In *Field Programmable Logic and Applications (FPL), 2013 23rd International Conference on*, pages 1–8, Sept 2013.

[3] L. Gantel, M. Benkhelifa, F. Lemonnier, and F. Verdier. Module Relocation in Heterogeneous Reconfigurable Systems-on-Chip using the Xilinx Isolation Design Flow. In *Reconfigurable Computing and FPGAs (ReConFig), 2012 International Conference on*, pages 1–6, Dec 2012.

[4] T. Haroldsen, B. Nelson, and B. White. Rapid FPGA Design Prototyping through Preservation of System Logic: A Case Study. In *Field Programmable Logic and Applications (FPL), 2013 23rd International Conference on*, pages 1–7, Sept 2013.

[5] E. Hung, F. Eslami, and S. Wilton. Escaping the Academic Sandbox: Realizing VPR Circuits on Xilinx Devices. In *Field-Programmable Custom Computing Machines (FCCM), 2013 IEEE 21st Annual International Symposium on*, pages 45–52, April 2013.

[6] B. L. Hutchings and J. Keeley. Rapid Post-Map Insertion of Embedded Logic Analyzers for Xilinx FPGAs. In *Field-Programmable Custom Computing Machines (FCCM), 2014 IEEE 22nd Annual International Symposium on*, pages 72–79, May 2014.

[7] B. L. Hutchings, J. Monson, D. Savory, and J. Keeley. A Power Side-channel-based Digital to Analog Converterfor Xilinx FPGAs. In *Proceedings of the 2014 ACM/SIGDA International Symposium on Field-programmable Gate Arrays*, FPGA '14, pages 113–116, New York, NY, USA, 2014. ACM.

[8] C. Lavin, B. Nelson, and B. Hutchings. Impact of Hard Macro Size on FPGA Clock Rate and Place/Route Time. In *Field Programmable Logic and Applications (FPL), 2013 23rd International Conference on*, pages 1–6, Sept 2013.

[9] C. Lavin, M. Padilla, J. Lamprecht, P. Lundrigan, B. Nelson, and B. Hutchings. RapidSmith: Do-It-Yourself CAD Tools for Xilinx FPGAs. In *Field Programmable Logic and Applications (FPL), 2011 International Conference on*, pages 349–355, Sept 2011.

[10] K. Murray, S. Whitty, S. Liu, J. Luu, and V. Betz. Titan: Enabling Large and Complex Benchmarks in Academic CAD. In *Field Programmable Logic and Applications (FPL), 2013 23rd International Conference on*, pages 1–8, Sept 2013.

[11] A. Otero, E. de la Torre, and T. Riesgo. Dreams: A Tool for the Design of Dynamically Reconfigurable Embedded and Modular Systems. In *Reconfigurable Computing and FPGAs (ReConFig), 2012 International Conference on*, pages 1–8, Dec 2012.

[12] D. Peterson, O. Bringmann, T. Schweizer, and W. Rosenstiel. StML: Bridging the Gap between FPGA Design and HDL Circuit Description. In *Field-Programmable Technology (FPT), 2013 International Conference on*, pages 278–285, Dec 2013.

[13] H.-M. Pham, S. Pillement, and S. Piestrak. Low-overhead Fault-tolerance Technique for a Dynamically Reconfigurable Softcore Processor. *Computers, IEEE Transactions on*, 62(6):1179–1192, June 2013.

[14] J. Rose, J. Luu, C. W. Yu, O. Densmore, J. Goeders, A. Somerville, K. B. Kent, P. Jamieson, and J. Anderson. The VTR Project: Architecture and CAD for FPGAs from Verilog to Routing. In *Proceedings of the ACM/SIGDA International Symposium on Field Programmable Gate Arrays*, FPGA '12, pages 77–86, New York, NY, USA, 2012. ACM.

[15] A. Sari, D. Agiakatsikas, and M. Psarakis. A Soft Error Vulnerability Analysis Framework for Xilinx FPGAs. In *Proceedings of the 2014 ACM/SIGDA International Symposium on Field-programmable Gate Arrays*, FPGA '14, pages 237–240, New York, NY, USA, 2014. ACM.

[16] O. Soll, T. Korak, M. Muehlberghuber, and M. Hutter. EM-based Detection of Hardware Trojans on FPGAs. In *Hardware-Oriented Security and Trust (HOST), 2014 IEEE International Symposium on*, pages 84–87, May 2014.

[17] N. Steiner, A. Wood, H. Shojaei, J. Couch, P. Athanas, and M. French. Torc: Towards an Open-source Tool Flow. In *Proceedings of the 19th ACM/SIGDA International Symposium on Field Programmable Gate Arrays*, FPGA '11, pages 41–44, New York, NY, USA, 2011. ACM.

[18] M. Wirthlin, J. Jensen, A. Wilson, W. Howes, S.-J. Wen, and R. Wong. Placement of Repair Circuits for In-field FPGA Repair. In *Proceedings of the ACM/SIGDA International Symposium on Field Programmable Gate Arrays*, FPGA '13, pages 115–124, New York, NY, USA, 2013. ACM.

# Technology Mapping into General Programmable Cells

Alan Mishchenko   Robert Brayton
Department of EECS, University of California, Berkeley
{alanmi, brayton}@berkeley.edu

Wenyi Feng   Jonathan Greene
Microsemi Corporation SOC Products Group
{wenyi.feng, jonathan.greene}@microsemi.com

## ABSTRACT

*Field-Programmable Gate Arrays (FPGA) implement logic functions using programmable cells, such as K-input lookup-tables (K-LUTs). A K-LUT can implement any Boolean function with K inputs and one output. Methods for mapping into K-LUTs are extensively researched and widely used. Recently, cells other than K-LUTs have been explored, for example, those composed of several LUTs and those combining LUTs with several gates. Known methods for mapping into these cells are specialized and complicated, requiring a substantial effort to evaluate custom cell architectures. This paper presents a general approach to efficiently map into single-output K-input cells containing LUTs, MUXes, and other elementary gates. Cells with to 16 inputs can be handled. The mapper is fully automated and takes a logic network and a symbolic description of a programmable cell, and produces an optimized network composed of instances of the given cell. Past work on delay/area optimization during mapping is applicable and leads to good quality of results.*

## 1. INTRODUCTION

Technology mapping for traditional FPGAs transforms a design into a network of K-input LUTs [7]. Since a K-LUT can implement any Boolean function of up to K inputs, mapping into LUTs can be structural, without any functional matching needed for standard cells and programmable cells.

**Categories and Subject Descriptors:** B.6.3 [**Logic Design**]: Design Aids – Optimization; B.7.1 [**Integrated Circuits**]: Types and Design Styles – Gate arrays

**General Terms:** Algorithms, Performance, Design, Experimentation, Modelling

**Keywords:** FPGA, technology mapping, programmable cells, Boolean matching, Boolean function

Novel FPGA architectures based on programmable cells have been proposed. For example, LUT structures combine two or more LUTs in one cell [5][17]. Other extensions include cells based on LUTs and AND gates [1], LUTs and MUXes [4][16], and cones of elementary gates [20].

A common difficulty in evaluating any such architecture is the need to develop a dedicated mapper, or at least modify a traditional LUT mapper often using ad hoc and suboptimal

methods. This task is difficult because matching into the given cell often requires sophisticated programming to fairly evaluate a proposed architecture. As a result, custom mappers are often inflexible (a change of the cell structure may lead to a non-trivial redesign of the mapper) and slow (in our experience, a 10x slow-down is common and expected when a modified LUT mapper performs on the fly matching against the cell).

To facilitate research in FPGA architecture evaluation, a general technology mapper ideally takes any design and programmable cell and produces a mapped network composed of multiple instances of the given cell, each with its own configuration parameters. These specify an assignment of variables of the original function to the cell inputs, and bits used to program LUTs present in the cell, so that the cell can realize a given Boolean function.

The present paper answers this need by proposing a general mapper into K-input programmable cells, where K can be up to 16, although computation is more efficient when K does not exceed 12, covering many of the practically interesting cell architectures.

The proposed mapper does not require manual tuning, other than providing a description of the cell. The time-consuming Boolean matching is replaced by a pre-computation, which can be carried out concurrently, reducing this one-time preparation from hours to minutes.

Finally, the quality of results produced by the mapper is on par with that of results produced by state-of-the-art LUT mappers, because the same mapping heuristics are used.

The paper is organized as follows. Section 2 reviews background. Section 3 shows a way to characterize a general programmable cell. Section 4 describes the process of pre-computing Boolean functions to be matched against the cell. Section 5 describes the Boolean matching. Section 6 describes modifications to a LUT mapper needed for mapping into programmable cells. Experimental results are described in Section 7, while Section 8 concludes the paper.

## 2. BACKGROUND

### 2.1 Boolean network

A *Boolean network* (or *circuit*) is a directed acyclic graph (DAG) with nodes corresponding to logic gates and edges corresponding to wires connecting the nodes.

A node $n$ has zero or more fanins, i.e. nodes driving $n$, and zero or more fanouts, i.e. nodes driven by $n$. The primary inputs (PIs) are nodes without fanins. The primary outputs (POs) are a subset of nodes of the network, connecting it to the environment. A fanin (fanout) cone of node $n$ is a subset of nodes of the network, reachable through the fanin (fanout) edges of the node.

### 2.2 And-Inverter Graph

*And-Inverter Graph* (AIG) is a Boolean network whose nodes can be classified as follows:

- One constant 0 node.
- Combinational inputs (primary inputs, flop outputs).
- Internal two-input AND nodes.

- Combinational outputs (primary outputs, flop inputs).

The fanins of internal AND nodes and combinational outputs can be complemented. The complemented attribute is represented as a bit mark on a fanin edge, rather than a single-input node. Due to their compactness and homogeneity, AIGs have become a de-facto standard for representing circuits in technology mappers.

## 2.3 Structural cut

A cut $C$ of a node $n$ is a set of nodes of the network, called *leaves* of the cut, such that each path from a PI to $n$ passes through at least one leaf. Node $n$ is called the root of cut $C$. The cut *size* is the number of its leaves. A trivial cut is the node itself. A cut is *K-feasible* if the number of leaves does not exceed $K$. A local function of a node $n$, denoted $f_n(x)$, is a Boolean function of the logic cone rooted in $n$ and expressed in terms of the leaves, $x$, of a cut of $n$.

Cut enumeration [15] is a technique used by a cut-based technology mapper to compute cuts using dynamic programming, starting from PIs and ending at POs.

## 2.4 Boolean function

Let $f(X): B^n \rightarrow B$, $B = \{0,1\}$, be a completely specified Boolean function, or *function* for short. The *support* of $f$, $supp(f)$, is the set of variables $X$ influencing the output value of $f$. The support size is denoted by $|X|$.

Two functions are NPN-equivalent if one of them can be obtained from the other by negation (N) and permutation (P) of the inputs and outputs. Consider the set of all Boolean functions derived from a given function $F$ by a sequence of these transforms. These functions constitute the *NPN class* of function $F$. The *NPN canonical form* of function $F$ is one function belonging to its NPN class, also called the *representative* of this class. Selection of the representative is algorithm-specific. For example, in some cases, the representation is the function whose truth table has minimum (or maximum) integer value among all the truth tables of functions belonging to the NPN class.

## 3. CELL DESCRIPTION

It is assumed that a programmable cell is composed of LUTs, MUXes and the elementary gates, AND and XOR. Other gates types can be expressed using these primitives.

The proposed matcher takes a character string expressed using the notation from [13][14]: parentheses represent an AND, square braces represent an XOR, angular braces represent a 2:1-MUX, curly braces represent a LUT, and an exclamation mark is NOT. For example, $(abc)$ is AND$(a, b, c)$, and $<abc>$ is MUX$(a, b, c) = ab + !ac$. For example, a 7-input cell composed of a 6-LUT feeding a 2-input AND [1] is represented as: $h=\{abcdef\};i=(gh)$. The lower-case characters ($a, b, c$, etc) are reserved for primary inputs. Internal variables (in this case, $h$ and $i$) follow without gaps in the alphabetical order. Spaces are disallowed in the description.

## 4. HARVESTING FUNCTIONS

During mapping into K-input cells, Boolean functions considered by an AIG-based mapper are those appearing as functions of K-input cuts in the AIG. Industrial designs often contain different types of logic and may vary greatly in terms of the functions found at their structural cuts. The matcher is applied to only those functions appearing at some cut in the design. Such functions can be collected and stored for future use.

An efficient method [19] to pre-compute Boolean functions of cuts in a design, or a suite of designs relies on fast algorithms to compute NPN-canonical forms [9] and compactly store them in a data-structure called the DSD manager [13][14]. The manager stores representatives of each NPN class as a shared tree,

providing a convenient way of checking functional properties, such as symmetry, unateness, decomposability, etc.

## 5. BOOLEAN MATCHING

SAT-based evaluation of programmable cells was introduced in [11] and further developed in [6][8]. Our implementation uses a dedicated Quantified Boolean Formula (QBF) solver, which performs iterative counterexample-guided refinement [18][10].

In this case, the problem of matching a function $F(x)$ with a cell $C(x, p)$, is equivalent to checking satisfiability of the formula: $\exists p \forall x[C(x, p) == F(x)]$. In addition, if a satisfying solution exists, it shows how to configure the cell using parameters $p$ to realize function $F(x)$.

The iterative approach finds one SAT assignment, $(x_0, p_0)$, of the formula $C(x, p) == F(x)$. For the given values of $p_0$, if $\forall x[C_{p0}(x) == F(x)]$ holds, then a solution, $p_0$, is found. Otherwise, $x_0$ is substituted into $C(x, p)$, and the resulting function, $C_{x0}(p)$, is used as an additional constraint for $\exists p[C(x, p) == F(x)]$. If at some point the formula is UNSAT, the QBF instance has no solution and the match does not exist. An upper bound on iterations required is $2^{|x|}$, but in practice it converges much faster. Additional speedup can be achieved by adding symmetry-breaking clauses and solving multiple QBF instances concurrently.

## 6. TECHNOLOGY MAPPING

We modified the priority-cut-based technology mapper [12] to enable processing K-input cuts whose functions are pre-computed and pre-matched. The mapper has access to the DSD manager storing each NPN class of Boolean functions appearing in the design along with its matching status (matchable/unmatchable) as well as the configuration parameters for the matchable functions.

In a typical LUT mapper, cuts are computed along with their truth tables using topological cut enumeration [15]. The cuts are then support-minimized by removing variables appearing in the structural support but not in the Boolean functions of the cut. NPN classes of the cut functions are computed [9]. These steps are performed as usual. Our modifications to the mapper concern handling of cuts whose functions have no match with the given cell. Such cuts are labeled and not allowed to be selected as best cuts. When prioritizing cuts, preference is given to matchable cuts, and if there is room left, some of the labeled cuts are stored and used to compute cuts for the fanouts. It is possible that, by merging two unmatchable cuts, a matchable cut is produced.

When the final mapping is derived, a subset of best cuts is selected and returned to the user as the final mapping. Since the best cuts are always matchable, the resulting mapping only contains the cuts that can be expressed using the target cell. At this point, the configuration parameters are retrieved and used to output the set of configured cells representing the given design. Optionally, a functional equivalence check can be performed to make sure that the network of configured programmable cells has the same functionality as the original Boolean network.

## 7. EXPERIMENTAL RESULTS

The proposed framework is implemented in ABC [2]. For a case-study, we a suite of 10 representative designs whose sizes are between 10K and 90K 6-LUTs.

### 7.1 Programmable cells

Figure 1 shows two programmable cells, which contain three 3-LUTs and two 2-ANDs. Our experiments indicate that the additional 2-LUT present in Cell B substantially increases its expressive power at the cost of only four additional configuration bits. Selecting these two cells is somewhat arbitrary but it allows us to illustrate the proposed method with Cell B having reconvergent paths, which is hard to handle using traditional Boolean methods.

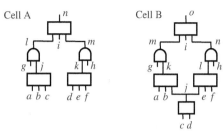

**Figure 1. Programmable cells used in this paper.**

Description of Cell A: $j=\{abc\};k=\{def\};l=(gj);m=(kh);n=\{lim\};AB;BC;DE;EF;GH$. Description of Cell B: $j=\{cd\};k=\{abj\};l=\{ef\};m=(gk);n=(lh);o=\{min\};AB;CD;EF;GH$. In both cases, an optional list of primary input symmetries is appended, which makes the SAT solver 2-4x faster. The lower-case characters are inputs and internal nodes. The upper-case characters are used for symmetries. (With some extra effort, symmetries can be computed automatically.)

## 7.2 Harvesting Boolean functions

As the first step, NPN classes of 9-input functions appearing in the selected benchmarks are pre-computed. Any logic synthesis script can be used for this task. In our experiments, the script (*&synch2; &if -n –K 9*) was iterated three times for each benchmark. This script performs logic synthesis with choices (*&synch2*), computes 9-input cuts together with their Boolean functions and saves them in the DSD manager (switch '-n'). The computation took about 20 minutes and the resulting manager contained about one million NPN classes together with their occurrence counters. The manager is saved into a file as follows: *dsd_save funcs9.dsd*. The size of the resulting file is 41MB.

All functions that are *not* collected by the script but appear in a design during mapping will be treated as unmatchable by the mapper. This limitation was addressed, but the description is outside of the scope of this paper, because ignoring a small fraction of complex functions, in our experience, does not impact the quality of results. This is why the next optional step is to filter out rare NPN classes. Such classes rarely appear during mapping; moreover, it is unlikely that they can be matched with the cell. Filtering them out tends to preserve quality and reduce runtime.

In our experiments, NPN classes appearing in the designs less than 10 times are removed: *dsd_load funcs9.dsd; dsd_filter -L 10; dsd_save funcs9filter.dsd*. The resulting file contains 130K classes and occupies only 4MB. We tried using unfiltered NPN classes, leading to a negligible (less than 1%) degradation of area/delay.

## 7.3 Boolean matching

Matching was performed by the following command: *dsd_load funcs9filter.dsd; set progressbar; dsd_match –S "<cell_description>" -P 30; dsd_save funcs9match.dsd; dsd_ps*. The last column printed by *dsd_ps* shows the number/percentage of classes unmatchable with the cell.

The runtime of concurrent matching (*dsd_match*) in our experiments was 450 sec for Cell A (1750 sec for Cell B) on a computer with 16 hyper-threaded cores. The argument "-P 30" limits the number of concurrent worker threads to 30, not counting the controller thread. The same computation for Cell A runs 8410 sec on one thread, which is 18.7x slower than the concurrent one.

## 7.4 Technology mapping

Given a pre-matched library of NPN classes of functions appearing in the sample designs, mapping can be performed using command *&if -k* after reading the library as follows: *dsd_load funcs9match.dsd*. Optionally, a custom LUT library (command *read_lut*) can be used to specify the LUT-size-specific area/delay.

In our experiment, we iterated the following script three times (*&synch2; &if –k –K 9*). Each node in the resulting netlists does not exceed 9 inputs and can be realized by the given programmable cell. Currently, the configuration parameters for the nodes are computed but not used. In general, a hierarchical mapped netlist can be produced where instances contain the logic of each cell defined by its configuration parameters.

The result of mapping into programmable cells is compared against mapping into traditional K-LUTs ($6 \le K \le 9$) produced by command *&if* in ABC [2]. Three iterations of the script (*&synch2; &if –m –K <num>*) were used with switch '-m' forcing truth table computation and cut minimization because these steps are required for mapping into programmable cells. In all cases, the results of mapping were verified using command *&cec*.

## 7.5 Summary of experiment

The experimental results are summarized in Table 1. Cell B outperforms Cell A in terms of both area and delay measured in terms of the number of cells and the number of cell levels. Area produced using Cell B is close to that for 9-LUTs, even though Cell B has only 28 configuration bits and two extra AND-gates, compared to the 512 bits needed for a 9-LUT! Delay produced by Cell B is between delays produced using 8-LUTs and 9-LUTs.

Table 1 shows that the synthesis flow based on Cell B is 48% slower than the flow based on the traditional 6-LUTs and only 20% slower than the flow based on 9-LUTs.

The good performance of Cell B motivates research into programmable cells containing reconvergent logic structure.

Another way to improve expressive power of the cells is to allow for constants and inverters at the free inputs of the AND-gates. For this, "g" and "h" in the cell description can be replaced by "{g}" and "{h}", respectively, where curly braces represent a 1-input LUT. Yet another way to boost the expressive power, is to replace 2-ANDs with 2-LUTs. In both cases, the matching and mapping stages of the flow can be repeated, resulting in more matches and improved quality of mapping, while the runtime of matching may degrade due to the increased cell complexity.

## 8. CONCLUSIONS

The paper presents an integrated approach to map logic netlists into arbitrary single-output programmable cells specified by the user. The approach is based on pre-computing typical Boolean functions appearing in a set of sample netlists and pre-matching them against the given cell. An available technology mapper is minimally modified to make use of the matching information. Because of the pre-computation, the runtime of the mapper is reasonable. The quality of results is good because the same efficient heuristics are used as during mapping into K-LUTs.

## 9. ACKNOWLEDGEMENTS

This work is supported in part by SRC contract 1875.001 and NSA grant "Enhanced equivalence checking in crypto-analytic applications". We also thank industrial sponsors of BVSRC: Altera, Atrenta, Cadence, Calypto, IBM, Intel, Jasper, Mentor Graphics, Microsemi, Real Intent, Synopsys, Tabula, and Verific for their continued support.

# 10. REFERENCES

[1] J. H. Anderson, Q. Wang, "Area-efficient FPGA logic elements: architecture and synthesis," *Proc. ASP-DAC'11*, pp. 369-375. http://janders.eecg.toronto.edu/pdfs/aspdac _2011.pdf

[2] Berkeley Logic Synthesis and Verification Group. *ABC: A System for Sequential Synthesis and Verification.* http://www-cad.eecs.berkeley.edu/~alanmi/abc

[3] V. Bertacco and M. Damiani, "Disjunctive decomposition of logic functions," *Proc. ICCAD '97*, pp. 78-82.

[4] S. Chin, J.H. Anderson, "A case for hardened multiplexers in FPGAs," *Proc. ICFPT'13, pp. 42-49.* http://janders.eecg.toronto.edu/ pdfs/xan.pdf

[5] J. Cong and Y. Hwang, "Boolean matching for LUT-based logic blocks with applications to architecture evaluation and technology mapping," *IEEE TCAD'01*, Vol. 20(9), pp. 1077-1090.

[6] J. Cong and K. Minkovich, "Improved SAT-based Boolean matching using implicants for LUT-based FPGAs", *Proc. FPGA'07*. http://cadlab.cs.ucla.edu/~kirill/fpga07.pdf

[7] R. J. Francis, J. Rose, and K. Chung, "Chortle: A technology mapping program for lookup table-based field programmable gate arrays", *Proc. DAC '90*, pp. 613-619.

[8] Y. Hu, V. Shih, R. Majumdar, and L. He. "Efficient SAT-based Boolean matching for heterogeneous FPGA technology mapping", *Proc. ICCAD'07*.

[9] Z. Huang, L. Wang, Y. Nasikovskiy, and A. Mishchenko, "Fast Boolean matching based on NPN classification", *Proc. ICFPT'13*. http://www.eecs.berkeley.edu/~alanmi/publica tions/2013/icfpt13_npn.pdf

[10] M. Janota, W. Klieber, J. Marques-Silva, and E. Clarke, "Solving QBF with counterexample-guided refinement", *Proc. SAT'12*. https://www.cs.cmu.edu/~wklieber/papers/ qbf-cegar-sat-2012.pdf

[11] A. Ling, D. Singh, and S. Brown. "FPGA PLB evaluation using Quantified Boolean Satisfiability", *Proc. FPGA'05*. http://www.eecg.toronto.edu/~brown/papers/fpl05-ling.pdf

[12] A. Mishchenko, S. Cho, S. Chatterjee, and R. Brayton, "Combinational and sequential mapping with priority cuts", *Proc. ICCAD '07*, pp. 354-361.

[13] A. Mishchenko and R. Brayton, "Faster logic manipulation for large designs", *Proc. IWLS'13*. http://www.eecs.berkeley. edu/ ~alanmi/publications/2013/iwls13_dsd.pdf

[14] A. Mishchenko, "Enumeration of irredundant circuit structures", *Proc. IWLS'14*. http://www.eecs.berkeley.edu/ ~alanmi/publications/2014/iwls14_dsd.pdf

[15] P. Pan and C.-C. Lin, "A new retiming-based technology mapping algorithm for LUT-based FPGAs", *Proc. FPGA '98*, pp. 35-42.

[16] M. Purnaprajna and P. Ienne, "A case for heterogeneous technology-mapping: soft vs hard multiplexers". *Proc. FCCM'13*, pp. 53-56.

[17] S. Ray, A. Mishchenko, N. Een, R. Brayton, S. Jang, and C. Chen, "Mapping into LUT structures", *Proc. DATE'12*.

[18] A. Solar-Lezama, Ch. G. Jones, and R. Bodik, "Sketching concurrent datastructures", *Proc. PLDI '08*. http://people.csa il.mit. edu/asolar/papers/pldi207_SketchingConcurrency.pdf

[19] W. Yang, L. Wang, and A. Mishchenko, "Lazy man's logic synthesis", *Proc. ICCAD'12*, pp. 597-604. http://www.eecs. berkeley.edu/~alanmi/publications/2012/iccad12_lms.pdf

[20] G. Zgheib, L. Yang, Z. Huang, D. Novo, H. Parandeh-Afshar, H. Yang, and P. Ienne, "Revisiting and-inverter cones". *Proc. FPGA'14*, pp. 45-54. http://lap.epfl.ch/files/ content/ sites/lap/files/shared/publications/ZgheibFeb14_ RevisitingAndInverterCones_FPGA14.pdf

**Table 1. Comparing traditional K-LUT mapping with mapping using the K-input programmable cells**

| Design | Area (number of instances) | | | | | | Delay (logic depth in terms of instances) | | | | | | Runtime (seconds) | | | |
|---|---|---|---|---|---|---|---|---|---|---|---|---|---|---|---|---|
| | 6-LUT | 7-LUT | 8-LUT | 9-LUT | Cell A | Cell B | 6-LUT | 7-LUT | 8-LUT | 9-LUT | Cell A | Cell B | 6-LUT | 9-LUT | Cell A | Cell B |
| 01 | 31246 | 28197 | 25734 | 24101 | 32408 | 25284 | 19 | 16 | 14 | 14 | 15 | 14 | 216 | 243 | 262 | 271 |
| 02 | 19808 | 19428 | 18998 | 18439 | 21694 | 18503 | 5 | 5 | 5 | 4 | 5 | 4 | 11 | 14 | 14 | 15 |
| 03 | 25528 | 23042 | 21314 | 20310 | 29071 | 20766 | 12 | 11 | 10 | 9 | 14 | 10 | 59 | 80 | 97 | 97 |
| 04 | 39366 | 36414 | 37315 | 35384 | 39548 | 33357 | 9 | 8 | 7 | 6 | 8 | 7 | 75 | 93 | 99 | 103 |
| 05 | 44426 | 41609 | 38232 | 36036 | 47810 | 36679 | 9 | 8 | 7 | 7 | 8 | 7 | 102 | 134 | 145 | 159 |
| 06 | 88964 | 83504 | 76317 | 72346 | 94669 | 72835 | 9 | 8 | 7 | 7 | 8 | 7 | 205 | 272 | 286 | 310 |
| 07 | 31048 | 27950 | 25042 | 24257 | 31769 | 24893 | 8 | 8 | 7 | 6 | 7 | 7 | 60 | 78 | 86 | 94 |
| 08 | 33154 | 29074 | 25268 | 26008 | 37626 | 26634 | 19 | 15 | 15 | 13 | 18 | 14 | 58 | 86 | 82 | 96 |
| 09 | 32684 | 32091 | 31485 | 31164 | 34709 | 31355 | 5 | 4 | 4 | 3 | 4 | 3 | 24 | 28 | 28 | 30 |
| 10 | 12909 | 12286 | 11688 | 11554 | 13165 | 11916 | 7 | 6 | 6 | 4 | 7 | 5 | 11 | 14 | 18 | 20 |
| Geomean | 1.000 | 0.929 | 0.870 | 0.841 | 1.065 | 0.852 | 1.000 | 0.885 | 0.820 | 0.707 | 0.919 | 0.759 | 1.000 | 1.282 | 1.381 | 1.487 |

# EURECA: On-Chip Configuration Generation for Effective Dynamic Data Access

Xinyu Niu
Department of Computing,
Imperial College London
niu.xinyu10@imperial.ac.uk

Wayne Luk
Department of Computing,
Imperial College London
w.luk@imperial.ac.uk

Yu Wang
Department of
Electronic Engineering,
Tsinghua University
yu-wang@tsinghua.edu.cn

## ABSTRACT

This paper describes Effective Utilities for Run-timE Configuration Adaptation (EURECA), a novel memory architecture for supporting effective dynamic data access in reconfigurable devices. EURECA exploits on-chip configuration generation to reconfigure active connections in such devices cycle by cycle. When integrated into a baseline architecture based on the Virtex-6 SX475T, the EURECA memory architecture introduces small area, delay and power overhead. Three benchmark applications are developed with the proposed architecture targeting social networking (Memcached), scientific computing (sparse matrix-vector multiplication), and in-memory database (large-scale sorting). Compared with conventional static designs, up to 14.9 times reduction in area, 2.2 times reduction in critical-path delay, and 32.1 times reduction in area-delay product are achieved.

## Categories and Subject Descriptors

C.0 [**Computer System Organization**]: System architectures

## General Terms

Design; performance

## Keywords

On-chip configuration generation; runtime reconfiguration; dynamic data access

## 1. INTRODUCTION

Field-Programmable Gate Arrays (FPGAs) provide a platform to implement customised data-paths for target applications. Orders-of-magnitude improvements in performance and power efficiency have been achieved over software designs, for applications such as financial modelling [21] and signal processing [15]. The applications that can maximally exploit the potential processing capability of FPGAs tend to favour static implementations: the connections between memory data and data-paths, as well as the operations in data-paths, are predefined during compile time and stay the same during runtime (see Figure 1(a)). In these applications, the static data connections and operators are often pipelined. At each clock cycle, all the implemented hardware resources are active, generating one result per data-path.

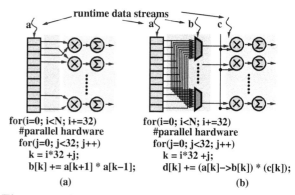

```
for(i=0; i<N; i+=32)          for(i=0; i<N; i+=32)
  #parallel hardware            #parallel hardware
  for(j=0; j<32; j++)           for(j=0; j<32; j++)
    k = i*32 +j;                  k = i*32 +j;
    b[k] += a[k+1] * a[k-1];      d[k] += (a[k]->b[k]) * (c[k]);
        (a)                           (b)
```

**Figure 1: Current FPGA support for applications with (a) static data access and (b) dynamic data access.**

While the processing capability of FPGAs has been demonstrated, the lack of support for dynamic operations, especially dynamic data access, limits the use of FPGAs as mainstream data processors. *Dynamic data access* refers to the capability of providing efficient parallel access to dynamic data structures such as linked lists. As shown in Figure 1(b), when data access operations a[k]->b[k] depend on runtime variable b instead of fixed offsets, each data access operation requires various connections between datapaths and memory. In hardware, all such connections need to be statically implemented, while only one of the connections is active in each cycle. As the number of connections for a dynamic data access operation increases, the benefit of hardware over software implementations diminishes.

Efficiently supporting such dynamic data access is a long-standing challenge for FPGA-based designs. Applications with dynamic data access are common in social networking (Memcached), scientific computing (sparse matrix-vector multiplication), graph traversal (breadth-first search), in-memory database (sorting, selection), and embedded systems (H.264). Previously, researchers proposed solutions to work around the dynamic data access in these applications, such as compromising memory management flexibility (Memcached [5]), replicating on-chip memory buffers (sparse matrix-vector multiplication [28]), and limiting parallelism (large-scale sorting [10]). As discussed in Section 5, these solutions either limit the market acceptance of the developed applications, or affect the application performance.

The objective of this work is to address the dynamic data access challenge in hardware designs, without affecting the

*FPGA'15*, February 22–24, 2015, Monterey, California, USA.
Copyright © ACM 978-1-4503-3315-3/15/02 ...$15.00.
http://dx.doi.org/10.1145/2684746.2689076.

current support for static applications. We propose a memory architecture known as EURECA that can be integrated with FPGAs, which meets the following requirements.

R1: to efficiently accommodate intensive dynamic data access (thousands of parallel wires, each with hundreds of possible runtime connections), without sacrificing application functionality or performance.

R2: to be compatible with existing synthesis tools and hardware languages, and to be transparent to applications without dynamic data access.

R3: to have overhead as small as possible when integrated with the relevant reconfigurable architectures.

Section 7 explains how these requirements are met by EURECA. The proposed memory architecture is underpinned by a novel runtime reconfiguration approach: instead of physically storing all possible configurations, the configurations are generated on-chip from user logic. At each cycle, the generated configurations update the implemented connections, ensuring implementation of only the active connections during runtime, while enabling applications with dynamic data access to be implemented with the same efficiency as static designs.

**Outline.** Section 2 discusses the related work. Section 3 presents an overview of the EURECA memory architecture in three aspects: (1) configuration flow, (2) architecture integration, and (3) EURECA-based designs. Section 4 shows the circuit details of a EURECA module. Section 5 studies the use of EURECA architectures in three benchmark applications: Memcached, sparse matrix-vector multiplication, and large-scale sorting. For each benchmark application, we discuss the design challenges, the improvements, and the impacts on applications with similar data access patterns. Section 6 evaluates the proposed architecture in terms of architecture efficiency, with the benchmark applications synthesised, placed and routed on a commercial FPGA enhanced with EURECA support. Measured results are based on EURECA circuits developed using Cadence Virtuoso with 65nm technology. Section 7 discusses the potential and the limitations of the proposed approach.

## 2. RELATED WORK

Previous work has explored communication operation support in reconfigurable system. Coarse-grain architectures such as Matrix [12], Tilera [23] and Ambric [3] implement distributed general-purpose processors and dedicated communication networks on-chip. Instruction execution of these architectures can involve dynamic data access, with the support of local memories and global communication networks. These architectures need new programming models to coordinate distributed processor execution, and fine-grain parallelism is not always captured in designs targeting these architectures. Another direction to improve communication efficiency in reconfigurable designs is to build high-level memory abstractions and optimisation tools. Memory abstractions such as CoRAM [7] decouple memory management from computation, and provide virtualised memory interfaces to users. However, CoRAM maps dynamic data access into separate local caches in processing elements, which can reduce data locality. While some high-level synthesis tools adopt polyhedral transformation [17] to improve memory bandwidth utilisation, such polyhedral approaches do not support dynamic data access. In contrast, this work enhances reconfigurable architectures with efficient support for dynamic data access, with fine-grain parallelism in reconfigurable designs preserved.

Runtime reconfiguration techniques provide opportunities to unfold dynamic data access in time dimension. In [27], partial reconfiguration is applied to update a wide crossbar

by reusing the routing multiplexers. It takes 220 $\mu s$ to reconfigure a crossbar running at 150MHz. For dynamic data access in high-performance applications, the implemented connections need to be updated every iteration. In this case, the reconfiguration time dominates the overall execution time of a reconfigurable design. To reduce reconfiguration time, DPGA [20] and time-multiplexed FPGAs [22] are proposed. In these architectures, configuration memories for reconfigurable logic are replicated to store multiple configurations on-chip. The 3D programmable architecture from Tabula [19] replicates the configuration of logic blocks as well as interconnect. Configurations of implemented designs thus can be updated within a cycle. The replicated configuration memories, however, introduce large area and power overhead. The inefficiency in previous runtime reconfiguration approaches is due to the need for storing all possible configurations, either on-chip or off-chip. The EURECA approach adopts a new configuration flow that only stores the active configurations in each cycle.

## 3. EURECA MEMORY ARCHITECTURE

The **configuration flow** in FPGAs defines how they can be reconfigured to implement different customised designs. As shown in Figure 2(d), the EURECA configuration flow includes Static Configuration Memory (SCM), Configuration Generator (CG), and Dynamic Configuration Memory (DCM), where the SCM defines the operations of the CG, the CG generates configuration data based on runtime variables, and the output of the CG writes into the DCM. In this work, we couple the DCM with routing multiplexers, and group the runtime reconfigurable multiplexers into EURECA modules. This new configuration flow brings three benefits: (1) the necessity to store all possible configurations is eliminated, since the DCM only stores the active configuration; (2) generating and adapting configurations on-chip significantly reduces reconfiguration time, allowing runtime reconfiguration operations to finish within one cycle; (3) implemented in user logic, CGs are customised to application requirements. For static designs without dynamic data access, no CGs will be necessary.

The configuration flow for static designs is demonstrated in Figure 2(a) and (b). Static Data-Paths (SDPs) are specified with a single configuration. Idle operators are introduced when dynamic operations are required.

In previous approaches, multiple configurations are prepared in advance, as shown in Figure 2(c). This configuration flow is inefficient because only one of the configurations is used. When stored off-chip (partial reconfiguration), the large reconfiguration time prohibits fine-grained reconfiguration [27]. When stored on-chip, the increase in memory capacity introduces large area overhead [20, 22]. Moreover, the additional memory area is fixed once FPGAs are fabricated. Static designs are implemented with the same area overhead, although only one of the replicated configuration memories is required.

**Architecture overview.** Integrating the EURECA memory architecture into an existing reconfigurable architecture, as demonstrated in Figure 3, includes three steps: (1) divide on-chip memory blocks into memory groups, and couple each memory group with a EURECA module; (2) implement on-chip memory controllers as hard blocks, and couple each memory controller with a EURECA module; (3) arrange the EURECA modules in columns, and insert the EURECA columns into existing routing and logic fabrics. A EURECA module is the basic building block in the EURECA memory architecture. The module provides I/O ports (1) to take CG output to update the DCMs in a EURECA module, and (2) to provide reconfigurable connections between user logic and memory elements. The EURECA modules, when cou-

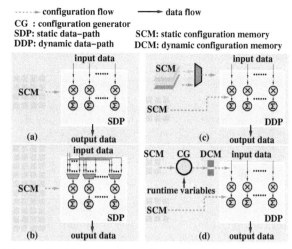

configuration flow ······▶  data flow ───▶

CG : configuration generator
SDP: static data–path    SCM: static configuration memory
DDP: dynamic data–path   DCM: dynamic configuration memory

**Figure 2: Data and configuration flow of (a) static design supporting static operations, (b) static design supporting dynamic operations, (c) dynamic design with prepared configurations, and (d) dynamic design reconfigured with EURECA approach.**

pled with memory groups, provide access to on-chip memory, while those coupled with memory controllers provide access to off-chip memory. The I/O ports of memory groups and memory controllers are hard-wired into EURECA modules, while the connections between user logic and EURECA modules are statically reconfigurable. In the current architecture, the interconnections between EURECA modules are mapped into routing channels.

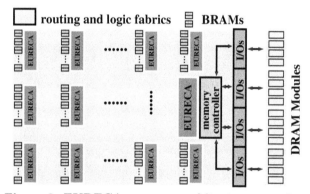

**Figure 3: EURECA memory architecture overview.**

**EURECA-based reconfigurable designs** are developed with hardware languages such as Verilog and VHDL, and synthesised with existing tool chains. A EURECA-based design contains SDPs, CGs and instantiated EURECA modules, where SDPs implement the static operations of an application, while CGs and EURECA modules support dynamic data access. Figure 4(a) and (b) respectively demonstrate the pseudocode and the hardware implementation of the algorithm in Figure 1(b). In this example, the SDPs are parallel multiply-and-accumulate modules, and the dynamic operations refer to the data access to **a**. We store **a** in a BRAM group, and instantiate the corresponding EURECA module. To reconfigure the EURECA module, we develop a CG that takes **b** as runtime input, and generates corresponding configurations **con**. As shown in Figure 4(a), the EURECA module takes **con** to update its DCM, and provides the SDPs the dynamic connections to **a**. This example design is a simplified sparse matrix-vector multiplication kernel. The application will be discussed in more detail in Section 5.2.

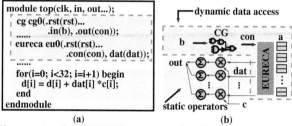

```
module top(clk, in, out...);
  cg cg0(.rst(rst)...
          .in(b), .out(con));
  ......
  eureca eu0(.rst(rst)...
          .con(con), dat(dat));
  for(i=0; i<32; i=i+1) begin
    d[i] = d[i] + dat[i] *c[i];
  end
endmodule
```

(a)      (b)

**Figure 4: A EURECA example design in Verilog, for the application in Figure 1(b).**

## 4. EURECA MODULE

The EURECA modules play a key role in our runtime reconfigurable design: to take runtime configurations and to update data connections correspondingly. As shown in Figure 5, a EURECA module consists of runtime reconfigurable multiplexers, configuration control units, and a configuration distribution network. A EURECA module supports both dynamic read and dynamic write. We use the dynamic read to illustrate the functionality of a EURECA module. The development of a EURECA module follows three principles: (1) grouping dynamic connections to reduce routing complexity; (2) sharing runtime configurations to minimise CG resource usage; (3) supporting both static data access and dynamic data access with various data widths

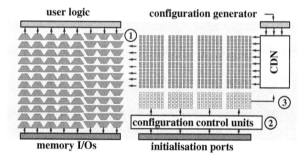

**Figure 5: A EURECA module with (1) runtime reconfigurable multiplexers, (2) configuration control units, and (3) Configuration Distribution Network (CDN).**

**Runtime reconfigurable multiplexers** refer to the dynamic connections between memory I/Os and user logic. A reconfigurable multiplexer contains a routing multiplexer and runtime writable SRAM cells (named as multiplexing SRAM cells) that define the implemented connection. We set the minimum data width supported in a EURECA module to be 1 byte, and divide the reconfigurable multiplexers into connection groups, with each group containing 8 multiplexers (bit-level dynamic connections are implemented with user logic due to the relatively small area usage). Figure 6 shows an example connection group with 256 input wires from memory, labelled as $i_0$ to $i_{255}$. The 256 input wires correspond to 32 input bytes. Correspondingly, routing multiplexers $m_0 \sim m_7$ in the connection group have 32 input wires. External designs use the output of the routing multiplexers $o_0 \sim o_7$ as an 8-bit dynamic connection.

We align the connections between memory elements and routing multiplexers, such that the multiplexers in a connection group can share the same multiplexing SRAM cells. For the example in Figure 6, the wires in the first input byte ($i_0 \sim i_7$) are correspondingly connected to the first input wires of $m_0 \sim m_7$. Similarly, the second input byte ($i_8 \sim i_{15}$) are connected to the second input wires of $m_0 \sim m_7$, in the same order. During runtime, to connect to the

76

second input byte, $m_0 \sim m_7$ share the same configuration value (00001). To dynamically reconfigure the connection, CGs only need to generate one configuration for a connection group, which reduces the resource usage of CGs by 8 times. The connections between EURECA modules and memory I/Os are fixed, while the connections to user logic are configurable. This reduces the routing complexity of EURECA-based designs, and preserves full configurability between user logic and dynamically accessed data.

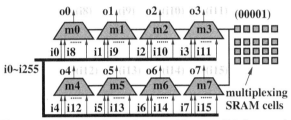

**Figure 6: 8 reconfigurable routing multiplexers in a EURECA module, sharing the same SRAM cells.**

**Configuration control units** operate EURECA modules in 4 different modes, to support static data access as well as dynamic data access with different data widths. In a EURECA module, we use SRAM cells to store configuration information, and organise the SRAM cells in rows. In the example case with 256 input wires, each row contains the multiplexing SRAM cells for 6 connection groups (30 SRAM bits). Figure 7 shows the SRAM organisation, and the circuit details of a multiplexing SRAM cell. In an SRAM cell, the WL port controls whether the cell value can be updated. A Write-Enable (WE) row is inserted below the multiplexing SRAM rows, and a column of shift registers is added. Each bit in the WE row controls the WL ports of an SRAM column, and each shift register controls the WL ports of an SRAM row. The input of an SRAM cell is multiplexed between the initialisation ports and the configuration ports. A EURECA module also contains a state bit, to indicate whether the current module operates in static or dynamic mode.

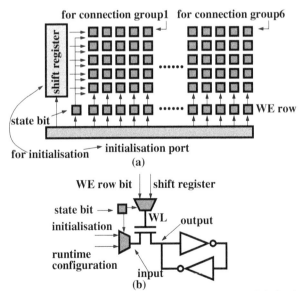

**Figure 7: (a) The control units for the multiplexing SRAM cells in a EURECA module. (b) The circuit details of a multiplexing SRAM cell.**

In the `initialisation mode`, the first 32-bit configuration data from the initialisation ports write the state bit to

'1', and push a '1' bit into the shift registers. In a multiplexing SRAM cell, the initialised state bit selects initialisation port data as input, and use shift register output as the WL signal. As the '1' bit shifts through the registers, the configuration data are written into SRAM cells row by row, which define the initial connections within a EURECA module. The state bit and the WE row are initialised last, with the values determined by the following operation mode.

To operate a EURECA module in the `static mode` during runtime, we set the state bit to '1', and push '0' into the shift registers, so that the connections between user logic and accessed data are fixed during runtime. This mode is used for applications with only static data access. No CG is implemented, and the EURECA modules become transparent to the implemented data-paths.

In the `dynamic mode`, all multiplexing SRAM cells are updated by CG output in parallel. The state bit is set to be '0' to select runtime reconfigurations as input, and use WE row bits to control the WL ports. All bits in the WE row are initialised to be '1'. In this mode, the dynamic connections in a EURECA module get full reconfigurability, i.e., the connections can be connected to all input bytes. The dynamic mode is used when the data involved in dynamic data access are 8-bit wide. As an example, in Memcached, due to the flexible key width, dynamic pointers implemented in hardware can point at any byte in the fetched off-chip memory data. The dynamic mode is therefore used.

In the `partially dynamic mode`, part of the multiplexing SRAM cells are updated during runtime, while the others remain static. In this mode, certain bits in the WE row are configured to be '0', turning off the WL ports of the corresponding SRAM columns. The partially dynamic mode is used when application data width is larger than 8 bits, and therefore not all possible connections for 8-bit data are required. More details for this mode will be given next.

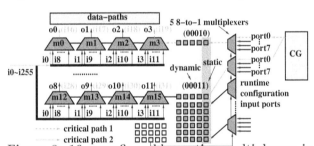

**Figure 8: 16 reconfigurable routing multiplexers in partially dynamic mode, providing a 16-bit dynamic connection.**

**Configuration distribution network (CDN)** shares runtime configurations among connection groups, when application data width is wider than 8 bits. As data width increases, a dynamic connection contains multiple connection groups. These connection groups are connected to the same input data during runtime, with static offsets. Therefore, we operate EURECA modules in the `partially dynamic mode`, to fix the static configuration bits, and share the remaining dynamic bits in the connection groups. Figure 8 shows the data connections for a 16-bit dynamic data access, which contains two connection groups $m_0 \sim m_7$ and $m_8 \sim m_{15}$. In the dynamic data access, $m_0 \sim m_7$ provide the lower 8 bits, and $m_8 \sim m_{15}$ provide the higher 8 bits. In other words, there is a 1 byte offset between the two connection groups. We thus fix the lowest configuration bit for the first and the second connection group to be '0' and '1', respectively. As an example, to dynamically connect to the second input data ($i_{16} \sim i_{31}$), $m_0 \sim m_7$ are configured with "00010", and $m_8 \sim m_{15}$ are configured with "00011". Since the lowest bit is fixed, the same runtime configuration "0001"

**Algorithm 1** Key searching algorithm in Memcached.

**input:** char *key, nkey
**output:** item *it
1: hv = hash(key, nkey);
2: it = primary_table[hv];
3: **while** it **do**
4:  **if** nkey==it→nkey && strcmp(key, it→key) **then**
5:   return it;
6:  **end if**
7:  it = it→next;
8: **end while**
9: return NULL;

can be shard via the CDN, from port0. In this work, we use 8-to-1 multiplexers in a CDN, to support applications with 8-bit to 64-bit data width. The configurations for the CDN are static, and are initialised in the initialisation mode.

**Critical path.** For a EURECA-based design, the execution process within a clock cycle is as follows. First, CGs output configuration information based on runtime variables. Second, the CDN distributes the configuration information to the multiplexing SRAMs in a EURECA module, which reconfigures the implemented connections. Third, when the connections are reconfigured and memory data appear at the EURECA I/O ports, SDPs start data processing. Therefore, as shown in Figure 8, there are two potential critical paths in a EURECA module: (1) between CG, multiplexers in CDN, multiplexing SRAMs, and routing multiplexers; and (2) between memory data and routing multiplexers.

# 5. CASE STUDIES

## 5.1 Memcached

Our first benchmark application, Memcached, is a distributed memory caching system widely used in the servers of web service companies (Facebook, Twitter, YouTube, Wikipedia, etc.). A Memcached server stores frequently accessed data in memory to provide quick responses to web requests. Memcached uses hash tables to index stored data, and uses slab allocation to allocate data chunks. Each hash bucket contains one to multiple hash entries, and each hash entry stores the address of its slab data. In hardware, as shown in Figure 9(a), we store a primary hash table on-chip to keep track of hash bucket addresses, and keep the hash data and the slab data in off-chip memory. Algorithm 1 presents the kernel operations to search for a hash entry. Once a request packet arrives, the packet decipher takes the Memcached command (e.g. get news21), and the hash function generates a hash value hv based on the key value (news21) and key length (6) (line 1). The algorithm then fetches the hash bucket address it based on hv (line 2), and traverses all hash entries in the bucket (line 3∼8). Once a hash entry with matched key value and key length is found, the corresponding slab data are fetched, and Memcached returns a response packet.

**Design challenge.** In Memcached, the key length varies from 1 byte to 256 bytes. When pointed to by dynamic pointers, the hash data have unaligned starting addresses, which lead to design challenges in hashed item search. As an example, if we assume a 6-byte memory channel, and data address it aligns with the channel width (i.e. $it\%6 = 0$), the data can be directly fetched and compared (see Figure 9(b)). Due to the variable key length, the accessed data are unaligned during runtime. As shown in Figure 9(c), when $it\%6 = 2$, the loaded data are in wrong order 21news. The search module continues searching as 21news != news21, although this hash entry stores the target hash data.

**Previous solutions.** In an FPGA implementation [4], the key size nkey is fixed at 64 bytes. Fixing the key size

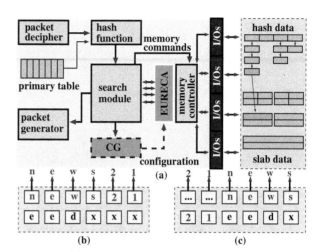

**Figure 9: (a) A EURECA-based Memcached design. Off-chip data access operations with (b) aligned and (c) unaligned starting addresses.**

aligns the runtime data. However, this design compromises functionality as keys smaller than 64 bytes need to be padded, and keys larger than 64 bytes cannot be supported. It is argued in [11] that this restrictive memory management will limit the market acceptance, based on recent industry trends. An architecture with soft processors and reconfigurable fabric is proposed in [11]. Parallel processing is implemented in hardware, and memory data are managed in soft processors. This approach consumes large on-chip area to integrate the processors, and introduces intensive communication between hardware and software.

**EURECA solution.** In a EURECA architecture, we instantiate a EURECA module to align the off-chip data access $it \rightarrow (nkey, key)$. The EURECA module is coupled with a memory controller. Since Memcached accesses data at byte level, we operate the EURECA module in the dynamic mode. As shown in Figure 9(a), the search module takes the initial it from Memcached commands, and updates it with the fetched data when traversing the hash buckets, until the matched hash entry is found. The memory controller fetches off-chip data pointed by it. The CG generates configurations for byte-level dynamic connections based on it as well as the position of a byte in off-chip memory channels. The CG operations can be expressed as $con_i = (it + i)\%N$, where $i$ indicates the $i$-th byte in data bus, and $N$ is the memory channel width ($N=6$ in the example in Figure 9(b)). The generated configurations therefore are updated cycle by cycle in the search process.

**Table 1: Comparison of Memcached solutions.**

| solution | complexity | functionality | throughput |
|----------|------------|---------------|------------|
| static | $N^2$ | full | $N$ |
| [4] | $N$ | compromised | $< N$ |
| [11] | $N + C_{cpu}$ | full | n/a |
| EURECA | $N + C_{eureca}$ | full | $N$ |

$N$: on-chip data bus width (byte).
$C_{cpu}, C_{eureca}$: constant overhead.

**Discussion.** Unaligned data access is common in applications with complex data structures. The unaligned data addresses come from variable data length, such as the hash key in Memcached, the chromosomes in genetic algorithm, and the FM-index in DNA sequencing. Table 1 compares the various solutions. Statically implementing all possible connections introduces $N^2$ area usage, where $N$ is the data stream width in bytes. For reconfigurable designs with high memory bandwidth, this is infeasible to implement. Sacrificing application functionality affects the market acceptance of the product, and integrating general processors introduces large area and communication overhead. The EURECA architecture enables applications with unaligned data access to be efficiently implemented, without sacrificing functionality or requiring general-purpose instruction processors

## 5.2 Sparse Matrix-Vector Multiplication

Our second benchmark application, Sparse Matrix-Vector multiplication (SpMV), is widely used in scientific computing and industrial development. SpMV multiplies a sparse matrix M with a dense vector vec, as shown in Figure 10(a). A sparse matrix can be stored in Compressed Sparse Row (CSR) format. Figure 10(b) illustrates the CSR format for the sparse matrix in Figure 10(a). The CSR data contain three vectors: val, col and offset. val stores all the nonzero elements of a sparse matrix, col indicates which column each val is in, and offset points to the starting data of each row. In this example sparse matrix, item A is stored in the first column of the second row. col[2]=0 indicates A is in the first column, and offset[1]=2 indicates the second row starts from the third non-zero element.

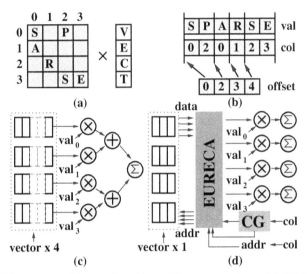

**Figure 10:** (a) An SpmV problem, stored in (b) CSR format. SpMV architectures with (c) replicated vector memory and (d) shared EURECA-based vector memory.

**Challenge.** The design challenge comes from the random data access to the dense vector. As shown in Algorithm 2, in each row, SpMV multiplies the val[j] with corresponding vector value vec[col[j]] (line 4). Since col are runtime data, the vector data access becomes random. To avoid the long latency of off-chip random data access, designers normally buffer vec on-chip. In FPGAs, the distributed BRAMs can be grouped as a unified memory architecture, which provides replicated SpMV data-paths the parallel data access to vec. Due to the randomness of the vector data access, each data-path needs to be able to access all BRAMs in the memory architecture. As an example, if a shared vector memory provides 4 output ports to 4 parallel data-paths, each data-path needs to connect to all the memory blocks in this vector memory, i.e., all of the 4 output ports. For an SpMV design with $N$ data-paths, this leads to $N^2$ possible runtime connections.

**Previous solution.** To address this issue, the SpMV architecture in [28] assigns each data-path a separate copy of the vector data, as shown in Figure 10(c). Given an FPGA with $mem$ on-chip memory capacity, the architecture supports vector size up to $mem/N$, and needs to block the sparse matrix data access when the vector size exceeds

**Algorithm 2** Sparse matrix-vector multiplication.

```
1: for i ∈ 0 → num_rows do
2:    res[i]=0;
3:    for j ∈ offset[i] → offset[i+1] do
4:       res[i] += val[j] * vec[col[j]];
5:    end for
6: end for
```

this limit. This architecture is sensitive to matrix sparsity. When the blocked matrix rows contain fewer than $N$ non-zeros in the data-paths. In Table 2, we calculate the efficiency as the ratio between measured performance and the theoretical peak performance. In [28], the idle cycles reduce the average efficiency to 42%. As $N$ increases, the efficiency will further reduce.

**EURECA solution.** Our EURECA-based SpMV design instantiates a EURECA module coupled with a memory group with $N$ memory blocks. The EURECA module operates at the partially dynamic mode, as the design uses 32-bit data. We save the vector data into a shared on-chip memory architecture, which is connected with $N$ data-paths. The data-paths stream CSR data from off-chip memory. A CG generates the runtime configurations for memory address and vector data, based on the value of col, as shown in Figure 10(d). For a vector data request, the CG first reconfigures the address connection to direct the address input into the right memory block, and reconfigures the data connection when the requested data appear at the memory output ports. The address input and the data output are pipelined. In this work we use 10 sparse matrices from [8] to simulate the computation. The average efficiency for the EURECA solution reaches 85%, when $N = 64$. The idle cycles in this solution mainly come from memory conflicts, where multiple data-paths are accessing data in the same memory block. As $N$ increases, the memory conflict ratio decreases, and the computational efficiency increases.

**Table 2: Comparison of SpMV solutions.**

| solution | complexity | vector size | efficiency |
|----------|-----------|-------------|------------|
| static | $N^2$ | $mem$ | 85% ($\propto N$) |
| [28] | $N$ | $mem/N$ | 42% ($\propto 1/N$) |
| EURECA | $N + C_{eureca}$ | $mem$ | 85% ($\propto N$) |

**Discussion.** Random access to parallel data is common in complex computational kernels such as sparse matrix processing and graph traversal. In these applications, the frequently accessed data (dense vector and bit-mask matrix) are normally stored on-chip to reduce data access latency. In modern reconfigurable computing platforms, hundreds of data-paths are implemented to process data in parallel ($N$=128 in [6]). Statically implementing a shared memory architecture for these applications is not feasible, due to the $N^2$ area complexity. Replicating on-chip data significantly reduces the effective cache size. The EURECA architecture enables a shared on-chip memory architecture to be implemented in reconfigurable designs, to support parallel random data access. The cache miss rate and the data-path idle cycles can thus be reduced.

## 5.3 Large-Scale Sorting

Our third benchmark application, sorting, is one of the most extensively researched subjects because of the need to quickly organise millions to billions data items in a database. As shown in Figure 11(a), sorting networks [1, 16] sort small data set in parallel. When targeting large-scale data, the sorting operations are divided into a sorting phase and a merging phase. In the merging phase, as shown in Figure 11(b), select-and-pop units merge small sorted data chunks step by step. In each step, the data chunks are

**Algorithm 3** Parallel merging of sorted data chunks.

**input:** sorted data chunk A, B, with size n
**output:** merged data chunk C, with size 2n
1: a=&A[0]; b=&B[0]; c=&C[0];
2: **while** c ≤ 2n **do**
3:   **for** i ∈ 0 → N **do**
4:     **if** a[i] < b[N-1-i] && a[i+1] > b[N-2-i] **then**
5:       commit = i+1; break;
6:     **end if**
7:   **end for**
8:   `assign`(c, a, commit);
9:   `assign`(c+commit, b, N-commit);
10:   `sort`(c, N);
11:   a+= commit; b+= N-commit; c+=N;
12: **end while**

buffered in on-chip FIFOs followed by the select-and-pop units.

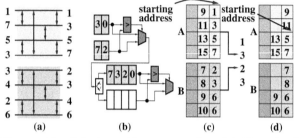

**Figure 11: (a) A sorting network. (b) Two basic select-and-pop units to merge sorted data. FIFOs starting addresses in (c) the first cycle and (d) the second cycle.**

**Challenge.** The main challenge is to commit multiple sorted data in each cycle when parallelising the merging operations. Algorithm 3 presents a parallel merging algorithm, where $N$ data are merged every iteration. The algorithm first compares the first $N$ data from both A and B, and labels the index for the smallest $N$ data as *commit* (line 3∼7). *commit* indicates the first *commit* data from A and the first $N - commit$ from B should be committed into C (line 8∼9). Finally, we sort the committed $N$ data, and increase array indices correspondingly (line 10∼11).

When implemented in hardware, the data connections between sorted data chunks (A, B) and comparators depend on runtime computation results. In the example in Figure 11(c), each sorted data chunk is stored in a FIFO with 4 output ports, and *commit*=2 in the first cycle. After reading the first two data from A and B, the starting addresses change from 0 to 2. As shown in Figure 11(d), the output data from FIFO A become (9,11,5,7) in the second cycle, although the right order is (5,7,9,11). If we statically configure the connections between FIFO output and comparator input, the comparison operations (line 3∼7) will return wrong results. During runtime, for a FIFO with $N$ output ports, the FIFO output data have $N$ different starting addresses.

**Previous solutions.** In a software implementation, the committed data are read sequentially, which eliminates the impact of variable starting addresses. In order to read multiple data per cycle with correct functionality, a hardware implementation needs to cover all possible runtime scenarios, which leads to $O(N^2)$ complexity for FIFOs with $N$ output ports. [10] proposes a select-and-pop unit with 2 data committed each cycle. However, the approach is not scalable for higher parallelism due to the quadratic design complexity.

**EURECA solution.** In our solution, we implement 2 EURECA modules, each coupled with a BRAM group. A BRAM group is implemented as a FIFO with $N$ inputs and

$N$ outputs, where $N$ is the number of committed data in each cycle. During runtime, we load the sorted data from the FIFOs, and reorganise the loaded data in the EURECA modules. A comparison module compares the reorganised data, commits the smallest $N$ data, updates the *commit* variable, and outputs FIFO read enable signals to shift the committed data out of the FIFOs. CGs for the EURECA modules calculate the configurations based on the current starting address, *commit*, and the position of the reconfigured connections in a FIFO. The CGs and the comparators in the comparison module form a feedback loop. Operations in this feedback loop are not pipelined.

**Table 3: Comparison of sorting solutions.**

| solution | complexity | data size | throughput |
|---|---|---|---|
| sorting network | $C \cdot N \log_2(N)$ | small | $N$ |
| merger | $N^2$ | large | $N$ |
| EURECA | $N + C_{eureca}$ | large | $N$ |

**Discussion.** The sorting problem is an example of applications in which data access operations in the current cycle depend on the computation results from previous cycles. When developed in parallel programming models for hardware, such a data access operation unfolds into multiple possible connections. Table 3 compares different solutions for the sorting application. Sorting networks [1, 16] are only applicable to small-scale data sets, as the design complexity is proportional to data size. Combining sorting networks and data mergers solves the data size limitation. However, a merger with $N$ parallel units suffers $O(N^2)$ complexity due to the $N$ possible starting addresses for read operations. Our EURECA solution solves both the data size limitation and the quadratic area complexity, by generating configurations for the next cycle based on the computation results in the current cycle.

## 6. EVALUATION

This section evaluates the EURECA architecture. First, we enhance a baseline architecture with EURECA support, and set up an experiment environment to synthesise designs into the enhanced architecture. Second, we evaluate the general benefits and the overhead of the enhanced architecture, and compare the EURECA approach with previous runtime reconfiguration techniques, for supporting dynamic data access. Third, for the benchmark applications, we develop both EURECA-based dynamic designs and static designs based on the baseline architecture, which are synthesised, placed and routed in the corresponding architectures, to measure the impacts on application performance.

### 6.1 Experiment Methodology

**Baseline system.** The experiment setup simulates a commercial reconfigurable system in terms of FPGA specification and off-chip memory systems, to capture the design realisation in practice. We assume the baseline system to be the Max3424A from Maxeler Technologies, which contains a Xilinx Virtex-6 SX475T FPGA and provides up to 38.4 GB/s memory bandwidth. As listed in Table 4, the off-chip memory system contains 4 128-bit DDR3 data channels, which operate at 303 MHz. We adapt the detailed architecture file developed in [9] to describe the baseline architecture. A CLB in this architecture contains two slices, each of which contains four Basic Logic Elements (BLEs), and a BLE contains a fracturable 6-input LUT and two FFs. We modify the architecture file to align with the architectural details of Virtex-6 SX475T shown in Xilinx FPGA Editor. The measured average channel width in FPGA Editor is 150. However, VTR [18], the synthesis tool used in our experiments, assumes a simplified routing model. Routing features in commercial FPGAs, such as non-unified channel width and diagonal wires, are not supported by VTR. In [13], the channel width is set to be 300 for Stratix IV. In this work, we inflate the channel width to 256 to approximate the actual routing capacity.

**EURECA implementation**. We develop the EURECA module full-custom at the transistor level in the Cadence Design Platform Virtuoso, with a 65-nm CMOS technology from UMC. Inside a EURECA module, multiplexers are implemented with pass transistors, 5T SRAM cells are used to dynamically configure routing multiplexers, and 6T SRAM cells are used to statically configure the 8-to-1 multiplexers in the CDN. In terms of area, the routing multiplexers and the 5T SRAM cells occupy most of a EURECA module. In terms of delay, as discussed in Section 4, the 8-to-1 multiplexers, the 5T SRAM cells, and the routing multiplexers are in the critical paths. To balance the module area and delay, we size the routing multiplexers to minimum width, optimise the 8-to-1 multiplexers for speed, and insert 4-time drivers between the 8-to-1 multiplexers and the 5T SRAM cells. The sizing approach for 5T SRAM in [14] is adopted to ensure robust read and write operations during runtime. Circuits outside the critical paths, such as the shift registers and the 6T SRAM cells, are optimised for area.

**Table 4: EURECA architecture parameters.**

| baseline FPGA | CLB: 37,200 | BRAM36: 1064 |
| | DSP48x2: 1008 | tile: 136x360 |
| | channel width: 256 | |
| DDR3 memory | width: 128*4 bits @ 303 MHz | |
| a EURECA module | data I/Os: 1024 | con I/Os: 896 |
| | address I/Os: 480 | con I/Os: 160 |
| | area: 593,210 (325,754) | |
| | delay: 0.17 ns | |
| | power: 96.56 mw @ 150 MHz | |
| on-chip memory | width: 1024*2 @ 150 MHz | |
| | memory group: 32 BRAM36 | |
| EURECA layout | BRAMs: 7 columns * 4 modules | |
| | memory controller: 2 modules | |

**Architecture integration**. EURECA modules are integrated with BRAMs and memory controllers. Given the parallelism in recent reconfigurable designs, we set each BRAM group to contain 32 BRAMs. The baseline architecture contains 1064 36Kb BRAMs, which are organised in 15 columns. Each of the BRAM groups is coupled with a EURECA module, which provides dynamic access to up to 32 memory blocks, or 128 different input bytes. The enhanced architecture therefore contains 7 EURECA columns. A EURECA column contains 4 EURECA modules, and sits in the middle of two BRAM columns. The left BRAMs are not connected to EURECA modules due to BRAM group granularity: a BRAM column contains 72 BRAMs, and the upper 8 BRAMs cannot construct a complete BRAM group.

The on-chip data-paths are set to operate at 150 MHz. The 38.4 GB/s memory bandwidth therefore corresponds to 2 1024-bit on-chip streams. We implement 2 memory controllers to connect the off-chip and on-chip data streams. Each memory controller is coupled with a EURECA module. As listed in Table 4, the off-chip memory system contains 4 128 bit (64 byte) DDR3 data channels. Along with the 303 MHz bandwidth and double data rate of DDR3, the 64-byte off-chip memory channel provides 38.4 GB/s bandwidth. Therefore, the maximum dynamic offset in off-chip data access is 64 bytes, i.e., a dynamic connection to off-chip data has up to 64 different input bytes. The routing multiplexers and 5T SRAMs in the 2 EURECA modules are customised for the reduced dynamic degree.

**Synthesis environment**. We use the VTR tool chain to synthesise designs into the EURECA architecture, with updated area and delay models. Carry chain is not supported in the current work. To model the design delay, we extract the delay information of CLBs, DSPs and BRAMs from the Xilinx TRCE results for the baseline architecture in speed grade -3, and use the routing delay information in [13], which is based on the same 40-nm technology node. The delay information for EURECA modules is measured from Cadence designs (room temperature and nominal voltage). The area information is expressed in the unit of minimum-width transistor area. We use the area model in [2] to estimate silicon area based on the drive strength of implemented transistors. The drive strength of the transistors in EURECA modules is collected from the implemented circuits. Table 4 lists the EURECA module areas (the area number in brackets is for the EURECA modules coupled with memory controllers). We estimate the CLB area based on the circuit specifications in [26], and adapt the area models for logic blocks based on those in [2]. To reduce routing complexity, for a EURECA module, we fix the configuration pins at the middle of the left and right sides, and spread the data I/O pins. The placement algorithm is modified such that once a EURECA module is placed, the coupled BRAMs are labelled as occupied.

## 6.2 Dynamic Connection Efficiency

This section evaluates the efficiency of the EURECA architecture, when supporting dynamic data access. We define the dynamic connection efficiency $E$ as the ratio between the number of different runtime connections $R$ supported by the same routing resources, and the overhead $O$ for enabling such connections.

$$E = \frac{R}{O} = \frac{R}{o_a \cdot o_t} \quad (1)$$

For an architecture with enhanced runtime reconfigurability ($R > 1$), the overhead $O$ includes (1) additional silicon area $O_a$ consumed by reconfiguration infrastructure, (2) additional execution time $O_t$ due to reconfiguration time, and (3) impacts on static designs. The third overhead is application-dependent, and therefore is difficult to generally quantify. Figure 12 compares the maximum channel width and the critical path of various applications targeting the baseline and the EURECA architectures. For static designs, using the EURECA architecture increases the channel width and the delay by less than 2% in average.

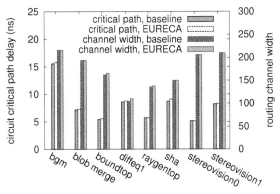

**Figure 12: Impacts of the EURECA memory architecture on static designs, in terms of critical path delay and channel width.**

An ideal architecture supports unlimited reconfigurability without area overhead ($o_a = 1$) or time overhead ($o_t = 1$). The efficiency $E$ increases linearly with the number of possible connections for a dynamic data access operation, as shown in Figure 13. Based on the area information in Table 4, integrating the EURECA architecture increases the overall area of the baseline architecture by 1.17% ($o_a$=1.017). For the reconfiguration time, since in the same cycle, the connections in EURECA modules are reconfigured, and data are loaded through the reconfigured connections, $o_t$=1. The efficiency of EURECA architecture approximates the optimal level.

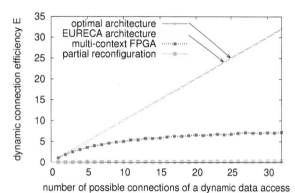

**Figure 13: Dynamic connection efficiency $E$ when the number of possible connections for a dynamic data access operation increases.**

Partial reconfiguration provides unlimited $R$, as designers can store all partial configurations off-chip. The efficiency is limited by reconfiguration time. Given the smallest addressable configuration size (3232 bits) and the maximum reconfiguration throughput (400 MB/s) in the latest devices [24, 25], the minimum reconfiguration time is 1.01 $\mu$s (151 clock cycles for the 150 MHz operating frequency). When the implemented configurations need to be updated every cycle, 1 result is generated every 152 cycles ($o_t$=152). The efficiency for partially reconfiguring the routing fabric, as shown in Figure 13, is far from optimal.

Multi-context FPGAs enable new configurations to be applied within a cycle, since possible configurations are stored on-chip. In this experiment, we replicate the configuration memory of routing multiplexers in the connection blocks of the baseline architecture. The number of replicated configuration memory increases with $R$. As $R$ increases, the area overhead quickly outweighs the increase in runtime reconfigurability. As shown in Figure 13, the efficiency of multi-context FPGAs reduces to 7.2 when $R = 32$, which indicates an area overhead of 4.42. To achieve the same reconfigurability of a EURECA module, the multi-context FPGAs need to replicate 128 configuration memory sets.

## 6.3 Application Evaluation

To further evaluate the EURECA approach, we develop a static design and a dynamic design for each benchmark application. The static design and the dynamic design share the same SDPs. In the static design, all the possible connections for dynamic data access are statically implemented into the baseline architecture, with `if-else` expressions. The dynamic design adopts the EURECA solutions proposed in Section 5, and targets the EURECA architecture. Except the feedback loop in the sorting design, operations in the benchmark applications are pipelined to reduce critical path delay. Table 5 presents the measured design properties. Given the 64-byte off-chip memory channel, the Memcached application has 64 possible connection sets, each 128 bytes wide. The parallelism for SpMV and large-scale sorting is set to be 32.

The resource usage and the critical-path delay of SDPs indicate the initial design properties, when dynamic data access operations are not required. The design properties of the dynamic designs are at the same level as the initial design properties. The critical-path delay of dynamic designs is slightly reduced as the EURECA module aggregates the distributed memory I/O connections into a single module, which eliminates some long connections in the SDPs. When statically implementing the possible connections, the resource usage is increased by up to 14.9 times, and the delay is doubled. In the sorting design, two memory groups are used to build the two input FIFOs, the intensive connections between the memory groups and comparators introduce a comparatively large initial delay. Overall, the dynamic designs reduce the area-delay product by up to 32.1 times.

Statically implementing all possible connections significantly increases the routing complexity of the benchmark designs, since thousands of $N$-to-1 connections need to be routed, where where $N = 64$ for Memcached, and $N$=32 for SpMV and for large-scale sorting. As shown in Table 5, all the three static designs cannot be routed under the current routing infrastructure. The average channel width for the static designs is 356, which indicates the routing difficulty of the static designs, even on large-scale commercial FPGAs. In other words, with the EURECA architecture, applications and design approaches previously considered not suitable for hardware acceleration can be efficiently implemented. As discussed in Section 5 and Table 1~3, the enabled features include flexible memory management, shared memory architecture supporting random and parallel data access, and parallel merging.

## 7. DISCUSSION AND CONCLUSION

This work is an initial investigation into the EURECA approach. We have only scratched the surface in this investigation, and more questions need to be answered. We discuss below the potential of the EURECA approach that has not been addressed in this work, and the limitations of the current research.

**Potential.** *(1) Supporting a wide range of applications.* Our initial investigation divides the applications with dynamic data access into 4 categories: (a) unaligned data access, such as the hash key in Memcached, the chromosomes in genetic algorithms and the FM-index in genetic sequence alignment; (b) random parallel data access, such as the dense vector in SpMV and the breadth-first traversal; (c) data-dependent data access, such as in-memory database operations (selection, merge join, etc); (d) pre-defined access patterns, such as the intra-prediction modes in H.264 and the orientations in histogram of oriented gradients. *(2) Enhancing FPGA programmability.* In existing memory abstractions and high-level synthesis tools such as CoRAM, LegUp and Vivado HLS, memory access of the replicated data-paths is restricted to avoid inefficient hardware. With the EURECA architecture, more programmer-friendly languages can be developed. *(3) Applying the EURECA approach to other reconfigurable architectures.* Given the area complexity of CGs, the EURECA approach is more suitable to coarse-grain computational units than fine-grain computational units, to rapidly switch between different runtime computational operations.

**Limitations.** *(1) Large-scale EURECA-based designs.* When a large number of EURECA modules are used in a reconfigurable design, the communication operations between the EURECA modules could potentially increase the critical-path delay. This problem can be solved by integrating a Network-on-Chip (NoC) with the memory architecture, where the communication operations between EURECA modules are mapped into the NoC. *(2) Experiment*

Table 5: Benchmark application performance. Each application contains SDPs and dynamic data access operations. baseline: a static design implemented in the baseline architecture, with dynamic data access operations expressed as if-else expressions. EURECA: a EURECA-based dynamic design.

| | Memcached | | | SpMV | | | Large-scale Sorting | | |
|---|---|---|---|---|---|---|---|---|---|
| | SDPs | baseline | EURECA | SDPs | baseline | EURECA | SDPs | baseline | EURECA |
| CLB | 227 | 4399 | 234 | 459 | 3521 | 465 | 550 | 4875 | 561 |
| DSP48x2 | 0 | 0 | 0 | 64 | 64 | 64 | 0 | 0 | 0 |
| RAM36Kb | 64 | 64 | 64 | 1024 | 1024 | 1024 | 64 | 64 | 64 |
| EURECA | 0 | 0 | 1 | 0 | 0 | 1 | 0 | 0 | 2 |
| area[1] $(10^6)$ | 1.185 | 22.97 | 1.54 | 2.396 | 18.39 | 3.02 | 2.872 | 25.46 | 3.52 |
| critical-path delay (ns) | 6.7 | 13.94 | 6.46 | 6.54 | 12.74 | 6.17 | 9.51 | 11.56 | 9.51 |
| area-delay product | | **32.14x** | 1x | | 12.57x | 1x | | 8.792x | 1x |
| routable[2] | ✓ | ✗ | ✓ | ✓ | ✗ | ✓ | ✓ | ✗ | ✓ |
| channel width | 202 | 382[3] | 211 | 215 | 317[3] | 221 | 211 | 368[3] | 204 |
| throughput (per cycle) | 128 bytes | | | 32 partial results | | | 32 sorted data | | |
| enabled feature | flexible memory management | | | shared memory architecture | | | parallel merging | | |

[1] The design area is estimated by the minimum-width transistor area of consumed CLB and EURECA blocks. The areas of DSPs and RAM blocks are not included due to the lack of area information.

[2] Routable indicates whether the designs can be routed under the current routing infrastructure (channel width 256).

[3] Unroutble designs are re-synthesised with variable channel width.

*setup.* Architecture evaluation involves estimations which can affect the outcome of our experiments: (a) the VTR routing model inflates the channel width to match the routing capability of the actual FPGAs; (b) the minimum-width transistor area model [18] does not include wire area; (c) the baseline architecture area does not include the area of DSP and RAM blocks, due to lack of their area information; (d) the EURECA module is developed in 65-nm technology, while the baseline architecture is in 40-nm technology. The second limitation leads to underestimated module area, while the last two limitations overestimate the architecture overhead. Given the large improvements in design properties, we expect the impacts of these issues to be minor.

**Conclusion.** This paper proposes a novel memory architecture that supports dynamic data access. Instead of physically storing configurations during runtime, EURECA generates the active configuration at each time using reconfigurable logic, which eliminates inefficiency in previous runtime configuration approaches. In addressing the requirement R1 in Section 1, significant reductions in area and critical-path delay are achieved for three benchmark applications with intensive dynamic data access. For R2, static and dynamic designs are developed in Verilog and synthesised with VTR, into the EURECA architecture. For R3, we show that a Virtex-6 SX475T device enhanced by EURECA has 1% area overhead. Current and future work includes laying out the EURECA architecture, enhancing the EURECA architecture with NoC and coarse-grain computational units, developing more applications, and building high-level tools to enable automatic development of applications targeting devices enhanced by EURECA.

**Acknowledgement.** This work was supported in part by the UK EPSRC, the European Union Seventh Framework Programme under Grant agreement number 257906, 287804 and 318521, the 973 project 2013CB329000, the National Science Foundation of China (No. 61373026), the HiPEAC NoE, the Maxeler University Program, and Xilinx.

# 8. REFERENCES

[1] K. E. Batcher. Sorting networks and their applications. In *AFIPS*, pages 307–314, 1968.

[2] V. Betz, J. Rose, and A. Marquardt. *Architecture and CAD for deep-submicron FPGAs.* Kluwer Academic Publishers, 2002.

[3] M. Butts et al. A structural object programming model, architecture, chip and tools for reconfigurable computing. In *FCCM*, pages 55–64, 2007.

[4] S. R. Chalamalasetti et al. An FPGA memcached appliance. In *FPGA*, pages 245–254, 2013.

[5] S. R. Chalamalasetti, K. T. Lim, M. Wright, A. AuYoung, P. Ranganathan, and M. Margala. An FPGA memcached appliance. In *FPGA*, pages 245–254, 2013.

[6] G. C. Chow et al. An efficient sparse conjugate gradient solver using a benes permutation network. In *FPL*, pages 151–160, 2014.

[7] E. S. Chung et al. CoRAM: an in-fabric memory architecture for FPGA-based computing. In *FPGA*, pages 97–106, 2011.

[8] T. A. Davis and Y. Hu. The university of florida sparse matrix collection. *ACM Trans. Math. Softw.*, 38(1):1, 2011.

[9] E. Hung et al. Escaping the academic sandbox: Realizing VPR circuits on xilinx devices. In *FCCM*, pages 45–52, 2013.

[10] D. Koch and J. Torresen. FPGASort: a high performance sorting architecture exploiting run-time reconfiguration on FPGAs for large problem sorting. In *FPGA*, pages 45–54, 2011.

[11] K. T. Lim et al. Thin servers with smart pipes: designing SoC accelerators for memcached. In *ISCA*, pages 36–47, 2013.

[12] E. Mirsky and A. DeHon. Matrix: A reconfigurable computing architecture with configurable instruction distribution and deployable resources. In *FCCM*, pages 157–166, 1996.

[13] K. E. Murray et al. Titan: Enabling large and complex benchmarks in academic CAD. In *FPL*, pages 1–8, 2013.

[14] S. Nalam and B. H. Calhoun. Asymmetric sizing in a 45nm 5t SRAM to improve read stability over 6t. In *CICC*, pages 709–712, 2009.

[15] X. Niu et al. Exploiting run-time reconfiguration in stencil computation. In *FPL*, pages 173–180, 2012.

[16] I. Parberry. The pairwise sorting network. *Parallel Processing Letters*, 2:205–211, 1992.

[17] L.-N. Pouchet et al. Polyhedral-based data reuse optimization for configurable computing. In *FPGA*, pages 29–38, 2013.

[18] J. Rose et al. The VTR project: architecture and CAD for FPGAs from verilog to routing. In *FPGA*, pages 77–86, 2012.

[19] Tabula. Tabula corporate backgrounder. http://www.tabula.com/about/Tabula_CorpBackgrounder4_13.pdf.

[20] E. Tau et al. A first generation DPGA implementation. In *FPD*, pages 138–143, 1995.

[21] D. B. Thomas and W. Luk. Credit risk modelling using hardware accelerated monte-carlo simulation. In *FCCM*, pages 229–238, 2008.

[22] S. Trimberger et al. A time-multiplexed FPGA. In *FCCM*, pages 22–29, 1997.

[23] D. Wentzlaff et al. On-chip interconnection architecture of the tile processor. *IEEE Micro*, 27(5):15–31, 2007.

[24] Xilinx. 7 series FPGAs configuration user guide. http://www.xilinx.com/support/documentation/user_guides/ug470_7Series_Config.pdf.

[25] Xilinx. LogiCORE IP AXI HWICAP (v2.01.a). http://www.xilinx.com/support/documentation/ip_documentation/axi_hwicap/v2_01_a/ds817_axi_hwicap.pdf.

[26] Xilinx. Virtex-6 FPGA configurable logic block. http://www.xilinx.com/support/documentation/user_guides/ug364.pdf.

[27] S. Young et al. A high I/O reconfigurable crossbar switch. In *FCCM*, pages 3–10, 2003.

[28] L. Zhuo and V. K. Prasanna. Sparse matrix-vector multiplication on FPGAs. In *FPGA*, pages 63–74, 2005.

# Energy-Efficient Discrete Signal Processing with Field Programmable Analog Arrays (FPAAs)

Yu Bai and Mingjie Lin
Department of Electrical Engineering and Computer Science
University of Central Florida, Orlando, FL, 32765, USA
{yu.bai, mingjie.lin}@ucf.edu

## ABSTRACT

Large-scale field programmable analog array (FPAA) devices have made analog and analog-digital signal processing techniques accessible to a much wider community. However, largely due to its severe resource constraints, high noise sensitivity, and enormous design space, reconfigurable analog computing remains a niche in the DSP application space. In this paper, we develop a probabilistic-based methodology for designing and implementing the analog computing engines that specifically target at energy-efficient signal processing systems. We will first demonstrate how to decompose a given DSP application into various functional modules within the framework of probabilistic-based processing. Furthermore, we will show how these individual functional modules can be easily mapped to the limited selection of analog blocks found in an commercially available FPAA device: the PSoC chip platform from Cypress. To keep our study concrete, our implementation example focuses on the 1-D convolution module, a fundamental algorithmic building block in many applications of computer vision and artificial intelligence. In the end, we construct a complete image processing system based on the PSoC chip platform, and use the application of image key point extraction to demonstrate that our proposed approach to reconfigurable analog computing has considerable advantages in hardware usage, energy efficiency, and computing robustness over the traditional DSP approaches.

## 1. WHY RECONFIGURABLE ANALOG COMPUTING?

Modern computing is predominantly governed by digital principles because a judiciously designed CMOS transistor network can flawlessly emulate any given Boolean equation with great efficiency. Such an advantage is further amplified by the emergence of reconfigurable digital computing devices such as FPGA, which presented engineers with much-coveted run-time diagnosis and implementation flexibility. However, it is well-known that analog computation is significantly more efficient in its use of resources, such as energy

consumption, than deterministic digital computation even at relatively high levels of precision for some important applications. For example, the results of some recent studies have shown that subthreshold analog signal processor (ASP) systems are 1000 times more efficient than comparable digital signal processors when it comes to the power needed per a million multiply accumulate cycles a second, effectively a 20-year leap on the Gene's law curve [1, 2]. Today, even with some of the most remarkable improvements in digital computing, many digital signal processing algorithms still can not achieve real-time performance within the power budget constraints required for many portable applications. Moreover, with the CMOS transistor dimension quickly approaching the physical limit, quantum-induced stochastic switching will sooner or later becomes so overwhelming that robust digital switching will become unattainable at a reasonable cost. At that point, analog computing may become more appealing. All these calls for a possible resurgence of analog computing.

Unfortunately, although the potential of analog signal processing has long been recognized, it is still quite limited in the scale and applicability, thus remaining to be a niche in computing. One major hurdle to fully unleashing the power of analog computing is the lack of user-friendly prototyping platforms. As such, various programmable analog technologies have since been proposed. Among them, large-scale field programmable analog arrays (FPAAs), the analog counterpart of FPGA, aims at enabling rapid and flexible analog circuit implementation for low power signal processing [3]. A single FPAA device typically contains hundreds of configurable analog blocks (CABs) and a limited supply of available interconnects. However, current FPAA technology poses several challenges in its applicability and versatility. Specifically, at least three hurdles significantly hinder the FPAA's wide-spread use for analog computations:

- **Severe Resource Constraints**—All existing programmable analog devices have a quite limited selection of different programmable elements (e.g., OTA, comparators, and integrator) and interconnection possibilities. Unlike the FPGA technology, the traditional FPAA devices don't have a universal programmable structure like a loop-up table (LUT). As such, traditional FPAA devices are typically used to implement small analog modules with restricted functionality, such as low-ordering filtering, amplification, and signal conditioning [4]. How to map an empirically-sized algorithm entirely to an FPAA device remains to be challenging.

- **High Noise Sensitivity**—It is well known that analog signals are far more sensitive to noise than digital signals because digital quantization, binary numbering, and Boolean algebra jointly increases error margins during computing. In contrast, analog signals are represented as continuous voltages or currents, whose precision can be affected directly if any noises occur. Furthermore, in reconfigurable digital fabric, different switch and interconnect configurations can only affect timing correctness and path delays. However, in programmable analog circuits, signal paths implemented with networks of switches will unavoidably change capacitance, resistance, and transistor leakage current along internal signal paths. Unfortunately, noise coupling to various isolated device structures is essentially proportional to the capacitance from that device to chip substrate, therefore no effective noise shielding techniques exist for FPAA devices.

- **Enormous Design Space**—Reconfigurable analog devices encompasses a much larger design space than traditional reconfigurable digital devices. This is because that the functionality of digital circuits can be readily expressed with a few of basic combinational and sequential primitives. Therefore, read only memory (ROM) primitive can be used to implement any combinational functions according to Boolean algebra and Shannon's logic expansion theorem. Furthermore, most of modern FPGAs use asynchronous ROMs to synthesize the combinational logic and D-type flip-flop for implementing the memory/sequential logic [4]. However, such an unified theoretic framework doesn't exist in order to implement a wide-range of analog circuits. Traditionally, designing and implementing an application-specific analog circuit requires a large number of discrete components such as transistors, resistors, diodes, and capacitors in addition to amplifiers, comparators, and integrator. These primitives are often quite fine in logic granularity, thus requiring a large number of them to implement any reasonably sized analog module.

In this paper, we propose a unified architectural framework to achieve energy-efficient DSP with field programmable analog arrays (FPAAs). While in the traditional DSP systems, analog processing is primarily used for front-end amplification and data conversion, and digital signal processing (DSP) units handle the algorithmic operations [3], our proposed framework aims at offloading the bulk of computations directly to analog functional blocks. In order to mitigate the high noise sensitivity often found in analog processing, we based our methodology on probabilistic-based computing. We will also demonstrate how to decompose a given DSP application into various functional modules within the framework of probabilistic-based processing. Furthermore, we will show how these individual functional modules can be easily mapped to the limited selection of analog blocks found in an FPAA device. In the end, we aim to show that our proposed approach to reconfigurable analog computing has considerable advantages in hardware usage, energy efficiency, and computing robustness over the traditional DSP approaches.

In Section 2, we formally introduce the concept and the overall structure of probabilistic domain transformation (PDT). We then, in Section 3, tackle the challenges of implementing three consisting modules of PDT methodology, i.e., probabilistic encoding, light-weight algorithmic operations, and probabilistic decoding, with analog circuit means. Specifi-

cally, we discuss in detail how to conduct Gaussian mixture modeling to encode any given signal with a mixture of Gaussian probability density functions. Subsequently in Section 4 and 5, we discuss how we perform probabilistic computing through FPAA. Additionally, we will take discrete convolution as an example to demonstrate the performance benefits and robustness improvements in our multiplier-less convolver on PSoC when compared with other standard approaches. Finally in Section 7, to illustrate the overall benefits of our FPAA-based approach, we choose a real-world DSP application, computing image keypoint extraction, to conclude our study.

## 2. PROBABILISTIC DOMAIN TRANSFORMATION (PDT)

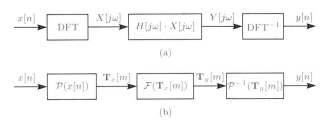

Figure 1: Two domain transformation paradigms. (a) Discrete Fourier transform. (b) Probabilistic domain transform. Note the striking conceptual resemblance between (a) and (b).

In discrete signal processing (DSP), domain transformations can yield equivalent results to input signals that would be hard to obtained if its original domain is used. For example, Fourier transform, arguably the most prominent domain transformation in DSP, considers the representation and analysis of analog signals and systems in the frequency domain. This is because the frequency domain can reveal further characteristics of signals and systems, i.e., the frequency content of an arbitrary aperiodic (or non-periodic) signal often referred to as the spectrum.

The *Probabilistic Domain Transform* (PDT) is a new domain transformation inspired by the Fourier transform first developed in [5]. In this method, as shown in Fig. 1(b), the input discrete signal $x[n]$ will be first converted into a serial of random samples $\mathbf{T}_x[m]$ through the transform $\mathcal{P}(\cdot)$. Corresponding to the system function $H[j\omega]$ in the Fourier transform shown in Fig. 1(a), the random samples $\mathbf{T}_x[m]$) are processed by $\mathcal{F}(\cdot)$, subsequently generating new random samples $\mathbf{T}_y[m]$. Finally, these newly generated random samples $\mathbf{T}_y[m]$) can be decoded as the final results $y[n]$ by $\mathcal{P}^{-1}(\cdot)$. Obviously, in order to successfully perform the proposed PDT, we need to clearly define what $\mathcal{P}(\cdot)$, $\mathcal{P}^{-1}(\cdot)$, and $\mathcal{F}(\cdot)$ represent, respectively.

Fig. 2 conceptually illustrates the scheme of using probabilistic domain transform. To make our study more concrete, we now take discrete convolution as an example. Formally, the discrete convolution of $f$ and $g$ is defined as $(f * g)[n] = \sum_{m=-\infty}^{\infty} f[m]g[n-m] = \sum_{m=-\infty}^{\infty} f[n-m]g[m]$, where $f$, $g$ are two functions defined on the set $\mathcal{Z}$ of integers. For two $N$-sized vectors $x[n]$ and $y[n]$, fully evaluating $(f * g)[n]$ needs approximately $n^2$ multiplications and $n^2$ additions, which is quite computationally intensive. To apply the scheme of probabilistic domain transformation to computing convolution, we can treat the input signals $f[n]$

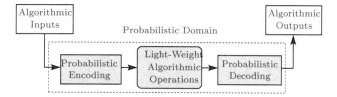

Figure 2: Conceptual picture of our proposed probabilistic computing paradigm. All operations within gray blocks will be realized by leveraging basic stochastic operations.

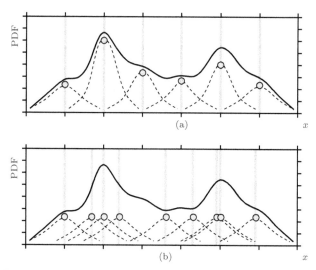

Figure 3: Two special cases of Gaussian mixture decomposition. (a) Type I Gaussian decomposition: Gaussian components with equally-spaced $\mu_k$s and variable $\sigma_k$s. (b) Type II Gaussian decomposition: Gaussian components with variable $\mu_k$s and constant $\sigma_k$s.

and $g[n]$, not in their original forms. Instead, we interpret their waveforms as two probability density functions (PDF) or histograms of their sample index. In other words, $f[n]$ and $g[n]$ will be become $m_{\mathbf{F}}[n]$ and $m_{\mathbf{G}}[n]$, the PDF of two discrete random variables $\mathbf{F}$ and $\mathbf{G}$, respectively. Subsequently, we can generate a large ensemble of random samples from $\mathbf{F}$ and $\mathbf{G}$. If we add these two groups of random samples pairwise, we will obtain a new set of random samples for a new random variable $\mathbf{W}$, which actually mimics the process of adding two independent random variables: $\mathbf{W} = \mathbf{F} + \mathbf{G}$. According to the well known probabilistic theorem [6] of summing independent random variables, the probability distribution function $m_{\mathbf{W}}[n]$ can be proven to be $m_{\mathbf{W}}[n] = \sum_{k=1}^{N} m_{\mathbf{F}}[k] m_{\mathbf{G}}[n-k] = m_{\mathbf{F}}[n] * m_{\mathbf{G}}[n]$, where $n = 1, 2, \cdots, N$. Therefore, by exploiting this principle and extracting the PDF of resulting random variable $\mathbf{W}$, we can compute the discrete convolution of two input vectors $f[n]$ and $g[n]$. In other words, $\mathcal{P}(\cdot)$, $\mathcal{P}^{-1}(\cdot)$, and $\mathcal{F}(\cdot)$ in Figure 1(b) correspond to interpreting as PDF, extracting PDF, and pair-wise addition, respectively.

## 3. PROBABILISTIC ENCODING AND DECODING

The standard design and implementation of PDT consists of three interconnecting modules shown in Fig. 2. Among these three modules, probabilistic encoding is the most difficult one to design because first, whatever the probabilistic encoding scheme may be, it has to be general enough to handle any given waveform. Second, the probabilistic encoding scheme must be simple enough for hardware implementation. Finally, the selection of probabilistic encoding scheme will, to a large extend, determine how efficient its associated probabilistic decoding stage will be.

In this paper, we propose to utilize the well-known Gaussian mixture modeling (GMM) method for probabilistically encoding, which aims at representing a parametric probability density function as a weighted sum of Gaussian component densities. GMM is appealing because Gaussian distribution possesses many beneficial properties that enable many important signal processing algorithms. As such, Gaussian mixture density modeling and decomposition has been widely applied in a variety of disciplines that require signal or waveform characterization for classification and recognition, including remote sensing, target identification, spectroscopy, electrocardiography, speech recognition, or scene segmentation [7, 8, 9].

Mathematically, GMM states that a multi-dimensional probability density function $p(\mathbf{x})$ can be represented as a sum of Gaussian components, i.e., $\sum_{k=1}^{K} \mathbf{a_k} \mathbf{g}(\mathbf{x}|\mu_\mathbf{k}, \Sigma_\mathbf{k})$, where integer $\mathbf{K}$ is the number of components and $\mathbf{a}_k | \mathbf{a}_k \geq 0, \sum_{k=1}^{K} \mathbf{a}_k =$ is the set of mixing proportion. In addition, $\mu_k$ and $\Sigma_k$ de-

note the vector of mean values and covariance matrix. In general, the Gaussian mixture model is a non-regular statistical model, therefore its parameters are non-identifiable. Fortunately, as shown in Fig. 3, there are two restricted cases of Gaussian mixture decomposition. In Type I Gaussian decomposition shown in Fig. 3(a), any given form of probabilistic density function $f_{\mathbf{x}}(x)$ can be decomposed into a weighted sum of Gaussian components with equally-spaced $\mu_k$s and variable $\sigma_k$s. In this method, the mean values of different Gaussian components, $\mu_k$s, are uniformly distributed, while the weight coefficients, $\mathbf{a}_k$s, are different. In Type II Gaussian decomposition shown in Fig. 3(b), the weight coefficients, $\mathbf{a}_k$s, are kept as constants, while the mean values of different Gaussian components, $\mu_k$s, are computed as variables according to the given waveform $f_{\mathbf{x}}(x)$.

Currently, the type I GMM decomposition is more widely used. However, in this approach, GMM parameters are typically estimated from training data using the iterative Expectation-Maximization (EM) algorithm or Maximum A Posteriori (MAP) estimation from a well-trained prior model. Unfortunately, these approaches are quite demanding in computation because complicated algorithmic steps of unsupervised learning or clustering procedures are required, thus making simple circuit means quite challenging to achieve. On the other hand, the type II GMM decomposition not only is simple conceptually, but also making hardware implementation rather convenient.

The basic idea of the type II GMM decomposition is that a given PDF $f_{\mathbf{x}}(x)$ can be approximated, to any specified accuracy, as an equally weighted sum of a number of Gaussian PDFs with the same variance $\sigma$, but different expected values $\mu_k$. Mathematically, the following holds true:

$$\mathbf{p}(\mathbf{x}|\Theta) = \sum_{\mathbf{k}=1}^{K} \frac{1}{\sqrt{2\pi\sigma_k^2}^M} exp(-\frac{|x - \mu_k|^2}{2\sigma_k^2}), \quad (1)$$

where $\sigma_k > 0$ is a constant. More details of the theoretic proof of the type II GMM decomposition can be found in relative papers. In Fig. 4, we depicted the concept of the type

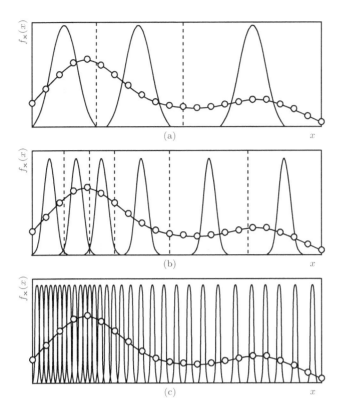

Figure 4: Gaussian mixture decomposition with different number of Gaussian components $K$. (a) $K = 3$. (b) $K = 6$. (c) $K = 30$.

II GMM decomposition using different number of Gaussian components. There are two observations. First, the more Gaussian components are used, the more accurate the resulting GMM will be in comparison with the given $f_{\mathbf{x}}(x)$. Second, the density of the GMM components will be in direct correspondence with the curvature and the shape of the given $f_{\mathbf{x}}(x)$. In fact, the higher the magnitude of the given $f_{\mathbf{x}}(x)$, the denser the concentration of Gaussian components is.

We now derive, for a given $K$, how to determine the different expected values $\mu_k$ in the Equation 1. Because $f_{\mathbf{x}}(x)$ is a well-defined probability density function, it is known that $\int_{\mathbf{R}} f_{\mathbf{x}}(x)dx = 1$, i.e., the area below the $f_{\mathbf{x}}(x)$ curve equals to 1. Because all GMM components have the same variance $\sigma$, $\int_{\mu_k - \frac{1}{2}\Delta}^{\mu_k + \frac{1}{2}\Delta} g_k(x)dx \approx 1$. Based on above equation, we are going to show the modified Gaussian mixture through simulation example. Given a input vector $\mathbf{X}$ is a continuous signal. In the beginning, the system sets up criteria to decompose PDF area under curve to several sub-areas. According to the Gaussian distribution mathematical theorem, the area under curve can be obtained from standard deviation. We rewrite Gaussian distribution for a peak in the chromatogram as

$$\mathbf{f}(\mathbf{x}) = \frac{A}{\sigma\sqrt{2\pi}}\mathbf{e}^{-\frac{(x-\mu)^2}{2\sigma^2}} \tag{2}$$

where A is the area under the curve. The maximum peak height H is easily proven to be found at $\mathbf{x} = \mu$, hence the exponential part is equal to 1. the equation can be simplified

as

$$\mathbf{H} = \mathbf{f}(\mu) = \frac{A}{\sigma\sqrt{2\pi}}\mathbf{e}^{-\frac{(x-\mu)^2}{2\sigma^2}} = \frac{A}{\sigma\sqrt{2\pi}} = \frac{0.3989\mathbf{A}}{\sigma} \tag{3}$$

The area is given by

$$\mathbf{A} = \frac{\mathbf{H}\sigma}{0.3989} \tag{4}$$

From the above formula, it is clear that the area of Gaussian distribution can be calculated by standard deviation. By setting the area criteria, the complex signal PDF can be approximately decomposed to several Gaussian distribution. The complex signal PDFs can be accumulated and decomposed by using area criteria. when the system reaches the maximum criteria, the mean value of input is generated. Hence, the continuous complex signal can be easily transferred to sequence of mean value. Finally, by given mean and constant standard deviation, the Gaussian random sample generator can readily generate the random samples that satisfy the input PDFs.

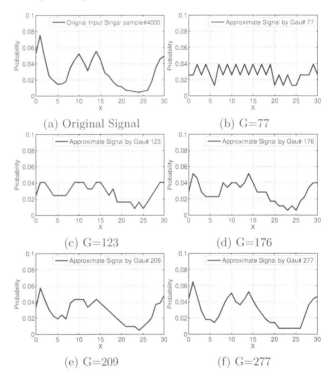

Figure 5: Results of different numbers of Gaussian components (G).

Using our modified Gaussian mixture model, a given input PDF signal can be approximated effectively. In Fig. 5, we illustrate the approximation quality of such a method. As the number of processed random samples $G$ increases from 77 to 277, the approximation quality significantly improves. For this 4000-sample signal, a mere 277-Gaussian-component approximate can reduce the approximation error to less than 1%. Such results also shows that, the larger the number of Gaussian mixture components is, the more accurate the approximation results will be.

## 4. ANALOG CIRCUIT MODULES FOR PDT

In this section, we present our analog circuit designs for each key component of implementing probabilistic domain transformation in hardware. Later in Section 5, we show that all these circuit modules, mainly consisting of amplifiers and comparators, can be conveniently implemented with the PSoC device.

## 4.1 Analog Circuit for Gaussian Decomposition

As discussed in Section 3, the type II GMM decomposition can approximate any given probability density function (PDF) $f_\mathbf{x}(x)$ by summing a number of equally weighted Gaussian components. Fortunately, one unique property of a PDF curve is that, for any value range $[x_i, x_{i+1}]$ of $\mathbf{x}$, its marginal probability equals to the area under the corresponding PDF curve for the same range. Because on our proposed approach of Probabilistic Domain Transformation (PDT) discussed in Section 2, we treat both input and output signal waveforms as specific probability density functions represented as voltage values. As such, we will design an analog circuit that performs current integration and voltage comparison in order to mimic our type II Gaussian mixture decomposition algorithm.

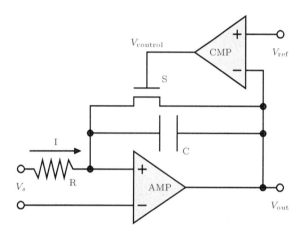

Figure 6: Analog circuit of Gaussian mixture decomposition.

Figure 6 depicts our designed circuit for Gaussian mixture decomposition. Its basic idea is to generate a ramp voltage The proposed integrator is generating a ramp voltage which is controlled and cleared by a comparator. With the flowing current $I$ passes though $R$, the input voltage $V_s$ is integrating at capacitor $C$. Meanwhile, the comparator send control signal to switch by comparing the output voltage with reference voltage $V_{\mathrm{ref}}$, if voltage $V_{\mathrm{out}}$ is equal or more than reference voltage, the pass transistor $S$ will be switched on and consequently discharge capacitor voltage $V_{\mathrm{out}}$ when receiving the control signal $V_{\mathrm{control}}$ from comparator. Analytically, the integrator output voltage $V_{\mathrm{out}}$ is given as

$$V_{\mathrm{out}} = -\frac{1}{C} \int_0^T \frac{V_{\mathrm{in}}}{R} dt. \qquad (5)$$

As such, faster voltage integration process requires a smaller capacitor $C$. The distance of Gaussian components after decomposition is determined by the choice of reference voltage $V_{\mathrm{ref}}$. Note that all circuit components in Figure 6, except capacitors and resistors, can be readily found in our targeted programmable analog device, PSoC.

To further verify the functionality of our Gaussian decomposition circuit shown in Figure 6, we have run extensive Spice simulations. Our results are shown in Figure 7. The

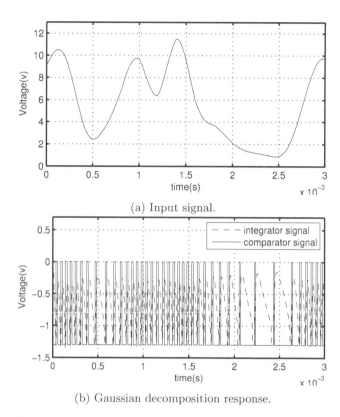

(a) Input signal.

(b) Gaussian decomposition response.

Figure 7: Spice simulation results of Gaussian decomposition circuit.

input signal $V_s$ has been ramped with the integrator as time increases. Whenever the signal $V_{\mathrm{out}}$ reaches a predefined $V_{\mathrm{ref}}$, its will be reset to zero and the integration restarts. As a result, the output signal $V_{\mathrm{out}}$ will be pulse-like, with each occurrence of a peak signaling the center point of one Gaussian component. It is clear that, as we reduce the value of $V_{\mathrm{ref}}$, the total number of pulses will increase. As expected, the density of the peaks of $V_{\mathrm{out}}$ directly corresponds to the voltage magnitude of the input signal $V_s$ in Figure 7(a). In other words, for any value range of a probability density function, if its probability value is high, more Gaussian components will be needed to achieve a good accuracy.

## 4.2 Analog Circuit for Programmable Adders

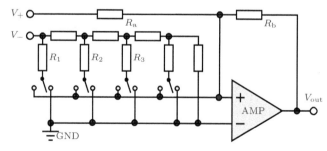

Figure 8: Programmable analog adder and gain block [10].

In order to evaluate convolution in probabilistic domain, we need to add a large number of random samples pairwise. Obviously, high speed and low cost in both hardware and energy consumption are desired in this case. The design of our analog adder is depicted in Figure 8 and mainly consists of an operational amplifier. To obtain accurate transfer function, it is necessary to use ratios of passive device value, rather than the absolute values alone. The control parameter for our analog adder is achieved by appropriate use of passive and switch networks. Moreover, this adder in Figure 8 is also programmable by setting appropriate resistor values. Specifically, in Fig. 8, one signal $V_{in,a}$ is given a fixed gain and combined with another signal $V_{in,b}$ in a programmable ratio, which is called R-2R CMOS DAC. In our case, we used five bits as the number resolution in order to achieve 8 bit linearity. Its programmable parameters can be obtained by appropriate use of passive and switch network [10]. In our architecture, the random samples will first be generated by combining all Gaussian components. Subsequently, these random sample from two groups of decomposed Gaussian components will be added pairwise using this analog adder. Our circuit design is largely based on [10], where more architectural details and parameter selection guidelines can be found. Once again, all circuit components in Figure 8, except all necessary resistors, can be readily found in our targeted programmable analog device, PSoC.

## 4.3 Analog Circuit for Probabilistic Decoding

The final key step of our proposed probabilistic domain transformation (PDT), probabilistic decoding, needs to extract the probability density function from a large number resulting random samples generated by the analog adder discussed above. Since probability density function describes the relative likelihood for a random variable to take on a given value, we need to design a circuit that counts the numbers of input data sample which is falling in various value ranges. In digital domain, it is quite easy to perform such a task by using logic comparators and integer counters, which together behave like a histogram builder logically. Unfortunately, the digital approach is relatively expensive in hardware usage and energy consumption. In this study, we will design a pure analog circuit to extract the probability density function from a large number of random samples.

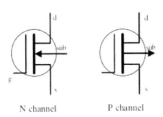

N channel          P channel

Figure 9: Monolithic MOSFETs

Before we present the details of our probabilistic decoding circuit design, we first introduce the working mechanism of monolithic MOSFET devices widely used in low power circuit design. Such devices will be used as the main building blocks for our circuit design. Our basic idea is to use the technology of scaling threshold voltage on monolithic MOSFETs by body effect to construct probabilistic decoding circuit. As shown in Figure 9, each monolithic MOSFET has four terminals: the drain $d$, gate $g$, source $source$, and bulk $sub$, among which, the additional terminal of the body

(bulk) is not normally used as an input or an output. Instead, the bulk terminal $sub$ usually connects to the drain-source channel through a diode junction. For discrete MOSFETs, the body lead is connected internally to the source.

We now analytically discuss the switch characteristics of a given MOSFET. According to the CMOS device physics, the threshold voltage of a monolithic MOSFET is equal to the sum of its flat-band voltages, which are twice of the bulk potential and the voltage across the oxide due to the depletion layer charge, the threshold voltage of n-type MOSFETs is given by:

$$\mathbf{V}_T = V_{FB} + 2\phi_F + \frac{\sqrt{2\xi_s q N_a(2\phi_F + V_{SB})}}{C_i}, \qquad (6)$$

where the flat-band voltage, $V_{FB}$ is given by

$$\mathbf{V}_{FB} = \Phi_{MS} - \frac{Q_f}{C_i} - \frac{1}{C_i}\int_0^{t_i}\frac{x}{x_i}\rho_i(x)dx, \qquad (7)$$

$\Phi_{MS}$ is given by

$$\mathbf{\Phi}_{MS} = \Phi_M - \Phi_S = \Phi_M - (\chi + \frac{E_g}{2q} + \phi_F), \qquad (8)$$

and $\phi_F$ is given by

$$\phi_F = V_t \ln \frac{N_a}{n_i}. \qquad (9)$$

The threshold voltage of a p-type MOSFET with an n-type substrate is obtained using the following equations

$$\mathbf{V}_T = V_{FB} + |2\phi_F| + \frac{\sqrt{2\xi_s q N_d(\|2\phi_F - V_{SB})}}{C_i}, \qquad (10)$$

where the flat-band voltage, $V_{FB}$ is given by

$$\mathbf{V}_{FB} = \Phi_{MS} - \frac{Q_f}{C_i} - \frac{1}{C_i}\int_0^{t_i}\frac{x}{x_i}\rho_i(x)dx, \qquad (11)$$

$\Phi_{MS}$ is given by

$$\mathbf{\Phi}_{MS} = \Phi_M - \Phi_S = \Phi_M - (\chi + \frac{E_g}{2q} + \|\phi_F|), \qquad (12)$$

and $\phi_F$ is given by

$$|\phi_F\| = V_t \ln \frac{N_d}{n_i}. \qquad (13)$$

From equations given above, the threshold voltage of a MOSFET is affected by the voltage which is applied to the back contact. The voltage difference between the source and the bulk is defined as $V_{BS}$. The $V_{BS}$ changes the width of the depletion layer so that the voltage across the oxide is due to the change of the charge in the depletion region. This results in a difference in threshold voltage which equals to the difference in charge in the depletion region divided by the oxide capacitance [11]. The theory on above shows a way to change threshold voltage by applying different voltage. In this study, we exploit this property to construct our probabilistic decoding circuit. Specifically, we use a single monolithic MOSFET device together with an analog integrator to implement classifying and counting functions. The monolithic MOSFETs can increase or decrease body effect character though scalable threshold. The simplified equation of scalable threshold voltage is given as

$$V_t = V_{to} + \gamma(\sqrt{\phi + |V_{sb}|} - \sqrt{\phi}) \qquad (14)$$

Figure 10 depicts the circuit design of our probabilistic decoding module. Because the transistor switch depend

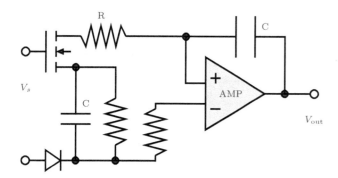

Figure 10: Probabilistic decoding circuit.

on difference of gate-source voltage and threshold voltage, when the zero threshold voltage $V_t$ is given, the NMOS will switch on if the $V_{gs} - V_t < 0$, PMOS will switch on if $V_{gs} - V_t > 0$. So that this specific MOSFETs with $V_t = 0$ will perform as a voltage range limiter. When input is higher than given source voltage applied to PMOS, the PMOS is on and pulling down voltage to given source voltage. The reason of using this PMOS is keeping input voltage, so that the integrator will not count so many times when input is several times bigger than value in the range. The lower limiter is made by diode. This diode limiter is also called "voltage clipper" in circuit design because this structure is often used to limit the input voltage. A basic diode limiter circuit is composed of a diode and a resistor. Depending upon the circuit configuration and bias, the circuit may clip or eliminate part of an input waveform. After choosing the voltage limiter made of PMOS monolithic MOSFETs as high voltage limiter and the diode as lower voltage limiter, the integrator will perform counter functions.

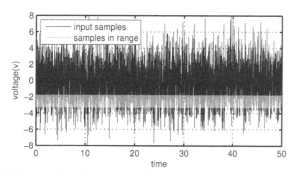

(a) High and low limiter simulation results with 4000 sample voltages

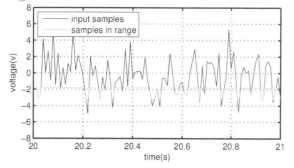

(b) High and low limiter simulation results with 100 sample voltages

To verify the functionality of probabilistic decoding circuit depicted in Figure 10, we have run extensive Spice circuit simulations. Figure 11a presents one set of 4000 random samples fed into the probabilistic decoding circuit. When we set the high and low voltage limits as $-2.2$ V and $-3.8$ V respectively, all random samples within such a voltage range will be filtered out and marked in red in Figure 11a. To see more details, we zoom in a 100-sample segment presented in Figure 11b, we can clearly see that the output voltage $V_{\text{out}}$ will only following the input voltage waveform $V_s$ if $V_{\text{Low}} \leq V_s \geq V_{\text{High}}$. Otherwise, the output voltage will become flat as $V_{\text{Low}}$.

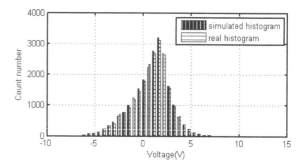

Figure 12: Simulation of MATLAB counts results and proposed architecture counts results

Because the time intervals between random samples are constant, the voltage integration of $V_{\text{out}}$ for a given range $[V_{\text{Low}}, V_{\text{High}}]$ will be linearly proportional to the number of occurrences of any random numbers whose voltage values fall into this given range. After integration, for the 4000 random samples in Figure 11a, its PDF is presented in Figure 12, which shows a clear match with the PDF results from a direct MATLAB calculations also presented in the same figure.

## 5. PSOC IMPLEMENTATION OF PDT

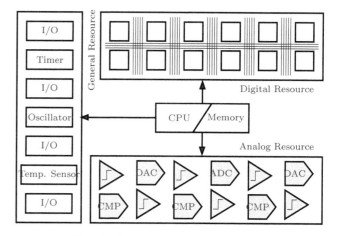

Figure 13: Sketch of available hardware resources in a PSoC device.

To validate our methodology of probabilistic-based analog computing, we choose the PSoC (Programmable Embedded System-on-Chip) platform to design, implement, and measure benchmarking applications. The PSoC device is a commercially-available programmable system-on-chip that integrates configurable analog and digital functions, memory and an embedded processor on a single chip. The original purpose of PSoC is to allow fast prototyping of various small-scale analog circuits within a reconfigurable chip. As shown in Fig. 13, a typical PSoC consists of both digital resource and analog resource, as well as an embedded CPU with its associated memory. The digital part of a PSoC greatly resembles the architecture of a modern FPGA, basically an array of configurable logic blocks connected with programmable interconnects. Its analog part consists of a limited selection of commonly-used analog functional modules, such as digital-to-analog converter (DAC), analog-to-digital converter (ADC), comparator, and amplifier. In addition, its global resource provides some shared components, such as I/O blocks, timer, and oscillator.

In a PSoC device, most of common analog and digital components are provided. However, they are not enough to feed various design needs. So that, the off-chip library in the component catalog of PSCOS creator provides a way for you to mix external and internal components on the same schematic. The components in this library cover the most common components that are most likely to be placed on the periphery of a PSoC device, which include resistors, capacitors, transistors, inductors, switches, and others. The library is not intended to supply every possible part, but can support a wide range of designs. Furthermore, user own part or parts library can be created if the design includes a custom or unique component.

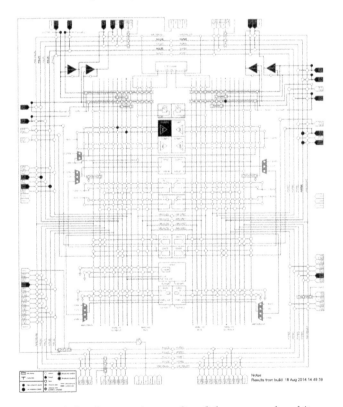

Figure 14: Implementation results of the proposed architecture with PSoC.

Figure 13 presents our final placed and routed circuit design for a probabilistic based convolution engine unit, where all used discrete analog components, such as amplifier and capacitor, are marked in black. The external devices such as resistors, capacitors, transistors, inductors, switches, and others are not shown in Figure 13. However, the PSoC platform provides external Pins assigned to connect internal devices with external devices. The Pins component in our synthesized design allows extra hardware resources to connect to a physical port-pin. It also provides signal accesses to external signals through an appropriately configured physical I/O pin. Additionally, specific electrical characteristics (e.g., Drive Mode) can be chosen for one or more pins; these characteristics are then used by PSoC Creator to automatically place and route the signals within the component. Pins can be used with schematic wire connections, software, or both.

## 6. PERFORMANCE MEASUREMENT

To facilitate the performance comparison between our PSoC-based implementation and others, we measure three performance metrics: hardware usage, power consumption, and execution time for the same given input.

### 6.1 Execution time Analysis

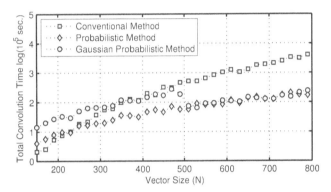

Figure 15: Execution time comparison between our proposed PSoC-based design and the conventional FPGA-based design.

We compare three different hardware implementations of a 1D convolution unit with different vector sizes. All execution times are experimentally measured. In addition to our PSoC-based design, we implemented two versions of 1D convolution unit. One is completely based on the conventional multiplier-based design, while the other is the probabilistic-based multiplierless 1D convolver based on [5]. As shown in Figure 15, for a conventional FPGA-based convolver, the execution time increases with input vector size almost exponentially, which indicates that the execution time will be exceedingly long when the input vector is long. The probabilistic FPGA-based convolver with $K = 16$ adders will have much less execution time when the input vector size is more than 110. When input vector is less than 110, the probabilistic method scalable scheme actually is slightly worse than the conventional FPGA-based convolver. Both of these FPGA-based convolvers are implemented with Virtex 6 devices at clock frequency of 100 MHz. Although running only at 67 MHz, our PSoC-based probabilistic convolver performs much better than the two FPGA-based implementations on average. Specifically, when input vector is less than 512, the probabilistic Gaussian mixture algorithm is not helping to decrease operation processes, but accuracy of signal estimation is bad due to its less samples probability estimation. The execution time of probabilistic

Gaussian method is longest among three methods. On the contrast, when input vector is more than 512, the enough input samples will be decreased to mean value vector which has smaller size than original input. However, even with help of efficiency algorithm, the execution time of probabilistic Gaussian method will have better performance than conventional method. Since the probabilistic method has fast clock, the execution time of probabilistic method has best performance.

## 6.2 Hardware Usage and Power Consumption Analysis

Power consumption is a key issue for most DSP applications. For an IC chip like the PSoC that consists of a mixed-signal array, accurately estimating its power consumption, which depends on a number of parameters used, can be challenging. Fortunately, Cypress provides an associated Microsoft Excel spreadsheet for power consumption in the families of various PSoC devices. Based on empirically measured data, the power consumption of a PSoC device can be calculated given different configurations, which typically involve the operating frequency and specific hardware resource usage. For FPGA-based designs, we estimate power consumption using the ISE XPower power estimation tool for Virtex 6 platforms we have used.

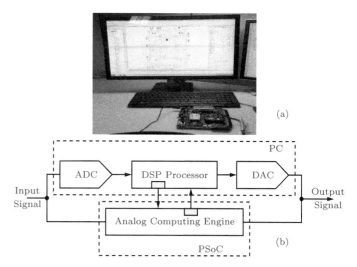

(a)

(b)

Figure 16: Overall image processing system consisting of PSoc chip platform and PC system.

| | | FPGA-Based | | | PSoC-Based | | |
|---|---|---|---|---|---|---|---|
| | | 64 | 1024 | 4096 | 64 | 1024 | 4096 |
| Area | Slice LUT | 950 | 3308 | 13232 | | | |
| | Slice Registers | 426 | 1436 | 5744 | | | |
| | Slice | 310 | 1036 | 4144 | | | |
| | Opamp | | | | 4 | 6 | 8 |
| | comparator | | | | 1 | 1 | 1 |
| | capacitor | | | | 4 | 8 | 12 |
| | resistor | | | | 5 | 9 | 14 |
| | diode transistor | | | | 4 | 7 | 13 |
| Power | Dynamic Power (mW) | 107.82 | 137.87 | 186.28 | 46.66 | 55.29 | 64.88 |
| | Energy Consumption (nJ) | 1196.80 | 1098.82 | 830.81 | 427.24 | 392.43 | 153.86 |

Table 1: Hardware usage and power consumption comparison between FPGA-based and PSoC-based convolution unit.

Table 1 presents the comparison results in hardware usage and power consumption Because Virtex 6 and PSoC 5 are quite difference chip devices, it is very hard to compare hardware usage. However, as Table 1 shows, the number of LUT, registers, and slices used in FPGA-based convolver is quite large. In contrast, the number of used operational amplifiers and comparators is relatively much smaller. consumes huge increasing hardware numbers. In terms of power consumption, our PSoC-based convolver consistently achieves about 3 to 4 times less dynamic power consumption than the FPGA-based convolver. We believe that such a significant reduction in power consumption is mostly due to the significantly less hardware usage, which can be contributed to the fundamental difference between analog and digital computing.

## 7. DEMO APPLICATION: IMAGE KEYPOINT EXTRACTION

To further validate the applicability of our probabilistic PSoC-based approach, we have designed and implemented a complete image processing system using one PC and one PSoC evaluation board as shown in Figure 16(a). We also draw a system block diagram in Figure 16(a) to illustrate different function blocks. In this system, the core functionality lies in the analog computing engine capable of performing high-speed 1D convolution with a low power budget. Because 1D convolution is a fundamental building block for many image and video processing algorithm, our image processing system is quite versatile in its processing capability.

We choose local feature extraction as our benchmark application, which is heavily researched in computer vision community. Local feature extraction plays a crucial role in many vision tasks, such as wide-baseline stereo matching, content-based image retrieval [12], content-based image retrieval [13], object class recognition [14], camera calibration [15], and symmetry detection [16]. All these applications attempt to exploit local features to represent the image content by a sparse set of salient regions or key points. Therefore, local feature extraction is quite sensitive to performance and energy consumption. The source code of our local feature extraction is written in Matlab language. Currently, only gray level images can be taken as inputs. The output points are made of $N$ rows of key-points extracted and three columns matrix. The first two columns give the position of the key-points. And the third column gives the feature scale of the key-points, which correspond to the radius of the local neighborhood to be considered. The core of this local feature extraction algorithm is the convolution of two matrix. We use the following equation to convert 2D convolution into 1D convolutions $y[m,n] = x[m,n] * h[m,n] = \sum_{j=-\infty}^{\infty} \sum_{i=-\infty}^{\infty} x[i,j] \times h[m-i,n-j]$ and $y[m,n] = h_1[m] * h_2[n] * x[m,n]$. In our PSoC-based image processing system depicted in Figure 16, all convolutions are offloaded to the analog computing engine implemented with the PSoc 5 device.

Figure 17 presents a set of different key feature extraction results for a given image. The number of key features detected represents the quality of results and processing accuracy. One interesting feature of our probabilistic-based computing scheme is its tunable accuracy by adjusting the number of decomposed Gaussian components as discussed in Section 3. As we increase the number of Gaussian com-

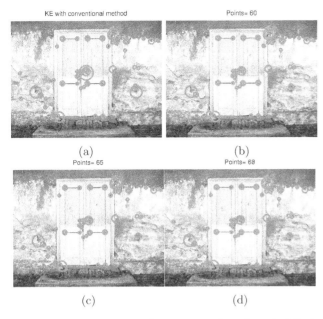

KE with conventional method    Points= 60

(a)                    (b)

Points= 65             Points= 68

(c)                    (d)

Figure 17: Comparison of conventional and probabilistic method in key point extraction application. (a) Conventional convolution method. (b) The probabilistic convolution with Gaussian#88 and feature points# 60. (c) The probabilistic convolution with Gaussian#154 and feature points# 65. (d) The probabilistic convolution with Gaussian#215 and feature points# 68.

ponents from 88 (Figure 17b) to 215 (Figure 17d), we can clearly see the improvement in the number of detected features increasing from 60 to 68.

## 8. CONCLUSIONS

We have presented a probabilistic-based analog computing framework that facilitates implementing many convolution-based image or video processing applications with the Field Programmable Analog Array (FPAA) devices. Our results have shown great potential in reducing power consumption for many important convolution-based DSP applications. More importantly, our probabilistic-based framework of analog computing mitigates two main challenges in implementing DSP algorithms with FPAA devices. First, our design methodology only requires a small number of common analog blocks, such as operational amplifiers and comparators, hence significantly reducing the overall design space. Second, because our computing strategy is based on probabilistic principles, the information to be processed is encoded with a large ensemble of random samples, therefore any local noise-induced data distortion has minuscule chance to affect overall results.

## Acknowledgments

This work was supported in parts by an ARO DURIP grant N16-22-6056, an NSF BRIGE grant ECCS-1342225 and an NSF CCF grant 1319884.

## 9. REFERENCES

[1] P. Hasler, "Low-power programmable signal processing," pp. 413–418, July 2005.

[2] G. Frantz, "Digital signal processor trends," *Micro, IEEE*, vol. 20, pp. 52–59, Nov 2000.

[3] C. Schlottmann and P. Hasler, "Fpaa empowering cooperative analog-digital signal processing," in *Acoustics, Speech and Signal Processing (ICASSP), 2012 IEEE International Conference on*, pp. 5301–5304, March 2012.

[4] T. Hall, C. Twigg, J. Gray, P. Hasler, and D. Anderson, "Large-scale field-programmable analog arrays for analog signal processing," *Circuits and Systems I: Regular Papers, IEEE Transactions on*, vol. 52, pp. 2298–2307, Nov 2005.

[5] M. Alawad, Y. Bai, R. DeMara, and M. Lin, "Energy-efficient multiplier-less discrete convolver through probabilistic domain transformation," in *Proceedings of the 2014 ACM/SIGDA International Symposium on Field-programmable Gate Arrays*, FPGA '14, (New York, NY, USA), pp. 185–188, ACM, 2014.

[6] W. Feller, *AN INTRODUCTION TO PROBABILITY THEORY AND ITS APPLICATIONS, 2ND ED.* No. v. 1 in Wiley publication in mathematical statistics, Wiley India Pvt. Limited, 2008.

[7] J. D. M. Rennie, "A short tutorial on using expectation-maximization with mixture models," 2004.

[8] D. A. Reynolds, T. F. Quatieri, and R. B. Dunn, "Speaker verification using adapted gaussian mixture models," *Digital Signal Processing*, vol. 10, no. 1âĂŞ3, pp. 19 – 41, 2000.

[9] H. Permuter, J. Francos, and H. Jermyn, "Gaussian mixture models of texture and colour for image database retrieval," in *Acoustics, Speech, and Signal Processing, 2003. Proceedings. (ICASSP '03). 2003 IEEE International Conference on*, vol. 3, pp. III–569–72 vol.3, 2003.

[10] C. A. Looby and C. Lyden, "A cmos continuous-time field programmable analog array," in *Proceedings of the 1997 ACM Fifth International Symposium on Field-programmable Gate Arrays*, FPGA '97, (New York, NY, USA), pp. 137–141, ACM, 1997.

[11] B. V. Zeghbroeck, *Principles of Semiconductor Devices*. University of Colorado, 2011.

[12] T. Tuytelaars and L. Van Gool, "Matching widely separated views based on affine invariant regions," *Int. J. Comput. Vision*, vol. 59, pp. 61–85, Aug. 2004.

[13] M. Mirmehdi and R. Periasamy, "Cbir with perceptual region features," in *Proceedings of the 12th British Machine Vision Conference*, pp. 511–520, BMVA Press, 2001.

[14] P. Schnitzspan, S. Roth, and B. Schiele, "Automatic discovery of meaningful object parts with latent crfs," in *Computer Vision and Pattern Recognition (CVPR), 2010 IEEE Conference on*, pp. 121–128, June 2010.

[15] W. FoĬLrstner, T. Dickscheid, and F. Schindler, "Detecting interpretable and accurate scale-invariant keypoints," in *Computer Vision, 2009 IEEE 12th International Conference on*, pp. 2256–2263, Sept 2009.

[16] P. Martins, P. Carvalho, and C. Gatta, "Context-aware features and robust image representations," *J. Vis. Comun. Image Represent.*, vol. 25, pp. 339–348, Feb. 2014.

# Expanding OpenFlow Capabilities with Virtualized Reconfigurable Hardware

Stuart Byma, Naif Tarafdar, Talia Xu, Hadi Bannazadeh
Alberto Leon-Garcia, Paul Chow
Department of Electrical and Computer Engineering
University of Toronto
Toronto, Ontario, Canada M5S 3G4
{bymastua, tarafda1}@eecg.toronto.edu
{talia.xu, hadi.bannazadeh, alberto.leongarcia}@utoronto.ca, pc@eecg.toronto.edu

## ABSTRACT

We present a novel method of using cloud-based virtualized reconfigurable hardware to enhance the functionality of OpenFlow Software-Defined Networks. OpenFlow is a capable and popular SDN implementation, but when users require new or unsupported packet-processing, software processing in the OpenFlow controller cannot provide multi-gigabit rates. Our method sees packet flows redirected through virtualized hardware with custom-designed packet-processing engines that can add new capabilities to an OpenFlow network, while retaining line-rate processing. A case study shows this can be achieved with virtually no loss in throughput and minimal latency overheads.

## Categories and Subject Descriptors

B.0 [**Hardware**]: General

## Keywords

Cloud Computing, Software-Defined Networking

## 1. INTRODUCTION

Software-Defined Networking (SDN) is a new networking paradigm that has been gaining popularity in the past few years [1]. The key to SDN is the separation of the network control plane from the data plane, where the control of network nodes is moved to a centralized system defined by software applications. Network nodes become "dumb" programmable switches that are told what to do with incoming packets by the central controller that has full view of the entire network topology. This allows network administrators to write software to achieve extensive fine-grain control over the entire network.

A problem arises when switches do not implement desired features in hardware. This can cause packets to traverse a much slower software path in the switch or through the SDN controller, which usually runs on a commodity server.

In this paper we introduce a novel method for circumventing this slow software path, keeping all desired packet-processing in fast hardware datapaths. We leverage existing work that provides virtualized in-network reconfigurable hardware accelerators, which can be brought up on the fly much like virtual machines [2]. We use these accelerators to implement the desired packet-processing features, and then redirect packet flows through the accelerators to integrate their functionality into the network.

## 2. BACKGROUND

In this section we introduce relevant background material on OpenFlow, as well as the cloud-based FPGA infrastructure that we make use of.

### 2.1 OpenFlow

OpenFlow [3] is a Software-Defined Networking protocol. OpenFlow operates by programming *flows* into OpenFlow-compatible network switches, which match packets against the flows and perform associated actions such as Forward or Drop. Current OpenFlow switches generally support a limited subset of the protocol in hardware. Therefore, a user operating an OpenFlow network at this point in time may come across two roadblocks: 1) An OpenFlow switch does not support a particular optional feature; 2) The user desires a custom rule match or action that OpenFlow does not specify.

### 2.2 Heterogeneous Cloud Infrastructures

Cloud computing is a paradigm in which physical resources are virtualized so that they can be shared between users in a flexible, scalable manner.

In this paper we will focus on Infrastructure as a Service (IaaS) type clouds. The resources provided in IaaS clouds are typically Virtual Machines (VM), storage, and networking resources, a well-known example being Amazon Web Services. Emerging next generation cloud architectures also include more heterogeneous computing resources such as GPUs, and more recently, FPGAs, as well as virtualized network resources. Figure 1 shows this architecture, components of which are described below.

#### 2.2.1 FPGA Resources (VFRs)

FPGAs typically do not map well to existing cloud systems because there is no straightforward way to abstract and virtualize them. Recent work, however, has used partial reconfiguration to partition a single FPGA device into several reconfigurable regions that are then offered as individual cloud resources [2]. A provided automated compile system allows a user to simply write HDL code and have it run, via the cloud management system, inside one of these reconfigurable regions, which are termed *Virtualized FPGA Resources* or VFRs. From our perspective (the user), we can

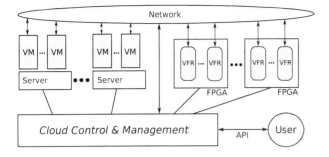

Figure 1: Cloud infrastructure showing VMs and VFRs.

view VFRs just as we view virtual machines – part of the infrastructure used to implement our cloud-based systems.

### 2.2.2 Network Resources

Our infrastructure contains a networking system that is also virtualized. This allows us to allocate networks as cloud resources, and attach other resources to these networks as well. These networks are also software-defined, and support the attachment of custom OpenFlow controllers. We make use of the Smart Applications on Virtual Infrastructure (SAVI) network Testbed [4] for our prototyping, which supports this network virtualization, as well as the VFRs discussed above.

## 3. PROPOSED METHOD

In this section we describe our method of using virtualized reconfigurable hardware to expand the functionality of an OpenFlow network. VFRs are used to implement desired packet-processing features, while *flow redirection* is used to direct packet flows through these VFR-based processors.

### 3.1 Customizing OpenFlow with VFRs

In a regular, homogeneous IaaS system, customizing an OpenFlow network would invariably involve software packet-processing using virtual machines. However, in our infrastructure, we can use VFRs to accomplish this packet-processing at line rate. The hardware can be booted via the cloud controller, and packet flows can be *redirected* using the programmable SDN that connects all resources.

#### 3.1.1 Flow Redirection

We use the term *Flow Redirection* to describe the process of moving desired packet flows through a VFR. A VFR can be seen as a single port Layer Two network device attached to a specific switch port. Packets need to be sent to the VFR for processing, and packets coming out of the VFR also need to be handled correctly. The scenario is shown in Figure 2. Normally, packets are simply forwarded according to existing flows in the OpenFlow Switch. In flow redirection, packets are redirected to the VFR and processed by custom hardware. Some may be dropped, and some or all may come back out of the VFR's single port. Packets exiting the VFR may also require redirection.

Whatever redirection is required is handled by programming additional flows into the OpenFlow switches, through the user's OpenFlow controller. In general, two sets of flows need to be added – one set redirecting packets into a VFR, and another set routing packets coming out of a VFR.

This flow redirection adds an additional hop to certain paths in the network. This will add latency, however throughput is relatively unaffected, as long as the VFR hardware is designed well. Compared with full network path latencies,

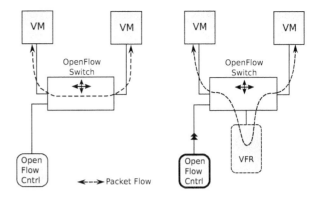

Figure 2: OpenFlow can be used to redirect packet flows through a VFR for additional custom processing.

which are usually in the millisecond range, the additional latency is comparatively small.

## 4. APPLICATION CASE STUDY

We present a case study demonstrating our method of enhancing the functionality of OpenFlow networks using reconfigurable hardware, focusing on the domain of network tunnels. We show that additional, even exotic funcionality can be added to an SDN at a low latency cost and negligible throughput overhead.

### 4.1 VXLAN

The Virtually eXtensible Local Area Network protocol, or VXLAN, is a network tunneling protocol that can connect two local area networks over IP. Entire Ethernet packets are encapsulated inside IP packets, creating a bridge between two physically separate Layer 2 networks. VXLAN is an application layer protocol, running on top of UDP. OpenFlow cannot "see" inside the payload of a UDP packet, meaning that OpenFlow cannot see what kinds of packets are flowing through a VXLAN tunnel. Since VXLAN operates on a designated port, 4789, an OpenFlow network could detect that VXLAN tunnels exist, but it is not capable of anything more than dropping the packets or forwarding them along a certain route. To "see" inside the tunnel requires extending OpenFlow to be able to match and perform actions on new packet fields, which is now possible using flow redirection and virtualized reconfigurable hardware.

### 4.2 OpenFlow VXLAN Firewall

A custom, OpenFlow-controlled in-network VXLAN Firewall implements the ability to perform matches and actions on the IP addresses, and source and destination ports of an encapsulated packet, and either drop or forward the packet. A user can control forwarding by sending control packets to the firewall hardware to configure it at runtime.

Figure 3 shows a high-level view of the firewall design. The firewall hardware contains two Content Addressable Memory blocks with a depth of 128 each, which store blacklisted IP addresses and port numbers. The hardware parses packets to detect destination UDP port 4789, signifying that the packet is a VXLAN packet. If this port is not detected, the packet is simply dropped. The hardware then tests if the destination transport layer port or the destination IP address of the encapsulated packet matches any currently stored in the CAM blocks. If either the port or the IP address matches, the packet is dropped. Values are written into the CAMs via control packets. The firewall hardware is limited in complexity due to the area constraints of the current VFRs.

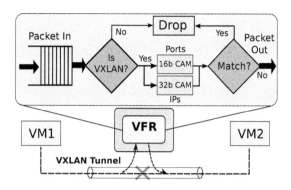

**Figure 3: VXLAN Firewall with CAM blocks**

### 4.2.1 Experimental Results

We set up an experiment to test the firewall as shown in Figure 2. Two virtual machines are booted on two separate physical machines along with the VXLAN firewall that has been compiled for the virtualized hardware system. Flows are added to the OpenFlow switch connecting these components to perform the redirection of packets traversing the network between the two VMs. The firewall filters the packets according to the rules programmed into it via control packets. Packets forwarded out of the firewall are sent on to their original destination. No modifications need to be made to the VMs; they operate unaware of what is happening in the network. The links of network physical layer are 1G Ethernet. The VMs are Ubuntu machines, with 2GB of RAM and one virtual processor at 1.2 GHz.

The performance utility `iperf` is used to measure throughput from one VM to another, and `ping` is used to measure latency. First, a baseline measurement is taken, that is with no additional flows installed, to see what the throughput and latency are between the VMs without the VFR in the network path. The `iperf` utility is run five times and an average is taken, while `ping` is run until 20 pings are completed. These tests are run both with and without VXLAN tunnelling. Results are shown under No Tunnel and VXLAN Tunnel in Table 1.

**Table 1: Throughput and Latency for VXLAN Firewall**

|  | Throughput | Latency |
|---|---|---|
| No Tunnel | 941 Mb/s | 0.465 ms |
| VXLAN Tunnel | 517.4 Mb/s | 0.532 ms |
| VXLAN through VFR | 513.2 Mb/s | 0.600 ms |

Without tunneling the throughput is near line rate (1 Gb/s) as expected. When tunneling using VXLAN, throughput takes a large performance hit due to the software implementation of the tunnel, though the specific loss depends on the VM specs.

Flows are then installed to reroute VXLAN traffic to the running VFR and `iperf` is run again to determine the overhead of rerouting the VXLAN traffic through the VFR firewall. An average of five runs gives a throughput of 513.2 Mb/s, slightly less than the 517.4 Mb/s achieved without the VFR in the network path. This is not a large difference and we can conclude that this technique introduces little

to no overhead in terms of throughput. We run the `ping` test again, and results show that rerouting to the VFR introduces a small increase in latency ($\sim$ 12%), but this is expected when adding an additional hop. These results are also summarized in Table 1 under VXLAN through VFR.

## 4.3 OpenFlow VXLAN Implementation

Our application involves sending a packet between two machines on two different Local Area Networks. The software implementation of encapsulating and decapsulating the packet through a VXLAN tunnel in OpenVSwitch introduces overhead and reduces our line rate throughput of 941 Mb/s to 517.4 Mb/s (Table 1).

We eliminate this software overhead by implementing the encapsulation and decapsulation of packets directly in hardware. The system is shown in Figure 4. Flows are set to forward packets to an *encapsulator* VFR where they enter the tunnel (i.e. encapsulated in a VXLAN packet), after which they are forwarded over the Internet to another VFR, the *decapsulator*, which implements the tunnel egress (i.e. popping the tunneled packet). Control packets are used to set the header information used by the encapsulator, such that the VXLAN packets are destined to the decapsulator. Thus a VXLAN tunnel is created without involving any software packet-processing.

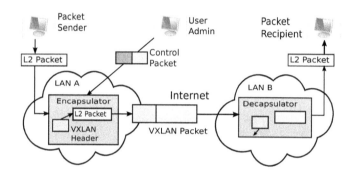

**Figure 4: Two hosts on two different LANs communicating using VXLAN.**

### 4.3.1 Hardware Microarchitecture

The encapsulator takes an L2 packet and encapsulates it with the entire VXLAN packet header. This packet header consists of 3 portions: MAC header, IP header, and UDP header. The MAC header specifies the source and destination MAC address, where the source is the encapsulator VFR and the destination is the decapsulator VFR. These three packet portions are constant fields that are programmed into the encapsulator with the use of control packets. The encapsulator must first be programmed by the use of three control packets, one specifying each portion of the VXLAN packet header. After the encapsulator has been programmed, it can accept general L2 packets for encapsulation, and entry into the tunnel.

The decapsulator receives an encapsulated packet and pops the original L2 frame/packet. This does not require any additional programming via control packets, since the VXLAN header is a constant size. The hardware does not handle variable IP options fields. The decapsulator checks to see if the packet is a VXLAN packet, and if so, strips off the the header (50 bytes).

### 4.3.2 Experimental Results

The overhead that a software-based tunnel experiences can be quite high, as shown in the first experiment. We set up another experiment to determine if the VFR-based VXLAN tunnel can indeed alleviate this overhead. We also wish to see how much latency the additional hops in the forwarding path add (through the encapsulator and decapsulator).

We measure the latency and throughput of the round-trip path between the initial sender and final destination, through the encapsulator and decapsulator. All of the nodes are on the same network. We know from the previous firewall application that one redirection added approximately a 12% latency penalty, and therefore we expect to see a similar result here.

The `ping` test is run with the redirection flows installed, and the resulting round trip latency is 0.509 ms, an increase of only 9% from the baseline (non-tunneled) latency of 0.465 ms. This is less than the one-hop redirection in the previous experiment since the latency penalty for the software VXLAN tunnel is not being paid since the tunnel is now implemented entirely in custom hardware. Throughput is nearly unaffected, measured using `iperf` at 938 Mb/s, only a 0.3% difference – verifying that flow redirection with VFRs can nearly eliminate the software overheads of VXLAN tunnels in OVS.

## 5. RELATED WORK

Related work has looked into using FPGAs with Open-Flow. Some efforts have been made to implement OpenFlow switches on FPGA-based cards – Naous et. al. have used the NetFPGA platform [5] and Khan et. al. have used the NetFPGA10G platform [6]. Their goal was to enable experimental exploration of SDN control and data planes, whereas the work we present here uses available cloud-based FPGAs to enhance existing OpenFlow networks with custom functions.

Much work has been done in the area of utilizing FPGAs to implement custom high-speed packet-processing hardware as well. Packet classification [7, 8], flow matching [9], and deep packet inspection [10] are just a few examples. These approaches may map well into our system to provide these specialized capabilities and algorithms to an existing Open-Flow network.

## 6. FUTURE WORK

One problem this type of system may face is that of usability and adoption – many potential end-users may not consider it given that it involves complex hardware design. The key may be to provide a high-level specification or domain specific language for describing rules, matches and actions to execute on packets. Recent work and developments in this area could be leveraged to provide a friendly, convenient way to create hardware engines that will work well with flow redirection [11, 12]. Libraries of different VFR compatible hardware engines could be created for use in a cloud system as well.

There are other applications of our method as well – line-rate deep packet inspection could be carried out on flows, with the hardware tailored to detect whatever the user is looking for. Virtualized hardware could realize the routing and forwarding protocols for an overlay network, avoiding the need to implement these nodes on Virtual Machines, thereby likely enhancing system performance.

## 7. CONCLUSION

In our view, redirecting packet flows through custom in-network hardware presents a compelling case. We have shown that additional, even exotic, functionality can be added to an OpenFlow Software-Defined Network with little to no penalty in throughput, in exchange for a small increase in end to end latency due to the additional hop that flow redirection adds. Recent developments in Domain Specific Languages and high-level synthesis will also make this approach to specialized functionality more palatable to the many potential users who do not have a background in digital hardware design.

## 8. ACKNOWLEDGEMENTS

We would like to thank members of the SAVI testbed Thomas Lin and Eric Lin for their help in running our experiments. This work was also supported in part by the SAVI Network, NSERC and Xilinx Inc.

## 9. REFERENCES

[1] Nick McKeown. Software-Defined Networking. *INFOCOM Keynote Talk*, 2009.

[2] Stuart Byma, J Gregory Steffan, Hadi Bannazadeh, Alberto Leon-Garcia, and Paul Chow. FPGAs in the Cloud: Booting Virtualized Hardware Accelerators with OpenStack. In *Field-Programmable Custom Computing Machines (FCCM)*. IEEE, 2014.

[3] Nick McKeown, Tom Anderson, Hari Balakrishnan, Guru Parulkar, Larry Peterson, Jennifer Rexford, Scott Shenker, and Jonathan Turner. OpenFlow: Enabling Innovation in Campus Networks. *ACM SIGCOMM Computer Communication Review*, 38(2):69–74, 2008.

[4] J.M. Kang, H. Bannazadeh, and A. Leon-Garcia. SAVI Testbed: Control and Management of Converged Virtual ICT Resources. In *International Symposium on Integrated Network Management*, pages 664–667. IEEE, 2013.

[5] Jad Naous, David Erickson, G. Adam Covington, Guido Appenzeller, and Nick McKeown. Implementing an OpenFlow Switch on the NetFPGA Platform. In *ACM/IEEE Symposium on Architectures for Networking and Communications Systems*, pages 1–9. ACM, 2008.

[6] A Khan and N. Dave. Enabling Hardware Exploration in Software-Defined Networking: A Flexible, Portable OpenFlow Switch. In *Field-Programmable Custom Computing Machines (FCCM)*, pages 145–148, April 2013.

[7] J. Fong, Xiang Wang, Yaxuan Qi, Jun Li, and Weirong Jiang. ParaSplit: A Scalable Architecture on FPGA for Terabit Packet Classification. In *High-Performance Interconnects (HOTI)*, pages 1–8, Aug 2012.

[8] Weirong Jiang and V.K. Prasanna. Scalable Packet Classification on FPGA. *IEEE Transactions on Very Large Scale Integration Systems*, 20(9):1668–1680, Sept 2012.

[9] Weirong Jiang, V.K. Prasanna, and N. Yamagaki. Decision Forest: A Scalable Architecture for Flexible Flow Matching on FPGA. In *Field Programmable Logic and Applications (FPL)*, pages 394–399, Aug 2010.

[10] Sarang Dharmapurikar, Praveen Krishnamurthy, T. Sproull, and J. Lockwood. Deep Packet Inspection Using Parallel Bloom Filters. In *High Performance Interconnects*, pages 44–51, Aug 2003.

[11] G. Brebner and Weirong Jiang. High-Speed Packet Processing using Reconfigurable Computing. *IEEE Micro*, 34(1):8–18, Jan 2014.

[12] Xilinx Inc. Xilinx SDNet. http://www.xilinx.com/applications/wired-communications/sdnet.html, 2014.

# Take the Highway: Design for Embedded NoCs on FPGAs

Mohamed S. Abdelfattah, Andrew Bitar, Vaughn Betz

Department of Electrical and Computer Engineering
University of Toronto, Toronto, ON, Canada
{mohamed, bitar, vaughn}@eecg.utoronto.ca

## ABSTRACT

We explore the addition of a fast embedded network-on-chip (NoC) to augment the FPGA's existing wires and switches, and help interconnect large applications. A flexible interface between the FPGA fabric and the embedded NoC allows modules of varying widths and frequencies to transport data over the NoC. We study both latency-insensitive and latency-sensitive design styles and present the constraints for implementing each type of communication on the embedded NoC. Our application case study with image compression shows that an embedded NoC improves frequency by 10–80%, reduces utilization of scarce long wires by 40% and makes design easier and more predictable. Additionally, we leverage the embedded NoC in creating a programmable Ethernet switch that can support up to 819 Gb/s on FPGAs.

## Categories and Subject Descriptors

B.4.3 [**Input/Output and Data Communications**]: Interconnections (Subsystems)

## 1. INTRODUCTION

Field-programmable gate-arrays (FPGAs) are increasing in both capacity and heterogeneity. Over the past two decades, FPGAs have evolved from a chip with thousands of logic elements (and not much else) to a much larger chip that has millions of logic elements, embedded memory, multipliers, processors, memory controllers, PCIe controllers and high-speed transceivers [26]. This incredible increase in size and functionality has pushed FPGAs into new markets and larger and more complex systems [24].

Both the FPGA's logic and I/Os have had efficient embedded units added to enhance their performance; however, the FPGA's interconnect is still basically the same. Using a combination of wire segments and multiplexers, a single-bit connection can be made between any two points on the FPGA chip. While this traditional interconnect is very flexible, it is becoming ever-more challenging to use in connecting large systems. Wire-speed is scaling poorly compared to transistor speed [19], and a larger FPGA device means that a connection often consists of multiple wire segments and multiplexers thus increasing overall delay. This makes it difficult to estimate the delay of a connection before placement and routing,

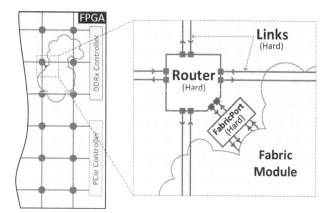

Figure 1: Embedded hard NoC connects to the FPGA fabric and hard I/O interfaces.

forcing FPGA designers to wait until design compilation is completed, then identify the critical path and manually add pipeline registers in an attempt to improve frequency – a time-consuming process. Furthermore, the high bandwidth of embedded I/O interfaces requires fast and very wide connections that distribute data across the whole chip. This utilizes much FPGA logic and a multitude of its single-bit wires and multiplexers; consequently, it is difficult to run these wide connections fast enough to satisfy the stringent delay constraints of interfaces like DDR3.

System-level interconnect has been proposed to augment the FPGA's bit-level interconnect to better integrate large systems. Some have suggested the use of bus-based FPGA interconnect to save area [27], while others have investigated embedded NoCs [5, 15, 17]. In this work we focus on the latter; specifically, how to interface the FPGA fabric to an embedded NoC, and how to use an embedded NoC for different design styles that are common to FPGAs. Previous work has investigated how to use an embedded NoC to create a multiprocessor-like memory abstraction for FPGAs [9]. In contrast, we focus on *adapting* an embedded NoC to the currently used FPGA design styles. To this end, we make the following contributions:

1. Present the FabricPort: a flexible interface between the FPGA fabric and a packet-switched embedded NoC.

2. Investigate the requirements of mapping the communication of different design styles (latency-insensitive and latency-sensitive) onto an embedded NoC.

3. Analyze latency-sensitive parallel JPEG compression both with and without an embedded NoC.

4. Design an Ethernet switch capable of 819 Gb/s using the embedded NoC; 5× more switching than previously demonstrated on FPGAs.

Table 1: NoC parameters and properties for 28 nm FPGAs.

| NoC Link Width | # VCs | Buffer Depth | # Nodes | Topology |
|---|---|---|---|---|
| 150 bits | 2 | 10 flits/VC | 16 nodes | Mesh |

| Area[†] | Area Fraction[*] | Frequency |
|---|---|---|
| 528 LABs | 1.3% | 1.2 GHz |

[†]LAB: Area equivalent to a Stratix V logic cluster.
[*]Percentage of core area of a large Stratix V FPGA.

## 2. EMBEDDED HARD NOC

Before presenting our embedded NoC, we define some of the NoC terminology [12] that may be unfamiliar to the reader:

- Flit: The smallest unit of data that can be transported on the NoC; it is equivalent to the NoC link width.

- Packet: One or more related flits that together form a logical meaning.

- Virtual channels (VCs): Separate FIFO buffers at a NoC router input port; if we use 2 VCs in our NoC, then each router input can store incoming flits in one of two possible FIFO buffers.

- Credit-based flow control: A backpressure mechanism in which each NoC router keeps track of the number of available buffer spaces (credits) downstream, and only sends a flit downstream if it has available credits.

Our embedded packet-switched NoC targets a large 28 nm FPGA device. The NoC presented in this section is used throughout this paper in our design and evaluation sections. Fig. 1 displays a high-level view of an NoC embedded on an FPGA. We base our router design on a state-of-the-art full-featured packet-switched router [10].

In designing the embedded NoC, we must over-provision its resources, much like other FPGA interconnect resources, so that it can be used in connecting *any* application. We therefore look at high bandwidth I/Os to determine the required NoC link bandwidth. The highest-bandwidth interface on FPGAs is usually a DDR3 interface, capable of transporting 64 bits of data at a speed of 1067 MHz at double-data rate (~17 GB/s). We design the NoC such that it can transport the entire bandwidth of a DDR3 interface on one of its links; therefore, we can connect to DDR3, or to one of the masters accessing it using a single router port. Additionally, we must be able to transport the control data of DDR3 transfers, such as the address, alongside the data. We therefore choose a width of 150 bits for our NoC links and router ports, and we are able to run the NoC at 1.2 GHz[1] [1]. By multiplying our width and frequency, we find that our NoC is able to transport a bandwidth of 22.5 GB/s on each of its links.

Table 1 summarizes the NoC parameters and properties. We use 2 VCs in our NoC. Previous work has shown that a second VC reduces congestion by ~30% [3]. We also leverage VCs to avoid deadlock, and merge data streams as we discuss in Sections 3 and 4. Additionally, we believe that the capabilities offered by VCs – such as assigning priorities to different messages types – would be useful in future FPGA designs. The buffer depth per VC is provisioned such that it is not a cause for throughput degradation (see Section 4.3.1). With the given parameters, each embedded router occupies an area equivalent to 35 logic clusters (Stratix-V LABs),

---

[1]We implement the NoC in 65 nm standard cells and scale the frequency obtained by 1.35× to match the speed scaling of Xilinx's (also standard cell) DSP blocks from Virtex5 (65 nm) to Virtex7 (28 nm) [26].

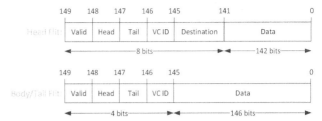

Figure 2: NoC packets consist of a head flit and zero-or-more body flits. The figure shows flits for a 16-node 150-bit-width NoC with 2 VCs. Each flit has control data to indicate whether this flit is valid, and if it is the head or tail flit (or both for a 1-flit packet). Additionally each flit must have the VC number to which it is assigned and a head flit must contain the destination address.

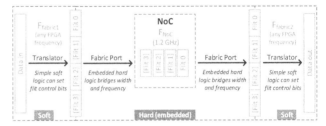

Figure 3: Data on the FPGA with any protocol can be translated into NoC flits using application-dependent soft logic (translator). A FabricPort then adapts width (1-4 flit width on fabric side and 1 flit width on NoC) and frequency (any frequency on fabric side and 1.2 GHz on NoC side) to inject flits into the NoC.

including the interface between the router and the FPGA fabric, and including the wire drivers necessary for the hard NoC links [4]. As Table 1 shows, the whole 16-node NoC occupies 528 LABs, a mere 1.3% of a large 28 nm Stratix-V FPGA core area (excluding I/Os).

## 3. FABRICPORT: INTERFACE BETWEEN FPGA AND NOC

### 3.1 Packet Format

Fig. 2 shows the format of flits on the NoC; each flit is 150 bits making flit width and NoC link width equivalent (as most on-chip networks do) [12]. One flit is the smallest unit that can be sent over the NoC, indicating that the NoC will be used for coarse-grained wide datapath transfers. This packet format puts no restriction on the number of flits that form a packet; each flit has two bits for "head" and "tail" to indicate the flit at the start of a packet, and the flit at the end of a packet. The VC identifier is required for proper virtual-channel flow control, and finally, the head flit must also contain the destination address so that the NoC knows where to send the packet. The remaining bits are data, making the control overhead quite small in comparison; for a 4-flit packet, control bits make up 3% of transported data.

### 3.2 FabricPort Functionality

Each NoC port can sustain a maximum input bandwidth of 22.5 GB/s; however, this is done at the high frequency of 1.2 GHz for our NoC. The main purpose of the Fabric-Port is therefore to give the FPGA fabric access to that communication bandwidth, at the range of frequencies at which FPGAs normally operate. How does one connect a module configured from the FPGA fabric to the embedded NoC running at a different width and frequency?

Fig. 3 illustrates the process of conditioning data from any FPGA module to NoC flits, and vice versa. A very simple translator takes incoming data and appends to it the neces-

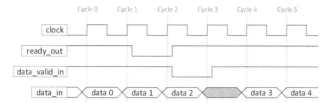

Figure 4: Waveform of ready/valid signals between soft module → FabricPort input, or FabricPort output → soft module. After "ready" signal becomes low, the receiver must accept one more cycle of valid data (data 2) after which the sender will have processed the "ready" signal and stopped sending more valid data.

sary flit control information. For most cases, this translator consists only of wires that pack the data in the correct position and sets the valid/head/tail bits from constants. Once data is formatted into flits, we can send between 0 and 4 flits in each fabric cycle, this is indicated by the valid bit on each flit. The FabricPort will then serialize the flits, one after the other, and inject the valid ones into the NoC at the NoC's frequency. When flits are received at the other end of the NoC, the frequency is again bridged, and the width adapted using a FabricPort; then a translator strips control bits and injects the data into the receiving fabric module.

This FabricPort plays a pivotal role in adapting an embedded NoC to function on an FPGA. We must bridge the width and frequency while making sure that the FabricPort is never a source of throughput reduction; furthermore, the FabricPort must be able to interface to different VCs on the NoC, send/receive different-length packets and respond to backpressure coming from either the NoC or FPGA fabric. We enumerate the essential properties that this component must have:

1. **Rate Conversion**: Match the NoC bandwidth to the fabric bandwidth. Because the NoC is embedded, it can run ~4× faster than the FPGA fabric [2, 4]. We leverage that speed advantage to build a narrow-link-width NoC that connects to a wider but slower FPGA fabric.

2. **Stallability**: Accept/send data on every NoC cycle in the absence of stalls, and stall for the exact number of cycles when the fabric/NoC isn't ready to send/receive data (as Fig. 4 shows). The FabricPort itself should never be the source of throughput reduction.

3. **Virtual Channels**: Read/write data from/to multiple virtual channels in the NoC such that the FabricPort is never the cause for deadlock.

4. **Packet Length**: Send/receive packets of different lengths.

5. **Backpressure Translation**: Convert the NoC's credit-based flow-control system into the more FPGA-familiar ready/valid signals.

## 3.3 FabricPort Circuitry

### 3.3.1 FabricPort Input: Fabric→NoC

Fig. 5 shows a schematic of the FabricPort with important control signals annotated. The FabricPort input (Fig. 5a) connects the output of a module in the FPGA fabric to an embedded NoC input. Following the diagram from left to right: data is input to the time-domain multiplexing (TDM) circuitry on each fabric clock cycle and is buffered in the "main" register. The "aux" register is added to provide elasticity. Whenever the output of the TDM must stall there is a clock cycle before the stall signal is processed by the fabric module. In that cycle, the incoming datum may still

be valid, and is therefore buffered in the "aux" registers. To clarify this ready-valid behavior, example waveforms are illustrated in Fig. 4. Importantly, this stall protocol ensures that every stall (ready = 0) cycle only stops the input for exactly one cycle ensuring that the FabricPort input does not reduce throughput.

The TDM unit takes four flits input on a slow fabric clock and outputs one flit at a time on a faster clock that is 4× as fast as the FPGA fabric – we call this the intermediate clock. This intermediate clock is only used in the FabricPort between the TDM unit and the asynchronous FIFO (aFIFO) buffer. Because it is used only in this very localized region, this clock may be derived locally from the fabric clock by careful design of circuitry that multiplies the frequency of the clock by four. This is better than generating 16 different clocks globally through phase-locked loops, then building a different clock tree for each router's intermediate clock (a viable but more costly alternative).

The output of the TDM unit is a new flit on each intermediate clock cycle. Because each flit has a valid bit, only those flits that are valid will actually be written in the aFIFO thus ensuring that no invalid data propagates downstream, unnecessarily consuming power and bandwidth. The aFIFO bridges the frequency between the intermediate clock and the NoC clock ensuring that the fabric clock can be completely independent from the NoC clock frequency and phase.

The final component in the FabricPort input is the "NoC Writer". This unit reads flits from the aFIFO and writes them to the downstream NoC router. The NoC Writer keeps track of the number of credits in the downstream router to interface to the credit-based backpressure system in the embedded NoC, and only sends flits when there are available credits. Note that credit-based flow control is by far the most-widely-used backpressure mechanism in NoCs because of its superior performance with limited buffering [12].

### 3.3.2 FabricPort Output: NoC→Fabric

Fig. 5b details a FabricPort output; the connection from an NoC output port to the input of a module on the FPGA fabric. Following the diagram from right to left: the first component is the "NoC Reader". This unit is responsible for reading flits from an NoC router output port and writing to the aFIFO. Note that separate FIFO queues must be kept for each VC; this is very important as it avoids scrambling data from two packets. Fig. 6 clarifies this point; the upstream router may interleave flits from different packets if they are on different VCs. By maintaining separate queues in the NoC reader, we can rearrange flits such that flits of the same packet are organized one after the other.

The NoC reader is then responsible for arbitrating between the FIFO queues and forwarding one (entire) packet – one flit at a time – from each VC. We currently implement fair round-robin arbitration and make sure that there are no "dead" arbitration cycles. That means that as soon as the NoC reader sees a tail flit of one packet, it has already computed the VC from which it will read next. The packet then enters the aFIFO where it crosses clock domains between the NoC clock and the intermediate clock.

The final step in the FabricPort output is the time-domain demultiplexing (DEMUX). This unit reassembles packets (or packet fragments if a packet is longer than 4 flits) by combining 1-4 flits into the wide output port. In doing so, the DEMUX does not combine flits of different packets and will instead insert invalid zero flits to pad the end of a packet that doesn't have a number of flits divisible by 4 (see Fig. 6). This is very much necessary to present a simple interface for designers allowing them to connect design modules to the FabricPort with minimal soft logic.

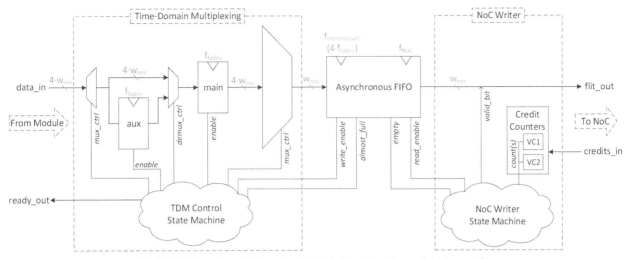

(a) FabricPort input: from the FPGA fabric to the embedded NoC.

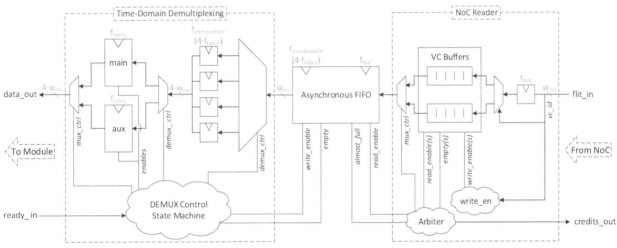

(b) FabricPort output: from the embedded NoC to the FPGA fabric.

Figure 5: The FabricPort interfaces the FPGA fabric to an embedded NoC in a flexible way by bridging the different frequencies and widths as well as handling backpressure from both the FPGA fabric and the NoC.

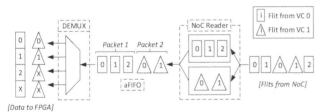

[Data to FPGA]

Figure 6: "NoC Reader" sorts flits from each VC into a separate queue thereby ensuring that flits of each packet are contiguous. The DEMUX then packs up to four flits together and writes them to the wide output port but never mixes flits of two packets.

## 3.4 FabricPort Discussion

### 3.4.1 Module Connectivity

The FabricPort converts 22.5 GB/s of NoC link data bandwidth (150 bits, 1.2 GHz) to 600 bits and any fabric frequency on the fabric side. An FPGA designer can then use any fraction of that port width to send data across the NoC. However, the smallest NoC unit is the flit; so we can either send 1, 2, 3 or 4 flits each cycle. If the designer connects data that fits in one flit (150 bits or less), all the data transported by the NoC

is useful data. However, if the designer want to send data that fits in one-and-a-half flits (225 bits for example), then the FabricPort will send two flits, and half of the second flit is overhead that adds to power consumption and worsens NoC congestion unnecessarily. Efficient "translator" modules (see Fig. 3) will therefore try to take the flit width into account when injecting data to the NoC.

A limitation of the FabricPort output is observed when connecting two modules. Even if each module only uses half the FabricPort's width (2 flits), only one module can receive data each cycle because the DEMUX only outputs one packet at a time by default as Fig. 6 shows. To overcome this limitation, we create a *combine-data* mode as shown in Fig. 7. For this combine-data mode, when there are two modules connected to one FabricPort, data for each module must arrive on a different VC. The NoC Reader arbiter must strictly alternate between VCs, and then the DEMUX will be able to group two packets (one from each VC) before data output to the FPGA. This allows merging two streams without incurring serialization latency in the FabricPort.

CONDITION 1. *To combine packets at a FabricPort output, each packet must arrive on a different VC.*

101

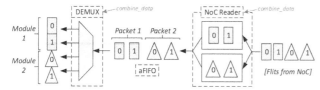

Figure 7: FabricPort output merging two packets from separate VCs in *combine-data* mode, to be able to output data for two modules in the same clock cycle.

Note that we are limited to the merging of two packets with 2 VCs but we can merge up to four 1-flit packets if we increase the number of VCs to four in the embedded NoC.

### 3.4.2 Frequency and Latency

Fig. 8 plots the zero-load latency of the NoC (running at 1.2 GHz) for different fabric frequencies that are typical of FPGAs. We measure latency by sending a single 4-flit packet through the FabricPort input→NoC→FabricPort output. The NoC itself is running at a very fast speed, so even if each NoC hop incurs 4 cycles of NoC clocks, this translates to approximately 1 fabric clock cycle. However, the FabricPort latency is a major portion of the total latency of data transfers on the NoC; it accounts for 40%–85% of latency in an unloaded embedded NoC. The reason for this latency is the flexibility offered by the FabricPort – we can connect a module of any operating frequency but that incurs TDM, DEMUX and clock-crossing latency. Careful inspection of Fig. 8 reveals that the FabricPort input always has a fixed latency for a given frequency, while the latency of the FabricPort output varies by one cycle sometimes – this is an artifact of having to wait for the *next* fabric (slow) clock cycle on which we can output data in the DEMUX unit.

## 4. FPGA-DICTATED NOC DESIGN

Fig. 9 shows the two possibilities of synchronous design styles, as well as two communication protocols that are common in FPGA designs. In a latency-insensitive system, the design consists of *patient* modules that can be stalled, thus allowing the interconnect between those modules to have arbitrary delay [8]. Latency-sensitive design, on the other hand, does not tolerate variable latency on its connections, and assumes that its interconnect always has a fixed latency. In this section we investigate how to map applications that belong to either design style (and any communication protocol) onto the NoC; Fig. 10 illustrates this. We are effectively augmenting the FPGA with a wide stallable network of buffered interconnect that can do flexible switching – how can we best leverage that new interconnection resource for different design styles? And can this embedded NoC be used for both latency insensitive/sensitive design styles, and both communication protocols?

### 4.1 Packet Ordering and Dependencies

#### 4.1.1 Ordering

Packet-switched NoCs like the one we are using were originally built for chip multiprocessors (CMPs). CMPs only perform **memory-mapped** communication; most transfers are cache lines or coherency messages. Furthermore, processors have built-in mechanisms for reordering received data, and NoCs are typically allowed to reorder packets.

With FPGAs, memory-mapped communication can be one of two main things: (1) Control data from a soft processor that is low-bandwidth and latency-critical – a poor target for embedded NoCs, or (2) Communication between design modules and on-chip or off-chip memory, or PCIe links – high

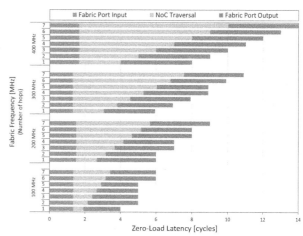

Figure 8: Zero-load latency of the embedded NoC (including FabricPorts) at different fabric frequencies. Latency is reported as the number of cycles at each frequency. The number of hops varies from 1 hop (minimum) to 7 hops (maximum – chip diagonal).

Figure 9: Design styles and communication protocols.

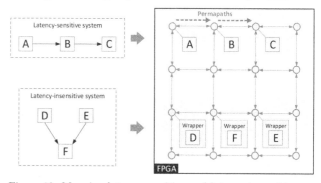

Figure 10: Mapping latency-sensitive and latency-insensitive systems onto an embedded NoC. We reserve *Permapaths* on the NoC to guarantee a fixed latency and perfect throughput for a latency-sensitive application. For latency-insensitive systems, modules must be encapsulated with wrappers to add stall functionality.

bandwidth data suitable for our proposed NoC. Additionally, FPGAs are very good at implementing **streaming**, or data-flow applications such as packet switching, video processing, compression and encryption. These streams of data are also prime targets for using our high-bandwidth embedded NoC. Crucially, neither memory-mapped nor streaming applications tolerate packet reordering on FPGAs, nor do FPGAs natively support it. While it may be possible to design reordering logic for simple memory-mapped applications, it becomes *impossible* to build such logic for streaming applications without hurting performance – we therefore choose to restrict the embedded NoC to perform in-order data transfers only. Specifically, an NoC is not allowed to reorder packets on a single connection.

DEFINITION 1. *A **connection (s, d)** exists between a single source (**s**) and its downstream destination (**d**) to which it sends data.*

DEFINITION 2. *A **path** is the sequence of links from **s** to **d** that a flit takes in traversing an NoC.*

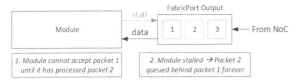

(a) Standard FabricPort output.

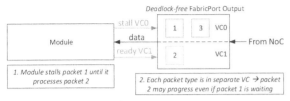

(b) Deadlock-free FabricPort output.

Figure 11: Deadlock can occur if a dependency exists between two message types going to the same port. By using separate VCs for each message type, this deadlock can be broken thus allowing two dependent message types to share a FabricPort output.

There are two causes of packet reordering. Firstly, an adaptive route-selection algorithm would always attempt to choose a path of least contention through the NoC; therefore two packets of the same source and destination (same connection) may take different paths and arrive out of order. Secondly, when sending packets (on the same connection) but different VCs, two packets may get reordered even if they are both taking the same path through the NoC.

To solve the first problem, we only use routing algorithms, in which routes are the same for all packets that belong to a connection.

CONDITION 2. *The same **path** must be taken by all packets that belong to the same **connection**.*

Deterministic routing algorithms such as dimension-ordered routing [12] fulfill Condition 2 as they always select the same route for packets on the same connection.

Eliminating VCs altogether would fix the second ordering problem; however, this is not necessary. VCs can be used to break message deadlock, merge data streams (Fig. 7), alleviate NoC congestion and may be also used to assign packet priorities thus adding extra configurability to our NoC – these properties are desirable. We therefore impose more specific constraints on VCs such that they may still be used on FPGA NoCs.

CONDITION 3. *All packets belonging to the same **connection** must use the same VC.*

To do this in NoC routers is simple. Normally, a packet may change VCs at every router hop – VC selection is done in a VC allocator [12]. We replace this VC allocator with a lightweight VC *facilitator* that cannot switch a packet between VCs; instead, it inspects a packet's input VC and stalls that packet until the downstream VC buffer is available. At the same time, other connections may use other VCs in that router thus taking advantage of multiple VCs.

### 4.1.2 Dependencies and Deadlock

Two *message types* may not share a standard FabricPort output (Fig. 5b) if a dependency exists between the two message types. An example of dependent message types can be seen in video processing IP cores: both control messages (that configure the IP to the correct resolution for example) and data messages (pixels of a video stream) are received on the same port [6]. An IP core may not be able to process the data messages correctly until it receives a control message.

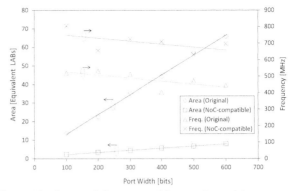

Figure 12: Area and frequency of latency-insensitive wrappers from [23] (original), and optimized wrappers that take advantage of NoC buffering (NoC-compatible).

Consider the deadlock scenario in Fig. 11a. The module is expecting to receive packet 2 but gets packet 1 instead; therefore it stalls the FabricPort output and packet 2 remains queued behind packet 1 forever. To avoid this deadlock, we can send each message type in a different VC [25]. Additionally, we created a deadlock-free FabricPort output that maintains separate paths for each VC – this means we duplicate the aFIFO and DEMUX units for each VC we have. There are now two separate "ready" signals; one for each VC, but there is still only one data bus feeding the module. The module can therefore *either* read from VC0 or VC1. Fig. 11b shows that even if there is a dependency between different messages, they can share a FabricPort output provided each uses a different VC.

CONDITION 4. *When multiple message types can be sent to a FabricPort, and a dependency exists between the message types, each type must use a different VC.*

## 4.2 Latency-Insensitive Design with NoC

Latency-insensitive design is a design methodology that decouples design modules from their interconnect by forcing each module to be *patient*; that is, to tolerate variable latency on its inputs [8]. This is typically done by encapsulating design modules with wrappers that can stall a module until its input data arrives. This means that a design remains functionally correct, by construction, regardless of the latency of data arriving at each module. The consequence of this latency tolerance is that a CAD tool can automatically add pipeline stages (called *relay stations*) invisibly to the circuit designer, late in the design compilation and thus improve frequency without extra effort from the designer [8].

Our embedded NoC is effectively a form of latency-insensitive interconnect; it is heavily pipelined and buffered and supports stalling. We can therefore leverage such an NoC to interconnect patient modules of a latency-insensitive system as illustrated in Fig. 10. Furthermore, we no longer need to add relay stations on connections that are mapped to NoC links, avoiding their overhead.

Previous work that investigated the overhead of latency-insensitive design on FPGAs used FIFOs at the inputs of modules in the stall-wrappers to avoid throughput degradation whenever a stall occurs [23]. When the interconnect is an embedded NoC; however, we already have sufficient buffering in the NoC itself (and the FabricPorts) to avoid this throughput degradation, thus allowing us to replace this FIFO – which is a major portion of the wrapper area – by a single stage of registers. We compare the area and frequency of the original latency-insensitive wrappers evaluated in [23], and the NoC-compatible wrappers in Fig. 12 for wrappers that support one input and one output and a width between

100 bits and 600 bits. As Fig. 12 shows, the lightweight NoC-compatible wrappers are 87% smaller and 47% faster.

We envision a future latency-insensitive design flow targeting embedded NoCs on FPGAs. Given a set of modules that make up an application, they would first be encapsulated with wrappers, then mapped onto an NoC such that performance of the system is maximized.

## 4.3 Latency-Sensitive Design with NoC (Permapaths)

Latency-sensitive design requires predictable latency on the connections between modules. That means that the interconnect is not allowed to insert/remove any cycles between successive data. Prior NoC literature has largely focused on using circuit-switching to achieve quality-of-service guarantees but could only provide a bound on latency rather than a guarantee of fixed latency [16]. We analyze the latency and throughput guarantees that can be attained from an NoC, and use those guarantees to determine the conditions under which a latency-sensitive system can be mapped onto a packet-switched embedded NoC. Effectively, our methodology creates permanent paths with predictable latencies (Permapaths) on our packet-switched embedded NoC.

### 4.3.1 Latency and Throughput Guarantees

To ensure that the NoC doesn't stall due to unavailable buffering, we size NoC buffers for maximum throughput, so that we never stall while waiting for backpressure signals within the NoC. This is well-studied in the literature and is done by sizing our router buffers to cover the *credit round-trip latency* [12] – for our system, a buffer depth of 10 suffices.

Fig. 13 plots the throughput between any source and destination on our NoC in the absence of contention. The NoC is running at 1.2 GHz with 1-flit width; therefore, if we send 1 flit each cycle at a frequency lower than 1.2 GHz, our throughput is always perfect – we'll receive data at the same input rate (one flit per cycle) on the other end of the NoC path. In fact, the NoC connection acts as a simple pipelined wire; the number of pipeline stages are equivalent to the zero-load latency of an NoC path; however, it is irrelevant because that latency is only incurred once at the very beginning of data transmission after which data arrives on each fabric clock cycle. We call this a **Permapath** through the NoC: a path that is free of contention and has perfect throughput. As Fig. 13 shows, we can create Permapaths of larger widths provided that the input bandwidth of our connection does not exceed the NoC port bandwidth of 22.5 GB/s. This is why throughput is still perfect with 4 flits×300 MHz for instance. To create those Permapaths we must therefore ensure two things:

CONDITION 5. *(Permapaths) The sending module data bandwidth must be less than or equal to the maximum FabricPort input bandwidth.*

CONDITION 6. *(Permapaths) No other data traffic may overlap the NoC links reserved for a Permapath to avoid congestion delays on those links.*

Condition 6 be determined statically since our routing algorithm is deterministic; therefore, the mapping of modules onto NoC routers is sufficient to identify which NoC links will be used by each module.

## 4.4 Multicast, Reconvergence and Feedback

A complex FPGA application may include multicast, reconvergence and feedback as shown in Fig. 14 – we discuss these aspects briefly here but leave the in-depth analysis

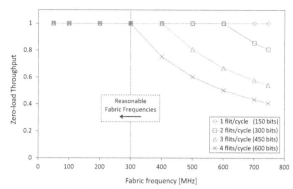

Figure 13: Zero-load throughput of embedded NoC path between any two nodes, normalized to sent data. A throughput of "1" is the maximum; it means that we receive $i$ flits per cycle, where $i$ is the number of flits we insert in the FabricPort each cycle.

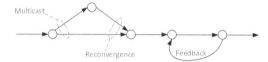

Figure 14: Aspects of complex FPGA applications.

for future work. Prior NoC research has shown that packet-switched routers can be augmented with multicast capability at very low area overhead [14]. As for reconvergence, the two branches of a reconvergent path may have different latencies on the embedded NoC with different implications for latency-sensitive and latency-insensitive systems. A latency-sensitive system may become functionally incorrect in that case; the designer must therefore ensure that the paths are balanced. For a latency-insensitive system functional correctness is guaranteed but throughput degradation may occur if latencies of the two paths differ by a large amount; prior work has investigated path balancing for latency-insensitive systems [22]. Balancing can be done by selecting two paths of the same length through the NoC (hence same latency) and using registers in the FPGA fabric for fine-grained latency adjustment. Feedback paths are also tricky to implement on embedded NoCs; this stems from the fact that these connections are typically latency-critical and require very low latency so as not to impede throughput.

While some of these connections can be mapped onto the NoC, not all of them have to be; the embedded NoC is not meant to be an interconnect capable of connecting everything on the FPGA; rather a flexible low-cost (but high bandwidth) interconnect resource that *augments* the current FPGA traditional interconnect. Remember that the embedded NoC is 1.3% of FPGA core area while the FPGA's traditional interconnect accounts for ~50% [21]. Traditional interconnect can still be used for latency-critical connections while the embedded NoC can be leveraged for connections on which timing closure is difficult or those that require buffering, stallability, or heavy switching.

## 5. APPLICATION CASE STUDIES

### 5.1 Simulator

To evaluate the performance of embedded NoCs, we created RTL2Booksim[2]: a simulation framework which allows the co-simulation of hardware description languages (HDL) such as Verilog and VHDL, and a widely-used cycle-accurate NoC simulator called Booksim [20].

---
[2]RTL2Booksim is available for download at www.eecg.utoronto.ca/~mohamed/rtl2booksim.html

Figure 15: Single-stream JPEG block diagram.

## 5.2 JPEG Compression

*(Latency-sensitive, streaming)*

We use a streaming JPEG compression design from [18]. The application consists of three modules as shown in Fig. 15; discrete cosine transform (DCT), quantizer (QNR) and run-length encoding (RLE). The single pipeline shown in Fig. 15 can accept one pixel per cycle and a data strobe that indicates the start of 64 consecutive pixels forming one (8×8) block on which the algorithm operates [18]. The components of this system are therefore latency-sensitive as they rely on pixels arriving every cycle, and the modules do not respond to backpressure.

We parallelize this application by instantiating multiple (10–40) JPEG pipelines in parallel; which means that the connection width between the DCT, QNR and RLE modules varies between 130 bits and 520 bits. Parallel JPEG compression is an important data-center application as multiple images are often required to be compressed at multiple resolutions before being stored in data-center disk drives; the back-end of large social networking websites and search engines. We implemented this parallel JPEG application using direct point-to-point links, then mapped the same design to use the embedded NoC between the modules using **Permapaths** similarly to Fig. 10. Using the `RTL2Booksim` simulator, we connected the JPEG design modules through the FabricPorts to the embedded NoC and verified functional correctness of the NoC-based JPEG. Additionally, we verified that throughput (in number of cycles) was the same for both the original and NoC versions; however, there are ~8 wasted cycles (equivalent to the zero-load latency of three hops) at the very beginning in the NoC version while the NoC link pipeline is getting populated with valid output data – these 8 cycles are of no consequence.

### 5.2.1 Frequency

To model the physical design repercussions (placement, routing, critical path delay) of using an embedded NoC, we emulated embedded NoC routers on FPGAs by creating 16 design partitions in Quartus II that are of size 7×5=35 logic clusters – each one of those partitions represents an embedded hard NoC router with its FabricPorts and interface to FPGA (see Fig. 18 for chip plan). We then connected the JPEG design modules to this emulated NoC. Additionally, we varied the physical location of the QNR and RLE modules (through location constraints) from "close" together on the FPGA chip to "far" on opposite ends of the chip. Note that the DCT module wasn't placed in a partition as it was a very large module and used most of the FPGA's DSP blocks.

Using location constraints, we investigated the result of a stretched critical path in an FPGA application. This could occur if the FPGA is highly utilized and it is difficult for the CAD tools to optimize the critical path as its endpoints are forced to be placed far apart, or when application modules connect to I/O interfaces and are therefore physically constrained far from one another. Fig. 16 plots the frequency of the original parallel JPEG and the NoC version. In the "close" configuration, the frequency of the original JPEG is higher than that of the NoC version by ~5%. This is because the JPEG pipeline is well-suited to the FPGA's traditional row/column interconnect. With the NoC version, the wide point-to-point links must be connected to the smaller area of 7×5 logic clusters (area of an embedded router); making the

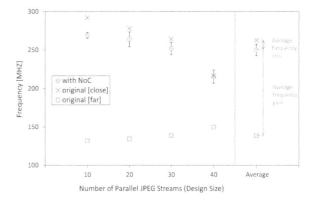

Figure 16: Frequency of the parallel JPEG compression application with and without an NoC. The plot "with NoC" is averaged for the two cases when it's "close" and "far" with the standard deviation plotted as error bars. Results are averaged over 3 seeds.

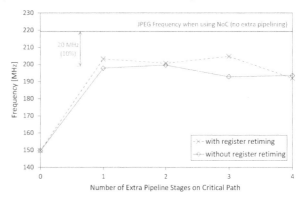

Figure 17: Frequency of parallel JPEG with 40 streams when we add 1-4 pipeline stages on the critical path. Frequency of the same application when connected to the NoC is plotted for comparison. Results are averaged over 3 seeds.

placement less regular and on average slightly lengthening the critical path.

The advantage of the NoC is highlighted in the "far" configuration when the QNR and RLE modules are placed far apart thus stretching the critical path across the chip diagonal. In the NoC version, we connect to the closest NoC router as shown in Fig. 18 – on average, the frequency improved by ~80%. Whether in the "far" or "close" setups, the NoC-version's frequency only varies by ~6% as the error bars show in Fig. 16. By relying on the NoC's predictable frequency in connecting modules together, the effects of the FPGA's utilization level and the modules' physical placement constraints become localized to each module instead of being a global effect over the entire design. Modules connected through the NoC become timing-independent making for an easier CAD problem and allowing parallel compilation.

With additional design effort, a designer of the original (without NoC) system would identify the critical path and attempt to pipeline it so as to improve the design's frequency. This design→compile→repipeline cycle hurts designer productivity as it can be unpredictable and compilation could take days for a large design [23]. We plot the frequency of our original JPEG with 40 streams in the "far" configuration after adding 1, 2, 3, and 4 pipeline registers on the critical path, both with and without register retiming optimizations, and we compare to the NoC version frequency in Fig. 17. The plot shows that the frequency of the pipelined version never becomes as good as that of the NoC version even with 4 pipeline stages – the NoC version is 10% better than original JPEG with pipelining.

Table 2: Interconnect utilization for JPEG with 40 streams in "far" configuration. Relative difference between NoC version and the original version is reported.

| Interconnect Resource | | Difference | Geomean |
|---|---|---|---|
| Short | Vertical (C4) | +13.2% | +10.2% |
| | Horizontal (R3,R6) | +7.8% | |
| Long | Vertical (C14) | -47.2% | -38.6% |
| | Horizontal (R24) | -31.6% | |

Wire naming convention: C=column, R=row, followed by number of logic clusters of wire length.

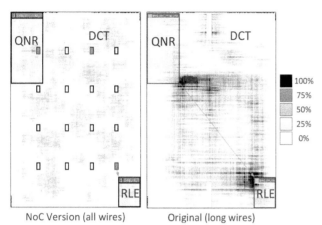

NoC Version (all wires)          Original (long wires)

Figure 18: Heat map showing total wire utilization for the NoC version, and only long-wire utilization for the original version of the JPEG application with 40 streams when modules are spaced out in the "far" configuration. In hot spots, utilization of scarce long wires in the original version goes up to 100%, while total wire utilization never exceeds 40% for the NoC version.

### 5.2.2 Interconnect Utilization

Table 2 quantifies the FPGA interconnect utilization difference for the two versions of 40-stream "far" JPEG. The NoC version reduces long wire utilization by ~40% but increases short wire utilization by ~10%. Note that long wires are scarce on FPGAs, for the Stratix V device we use, there are 25× more short wires than there are long wires. By offloading long connections onto an NoC, we conserve much of the valuable long wires.

Fig. 18 shows wire utilization for the two versions of 40-stream "far" JPEG and highlights that using the NoC does not produce any routing hot spots around the embedded routers. As the heat map shows, FPGA interconnect utilization does not exceed 40% in that case. Conversely, the original version utilizes long wires heavily on the long connection between QNR→RLE, with utilization going up to 100% in hot spots at the terminals of the long connection as shown in Fig. 18.

### 5.3  Ethernet Switch *(Latency-insensitive, streaming)*

One of the most important and prevalent building blocks of communication networks is the Ethernet switch. The embedded NoC provides a natural back-bone for an Ethernet switch design, as it includes (1) switching and (2) buffering within the NoC routers, and (3) a built-in backpressure mechanism for flow control. Recent work has revealed that an Ethernet switch achieves significant area and performance improvements when it leverages an NoC-enhanced FPGA [7]. We describe here how such an Ethernet switch can take full advantage of the embedded NoC, while demonstrating that it considerably outperforms the best previously proposed FPGA switch fabric design [11].

Table 3: Hardware cost breakdown of an NoC-based 10-Gb Ethernet switch on a Stratix V device.

| | 10GbE MACs | I/O Queues | Translators | **Total** |
|---|---|---|---|---|
| ALMs | 24000 | 3707 | 3504 | **31211** |
| M20Ks | 0 | 192 | 0 | **192** |

The embedded NoC is used in place of the switch's crossbar. For a 16×16 switch, each of the 16 transceiver nodes are connected to one of the 16 NoC routers via the FPGA's soft fabric. Fig. 19 shows the path between transceiver 1 and transceiver 2; in our 16×16 switch there are 256 such paths from each input to each output. On the receive path ($Rx$), Ethernet data is packed into NoC flits before being brought to the FabricPort input. The translator sets NoC control bits such that one NoC packet corresponds to one Ethernet frame. For example, a 512-byte Ethernet frame is converted into 32 NoC flits. After the NoC receives the flit from the FabricPort, it steers the flit to its destination, using dimension-order XY routing. On the transmit path ($Tx$), the NoC can output up to four flits (600 bits) from a packet in a single system clock cycle – this is demultiplexed in the output translator to the output queue width (150 bits). This demultiplexing accounts for most of the translators area in Table 3. The translator also strips away the NoC control bits before inserting the Ethernet data into the output queue. The design is synthesized on a Stratix V device. A breakdown of its FPGA resource utilization is shown in Table 3. Because we take advantage of the NoC's switching and buffering our switch is ~3× more area efficient than previous FPGA Ethernet switches [11].

Two important performance metrics for Ethernet switch design are bandwidth and latency [13]. The bandwidth of our NoC-based Ethernet switch is limited by the supported bandwidth of the embedded NoC. As described in Section 2, the NoC's links have a bandwidth capacity of 22.5 GB/s (180 Gb/s). Since some of this bandwidth is used to transport packet control information, the NoC's links can support up to 153.6 Gb/s of Ethernet data. Analysis of the worst case traffic in a 16-node mesh shows that the NoC can support a line rate of one third its link capacity, i.e. 51.2 Gb/s [7]. While previous work on FPGA switch design has achieved up to 160 Gb/s of aggregate bandwidth [11], our switch design can achieve 51.2×16 = 819.2 Gb/s by leveraging the embedded NoC. We have therefore implemented a programmable Ethernet switch with 16 inputs/outputs that is capable of either 10 Gb/s, 25 Gb/s or 40 Gb/s – three widely used Ethernet standards.

The average latency of our Ethernet switch design is measured using the RTL2Booksim simulator. An ON/OFF injection process is used to model bursty, uniform random traffic, with a fixed Ethernet frame size of 512 bytes (as was used in [11]). Latency is measured as the time between a packet head being injected into the input queue and it arriving out of the output queue. Fig. 20 plots the latency of our Ethernet switch at its supported line rates of 10 Gb/s, 25 Gb/s and 40 Gb/s. Surprisingly, the latency of a 512 byte packet improves at higher line rates. This is because a higher line rate means a faster rate of injecting NoC flits, and the NoC can handle the extra switching without a large latency penalty thus resulting in an improved overall latency. No matter what the injection bandwidth, the NoC-based switch considerably outperforms the Dai/Zhu switch [11] for all injection rates. By supporting these high line rates, our results show that an embedded NoC can push FPGAs into new communication network markets that are currently dominated by ASICs.

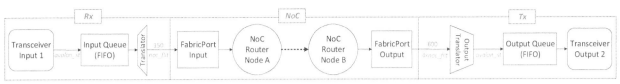

Figure 19: Functional block diagram of one path through our NoC Ethernet switch.

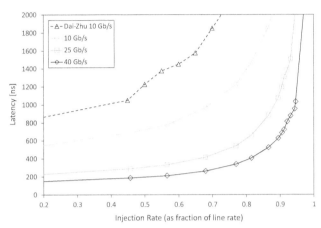

Figure 20: Latency vs. injection rate of the NoC-based Ethernet switch design given line rates of 10, 25, and 40 Gb/s, and compared to the Dai/Zhu 16×16 10 Gb/s FPGA switch fabric design [11]. Our switch queues and Dai/Zhu's switch queues are of size 60kb and 16kb, respectively.

# 6. CONCLUSION

We proposed augmenting FPGAs with an embedded NoC and focused on how to use the NoC for transporting data in FPGA applications of different design styles. The FabricPort is a flexible interface between the embedded NoC and the FPGA's core; it can bridge any fabric frequency and data width up to 600 bits to the faster but narrower NoC at 1.2 GHz and 150 bits. We have shown that latency-insensitive systems can be interconnected using an embedded NoC with lower hardware overhead by taking advantage of the NoC's built-in buffering. Additionally, we showed how latency-sensitive systems can be guaranteed fixed delay and throughput through the NoC by using Permapaths.

We investigated two streaming applications; latency-sensitive JPEG that only requires wires between modules, and a latency-insensitive Ethernet switch that requires heavy arbitration and switching between its transceiver modules. With an embedded NoC, JPEG's frequency can be improved by 10–80%. Wire utilization is also improved, as the embedded NoC avoids wiring hotspots and reduces the use of scarce long wires by 40% at the expense of a 10% increase of the much more plentiful short wires. Finally, we showed that high-bandwidth Ethernet switches can be efficiently constructed on the FPGA; by leveraging an embedded NoC we created an 819 Gb/s programmable Ethernet switch – a major improvement over the 160 Gb/s achieved by prior work in a traditional FPGA.

# 7. ACKNOWLEDGMENTS

We are indebted to Prof. Natalie Enright-Jerger and her research team (Shehab Elsayed, Mario Badr and Robert Hesse) for NoC discussions and for providing some of the code used to build RTL2Booksim. We would also like to thank David Lewis, Mike Hutton, Dana How and Desh Singh for feedback on FPGAs, and Kevin Murray for feedback on latency-insensitive design. This work is funded by Altera, NSERC and Vanier CGS.

# 8. REFERENCES

[1] M. S. Abdelfattah. FPGA NoC Designer. www.eecg.utoronto.ca/~mohamed/noc_designer.html.

[2] M. S. Abdelfattah and V. Betz. Design Tradeoffs for Hard and Soft FPGA-based Networks-on-Chip. In *FPT*, pages 95–103, 2012.

[3] M. S. Abdelfattah and V. Betz. The Power of Communication: Energy-Efficient NoCs for FPGAs. In *FPL*, pages 1–8, 2013.

[4] M. S. Abdelfattah and V. Betz. Networks-on-Chip for FPGAs: Hard, Soft or Mixed? *TRETS*, 7(3):20:1–20:22, 2014.

[5] M. S. Abdelfattah and V. Betz. The Case for Embedded Networks-on-Chip on Field-Programmable Gate Arrays. *IEEE Micro*, 34(1):80–89, 2014.

[6] Altera Corp. Video and Image Processing Suite, 2014.

[7] A. Bitar et al. Efficient and programmable Ethernet switching with a NoC-enhanced FPGA. In *ANCS*, 2014.

[8] L. Carloni and A. Sangiovanni-Vincentelli. Coping with latency in SOC design. *IEEE Micro*, 22(5):24–35, 2002.

[9] E. S. Chung, J. C. Hoe, and K. Mai. CoRAM: An In-Fabric Memory Architecture for FPGA-based Computing. In *FPGA*, pages 97–106, 2011.

[10] D. U. Becker. *Efficient Microarchitecture for Network on Chip Routers*. PhD thesis, Stanford University, 2012.

[11] Z. Dai and J. Zhu. Saturating the Transceiver BW: Switch Fabric Design on FPGAs. In *FPGA*, pages 67–75, 2012.

[12] W. J. Dally and B. Towles. *Principles and Practices of Interconnection Networks*. Morgan Kaufmann Publishers, Boston, MA, 2004.

[13] I. Elhanany et al. The network processing forum switch fabric benchmark specifications: An overview. *IEEE Network*, 19(2):5–9, 2005.

[14] N. Enright Jerger, L.-S. Peh, and M. Lipasti. Virtual circuit tree multicasting: A case for on-chip hardware multicast support. In *ISCA*, pages 229–240, 2008.

[15] R. Francis and S. Moore. Exploring Hard and Soft Networks-on-Chip for FPGAs. In *FPT*, pages 261–264, 2008.

[16] K. Goossens, J. Dielissen, and A. Radulescu. Aethereal network on chip: Concepts, architectures, and implementations. *IEEE Design and Test*, 22(5), 2005.

[17] K. Goossens et al. Hardwired Networks on Chip in FPGAs to Unify Functional and Configuration Interconnects. In *NOCS*, pages 45–54, 2008.

[18] A. Henson and R. Herveille. Video Compression Systems. www.opencores.org/project,video_systems, 2008.

[19] R. Ho, K. W. Mai, and M. A. Horowitz. The Future of Wires. *Proceedings of the IEEE*, 89(4):490–504, 2001.

[20] N. Jiang et al. A Detailed and Flexible Cycle-Accurate Network-on-Chip Simulator. In *ISPASS*, pages 86–96, 2013.

[21] D. Lewis et al. Architectural Enhancements in Stratix V. In *FPGA*, pages 147–156, 2013.

[22] R. Lu and C.-K. Koh. Performance optimization of latency insensitive systems through buffer queue sizing of communication channels. In *ICCAD*, pages 227–231, 2003.

[23] K. E. Murray and V. Betz. Quantifying the Cost and Benefit of Latency Insensitive Communication on FPGAs. In *FPGA*, pages 223–232, 2014.

[24] A. Putnam et al. A reconfigurable fabric for accelerating large-scale datacenter services. In *ISCA*, pages 13–24, 2014.

[25] D. J. Sorin et al. A Primer on Memory Consistency and Cache Coherence. *Synthesis Lectures on Computer Architecture*, 6(3):1–212, 2011.

[26] Xilinx Inc. Virtex-5,6,7 Family Overview, 2009-2014.

[27] A. Ye and J. Rose. Using Bus-based Connections to Improve Field-programmable Gate-array Density for Implementing Datapath Circuits. *TVLSI*, 14(5):462–473, 2006.

# Enhancements in UltraScale CLB Architecture

Shant Chandrakar
Xilinx Inc.
Hyderabad, India
shantc@xilinx.com

Dinesh Gaitonde
Xilinx Inc.
San Jose, CA
dineshg@xilinx.com

Trevor Bauer
Xilinx Inc.
Longmont, CO
trevor@xilinx.com

## ABSTRACT

Each generation of FPGA architecture benefits from optimizations around its technology node and target usage. In this paper, we discuss some of the changes made to the CLB for Xilinx's 20nm UltraScale product family. We motivate those changes and demonstrate better results than previous CLB architectures on a variety of metrics. We show that, in demanding scenarios, logic placed in an UltraScale device requires 16% less wirelength than 7-series. Designs mapped to UltraScale devices also require fewer logic tiles. In this paper, we demonstrate the utilization benefits of the UltraScale CLB attributed to certain CLB enhancements. The enhancements described herein result in an average packing improvement of 3% for the example design suite. We also show that the UltraScale architecture handles aggressive, tighter packing more gracefully than previous generations of FPGA. These significant reductions in wirelength and CLB counts translate directly into power, performance and ease-of-use benefits.

## Categories and Subject Descriptors

B.5.2 [**REGISTER-TRANSFER-LEVEL IMPLEMENTATION**]: Design Aids—*Optimization*; B.6.1 [**LOGIC DESIGN**]: Design Styles—*Logic arrays*; B.7.2 [**INTEGRATED CIRCUITS**]: Design Aids—*Placement and routing*

## Keywords

FPGA, CLB, packing, placement, routing, logic array, control set, wirelength

## 1. INTRODUCTION

At each technology node, the architecture of an FPGA fabric needs to be reconsidered. Customer use models and physical implementation algorithms also play a significant role in the design and evaluation of the FPGA fabric. Xilinx recently introduced the UltraScale architecture for TSMC's 20nm process. In this paper, we compare several key aspects of the UltraScale CLB with the previous generation, 7-series CLB. Through experimental results, we motivate some of the changes made between these two CLB definitions. We describe how these decisions were informed by the technology constraints and opportunities. We also describe what modifications were performed to support the increasingly complex demands customers place on their FPGAs. This paper is focused on a subset of the changes made to the CLB structure. A small change to the CLB is shown to make a large impact in the resources required to route difficult designs. Using fewer routing resources enables lower congestion, improved power and higher performance. More information about other aspects of the FPGA fabric and other blocks in UltraScale has been published elsewhere[10].

We demonstrate the benefits of the changes using large designs representing real customer use cases.

## 2. 7-SERIES CLB & SLICE DEFINITION

The Configurable Logic Block (CLB) is the FPGA's main logic resource for implementing combinatorial and sequential logic functions. Each CLB is connected to the general routing fabric through a switch matrix. The Xilinx 7-series CLB, shown in Figure 1, consists of two slices. Figure 2 represents a typical SLICEL found in 7-Series CLBs. The SLICEL is built from Basic Logic Elements (BELs) such as Look up Tables (LUTs), flops, carry logic and wide-function multiplexers. Each slice consists of four 6-input LUTs, each of which can implement any combinatorial function of up to six inputs. The 6-input LUT can also be used as two 5-input LUTs, provided the combined number of unique inputs is less than six. Each slice also contains eight flops, four of which are primary, having direct connectivity to and from the switch matrix; the other four are secondary with indirect fabric connectivity only through LUTs. Another type of slice, called SLICEM, enables distributed memories and shift registers in addition to SLICEL capability.

There are two types of flops in the SLICEL, primary and secondary, differentiated by their connectivity. Primary flops have direct connectivity to the switch matrix through their respective Q pins (i.e. AQ, BQ, CQ, DQ). The secondary flop outputs do not have direct connectivity to the switch matrix; rather, they are required to share an output with other SLICEL signals. Further, each primary/secondary pair of flops shares a single bypass input (i.e. AX, BX, CX, DX). Thus, only one flop in each pair can be driven directly from the switch matrix; the other requires a LUT configured as a logic function or buffer. This

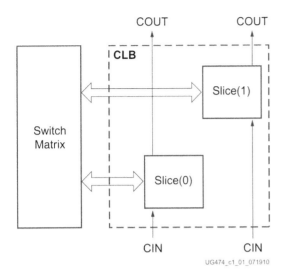

Figure 1: Arrangement of Slices within the CLB taken from Virtex 7 User Guide [6]

connectivity biases the packer to use only one of the two flops for independent registering.

Another factor determining the usage of flops in CLBs is control set resolution. The signals that control a flop are the clock(CLK), set/reset(SR) and clock enable(CE). The collection of these three signals is called the control set of a flop. Two flops are said to have compatible control sets if they share the same CLK, SR and CE nets. Figure 3 shows the connectivity of the control sets to all the flops in a 7-series CLB. Only one control set can exist in each slice. So, for example, two distinct clock signals cannot drive flops within the same slice. Since a 7-series CLB has two slices, flops that get mapped to one CLB have to be partitionable to at most two control sets, each of which cannot exceed eight flops.

## 3. FPGA FABRIC TRENDS

CLBs and interconnect are key resources in each FPGA fabric. Overall system performance, cost and power are impacted by the characteristics of these ubiquitous resources. The CLB and interconnect design needs to support the latest technology requirements and new user demands. Moreover, the tools and architecture must work effectively together.

### 3.1 Routability

As has been documented [1], interconnect is a key bottleneck to technology scaling. Wires are not scaling as well as gates. Increased bandwidth demands in customer designs translate into wider buses, meaning more wires are required. This trend will continue. Thus, anything that can be done in an FPGA fabric or physical implementation tool to reduce the number of routing resources required for a given design will help respond to this trend.

### 3.2 Performance

Similar to routability, design performance is also, to a large extent, determined by interconnect use. Interconnect delay has come to be a significant fraction of total delay

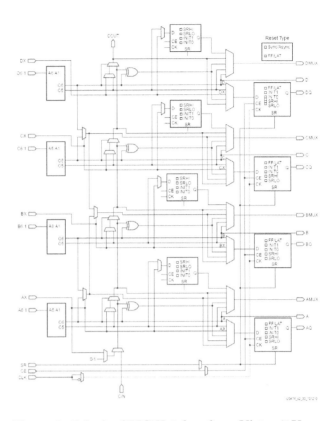

Figure 2: 7-Series SLICEL taken from Virtex 7 User Guide [6]

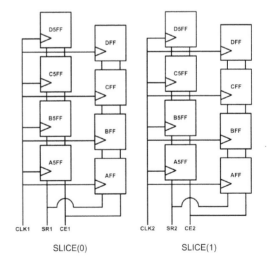

Figure 3: Connectivity of control set signals to the flops of 7-Series CLB

in critical paths. The UltraScale CLB architecture is optimized to aid placement and routing algorithms achieve critical paths with fewer interconnect resources. Another technique often used to improve performance is pipelining. Achieving the maximum benefit from pipelining requires the pipeline flops to be placed in ideal locations. Any perturbation in flop placement due to architectural restrictions will impact the benefit of pipelining.

## 3.3 Power

Power consumption is also important. In recent FPGA generations, more designs have been limited by their power budgets. One technique that has achieved good results is aggressive clock gating. Algorithms exist [3], supported by implementation tools [5], which can synthesize aggressive dynamic clock gating conditions to save power. Synthesis of these structures results in fragmented control sets for flops, further impacting packing density.

## 3.4 Software Tools

A CLB architecture definition has implications on software tools. Consider, for example, the disparate demands on the slice structure. Due to shared connectivity within a slice, there are restrictions on what logic can be packed into a single slice. At the level above a slice, few restrictions exist on placement. Questions about whether a given placement of slices is legal, in terms of whether it violates any FPGA restrictions, are easy to answer. Whether a collection of BELs that are packed into a slice is legal is a much tougher question to answer [4]. Fewer restrictions on what logic can be packed into a slice improves tool run-time, tool predictability and design performance.

## 4. ULTRASCALE CLB

The UltraScale CLB is designed to improve routability, performance and power. It also helps improve tool runtime and predictability. The changes primarily involved making the flops in a slice more accessible. This increased usability is provided via two key changes in the architecture. First, independent access to all flop inputs and from all flop outputs is possible in UltraScale. Second, more unique control sets are legally placeable in the same slice.

The UltraScale CLB has the same number of LUTs and flops as a 7-series CLB. However, the UltraScale CLB is organized as a single, coarser slice having the same capacity as two 7-series slices. The functionality of the LUTs and flops has been retained. Figure 5 shows one of the eight LUT-flop pairs available in the UltraScale CLB.

In contrast to the 7-series CLB, which has one bypass input for every two flops, the UltraScale CLB has just as many bypass inputs as flops. This allows direct access to all CLB flops without consuming the corresponding LUTs. Additionally, while secondary flops in 7-series share an output with other slice functionality, all flops in UltraScale slices have their own, direct and independent output pins connecting to the switch matrix. Normally, adding extra pins is expensive since the switch matrix also has to be scaled to accommodate the new pins. In UltraScale, however, this cost has been amortized over the other pins. There have been significant changes to the architecture in UltraScale compared to 7-series. What we describe here are UltraScale modifications relevant to the changes described above. As shown in Figure 6, general interconnect wires drive CLB in-

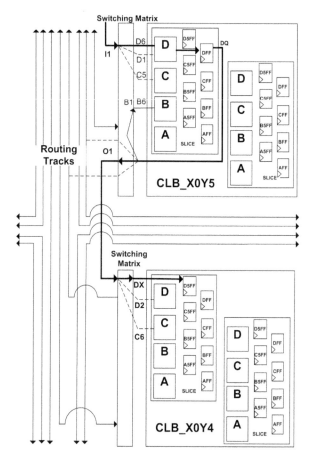

**Figure 4: A simplified representation of routing in 7-series**

puts and are in turn driven by CLB outputs. In 7-series, the general interconnect drives 56 inputs in a CLB made of just SLICELs and 60 inputs in a CLB made of SLICEL and SLICEM. The general interconnect is driven by 24 outputs from the CLB. In UltraScale, the general interconnect connects to each CLB through 64 inputs and 32 outputs.

Although the number of input and output pins on the CLB increased from 7-series to Ultrascale, the number of general interconnect signals (singles, doubles) driving the CLB did not. A simple implementation of the input change would require 8 more input muxes for SLICELs to accommodate the extra inputs and the associated cost of a more complicated switch matrix. Instead of incurring this cost, we repurposed existing muxes in the 7-series. As a result, some amount of the flexibility at the input switch matrix is lost. Experiments showed that the marginal loss in flexibility was a price worth paying for all the other benefits of this change (details of the benefits are described later on in the paper). Characteristics of designs mapped to UltraScale are expected to be different than in 7-series. The CLB architecture was changed to accomodate the new design styles.

The number of CLB outputs increased from 24 in 7-series to 32 in UltraScale. The extra outputs support the independent flip-flop outputs. This increase did not drive any downstream modifications to the general interconnect; rather, flexibility in the reach of each output was reduced proportionally. In short, both for non-control inputs and outputs, extra CLB flexibility was introduced at the expense of flexibility with respect to general interconnect.

These changes have made the job of placing flops on a device easier. Consider the objective of a placer. The placer tries to create a legal, routable placement which meets a design's timing constraints and minimizes wirelength. In order to do this, the placer needs to have an idea of how much capacity each slice has. In 7-series, the number of LUTs available in the slice depends on how many flops in the slice require a LUT route-thru and the number of flops available in the slice depends on how many LUTs are prevented from being used as route-thrus. This makes accounting for capacity cumbersome for the placer. Specifically, it is not easy for the placer to decide whether it should replace a logical LUT with a route-thru LUT to accommodate an additional flop or remove an existing flop to replace a route-thru LUT with a logical LUT. The UltraScale CLB solves this problem with bypass inputs and independent outputs for all flops. This enhancement benefits highly pipelined designs, allowing the device to support high performance designs. It also reduces the number of resources wasted - LUTs used as route-thrus or flop locations left empty.

One other enhancement from the 7-series CLB to the UltraScale CLB is the ability to pack more diverse control sets in one CLB. Specifically, flops that have more unique clock enables and reset nets can now be packed together in one CLB, as shown in Figure 7. Figure 8 shows the connectivity of the control sets to the 7-Series and UltraScale CLB. The control set signals of adjacent CLBs are driven primarily by common global control wires. There are 12 control set signals for a pair of adjacent 7-Series CLBs which are driven by global control wires. In order to accommodate extra clock enables in the UltraScale CLB, the number of control muxes was increased by 6.

This change of having flops with more diverse control sets packable in the same CLB also benefits power consumption.

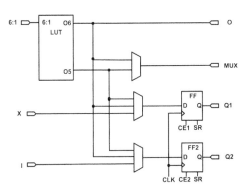

Figure 5: 1 of the 8 LUT-flop pair from UltraScale CLB [8]

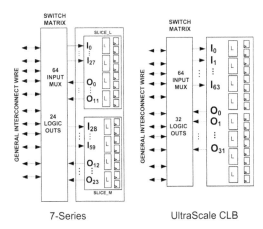

Figure 6: Interface between CLB input and output with general interconnect wires

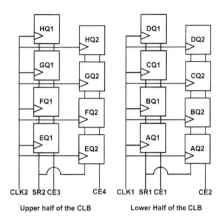

**Figure 7: Connectivity of control set signals to the flops of UltraScale CLB**

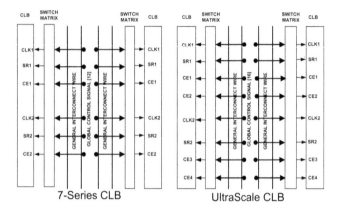

**Figure 8: Interface between CLB's control set signals with general interconnect wires and global control signals.**

One very effective way of reducing dynamic power in the fabric is by synthesizing clock gating logic. This saves unnecessary clock and data switching. Both 7-series and UltraScale CLBs and tools support power reduction this way in Vivado [9]. More clock enables imply more control sets for the flops, thereby reducing the likelihood that two randomly chosen flops can coexist in a slice. If the wirelength of a placed design increases due to the synthesis of more control sets, then the power savings from reduced switching on the clock tree would be squandered due to longer routes.

In summary, changes were made to the UltraScale CLB to enable tighter packing. This reduces power consumption, both due to shorter wirelengths and enabling more aggressive clock gating. This also improves performance and reduces demand on interconnect. In the next section we show experimental results that validate these claims.

## 5. RESULTS

### 5.1 Experimental Setup

We now describe experiments we performed to validate the advantages of UltraScale CLBs. Since these CLB enhancements are not the only thing that changed from 7-series, we extract the effect of these changes by designing targeted experiments. For example, one would expect UltraScale de-

signs to be faster than 7-series due to technology scaling or a variety of other architectural enhancements. As a result, we don't compare 7-series metrics directly with UltraScale. Instead we compute how metrics are impacted by different kinds of stress in 7-series and UltraScale.

The designs we chose for this work are all customer designs or IPs. Their identifying characteristics have been removed from our results. These designs include a variety of FPGA resources in addition to flops and LUTs, such as Block RAMs, DSPs, etc... These designs are implemented on comparable 7-Series and UltraScale devices. We have used the Vivado Design Suite for implementing the designs [9].

Designers want to use as many resources as possible from a given device. Therefore, while implementing a design, they would target close to 100% device utilization if possible. In order to force the placer to pack aggressively, we create several scenarios for each design. Each scenario represents an increasingly aggressive packing requirement. This is achieved by imposing a series of increasingly tightened area constraints. Figure 9 shows the flow used to achieve the increasingly aggressive scenarios.

As the placeable area reduces, the tools struggle to pack the design. While doing this, the tools have to trade off some design metric, wirelength or performance, to achieve legal packing. At the extreme, if we force the design to fit in an area which does not have enough resources, then the placer will simply fail. These area constraints are imposed on the Vivado placer using pblocks.

UltraScale architecture is different from 7-series in more than just the CLB changes. We isolated the impact of just the CLB changes by modifying Vivado's flow for placing a design. Placers in general and Vivado's placer in particular, use an approximate view of the targeted architecture when placing a design. Specifically, placers use bounding box as a metric (or some variant thereof) to estimate how much routing resources a specific placement will take. They also employ simple metrics to judge whether a given placement will meet timing and route succesfully. All these metrics are very architecture dependent, except possibly the bounding box metric. In our experiments, we turn off all response from Vivado to any architecture specific tuning, except for the new CLB structure. We do this to ensure that the tool is not optimizing for any feature of UltraScale besides the CLB changes. Secondly, during placement, in order to meet timing constraints, the Vivado placer estimates the delay for each connection. This estimate depends on other aspects of the architecture. We force Vivado to use the same delay estimates irrespective of which architecture is targeted. Finally, unless otherwise stated, the results reported represent the placer's predictions. In order to avoid favoring any one architecture, we don't run the router. Results reported post placement are purely a function of CLB logic changes and reflect no benefit of any other architectural changes.

In all the scenarios, we try to keep the aspect ratio of the pblocks as square as possible. By doing this we ensure that the shape does not affect the wirelength in either horizontal or vertical direction. Since we don't bias the pblock in any direction, we don't favor the particular characteristics of any one architecture. We show in subsequent sections how the UltraScale CLB is able to handle this stress more gracefully than 7-series, achieving higher utilization and lower wirelength.

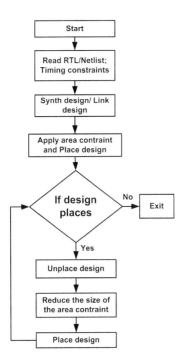

**Figure 9: Methodology to create aggressive packing scenario**

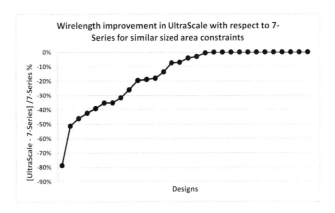

**Figure 10: Percentage improvement in wirelength for UltraScale compared to 7-series**

In order to measure the UltraScale and 7-Series CLB response to aggressive packing, there is a need to identify the smallest possible region below which the design would fail. Since we are interested in understanding CLB changes only, we did not constrain the placement of non CLB resources to within the pblock. If we did try to do this, placement would fail due to particular characteristics of the device chosen rather than anything inherent in the CLB architecture. Therefore, the area constraint is only applied on the CLB resources.

## 5.2 Routability

One predictor for the number of routing resources required for a given design is the wirelength of the placement that the software generates. Wirelength is not a metric with complete fidelity to routability, but it is a close proxy. Most placement tools, all else being equal, attempt to minimize wirelength for a given design [2]. Improvements in placement and routing algorithms have a huge impact on total wirelength. Similarly, improvements in architecture, all else being equal, impact routability and wirelength. In an attempt to isolate the impact of the CLB changes, the same design suite and same software were used.

The extent to which the tool has to sacrifice wirelength in the interests of legality is an indication of how flexible the CLB architecture is. Figure 10 shows the improvement in wirelength generated by tools on UltraScale devices compared to 7-series under similar packing constraints, i.e. similar sized area constraints. The size of each area constraint chosen is the one that corresponds to the smallest succesful 7-series placement. Wirelength of a placed design is computed as the sum of the Manhattan bounding box of each net in the design. For each net, Manhattan bounding box is computed in tile based units. This ensures that the wirelengths for the two experiments are comparable. We see an

average wirelength reduction of 16% in UltraScale compared to 7-series.

Since we only report bounding box wirelength, the improvement in wirelength is primarily explained by changes to the CLB logic architecture. Since wirelength is a primary metric optimized by placers to help routability, these results show that designs on UltraScale devices would be easier to route than 7-series even if the area constraints are tight. Smaller wirelength is also correlated with better performance and lower power consumption.

## 5.3 Effective Packing

We demonstrate the packing benefits of the UltraScale CLB by considering how densely we can pack our designs and still have successful placement. Given a design and an unconstrained FPGA device, the tools are free to use the entire device to place and route. Getting the densest packing is not one of the primary cost functions that the Vivado software optimizes. Instead, by not forcing the densest placement, the software is able to optimize for the best performance and power of a given design in the selected device. As a result, dense area constraints are required to demonstrate the minimal number of CLBs required for a design. Figures 11 and 12 show examples of placements achieved through unconstrained and constrained implementation of a design on 7-series using the above methodology.

Figure 13 shows the percentage of fewer CLBs UltraScale requires compared to 7-series under the tightest area constraints. The tightest area constraints represent the smallest number of CLBs used to achieve legal placement in both the architectures. Designs required as much as 14% fewer CLBs in UltraScale compared to 7-Series. On average, these CLB changes resulted in a 3% CLB reduction in UltraScale compared to 7-series. The UltraScale architecture provides many other improvements in density thanks to other changes from 7-series to UltraScale, including clocking, routing and IP [7].

As the graph in Figure 13 shows, the reduction in the number of CLBs achieved by UltraScale is not uniform. It depends on the design characteristics. The connectivity to and from secondary flops and control set restrictions impose constraints on the placer. Designs for which these restrictions impose a burden show more improvement in UltraScale compared to 7-series.

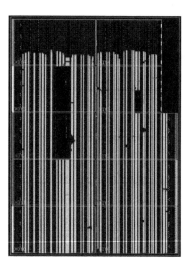

Figure 11: Default placement for a design on 7-series, taken from floorplanning view of Vivado [9]

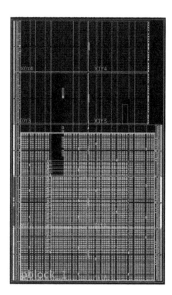

Figure 12: Constrained placement for a design in the smallest area on 7-series, taken from floorplanning view of Vivado [9]

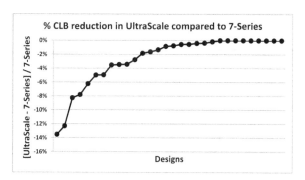

Figure 13: Percentage improvement in number of CLBs used by UltraScale compared to 7-series

In both 7-series and UltraScale, two "smaller" LUTs can be placed in one LUT6 location as long as the number of unique inputs from the two LUTs is less' than six. This provides an opportunity to place flops in a CLB even if a secondary input is not available. As a result, the amount of usable flexibility offered by UltraScale CLB changes depends on the distribution of LUT sizes in the design. As the packer tries to merge small LUTs, it is successful more often in UltraScale than in 7-series. This is because the merging operation is not possible if the flop also requires the LUT to be configured as a route-through buffer.

Designs which are LUT-dominated and have a distribution of LUT sizes permitting extensive LUT merging show improved packing in UltraScale. For flop dominated designs, two different aspects of the design determine how effective our changes are. If the design has a lot of unique control sets, or if a design is flop dominated with a large fraction requiring independent access, the UltraScale CLB achieves improved packing efficiency. We expect that high performance design techniques such as aggressive pipelining and low power design techniques such as clock gating will result in more designs benefiting from UltraScale changes.

### 5.4 Performance

Similar to the previous experiments, we constrained each design to be placed in as small a region as possible. We expect a trend in predicted performance similar to what we see for predicted wirelength. As we tighten the region given to the placer performance suffers as the placer struggles to accommodate the design in the region. As the region is constrained further, the design fails to place. One measure of how forgiving the architecture is, is the ratio of the frequency achieved for a given area constraint as a percentage of the frequency achieved with 80% LUT utilization (baseline frequency). Figure 14 shows how the frequency of one particular design changes during this experiment. This particular design had 97K flops, 70K LUTs and 1100 control sets. While many other designs do not have trouble achieving much higher utilizations than 80% in 7-series, already a noticeable improvement over previous architectures, UltraScale is able to achieve close to maximum LUT utilization. Further, at the tightest achieved packing, UltraScale maintains performance within 12% of the baseline frequency. The same design when packed tightly into 7-series, shows about 20% degradation before struggling to pack.

Figure 15 shows the performance degradation across multiple designs in UltraScale and 7-Series for similar sized area

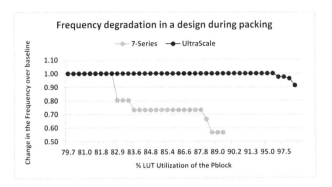

Figure 14: How frequency of one design changes in UltraScale and 7-series during the packing experiment

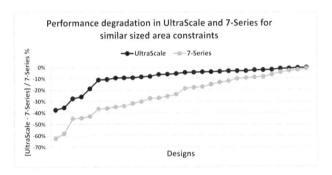

Figure 15: How performance changes For UltraScale and 7-series as design is constrained to tighter regions

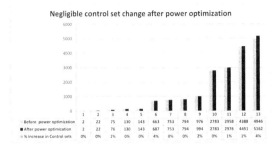

Figure 16: No effect of power optimization on the control set count

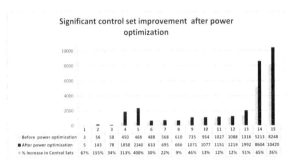

Figure 17: Marked increase in the number of control sets with power optimization

constraints. The average performance degradation of these designs in UltraScale is 9% and in 7-Series is 24%. This implies that the performance of the UltraScale CLB architecture is maintained over more aggressive packing i.e. higher CLB utilizations.

It is important to restate here that these experiments were done in order to isolate the effect of CLB changes. In Figures 14 and 15, we do not report results after routing. Results reported after routing would have been contaminated with non-CLB architecture changes as well. We only report results post-placement. All results quoted are assuming the same delay model for interconnect delay across the two architectures. Needless to say, the improvements reported here are sustained through routing.

## 5.5 Power Optimization

In order to achieve more power reduction benefits from clock gating, we expect more diverse control sets in the future. Reducing power consumption has become an important optimization goal for FPGA users. We mimic a customer implementing clock gating for dynamic power reduction. We reduce power by using the *power_opt_design* [9] command. This command synthesizes extra clock enables for flops whose clocks can be safely gated.

In this experiment we observe that in some designs, power optimization does not create new clock enables (Figure 16). In other designs, it does (Figure 17). Figure 18 shows that, with power optimization, the UltraScale architecture can handle the increase in control sets. In the context of

power optimization, Vivado is able to gate clocks more aggressively in UltraScale without having adverse impacts on CLB utilization, wirelength and design performance.

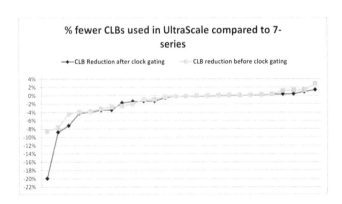

Figure 18: Percentage improvement in number of CLBs used by UltraScale compared to 7-series after power optimization

# 6. CONCLUSIONS

We've compared the CLBs from UltraScale and 7-series, specifically with respect to the connectivity of their flops. Analysis has shown that the independent access provided to the flop inputs, outputs and control sets can improve the quality of a design's placement, including reductions in wirelength and increases in utilization. Increases in design complexity require more routing resources. We've shown here that there are ways of dealing with this besides just increasing the number of routing resources in the interconnect. Changes to the CLB logic can address the interconnect demand side of the problem as well.

# 7. ACKNOWLEDGEMENTS

We would like to thank several colleagues at Xilinx, too many to be individually named, for helping run some of the experiments and in discussing their implications. We also appreciate the constructive feedback from the anonymous reviewers.

# 8. REFERENCES

[1] X. Chen, J. Liang, and H.-S. P. Wong. Interconnect scaling into the sub-10nm regime. In *Proceedings of the International Workshop on System Level Interconnect Prediction*, SLIP '12, pages 2–2, New York, NY, USA, 2012. ACM.

[2] J. Cong, J. R. Shinnerl, M. Xie, T. Kong, and X. Yuan. Large-scale circuit placement. *ACM Trans. Des. Autom. Electron. Syst.*, 10(2):389–430, Apr. 2005.

[3] A. P. Hurst. Automatic synthesis of clock gating logic with controlled netlist perturbation. In L. Fix, editor, *DAC*, pages 654–657. ACM, 2008.

[4] J. Luu, J. H. Anderson, and J. Rose. Architecture description and packing for logic blocks with hierarchy, modes and complex interconnect. In *Proceedings of the ACM/SIGDA 19th International Symposium on Field Programmable Gate Arrays, FPGA 2011, Monterey, California, USA, February 27, March 1, 2011*, pages 227–236, 2011.

[5] F. Rivoallon and J. Balasubramanian. *Reducing Switching Power with Intelligent Clock Gating*. Xilinx.

[6] Xilinx. *7 Series FPGAs Configurable Logic Block - User Guide*.

[7] Xilinx. *UltraScale Architecture and Product Overview*.

[8] Xilinx. *UltraScale Architecture Configurable Logic Block Advance Specification User Guide*.

[9] Xilinx. *Vivado Design Suite User Guide*.

[10] S. Young, D. Gaitonde, and T. Bauer. Xilinx FPGAs case study: High capacity and performance 20nm FPGAs. HotChips, 2014.

# DISCLAIMER

# Floating-Point DSP Block Architecture for FPGAs

Martin Langhammer
Altera European Technology Centre, UK

Bogdan Pasca
Altera European Technology Centre, UK

## ABSTRACT

This work describes the architecture of a new FPGA DSP block supporting both fixed and floating point arithmetic. Each DSP block can be configured to provide one single precision IEEE-754 floating multiplier and one IEEE-754 floating point adder, or when configured in fixed point mode, the block is completely backwards compatible with current FPGA DSP blocks. The DSP block operating frequency is similar in both modes, in the region of 500MHz, offering up to 2 GMACs fixed point and 1 GFLOPs performance per block. In floating point mode, support for multi-block vector modes are provided, where multiple blocks can be seamlessly assembled into any size real or complex dot products. By efficient reuse of the fixed point arithmetic modules, as well as the fixed point routing, the floating point features have only minimal power and area impact. We show how these blocks are implemented in a modern Arria 10 FPGA family, offering over 1 TFLOPs using only embedded structures, and how scaling to multiple TFLOPs densities is possible for planned devices.

## 1. INTRODUCTION

FPGAs are increasingly being used as compute platforms, whether in traditional computing applications, or in more complex embedded functions. Floating-point (FP) arithmetic is required for many of these use cases, which often include algorithms such as matrix decompositions. Mainstream adoption of FPGAs as compute accelerators requires FP capabilities ranging from basic operators to elementary functions. It was shown that FPGAs can outperform competing platforms when computing elementary functions [15, 16]; however, operations such as matrix decompositions require simpler standard operators, such as adders and multipliers, but in great numbers. Implementing these large datapaths requires significant logic resources which impact area, power and latency.

Embedded floating-point units are therefore required, but in the context of an FPGA and not an Application Specific Standard Product (ASSP). To make FPGAs floating-point usable while maintaining the economies of scale of a standard FPGA product, such units must have minimal impact on area, power, and fixed-point functionality. This is one key factor often overlooked in previous works

which embedded FP functionality in the FPGA fabric. Many device families from both major vendors [8, 6] have several product groupings, each with different ratios of embedded functions to soft logic, such as transceivers in the case of wireline targeted devices, and DSP blocks in the case of signal processing targeted devices. The cost of the DSP blocks for a given device is determined by percentage of core area, from less than 1% for a transceiver focused device to 5% for a DSP focused device. Therefore, the addition of floating-point functionality to DSP blocks is worthy goal; if a modest area penalty is applied to every DSP block, there will be essentially a negligible impact to non-DSP users.

The problem is in finding an effective DSP architecture that supports both useful fixed and floating-point implementations. Ideally, the fixed-point functionality will be backwards compatible to current DSP blocks, with the floating point features introducing no performance, latency, or power penalty. Conversely, the floating-point features must also offer the same clock rates and power consumption as the fixed point modes. In many DSP or arithmetic algorithms, one multiplier output is added to another, which is well supported by existing DSP block architectures; for example, cascade chains from one DSP block to another to support FIR filters in direct form I or systolic modes. These types of features must also be considered for floating-point DSP blocks, but the different bus width to function densities will require new types of inter-function connection structures.

The contributions of this paper are two-fold: (a) embedding high performance FP capabilities into the DSP blocks by reusing the fixed-point hardware, keeping full fixed-point backwards compatibility and maintaining fixed-point performance, and (b) cascading DSP block structures in FP mode that allow for efficient mapping of scalar-product operations. The efficient reuse of existing fixed-point hardware, combined with the low-area and low-latency design for the FP cores, requires an approximate 10% DSP area overhead to provide a fully functional single-precision floating-point unit (adder and multiplier), supporting rounding to nearest (RNE) and with subnormal flushing to zero on inputs and outputs. This has a maximum of 0.5% silicon penalty for applications not using this feature, even in the case of a DSP targeted device with 5% of total die core area used for DSP blocks. Embedding FP blocks as separate units, which is suggested by previous works, would lead to significantly larger area penalties in non-FP applications.

The rest of the paper is organized as follows. Section 2 briefly reviews floating point terminology. Section 3 reviews prior work on embedded floating-point functions in FPGAs. Section 4 introduces the new DSP block architecture that supports both fixed and FP arithmetic, as well as discussing the multi-block, or vector, mode. Section 5 gives a more detailed description of the micro-architecture of the arithmetic structures used in the block. Sec-

*FPGA'15*, February 22–24, 2015, Monterey, California, USA.
Copyright © ACM 978-1-4503-3315-3/15/02 ...$15.00.
http://dx.doi.org/10.1145/2684746.2689071.

tion 6 presents results for common applications, including FFTs, FIR filters, matrix-matrix multiplies, and matrix decompositions. It also includes a qualitative results comparison to previous works. Finally, conclusions and the references are presented.

## 2. BACKGROUND

The IEEE-754 standard for floating-point arithmetic (revised in 2008) [4] uses a triplet to represent a FP value $x$: $s$ – sign bit (0 for positive, 1 for negative), $e$ – exponent (an integer value) and $m$ – the significand. The value of $x$ is $x = (-1)^s 2^e m$. In order to avoid duplicate representations of the same value, the standard uses a normalized significand – usually $m \in [1, 2)$. This allows writing $x = (-1)^s 2^e 1.f$ where $f$ is a fraction $\in [0, 1)$. The number of bits used to represent the exponent (wE) and fraction (wF) define the formats of the standard. For instance single-precision uses wE=8 and wF=23.

Representing values that require an exponent smaller than $e_{\min}$ exponent (for that particular format) may be done by denormalising the significand. The property of denormalizing the significand for numbers very close to zero is often referred to as subnormal support (gradual underflow). Subnormal support is often not available in the embedded context since it adds significant resources to the hardware implementation of basic operators.

The IEEE-754 standard proposes several rounding modes for choosing the point on the grid to use for a specific real value: round to nearest (even, away), towards 0 and towards $+\infty$ or $-\infty$. The round to nearest modes are the most commonly used since they introduce the smallest error.

In this work both the floating point multiplier and adder support IEEE-754 arithmetic, with the following limitations. The only rounding mode supported is round to nearest tie-breaks-to-even (RNE). Subnormals are flushed to zero on both inputs and outputs. All other signalling and exception modes, such as zero, NaN, and infinity are properly handled on input, and correctly encoded on the output, although all NaNs are handled as quiet NaNs. Flags are not currently supported, as we felt traps were unlikely to be needed in large, parallel datapath applications such as those for which this core is optimized.

## 3. PREVIOUS WORK

Several earlier papers describe adding embedded floating point features to FPGAs [26, 11, 19, 12]. In [11], Beauchamp et.al. compare three alternate methods for implementing efficient floating-point computations in FPGA devices. One of these methods involves embedding a dedicated double-precision floating-point DSP block into the fabric, supporting a floating-point multiply-add operation. The performance and silicon area are estimated from published microprocessor FPU data. They conservatively estimate the FPU to be equivalent in area to 161 Xilinx Virtex 2 CLBs (1288 4-LUTs). The area of a single-precision implementation can be roughly approximated based on the single to double interface (1:2) or gate complexity (1:4) ratio, to 40-80 CLBs (300-600 4-LUTs) using their methodology. The resource savings when using the embedded floating-point block was assessed against traditional logic and multiplier-based implementations on a number of floating point benchmarks (common DSP and linear algebra algorithms). Using this methodology, they report that the embedded FPU FPGA uses 58% fewer logic elements. Unfortunately, no details are given on the architectures of the benchmarks, but since there are relatively few FPUs available, we assume that these are processing element (PE)-based implementations. PE based implementations suffer from interface and control overhead required for recirculat-

ing data to the compute units. The performance of vector-based operations, common in linear algebra algorithms, would therefore be negatively impacted.

In [19] Ho, et.al. evaluate embedding FP cores into an FPGA architecture using simple function benchmarks, such as an FFT butterfly, a 4 tap FIR filter, and 3x3 matrix multiply. They use published data from the IBM Power PC to estimate the FPU size at 570 4-LUTs (the estimation is based on a 5-level pipeline stage datapath of the processor; the potentially simpler FPGA FP blocks are likely to require less area). Reported results show that the small number of embedded FPUs added to the fabric can bring up to 18X area savings compared to traditional implementations on the simplistic set of benchmark designs. Unfortunately, the analysis does not consider more realistic benchmarks that require hundreds of operators. The size of the FPU only allows the integration of a reduced number per device (even scaling to larger, current devices the FPU count would still be low) so unrolled structures such as long scalar products would have to be mapped to the same few units, in a PE fashion. This leads to throughput degradation due to the overhead of data recirculation. Moreover, their proposed unit may only issue one multiplication or one addition per clock cycle; this is suboptimal since the size of the unit would provide sufficient routing resources to simultaneously use the two operators.

Ho, et.al. update their work in [21, 20] where both single and double precision FPUs are proposed. They propose a hybrid FPGA architecture embedding coarse-grain blocks consisting of floating-point operators into the FPGA fabric. The number of coarse-grain blocks as well as the number of FP blocks within the unit are parametrizable. For comparison with this work, we will focus on the single precision results only. They propose a Xilinx XC2V3000 (28772 4-LUTs) device with 16 single precision FPUs, with each FPU containing two floating point multipliers and two floating point adders. Cost is given at 7% die area total, with each FPU equivalent to 122 LUTs. Scaling to the current mid-range 20nm devices containing in the region of about 700K 4-LUT equivalents, we would expect a total of 1600 single precision operators. Fixed point scaling follows this pattern - the 96 18x18 multipliers in the XC2V3000 would translate to 2400 multipliers in a current device- the Altera Arria 10 660 [9] has 3356 19x18 multipliers and the Xilinx Kintex Ultrascale 756 [10] contains 2592 27x18 multipliers. The improved size of the FPU would allow running large realistic benchmarks in today's devices. Several architectural limitations would impact system performance and utility: (a) lack of local interconnect between FPUs would not support cascade modes, (b) inability to simultaneously utilize the FP cores in the FPU, and (c) the floating point only nature of the design.

In [12], Chong and Parameswaran improve on Ho's work by designing, rather than estimating, the double precision FPU. Their FPU is configurable as one double precision floating point multiplier-adder pair, or two single precision pairs. Their design is only 74 4-LUTs in area, although they have to scale the aspect ratio to ensure enough routing resources for the interface. As a result, their FPU grows to 288 4-LUTs in area. The authors state that they hope that their multimode design will justify commercial use of FPGA FPUs. Although their results are better than Ho's, their proposal still suffers from the application specific nature of the FPU (although they also support some integer operations, standard fixed point DSP elements are still included in the FPGA), as well as only small number of the FPUs because of their routing requirements.

In [23] an alternate approach for enhancing floating point performance on FPGAs is presented. Rather than embedding dedicated FP units in the fabric, the work focuses on how to use the existing resources more efficiently. The approach focuses on fusing a

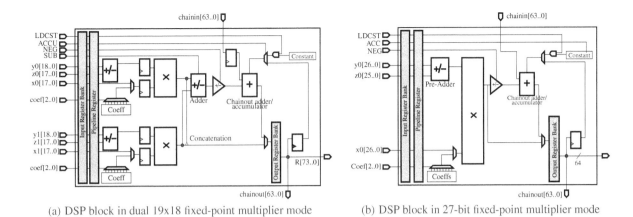

(a) DSP block in dual 19x18 fixed-point multiplier mode    (b) DSP block in 27-bit fixed-point multiplier mode

**Figure 1: DSP block in two fixed-point configurations**

cluster of multiple floating point operators together, by recognizing that: (a) two connected floating point operations will have a redundant normalize-denormalize pair, and (b) wider internal datapaths can compensate the accuracy impact of skipping some rounding stages. Results show that logic can be reduced by approximately 50%; in [17] it is shown that the approach is actually more accurate than single-precision IEEE-754 in 75% of the cases, using a Cholesky matrix decomposition example. Although this soft floating point method is more efficient, it still has significant latency if many operators are used in a datapath. There is still a considerable amount of logic used, and system speed for large designs is typically 50% lower than the speed of a DSP block.

The embedded FPU works acknowledge the application specific nature of their designs; "potential to waste significant silicon for non-floating-point applications" [16], "Dedicated FPUs are wasted resources for designs that do not make use of them" [21], and "However, if unutilized, embedded FPUs waste space on the FPGA die" [12]. Consequently, from a commercial perspective FPU units are only viable if their overhead is significantly small for designs not using them.

## 4. ARCHITECTURE

### 4.1 Why not another FPU?

Many things need to be considered when including embedded floating-point features in an FPGA: (a) Size – routing density, routing congestion, and device redundancy, (b) Performance – the floating point function must run as fast as the maximum possible system speed, and in no way affect the performance of the existing fixed-point functions; (c) Utility – all fixed point functions must remain backwards compatible, or possibly align with a natural evolution of the DSP block, and (d) Tool support – the cost to support new synthesis and Place & Route tools, as well as the cost of IP migration all need to be taken into account. All of these underscore the need to include the floating-point features as part of the fixed-point DSP block, rather than another embedded core.

A good starting point is the StratixV DSP block[6]. Firstly, it already contains the hardware required for a single-precision mantissa multiplier under the form of a 27x27-bit fixed-point multiplier Fig. 1(b). Secondly, it has a good routing density with 108 data inputs which will support up to three 32 bit single precision inputs. With three inputs, the single-precision multiply-add operation can be supported within one block. Finally, it contains wide local in-

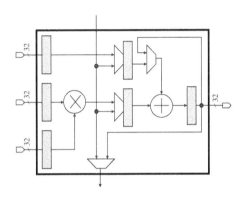

**Figure 2: DSP block in floating-point mode - simplified**

terconnect paths that may be reused for cascade operations when configured in FP mode.

The routing density could be increased to support two or three double precision inputs, but this would have knock-on effects on routing congestion. The aspect ratio of the block could be changed to increase the number of inputs per block while simultaneously reducing routing density, but other device features such as row-based redundancy would not be supported. These considerations strongly suggest that a single precision multiply-add structure is a good starting point for an FPGA floating-point architecture. Even when using the embedded fixed point multipliers, a single precision floating point multiply and add pair would consume in the region of 700 LUTs and registers [29, 7].

### 4.2 Floating-point multiplier

The fixed-point configuration modes for DSP block are shown in Figure 1. The two 19x18 multipliers can be used independently, summed (both in Fig. 1(a)), or combined to create a 27x27 multiplier (Fig. 1(b)), which can be used to implement the mantissa multiplier for an IEEE-754 floating point multiplier. The IEEE-754 exponent calculation is simple, and the exception handling is a straightforward combinatorial wrapper around the arithmetic datapath. Because of the additional cost in silicon area and power, we decided not to support subnormal numbers as they are rarely used in FPGA arithmetic operators [7]. In fact, subnormal numbers are optional in the single-precision implementation of the OpenCL

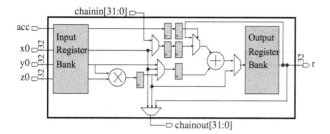

**Figure 3: DSP block in FP mode; balancing registers shown**

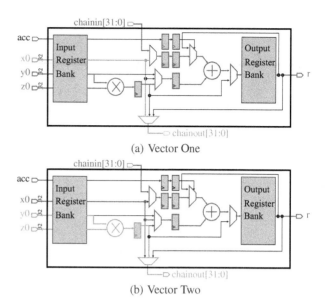

(a) Vector One

(b) Vector Two

**Figure 4: DSP block in floating-point vector modes**

[22] standard which is used in a much wider range of device targets (such as GPUs and DSPs). We therefore flush to zero on the input and output of our floating point operators.

The greatest challenge is the implementation of the IEEE-754 round-to-nearest tie breaks to even (RNE) mode for the multiplier. Whereas a traditional implementation would require two carry-prop-agate-adders (CPA) on the critical path – one for the multiplier par-tial products and one for the rounding – a VLSI implementation of this structure would yield a large area and delay. In Section 5, we introduce some of the structures that make an efficient implemen-tation possible such that overall, the inclusion of the FP multiplier has no impact on design performance, and only a 3% impact in DSP block area, including exponent and exception handling.

To complete the design of the floating point DSP block, a FP adder is also needed. Section 5 highlights some of the key imple-mentation techniques allowing for a reduced implementation size while allowing for a one cycle execution at DSP nominal frequency.

The addition of both the multiplier and the adder has to be done with sufficient connectivity flexibility such that (i) scalar operations are available, (ii) multiply-add operations can be completed within the DSP block, and (iii) DSP blocks can be cascaded to easily and efficiently map operations such as scalar products onto them.

### 4.3 Proposed DSP Block

Fig. 2 shows a logical block diagram of the connectivity (many of the registers used for performance or delay balancing have been omitted for clarity) supporting common arithmetic structures for both intra and inter block use. The latency for the DSP block in floating point mode is 2 (optionally 3 for performance) clocks for the FP multiplier and one additional clock when the adder follows the multiplier directly. An adder accessed independently of the multiplier will have a latency of 3 clocks. All or some pipeline stages can be optionally bypassed, but at the cost of a significant performance reduction.

Fig. 3 shows an alternate view of the DSP block, highlighting the balancing registers needed for the block to support all of the multi-row floating point modes at speed. All registers in the block are selectively by-passable, allowing any combination of multipli-ers and adders to be combined within a single block, or across two blocks, even though the maximum depth of the multiplier (three cycles) is different than the adder (combinatorial, with only an op-tional input and output pipeline). The adder can also be configured as a floating point accumulator, enabled by the multiplexer imme-diately preceding the right hand side input.

The circuit design of the FP adder is critical for success. The fixed point DSP Block is highly optimized to fit into a row height (LAB/M20K height) in order to support redundancy. In a mid-range device there are almost 2000 DSP blocks, so the impact of the FP adder may be significant in terms of area, device architecture, and power consumption. The FP adder select inputs from a number

of sources, including inside the DSP block, from outside the DSP block through general purpose routing, and from the adjacent DSP blocks though the chainin/chainout connection.

### 4.4 Dedicated vector structures

Vector structures are particularly useful for many unrolled DSP algorithms, such as FIR filters and matrix manipulations. New al-gorithms for common matrix decompositions such as Cholesky and QR have been introduced [17]. These algorithms work by reducing or eliminating data dependencies within rows and columns such that entire rows can be processed in parallel. The decomposition process is still an iterative process (though at a higher granularity) and low latency vector kernels are essential for enhanced perfor-mance. The multi-row DSP structure proposed in this work allows for a straightforward efficient logarithmic latency to kernel length ratio mapping.

Fig. 4 illustrates two path configurations supported by the DSP block, which we will refer to as vector modes one and two, respec-tively. In vector mode one, the result of the floating point mul-tiplication is directly fed to one input of the floating point adder, and the other input to the adder comes from the immediately ad-jacent block. In vector mode two, the multiplier is fed directly to the chainout connection (typically to the chainin connection of a DSP block configured as vector mode one); the two inputs to the adder come from outside the block, the left input through the input register bank, and the right input from the chainin connection.

The modes shown in Fig. 4 can be used to create a recursive tree structure of any size by using general purpose routing (but without soft logic). A logical block diagram (omitting many of the balanc-ing register for illustrative simplicity) is shown in Fig. 6.

The basic building block is the addition of two products – in this figure AB + CD (in the first two DSP blocks from the left) and EF + GH (in the next two DSP blocks). The AB+CD result is routed (via general purpose routing) into the third input of the second block from the left, and multiplexed into the left input of the floating point adder in that block. The EF+GH result is routed (again, via general purpose routing) to the third input of the third block from the left, and routed via the chainout/chainin connection to the second block from the left, and into the right input of the

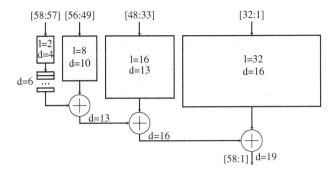

**Figure 5: Structure of a 58 Element Vector**

adder, producing AB+CD+EF+GH at the output of the DSP block. This process can be repeated to any degree to create any length of dot product. As there will be N FP adders and N FP multipliers in any collection of N DSP blocks, and only N-1 adders are required for a tree, there will be no function or connection shortage. While a floating adder inside a DSP block, i.e. following a multiply, has an additional latency of one clock cycle, an adder used for the recursive tree addition after the first level will add three clock cycles. Again counting from left block to right block, the first block is in vector mode one, the next block is in vector mode two, the next block in vector mode one, and the last two continuing in this alternating pattern. In general, this mode one/mode two pattern can be used to build any size reduction tree, although the connection length between two nodes in the later stages of the tree will tend to become very long.

For very large vectors, some of these general purpose routing connections may become the critical path, especially for a heavily utilized design. By inspection, the general purpose routing connections can be pipelined to any degree, as long as all connections at the same level of recursion are pipelined identically. Pipelining of the general purpose connections is also required if the length of the vector is not a power of two. The most efficient way to implement such a vector would be to decompose the structure into increasing powers of two, balancing the latency between the first two sub-structures and adding them, and then balancing the delay of the addition output with the subsequent sub-structure before addition, and so on. For example, a vector length of 58 would be decomposed in the following substructure sizes: 2, 8, 16, and 32, with latencies of 4, 10, 13, and 16, respectively, and a total delay of 19 clocks. Fig. 5 shows this structure.

Supporting a an efficient mapping of this recursive computing structure is key for many of the application types, such as matrix decompositions.

# 5. ARITHMETIC MICRO-ARCHITECTURE

## 5.1 FP Multiplier

The greatest challenge is the implementation of the IEEE-754 round-to-nearest-even (RNE) mode, as the pedantic implementation consists of one CPA on the output of the multiplier, a 1 bit normalization circuit, and a final CPA for rounding. This is prohibitively expensive as the CPA is a significant portion of the multiplier in terms of both area and propagation delay, and a second adder would significantly affect both the fixed and floating point datapaths. The solution cannot be fully explained in space available in this paper. In summary, all possible rounded and normalized values for the output mantissa are calculated in the portion of

the multiplier carry prefix structure corresponding to mantissa output position. These pre-calculated values are also used by the fixed point multiplier datapath; the carry prefix structures are distributed across the various fixed point decomposition points of the 74 bit CPA, and some of the larger fixed point additions are generated using carry select adders, choosing between some of the possible rounded floating point mantissa values for a certain range of the output. A detailed description of the FP multiplier mapping can be found in [24].

The only remaining multiplexer that may affect the fixed point performance is the final 2:1 multiplexer, selecting between fixed-point and the floating-point value post-exception handling. This will be a short path, as the exception handling conditions are largely calculated before the final output. Overall, the inclusion of the FP multiplier has no impact on design performance, and only a 3% impact in DSP block area, including exponent and exception handling.

## 5.2 FP Adder

We evaluated multiple FP adder architectures, finally choosing a dual path design. Like the FP multiplier, the RNE was the critical path, which we implemented by calculating all rounded possibilities of the mantissa before the final selection. The dual path FP adder is well known [18], preceding even the original IEEE-754 specification [3]. Many enhancements have been proposed since [27, 28], so we will not describe the architecture in detail beyond our RNE implementation.

The FP adder is logically and physically separate from the FP multiplier (the multiplier block also includes fixed point accumulators), so fused-multiply-add (FMA) is not supported, only multiply-add. We only needed to obtain a sufficient area and performance result; as the multiplier pipeline was much more complex in both gate numbers and functionality (supporting both floating-point, as well as many fixed-point modes), we decided to try a completely synthesizable approach to the adder, to allow a very malleable design during place and route. In common with many dual path architectures, the near path only implements subtraction; the far path also supports the near path addition. Consequently, the far path can have three ranges of values: $4 > x \geq 2$, $2 > x \geq 1$, and $1 > x \geq 0.5$. The rounding decision points for the three possible results can be calculated in parallel using three behaviourally described additions, with the actual result being selected based on the upper bits of the first adder ($x \geq 2$). The FP adder area is approximately 10% of the final DSP block core.

## 5.3 Integration and Verification

The base case DSP block and proposed additions were implemented in Verilog and synthesized with Design Compiler to a TSMC 28nm library. The functions were functionally verified using VCS to ensure no functionality was lost during the additions. Final area numbers are post-place-and-route, which was performed using Synopsys ICC and the design was DRC-clean. PrimeTime was used to verify that the block closes timing at 500MHz across standard process corners. The aspect ratio of the Block was determined by the Altera Arria 10 LAB height, as the DSP block was pitch matched to it, so that the row based redundancy could be applied to all features of the device. The DSP block is 2.5 times the width of the LAB.

We performed an extensive verification process, with one set of test vectors based on the methodology described in several different sources [13, 25] to verify a black-box view of the block. We also performed a white-box test, using a large set of internally generated vectors, which were designed to exercise areas of the architecture

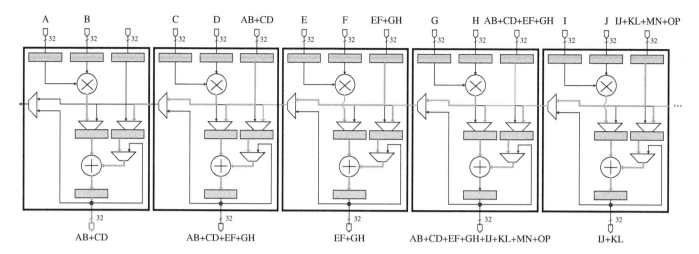

**Figure 6: DSP block in Recursive Vector Mode**

# 6. RESULTS

## 6.1 Application benchmarks

*Methodology*

We use a number of benchmark circuits to show the advantages of this new DSP block: a FIR filter, a FFT, a scalar product, a matrix-matrix multiply and a Cholesky decomposition. Each uses a different ratio of logic, memory and DSP blocks, a different DSP block to DSP connection pattern, and a different data flow pattern. All benchmarks use single-precision FP arithmetic, round to nearest (RNE) mode, with full support for infinities and NaNs but without subnormal support. Where possible, we compare the same design with and without FP DSP blocks enabled. Some of our example designs cannot be supported on any current FPGA without hard FP due to insufficient logic resources. Our soft FP implementations use the fused FP datapath synthesis supported by DSP Builder Advanced, and will give a more efficient soft logic only implementation than previous works.

For the FIR filter we present results for both a 1518 taps in order to highlight the top performance of the Arria 10 device, as well as a 128 taps FIR, which we use to show the resource improvements over a Stratix V device.

For the FFT we use two architectures. First, a 32K point FFT (32-way parallel) is performed in 1K cycles. The FFT uses radix 32, with each fully parallel 32-point FFT implemented using the split radix method. This architecture uses in excess of 1300 DSPs in FP configuration, and only fits in its current form on FP enabled Arria 10 devices. We report Flops performance using the conventional FFT flops metric which presumes that a size $N$ FFT costs $5N\log_2(N)$ FP operations. Using this metric we obtain roughly $(5 \times 32K \times 15)/1K$ (FP operations/cycles). The second FFT archi-

tecture is a 64K point, 4-way parallel implementation consisting of 4-serial pipelines of depth 6 (each implemented as 3 radix $2^2$ stages) feeding a 4-way parallel pipeline of depth 10 (implemented as 5 radix-4 stages) with a ROM implementation of the top-level twiddle factors. This architecture is used to highlight the advantages of using the embedded FP units as opposed to a soft floating point implementation (which is implemented on a Stratix V C2 device). The architectures have been generated using Altera DSP Builder Advanced Blockset 14.1 [2].

The scalar product family of tests include a 16-element dot product, and matrix-matrix multiply (MMM) of a $1280^2$ matrix. We compare these architectures both with and without embedded FP support. The MMM uses a blocking decomposition of $128^2$, with 8 separate scalar products of size 128. We also report an embedded FP only MMM chip-filling Arria 10 design, processing a $1600^2$ matrix, with a blocking decomposition of $160^2$, implemented using 8 scalar products of size 160. Both MMM benchmarks have been implemented using Altera OpenCL SDK 14.1 [1] and are fully functional architectures including all required communication interfaces.

Finally, we benchmark a Cholesky matrix decomposition of size $254^2$. The architecture used is similar to the previously presented works in [17, 5] and was implemented in DSP Builder Advanced (and is also part of the example designs). This benchmark compares the resource consumption of the Arria 10 and Stratix V implementations.

*Discussion*

The benchmarks results are grouped in Table 1. The left column presents the benchmark, then subsequent columns present the resources and performance for designs without and with embedded FP support.

Firstly, the 1518 tap FIR filter shows the maximum attainable performance when only FP DSPs are used. The number of taps equals the number of DSPs of a large Arria 10 device (10AX115U5F45I3SP). The device has a layout similar to Fig. 7(a) and has 7 DSP columns of various length. The filter is therefore split into 7 corresponding sections with data delay chains running vertically. The jumps between columns span across the full height of the device and therefore require several stages of pipeline (we used 5 stages) to achieve the DSP block limited frequency of 470MHz, which translates to over 1.4TFlops.

122

**Table 1: Performance comparison for embedded floating-point feature DSP block vs. traditional implementations**

| Algorithm | Perf. w/o FPDSP (Stratix V except MMM (1280) – Arria 10) | Perf. w FPDSP (Arria 10) |
|---|---|---|
| FIR 1518 | no fit | 470MHz (>1.4TFlops) |
| FIR 128 | 60881ALMs, 128 DSPs, 353 MHz | 1676 ALMs, 131 DSPs, 365MHz |
| FFT 32K | no fit | 78244 ALMs, 1364 DSPs, 356 M20K, 290MHz ($\approx$700GFlops) |
| FFT 64K | 92923 ALMs, 96 DSPs, 508M20K, 330MHz | 13993 ALMs, 256 DSPs, 508 M20K, 360MHz |
| Vector (16) | 7781 ALMs, 16 DSPs, 450MHz, 54 cycles | 263 ALMs, 16 DSPs, 385MHz, 14 cycles |
| MMM (1600) | no fit | 141442 ALMs, 1280 DSPs 1967 M20K, 285 MHz (730GFlops) |
| MMM (1280) | 315061 ALMs, 1034 DSPs, 1732 M20K, 249MHz | 61293 ALMs, 1034 DSPs, 1732 M20K, 280 MHz |
| Cholesky (254) | 109914 ALMs, 260 DSPs, 333M20K, 275 MHz | 12716 ALMs, 270 DSPs, 332 M20K, 277MHz |

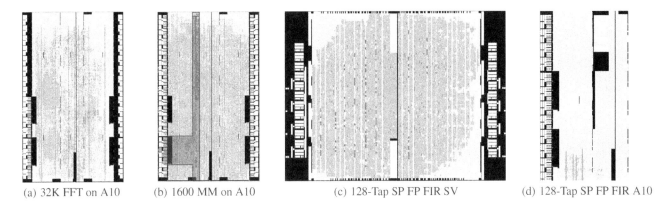

(a) 32K FFT on A10    (b) 1600 MM on A10    (c) 128-Tap SP FP FIR SV    (d) 128-Tap SP FP FIR A10

**Figure 7: ChipPlanner views of mapped designs on Arria10 devices and corresponding StratixV devices where available**

The 128 tap FP FIR filter is presented in order to contrast the logic utilization reduction between a Stratix V device and the Arria 10 device. The logic reduction is more than 97% as virtually all of the logic in the filter is mapped to the DSP blocks. The number of DSP blocks increases from 128 to 131 in the hard FP case, as DSP Builder Advanced uses a default chunk size of 32 when splitting long dot-products. As a result, 3 additional adders are used to sum the 4 chunks together. Figures 7(c) and 7(d) visually present the device utilization ratio between the two architectures.

The 32K point FFT (32-way parallel) is used as an example of the capabilities of the new hard FP enabled devices. The number of DSPs used is close to the maximum count. Logic resources are used for constant (twiddle) multipliers and synchronization paths. The performance is close to 700 GFlops which is particularly interesting since FFTs have an imbalanced use of adders to multipliers. The logic utilization in the large device is less than 20%. Fig. 7(a) shows the relatively low logic resource utilization when FP DSP blocks are used. The smaller FFT demonstrates the implementation possibilities between hard and soft FP designs. Because of the non 1:1 multiplier:adder ratio in an FFT, the 85% logic savings are partially offset by a 2.66x increase in DSP blocks.

The next benchmark is a small 16-element real scalar. In this relatively trivial example, the logic savings of the FP DSP block approach 96% while also reducing latency by approximately 75%. A more complex MMM example provides a maximum performance of 730GFlops on multiplying square matrices of size 1600. The 8 vector products of size 160 used in the architecture are mapped to the 7 available DSP columns. Fig. 7(b) shows the device utilization for this design. A smaller example running on matrices of size $1280^2$ and using 8 vector products of size 128 highlights the advantage of using the embedded FP DSP blocks. The non FP DSP

design uses 315K ALMs, mapped to an Arria 10 device with no FP DSPs active for comparison. The logic savings in this case are close to 80%.

Finally, a DSP Builder Advanced Cholesky matrix decomposition example (part of the example degins) shows a push-button 88% improvement in logic resources over the equivalent Stratix V design.

## 6.2 Performance comparison with related works

The comparison of our results to the previous works is not straightforward. Some newer techniques have been introduced recently for FP datapath construction [23], which reduce the logic and latency of a dot product in the order of 50%, as well as new methods for matrix decompositions [17]. The use of these methods would change the area and performance improvement analysis in the three previous papers. We also decided to normalize our results to the each of the three previous works individually. We believe that the area numbers previously reported do not completely correctly reflect the implementation in actual FPGA architectures, although we will not make an adjustment for this in our analysis for simplicity.

Beauchamp,et.al. [11] estimate the FPU area and performance from other published work. As the referenced work uses a more complex 5 stage pipeline, and is based on a commercial device, the FPGA scaling numbers are probably pessimistic; the integration overhead would be included in the reported area, and the 5 stage, higher performance, pipeline would likely be larger than the shorter FPGA embedded block.

Five benchmarks are used: matrix multiply, matrix-vector multiply, for product, FFT, and LU decomposition. No information on data sizes or algorithms, such as radix for the FFT, are given. There is no information on the architectures used – which will have a significant influence on the mapping to FPGA – for example, if dot product structures are used, or if a multiple PEs architecture is used. They state that division is mapped to logic, which may mean bit recurrence implementation, which will have a negative impact on performance with the associated long latency and routing stress.

Our methodology and results have been widely reported [17, 5] , including independent verification. We will compare dot product, FFT, and substitute a Cholesky decomposition for the LU decomposition. The Cholesky and LU algorithms are similar in complexity, and both use division. We will not attempt to normalize the comparison results – there is not enough implementation information given in [11].

Our logic reduction is typically 80%, in comparison to the 54% reported in [11]. This may be due to several reasons: a PE architecture will not scale as well as vector mapping, the FIR filter maps directly to our DSP blocks, and the recursive vector mode reduces overall routing congestion because of dedicated DSP to DSP connections. Newer algorithms for Cholesky decomposition allow long latency dot products to be used for matrix decompositions such as LU, Cholesky, and QR, because data dependencies are no longer the bottleneck. Beauchamp reports a 17% FPU device area – there are no details on how this was calculated, so we cannot normalize this to a current device – but in any case prohibitive for a mainstream FPGA. His estimates appear to require more area than the equivalent blocks implemented in [12] and [20].

Ho, et. al. [20] use a number of benchmarks. The three that are described in enough detail to implement are trivial - even in comparison to the contemporary FPGA used - matrix multiply, FIR, and FFT butterfly.

The matrix multiply is a 3 element vector, consisting of 3 multipliers and 2 adders. The FIR filter is a 4 tap FIR filter, assuming it consists of 4 multipliers and a binary tree of 3 adders, or perhaps it is of the alternate form, also requiring 4 multipliers, and 3 adders, with each adder summing the previous tap with the current tap. The FFT is a complex multiplier, followed by a complex adder. Ho gives an expected area for all of these in their Table IV(a), and reports an average of a 96% area reduction for these three functions. This is not a totally fair comparison, as their reported baseline numbers are for FP functions completely implemented in soft logic, with no use of the available embedded 18x18 multipliers.

These simple benchmarks can be directly mapped to our DSP blocks, using no soft logic other than registers needed to balance the datapath delays. We can implement the FIR filter directly using both forms: the direct form two structure with the following binary tree reduction is supported with the recursive vector mode of Fig. 4, and the direct form 1 structure is supported with the systolic mode connections, in a similar fashion to the existing fixed point FIR filter modes. Our implementation is more efficient from a whole chip perspective, as the FP functions are implemented in the existing DSP blocks, and DSP block to DSP block direct connections are available – and optimized for – common DSP structures, without using soft logic or routing.

Normalizing the reported FPU area into a current 700K LUT equivalent device would require 14% die area for 1600 DSP blocks, or approximately 4 times the cost of our design, but without the integer support. The difference is likely due to two reasons: the use of externally developed FP operators, which may not have been optimal for the area/performance requirements of this design, and the routing interface design, which would force a potentially difficult FPU aspect ratio.

Chong and Parameshawan in [12] built a configurable FPU structure that can be dynamically configured to support integer, single precision, and double precision arithmetic. They also built a double precision only FPU to understand the cost of providing multimode operation, which they reported as a 31% area and 21% delay increase. We believe that these numbers reasonably mirror that of the cost of configurability for commercial devices, although the incremental cost of adding single precision FP to our integer DSP blocks was in the range of 15% logic, without any performance reduction. Their FPU uses more complex double precision arithmetic, but the number of integer modes in a commercial device [9, 10] is very large, and not reflected in the modes supported in Chong. We disagree with their choice of a single path FP adder based on their stated reasons of design complexity and area, as the dual path architecture will typically synthesize to a much better area-performance result, which may impact the size of their FPU. Chong and Parameshawan use the same simple benchmarks as Ho, et. al. Their analysis shows a 68% reduction, rather than the 96% area reduction of Ho, because they include the embedded 18x18 multipliers in their calculations. Also, they use more soft logic around the FIR and matrix multiply benchmarks, presumably for data and coefficient storage. Again, we are able to map all of the arithmetic circuits directly to our DSP block, using only registers to balance delays, such as shown in our Fig. 5, or to store data and coefficients. Interestingly, normalizing their reported area results into a current 700K LUT device will require 17% for the equivalent of 1600 DSP blocks, although in this case, double precision is also supported.

In all three previous works, the system cost of the FPU blocks, normalized to current devices with DSP blocks supporting FP is similar in area; the interface density required seemingly the single most important influence.

Area is examined in all three previous works, but not routing optimization. In fact, all three designs are modified to allow full connectivity to the arithmetic structures.

## 7. CONCLUSION

We presented a new DSP block that can be configured to provide both and fixed and FP functions. Compared to earlier works, the proposed DSP block is truly integrated into the FPGA fabric, with high performance and efficient routing usage. It allows for a very high density of over 1600 single precision FP DSP blocks on a mid-range 20nm device, supporting up to 1.6 TFLOPs using only the newly embedded features. The proposed floating-point solution builds upon the existing fixed-point DSP block, and has lower routing requirements that the fixed-point modes. No degradation of fixed point performance or density occurs, and any mix of fixed and floating-point operations can be configured. In fact, this FP enhanced FPGA behaves just like a traditional FPGA architecture with fixed-point only capability, with essentially no cost or power impacts to non-floating point users.

## Acknowledgements

We kindly thank Simon Finn and Tomasz Czajkowski for their contributions to application benchmarking.

## 8. REFERENCES

[1] Altera OpenCL SDK. http://www.altera.co.uk/products/software/opencl/opencl-index.html.

[2] DSP Builder Advanced Blockset. http://www.altera.com/technology/dsp/advanced-blockset/dsp-advanced-blockset.html.

[3] IEEE Standard for Binary Floating-Point Arithmetic. *ANSI/IEEE Standard, Std 754-1985, New York*, 1985.

[4] IEEE Standard for Floating-Point Arithmetic. *IEEE Std 754-2008*, pages 1–58, 29 2008.

[5] An Independent Analysis of Altera's FPGA Floating-point DSP Design Flow, 2011.

[6] *StratixV Device Handbook*, 2011. http://www.altera.com/literature/hb/stratix-v/stratix5_handbook.pdf.

[7] *LogiCORE IP CORDIC v7.0*, 2013. http://www.xilinx.com/support/documentation/ip_documentation/floating_point/v7_0/pg060-floating-point.pdf.

[8] *7 Series FPGAs Overview - Product Specification*, 2014.

[9] *Arria10 Device Overview*, 2014. http://www.altera.com/literature/hb/arria-10/a10_overview.pdf.

[10] *UltraScale Architecture and Product Overview - Advance Product Specification*, 2014. http://www.xilinx.com/support/documentation/data_sheets/ds890-ultrascale-overview.pdf.

[11] M. Beauchamp, S. Hauck, K. Underwood, and K. Hemmert. Architectural modifications to enhance the floating-point performance of FPGAs. *VLSI*, 16(2):177–187, Feb 2008.

[12] Y. J. Chong and S. Parameswaran. Configurable multimode embedded floating-point units for FPGAs. *VLSI*, 19(11):2033–2044, Nov 2011.

[13] J. T. Coonen. *Contributions to a Proposed Standard for Binary Floating-point Arithmetic (Computer Arithmetic)*. PhD thesis, 1984. AAI8512788.

[14] T. S. Czajkowski. Silicon verification using high-level design tools. In *ACM/SIGDA International Symposium on Field Programmable Gate Arrays*. ACM, 2015.

[15] F. de Dinechin, J. Detrey, I. Trestian, O. Creţ, and R. Tudoran. When FPGAs are better at floating-point than microprocessors. Technical Report ensl-00174627, ENS Lyon, 2007. http://prunel.ccsd.cnrs.fr/ensl-00174627.

[16] F. de Dinechin and B. Pasca. Floating-point exponential functions for DSP-enabled FPGAs. In *FPT*. IEEE, 2010.

[17] S. Demirsoy and M. Langhammer. Cholesky decomposition using fused datapath synthesis. In *FPGA*, pages 241–244, 2009.

[18] P. M. Farmwald. *On the Design of High Performance Digital Arithmetic Units*. PhD thesis, Stanford, CA, USA, 1981.

[19] C. Ho, P.-W. Leong, W. Luk, S. J. E. Wilton, and S. Lopez-Buedo. Virtual embedded blocks: A methodology for evaluating embedded elements in FPGAs. In *FCCM*, pages 35–44, April 2006.

[20] C. H. Ho, C. W. Yu, P. Leong, W. Luk, and S. J. E. Wilton. Floating-point FPGA: Architecture and modeling. *VLSI*, 17(12):1709–1718, Dec 2009.

[21] C. H. Ho, C. W. Yu, P.-W. Leong, W. Luk, and S. J. E. Wilton. Domain-specific hybrid FPGA: Architecture and floating point applications. In *FPL*, pages 196–201, Aug 2007.

[22] Khronos OpenCL Working Group. *The OpenCL Specification, version 1.2.19*, November 2012.

[23] M. Langhammer. Floating point datapath synthesis for FPGAs. In *FPL*, pages 355 –360, sept. 2008.

[24] M. Langhammer and B. Pasca. Design and Implementation of an Embedded FPGA Floating Point DSP Block. Research report, Altera, Dec. 2014.

[25] Z.-S. A. Liu. Berkeley elementary function test suite. Technical report, Department of EE and CS, UC at Berkeley, Dec. 1988.

[26] E. Roesler and B. E. Nelson. Novel optimizations for hardware floating-point units in a modern FPGA architecture. In *FPL'02*, pages 637–646, London, UK, UK, 2002.

[27] P.-M. Seidel and G. Even. On the design of fast IEEE floating-point adders. In *ARITH*, pages 184–194, 2001.

[28] P.-M. Seidel and G. Even. Delay-optimized implementation of IEEE floating-point addition. *IEEE Trans. Comput.*, 53(2):97–113, Feb. 2004.

[29] K. Underwood. FPGAs vs. CPUs: trends in peak floating-point performance. In *FPGA*, pages 171–180. ACM, 2004.

# Superoptimized Memory Subsystems for Streaming Applications

Joseph G. Wingbermuehle, Ron K. Cytron, and Roger D. Chamberlain
Dept. of Computer Science and Engineering
Washington University in St. Louis
{wingbej,cytron,roger}@wustl.edu

## ABSTRACT

Because main memory is many times slower than modern processor cores, deep, multi-level cache hierarchies are ubiquitous in computers today. Similarly, applications deployed on ASICs and FPGAs are often hindered by slow external memories. Therefore, to achieve good performance, hardware designers must optimize main memory usage. Unfortunately, this process is often labor intensive and fails to explore the full range of potential memory designs. To address this issue for applications expressed in a streaming manner, we show that it is possible to generate automatically a *superoptimized* memory subsystem that can be deployed on an FPGA such that it performs better than a general-purpose memory subsystem. Rather than explore only simple memory subsystems, our superoptimizer is capable of exploring extremely complex designs consisting of multi-level caches and other components. Finally, we show that it is possible to deploy applications with superoptimized memory subsystems with minimal additional effort while achieving significant performance improvements over a naive memory subsystem.

## Categories and Subject Descriptors

B.6.3 [**Logic Design**]: Design Aids; B.3.2 [**Memory Structures**]: Design Styles

## 1. INTRODUCTION

Due to the large disparity in performance between main memory and processor cores, large cache hierarchies are a necessary feature of modern computer systems. By exploiting locality in memory references, these cache hierarchies attempt to reduce the amount of time an application spends waiting on memory accesses. Although cache hierarchies are most common, one can extend this notion to a generalized on-chip memory subsystem, which acts as an interface between the computation elements and off-chip main memory.

For general-purpose computers, memory subsystems are designed to have the best performance across a large range of applications. However, due to the general-purpose nature of these memory subsystems, such a memory subsystem may not be optimal for a particular application. Because of the potential performance benefit with a custom memory subsystem, we propose the use of memory subsystems tailored to a particular application. Such custom memory subsystems have been used for years for applications deployed on ASICs and FPGAs [3,10,19]. Further, it is conceivable that general-purpose computer systems may one day be equipped with a more configurable memory subsystem if the configurability provided enough of a performance advantage.

Although selecting the parameters for custom cache hierarchies optimally is an active area of research, most previous work focuses on a fixed topology. Recently, superoptimization has been employed to expand the search space for memory subsystems to contain multiple memory subsystem components such as caches, scratchpads, and address transformations, allowing for these components to be combined arbitrarily [27]. However, that work only considers single-threaded applications. Here we extend that work by considering custom memory subsystems for pipelined, streaming applications.

Streaming is a parallel programming paradigm in which application kernels communicate over fixed communication channels. The streaming paradigm is used in systems such as ScalaPipe [26] and StreamIt [23], among many others [4,21]. Within the streaming paradigm, conceptually, each kernel has its own independent memory address space. Communication between kernels is performed via communication channels implemented as FIFO buffers. Unlike a single-threaded application, which has a single memory subsystem to optimize, a streaming application can potentially have a separate memory subsystem for each kernel. In addition, each communication channel or FIFO between kernels is yet another memory subsystem to be optimized.

The concept of superoptimization was introduced with the goal of finding the smallest instruction sequence to implement a function [15]. This differs from traditional program optimization in that superoptimization attempts to find the best sequence at the expense of a potentially long search process rather than simply improving code. In a similar vein, we are interested in finding the best memory subsystem at the expense of a potentially long search process rather than a generic memory subsystem.

*FPGA'15*, February 22–24, 2015, Monterey, Califirnia, USA.
Copyright is held by the owner/author(s). Publication rights licensed to ACM.
ACM 978-1-4503-3315-3/15/02...$15.00.
http://dx.doi.org/10.1145/2684746.2689069

Traditionally, superoptimizers have used exhaustive search; however, exhaustively searching for the best memory subsystem would be prohibitively time-consuming. This is because in evaluating a particular memory subsystem, we simulate an address trace from the application. Due to the size of these traces, the simulation time can be extremely time consuming. Therefore, as in [20] and [27], we use a stochastic search technique instead of exhaustive search.

Due to the number of memory subsystems in a streaming application, the already complex problem of superoptimizing a single-threaded address trace is compounded. This is because, in addition to a shared resource constraint, the performance of one kernel can affect another both directly, by moving the bottleneck, and indirectly, by consuming excessive main memory bandwidth. Thus, we use a heuristic to guide the search to those memory subsystems that are most likely to benefit the application.

To evaluate our superoptimized memory designs, we target an FPGA with an external LPDDR main memory. The FPGA device is a Xilinx Spartan-6 LX45 clocked at 100 MHz. The external LPDDR is a 512 Mib device clocked at 100 MHz. All memory subsystems share access to the external LPDDR memory device. The Spartan-6 LX45 has 116 block RAMs (BRAMs), which we use to implement our custom memory subsystems. Each BRAM is 18 Kib, providing a total of 2,088 Kib on-chip memory.

By evaluating our applications on a physical device, we show that it is possible to achieve real performance improvements over a generic memory subsystem with minimal extra effort.

## 2. RELATED WORK

Here we extend the work on superoptimized memory subsystems for single-threaded applications [27] by considering streaming applications. Further, we show actual performance improvements for applications implemented on an FPGA device in addition to simulated reductions in execution time.

There is related work in making off-chip memory easier to use. LEAP scratchpads [1] provide a portable memory abstraction for hardware kernels. These memory abstractions may contain caching and can be backed by a larger main memory. CoRAM [6] is a technology similar to LEAP scratchpads, but lower-level, that provides an SRAM-style interface to memory. Unlike block RAM resources embedded in the FPGA, however, CoRAMs can be backed by a larger main memory. Both LEAP scratchpads and CoRAMs provide a similar function to our memory subsystem generator. However, unlike these works, we are concerned with automatic discovery of memory subsystems rather than an explicit description.

Prefetching [29] has been considered to improve the performance of applications deployed on an FPGA when combined with a memory abstraction such as LEAP scratchpads or CoRAM. Unlike our work, that prefetching mechanism is generic and dynamically discovers strided accesses.

MPack [24] attempts to optimize the packing of data into block RAM resources. In our work we do not consider packing multiple subsystem components, though doing so could allow for a higher utilization of block RAM resources.

Another source of related work comes from the automatic selection of cache parameters. Such optimization has been demonstrated for single-level caches [9] and two-level cach-

es [10,11]. In addition, there have been approaches to changing certain cache parameters dynamically [2, 22, 25]. However, these techniques do not consider the potential for a more complex memory subsystem.

An approach to optimizing both the computation and communication between kernels in streaming applications is presented in [7]. In [28], an approach to improving the memory behavior for FPGA applications implemented in a high-level language such as C or C++ is presented. Unlike these works, we treat the computation as fixed, but consider a wider search space for memory subsystems.

Finally, non-traditional memory subsystems, such as victim caches [13], combinations of caches and scratchpads [18, 19], and split caches [17] have been considered. However, these techniques represent specific modifications to the memory subsystem that are intended to be generic rather than customized for a particular application.

## 3. METHOD

Given an application to be deployed on either an ASIC or FPGA, the process to create a custom memory subsystem consists of several steps. First, the design without a memory subsystem is evaluated to determine what ASIC or FPGA resources are not used and, therefore, available for the memory subsystem. Next, an address trace is gathered for a single run of the application. This address trace is then fed into the memory subsystem superoptimizer, which proposes memory subsystems and simulates them to determine their performance. Finally, the memory subsystem generator is used to generate a custom HDL design for the application to use.

### 3.1 Address Traces

To superoptimize a memory subsystem, we first require an address trace. Unlike single-threaded address traces, we require a separate trace per kernel (note that each kernel has its own memory subsystem). In addition, communication between kernels must be recorded to allow us to model accurately the parallel kernels and optimize the size of the FIFOs between the kernels. Finally, some notion of the computation time between memory accesses must be recorded to predict accurately how long each kernel will run relative to other kernels.

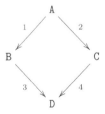

**Figure 1: Split-Join Topology**

Consider the simple streaming application topology shown in Figure 1. The vertices of the graph represent kernels and the edges represent communication channels. Here we have four kernels (A, B, C, and D) where kernel A produces data on two channels (1 and 2) and kernel D consumes data on two channels (3 and 4).

Each kernel has a separate address trace. For example, the trace for kernel B might look something like:

| Component | Description | Parameters ($n \in \mathbb{Z}_+$) | Latency (cycles) |
|---|---|---|---|
| Cache | Parameterizable cache | Line size ($2^n$) Line count ($2^n$) Associativity ($1 \ldots line\_count$) Replacement (LRU, MRU, FIFO, PLRU) Write policy (write-back, write-through) | 3 |
| FIFO | FIFO implemented in BRAM | Depth ($2^n$) | 1 |
| Offset | Address offset | Value ($\pm n$) | 0 |
| Prefetch | Stride prefetcher | Stride ($\pm n$) | 0 |
| Rotate | Rotate address transform | Value ($\pm n$) | 0 |
| Scratchpad | Scratchpad memory | Size ($2^n$) | 2 |
| Split | Split memory | Location ($n$) | 0 |
| XOR | XOR address transform | Value ($n$) | 0 |

Table 1: Memory Subsystem Components

```
Consume an element from channel 1
Read 4 bytes from address 0x1234
Perform a computation taking 8 cycles
Write 8 bytes to address 0x200
Produce an element on channel 3
```

Recording the interaction over the communication channels as *produce* and *consume* allows the superoptimizer to size the the FIFOs used for the communication channels without affecting correctness of the application, provided the FIFOs are at least as large as the application requires.

Although recording an address trace for *split* kernels (such as kernel A in Figure 1) and *join* kernels (such as kernel D) would provide a valid trace, such a trace may not give the superoptimizer sufficient freedom to size the FIFOs. For example, if kernel A were a load balancer, it might output more items to one channel than the other depending on its ability to write to the channel. To handle such situations, our simulator is capable of modeling certain *split* and *join* kernels intrinsically without using an address trace.

There are several ways to obtain address traces. Because our benchmarks are implemented in ScalaPipe, we modified ScalaPipe to have the ability to dump an address trace for kernels mapped to processor cores. This allows us to run the application first on general-purpose processor cores to gather the address traces. After an address trace is gathered, the application can be mapped to an FPGA device for deployment.

An additional benefit to using ScalaPipe to gather the traces is that, since ScalaPipe is capable of high-level synthesis, we can also record the number of cycles that the computation will take between memory accesses in the address trace. This information allows the superoptimizer to divide the memory resources among the kernels more effectively.

For benchmarks not implemented in ScalaPipe, it is possible to instrument the application manually to generate the required trace data. For example, an application implemented in a hardware description language (HDL) could be manually instrumented and then run in a simulator.

## 3.2 Simulation

To evaluate the performance of the memory subsystems proposed by the superoptimizer, we use a custom trace-based memory simulator. We use a custom memory subsystem simulator for three reasons. First, we need to simulate complex memory subsystems beyond simple caches. Second, rather than the number of cache misses, we are interested

| Parameter | Description | Value |
|---|---|---|
| Frequency | DRAM I/O frequency | 100 MHz |
| CAS | Cycles to select a column | 3 |
| RCD | Cycles from open to access | 3 |
| RP | Cycles required for precharge | 3 |
| Page size | Size of a page in bytes | 1024 |
| Page count | Number of pages per bank | 8192 |
| Width | Channel width in bytes | 2 |
| Burst size | Number of columns per access | 8 |
| Page mode | Open or closed page mode | closed |
| DDR | Double data rate | true |

Table 2: Main Memory Parameters

in the total run time of the application: cache misses alone would not provide enough information to the superoptimizer for it to decide between a single level and a multi-level cache and memory access time is insufficient for deciding how to divide up the memory resources among multiple memory subsystems. Finally, the simulator must be fast enough to simulate large traces for many thousands of repetitions in a reasonable amount of time.

For the results presented here, our simulator accommodates the memory subsystem components shown in Table 1. The simulator reports the total cycles that the application would take to run on our target platform. For the main memory, the simulator assumes that there is a priority arbiter in front of the main memory with a single read/write port. The main memory is modeled as a DRAM device with the parameters shown in Table 2, which were chosen to closely model our experimental platform.

## 3.3 Optimization

We use *old bachelor acceptance* [12] to explore the search space of memory subsystems. Old bachelor acceptance extends threshold acceptance [8], which is a stochastic hill-climbing technique similar to simulated annealing [14]. Old bachelor acceptance provides a compromise between search space exploration and hill climbing. Thus, although we may not obtain the best possible memory subsystem with this technique, we do see fairly good results in much less time than it would take to perform an exhaustive search.

As in [27], a proposal for a particular memory subsystem involves (1) the insertion of a memory subsystem component, (2) the removal of a component, or (3) a change to one of the component's parameters. This allows the generation of arbitrarily complex memory subsystems. The components supported by the superoptimizer are shown in Table 1.

The search space is much larger when multiple kernels are considered than it is for single-threaded applications. Because of this, in addition to the address-selection heuristic presented in [27], our superoptimizer employs a heuristic to guide it to spend more effort exploring the memory subsystems that are most likely to benefit the application. To do this, the subsystems for each kernel and FIFO are weighted by the product of their resource usage and their total memory access time. The superoptimizer then randomly selects a subsystem to modify based on these weights. This causes the superoptimizer to spend more time on those memory subsystems that consume a large portion of the resources and those with the most room for improvement.

Since our target device is an FPGA, we constrain the superoptimization process by FPGA resources. Specifically, we constrain the superoptimization process such that the final application uses no more than 80% of the slices and no more than 80% of the BRAMs available on the FPGA. By constraining the resources to 80%, we prevent the design from becoming too congested, which could prevent the design from being routed or meeting timing closure. In addition to the resource constraints, we place a lower bound of 100 MHz on the system clock for the design. The clock constraint prevents the superoptimizer from slowing down the computation with an overly-complex memory subsystem.

To enforce the resource constraints, rather than build each proposed memory subsystem, the superoptimizer tracks the resource usage of each memory subsystem component by storing synthesis results in a database. The sum of the resources used for each component are then used in the superoptimization process. To ensure the design will run at the required frequency, memory subsystem components whose synthesis estimates are less than 100 MHz are discarded.

Although the constraints on BRAMs and slices are fairly conservative, the constraint on frequency could easily be broken with too complex of a design. To address this, we maintain an estimate of the maximum path length in the superoptimizer and use the estimate as an additional constraint.

## 3.4 Subsystem Generation

Once a memory subsystem has been superoptimized, we use an automatic memory subsystem generator to generate a VHDL description of the memory subsystem. This subsystem generator is capable of generating all of the memory subsystems shown in Table 1. Each subsystem has a simple SRAM-style interface with per-byte write enables. The subsystems are connected to the main memory using a priority arbiter capable of allowing multiple outstanding main memory requests (one for each subsystem).

The word size of various components in the memory subsystem can differ. To handle this, an adapter is inserted between each component in the memory subsystem. For example, if there is a two-level cache where the first level has a word size of 8 bytes and the second level has a word size of 16 bytes, the adapter will direct the reads to the correct part of the larger word and set the byte mask appropriately for writes. If the second level cache has the smaller word size, each access from the first level cache will be turned into multiple accesses. For simplicity, the word size is restricted to a power of two.

## 4. BENCHMARKS

Following is a description of the benchmarks used to evaluate our custom memory subsystems. All of the benchmarks are implemented in ScalaPipe [26]. ScalaPipe is a streaming application generator that allows one to author an application in a high-level language and then generate code for deployment on traditional processors and FPGAs.

We have enhanced ScalaPipe with the ability to generate applications that output memory address traces for kernels deployed on standard processor cores and to use our custom memory subsystems for kernels deployed on FPGAs. This allows us to deploy the application first on processor cores to generate the address traces and then generate the application on FPGA cores for deployment with our custom memory subsystems.

### 4.1 Merge Sort

The first application we consider is a merge sort capable of sorting up to one million 32-bit integers [5]. This application makes use of a generic merge kernel with a single input channel and a single output channel. The kernel is replicated $\lceil \lg n \rceil$ times to sort $n$ elements, as shown in Figure 2. Each kernel in the pipeline sorts sequences of elements $2\times$ longer than the sequences from the preceding kernel by using an internal buffer to store half the elements.

**Figure 2: Merge Application Topology**

Due to the memory requirements of sorting one million integers, this application requires off-chip memory. However, exactly how the BRAM resources of the FPGA should be divided up among the kernels and FIFOs is not immediately apparent and is the subject of investigation.

### 4.2 n-Body

The next benchmark we consider is an application to simulate the 3-dimensional n-body problem using the naive $O(n^2)$ algorithm. An n-body simulation predicts the positions and velocities of point masses in space at various times. The naive algorithm updates each point by considering the gravitational effect of all other points. The topology of the n-body application is shown in Figure 3.

In the n-body application, the `Input` kernel reads the initial positions of each particle to be simulated. The `Buffer` kernel buffers the points for the next iteration (or from input on the first iteration). Next, the `Streamer` kernel sends the particles past the `Force` kernel, which computes the forces on

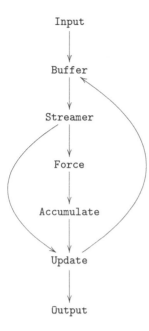

**Figure 3: n-body Application Topology**

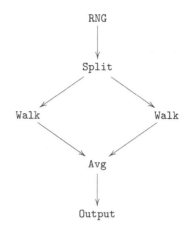

**Figure 4: Laplace Application Topology**

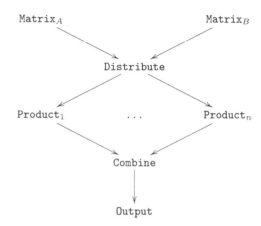

**Figure 5: Matrix-Matrix Multiplication Topology**

each particle. The `Accumulate` kernel then sums the forces on each particle. Once the total force on a particle has been computed, the `Update` kernel updates the particle's position and velocity, sending the results to both the `Output` and `Buffer` kernels. Finally, the `Output` kernel saves the results.

In this application, there are two kernels that use off-chip memory: the `Buffer` kernel and the `Streamer` kernel. In addition to the memory subsystems used by these two kernels, there are eight FIFOs to be optimized. Although it would be possible to simulate a small number of particles without using off-chip memory, larger problems necessitate the use of off-chip memory, leaving us to determine how to best use the BRAM resources.

### 4.3 Laplace

The Laplace benchmark is an application to solve Laplace's equation using a Monte-Carlo technique [26]. Laplace's equation is a partial differential equation that can be used to model steady-state heat diffusion. The topology of this application is shown in Figure 4.

In the Laplace application, random numbers are generated using the Mersenne twister [16] random number generator in the `RNG` kernel. The `Split` kernel divides the random numbers among two `Walk` kernels, which perform a random walks from each position of interest. Next, the `Avg` kernel averages the results of the random walks and sends the output to the `Output` kernel.

The only kernel in this application to use a memory array is the `RNG` kernel, which uses 2,496 bytes of memory. So although this application does not require the use of off-chip memory, off-chip memory could potentially be used effectively for the `RNG` kernel and one or more of the FIFOs.

### 4.4 Matrix-Matrix Multiply

The matrix-matrix multiply benchmark is a streaming application to perform matrix-matrix multiplication on two 256x256 matrices of 32-bit floats. The topology is shown in Figure 5.

In the matrix-matrix multiply benchmark, the source matrices are provided by the `Matrix`$_A$ and `Matrix`$_B$ kernels. The `Distribute` kernel holds the matrix data and streams it past the `Product` kernels. Each `Product` kernel performs a dot product. In our experiments, we use two `Product` kernels. Next, the `Product` kernels send the dot products to the `Combine` kernel, which collects the results in the correct order. Finally, the `Output` kernel outputs the results.

With this benchmark, only the `Distribute` kernel uses a memory array: one to store the matrices totaling 524,288 bytes. In addition to this memory subsystem, there are FIFOs connecting all of the kernels, which could potentially be resized.

### 4.5 Median

Finally, we consider an application to find the median of a stream of up to one million unique integers. This benchmark is a simple two-stage pipeline, shown in Figure 6, where the `Hash` stage removes duplicates using an open-address hash table and the `Heap` stage uses a binary heap to recover the median value.

In the median application, both the `Hash` and the `Heap` kernels require more memory the FPGA has available. The `Hash` kernel uses 8 MiB and the heap kernel uses 4 MiB. In addition to the memory subsystems for the kernels, the

Figure 6: Median Application Topology

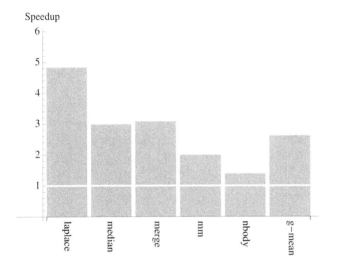

Figure 7: Simulated Speedup

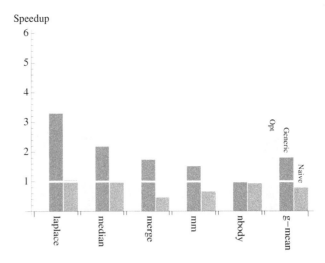

Figure 8: Actual Speedup

FIFO between the kernels is another subsystem whose size and implementation is to be optimized.

## 5. RESULTS

Our results are presented with respect to the following baseline: we implement all FIFOs as registers (FIFOs that can hold a single element). All memory subsystems for kernels are connected directly to the arbiter for the main memory. This type of memory structure uses the least amount of area on the FPGA device and requires the least amount of effort to implement. Thus, although it might not be the final design for a particular application, it does represent a likely starting point.

Figure 7 shows the speedup of the superoptimized memory subsystems over the baseline for each benchmark as reported by the memory simulator (the *g-mean* bar shows the geometric mean). Because the simulator takes into account computation time as well as memory access time, the simulated speedup should be an accurate representation of the actual speedup one would expect to obtain by running the application on the physical device. However, there are two potential sources of error. The first is the main memory model, which does not take all possible parameters into account (for example, refresh is not included in the simulated memory model). The other source of error is the application input and output, which is done over a USB interface.

Figure 8 shows the actual speedup from running each benchmark on the FPGA device described in Section 1. The first bar in each group shows the speedup over the baseline for the superoptimized memory subsystem. As before, the *g-mean* group shows the geometric mean.

In addition to a comparison of the superoptimized memory subsystem against the baseline, we also compare a generic memory subsystem as well as a naive memory subsystem to the same baseline. For the *generic* memory subsystem (the second bar in each group in Figure 8), each kernel memory subsystem has a 8 KiB direct-mapped cache and each FIFO is 256 items deep and implemented in BRAM. This generic memory subsystem demonstrates the performance one might expect from a memory subsystem that was selected without considering the implementation details of the kernels.

For the *naive* memory subsystem (the last bar in each group in Figure 8), no BRAM is used for the kernel memory subsystems and each FIFO is 256 items deep implemented in main memory instead of BRAM. The naive memory subsystem attempts to demonstrate a worst-case memory subsystem where every access contends for main memory.

Comparing the actual results to the simulated results, we see that in most cases the actual speedup was slightly higher than the simulated speedup. This is due to the fact that reducing the number of main memory accesses improves performance more than the simulated memory model predicts. However, for the Laplace benchmark, the actual speedup is less than predicted. Again, this is due to the main memory model since, as we will see later, two of the FIFOs between kernels were moved into main memory rather than using BRAMs.

### 5.1 Laplace

The Laplace benchmark exhibits a smaller speedup than the simulation would imply. For the Laplace benchmark, the superoptimizer selected a 4,096-byte scratchpad for the RNG kernel. This moves all memory accesses RNG into the faster BRAM, avoiding the main memory completely. In addition, several of the FIFO sizes were adjusted, as shown in Table 3.

Because the superoptimizer tries to find the memory subsystem that provides the lowest execution time using as few resources as possible, several of the FIFOs are implemented

| FIFO | Depth | Implementation |
|---|---|---|
| RNG → Split | 1 | register |
| Split → Walk$_1$ | 256 | main memory |
| Split → Walk$_2$ | 256 | BRAM |
| Walk$_1$ → Avg | 64 | main memory |
| Walk$_2$ → Avg | 8 | BRAM |
| Avg → Output | 1 | register |

Table 3: Laplace FIFO Implementations

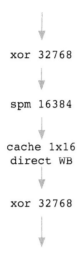

```
xor 32768

spm 16384

cache 1x16
direct WB

xor 32768
```

Figure 9: Subsystem for the Hash kernel

in main memory rather than directly in BRAM. According to the simulation model, this does not slow down the benchmark since the computation time is able to hide the memory latency. However, since the main memory model is imprecise, there is a benefit to implementing the FIFOs in BRAM that is unknown to the superoptimizer. By implementing all of the FIFOs in BRAM, we are able to obtain a speedup slightly better than the simulation model estimates.

For the Laplace benchmark, the superoptimized memory subsystem provides more than a 3× speedup over the baseline. However, the generic memory subsystem provides a similar speedup. This is because this benchmark is very sensitive to the size of the FIFOs. Thus, even the naive memory subsystem offers a performance improvement over the baseline due to the increased FIFO sizes.

## 5.2 Median

For the median benchmark, the superoptimized memory subsystem for the Hash kernel is shown in Figure 9. In the figure, memory accesses from the kernel enter the top and memory accesses to the main memory exit the bottom. In this particular memory subsystem, the address is transformed by flipping a bit (xor). The address transformation is followed by a 16,384-byte scratchpad, which is followed by a single-entry cache having a single line that is 16 bytes (the WB in Figure 9 stands for write-back). Finally, the last address transformation reverses the first transformation. Note that the superoptimizer automatically inserts address transformations in pairs like this to ensure the correct section of main memory is accessed.

The effect of the address transformation is to move certain parts of the hash table into the scratchpad. The cache can

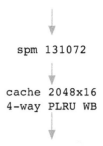

```
spm 131072

cache 2048x16
4-way PLRU WB
```

Figure 10: Subsystem for the Heap kernel

be helpful here since the main memory interface is 16-bytes wide and we only access 4 bytes at a time. Therefore, the cache allows us to avoid main memory accesses when multiple words are requested within the same 16-byte range.

The superoptimized memory subsystem for the Heap kernel is shown in Figure 10. Again, we have a scratchpad followed by a cache. This is logical for a binary heap structure since the early addresses are accessed much more frequently than later addresses.

Finally, the FIFO between the Hash and Heap kernels is 16 entries deep and implemented in BRAM. This allows the Hash kernel to keep running even if the Heap kernel backs up. The other FIFOs are 1 entry deep.

## 5.3 Merge Sort

The merge benchmark has 15 memory subsystems for the Merge kernels and 23 memory subsystems for FIFOs, giving a total of 38 memory subsystems. Although there are 20 Merge kernels, only 15 have memory subsystems since ScalaPipe does not generate memory subsystems if the size of the memory is less than 1,024 bytes.

For the Merge kernels with smaller memory subsystems that need to store fewer than 32,768 bytes, the superoptimizer selects scratchpads. However, for the larger memory subsystems, the superoptimizer selects small, direct-mapped caches. The scratchpads allow the smaller memory subsystems to run without accessing main memory at all. The small direct-mapped caches, on the other hand, reduce the number of accesses going to main memory since the main memory is 16 bytes wide and each access is only 4 bytes.

Most of the FIFOs between kernels were selected to be a single element deep and implemented as a register. However, several of the FIFOs between the later stages are 1,024 and 2,048 elements deep implemented in BRAM. This is because the access latency between the later stages will vary since not all the accesses will hit in cache.

In terms of performance, the superoptimized memory subsystem for the merge sort benchmark is over 3× the baseline memory subsystem and closely matches what the simulation predicted. In this case, the generic memory subsystem provides a performance improvement, but just over 2× the performance of the baseline memory subsystem.

## 5.4 Matrix-Matrix Multiply

As shown in Figure 8, the superoptimized memory subsystem for the matrix-matrix multiply benchmark (mm) provides about a 2× speedup over the baseline benchmark. For this benchmark, only the Distribute kernel uses external

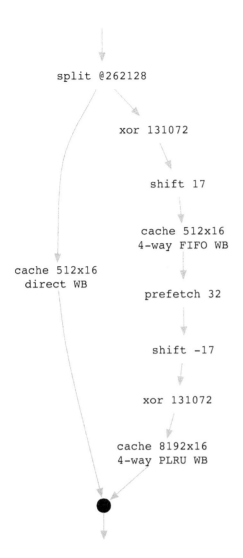

Figure 11: Subsystem for the `Distribute` kernel

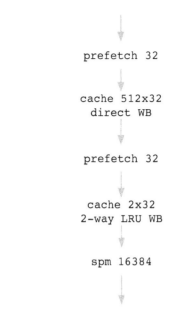

Figure 12: Subsystem for the `Buffer` kernel

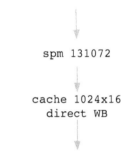

Figure 13: Subsystem for the `Streamer` kernel

memory. The superoptimized memory subsystem for the `Distribute` kernel is shown in Figure 11.

There are several interesting features of the memory subsystem shown in Figure 11. The first observation is the split. The split causes the memory accesses for the two source matrices to go to separate caches. The left side of the split handles the matrix that is accessed in column-major order whereas the right side handles the matrix that is accessed in row-major order. After the split, the first matrix is stored in a cache, whereas the second matrix is transposed from the memory subsystem's perspective before entering a cache.

All but four FIFOs are implemented as registers in the superoptimized memory subsystem for the mm benchmark. The two FIFOs between the `Distribute` kernel and the `Product` kernels are 256 entries and implemented in BRAM. The FIFOs between the `Product` kernels and `Combine` kernel are 128 entries deep and implemented in BRAM as well.

## 5.5 n-body

For the n-body benchmark, neither the simulated nor actual speedup are very large. This is because the n-body benchmark is compute-bound. However, we note that there is a performance gain even in this case. For this benchmark, all of the FIFOs are implemented as single-element registers. This allows all of the memory resources to be dedicated to the two kernel memory subsystems.

The superoptimized memory subsystem for the `Buffer` kernel is shown in Figure 12. This memory subsystem contains two prefetch components, two caches, and a scratchpad. The first prefetch requests the value 32 bytes after the current address, which causes the first cache to request the next line after the current access. Likewise, the second prefetch has the same effect on the second cache. Finally, the scratchpad stores the first elements rather than storing everything in main memory.

The memory subsystem for the `Streamer` kernel, shown in Figure 13, is a scratchpad followed by a cache. Unlike the previous memory subsystem, here the scratchpad comes first. This is likely due to the fact that placing the scratchpad after a cache, as is done for the memory subsystem for the `Buffer` kernel, incurs extra latency and poisons the cache. However, the prefetch components used for the `Buffer` kernel memory subsystem reduce this effect.

Given the way the benchmark works, it is not intuitive that the superoptimized memory subsystem for the `Buffer` kernel would be more complex than the subsystem for the

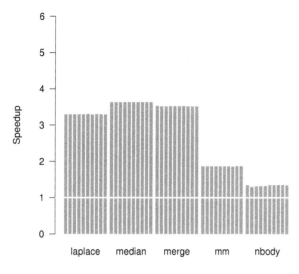

Figure 14: Input Specificity

Streamer kernel since the Streamer kernel streams the data past the Force kernel. However, because the Force kernel is computationally intensive, the memory delays that the Streamer kernel experiences contribute little to the overall run time. Instead, reducing the memory access times for the Buffer kernel provides a greater performance advantage than reducing the access times for the Streamer kernel.

## 5.6 Input Specificity

Although we are able to obtain a performance improvement for each of the benchmarks, we note that this improvement is not for the benchmark, but for a particular data set used with the benchmark. Because we are using only a single address trace for the optimization, it is possible that the memory subsystems could be over-fitted. Indeed, this appears to have happened for the Hash kernel for the median benchmark (Figure 9), which contains an address transformation to move parts of the hash table into a scratchpad.

To determine to what extent over-fitting affects the results, we re-ran each of the benchmarks with ten separate inputs. The results are shown in Figure 14. Here each bar shows the speedup of the superoptimized memory subsystem over the baseline memory subsystem for a particular data set. The left-most bar in each group shows the result from the original data set presented above. The nine remaining bars show the speedup for different data sets.

To change the input for the Laplace benchmark, we used a different random number seed. As shown in Figure 14, using a different random number seed has little effect on the speedup. For both the median and merge benchmarks, we used different data sets of the same size as the original. Finally, for the n-body benchmark, we used a different input size for each run (1,000 to 10,000 in increments of 1,000).

As Figure 14 shows, there is very little difference in the performance gain with different input data sets. This suggests that the superoptimized memory subsystems are not over-fitted. Nevertheless, it is conceivable that some superoptimized memory subsystems could be overly specific for a particular data set. In some cases, this could be desirable. For example, if an application used a hash table and the data stored in the hash table never changed. Generally, overfitting is something we would likely want to avoid.

## 5.7 Discussion

As the above results indicate, it is possible to superoptimize memory subsystems for streaming applications. The structure of some of the superoptimized memory subsystems are not surprising. For example, the memory subsystem for the Laplace benchmark is likely very similar to what one would select manually. On the other hand, some of the memory subsystems are logical, but would likely require manual experimentation to discover. For example, the memory subsystems for the median and the merge benchmarks are fairly standard, but require the tuning of many parameters. Finally, the superoptimizer is able to discover memory subsystems that are very unusual, such as those for the matrix-matrix multiply and n-body benchmarks.

The superoptimization process can take a long time, depending on the number of memory subsystems and the length of the memory address traces. The superoptimized memory subsystems presented here were generated by running the superoptimizer for between 10,000 and 200,000 simulation runs, depending on the benchmark. Applications with only a few memory subsystems, such as the Laplace benchmark, require far fewer simulation runs than those with many memory subsystems, such as the merge benchmark.

The run time of each simulation depends on the length of the address trace as well as the complexity of the memory subsystem. For the benchmarks presented here, the time for a single simulation is in the range of 5 to 15 minutes. To reduce the total run time for the superoptimization process, we made use of multiple processing cores and stored the results from each simulation in a database shared among the processing cores. The database allows the superoptimizer to revisit prior results without simulation.

As the superoptimization process runs, the memory subsystem it discovers never gets worse and is at all times usable. Thus, it is possible to terminate the process as soon as a satisfactory memory subsystem is discovered. The use of of multiple cores allowed us to obtain the results presented here in a week.

## 6. CONCLUSION AND FUTURE WORK

We have described a technique for creating superoptimized memory subsystems for streaming applications. We have shown that not only do these superoptimized memory subsystems perform well in simulation, but, by deploying the applications on an FPGA device, we have shown that these memory subsystems perform well in actual hardware. Through the use of ScalaPipe with our superoptimizer, we were able to create a design implemented on an FPGA device using a customized memory subsystem with minimal effort and without writing HDL.

In the future, we would like to explore the use of superoptimized memory subsystems with existing HDL designs. In addition, we would like extend this approach to optimize the memory subsystem for objectives other than performance, such as minimizing writes or energy consumption.

## 7. ACKNOWLEDGMENTS

This work was supported by Exegy, Inc., and VelociData, Inc. Washington University in St. Louis, R. Chamberlain, and R. Cytron receive income based on a license of technology by the university to Exegy, Inc., and VelociData, Inc.

# 8. REFERENCES

[1] M. Adler, K. E. Fleming, A. Parashar, M. Pellauer, and J. Emer. LEAP scratchpads: automatic memory and cache management for reconfigurable logic. In *Proc. of 19th Int'l Symp. on Field Programmable Gate Arrays*, pages 25–28, 2011.

[2] R. Balasubramonian, D. H. Albonesi, A. Buyuktosunoglu, and S. Dwarkadas. A dynamically tunable memory hierarchy. *IEEE Trans. on Computers*, 52(10):1243–1258, Oct. 2003.

[3] R. Banakar, S. Steinke, B.-S. Lee, M. Balakrishnan, and P. Marwedel. Scratchpad memory: design alternative for cache on-chip memory in embedded systems. In *Proc. of 10th Int'l Symp. on Hardware/Software Codesign*, pages 73–78, 2002.

[4] R. D. Chamberlain, M. A. Franklin, E. J. Tyson, J. H. Buckley, J. Buhler, G. Galloway, S. Gayen, M. Hall, E. B. Shands, and N. Singla. Auto-Pipe: Streaming applications on architecturally diverse systems. *Computer*, 43(3):42–49, Mar. 2010.

[5] R. D. Chamberlain and N. Ganesan. Sorting on architecturally diverse computer systems. In *Proc. of 3rd Int'l Workshop on High-Performance Reconfigurable Computing Technology and Applications*, Nov. 2009.

[6] E. S. Chung, J. C. Hoe, and K. Mai. CoRAM: an in-fabric memory architecture for FPGA-based computing. In *Proc. of 19th Int'l Symp. on Field Programmable Gate Arrays*, pages 97–106, 2011.

[7] J. Cong, M. Huang, and P. Zhang. Combining computation and communication optimizations in system synthesis for streaming applications. In *Proc. of 22nd Int'l Symp. on Field Programmable Gate Arrays*, pages 213–222. ACM, 2014.

[8] G. Dueck and T. Scheuer. Threshold accepting: a general purpose optimization algorithm appearing superior to simulated annealing. *Journal of Computational Physics*, 90(1):161–175, 1990.

[9] A. Ghosh and T. Givargis. Cache optimization for embedded processor cores: An analytical approach. *ACM Trans. on Design Automation of Electronic Systems*, 9(4):419–440, Oct. 2004.

[10] A. Gordon-Ross, F. Vahid, and N. Dutt. Automatic tuning of two-level caches to embedded applications. In *Proc. of the Conf. on Design, Automation and Test in Europe*, page 10208, 2004.

[11] A. Gordon-Ross, F. Vahid, and N. Dutt. Fast configurable-cache tuning with a unified second-level cache. In *Proc. of Int'l Symp. on Low Power Electronics and Design*, pages 323–326, 2005.

[12] T. C. Hu, A. B. Kahng, and C.-W. A. Tsao. Old bachelor acceptance: A new class of non-monotone threshold accepting methods. *ORSA Journal on Computing*, 7(4):417–425, 1995.

[13] N. P. Jouppi. Improving direct-mapped cache performance by the addition of a small fully-associative cache and prefetch buffers. In *Proc. of 17th Int'l Symp. on Computer Architecture*, pages 364–373, 1990.

[14] S. Kirkpatrick, C. D. Gelatt, and M. P. Vecchi. Optimization by simmulated annealing. *Science*, 220(4598):671–680, 1983.

[15] H. Massalin. Superoptimizer: a look at the smallest program. In *Proc. of 2nd Int'l Conf. on Architectural Support for Programming Languages and Operating Systems*, pages 122–126, 1987.

[16] M. Matsumoto and T. Nishimura. Mersenne twister: a 623-dimensionally equidistributed uniform pseudo-random number generator. *ACM Trans. on Modeling and Computer Simulation*, 8(1):3–30, 1998.

[17] A. Naz. *Split Array and Scalar Data Caches: A Comprehensive Study of Data Cache Organization*. PhD thesis, Univ. of North Texas, 2007.

[18] P. R. Panda, N. D. Dutt, and A. Nicolau. Local memory exploration and optimization in embedded systems. *IEEE Trans. on Computer-Aided Design of Integrated Circuits and Systems*, 18(1):3–13, 1999.

[19] P. R. Panda, N. D. Dutt, A. Nicolau, F. Catthoor, A. Vandecappelle, E. Brockmeyer, C. Kulkarni, and E. De Greef. Data memory organization and optimizations in application-specific systems. *IEEE Design & Test of Computers*, 18(3):56–68, 2001.

[20] E. Schkufza, R. Sharma, and A. Aiken. Stochastic superoptimization. In *Proc. of 18th Int'l Conf. on Architectural Support for Programming Languages and Operating Systems*, pages 305–316, 2013.

[21] J. H. Spring, J. Privat, R. Guerraoui, and J. Vitek. StreamFlex: high-throughput stream programming in Java. *ACM SIGPLAN Notices*, 42(10):211–228, 2007.

[22] K. T. Sundararajan, T. M. Jones, and N. P. Topham. Smart cache: A self adaptive cache architecture for energy efficiency. In *Proc. of Int'l Conf. on Embedded Computer Systems*, pages 41–50, 2011.

[23] W. Thies, M. Karczmarek, and S. Amarasinghe. StreamIt: A language for streaming applications. In *Proc. of 11th Int'l Conf. on Compiler Construction*, pages 179–196, 2002.

[24] J. Vasiljevic and P. Chow. MPack: global memory optimization for stream applications in high-level synthesis. In *Proc. of Int'l Symp. on Field Programmable Gate Arrays*, pages 233–236, 2014.

[25] A. Veidenbaum, W. Tang, R. Gupta, A. Nicolau, and X. Ji. Adapting cache line size to application behavior. In *Proc. of 13th Int'l Conf. on Supercomputing*, pages 145–154, 1999.

[26] J. G. Wingbermuehle, R. D. Chamberlain, and R. K. Cytron. ScalaPipe: A streaming application generator. In *Proc. of 2012 Symp. on Application Accelerators in High-Performance Computing*, pages 244–254, 2012.

[27] J. G. Wingbermuehle, R. K. Cytron, and R. D. Chamberlain. Superoptimization of memory subsystems. In *Proc. of Conf. on Languages, Compilers, and Tools for Embedded Systems*, 2014.

[28] F. Winterstein, S. Bayliss, and G. Constantinides. Separation logic-assisted code transformations for efficient high-level synthesis. In *Proc of 22nd Int'l Symp. on Field Programmable Custom Computing Machines*, pages 1–8, 2014.

[29] H.-J. Yang, K. Fleming, M. Adler, and J. Emer. Optimizing under abstraction: Using prefetching to improve FPGA performance. In *Proc. of 23rd Int'l Conf. on Field Programmable Logic and Applications*, pages 1–8, 2013.

# MATCHUP: Memory Abstractions for Heap Manipulating Programs

Felix Winterstein
European Space Agency
Ground Systems Eng. Dept.
f.winterstein12@ic.ac.uk

Kermin Fleming
Intel Corporation
VSSAD Group
kermin.fleming@intel.com

Hsin-Jung Yang
Massachusetts Institute of
Technology, CSAIL
hjyang@csail.mit.edu

Samuel Bayliss
Imperial College London
Circuits and Systems Group
s.bayliss08@ic.ac.uk

George Constantinides
Imperial College London
Circuits and Systems Group
g.constantinides@ic.ac.uk

## ABSTRACT

Memory-intensive implementations often require access to an external, off-chip memory which can substantially slow down an FPGA accelerator due to memory bandwidth limitations. Buffering frequently reused data on chip is a common approach to address this problem and the optimization of the cache architecture introduces yet another complex design space. This paper presents a high-level synthesis (HLS) design aid that generates parallel application-specific multi-scratchpad architectures including on-chip caches. Our program analysis identifies non-overlapping memory regions, supported by private scratchpads, and regions which are shared by parallel units after parallelization and which are supported by coherent scratchpads and synchronization primitives. It also decides whether the parallelization is legal with respect to data dependencies. The novelty of this work is the focus on programs using dynamic, pointer-based data structures and dynamic memory allocation which, while common in software engineering, remain difficult to analyze and are beyond the scope of the overwhelming majority of HLS techniques to date. We demonstrate our technique with three case studies of applications using dynamically allocated data structures and use Xilinx Vivado HLS as an exemplary HLS tool. We show up to $10\times$ speed-up after parallelization of the HLS implementations and the insertion of the application-specific distributed hybrid scratchpad architecture.

## Categories and Subject Descriptors

B.5.2 [**Design Aids**]: Automatic synthesis

## General Terms

Algorithms, Design

## Keywords

High-Level Synthesis, Caching Schemes, Separation Logic

## 1. INTRODUCTION

High-level synthesis (HLS) raises the abstraction level from register transfer level (RTL) to high-level languages, such as C/C++, and can significantly shorten the design cycle when developing applications for field-programmable gate arrays (FPGAs) as compared with an RTL-based specification. State-of-the-art C-to-FPGA tools such as Xilinx Vivado HLS, ROCCC [2] or LegUp [1] can deliver a quality of results (QoR), measured in terms of latency and resource utilization, close to hand-written RTL implementations [12, 17]. The extraction of parallelism is crucial for achieving a good QoR. Computational parallelism also requires that the memory system is not a sequential bottleneck to performance. The distributed memory architecture in FPGAs can provide impressive memory bandwidth if the program data can be partitioned and distributed over multiple on-chip memory banks. Parallel on-chip memory capacity remains a scarce resource and many FPGA applications that process large data sets require access to a large off-chip memory. Accessing external memory, however, can substantially slow down an FPGA accelerator due to memory bandwidth limitations and, in the worst case, the contention on the external memory bus eliminates the gain of parallelization. An application-specific optimization of the on-chip/off-chip memory architecture is thus crucial for mapping a program to an efficient FPGA implementation.

Caching frequently reused data is a common approach to reduce the number of expensive accesses to an external memory. FPGAs allow the implementor to tailor the memory interface according to the requirements of the application. An application-specific optimization of this architecture introduces yet another complex design space and remains a complex task for a developer. Furthermore, automatic cache design in an HLS context requires the extraction of application-specific properties from program descriptions and remains foreign to most HLS flows. This work seeks to bridge this gap. We present an HLS design aid that inserts multiple on-chip caches into the interface to an off-chip memory which results in an application-specific high-performance memory hierarchy. Our technique leverages recent memory abstractions [9,10], which build an on-chip/off-chip memory hierarchy underneath a uniform interface and which we refer to as *scratchpads* (SPs) in this paper. Each single SP contains an optional on-chip cache and automatically ensures coherency between the cache contents and data in off-chip memory for an arbitary memory access pattern [9]. SPs also provide an optional mechanism to maintain coherency between the on-chip caches in multiple, parallel SPs [10]. In this work, we leverage a program analysis to determine whether or not such an inter-scratchpad coherency mechanism is required in the generated multi-scratchpad architecture.

This work is based on a static program analysis that extracts memory access information. It focuses on heap-manipulating C/C++ programs, making this work a complement to existing work based on run-time profiling [15], manual code annotations [20] or automated analyses that target explicitly static arrays referenced in static loop nests (leveraging the *polyhedral model*) [11, 16, 19]. Our motivation is driven by the fact that pointer-based memory references and dynamic memory allocation are well established and widely used features of high-level languages such as C++, their analysis and automated program optimizations resulting from it, however, are beyond the scope of the most HLS techniques to date. The memory model in C/C++ assumes the presence of a *heap*, a large monolithic memory space and the identification of independent and shared portions in heap remains complicated because of the difficulty of disambiguating aliases and predicting the referenced memory locations.

The heap analysis used in this work is based on *separation logic* [18], a theory for reasoning about the behavior of programs that finds its main application in modern software verification tools. We build on a baseline analysis presented in [7] which determines whether (parts of) the accessed heap memory can be completely partitioned into disjoint, non-overlapping portions, which we refer to as *heaplets*. Finding a solution to this question is a pre-requisite for parallelizing the loop by splitting it into parallel sub-loops and partitioning the on-chip memory space. The analysis guides automated code transformations which ensure the synthesizability of heap-manipulating C++ programs by off-the-shelf HLS tools and implement the partitioning and parallelization. The applicability of the baseline technique in [7] is limited to cases where the on-chip memory capacity is sufficient and the accessed memory space can be split into independent, private partitions. In this paper we extend it to shared resources and apply it to the synthesis of efficient interfaces to an off-chip memory. To the best of our knowledge, this is the first application of a separation logic-based analysis to an automated optimization of the on-chip/off-chip memory hierarchy for FPGA accelerators. The contributions are:

○ In addition to the identification of disjoint heap regions, we extend the baseline analysis in [7] by an identification of heaplets that would be shared by the parallel loop kernels after parallelization by the source-to-source translator. Our analysis inserts additional synchronization primitives for program parts that access shared resources.

○ Even if coherency is ensured, updates to the shared resource may happen in a different order after parallelization compared to the sequential program. This paper presents a *commutativity analysis* for the shared heap update in order to prove that the parallelization is semantics-preserving.

○ The framework targets FPGA accelerators with access to an off-chip memory. The disjointness and sharing infor-

```
1  //main kernel function
2  void traverse(TR *root, CI *z) {
3    CS* c0 = new CS;
4    *c = ...;
5    ST *s = push(root, c0, true, NULL);
6    while (s != NULL) {
7      TR *u; CS *c; bool d;
8      s = pop(&u, &c, &d, s);
9      TR tn = *u;
10     CS cs = *c;
11     if (d) {
12       delete c;
13     }
14     CS *cnew = new CS;
15     *cnew = subfunction1(cs);
16     if  (tn.left!=NULL) && (tn.right!=NULL)
              && subfunction2(cs) {
17       s = push(tn.left, cnew, true, s);
18       s = push(tn.right, cnew, false, s);
19     } else {
20       delete cnew;
21       CI w = tn.wgtCent;
22       CI wprev = z->wgtCent;
23       z->wgtCent = wprev+ w;
24     }
25     delete u;
26   }
27 }
28 //auxiliary function push (create new entry)
29 ST* push(TR *u, CS *c, bool d, ST *s){
30   ST *t = new ST;
31   t->u=u; t->c=c; t->d=d; t->n=s;
32   return t;
33 }
34 //auxiliary function pop (delete list head)
35 ST* pop(TR **u, CS **c, bool *d, ST *s){
36   *u=s->u; *c=s->c; *d=s->d; ST *t=s->n;
37   delete s; return t;
38 }
```

**Listing 1: C-like pseudo code from a $K$-means clustering kernel [5].**

mation provided by our analyses are used to break the heap (residing in off-chip memory by default) into heaplets, to generate an application-specific parallel multi-scratchpad architecture containing on-chip caches and (if needed) coherency mechanisms: We synthesize parallel private scratchpads for disjoint heap regions and (inherently more expensive) coherent parallel scratchpads for shared regions.

○ We demonstrate the effectiveness of our technique using three applications as test cases which dynamically allocate memory and traverse and update heap-allocated data structures. We use Xilinx Vivado HLS as an exemplary back-end HLS tool in our case studies. We use the open-source LEAP infrastructure [8] and implement our test cases on a Virtex 7 FPGA connected to a DDR3 memory.

Section 2 presents a motivating example for this work. Section 3 describes our program analyses. Section 4 gives a brief overview of the implementation followed by a presentation of our experimental results in Section 5. Section 6 discusses related work and Section 7 concludes the paper.

## 2. MOTIVATING EXAMPLE

This section reviews a motivating example in the context of our previous work in [7] and explains how the extensions of baseline analysis in [7] are applied to generate a multi-

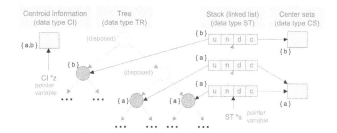

**Figure 1: Snapshot of the pointer-linked dynamic data structures accessed by the loop in Listing 1.**

scratchpad architecture for both private and shared heap regions. Listing 1 shows C-like pseudo code taken from (a modified version of) a tree-based $K$-means clustering implementation [5]. The `while`-loop in `traverse` accesses four heap-allocated data structures: the binary tree (type `TR`), the sets of candidate centers (type `CS`), the stack (type `ST`) and the centroid (type `CI`). The tree has been built up from the data set to be clustered. The center sets are intermediate solutions propagated through the call graph. The stack data structure is a pointer-linked list which manages the tree traversal. It stores the pointers to left and right sub-trees and the center sets. Retrieving these pointers from it and `new`/`delete` operations on its head are performed by the auxiliary functions `push` (lines 5, 17 and 18) and `pop` (line 8). If the data-dependent conditional (line 16) evaluates to false (dead end of the tree traversal) the centroid data structure is updated (lines 22 and 23) which contains the information from which the final clustering result is calculated.

All data structures accessed by this program are created at run-time using dynamic memory allocation. Allocating memory at run-time results in efficient memory usage if the average-case amount of required memory is much smaller than the worst-case amount. An efficient memory architecture for this program provides fast access to this small amount of memory space and, at the same time, supports worst-case allocation by providing a large memory as a backup. Hence, our approach is to place, by default, all heap-allocated data in a large off-chip memory connected to the FPGA accelerator and to insert scratchpads including on-chip caches which mirror parts of the off-chip data and provide fast data access. We describe the baseline method in [7] and its extensions are described below.

## 2.1 Memory Partitioning and Parallelization

This section reviews the partitioning method in [7] and demonstrates its application to the novel multi-scratchpad synthesis. Fig. 1 shows an example of the data structures allocated in the heap after executing two `while`-loop iterations. The data structures are grouped according to their types. The loop is split into in parallel sub-loops as shown in Listing 2 (two in this example). If we ignore the centroid data structure (type `CI`) in the heap layout in Fig. 1 for a moment, the method in [7] can prove that the pointers dereferenced in any iteration of a sub-loop never refer to the data structures used by the other loop. We call these loop kernels 'communication free' with respect to each other, which satisfies the 'independence condition' that two parts of a program can operate in parallel if they access different data. A standard HLS tool can use the independence information to instantiate parallel hardware blocks. The analysis partitions

```
1  //main kernel function
2  void traverse(TR *root, CI *z) {
3      ...preamble (pointers access partitions a
          and b)
4      while (s_a != NULL) {
5      //parallel loop kernel a
6      ..access private SP for CS, partition a
7      ..access private SP for ST, partition a
8      ..access private SP for TR, partition a
9      acquireLock();
10     ..access coherent SP for CI, partition a
11     releaseLock();
12     }
13     while (s_b != NULL) {
14     //parallel loop kernel b
15     ..access private SP for CS, partition b
16     ..access private SP for ST, partition b
17     ..access private SP for TR, partition b
18     acquireLock();
19     ..access coherent SP for CI, partition b
20     releaseLock();
21     }
22  }
```

**Listing 2: Transformed program from Listing 1.**

the remaining tree data structure (dark gray nodes, type `TR`) into two sub-trees labeled with $\{a\}$ and $\{b\}$. It splits the linked list (type `ST`) into the uppermost node and the nodes below, and the pool of center sets (type `CS`) is partitioned accordingly. The generation of the multi-scratchpad architecture in this work uses the heap partitioning information from the baseline analysis. Each of the parallel sub-loops obtains its own interfaces to off-chip memory and the fact that the memory regions can be proven to be non-overlapping allows our setup to instantiate private SPs for each partition without the need to ensure coherency between them, greatly reducing hardware implementation cost.

## 2.2 Parallel Access to Shared Resources

Our baseline analysis in [7] cannot handle situations including the shared centroid information in Fig. 1. In this work, we present an extension which marks it as a shared resource, indicated by the label $\{a,b\}$, as both sub-loops would update it after parallelization. After the detection of a shared heap region, our framework instantiates a coherent memory interface [10] to this region in each of the sub-loops. The coherent interface consists of two parts: SPs with caches and a coherence mechanism that ensures data coherency between them and locks which enable atomic updates of the shared resource in the presence of multiple accessors. The detection of a shared resource triggers a second analysis as sharing invalidates the independence assumption that parallel units access different data. Assuming that coherency is ensured between parallel units, it remains to prove that the modified order in which the shared resource is updated after parallelization does not alter the program semantics. The shared centroid information is updated in line 23:

$$z \to \texttt{wgtCent} = w_{prev} + w;$$

where $w$ is the contribution of the tree nodes. In the original, sequential program $z$ receives the contributions of all nodes in the right sub-tree (labeled with $\{a\}$) before it receives the first contribution from the left sub-tree (labeled with $\{b\}$ in Fig. 1). However, in the parallelized version $z$ may be updated with data from left and right sub-tree in an arbitrarily interleaved fashion. In this example, the parallelization is legal because of the commutativity and associativity of the addition[1]. In general, we address this question with a commutativity analysis of the update function.

Listing 2 shows the final result of a source code transformation based on the result of all analyses above. The transformed source code, when run through a back-end HLS tool and RTL implementation, results in a custom configuration of multiple private/coherent scratchpads with a custom degree of parallelism. The on-chip memory blocks in modern FPGAs, a distinguishing feature compared to microprocessors, are aggregated accordingly in order to construct the application-specific parallel caching scheme. The difficult part of these memory system optimizations is the heap analysis: Heap-directed pointer expressions are not restricted to a particular scope and can reference any memory cell in the global heap, which may lead to dependencies between expressions in the program that are syntactically unrelated. Furthermore, the values of pointers change during runtime. A static analysis ruling out pointer aliasing relations is particularly challenging for pointer-linked data structures. Separation logic provides an efficient theoretical framework for expressing the heap layout and alias information during program execution as described below.

# 3. PROGRAM ANALYSIS

This section describes the program analyses enabling the source code transformations that turn a sequential heap-manipulating program into a parallelized HLS implementation with an application-specific off-chip memory interface. The following background section briefly reviews theoretical background of separation logic [18] and the heap analysis developed previously in [7], which we refer to the 'baseline analysis' and which this work builds on. New extensions of the baseline are described after Section 3.1.

## 3.1 Background

Our static analysis is based on the *symbolic execution* of an imperative program under test. The values assigned to program variables and memory cells accessed are referred to as *program state*. During execution, the state is modified by program statements (commands). Additionally, a program contains control parts such as conditionals and loops. The symbolic execution engine in our analysis propagates the program state through all paths of the program's control flow graph (CFG). Branching creates multiple control flow paths and loops additionally create a cycle.

The analysis uses a formal description of the program state. It describes the values assigned to program variables (*e.g.* $x = 3 \land y = 5$ means that variable $x$ and $y$ currently hold the value 3 and 5, respectively, where '$\land$' is the classical 'and'-conjunction). At each CFG node, the symbolic execution engine updates the current description of the program state, *e.g.* the assignment statement $x := 1$ results in the new state $x = 1 \land y = 5$. In addition to this, the state model consists of the *heap* which describes the values assigned to addressable memory locations (*e.g.* $v \mapsto 4$ means that the memory cell referenced by the pointer variable $v$ contains

the value 4). Reasoning about the program semantics in this way is substantially more complicated if a program uses heap-directed pointers. Assuming that the current program state is $u \mapsto 4 \land v \mapsto 6$ and we execute the heap update command $[u] := 1$, we may wish to conclude that the assignment does not affect the heap cell referenced by $v$, *i.e.* $u \mapsto 1 \land v \mapsto 6$. This, of course, can only be ensured if we explicitly rule out the potential aliasing of $u$ and $v$ by adding an additional contraint: $u \neq v \land u \mapsto 1 \land v \mapsto 6$. These constraints are required for each pair of pointers in the program which quickly limits the applicability of an automated heap analysis to real-life programs that arise in practice.

Separating logic solves this problem by extending the classical first order logic by a 'separating conjunction' ($*$): The formula $u \mapsto 4 * v \mapsto 6$ means that the heap is split into two disjoint portions $h_0$ and $h_1$, where $u \mapsto 4$ holds for $h_0$ and $v \mapsto 6$ holds for $h_1$. We call disjoint heap portions *heaplets*. The $*$-operator rules out aliasing of pointers $u$ and $v$ by definition, *i.e.* it implies $u \neq v$. Hence, each heap cell can be updated without any side effects for the other one. In addition to single values, $u \mapsto [\mathtt{f}_1 : x_1', .., \mathtt{f}_n : x_n']$ describes a heap-allocated record (*structs* in C/C++): $u$ points to a record containing the fields $\mathtt{f}_1, ..., \mathtt{f}_n$ with content $x_1', ..., x_n'$. In addition to program variables $u$, $v$, $x$ and $y$, the primed variables $x_1', ..., x_n'$ are symbolic replacements of values and are only used in formulae (not as program variables). The abbreviation $u \mapsto \_$ means that $u$ points to 'some' record.

In general, formulae in separation logic are of the form $\Pi \land \Sigma$, where $\Pi$ are assertions in classical logic (connected by '$\land$') and $\Sigma$ are spatial assertions such as $u \mapsto 4 * v \mapsto 6$. $\Sigma$ can also include the value *emp* which denotes an empty heap where nothing is allocated. Pointer variables may hold a special value $\mathtt{nil}$ corresponding to the $\mathtt{NULL}$ expression in C/C++. The effect of heap-manipulating program commands (*new*, *delete* and dereferencing for read/write) can be specified with concise separation logic formulae and used by the symbolic execution engine. Our symbolic execution implements a technique called *labeled symbolic execution* [21]. For each program statement, it assigns a unique label to the accessed heap portions of the current state. In the original work in [21], each program statement $C_i$ is assigned a unique label $l_i$. The technique thus propagates the 'heap footprint' of each statement through the CFG. Our heap access analyses use modified versions of labeled symbolic execution in order to find disjoint and shared heap regions.

Our baseline analysis for identifying private heap regions and memory partitioning [7] is the starting point for all subsequent analyses related to parallelization, shared resources and commutativity of shared resource updates. Loop parallelization and its follow-up analyses are only triggered if (at least parts of) the heap-allocated data structures accessed by the loop can be split into $P$ partitions, where $P$ is the desired parallelism degree. The inner do-while-loop in Algorithm 1 summarizes the baseline analysis in [7]. It starts with a symbolic execution of the loop preamble and a finite number of the first loop iterations (function SYMBEXELOOPBODY). In each step, it explores the separation logic formula describing the pre-state of the loop ($\Pi \land \Sigma$), *i.e.* the program state before executing the loop body. Our analysis is based on *cut-points*: A cut-point is a program variable pointing

---

[1]We focus on integer or fixed-point systems and ignore non-associativity caused by floating-point representations.

to a heaplet in the symbolic heap [7]. The algorithm inserts cut-points into the loop pre-state formulae (function CUTPINSERT) while it peels off loop iterations so as to find a valid cut-point assignment. We define a cut-point as valid if 1) it consists of $P$ cut-points, 2) these $P$ cut-points reference heaplets of the same shape, *i.e.* describe the same type of data structure, 3) the built-in proof engine, performing a *fix-point calculation* for the loop-under-analysis (function FIXPCALC) proves that the initial partitioning of the heap-allocated data structures is maintained for all subsequent loop iterations. Note that, for ease of explanation, we omit cases in Algorithm 1 where multiple alternative cut-point insertions for the same number of unrolled iterations are available and need to be checked as discussed in [7].

The proof of loop-invariant resource separation is generated by assigning a state to each inserted cut-point (function ASSIGNCPSTATES). The fix-point calculation assigns footprint labels to the accessed heaplets according to the current cut-point state, which changes once a heaplet referenced by a different cut-point is accessed during the symbolic execution. Complete partitioning of the heap accessed by the loop-under-test is proven by the absence of non-singleton label sets attached to the heaplets in the state formulae. A detailed description of the technique is given in [7]. If we ignore the centroid information in the motivating example, starting from the pre-state in Fig. 1 and with a second cut-point $s_b$ (in addition to $s$) referencing the uppermost stack record in Fig. 1, the proof of complete separability is generated by our baseline analysis, a prerequisite for parallelization.

## 3.2 Detecting Private and Shared Resources

The baseline analysis in [7] is limited to cases where the accessed memory space can be split into independent, private partitions. We aborted the analysis reporting a failed proof after a fixed parameter of $L$ unrollings if the program state cannot be completely partitioned. Here, we relax the constraint that the inherent parallelism of the application needs to be communication-free. Algorithm 1 shows the extended baseline analysis to identify disjoint and shared resources. If we include the centroid information in our motivating example and run the disjointness analysis, the proof engine always finds a non-singleton label set attached to it and never reports a valid proof. Our goal is to mark this heaplet as a shared resource. The shared resource analysis requires two extensions of the baseline analysis: 1) identifying shared heaplets and 2), once marked as shared, re-running the cut-point insertion and proof-engine invocations while excluding them from the search for separable heap regions.

In the first phase, we turn a failed proof of complete separability into the detection of shared resources. We run the cut-point insertion and fix-point calculation with the objective of splitting the heap into $P$ partitions as in [7], as shown in the inner **do-while**-loop in Algorithm 1. After peeling off the first loop iteration of the motivating example, the function FIXPCALC terminates unsuccessfully because it finds non-singleton label sets attached to a center set and the centroid information. After unrolling two iterations, the sharing of a center set disappears and the centroid information remains as the only shared resource. We use a heuristic approach to filter shared resources by declaring all heaplets which have a non-singleton label sets after $L$ unrollings as

**Algorithm 1** Detecting Private and Shared Resources.

Input:
Loop body specification (code)
Initial state formula $(\Pi \wedge \Sigma)_{\text{initial}}$
Output:
Assignment of pointer statements to heap partitions
Number of initial unrollings
Shared/private predicate for pointer statements
Variables:
$it$: Iteration counter (number of iterations to be unrolled)
$C$: Set of cut-points
$C_{shared}$: Set of cut-points referencing shared heaplets
$S_{cutpoints}$: Set of cut-point states
$\Pi \wedge \Sigma$: Loop pre-state formula
$StmtS$: Set of statement sets accessing shared heaplets
**procedure** HEAPANALYSIS
    $C_{shared} \leftarrow \emptyset$
    **do**
        $it \leftarrow 0$
        $C \leftarrow \emptyset$
        $\Pi \wedge \Sigma \leftarrow (\Pi \wedge \Sigma)_{\text{initial}}$
        $StmtsS \leftarrow \emptyset$
        $success \leftarrow$ **false**
        **do**
            **while** $C$ not valid **do**
                $\Pi \wedge \Sigma \leftarrow$ SYMBEXELOOPBODY$(\Pi \wedge \Sigma, it)$
                $\Pi \wedge \Sigma, C \leftarrow$ CUTPINSERT$(\Pi \wedge \Sigma, C_{shared})$
                $it \leftarrow it + 1$
            **end while**
            $S_{cutpoints} \leftarrow$ ASSIGNCPSTATES$(C)$
            $success, Stmts_{shared} \leftarrow$ FIXPCALC(
                $\Pi \wedge \Sigma, C, S_{cutpoints}, C_{shared})$
            $StmtsS \leftarrow StmtsS \cup \{Stmts_{shared}\}$
        **while** (not $success$) and $(it < L)$
        **if** $it = L$ **then**
            $C_{shared} \leftarrow$ EXTRCTCUTP$(\underset{Stmts \in StmtsS}{\operatorname{argmin}} |Stmts|)$
        **end if**
    **while** not $success$
    ... generate analysis output
**end procedure**

shared. The fix-point calculation is modified in that whenever it detects sharing on a heaplet, it collects the set of program statements that accessed the shared heaplet (each statement in the control flow graph has a unique identifier). During the course of the alternating iteration unrolling, cut-point insertion and fix-point calculation, the analysis builds a set of statement sets accessing shared heaplets ($StmtsS$).

After termination of the inner **do-while**-loop, the analysis is reset. From $StmtsS$, we pick the set $Stmts$ containing the fewest statements accessing shared resources, from which the function EXTRCTCUTP extracts all cut-points mentioned in at least one of these program statements ($C_{shared}$). The second phase begins by relaunching the analysis. We pass the set $C_{shared}$ to the to the modified function CUTPINSERT which excludes these cut-points during the search for cut-points in the loop pre-state. Similarly during the fix-point calculation we prevent the analysis from adding a partition label to a heaplet if the current program statement has been marked as excluded. Finally, we obtain a proof of separability for the tree, the stack and the pool of center sets, and the centroid heaplet is marked as a shared resource. The interface to the shared heap region residing in off-chip memory is then supported by a coherency protocol. The corresponding program statements accessing the shared resource are lines 22 and 23. The notion of these statements, extracted from the anaysis, is used by the source code transformation to insert *acquireLock* and *releaseLock* commands before and after the critical statements as shown in Listing 2 in order to ensure atomic updates of the shared heap region.

## 3.3 Commutativity Analysis

Parallelization in the presence of shared resources requires a second analysis step after detection of a shared heap region. We must verify that, after parallelization, the program semantics are not altered because the order in which the updates of the shared resource are made by the parallel version is altered. For example, during the execution of the original (unparallelized) loop in Listing 1, the shared centroid information receives all contributions from the right sub-tree before it receives any contribution from the left sub-tree, while it may be updated with data from left and right sub-tree in an arbitrarily interleaved fashion in the parallelized version. Enforcing the original order with barrier synchronization means re-sequentializing the parallelized implementation and is not a viable solution. Instead we want to determine that the modified order of state updates is legal. In the following walk-through, for ease of explanation, we define the function $F$ which reads and writes the shared state (lines 22 and 23 in Listing 1):

DEFINITION 1   (UPDATE FUNCTION).

> **function** $F(w)$
>   $w_{prev} = z \to \texttt{wgtCent}$;
>   $z \to \texttt{wgtCent} = w_{prev} + w$;
> **end function**

A commutativity analysis was proposed by Rinard and Diniz [25] and our approach builds on the same basic idea: We say two operations on the program state are commutable if their execution in sequence results in the same program state regardless of their execution order. In our case, $F$ is commutable if $\forall w_1, w_2, F(w_1); F(w_2)$ results in the same program state as $F(w_2); F(w_1)$. From the symbolic execution and detection of the shared resources as above, we extract the pre- and post-conditions on the program state:

$$\{w = w'_0 \wedge z \mapsto [\texttt{wgtCent} : w'_1]\} \qquad (1)$$
$$F$$
$$\{w = w'_0 \wedge w'_2 = w'_1 + w'_0 \wedge z \mapsto [\texttt{wgtCent} : w'_2]\}$$

The extraction phase brings the pre- and post-specification of $F$ into a canonical form $\Pi \wedge \Sigma$, where $\Pi$ are the pure formulae and $\Sigma$ are the spatial formulae referring to the shared heap resource. For example, the built-in symbolic execution engine ensures that arithmetic operations in the state formulae appear only in the pure part by creating a fresh primed variable $w'_2$. We test whether $F$ is commutable by symbolically executing two sequences of two calls to $F$:

$$w = w'_{0,1}; \ F(w); \ w = w'_{0,2}; \ F(w); \ w = w'_{0,3}; \qquad (2)$$
$$w = w'_{0,2}; \ F(w); \ w = w'_{0,1}; \ F(w); \ w = w'_{0,3}; \qquad (3)$$

Note the permuted assignment of symbolic values to $w$ in (3). In order to show that $F$ is commutable, we must prove that the post-states of the sequences in (2) and (3) describe the same program state. Their post-state formulae are:

$$w = w'_{0,3} \wedge w'_3 = w'_1 + w'_{0,1} + w'_{0,2} \wedge z \mapsto [\texttt{wgtCent} : w'_3] \qquad (4)$$
$$w = w'_{0,3} \wedge w'_4 = w'_1 + w'_{0,2} + w'_{0,1} \wedge z \mapsto [\texttt{wgtCent} : w'_4] \qquad (5)$$

The updated shared resource in (4) and (5) is described by $z \mapsto [\texttt{wgtCent} : w'_3]$ and $z \mapsto [\texttt{wgtCent} : w'_4]$, respectively. We want to prove that these predicates describe the same state. We first ask a separation logic theorem prover whether they match which recognizes their equality in shape and creates a new proof obligation:

$$w'_3 = w'_4 \qquad (6)$$

Next, we combine the verification condition (6) with the remaining pure parts of the formulae and aim to prove:

$$\forall w'_{0,2}, w'_{0,1}. \qquad (7)$$
$$w = w'_{0,3} \wedge w'_3 = w'_1 + w'_{0,1} + w'_{0,2} \wedge$$
$$w = w'_{0,3} \wedge w'_4 = w'_1 + w'_{0,2} + w'_{0,1} \Rightarrow (w'_3 = w'_4)$$

In the actual verification step, we use satisfiability modulo theories (SMT) solving [4] to decide (7). However, an SMT solver cannot deal with the universal quantification ($\forall$), so we rephrase (7) by negating the verification condition:

$$\exists w'_{0,2}, w'_{0,1}. \qquad (8)$$
$$w = w'_{0,3} \wedge w'_3 = w'_1 + w'_{0,1} + w'_{0,2} \wedge$$
$$w = w'_{0,3} \wedge w'_4 = w'_1 + w'_{0,2} + w'_{0,1} \wedge (w'_3 \neq w'_4)$$

The solver returns one of three possible results: 1) If (8) is satisfiable, we can find an assignment to the input variables $w'_{0,2}, w'_{0,1}$ of $F$ that makes the program states after executing both sequences different: $F$ is not commutable. 2) If (8) is not satisfiable, there is no such assignment: $F$ is commutable. 3) The solver may not be able to decide the question in which case we conservatively assume that $F$ is not commutable. For the running example and with the theory of linear arithmetic of integers it decides that $F$ is commutable. Commutativity has been shown to be an undecidable problem in general [14]. However, it can still be shown for many cases that arise in practice. Our analysis is conservative: If we cannot decide it, we declare the update function non-commutative and abort the parallelization.

## 3.4 Robustness of the Heap Analysis

The heap analysis is the core element of our framework. We briefly discuss its performance and identify weaknesses motivating future research. An advantage of our technique is that it can, beyond straightline code and deterministic static control parts such as unrollable `for`-loops, handle `while`-loops enclosing data-dependent conditionals, and with data-dependent loop condition and unknown iterations count. This feature requires us to describe data structures of unknown size to ensure convergence of the fix-point calculation. We achieve this with recursive predicates as discussed in [7]. For instance, an acyclic linked list is described by:

$$ls(x, y) \Leftrightarrow (x = y \wedge emp) \vee$$
$$(x \neq y \wedge x \mapsto [\texttt{n} : x'_1] * ls(x'_1, y) ) \qquad (9)$$

Our analysis is based on symbolic execution which mimics the actual program execution and heap accesses. In contrast to a *reachability analysis* [22], another common approach to disjointness detection, which relies on the reachability properties of certain pointer data structures (*e.g.* left and right sub-tree), the separation logic-based heap footprint analysis can also partition cyclic data structures, such as a circular linked list or a doubly linked list.

Folding singleton heaplets into recursive predicates is essential for the successful termination of the loop analysis. For example, our analysis automatically folds

$$s \mapsto [\mathbf{n} : s_1'] * s_1' \mapsto [\mathbf{n} : s_0'] * s_0' \mapsto [\mathbf{n} : \mathbf{nil}] \quad (10)$$

into $ls(s, \mathbf{nil})$. The recursive predicates are defined in logic rules used by the built-in theorem prover which automatically searches for applicable rules. We define a set of predicates for common data structures such as trees, lists, lists with additional pointers to singleton heaplets and sub-trees. These allow us to cover a large range of pointer-based programs. However, we may find applications using more exotic structures for which no folding rule in our current set applies. This limitation can be removed by integrating algorithms for automatic inference of recursive predicates, such as [24] in our tool. The decision under what conditions the folding is triggered builds on a heuristic [23] which 'gobbles up' heaplets by recursive predicates if their pointers are primed variables which do not appear in any other part of the formula except of the predicates involved in the folding. The heuristic works well in practice and we are not aware of a theorem prover implementing a more robust technique. However, in general, we cannot rule out situations where the folding fails due to the incompleteness of the heuristic. A code example where this is the case in given in [23]. The same holds for Algorithm 1 itself which uses a heuristic to distinguish private from shared heap regions. Our analysis may thus indicate sharing of a heaplet which in reality is private to a particular code section. Note that this does not compromise correctness but only performance as our tool instantiates an unnecessary coherency mechanism in this case. We argue that the benchmark applications in Section 5 are representative of common pointer-based programs.

The scalability of the analysis is determined by the fix-point calculation which performs repeated symbolic executions of the loop body until convergence. Non-deterministic branching (*e.g.* data dependent conditionals) in the loop body results in several disjunctive clauses describing the loop state as all control flow paths must be analyzed. In the worst case the number of these clauses can grow exponentially with the number of fix-point iterations. However, absorbing heaplets in recursive predicates contains the growth of the state formula. For moderate parallelism degrees, we observe a maximum of 28 disjunctive clauses which results in up to 7 minutes for the fix-point calculation.

The next section describes our compilation flow that uses the information provided by the above program analyses to generate application-specific multi-scratchpad architectures.

# 4. CODE GENERATION

We implemented a prototype tool of our technique consisting of three parts main parts: 1) The heap analyzer implements the analyses described in the previous section and interfaces the Z3 SMT solver [4]. 2) The source-to-source translator is built on the ROSE compiler infrastructure [3]

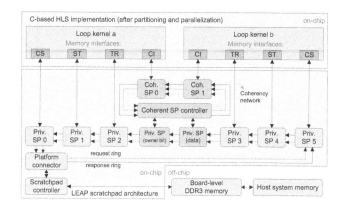

**Figure 2: Parallelized HLS implementation of the filtering algorithm with a hybrid cache architecture.**

and implements the loop parallelization and pointer access transformations. The heap analyzer and source translator are extensions of the baseline framework described in [7]. 3) We leverage the open-source LEAP (Latency-insensitive Environment for Application Programming) framework [8] to embed the C/C++-based HLS kernels in an environment that provides access to a physical FPGA device and memory.

Like an operating system, LEAP provides a unified layer of abstraction on top of device-specific drivers that interface the underlying FPGA device, on-board memory and the host system an FPGA card is plugged into. In particular, our setup uses LEAP's *scratchpads* (SPs), a memory interface abstraction for FPGA applications. SPs provide a simple read-request, read-response and write memory interface to the connected application. Internally, Leap scratchpads instantiate a memory hierarchy: an optional on-chip cache, board-level off-chip memory and finally the main memory of the attached host system as shown in Fig. 2. SPs without on-chip caches forward all requests to off-chip memory which results in longer response times. The same applies for cache misses. Evicted items are automatically flushed to the next memory level. The framework provides two types of SPs: 1) *Private scratchpads* [9] are instantiated when memory spaces are known to be disjoint from all regions accessed by other memory interfaces. 2) If several memory interfaces refer to a shared memory region we instantiate *coherent scratchpads* [10]. The latter feature consists of distributed caches backed by a coherence protocol. Multiple coherent SPs appear as independent interfaces to the application, while they are internally connected via a ring network that ensures coherency between them. The shared memory abstraction by coherent scratchpads hides the internals of the coherency mechanism. Coherent SPs are more expensive (in terms of FPGA resources) and slower (in terms of response time) than their private counterparts.

Our source translator replaces the basic C++ routines for dynamic memory allocation with custom implementations to ensure synthesizability by off-the-shelf HLS tools. Occurrences of **new** and **delete** statements are grouped according to the type of their operand and custom allocator functions are instantiated for each type. The fixed-size allocator is a standard implementation using a *free-list* which keeps track of occupied memory space [6]. Heap memory is replaced by arrays located in off-chip memory by default (a portion of

```
1  requestLock(access_critical_region0);
2  waitForLock(); //stalls until lock has been
       acquired
3  ...issueMemoryRequest //set memory fence
4  releaseLock(access_critical_region0);
```

**Listing 3: Lock-synchronized shared memory access.**

them resides on-chip via caches) and each heap access becomes an access to the external memory bus. The translator turns pointer dereferencing into array-based bus accesses and instantiates a memory interface for each data structure type and each of the $P$ heap partitions (private and shared). The heap analyzer provides information whether the memory bus points to a private or a shared heap region. We insert a generic Verilog wrapper for each interface that acts as a bridge between Vivado's native bus protocol and the LEAP memory interface. Vivado's scheduler ensures that, when the HLS kernel issues a memory request, it stalls execution until the memory request has been serviced by the SP.

Fig. 2 shows the integration of our running example after heap partitioning and parallelization with $P = 2$ into the LEAP framework and memory hierarchy. Each loop kernel (we omit the preamble here) has an interface to the memory system for the each type of heap-allocated data-structure: center sets (CS), stack records (ST), tree nodes (TR) and centroid information (CI). An additional coherency network is instantiated for the CI ports (shared memory). For shared heap regions, the source translator inserts synchronization signals in order to ensure fine-grain atomic updates to the shared heap cell. Listing 3 shows an example. The pass-by-reference argument `access_critical_region0` translates into a boolean signal in the generated RTL code and triggers lock acquisition and releasing. The lock service provided by LEAP ensures that no access to heap region 0 is granted before the lock is acquired (only one requestor can own the lock). The memory fence instruction ensures that the memory transaction has been completed before releasing the lock.

## 5. EXPERIMENTS

We run our experiments with three C++ applications that traverse, update, allocate and dispose dynamic data structures in heap memory. Our benchmark applications are:
**Merger** - The program builds up four linked lists from scratch performing a sorted insertion of input values, and subsequently merges and disposes the four lists to produce a single sorted output stream. The linked lists are disjoint, the parallelized program does not access shared heap memory as determined by our analysis. Four private scratchpads are inserted in the parallelized implementation.
**Tree Deletion** - This application traverses binary tree structure and deletes the visited tree nodes after some computation at each node. Our analysis splits the tree and stack (a linked list implementing the tree traversal) into $P$ disjoint sub-structures after peeling off the first loop iteration. During tree traversal, the program updates a running minimum which is heap-allocated and detected as a shared resource. Commutativity of the min-reduction can be shown. $P$ coherent scratchpads and a lock service are instantiated for the shared heap region.
**Filter** - This is our running example. The tree, center sets and linked list data structures are partitioned and supported

**Table 1: Parallelization and caching.**

| $P$ | $N_c$ | Slices | DSP | BRM | Clock | Lat. | $S$ |
|---|---|---|---|---|---|---|---|
| **Merger** ($4 \times 2048$ random input key-value pairs) | | | | | | | |
| scratchpads without on-chip caches | | | | | | | |
| 1 | 0 | 18080 | 3 | 42 | 10.0ns | 1257.9ms | **1.0** |
| 4 | 0 | 19338 | 3 | 62 | 10.0ns | 533.8ms | 2.4 |
| scratchpads with on-chip caches (32 KBytes) | | | | | | | |
| 1 | 1 | 20807 | 3 | 62 | 10.0ns | 757.6ms | 1.7 |
| 4 | 4 | 22961 | 3 | 72 | 10.0ns | 115.3ms | 10.9 |
| **Tree Deletion** (2048 tree nodes) | | | | | | | |
| scratchpads without on-chip caches | | | | | | | |
| 1 | 0 | 24711 | 15 | 52 | 10.0ns | 6575.2us | **1.0** |
| 2 | 0 | 26127 | 15 | 61 | 10.0ns | 3601.8us | 1.8 |
| 4 | 0 | 29293 | 15 | 91 | 10.0ns | 2207.9us | 3.0 |
| scratchpads with on-chip caches (32 KBytes) | | | | | | | |
| 1 | 3 | 31754 | 18 | 82 | 10.0ns | 5928.7us | 1.1 |
| 2 | 6 | 37740 | 19 | 111 | 10.0ns | 2604.3us | 2.5 |
| 4 | 12 | 41860 | 23 | 202 | 10.5ns | 711.0us | 9.2 |
| **Filter** (32767 kd-tree nodes, $K = 128$ clusters) | | | | | | | |
| scratchpads without on-chip caches | | | | | | | |
| 1 | 0 | 26508 | 39 | 69 | 10.0ns | 135.8ms | **1.0** |
| 2 | 0 | 30594 | 103 | 92 | 10.0ns | 81.9ms | 1.7 |
| 4 | 0 | 38362 | 235 | 125 | 10.0ns | 61.6ms | 2.2 |
| scratchpads with on-chip caches (32 KBytes) | | | | | | | |
| 1 | 4 | 34085 | 41 | 102 | 10.0ns | 93.4ms | 1.5 |
| 2 | 8 | 42410 | 110 | 147 | 10.0ns | 53.8ms | 2.5 |
| 4 | 16 | 51901 | 244 | 272 | 11.1ns | 41.8ms | 3.2 |

by private caches and the traversal loop is parallelized. The shared heap-allocated running sum is supported by coherent scratchpads and a lock service.

We use Xilinx Vivado HLS 2014.1 as a back-end C-to-FPGA tool. LEAP supports Altera FPGA boards as well as several boards with Xilinx FPGAs (Nallatech ACP, XUPV5, HTG-V5, ML605, VC707). Recently, support has been added for Xilinx VC709 boards with two board-level DDR3 memory modules. Here, the target platform is a VC707 evaluation board (Virtex 7 FPGA, 1GB on-board DDR3 SDRAM). We build the Bluespec-based LEAP framework with Bluespec 2014-07-A. The generated RTL code is integrated into the framework with Bluespec's `import BVI` statement. The complete FPGA designs are implemented in a hybrid flow with Synopsys Synplify 2013.09 and Xilinx ISE 14.5. The on-chip caches of the private and coherent scratchpads are direct-mapped with write-back policy and we set their size to 32 KBytes with 64 bit block size by default. We report FPGA slices, DSP48 slices, 36K Block RAMs (BRM), achieved clock period and total latency (cycle count $\times$ clock period) for the complete FPGA designs (HLS core and multi-scratchpad architecture). Table 1 quantifies the acceleration and resource consumption of parallelization and the multi-scratchpad architecture. $N_c$ is the number of inserted SPs.

**Table 2: Cost increase of all-coherent default compared to application-specific hybrid scratchpad architectures.**

| $P$ | $N_c$ | Slices | DSP | BRAM | Clock | Latency | Area-time product |
|---|---|---|---|---|---|---|---|
| **Merger** ($4 \times 2048$ random input key-value pairs) | | | | | | | |
| 4 | 4 | 31825 (38.6%) | 8 (166.7%) | 76 (5.6%) | 11.1 ns (11.0%) | 138.9 ms (20.5%) | 4421.0 slices×s (67.0%) |
| **Tree Deletion** (2048 tree nodes) | | | | | | | |
| 2 | 6 | 38296 (1.5%) | 25 (31.6%) | 132 (18.9%) | 11.1 ns (11.0%) | 4353.6 us (67.2%) | 166.7 slices×s (69.6%) |
| 4 | 12 | 52223 (24.8%) | 25 (8.7%) | 206 (2.0%) | 11.8 ns (12.4%) | 1311.1 us (84.4%) | 68.5 slices×s (130.0%) |
| **Filter** (32767 kd-tree nodes, $K = 128$ clusters) | | | | | | | |
| 2 | 8 | 45985 (8.4%) | 108 (-1.8%) | 169 (15.0%) | 11.1 ns (11.0%) | 84.7 ms (57.3%) | 3894.1 slices×s (70.6%) |
| 4 | 16 | 64330 (23.9%) | 242 (-0.8%) | 278 (2.2%) | 11.8 ns (6.3%) | 63.0 ms (50.7%) | 4051.7 slices×s (86.8%) |

For each benchmark, we set the unparallelized ($P = 1$) design with no caches as a reference (top row for each benchmark). The ratio $S$ is the speed-up of each configuration compared to the reference case ($S = 1$).

As expected, the speed-up by parallelization is moderate ($2.2\times$ - $3.0\times$) if the memory interface is not supported by caches. Adding single caches to the unparallelized implementations brings a speed-up of $1.1\times$ - $1.7\times$. We observe latency improvements when the applications are parallelized and multiple caches are inserted. The speed-up for Merger and Tree Deletion is significant in this case ($10.9\times$ and $9.2\times$) because the heap-allocated data, after partitioning by our analysis, fit almost entirely in the on-chip caches, as opposed to the tree data structure used by the filtering algorithm which achieves a moderate speed-up of $3.2\times$ due to the sub-tree size and limited reuse of tree node data.

Our analysis determines that Merger requires $P$ private SPs, while Filter and Tree Deletion require a hybrid architecture consisting of private and coherent SPs. We compare the implementation results of our application-specific architectures to an 'all-shared' scenario where no knowledge of disjoint heap regions is available to generate the multi-scratchpad system. Firstly, such a scenario requires a commutativity analysis for safe parallelization for all heap updates which significantly increases the burden of analysis. Secondly, all SPs must be supported with a coherency network by default. We focus on the second point here and quantify the additional cost of such an all-coherent architecture in terms of loss of efficiency: Table 2 lists the implementation results for the designs with all-coherent SPs. Each row also shows the increase in resource consumption, latency and the slices-latency product of the all-coherent (AC) default compared to the corresponding hybrid (HY) SP architecture in Table 1 which uses knowledge of private and shared heap regions ($\frac{AC-HY}{HY}$ in %). The AC versions use more logic and have longer latencies. We compare the efficiency of the implementations by the area-time product. Our disjointness analysis brings an overall improvement of the slices-latency product of 67.0% to 130.0% (84.8% on average).

## 6. RELATED WORK

There are several approaches to optimizing the on-chip/off-chip memory hierarchy in an HLS context. Cheng *et al.* [15] use run-time profiling to group program operations accessing the same memory addresses into partitions and to instanti-

ate separate on-chip caches assigned to disjoint memory regions accessed by the groups. This approach does not make any assumptions about the type of program to analyze. A disadvantage, however, is that it has to rely on representative test inputs and a simulation environment and requires a mechanism to take corner cases into account that have been missed during simulation. Similar to this work, the CHiMPS framework is a C-to-FPGA flow that generates a distributed multi-cache architecture [20]. A main difference to our work is that, sidestepping the coherence problem, shared memory regions are not supported by caches, while we address this issue with a sharing analysis and coherent caches. Another main difference is that independent memory regions must be manually indicated with source code annotations as opposed to an automated analysis in this work.

Significant advancements in the direction of automated static analyses have been made for loop analyses using the *polyhedral model*, an algebraic representation of the iteration space of static loop nests. The polyhedral model is applied to precisely analyze the accesses to static arrays referenced in such loop nests. For example, Liu *et al.* [16], and Bayliss and Constantinides [11] use the polyhedral model to determine the addresses of reused data items and buffer them in on-chip memories, whereas Pouchet *et al.* [19] present an on-chip buffer insertion in combination with automatic loop-level parallelization. The polyhedral model provides a powerful abstraction for the analysis of static loop kernels and array references, but it cannot analyze arbitrary memory accesses such as indirect array references or pointer accesses or capture dynamic memory allocation. The focus of our work on heap-allocated data-structures significantly increases the body of code for which automated parallelization and automatic memory-system optimizations can be applied.

## 7. CONCLUSION

Mapping dynamic memory operations to FPGAs is difficult, both in terms of analysis and implementation. In this work, we present an HLS design aid for synthesizing pointer-based C/C++ programs into efficient FPGA applications. We target applications that perform computation on large heap-allocated data structures and that require access to an off-chip memory. We leverage a separation logic-based static program analysis in [7] to determine whether different program parts access disjoint, non-overlapping regions in the monolithic heap space in which case we trigger automated source-to-source transformations that automatically parallelize the application. Our extended analyzer also detects heap regions that are shared by multiple accessors in the parallelized implementation. An additional commutativity analysis decides whether the parallelization in the presence of shared memory regions is semantics-preserving. The information provided by the heap analyses is used to optimize the interface between the parallelized HLS kernel and an off-chip memory: We generate an application-specific multi-scratchpad architecture where disjoint heap partitions are mirrored in private, independent on-chip caches and interfaces to shared heap regions are supported where necessary with on-chip caches backed by (inherently more expensive) coherency mechanisms and a synchronization service.

In our experiments with three heap-manipulating C++ benchmark applications, we observe a speed-up of up to $10.9\times$ after parallelization and generation of a multi-scratchpads architecture compared to the unparallelized application and uncached access to the off-chip memory. We also quantify the benefit of extracting application-specific knowledge about disjoint and shared heap memory regions: Our hybrid multi-scratchpads architecture consisting of private and coherent scratchpads outperforms a default all-coherent version by 84.8% on average in terms of the area-time product.

Future work will extend our static program analysis to detect data reuse during program execution. The outcome of this analysis is a binary decision whether to insert a cache. Beyond data reuse detection, we plan to integrate a prediction of memory access patterns into our analysis framework and to use this information to approximate the cache hit probability as another application-specific feature taken into account to optimize the cache architecture. Knowledge about access patterns will also be used to implement application-specific prefetching and request merging. We also plan to implement a quantification of the average amount of heap consumption to generate cache sizing information.

# 8. REFERENCES

[1] High-Level Synthesis with LegUp. [Online]. Available: http://legup.eecg.utoronto.ca/

[2] ROCCC 2.0. [Online]. Available: http://www.jacquardcomputing.com/roccc/

[3] ROSE compiler infrastructure. [Online]. Available: http://rosecompiler.org/

[4] Z3: An Efficient SMT Solver. [Online]. Available: http://z3.codeplex.com/

[5] F. Winterstein, S. Bayliss, and G. Constantinides. FPGA-Based K-Means Clustering using Tree-Based Data Structures. In *Proc. Field Programmable Logic and Appl.*, pages 362–365, 2013.

[6] F. Winterstein, S. Bayliss and G.A. Constantinides. High-level synthesis of dynamic data structures: A case study using Vivado HLS. In *Proc. Field-Programmable Technology*, pages 362–365, 2013.

[7] F. Winterstein, S. Bayliss and G.A. Constantinides. Separation logic-assisted code transformations for efficient high-level synthesis. In *Proc. Field-Program. Cust. Comput. Machines*, pages 1–8, 2014.

[8] K. Fleming, H.-J. Yang, M. Adler and J. Emer. The leap fpga operating system. In *Proc. Field Programmable Logic and Appl.*, pages 1–8, 2014.

[9] M. Adler, K. Fleming, A. Parahsar, M. Pellauer and J. Emer. Leap scratchpads: automatic memory and cache management for reconfigurable logic. In *Proc. Field Program. Gate Arrays*, pages 25–28, 2011

[10] H.-J. Yang, K. Fleming, M. Adler and J. Emer. LEAP shared memories: automating the construction of fpga coherent memories. In *Proc. Field-Programmable Custom Comput. Machines*, pages 117–124, 2014.

[11] S. Bayliss and G. Constantinides. Optimizing sdram bandwidth for custom fpga loop accelerators. In *Proc. Field Programmable Gate Arrays*, pages 195–204, 2012.

[12] BDTI. An independent evaluation of: the autoesl autopilot high-level synthesis tool, 2010.

[13] C. Calcagno and D. Distefano. Infer: an automatic program verifier for memory safety of C programs. In *Proc. NASA Formal Methods*, pages 459–465, 2011.

[14] A. Charlesworth. The undecidability of associativity and commutativity analysis. *ACM Trans. on Program. Lang. and Systems*, 24(5):554–565, Sept. 2002.

[15] S. Cheng, M. Lin, H. J. Liu, S. Scott, and J. Wawrzynek. Exploiting memory-level parallelism in reconfigurable accelerators. In *Proc. Field-Program. Cust. Comput. Machines*, pages 157–160, 2012.

[16] Q. Liu, G. Constantinides, K. Masselos, and P. Cheung. Combining data reuse with data-level parallelization for fpga-targeted hardware compilation: a geometric programming framework. *IEEE Trans. on Computer-Aided Design of Integrated Circuits and Systems*, 28(3):305–315, Mar. 2009.

[17] W. Meeus, K. Van Beeck, T. Goedemé, J. Meel, and D. Stroobandt. An overview of today's high-level synthesis tools. *Design Automation for Embedded Systems*, pages 1 – 21, Aug. 2012.

[18] P. O'Hearn, J. Reynolds, and H. Yang. Local reasoning about programs that alter data structures. In *Proc. Computer Science Logic*, pages 1–19, 2001.

[19] L.-N. Pouchet, P. Zhang, P. Sadayappan, and J. Cong. Polyhedral-based data reuse optimization for configurable computing. In *Proc. Field Programmable Gate Arrays*, pages 29–38, 2013.

[20] A. Putnam, S. Eggers, D. Bennett, E. Dellinger, J. Mason, H. Styles, P. Sundararajan, and R. Wittig. Performance and power of cache-based reconfigurable computing. *ACM SIGARCH Computer Architecture News*, 37(3):395, June 2009.

[21] M. Raza, C. Calcagno, and P. Gardner. Automatic parallelization with separation logic. In *Programming Lang. and Syst.*, pages 348–362, 2009.

[22] L.J. Hendren, A. Nicolau. Parallelizing Programs with Recursive Data Structures. In *IEEE Trans. Parallel Distrib. Syst.*, 1(1):35–47, Jan. 1990.

[23] S. Magill, A. Nanevski, E. Clarke, and P. Lee. Inferring invariants in separation logic for imperative list-processing programs. In *SPACE*, 2006.

[24] B. Guo, N. Vachharajani, and D. I. August. Shape analysis with inductive recursion synthesis. In *ACM SIGPLAN Notices*, 42(6):256–265, Jun. 2007.

[25] M. C. Rinard and P. C. Diniz. Commutativity analysis: a new analysis technique for parallelizing compilers. *ACM Transactions on Programming Languages and Systems*, 19(6):942–991, Nov. 1997.

# Impact of Memory Architecture on FPGA Energy Consumption

Edin Kadric
ekadric@seas.upenn.edu

David Lakata
dlakata@seas.upenn.edu

André DeHon
andre@acm.org

Department of Electrical and Systems Engineering
University of Pennsylvania
200 S. 33rd St., Philadelphia, PA 19104

## ABSTRACT

FPGAs have the advantage that a single component can be configured post-fabrication to implement almost any computation. However, designing a one-size-fits-all memory architecture causes an inherent mismatch between the needs of the application and the memory sizes and placement on the architecture. Nonetheless, we show that an energy-balanced design for FPGA memory architecture (memory block size(s), memory banking, and spacing between memory banks) can guarantee that the energy is always within a factor of 2 of the optimally-matched architecture. On a combination of the VTR 7 benchmarks and a set of tunable benchmarks, we show that an architecture with internally-banked 8Kb and 256Kb memory blocks has a 31% worst-case energy overhead (8% geomean). In contrast, monolithic 16Kb memories (comparable to 18Kb and 20Kb memories used in commercial FPGAs) have a 147% worst-case energy overhead (24% geomean). Furthermore, on benchmarks where we can tune the parallelism in the implementation to improve energy (FFT, Matrix-Multiply, GMM, Sort, Window Filter), we show that we can reduce the energy overhead by another 13% (25% for the geomean).

## Categories and Subject Descriptors

B.7.1 [**Integrated Circuits**]: Types and Design Styles

## Keywords

FPGA, Energy, Power, Memory, Architecture, Banking

## 1. INTRODUCTION

Energy consumption is a key design limiter in many of today's systems. Mobile devices must make the most of limited energy storage in batteries. Limits on voltage scaling mean that even wired systems are often limited by power density. Reducing energy per operation can increase the performance delivered within a limited power envelope.

Memory energy can be a significant energy component in computing systems, including FPGAs. This is particularly true when we assess the total cost of memories, including interconnect energy on wire segments that carry data to distant and distributed memory blocks or to off-chip memory.

This leads to an important architectural question: *How do we organize memories in FPGAs to minimize the energy required for a computation?* We have several choices: What are the sizes of memory blocks? Where (how frequently) are memory blocks placed in the FPGA? How are they activated? How are they decomposed into sub-block banks? Then, there are choices available to the RTL mapping flow: When mapping a logical memory to multiple blocks, should they each get a subset of the data width and be activated simultaneously? or should they each get a subset of the address range and be activated exclusively? In this paper, we first develop simple analytic relations to reason about these choices (Section 2). After reviewing some background in Section 3, we describe our methodology in Section 4. In Section 5, we perform an empirical, benchmark-based exploration to identify the most energy-efficient organization for memories in FPGAs and quantify the trade-offs between area- and energy-optimized mappings.

Section 6 takes the study from Section 5 one step further. For high-level tasks, we are not stuck with a single memory organization—the choice of parallelism in the design impacts the memory organization needed and, consequently, the total energy for the computation. A highly serial design might build a single processing element (PE) and store data in a single large memory; whereas a more parallel version would use multiple PEs and multiple, smaller memory blocks. The parallel version would then have lower memory energy, but may spend more energy on routing. Consequently, there is additional leverage to improve energy by selecting the appropriate level of parallelism. In Section 6, we explore how this selection allows energy savings and how it further drives the selection of energy-efficient FPGA memory architectures.

Contributions:

- Analytic characterization of the energy overhead that results from mismatches between the logical memory organization needed by a task and the physical memory organization provided by an FPGA (Section 2)
- First empirical exploration of memory architecture space for energy minimization (Section 5)
- VTR-compatible memory mapping for energy minimization (Section 4.2)
- Joint exploration of memory architecture space and high-level parallelism tuning (Section 6)

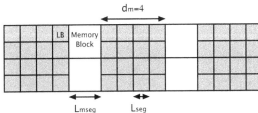

Figure 1: Column-Oriented Embedded Memories

# 2. ARCHITECTURE MISMATCH ENERGY

FPGA embedded memories generally improve area- and energy-efficiency [10]. When it perfectly matches the size and organization needed by the application, an FPGA embedded memory can be as energy-efficient as the same memory in a custom ASIC. Nonetheless, the FPGA has a fixed-size memory that is often mismatched with the task, and this mismatch can be a source of energy overhead.

First, let us consider just the memory itself. Memory energy arises almost directly from the energy to charge wire capacitance, which grows as the side length of the memory; that is, in an energy-minimizing layout, a memory block will roughly be square and the length of address lines, bit lines, and output wires grow as the square root of the memory capacity. A memory that is four times as large will require twice the energy. Therefore, when the FPGA memory block ($M_{arch}$) is larger than the application memory ($M_{app}$), there is an energy overhead that arises directly from reading from a memory bank that is too large ($E(M_{arch})/E(M_{app})$).

There is also a mismatch overhead when the memory block is smaller than the application memory. To understand this, we must also consider the routing segments needed to link up the smaller memory banks into a larger memory bank. To build a larger bank, we take a number of memory banks ($\lceil M_{app}/M_{arch} \rceil$) and wire them together, with some additional logic, to behave as the desired application memory block. In modern FPGAs it is common to arrange the memory blocks into periodic columns within the FPGA logic fabric (See Fig. 1). Assuming square memory and logic blocks, the set of smaller memory blocks used to realize the large memory block would roughly be organized into a square of side length $\left\lceil \sqrt{M_{app}/M_{arch}} \right\rceil$, demanding that each address bit and data line connected to the memory cross roughly $d_m \times \left\lceil \sqrt{M_{app}/M_{arch}} \right\rceil$ horizontal interconnect segments to address the memory, where $d_m$ is the distance between memory columns in the FPGA architecture. If $E_{seg}$ is the energy to cross a length-1 segment over a logic island in the FPGA and $E_{mseg}(M_{arch})$ is the energy to cross a length-1 segment over a memory block of capacity $M_{arch}$, the horizontal and vertical routing energy to reach across the memory is:

$$E_h = (d_m E_{seg} + E_{mseg}(M_{arch})) \times \left\lceil \sqrt{M_{app}/M_{arch}} \right\rceil \quad (1)$$

$$E_v = E_{mseg}(M_{arch}) \left\lceil \sqrt{M_{app}/M_{arch}} \right\rceil \quad (2)$$

Since the routing energy of wires comprises most of the energy in a memory read, and since each bit must travel the height of the memory block (bit lines) and the width (output select), per bit, the energy of a memory read is roughly the energy of the wires crossing it:

$$E_{bit}(M) \approx 2E_{mseg}(M) \quad (3)$$

Therefore:

$$E_{mseg}(M_{arch}) \left\lceil \sqrt{\frac{M_{app}}{M_{arch}}} \right\rceil \approx E_{mseg}(M_{app}) \approx 0.5 E_{bit}(M_{app})$$

This gives us the following mismatch ratio, driven by the ratio of the energy for routing between memory banks to the energy for routing over memory banks:

$$\frac{E_h + E_v}{E_{bit}(M_{app})} \approx 1 + \frac{d_m E_{seg}}{2 E_{mseg}(M_{arch})} \quad (4)$$

To illustrate the mismatch effects, Fig. 3a shows the result of an experiment where we quantify how the energy compares between various matched and mismatched designs. Each of the curves represents a single-processing-element matrix-multiply design that uses a single memory size; the size of the memory varies with the size of the matrices being multiplied. Each curve shows the energy mismatch ratio (Y-axis) between the energy required on a particular memory block size (X-axis) and the energy required at the energy-minimizing block size (typically the matched size); hence all curves go to 1.0 at one memory block size and increase away from that point. In contrast to the previous paragraph where we used deliberately simplified approximations to provide intuition, Fig. 3a is based on energy from placed-and-routed designs using tools and models detailed in the following sections; Fig. 3 also makes no *a priori* assumption about large memory mapping, allowing VTR [15] to place memories to minimize wiring. The figure shows how the energy mismatch ratio grows when the memory block size is larger or smaller than the matched memory block size. In practice, designs typically demand a mix of memory sizes, making it even harder to pick a single size that is good for all the memory needs of an application. Nonetheless, this single-memory size experiment is useful in understanding how each of the mismatched memories will contribute to the total memory energy overhead in a heterogeneous memory application.

There is also a potential energy overhead due to a mismatch in memory placement. Assuming we accept a column-oriented memory model, this can be stated as a mismatch between the appropriate spacing of memories for the application ($d_{m_{app}}$) and the spacing provided by the architecture ($d_{m_{arch}}$). If the memories are too frequent, non-memory routes may become longer due to the need to route over unused memories. If the memories are not placed frequently enough, the logic may need to be spread out, effectively forcing routes to be longer as they run over unused logic clusters. This gives rise to a mismatch ratio:

$$\frac{\left\lceil \frac{d_{m_{app}}}{d_{m_{arch}}} \right\rceil (d_{m_{arch}} E_{seg} + E_{mseg}(M_{arch}))}{d_{m_{app}} E_{seg} + E_{mseg}(M_{arch})} \quad (5)$$

Note that if we make $d_{m_{arch}} E_{seg} = E_{mseg}(M_{arch})$, the mismatch ratio due to route mismatch (Eq. 5) is never greater than 2×. Similarly, the mismatch ratio due to memories being too small (Eq. 4) is never greater than 1.5×. We can observe this phenomenon in Fig. 3a by looking at the 32Kb memory size that never has an overhead greater than 1.2×. In Fig. 3, we also identify the $d_{m_{arch}}$ that minimizes max-overhead (shown between square brackets for each memory size in Fig. 3). This approximately corresponds to the intuitive explanation above, where the energy for routing across memories is balanced with the energy for routing across

147

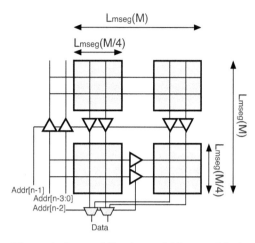

Figure 2: Internal Banking of Memory Block

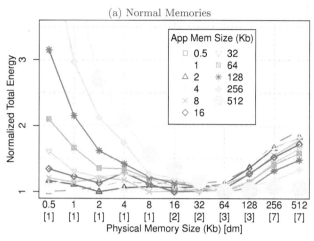

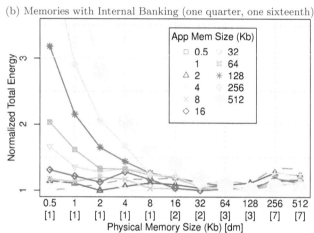

Figure 3: Energy Overhead due to Architectural Mismatch for Matrix-Multiply

logic. The 32Kb case has $E_{mseg}(M_{arch})/E_{seg} = 2.53$, suggesting a $d_{m_{arch}}$ of 2 or 3. For this 32Kb case, we found $d_{m_{arch}} = 2$ experimentally. Since segment energy is driven by wire length, $d_{m_{arch}}E_{seg} = E_{mseg}(M_{arch})$ roughly means $d_{m_{arch}}L_{seg} = L_{mseg}(M_{arch})$; when we populate memories this way, half the FPGA area is in memory blocks. This design point gives us an *energy-balanced* FPGA that makes no *a priori* assumptions about the mix of logic and memory in the design. In contrast, today's typical commercial FPGAs could be considered *logic-rich*, making sure the energy (and area) impact of added memories is small on designs that do not use memories heavily.

While the $d_{m_{arch}}E_{seg} = E_{mseg}(M_{arch})$ balance can limit the overhead when the memories are too small, we can still have large overhead when the memory blocks are too large ($E(M_{arch})/E(M_{app})$). One way to combat this problem is to use *internal banking*, or Continuous Hierarchy Memories (CHM) [8]: We can bank the memory blocks internally so that we do not pay for the full cost of a large memory block when we only need a small one. For example, if we cut the memory block into four, quarter-sized memory banks, and only use the memory bank closest to the routing fabric when the application only uses one fourth (or less) of the memory capacity, we only pay the memory energy of the smaller memory bank (See Fig. 2). In the extreme, we might recursively decompose the memory by powers-of-two so that we are never required to use a memory more than twice the size of the memory demanded by the application. There are some overheads for this banking which may suggest stopping short of this extreme. Fig. 3b performs the same experiment as Fig. 3a, except with memory blocks that can be decomposed into one-quarter and one-sixteenth capacity sub-banks. With this optimization, the curves flatten out for larger memory sizes. The physical size with smallest max-overhead is now shifted to 128Kb, still at 1.2×.

Another way to reduce the impact of memory block size mismatch is to include memory blocks of multiple sizes in the architecture. This way, the design can use the smallest memory block that will support the application memory. For example, if we had **both** 1Kb and 64Kb memories, we could map the 2Kb and smaller application memories to the 1Kb memory block and the 4Kb and larger application memories to the 64Kb block and reduce the worst-case overhead to 1.1× (Fig. 3a). However, this raises an even bigger question

about balance among logic and the multiple memory sizes. In particular, routes may now need to pass over the memory blocks of the unused size. We can generalize the previous observation about balancing routing over memories and logic to: $d_{m_1}E_{seg} = E_{mseg}(M_1)$, $d_{m_2}E_{seg} = E_{mseg}(M_2)$. However, since there are now three different resource types, in the worst-case, a route could need 3× the energy of the optimally-matched architecture instead of 2× when there were only two resource types (logic and one memory size).

Another point of mismatch between architecture and application is the width of the data read or written from the memory block. Memory energy also scales with the data-width. In particular, energizing twice as many bit lines costs roughly twice the energy. While FPGA memory blocks can be configured to supply less data than the maximum width, this is typically implemented by multiplexing the wider data down to smaller data **after** reading the full width—the same number of bit lines are energized as the maximum width case, so these smaller data reads are just as expensive as the maximum width read, and hence more expensive than they could have been with an optimally-configured memory. While width mismatch is another, important source of mismatch, it is beyond the scope of this paper. We stick to a single raw data-width of 32 bits throughout our experiments.

Another potential point of mismatch is the simultaneous ports provided by the memories. We assume all memories are dual-ported (2 read/write ports) throughout this paper.

# 3. BACKGROUND

## 3.1 FPGA Memory Architecture

We build on the standard Island-Style FPGA model [3]. The basic logic tile is a cluster of K-LUTs with a local crossbar providing connectivity within the cluster (*c.f.* Xilinx CLB, Altera LAB). These clusters are arranged in a regular mesh and connected by segmented routing channels.

To incorporate memories into this mesh, we follow the model used by VTR [15], Xilinx, and Altera, where select columns are designated as memory columns rather than logic columns (Fig. 1). Organizing the memory tiles into a homogeneous column rather than placing them more freely in the mesh allows them the freedom to have a different size than the logic tiles. For example, if the memory block requires more area than the logic cluster, we can make the memory column wider without creating irregularity within rows or columns. Altera uses this column memory model in their Cyclone and Stratix architectures, and the M9K blocks in the Stratix III [12] are roughly $3\times$ the area of the logic clusters (LABs) [20], while being logically organized in the mesh as a single tile. Large memories can span multiple rows, such as the M144K blocks in the Stratix III, which are 8-rows tall while remaining one logical row wide, accommodated by making the column wider as detailed above.

Within this architectural framework, we can vary the proportion of memory tiles to logic tiles by selecting the fraction of columns that are assigned to memory tiles rather than logic tiles. One way to characterize this is to set the number of logic columns between memory columns, $d_m$. VTR identifies this as a `repeat` parameter (`repeat`=$d_m + 1$). For two memory sizes, $d_m$ still gives the spacing between memory columns, but we first use $h_1/h_0$ memory columns with small memories of height $h_0$, followed by one column of large memories of height $h_1$, so that the area occupied by the small memories is equal to the area occupied by the large ones.

## 3.2 Energy Modeling and Optimization

Poon [17] developed energy modeling for FPGAs and identified how to size LUTs (4-LUTs), clusters (8–10), and segments (length 1) to minimize energy. However, Poon did not identify an energy-minimizing memory organization. FPGA energy modeling has since been expanded to modern direct-drive architectures and integrated into VTR [6].

Recent work on memory architecture has focused on area optimization rather than energy. Luu examined the area-efficiency of memory packing and concluded that it was valuable to support two different memory block sizes in FPGAs [14]. Lewis showed how to size memories for area optimization in the Stratix V and concluded that a single 20Kb memory was superior to the combination of 9Kb and 144Kb memories in previous Stratix architectures [13], but did not address energy consumption, leaving open the question of whether energy-optimized memory architectures would be different from area-optimized ones.

## 3.3 Memory Energy Modeling

We use CACTI 6.5 [16] to model the physical parameters (area, energy, delay) of memories as a function of capacity, organization, and technology. In addition to modeling capacity and datapath width, CACTI explores internal implementation parameters to perform trade-offs among area, delay, throughput, and power. We use it to supply the mem-

| Addresses | 0–63 | 64–255 | 256–1023 |
|---|---|---|---|
| Shape | 16×32 | 48×32 | 192×32 |
| Size ($\mu m^2$) | 38×15 | 52×31 | 94×58 |
| $E_{mem}$ (pJ) | 0.31 | 0.54 | 1.1 |
| $E_{wires}$ (pJ) | 0.0 | 0.46 | 0.84 |

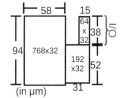

Figure 4: Internal Banking for 32K memory

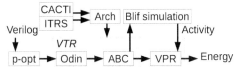

Figure 5: Energy Estimation Tool Flow

ory block characteristics for VTR architecture files at 22 nm. We set it to optimize for the energy-delay-squared product.

For internal banking (Fig. 2), CACTI gives us the area and energy ($E_{mem}$) of the memory banks, and we compute wire signaling energy ($E_{wires}$) to communicate data and addresses between the referenced memory bank and the memory block I/O. For example, consider the data in Fig. 4 for a $1024\times32$b (32Kb) internally-banked memory. A monolithic 32Kb memory block is $67\mu m\times113\mu m$, which is high enough to contain the $94\mu m$ required for the height of the $768\times32$ memory of size $58\mu m\times94\mu m$ (plus room for extra logic), as shown in Fig. 4. The total width in Fig. 4 is $58 + 31 = 89\mu m$, or $89/67 = 1.33\times$ that of the monolithic 32Kb memory block. We therefore adjust $E_{mseg}$(32K-banked)= $1.33 \times E_{mseg}$(32K). CACTI directly provides $E_{mem}$. For the largest bank, $E_{wires}$ is $(31\mu m)(1 + 10 + 64)C_{wire}(V_{dd})^2$. $C_{wire} = 180$pF/m, $V_{dd} = 0.95$V. $(1 + 10 + 64)$ corresponds to one signal for the enable, 10 for the address bits, 64 for the 32b input and 32b output. $31\mu m$ is the distance to reach the large bank. The medium-size bank has a similar $E_{wires}$ equation but with $38\mu m$ instead of $31\mu m$, and the small bank has $E_{wires} = 0$. Then, the energy of an internally-banked memory is given by $E_{banked} = E_{mem} + \alpha E_{wires}$, where $\alpha$ is the average activity factor over all signaling wires.

# 4. METHODOLOGY

Fig. 5 shows our tool flow. We developed and added several components on top of a stock VTR 7 release.

## 4.1 Activity Factor Simulation

Activity factors and static probabilities assigned to the nets of a design have a major impact on the estimated energy. Common ways to estimate activity include assigning a uniform activity to all nets (*e.g.*, 15%), or performing vectorless estimation with tools such as ACE [11], as done by VTR. For better accuracy, our flow obtains activity factors by simulating the designs. We run a logic simulation on the BLIF output of ABC (`pre-vpr.blif` file) on a uniformly random input dataset. For example, for the matched 32Kb-memory matrix-multiply design in Fig. 3a, the average simulated activity factor is 11%, whereas ACE estimates it to be 3%, resulting in an energy estimation that is off by $\approx 3.7\times$. The tunable benchmarks are designed in a streaming way that activates all memories all the time (independent of the random data), except Matrix Multiply (`MMul`), for which the clock-enable signal is on $\approx 1/3$ of the time. The VTR benchmarks do not come with clock-enable for the memories, so we set them to be always on.

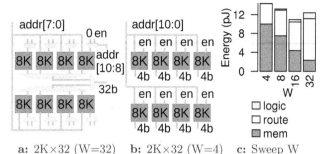

**a:** 2K×32 (W=32)  **b:** 2K×32 (W=4)  **c:** Sweep W

Figure 6: Effect of Memory Block Activation and Output Width Selection on Energy Consumption

## 4.2 Power-Optimized Memory Mapping

When mapping logical memories onto physical memories, FPGA tools can often choose to optimize for either delay or energy using power-aware memory balancing [19]. For example, when implementing a 2K×32b logical memory using eight 256×32b physical memories, the tool could choose to read $W = 4$b from each memory (delay-optimized, Fig. 6b). Since each memory internally reads at the full, native width, the cost of the memory operation is multiplied by the number of memory blocks used. Alternatively, it could read $W = 32$b from only one of the memories (Fig. 6a), in which case only one memory is activated at a time (reducing memory energy), but extra logic and routing overhead is added to select the appropriate memory and data. The power-optimized case often lies between these extremes. For example, as our experiment shows in Fig. 6c, the optimum is to activate 2 memories at once and read $W = 16$b from each.

Unfortunately, the VTR flow does not perform this kind of trade-off: it always optimizes for delay. Odin decomposes the memories into individual output bits [18], and the packer packs together these 1-bit slices as much as possible within the memory blocks to achieve the intended width [14]. In fact, VTR memories do not have a clock-enable so they must be activated all the time. Instead, we use VTR architectures with special memory block instantiations that contain a clock-enable, modify VTR's architecture-generation script (`arch_gen.py`) to support these blocks and to support two memory sizes, and add a `p-opt` stage before Odin to perform power-optimized memory mapping based on the memories available in the architecture. This includes performing memory sweeps as illustrated in Fig. 6c to select the appropriate mapping for each application memory. The impact of this optimization is shown for the best architectures in Tab. 2. We find that mapping without p-opt adds 4-19% geomean energy overhead for the optimum architectures, comparable to the 6% benefit reported in [19]. Not using p-opt adds 40–108% worst-case energy overhead, suggesting that this optimization is more important for the designs with high memory overhead. Our p-opt code and associated VTR architecture generation script can be found online [7].

## 4.3 Logic Architecture

The logic architecture uses k4n10 logic blocks (clusters of 10 4-LUTs) and 36×36 embedded multipliers (which can be decomposed into two 18×18 multiplies, or four 9×9 multiplies) with $d_{mpy}=10$ and the same shape and energy as in VTR's default 22 nm architectures (a height of 4 logic tiles, plus we use $L_{mpyseg} = 4L_{seg}$). The routing architecture uses direct-drive segments of length 1 with Wilton switch-boxes.

## 4.4 Technology

We use Low Power (LP) 22 nm technology [1] for logic evaluation and Low Stand-by Power (LSTP) for memories. We use ITRS parameters for constants such as the unit capacitance of a wire at 22 nm ($C_{wire} = 180$ pF/m). Then:

$$C_{metal} = C_{wire} \times \text{tile-length} \qquad (6)$$

We evaluate interconnect energy based on this $C_{metal}$, instead of the constant one that is provided in the architecture file. This way, the actual size of the low-level components of the given architecture and technology, as well as the computed channel width, are taken into account when evaluating energy. It is important to model this accurately since routing energy dominates total FPGA energy (See Fig. 6c).

## 4.5 Energy and Area of Memory Blocks

VTR assigns one type of block to each column on the FPGA (logic cluster, multiplier, or memory), and can give them different heights, but assumes the same horizontal segment length crossing each column. However, some memories can occupy a much larger area than a logic tile, and laying them out vertically to fit in one logic tile width would be inefficient. For energy efficiency, the memories should be closer to a square shape, and to that end, we allow the horizontal segment length crossing memories to be longer (which costs more routing energy, hence $E_{mseg}(M) \neq E_{seg}$ in Section 2). We fix the height of the memory ($h$) ahead of time, but keep the horizontal memory segment length ($L_{mseg}$) floating:

$$h = \left\lceil \frac{\sqrt{A_{sw}(W_0) + A_{mem}}}{\sqrt{A_{logic}(W_0)}} \right\rceil \qquad (7)$$

Here $W_0$ is a typical channel width for the architecture and benchmark set. We use $W_0 = 80$. Then, when VPR finds the exact channel width, $W_{act}$, and hence the tile-length and area ($A_{logic}$), we can adjust $L_{mseg}$ accordingly:

$$L_{mseg} = \frac{A_{sw}(W_{act}) + A_{mem}}{h\sqrt{A_{logic}(W_{act})}} \qquad (8)$$

$A_{mem}$ is the area for the memory obtained from CACTI, and $A_{sw}$ is the switch area required to connect the memory to the FPGA interconnect. We obtain $A_{sw}$ from VPR's low-level models, similar to the way it computes $A_{logic} = A_{luts} + A_{sw}$.

## 4.6 Benchmarks

To explore the impact of memory architecture, we use the VTR 7 Verilog benchmarks[1] [15] and a set of tunable benchmarks that allow us to change the parallelism level, $P$, in Section 6. Tab. 1 summarizes the benchmarks that have memories. We expect future FPGA applications to use more memory than the VTR 7 benchmarks. Some of them, such as stereovision, only model the compute part of the application and assume off-chip memory. We expect this memory to move on chip in future FPGAs. The tunable benchmarks provide better coverage of the large memory applications we think will be more typical of future FPGA applications. For this reason, we do not expect a simple average of the benchmarks, such as the geometric mean, to be the most meaningful metric for the design of future FPGAs—it is weighted too heavily by memory-free and memory-poor applications.

We implemented the tunable benchmarks in Bluespec SystemVerilog [4]; they are the following:

---

[1]Except **LU32PEEng** and **LU64PEEng** (similar to **LU8PEEng**) on which VPR routing did not complete after 10 days.

Table 1: Memory Requirements for the Benchmarks

| Benchmark | Mem Bits | # Memories | Largest Mem |
|---|---|---|---|
| **VTR** | | | |
| boundtop | 32K | 1 | 1K×32 |
| ch_intrinsics | 256 | 1 | 32×8 |
| LU8PEEng | 45.5K | 9 | 256×32 |
| mcml | 5088K | 10 | 64K×36 |
| mkDelayWorker32B | 520K | 9 | 1K×256 |
| mkPktMerge | 7.2K | 3 | 16×153 |
| mkSMAdapter4B | 4.35K | 3 | 64×60 |
| or1200 | 2K | 2 | 32×32 |
| raygentop | 5.25K | 1 | 256×21 |
| spree | 1538K | 4 | 32K×32 |
| **Tunable** | | | |
| MMul128 | 516K | 2P | (16K/P)×32 |
| GMM128 | 7680K | P | (16K/P)×480 |
| Sort8K | 1440K | (12-logP)+2P | (8K/P)×45 |
| FFT8K (-twiddle) | 1023K | 4P | (4K/P)×32 |
| WFilter128 (-line buffer) | 256K | P | (16K/P)×16 |

**GMM**: Gaussian Mixture Modeling [5] for an $N \times N$ pixel image, with 16b per pixel and $M = 5$ models. $P$ pixels are computed every cycle. This operation is embarrassingly parallel, since each PE is independent of the other ones.

**WFilter**: 5×5 Gaussian Window Filter for an $N \times N$ pixel image, with 16b per pixel and power-of-2 coefficients. $P = 1/5$ corresponds to a single PE that needs 5 main memory reads per pixel (storing the last 24 values read in registers). $P = 1$ adds line buffers so that only 1 main memory read and 4 line buffer reads translate into 1 pixel per cycle. $P = 2$ and $P = 4$ extend the filter's window, share line buffers, and compute 2 and 4 pixels per cycle, respectively. For $P > 4$, every time $P$ is doubled, the image is divided into two subimages, similar to the GMM benchmark.

**MMul**: $N \times N$ matrix-multiply ($A \times B = C$), with 32b integer values and datapaths (See Fig. 11).

**FFT**: $N$-point 16b fixed-point complex streaming Radix-2 Fast Fourier Transform, with $P \times \log(N/P)$-stage FFTs followed by $\log(P)$ recombining stages.

**Sort**: $N$-point 32b streaming mergesort [9], where each datapoint also has a $\log(N)$-bit index. One value is processed per cycle, and the parallelism comes from implementing the last $\log(P)$ stages spatially.

In Section 5, we use $P = 1$ for each of these benchmarks.

## 4.7 Limit Study and Mismatch Lower Bound

Section 5 shows the energy consumption for different applications and memory architectures (*e.g.*, Figs. 7, 8, 9). In order to identify bounds on the mismatch ratio, we also set up *limit study* experiments. Our limit study assumes that each benchmark gets exactly the physical memory depth it needs (the width stays at 32), as if the FPGA were an ASIC. Therefore, there is no overhead for using memories that are too small (no need for internal banking as in Section 2) or too large (no need to combine multiple memory blocks as in Section 4.2). We further assume that the limit study memories have the same height as that of a logic tile, making them widely available and keeping the interconnect energy low for vertical memory crossings. Finally, we place memory blocks every 2 columns ($d_m = 1$), so that place-and-route tools can always find a memory right where they need one. To avoid overcharging for unnecessary memory columns, we modify routing energy calculations, and ignore horizontal memory-column crossings for the limit study ($E_{mseg} = 0$). Some large-memory benchmarks drop slightly

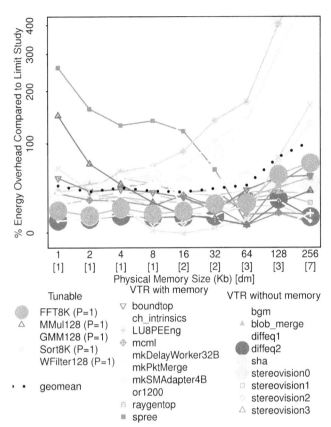

Figure 7: Single Memory Block Size Sweep

below the limit study. When the large memories are decomposed, they can see benefits similar to internal banking, where memory references to component memory blocks close to the output require less energy than references to the full, application-sized memory bank.

## 5. EXPERIMENTS

### 5.1 Memory Block Size Sweep

We start with the simplest memory organization that uses a single memory block size and no internal banking (Fig. 7), with the $d_m$ values from Fig. 3a. For comparison, energy is normalized to the lower-bound obtained using the limit study. Most of the curves have an energy-minimizing memory size between the two extreme ends (1Kb and 256Kb). Benchmarks with little memory have an energy-minimizing point at the smallest memory size (1Kb). Benchmarks with no memory have a close-to-flat curve, paying only to route over memories, but not for reads from large memories. The 16Kb memory architecture minimizes the geometric mean energy overhead of all the benchmarks at 37%. As noted (Section 4.6), the geometric mean is weighted heavily by the many benchmarks with little or no memory, so may not be the ideal optimization target for future FPGA applications. `spree` and `mkPktMerge` define the maximum energy overhead curve and suggest that a 4Kb memory minimizes worst-energy overhead at 130% the lower bound.

Fig. 8 shows the detailed breakdown of energy components for three benchmarks as a single memory block size is varied, both for the normal case (top row) and for the internally-banked memories (bottom row) described in Section 3.3.

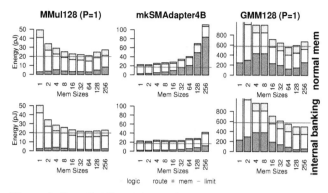

**Figure 8:** Detailed Breakdown of Energy Components When Sweeping Memory Block Size

We also show a blue line highlighting the optimistic lower bound obtained from the limit study Most benchmarks have the shape of MMul128, with an energy-minimizing memory size between 1Kb and 256Kb. Small benchmarks with small memories have the shape of mkSMAdapter4B, with large increases in memory energy with increasing physical memory size. Fig. 8 shows how internal banking reduces this effect. Sometimes this allows the minimum energy point to shift. For example, in GMM128 the minimum shifts from 64Kb to 256Kb, reducing total energy at the energy-minimizing block size from 553 pJ to 495 pJ, a reduction of 10%.

## 5.2 Full Parameter Sweep

In Section 2 we showed analytically why the spacing between memory columns, $d_m$, should be chosen to balance logic and memory in order to minimize worst-case energy consumption. For simplicity, we limited Fig. 7 to only use the $d_m$ values from our mismatch experiment (Fig. 3a). Since the optimal values of $d_m$ may vary among benchmarks, Fig. 9 shows geomean (a) and worst-case (b) energy overheads when varying both memory block size and $d_m$. In Tab. 2, we identify the energy-minimizing architectures for each of the four architectural approaches (1 or 2 memory sizes, internal-banking or not). We also compare to the lower-bound energy ratios for our closest approximation to the Cyclone (C with $d_m = 9$ and 8Kb blocks) and Stratix (S with $d_m = 9$ and 16Kb blocks) architectures.[2] The heatmap (Fig. 9) gives a broader picture than the specific energy minimizing points, showing how energy increases as we move away from the identified points. We see broad ranges of values that achieve near the lowest geometric mean point, with narrower regions, often single points, that minimize the worst-case overhead. The heatmap shows that overhead has a stronger dependence on memory block size than memory spacing. The commercial designs are appropriately on the broad energy-minimizing valley for geometric mean, but the large spacing, $d_m$, leaves them away from the worst-case energy-minimizing valley. Multiple memories and internal banking both reduce energy, and their combination achieves the lowest energies. Compared to the commercial architectures, we identify points that reduce the worst-case by 47% $((2.47-1.31)/2.47)$ while reducing the geomean by 13%. In all the energy minimizing cases, the memories are placed more frequently than the commercial architectures, closer to the balanced point identified analytically in Section 2.

---

[2] Modeled points have square logic clusters and memories, whereas real Stratix and Cyclone devices are rectangular.

Table 2: Energy Minimizing Architectural Parameters

| ID Fig. 10 | mem1 (Kb) | mem2 (Kb) | int bank | dm | Energy % Overhead geo | worst | +% w/o p-opt geo | worst | Area % Overhead geo | worst |
|---|---|---|---|---|---|---|---|---|---|---|
| | | | | best worst-case | | | | | | |
| 4f | 16 | 0 | no | 6 | 24 | 114 | 13 | 108 | 43 | 143 |
| 06b | 1 | 64 | no | 2 | 17 | 46 | 7.7 | 64 | 70 | 199 |
| 5b | 32 | 0 | yes | 2 | 25 | 52 | 8.0 | 70 | 151 | 384 |
| 38d | 8 | 256 | yes | 4 | 8.0 | 31 | 3.7 | 40 | 77 | 162 |
| | | | | best geomean | | | | | | |
| 3g | 8 | 0 | no | 7 | 21 | 204 | 17 | 93 | 37 | 303 |
| 06c | 1 | 64 | no | 3 | 14 | 48 | 7.0 | 58 | 52 | 180 |
| 5g | 32 | 0 | yes | 7 | 11 | 63 | 8.1 | 71 | 53 | 225 |
| 37e | 8 | 128 | yes | 5 | 7.0 | 48 | 3.7 | 41 | 63 | 490 |
| | | | | commercial-like | | | | | | |
| C(3i) | 8 | 0 | no | 9 | 22 | 216 | 19 | 74 | 46 | 361 |
| S(4i) | 16 | 0 | no | 9 | 24 | 147 | 11 | 52 | 41 | 172 |

## 5.3 Area-Energy Trade-off

Since there are valleys with many energy points at or close to the minimum energy, parameter selection merits some attention to area. Furthermore, it is useful to understand how much area we trade off for various energy gains. Fig. 10 shows the energy-area trade-off points when varying memory size and organization (1 vs. 2 memories, internal banking vs. not). To simplify the figure, we only show the pareto-optimal points of each set. Energy is normalized to the limit study, while area is normalized to the smallest area achieved.

The architectures with two memory sizes are particularly effective at keeping both worst-case area and worst-case energy overhead low. The architecture that minimizes worst-case area-overhead is a single 16Kb memory design with $d_m = 5$, requiring 80% more energy than the design that minimizes worst-case energy (which requires 33% more area). The designs that minimize geomean form a tight cluster spanning 28% area and 16% energy. Overall, the Stratix and Cyclone architectures fit into this geomean area- and energy-minimizing cluster, but are far from the pareto optimum values in the worst-case energy-area graph. This suggests the commercial architectures are well optimized for the logic-rich design mix captured in the VTR benchmark set. However, as FPGAs see more computing tasks with greater memory use and a larger range of logic-memory balance, our results suggest there are architectural options that provide tighter guarantees of low energy and area overhead.

## 5.4 Sensitivity

The best memory sizes and the magnitude of benefits achievable are sensitive to the relative cost of memory energy compared to interconnect energy. Since PowerPlay [2] estimates that the Altera memories are more expensive (about $3\times$ the energy—perhaps because the Altera memories are optimized for delay and robustness rather than energy) than the energy-delay-squared-optimized memories CACTI predicts are possible, it is useful to understand how this effect might change the selection of architecture. Therefore, we perform a sensitivity analysis where we multiply the energy numbers reported by CACTI by factors of $2\times$, $3\times$, and $4\times$. The results for a single memory block size are shown in Fig. 9c. Without internal banking, the relative overhead cost of using an oversized memory is increased, shifting the energy-minimizing bank size down to 4Kb or 2Kb. At $2\times$ the CACTI energy, the benefit of internal-banking is roughly the same at 30%, but drops to 19% by $4\times$.

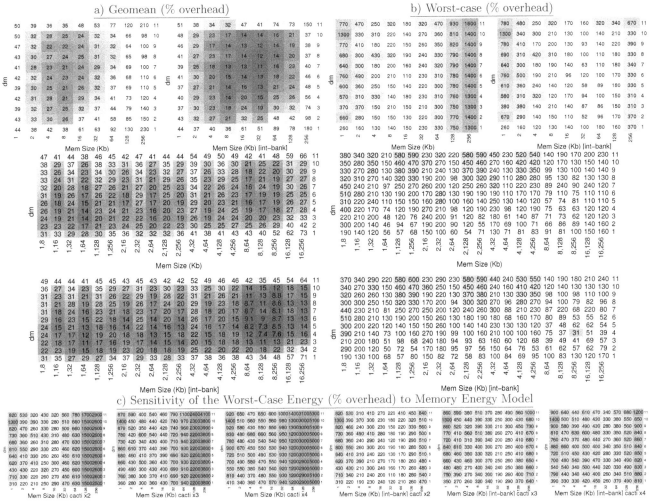

Figure 9: Energy overhead versus memory block size(s) and $d_m$

# 6. PARALLELISM TUNING

For many designs, we can choose either to serialize the computation on a single processing element (PE), requiring a large memory for the PE, or to parallelize the computation with many PEs, each with smaller memories. For the Stratix IV with two memory levels (9Kb and 144Kb), we previously showed [8] that parallel designs with many PEs improved the energy-efficiency over sequential designs. In this section, we ask: what is the optimal memory architecture, and minimum energy achievable, when we can vary the parallelism in the design to find the energy-minimizing configuration for each memory architecture?

## 6.1 Issues

When we increase the number of PEs, we can reduce the size of the dataset that must be processed by each PE, decomposing the memory needed by the application into multiple, smaller memories (smaller $M_{app}$) and thus lowering the energy per memory access. Specifically, doubling the number of PEs often halves the $M_{app}$ and hence reduces memory energy by $\sqrt{2}$. For most designs, increasing the number of PEs also increases the data that must be routed among PEs and hence increases inter-PE routing energy. As long as the fraction of energy in memory remains larger than the inter-PE routing energy, increasing the number of PEs results in a net reduction in total energy.

For example, Fig. 11 shows the shape of an $N \times N$ by $N \times N$ matrix-multiply $A \times B = C$ for different parallelism levels $P$ ($N = 4$ is shown). The computation is decomposed by columns, with each PE performing the computation for $N/P$ columns of the matrix. The $B$ data is streamed in first and stored in $P$ memories of size $N^2/P$, then $A$ is streamed in row major order. Each $A$ datapoint ($A[i,k]$) is stored in a register, data for each column ($j$) is read from each $B$ memory, a multiply-accumulate is computed ($C[i,j] = C[i,j] + A[i,k] \cdot B[k,j]$), and the result is stored in a $C$ memory of size $N/P$.[3] Once all the $A$ datapoints of a row have been processed, the results of the multiply-accumulates can be streamed out, and the $C$ memories can be used for the next row. When $P = N$, $C$ does not need memories. Either way, increasing $P$ keeps the total number of multiply-accumulates and memory operations constant. However, since the memories are organized in smaller banks, each memory access now costs less, and energy is reduced, as long as the interconnect-per-PE does not increase too much.

Fig. 12 shows how energy-efficiency changes with PE count for three tunable benchmarks. It shows how energy is reduced with additional parallelism up to an energy-minimizing

---

[3]This is different from the matrix-multiply in Section 2, where $C$ was stored in an output memory of size $N^2$ ($P = 1$), keeping only one size of memory for the application.

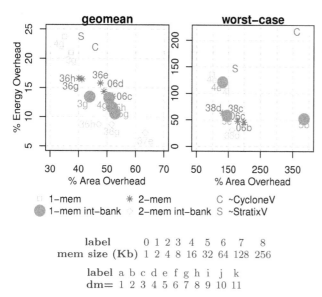

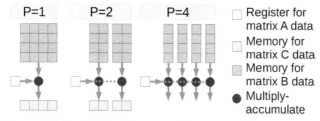

Figure 10: Energy-Area Trade-off

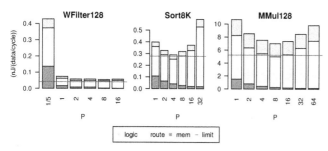

Figure 11: Parallelism Impact on Memory and Interconnect Requirements for a $(4 \times 4)^2$ matrix-multiply

number of PEs, with benefits of 86% (WFilter128), 27% (Sort8K), and 34% (MMul128).

## 6.2 Experiments

Once the memory architecture is fixed (with a given memory block size), being able to tune the parallelism level of the benchmarks as in Section 6.1 allows us to reduce potential mismatches between the application's memory requirements and the memory architecture. For example, consider Fig. 13, showing a sweep of both memory block size and parallelism for MMul128. The curves are normalized to the same limit study point as in Section 5 ($P = 1$), hence the curves can go below 0% overhead: the more parallel versions are different designs, and they can be more energy-efficient. For example, within the space of internally-banked, 1-memory-size architectures, Section 5 concluded that a memory size

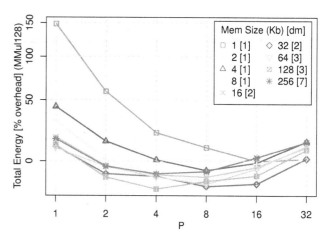

Figure 13: Energy versus P for MMul128 and varying mem sizes (int-bank) (normalized to the limit study for $P = 1$)

of 32Kb minimizes energy. In the case of MMul128, this gave an overhead of 10%. However, tuning the benchmark to $P = 8$ brings it down to -15%, a 23% reduction. This shows that parallelism can be a powerful optimization to reduce energy even when we do not have control over the memory architecture. In fact, MMul128 has a point at -17% overhead ($P = 4$ and a 128Kb memory), suggesting that the ability to tune $P$ may shift the optimum architecture.

Fig. 14 shows the effect of tuning to optimum $P$ for different memory sizes and $d_m$ values. Due to space constraints, we show only the 2-memory, internally banked designs, which contain the lowest energy points. We can observe three effects from parallelism tuning that the previous sections have set up: (1) reduce the absolute energies, and hence overheads, achievable; (2) shift the energy-minimizing parameter selections to smaller memories (e.g., 1Kb+64Kb vs. 8Kb+256Kb for worst-case); and (3) create broader near-minimum-energy valleys, making energy overhead less sensitive to the selection of memory block size.

## 7. CONCLUSIONS

We have shown how to size and place embedded memory blocks to guarantee that energy is within a factor of two of the optimal organization for the application. We focused on energy-balanced FPGA design points, which may be different from the logic-rich design points for current commercial architectures. On the benchmark set, we have seen that a two-memory design with 8Kb and 256Kb banks with internal banking and $d_m = 4$ keeps the worst-case mismatch energy overhead below 31% compared to an optimistic limit-study lower bound. Internal banking provided 19% of the energy savings. The optimal energy-balanced memory architecture for energy minimization differs from the logic-rich, area-minimizing points: we are driven to multiple memory sizes (8Kb and 256Kb vs. single 16Kb) and more frequent ($d_m$=4 vs. $d_m$=5–9) memories, spending 33% more worst-case area (28% more geomean area on logic-rich benchmarks) for 80% lower worst-case energy (16% lower geomean energy). Finally, tuning parallelism in the application can reshape the memory use, reducing the energy overhead by avoiding memory size mismatches. Joint optimization further reduces the worst-case energy overhead by 13%, and the geomean by 25%.

WFilter128    Sort8K    MMul128

Figure 12: Energy breakdown versus P for different tunable benchmarks (4Kb int-bank with $d_m = 2$)

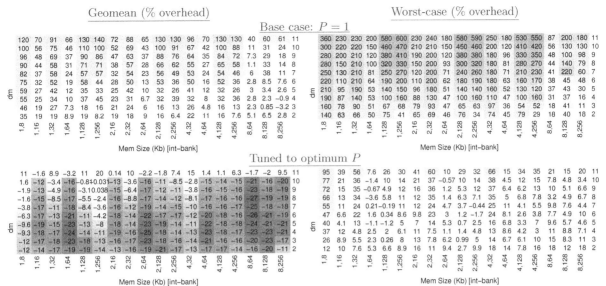

Figure 14: Energy overhead for the tunable benchmarks

## 8. ACKNOWLEDGMENTS

This research was funded in part by DARPA/CMO contract HR0011-13-C-0005. David Lakata was supported by the VIPER program at the University of Pennsylvania. Any opinions, findings, and conclusions or recommendations expressed in this material are those of the authors and do not reflect the official policy or position of the Department of Defense or the U.S. Government.

## 9. REFERENCES

[1] International technology roadmap for semiconductors. <www.itrs.net/Links/2012ITRS/Home2012.htm>, 2012. 4.4

[2] Altera Corporation. *PowerPlay Early Power Estimator*, 2013. 5.4

[3] V. Betz, J. Rose, and A. Marquardt. *Architecture and CAD for Deep-Submicron FPGAs*. Kluwer Academic Publishers, Norwell, MA, 02061 USA, 1999. 3.1

[4] Bluespec, Inc. Bluespec SystemVerilog 2012.01.A. 4.6

[5] M. Genovese and E. Napoli. ASIC and FPGA implementation of the gaussian mixture model algorithm for real-time segmentation of high definition video. *IEEE Trans. VLSI Syst.*, 22(3):537–547, March 2014. 4.6

[6] J. Goeders and S. Wilton. VersaPower: Power estimation for diverse FPGA architectures. In *ICFPT*, pages 229–234, 2012. 3.2

[7] E. Kadric. Power optimization (p-opt) code and architecture files. http://ic.ese.upenn.edu/distributions/meme_fpga2015/, 2015. 4.2

[8] E. Kadric, K. Mahajan, and A. DeHon. Kung fu data energy—minimizing communication energy in FPGA computations. In *FCCM*, 2014. 2, 6

[9] D. Koch and J. Torresen. FPGASort: A high performance sorting architecture exploiting run-time reconfiguration on FPGAs for large problem sorting. In *FPGA*, pages 45–54, 2011. 4.6

[10] I. Kuon and J. Rose. Measuring the gap between FPGAs and ASICs. *IEEE Trans. Computer-Aided Design*, 26(2):203–215, February 2007. 2

[11] J. Lamoureux and S. J. E. Wilton. Activity estimation for field-programmable gate arrays. In *FPL*, pages 1–8, 2006. 4.1

[12] D. Lewis, E. Ahmed, D. Cashman, T. Vanderhoek, C. Lane, A. Lee, and P. Pan. Architectural enhancements in Stratix-III and Stratix-IV. In *FPGA*, pages 33–42, 2009. 3.1

[13] D. Lewis, D. Cashman, M. Chan, J. Chromczak, G. Lai, A. Lee, T. Vanderhoek, and H. Yu. Architectural enhancements in Stratix V. In *FPGA*, pages 147–156, 2013. 3.2

[14] J. Luu, J. H. Anderson, and J. S. Rose. Architecture description and packing for logic blocks with hierarchy, modes and complex interconnect. In *FPGA*, pages 227–236, 2011. 3.2, 4.2

[15] J. Luu, J. Goeders, M. Wainberg, A. Somerville, T. Yu, K. Nasartschuk, M. Nasr, S. Wang, T. Liu, N. Ahmed, K. B. Kent, J. Anderson, J. Rose, and V. Betz. VTR 7.0: Next generation architecture and CAD system for FPGAs. *ACM Tr. Reconfig. Tech. and Sys.*, 7(2):6:1–6:30, July 2014. 2, 3.1, 4.6

[16] N. Muralimanohar, R. Balasubramonian, and N. P. Jouppi. CACTI 6.0: A tool to model large caches. HPL 2009-85, HP Labs, Palo Alto, CA, April 2009. Latest code release for CACTI 6 is 6.5. 3.3

[17] K. Poon, S. Wilton, and A. Yan. A detailed power model for field-programmable gate arrays. *ACM Tr. Des. Auto. of Elec. Sys.*, 10:279–302, 2005. 3.2

[18] J. Rose, J. Luu, C. W. Yu, O. Densmore, J. Goeders, A. Somerville, K. B. Kent, P. Jamieson, and J. Anderson. The VTR project: architecture and CAD for FPGAs from verilog to routing. In *FPGA*, pages 77–86, New York, NY, USA, 2012. ACM. 4.2

[19] R. Tessier, V. Betz, D. Neto, A. Egier, and T. Gopalsamy. Power-efficient RAM mapping algorithms for FPGA embedded memory blocks. *IEEE Trans. Computer-Aided Design*, 26(2):278–290, Feb 2007. 4.2, 4.2

[20] H. Wong, V. Betz, and J. Rose. Comparing FPGA vs. custom CMOS and the impact on processor microarchitecture. In *FPGA*, pages 5–14, 2011. 3.1

# Design Space Exploration of L1 Data Caches for FPGA-Based Multiprocessor Systems

Eric Matthews
Simon Fraser University
8888 University Drive
Burnaby BC V5A 1S6
Canada
ematthew@sfu.ca

Nicholas C. Doyle
Simon Fraser University
8888 University Drive
Burnaby BC V5A 1S6
Canada
ndoyle@sfu.ca

Lesley Shannon
Simon Fraser University
8888 University Drive
Burnaby BC V5A 1S6
Canada
lshannon@sfu.ca

## ABSTRACT

Combining multi-processing with the high level of configurability possible with FPGA-based soft-processors, this paper presents a multiprocessing framework based on the MicroBlaze soft-processor that provides multicore support and fully coherent, independently configurable Level 1 Caches with Linux multicore support. This architecture allows for finegrain configurability of the system, allowing for FPGA resources to be better optimized for a specific embedded application. We use our framework to explore the L1 Data Cache configuration, developing a metric for efficiency based on resource usage and static application runtime. We find that a Pseudo-Random replacement policy is consistently the more efficient choice for FPGA systems.

## Categories and Subject Descriptors

C.1.3 [**Other Architecture Styles**]: Adaptable architectures

## Keywords

Soft-Processor; Reconfigurable L1 Cache; MicroBlaze; PolyBlaze; Performance Efficiency Ratio; Cache Coherency

## 1. INTRODUCTION

As Field Programmable Gate Array (FPGA) devices have grown in capacity and sophistication, they have gained enough capacity to implement complicated microprocessor units in complex multicore configurations. Soft-processors, implemented on the FPGA fabric itself, allow for the flexibility of adding computing power as required for the application. For many low-power, low-cost embedded systems that do not require high operating speeds, soft-processors provide extensive capability to customize the system for the needs of the application

In this paper, we extend PolyBlaze [10], an SMP variant of the Xilinx MicroBlaze [13] soft-processor. We add fully

*FPGA'15*, February 22–24, 2015, Monterey, Califirnia, USA.
Copyright is held by the owner/author(s). Publication rights licensed to ACM.
ACM 978-1-4503-3315-3/15/02...$15.00.
http://dx.doi.org/10.1145/2684746.2689083.

coherent L1 Caches and support for extensive configuration of the L1 Data and Instruction Caches. After characterizing the resource usage and application performance of cache configurations across the design space, we develop a performance efficiency ratio for making trade-offs between application performance and resource usage. We find that replacement policy has a minimal impact on results, compared to cache size and associativity, and that Pseudo-Random was the most efficient choice for systems based on our design.

## 2. BACKGROUND

Memory latency and bandwidth act as significant performance bottlenecks for modern computing systems. L1 Caches are responsible for large improvements in system latency and bandwidth. This work focuses on write-through L1 Caches that are set-associative and configurable across a wide range of parameters. Instruction and data caches also often have different configurations, as all of the parameters offer different trade-offs in performance for applications, resource usage and operating frequency.

### 2.1 Existing Soft-Processors

Although FPGA-based soft-processors typically operate at much lower frequencies than their ASIC counterparts, caches are still required to compensate for the substantial memory system latency. The Xilinx MicroBlaze [13] and the Altera NIOS II [4] both provide direct-mapped caches that are highly configurable. However, neither processor supports cache coherency for multi-processor systems, hardware or operating system level support for multi-processing, or the set associative caches that are pervasive in today's commercial systems. The Open-SPARC T1 [12] has support for coherent L1 caches, but offers no configurability of its caches. Its large resource requirements and software emulated memory controller make it unsuitable for developing sophisticated embedded multi-core systems. The LEON3 processor [2], another SPARC based system, also has large resource requirements, and uses a bus snoop-based coherency mechanism with limited scalability as bus traffic increases. Some work has been undertaken to address memory coherency in FPGA platforms, including FCache [11] and LEAP shared memories [14], but they did not address asymmetric caches for soft-processors.

## 3. FPGA-BASED FRAMEWORK DESIGN

We selected the PolyBlaze processor [10] as the foundation for our asymmetric cache development. The PolyBlaze

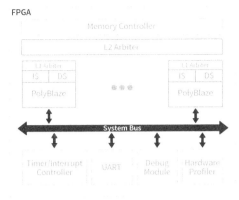

**Figure 1: PolyBlaze system diagram**

processor is an extension to version 8.00.b of Xilinx's MicroBlaze processor, adding multiprocessing support to MicroBlaze, along with SMP Linux support. While MicroBlaze provides support for direct-mapped L1 Caches, it does not support set-associative caches, and does not provide any multi-processor cache coherency mechanism, making it unsuitable for use in shared memory multicore systems. This work focuses on the addition of flexible write-through L1 Cache support to the PolyBlaze platform, including support for both set associativity and coherency.

In a PolyBlaze system, each processor includes an independent instruction and data cache supporting single-cycle read hits and writes. Instruction and data requests are passed through an L1 Arbiter in each core to reduce the number of connections into the L2 Arbiter. The L2 Arbiter arbitrates between the processor requests to the memory controller, and contains our coherency mechanism. To monitor the performance of the cache system as system parameters are adjusted, the framework includes a hardware profiling unit. Operating independently from the CPU, it monitors the performance of the CPUs and caches and stores them in internal counters. Fig. 1 shows the structure of the entire system.

## 3.1 Cache Structure

Our caches are partitioned into three logical blocks: tags, data, and replacement policy. By implementing the tag bank replacement policy as a separate module with a fixed interface, we allow for a range of policies to be readily developed without requiring knowledge of the inner workings of the cache. For set-associative configurations, tag banks in each way are mapped to separate BRAMs. Careful consideration has been taken in designing and integrating our caches into the PolyBlaze processor. As misses will always take multiple cycles to complete, update logic for the tag banks and replacement policies are pipelined to ensure that they do not contribute to the critical path in the cache.

### 3.1.1 Replacement Policies

To compare the effectiveness of different cache replacement policies, Clock (CLK) [6] Least Recently Used (LRU), and Pseudo-Random (PR) [9] have been implemented for use in our system. The Clock policy implementation is based on one used on recent Intel CPUs [7], requiring an N-bit counter for each line in the cache and resulting in a linear increase in memory usage as the size of the cache and number of ways increase. The LRU implementation uses one-hot encoding for speed, and maintains a buffer of N entries of N bits for each line in cache. The Pseudo-Random implemen-

tation consists primarily of a free-running 16-bit Fibonacci linear feedback register and requires no additional memory.

### 3.1.2 Cache Coherency

We selected a simple, yet highly flexible cache coherency mechanism. In our design, coherency is maintained by broadcasting write operations to all CPUs as they pass through the L2 Arbiter. This leverages the L2 Arbiter's existing behaviour and enables it to act as the serialization point for all memory requests in the system, as only a small amount of additional logic is required for coherency support. One of the primary benefits of the broadcast based system is that it is not tied to any particular cache architecture, readily supporting caches with different numbers of words per line and even non-cache-like structures in heterogeneous configurations. This approach is also transparent, requiring no additional software support to force coherency.

By choosing to broadcast writes to maintain coherency, a potential bottleneck in the scalability of our system becomes our ability to keep up with the rate at which broadcasts are generated. If any processor cannot match the rate of notifications, then the L2 Arbiter must stall until the notifications are handled, harming system throughput. Multi-pumping [5] is one of several techniques used to effectively double the number of ports on the memory [1], which we use to allow our system to double the number of reads and/or writes that can be executed per cycle. Multi-pumping allows us to integrate invalidation look-ups without impacting the normal operation of the cache.

## 3.2 Resource Comparison to MicroBlaze

To measure the overhead introduced by the multiprocessor and coherency support in PolyBlaze, a Xilinx MicroBlaze CPU (version 8.00.b) and a single-core PolyBlaze CPU were built, both with 4 kB direct-mapped caches. PolyBlaze saw a 7% and 2% increase in register and LUT usage, due to the registering of signals required to implement multi-pumping for invalidation support. A 23% decrease in BRAM usage arises from variations in our implementation of the cache structure.

## 4. CONFIGURATION ANALYSIS

In this section, we perform a thorough analysis characterizing how the performance, resource usage and coherency of our system scales as the cache configuration is varied. By comparing against previous studies [3][8], we can verify the functionality of the caches. This also provides us with insight into the unique design trade-offs for caches on FPGA-based systems. Due to space limitations, this study will focus on characterizing the configuration of the Data Cache.

All system testing is done on a Xilinx Virtex 5-based XUPV5-110T development board with 256 MB of DDR2 memory. Xilinx PetaLinux 12.12, a full operating system for the MicroBlaze platform based on the Linux 3.6.0 kernel, was modified to add PolyBlaze SMP support. The primary cache configurations under examination include: the number of ways, total cache size and replacement policy, with all caches configured with 4 words per line. Systems are built with a 80 MHz system clock and a 160 MHz L2 Arbiter and memory clock for easy place-and-route and faster build times. Test systems are configured with a fixed instruction cache (32 kB 4-way with a Pseudo-Random re-

**Table 1: 18Kb BRAM Allocations for Single Core PolyBlaze Cache Test Systems**

| Cache Size | Direct-Mapped | 2-Way | | | 4-Way | | |
|---|---|---|---|---|---|---|---|
| | | CLK | LRU | P-R | CLK | LRU | P-R |
| 4 kB | 51 | +7.84% | +9.80% | +5.88% | +19.61% | +25.49% | +17.65% |
| 8 kB | +3.92% | +7.84% | +9.80% | +5.88% | +19.61% | +25.49% | +17.65% |
| 16 kB | +13.73% | +15.69% | +17.65% | +13.73% | +19.61% | +25.49% | +17.65% |
| 32 kB | +29.41% | +35.29% | +37.25% | +33.33% | +35.29% | +41.18% | +33.33% |

placement policy) while the data cache is configuration is varied across its parameters with 4, 8, 16, and 32 kB sizes being investigated. For each cache size, the systems are built with Direct-Mapped, 2-way and 4-way caches. The set-associative caches are configured with Clock, LRU and Pseudo-Random (P-R) replacement policies, resulting in 28 total test systems.

## 4.1 Resource Usage and Operating Frequency

To understand the resource trade-offs for cache configurations, we build several systems and examine register, LUT, and BRAM resource usage. Between all configurations, *we found a maximum 3% variation in the usage of registers and LUTs*. Table 1 shows the BRAM usage for all configurations normalized to the 4kB Direct-Mapped configuration. Between the smallest (4 kB Direct-Mapped) and largest (32 kB 4-Way LRU) cache, we see a 41% increase in BRAM usage. In general, there is very little difference between replacement policies in terms of LUT and register usage. As expected, Direct-Mapped caches have the smallest BRAM usage, followed by Pseudo-Random, Clock, and then LRU.

In the set-associative caches, each way is mapped to its own BRAM to allow for parallel look-up. In Xilinx Virtex 5 devices, 4 kB assignments are the smallest BRAM block available. As a result, 4 kB 2-way caches are assigned 4 kB BRAM for each way, of which only 2 kB is used. A similar situation can be seen for 4 kB and 8 kB 4-way caches. As a result, *for this FPGA architecture and cache design, direct mapped caches should be at least 4 kB, 2-way caches should be at least 8 kB, and 4-way caches should be at least 16 kB, with the trend continuing as the associativity is increased.* The resource usage variation for all configurations of 32 kB caches relative to a direct mapped cache is less than 3% in LUTs and registers and between 4-12% for BRAMs. The resource cost of set associativity and replacement policies for 32 kB is relatively low, which could provide significant performance advantages.

We also examine the impact our design choices have on the maximum operating frequency of the system. For this investigation we using the Xilinx SmartXplorer tool to map single-core systems with several cache configurations using 20 different seeds to find the limiting factors in our maximum operating frequency. The Xilinx MicroBlaze with 4 kB direct-mapped caches is included for comparison, with a maximum clock speed of 131 MHz. We find the addition of coherency support and set-associativity for the caches incurs a cumulative cost in the maximum operating frequency. The addition of extra fan-out and levels of logic, coupled with the addition of multipumping, makes our data caches the critical paths in our system. This decreased the maximum clock frequency of a 4 kB direct-mapped system to 112 MHz. The additional logic for performing comparison and introducing replacement policies imposes a further penalty on the maximum clock frequency. A system with a 4-way 16 kB instruction cache operates at 103 MHz, while a 4-way 16 kB data cache operates at 103 MHz. A system with both 4-way 32 kB instruction and data caches operates at 101 MHz.

## 4.2 Application Performance Testing

To investigate the impact of different cache configurations on application performance, SPECCPU 2006 benchmarks were selected and built using the Xilinx PetaLinux toolchain. We used the integer benchmarks, as the test system is built without hardware floating point support to conserve system resources. Due to space limitations, we have focused on *bzip2, libquantum, h264ref*, and *specrand* for detailed analysis, as initial testing of the entire integer benchmark suite showed that these benchmarks provided a variety of sensitivities to data cache configurations.

To provide a measure of performance efficiency in terms of resource usage, we calculate the ratio between the improvement in the runtime and the increase in BRAM usage, using the 4 kB direct-mapped system as a baseline. This performance efficiency ratio allows a system designer to make informed decisions on which cache configurations make the most efficient use of BRAM for their workload. We consider only BRAM usage, as the systems experience little variation in LUT and register usage, and BRAMs are a scarce resource on FPGAs. The performance efficiency ratio takes the following form:

$$eff = \frac{\text{runtime decrease } (\%)}{\text{BRAM usage increase } (\%)}$$

The benchmarks varied in their sensitivity to data cache configuration, with *h264ref* showing strong sensitivity to Data Cache configuration, *bzip2* and *specrand* showing moderate sensitivity, and *libquantum* being insensitive to Data Cache configuration. Fig. 2 shows the difference in impact Data Cache configuration makes on the runtime between a highly sensitive (*h264ref*) and a relatively insensitive (*libquantum*) system. The solid bars show the benchmark runtime for different data cache configurations and sizes, while the outlines show the performance efficiency ratio for each system.

*h264ref* and *specrand* experienced peak runtime efficiency with a 2-way Pseudo-Random configuration for 8 kB caches. *bzip2* had peak efficiency with a Direct-Mapped configuration, followed by 2-way Pseudo-Random for 8 kB caches. All three benchmarks had peak efficiency for a 2-way Pseudo-Random configuration for 16 kB caches. As the cache size increases to 32 kB, the performance efficiency ratio for all

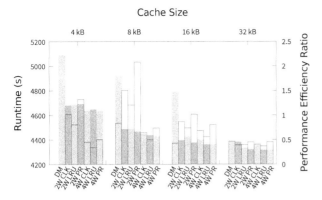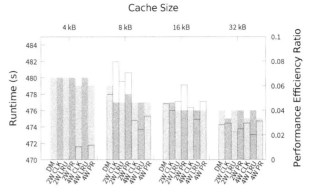

Figure 2: Runtime performance with varied cache configurations for h264ref (left) and libquantum (right)

benchmarks decreased substantially, showing diminishing performance returns for the larger caches. As discussed previously, 2-way caches less than 8 kB and 4-way caches less than 16 kB suffer from unused BRAM resources, which is reflected in the efficiency results.

Our results show that *h264ref* experiences the strongest reduction in runtime (15.16%), as well as the strongest peak performance efficiency ratio (2.079) with the correct cache configuration. *bzip2* and *specrand* showed moderate runtime reductions (8.92% and 4.55%), with moderate peak performance efficiency ratios (0.898 and 0.667). *libquantum* shows almost no sensitivity to the data cache configuration, with runtime varying by only 1.1%. A designer of an FPGA-based multicore system can use performance efficiency analysis of the intended applications, determine which are most sensitive to cache configuration, and select a cache configuration to maximize the efficient use of resources in the system.

As suggested by previous simulation-based studies [3][8], cache size has the biggest impact on performance, followed by the associativity, and then replacement policy. Replacement policy made less than a half percentage difference in execution time in the worst case (4 kB, 2-way caches), with even less of an impact for larger caches. As such, *these results suggest that, for most applications, the Pseudo-Random replacement policy is the most efficient choice for set associative L1 Cache systems running on FPGAs with limited BRAM resources.*

## 5. CONCLUSIONS

This paper describes the design of fully configurable and coherent L1 Cache support for the PolyBlaze soft-processor. Using this platform, we explore the design space of the L1 Data Cache and develop some clear design guidelines for FPGA-based systems based on this platform, including minimum cache sizes and a performance efficiency metric. We find that the Pseudo-Random replacement policy is consistently the most efficient choice for this FPGA-based platforms based on our cache design.

## 6. REFERENCES

[1] A. M. Abdelhadi and G. G. Lemieux. Modular multi-ported sram-based memories. In *Proceedings of the 2014 ACM/SIGDA International Symposium on Field-programmable Gate Arrays*, FPGA '14, pages 35–44, New York, NY, USA, 2014. ACM.

[2] Aeroflex Gaisler. *GRLIB IP Core User's Manual.* www.gaisler.com/products/grlib/grip.pdf.

[3] H. Al-Zoubi, A. Milenkovic, and M. Milenkovic. Performance evaluation of cache replacement policies for the spec cpu2000 benchmark suite. In *42nd Annual Southeast Reg. Conf.*, ACM-SE 42, pages 267–272, New York, NY, USA, 2004. ACM.

[4] Altera Corporation. *Nios II Core Implementation Details, Nios II Processor Reference Handbook.* www.altera.com/literature/hb/nios2/nc2cpunii51015.pdf.

[5] A. Canis, J. H. Anderson, and S. D. Brown. Multi-pumping for resource reduction in fpga high-level synthesis. In *Conf. on Design, Automation and Test in Europe*, DATE '13, pages 194–197, San Jose, CA, USA, 2013. EDA Consortium.

[6] F. J. Corbató. A paging experiment with the multics system. In Festschrift, editor, *In Honor of P. M. Morse*, pages 217–228. MIT Press, Cambridge, Massachusetts, 1969.

[7] D. Eklov, N. Nikoleris, D. Black-Schaffer, and E. Hagersten. Cache pirating: Measuring the curse of the shared cache. In *Parallel Processing (ICPP), 2011 Int. Conf. on*, pages 165–175, Sept 2011.

[8] A. Janapsatya, A. Ignjatović, and S. Parameswaran. Finding optimal l1 cache configuration for embedded systems. In *Design Automation, 2006. Asia and South Pacific Conference on*, pages 6 pp.–, Jan 2006.

[9] P. Kongetira, K. Aingaran, and K. Olukotun. Niagara: a 32-way multithreaded sparc processor. *Micro, IEEE*, 25(2):21 – 29, March 2005.

[10] E. Matthews, L. Shannon, and A. Fedorova. Polyblaze: From one to many bringing the microblaze into the multicore era with linux smp support. In *Field Programmable Logic and Applications (FPL), 2012 22nd Int. Conf. on*, pages 224–230, 2012.

[11] V. Mirian and P. Chow. Fcache: A system for cache coherent processing on fpgas. In *ACM/SIGDA Int. Symp. on Field Programmable Gate Arrays*, FPGA '12, pages 233–236, New York, NY, USA, 2012. ACM.

[12] Oracle Corporation. *OpenSPARC FPGA.* www.opensparc.net/fpga/index.html.

[13] Xilinx Inc. *MicroBlaze Processor Reference Guide.* www.xilinx.com/support/ documentation/sw_manuals/xilinx12_4/mb_ref_guide.pdf.

[14] H. J. Yang, K. Fleming, M. Adler, and J. Emer. Leap shared memories: Automating the construction of fpga coherent memories. In *Field-Programmable Custom Computing Machines (FCCM), 2014 IEEE 22nd Annual Int. Symp. on*, pages 117–124, May 2014.

# Growing a Healthy FPGA Ecosystem

John Lockwood
(Moderator)
Algo-Logic Systems, Inc.
Santa Clara, CA 95050
(408) 707-3740
JWLockwd@Algo-Logic.com

Michael Adler
Intel

Derek Chiou
Microsoft

Jason Cong
UCLA

Dan Mansur
Xilinx

Mike Strickland
Altera

Steve Teig
Tabula

## ABSTRACT

The personal computer market grew exponentially in the 1980's for vendors such as Apple, Microsoft, and Intel when there was a healthy mix of software, tools, and microprocessor devices.

At the time, killer applications that drove the market were spreadsheets, compilers, and games that ran on the personal computer.

Thirty years later, we now have a similar opportunity to grow a healthy ecosystem as developers and vendors bring killer applications, tools, and programmable logic devices to the market to accelerate datacenters for cloud computing.

**Categories and Subject Descriptors:** B.7.1 [**Logic Design**]: Integrated Circuits – *Algorithms implemented in hardware, gate arrays*; C.1.3 [**Computer System Organization**]: Other Architecture Styles – *adaptable architectures*

## General Terms

Algorithms, Design, Economics

## Keywords

Field Programmable Gate Array; microprocessor; datacenter; cloud computing

## QUESTIONS FOR THE PANELISTS

The panel poses four questions to the panelists for discussion and debate. Additional questions from the audience are welcome.

### 1.1 How large do you project that the ecosystem for programmable logic can become?

What is the market size (in Billions of US dollars of revenue) for programmable logic applications, devices, and tools? How is this market size justified and which segments are expected to grow in the next few years?

### 1.2 What are you doing to grow the FPGA ecosystem?

What steps have you and/or your company taken to expand the size of the FPGA market? What steps will be taken in the future?

### 1.3 How do you collaborate with partners and what do you ask of them to grow the FPGA ecosystem?

What steps can other companies or universities take to grow the FPGA market? Which contributions could have the most impact?

### 1.4 What is your call to action for the attendees of the FPGA 2015 conference?

What can company leaders, professors, and/or the students at this event do that would make how to grow the FPGA ecosystem?

*FPGA'15*, February 22–24, 2015, Monterey, California, USA.
ACM 978-1-4503-3315-3/15/02.
http://dx.doi.org/10.1145/2684746.2721404

# Optimizing FPGA-based Accelerator Design for Deep Convolutional Neural Networks

Chen Zhang[1]
chen.ceca@pku.edu.cn

Peng Li[2]
pengli@cs.ucla.edu

Guangyu Sun[1,3]
gsun@pku.edu.cn

Yijin Guan[1]
guanyijin@pku.edu.cn

Bingjun Xiao[2]
xiao@cs.ucla.edu

Jason Cong[2,3,1,*]
cong@cs.ucla.edu

[1]Center for Energy-Efficient Computing and Applications, Peking University, China
[2]Computer Science Department, University of California, Los Angeles, USA
[3]PKU/UCLA Joint Research Institute in Science and Engineering

## ABSTRACT

Convolutional neural network (CNN) has been widely employed for image recognition because it can achieve high accuracy by emulating behavior of optic nerves in living creatures. Recently, rapid growth of modern applications based on deep learning algorithms has further improved research and implementations. Especially, various accelerators for deep CNN have been proposed based on FPGA platform because it has advantages of high performance, reconfigurability, and fast development round, etc. Although current FPGA accelerators have demonstrated better performance over generic processors, the accelerator design space has not been well exploited. One critical problem is that the computation throughput may not well match the memory bandwidth provided an FPGA platform. Consequently, existing approaches cannot achieve best performance due to under-utilization of either logic resource or memory bandwidth. At the same time, the increasing complexity and scalability of deep learning applications aggravate this problem. In order to overcome this problem, we propose an analytical design scheme using the roofline model. For any solution of a CNN design, we quantitatively analyze its computing throughput and required memory bandwidth using various optimization techniques, such as loop tiling and transformation. Then, with the help of roofline model, we can identify the solution with best performance and lowest FPGA resource requirement. As a case study, we implement a CNN accelerator on a VC707 FPGA board and compare it to previous approaches. Our implementation achieves a peak performance of 61.62 GFLOPS under 100MHz working frequency, which outperform previous approaches significantly.

## Categories and Subject Descriptors

C.3 [**SPECIAL-PURPOSE AND APPLICATION-BASED SYSTEMS**]: Microprocessor/microcomputer applications

## Keywords

FPGA; Roofline Model; Convolutional Neural Network; Acceleration

## 1. INTRODUCTION

Convolutional neural network (CNN), a well-known deep learning architecture extended from artificial neural network, has been extensively adopted in various applications, which include video surveillance, mobile robot vision, image search engine in data centers, etc [6] [7] [8] [10] [14]. Inspired by the behavior of optic nerves in living creatures, a CNN design processes data with multiple layers of neuron connections to achieve high accuracy in image recognition. Recently, rapid growth of modern applications based on deep learning algorithms has further improved research on deep convolutional neural network.

Due to the specific computation pattern of CNN, general purpose processors are not efficient for CNN implementation and can hardly meet the performance requirement. Thus, various accelerators based on FPGA, GPU, and even ASIC design have been proposed recently to improve performance of CNN designs [3] [4] [9]. Among these approaches, FPGA based accelerators have attracted more and more attention of researchers because they have advantages of good performance, high energy efficiency, fast development round, and capability of reconfiguration [1] [2] [3] [6] [12] [14].

For any CNN algorithm implementation, there are a lot of potential solutions that result in a huge design space for exploration. In our experiments, we find that there could be as much as 90% performance difference between two different solutions with the same logic resource utilization of FPGA. It is not trivial to find out the optimal solution, especially when limitations on computation resource and memory bandwidth of an FPGA platform are considered. In fact, if an accelerator structure is not carefully designed, its computing throughput cannot match the memory bandwidth provided an FPGA platform. It means that the performance is degraded due to under-utilization of either logic resource or memory bandwidth.

*In addition to being a faculty member at UCLA, Jason Cong is also a co-director of the PKU/UCLA Joint Research Institute and a visiting chair professor of Peking University.

Unfortunately, both advances of FPGA technology and deep learning algorithm aggravate this problem at the same time. On one hand, the increasing logic resources and memory bandwidth provided by state-of-art FPGA platforms enlarge the design space. In addition, when various FPGA optimization techniques, such as loop tiling and transformation, are applied, the design space is further expanded. On the other hand, the scale and complexity of deep learning algorithms keep increasing to meet the requirement of modern applications. Consequently, it is more difficult to find out the optimal solution in the design space. Thus, an efficient method is urgently required for exploration of FPGA based CNN design space.

To efficiently explore the design space, we propose an analytical design scheme in this work. Our work outperforms previous approaches for two reasons. First, work [1] [2] [3] [6] [14] mainly focused on computation engine optimization. They either ignore external memory operation or connect their accelerator directly to external memory. Our work, however, takes buffer management and bandwidth optimization into consideration to make better utilization of FPGA resource and achieve higher performance. Second, previous study [12] accelerates CNN applications by reducing external data access with delicate data reuse. However, this method do not necessarily lead to best overall performance. Moreover, their method needs to reconfigure FPGA for different layers of computation. This is not feasible in some scenarios. Our accelerator is able to execute acceleration jobs across different layers without reprogramming FPGA.

The main contributions of this work are summarized as follows,

- We quantitatively analyze computing throughput and required memory bandwidth of any potential solution of a CNN design on an FPGA platform.

- Under the constraints of computation resource and memory bandwidth, we identify all possible solutions in the design space using a roofline model. In addition, we discuss how to find the optimal solution for each layer in the design space.

- We propose a CNN accelerator design with uniform loop unroll factors across different convolutional layers.

- As a case study, we implement a CNN accelerator that achieves a performance of 61.62 GFLOPS. To the best of our knowledge, this implementation has highest performance and the highest performance density among existing approaches.

The rest of this paper is organized as follows: Section 2 provides a background for CNN and roofline model. Section 3 presents our analytical approach for optimizing accelerator design. Section 4 describes implementation details. Section 5 shows our experiment result. Section 6 makes comparison between our implementation and existing work and Section 7 concludes the paper.

## 2. BACKGROUND

### 2.1 CNN Basics

Convolutional neural network (CNN) is first inspired by research in neuroscience. After over twenty years of evolution, CNN has been gaining more and more distinction in research fields, such as computer vision, AI (e.g. [11] [9]). As a classical supervised learning algorithm, CNN employs a feedforward process for recognition and a backward path for training. In industrial practice, many application designers train CNN off-line and use the off-line trained CNN to perform time-sensitive jobs. So the speed of feedforward computation is what matters. In this work, we focus on speeding up the feedforward computation with FPGA based accelerator design.

A typical CNN is composed of two components: a feature extractor and a classifier. The feature extractor is used to filter input images into "feature maps" that represent various features of the image. These features may include corners, lines, circular arch, etc., which are relatively invariant to position shifting or distortions. The output of the feature extractor is a low-dimensonal vector containing these features. This vector is then fed into the classifier, which is usually based on traditional artificial neural networks. The purpose of this classifier is to decide the likelihood of categories that the input (e.g. image) might belong to.

A typical CNN is composed of multiple computation layers. For example, the feature extractor may consist of several convolutional layers and optional sub-sampling layers. Figure 1 illustrates the computation of a convolutional layer. The convolutional layer receives $N$ feature maps as input. Each input feature map is convolved by a shifting window with a $K \times K$ kernel to generate one pixel in one output feature map. The stride of the shifting window is $S$, which is normally smaller than $K$. A total of $M$ output feature maps will form the set of input feature maps for the next convolutional layer. The pseudo code of a convolutional layer can be written as that in Code 1.

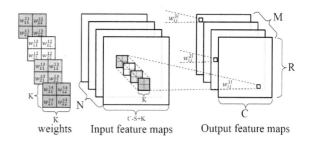

**Figure 1: Graph of a convolutional layer**

```
for(row=0; row<R; row++) {
 for(col=0; col<C; col++) {
  for(to=0; to<M; to++) {
   for(ti=0; ti<N; ti++) {
    for(i=0; i<K; i++) {
     for(j=0; j<K; j++) {
    L:  output_fm[to][row][col] +=
          weights[to][ti][i][j]*
          input_fm[ti][S*row+i][S*col+j];
} } } } } }
```

**Code 1: Pseudo code of a convolutional layer**

In the feedforward computation perspective, a previous study [5] proved that convolution operations will occupy over 90% of the computation time. So in this work, we will focus on accelerating convolutional layers. An integration with other optional layers, such as sub-sampling or max pooling layers, will be studied in future work.

## 2.2 A Real-Life CNN

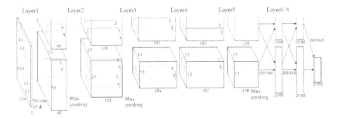

**Figure 2: A real-life CNN that won the ImageNet 2012 contest [9]**

Figure 2 shows a real-life CNN application, taken from [9]. This CNN is composed of 8 layers. The first 5 layers are convolutional layers and layers 6 ∼ 8 form a fully connected artificial neural network. The algorithm receives three 224x224 input images that are from an original 256x256 three-channel RGB image. The output vector of 1000 elements represents the likelihoods of 1000 categories. As is shown in Figure 2, Layer1 recieves 3 input feature maps in 224x224 resolution and 96 output feature maps in 55x55 resolution. The output of layer1 is partitioned into two sets, each sized 48 feature maps. Layer1's kernel size is 11x11 and the sliding window shifts across feature maps in a stride of 4 pixels. The following layers also have a similar structure. The sliding strides of other layers' convolution window are 1 pixel. Table 1 shows this CNN's configuration.

**Table 1: CNN configurations**

| Layer | 1 | 2 | 3 | 4 | 5 |
|---|---|---|---|---|---|
| input_fm (N) | 3 | 48 | 256 | 192 | 192 |
| output_fm (M) | 48 | 128 | 192 | 192 | 128 |
| fm row (R) | 55 | 27 | 13 | 13 | 13 |
| fm col. (C) | 55 | 27 | 13 | 13 | 13 |
| kernel (K) | 11 | 5 | 3 | 3 | 3 |
| stride (S) | 4 | 1 | 1 | 1 | 1 |
| set # | 2 | 2 | 2 | 2 | 2 |

## 2.3 The Roofline Model

Computation and communication are two principal constraints in system throughput optimization. An implementation can be either computation-bounded or memory-bounded. In [15], a roofline performance model is developed to relate system performance to off-chip memory traffic and the peak performance provided by the hardware platform.

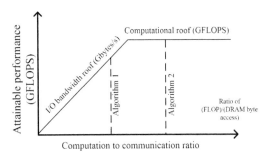

**Figure 3: Basis of the roofline model**

Eq. (1) formulates the attainable throughput of an application on a specific hardware platform. Floating-point performance (GFLOPS) is used as the metric of throughput. The actual floating-point performance of an application kernel can be no higher than the minimum value of two terms. The first term describes the peak floating-point throughput provided by all available computation resources in the system, or *computational roof*. Operations per DRAM traffic, or *computation to communication (CTC) ratio*, features the DRAM traffic needed by a kernel in a specific system implementation. The second term bounds the maximum floating-point performance that the memory system can support for a given computation to communication ratio.

$$Attainable\ Perf. = min \begin{cases} Computational\ Roof \\ CTC\ Ratio \times BW \end{cases} \quad (1)$$

Figure 3 visualizes the roofline model with computational roof and I/O bandwidth roof. Algorithm 2 in the figure has higher computation to communication ratio, or better data reuse, compared to Algorithm 1. From the figure, we can see that by fully-utilizing all hardware computation resources, Algorithm 2 can outperform Algorithm 1, in which computation resources are under-utilized because of the inefficient off-chip communication.

## 3. ACCELERATOR DESIGN EXPLORATION

In this section, we first present an overview of our accelerator structure and introduce several design challenges on an FPGA platform. Then, in order to overcome them, we propose corresponding optimization techniques to explore the design space.

### 3.1 Design Overview

As shown in Figure 4, a CNN accelerator design on FPGA is composed of several major components, which are processing elements (PEs), on-chip buffer, external memory, and on-/off-chip interconnect. A PE is the basic computation unit for convolution. All data for processing are stored in external memory. Due to on-chip resource limitation, data are first cached in on-chip buffers before being fed to PEs. Double buffers are used to cover computation time with data transfer time. The on-chip interconnect is dedicated for data communication between PEs and on-chip buffer banks.

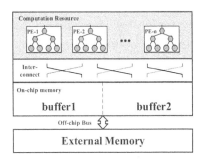

**Figure 4: Overview of accelerator design**

There are several design challenges that obstacle an efficient CNN accelerator design on an FPGA platform. First, loop tiling is mandatory to fit a small portion of data on-chip. An improper tiling may degrade the efficiency of data

```
for(row=0; row<R; row+=Tr) {
 for(col=0; col<C; col+=Tc) {
  for(to=0; to<M; to+=Tm) {
   for(ti=0; ti<N; ti+=Tn) {
   //load output feature maps
   //load weights
   //load input feature maps
```
External data transfer
To be discussed in Section 3.2

On-chip data computation
To be discussed in Section 3.1
```
   for(trr=row; trr<min(row+Tr,R); trr++){
    for(tcc=col; tcc<min(col+Tc,C); tcc++){
     for(too=to; too<min(to+Tm,M); too++){
      for(tii=ti; tii<min(ti+Tn,N); tii++){
       for(i=0; i<K; i++) {
        for(j=0; j<K; j++) {
        L: output_fm[too][trr][tcc] +=
            weights[too][tii][i][j]*
            input_fm[tii][S*trr+i][S*tcc+j];
   } } } } }
   //store output feature maps
} } } }
```

**Figure 5: Pseudo code of a tiled convolutional layer**

```
//on-chip data computation
for(trr=row; trr<min(row+Tr,R); trr++){
 for(tcc=col; tcc<min(col+Tc,C); tcc++){
  for(too=to; too<min(to+Tm,M); too++){
   for(tii=ti; tii<min(ti+Tn,N); tii++){
    for(i=0; i<K; i++) {
     for(j=0; j<K; j++) {
     L: output_fm[too][trr][tcc] +=
         weights[too][tii][i][j]*
         input_fm[tii][S*trr+i][S*tcc+j];
} } } } } }
```

**Code 2: On-chip data computation**

```
//on-chip data computation
for(i=0; i<K; i++) {
 for(j=0; j<K; j++) {
  for(trr=row; trr<min(row+Tr,R); trr++){
   for(tcc=col; tcc<min(col+Tc,C); tcc++){
    for(too=to; too<min(to+Tm,M); too++){
#pragma HLS UNROLL
     for(tii=ti; tii<min(ti+Tn,N); tii++){
#pragma HLS UNROLL
     L: output_fm[too][trr][tcc] +=
         weights[too][tii][i][j]*
         input_fm[tii][S*trr+i][S*tcc+j];
} } } } } }
```

**Code 3: Proposed accelerator structure**

reuse and parallelism of data processing. Second, the organization of PEs and buffer banks and interconnects between them should be carefully considered in order to process on-chip data efficiently. Third, the data processing throughput of PEs should match the off-chip bandwidth provided by the FPGA platform.

In this section, we start our optimization from Code 1 and present our methodology for exploring the design space to achieve an efficient design in successive steps. First, we apply loop tiling (Figure 5). Note that loop iterators $i$ and $j$ are not tiled because of the relatively small size (typically ranging from 3 to 11) of convolution window size $K$ in CNN. Other loop iterators (*row*, *col*, *to* and *ti*) are tiled into tile loops and point loops (*trr*, *tcc*, *too* and *tii* in Figure 5). Second, we discuss the computation engine optimization and formulate the computational performance with the tilling factors (Section 3.2). Third, We use data reuse technique to reduce external memory traffic and formulate the computation to communication ratio with tiling factors (Section 3.3). Forth, with the two variables defined above, we define the design space, in which we present the computation-memory-access-matched-design under FPGA board specification (Section 3.4). Fifth, We discuss how to select a best uniform accelerator for the entire multi-layer CNN application (Section 3.5).

## 3.2 Computation Optimization

In this section, we use standard polyhedral-based data dependence analysis [13] to derive a series of legal design variants of equivalently CNN implementations through loop scheduling and loop tile size enumeration. The objective of computation optimization is to enable efficient loop unrolling/pipelining while fully utilizing of all computation resources provided by the FPGA hardware platform. In this section, we assume that all required data are on-chip. Off-chip memory bandwidth constraints will be discussed in Section 3.3.

*Loop Unrolling.* Loop unrolling can be used to increase the utilization of massive computation resources in FPGA devices. Unrolling along different loop dimensions will generate different implementation varients. Whether and to

what extent two unrolled execution instances share data will affect the complexity of generated hardware, and eventually affect the number of unrolled copies and the hardware operation frequency. The data sharing relations between different loop iterations of a loop dimension on a given array can be classified into three categories:

- *Irrelevant.* If a loop iterator $i_k$ does not appear in any access functions of an array $A$, the corresponding loop dimension is *irrelevant* to array $A$.

- *Independent.* If the union of data space accessed on an array A is totally separable along a certain loop dimension $i_k$, or for any given two distinct parameters $p_1$ and $p_2$, the data accessed by $DS(A, i_k = p_1) = \bigcup Image\left(F_S^A, (\mathcal{D}_S \cap i_k = p_1)\right)$ is disjoint with $DS(A, i_k = p_2) = \bigcup Image\left(F_S^A, (\mathcal{D}_S \cap i_k = p_2)\right)$[1], the loop dimension $i_k$ is *independent* of array $A$.

- *Dependent.* If the union of data space accessed on an array A is not separable along a certain loop dimension $i_k$, the loop dimension $i_k$ is *dependent* of array $A$.

The hardware implementations generated by different data sharing relations are shown in Figure 6. An independent data sharing relation generates direct connections between buffers and computation engines. An irrelevant data sharing relation generates broadcast connections. A dependent data sharing relation generates interconnects with complex topology.

The data sharing relations of Figure 5 is shown in Table 2. Loop dimensions *too* and *tii* are selected to be unrolled to avoid complex connection topologies for all arrays. *Too* and *tii* are permuted to the innermost loop levels to simplify HLS code generation. The generated hardware implementation can be found in Figure 7.

---
[1]The polyhedral annotations used here can be found in [13]

164

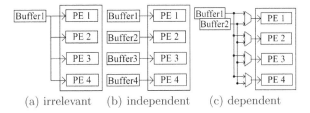

(a) irrelevant    (b) independent    (c) dependent

**Figure 6: Hardware implementations of different data sharing relations**

Table 2: Data sharing relations of CNN code

|  | input_fm | weights | output_fm |
|---|---|---|---|
| $trr$ | dependent | irrelevant | independent |
| $tcc$ | dependent | irrelevant | independent |
| $too$ | irrelevant | independent | independent |
| $tii$ | independent | independent | irrelevant |
| $i$ | dependent | independent | irrelevant |
| $j$ | dependent | independent | irrelevant |

*Loop Pipelining.* Loop pipelining is a key optimization technique in high-level synthesis to improve system throughput by overlapping the execution of operations from different loop iterations. The throughput achieved is limited both by resource constraints and data dependencies in the application. Loop-carried dependence will prevent loops to be fully pipelined. Polyhedral-based optimization framework [16] can be used to perform automatic loop transformation to permute the parallel loop levels to the innermost levels to avoid loop carried dependence. Code structure after optimization for loop unrolling and loop pipelining is shown in Code 3.

*Tile Size Selection.* Fixing the loop structure, design variants with different loop tile size will also have significantly different performance. The space of all legal tile sizes for Code 3 are illustrated by Equation (2).

$$\begin{cases} 0 < Tm \times Tn \leq (\# \ of \ PEs) \\ 0 < Tm \leq M \\ 0 < Tn \leq N \\ 0 < Tr \leq R \\ 0 < Tc \leq C \end{cases} \quad (2)$$

Given a specific tile size combination $\langle Tm, Tn, Tr, Tc \rangle$, the computational performance (or computational roof in the roofline model) can be calculated by Equation (3). From the equation, we can observe that the computational roof is a function of $T_m$ and $T_n$.

$$\begin{aligned} & computational\ roof \\ = \ & \frac{total\ number\ of\ operations}{number\ of\ execution\ cycles} \\ = \ & \frac{2 \times R \times C \times M \times N \times K \times K}{\lceil \frac{M}{T_m} \rceil \times \lceil \frac{N}{T_n} \rceil \times \frac{R}{T_r} \times \frac{C}{T_c} \times (T_r \times T_c \times K \times K + P)} \\ \approx \ & \frac{2 \times R \times C \times M \times N \times K \times K}{\lceil \frac{M}{T_m} \rceil \times \lceil \frac{N}{T_n} \rceil \times R \times C \times K \times K} \end{aligned} \quad (3)$$

where $P = pipeline\ depth - 1$.

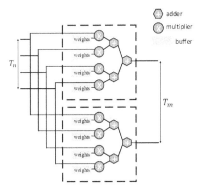

**Figure 7: Computation engine**

## 3.3 Memory Access Optimization

In Section 3.2, we discussed how to derive design variants with different computational roofs, assuming all data accessed by the computation engine are already buffered onchip. However, design variants with the higher computational roof does not necessarily achieve the higher performance under memory bandwidth constraints. In this section, we will show how to reduce communication volume with efficient data reuse.

Figure 9 illustrates the memory transfer operations of a CNN layer. Input/output feature maps and weights are loaded before the computation engine starts and the generated output feature maps are written back to main memory.

```
for(row=0; row<R; row+=Tr) {
  for(col=0; col<C; col+=Tc) {
    for(to=0; to<M; to+=Tm) {
      for(ti=0; ti<N; ti+=Tn) {
        //load output feature maps
        //load weights
        //load input feature maps

        L: foo(output_fm(to,row,col),
               weights(to,ti),
               input_fm(ti,row,col));
        //store output feature maps
      }

} } }
```

**Figure 9: Local memory promotion for CNN**

*Local Memory Promotion.* If the innermost loop in the communication part (loop dimension $ti$ in Figure 9) is *irrelevant* to an array, there will be redundant memory operations between different loop iterations. Local memory promotion [13] can be used to reduce the redundant operations. In Figure 9, the innermost loop dimension $ti$ is irrelevant to array *output_fm*. Thus, the accesses to array *output_fm* can be promoted to outer loops. Note that the promotion process can be iteratively performed until the innermost loop surrounding the accesses is finally *relevant*. With local memory promotion, the trip count of memory access operations on array *output_fm* reduces from $2 \times \frac{M}{T_m} \times \frac{N}{T_n} \times \frac{R}{T_r} \times \frac{C}{T_c}$ to $\frac{M}{T_m} \times \frac{R}{T_r} \times \frac{C}{T_c}$.

*Loop Transformations for Data Reuse.* To maximize the opportunities of data reuse through local memory promo-

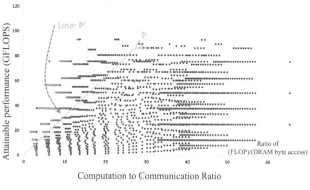

(a) Design space of all possible designs

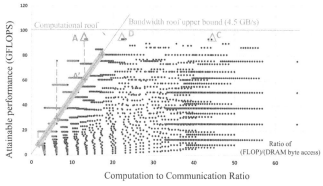

(b) Design space of platform-supported designs

Figure 8: Design space exploration

tions, we use polyhedral-based optimization framework to identify all legal loop transformations. Table 3 shows the data sharing relations between loop iterations and arrays. Local memory promotions are used in each legal loop schedule whenever applicable to reduce the total communication volume.

Table 3: Data sharing relations of communication part

|  | irrelevant dimension(s) |
| --- | --- |
| *input_fm* | *to* |
| *weights* | *row,col* |
| *output_fm* | *ti* |

*CTC Ratio.* Computation to communication (CTC) ratio is used to describe the computation operations per memory access. Data reuse optimization will reduce the total number of memory accesses, thus increase the computation to communication ratio. The computation to communication ratio of the code shown in Figure 9 can be calculated by Equation (4), where $\alpha_{in}, \alpha_{out}, \alpha_{wght}$ and $B_{in}, B_{out}, B_{wght}$ denote the trip counts and buffer sizes of memory accesses to input/output feature maps and weights respectively.

$$
\begin{aligned}
&\quad Computation\ to\ Communication\ Ratio \\
&= \frac{total\ number\ of\ operations}{total\ amount\ of\ external\ data\ access} \\
&= \frac{2 \times R \times C \times M \times N \times K \times K}{\alpha_{in} \times B_{in} + \alpha_{wght} \times B_{wght} + \alpha_{out} \times B_{out}} \quad (4)
\end{aligned}
$$

where

$$B_{in} = T_n(ST_r + K - S)(ST_c + K - S) \quad (5)$$

$$B_{wght} = T_m T_n K^2 \quad (6)$$

$$B_{out} = T_m T_r T_c \quad (7)$$

$$0 < B_{in} + B_{wght} + B_{out} \leq BRAM_{capacity} \quad (8)$$

$$\alpha_{in} = \alpha_{wght} = \frac{M}{T_m} \times \frac{N}{T_n} \times \frac{R}{T_r} \times \frac{C}{T_c} \quad (9)$$

Without *output_fm*'s data reuse,

$$\alpha_{out} = 2 \times \frac{M}{T_m} \times \frac{N}{T_n} \times \frac{R}{T_r} \times \frac{C}{T_c} \quad (10)$$

With *output_fm*'s data reuse,

$$\alpha_{out} = \frac{M}{T_m} \times \frac{R}{T_r} \times \frac{C}{T_c} \quad (11)$$

Given a specific loop schedule and a set of tile size tuple $\langle Tm, Tn, Tr, Tc \rangle$, computation to communication ratio can be calculated with above formula.

## 3.4 Design Space Exploration

As mentioned in Section 3.2 and Section 3.3, given a specific loop schedule and tile size tuple $\langle Tm, Tn, Tr, Tc \rangle$, the computational roof and computation to communication ratio of the design variant can be calculated. Enumerating all possible loop orders and tile sizes will generate a series of computational performance and computation to communication ratio pairs. Figure 8(a) depicts all legal solutions for layer 5 of the example CNN application in the rooline model coordinate system. The "x" axis denotes the computation to communication ratio, or the ratio of floating point operation per DRAM byte access. The "y" axis denotes the computational performance (GFLOPS). The slope of the line between any point and the origin point $(0, 0)$ denotes the minimal bandwidth requirement for this implementation. For example, design $P$'s minimal bandwidth requirement is equal to the slope of the line $P'$.

In Figure 8(b), the line of bandwidth roof and computational roof are defined by the platform specification. Any point at the left side of bandwidth roofline requires a higher bandwidth than what the platform can provide. For example, although implementation $A$ achieves the highest possible computational performance, the memory bandwidth required cannot be satisfied by the target platform. The actual performance achievable on the platform would be the ordinate value of $A'$. Thus the platform-supported designs are defined as a set including those located at the right side of the bandwidth roofline and those just located on the bandwidth roofline, which are projections of the left side designs.

We explore this platform-supported design space and a set of implementations with the highest performance can be collected. If this set only include one design, then this design will be our final result of design space exploration. However, a more common situation is that we could find several counterparts within this set, e.g. point $C$, $D$ and some others in Figure 8(b). We pick the one with the highest CI value because this design requires the least bandwidth.

This selection criteria derives from the fact that we can use fewer I/O ports, fewer LUTs and hardwired connections etc. for data transfer engine in designs with lower bandwidth requirement. Thus, point $C$ is our finally chosen design in this case for layer 5. Its bandwidth requirement is 2.2 GB/s.

## 3.5 Multi-Layer CNN Accelerator Design

Table 4: Layer specific optimal solution and cross-layer optimization

| | Optimal Unroll Factor $\langle Tm, Tn \rangle$ | Execution Cycles |
|---|---|---|
| Layer 1 | $\langle 48, 3 \rangle$ | 366025 |
| Layer 2 | $\langle 20, 24 \rangle$ | 237185 |
| Layer 3 | $\langle 96, 5 \rangle$ | 160264 |
| Layer 4 | $\langle 95, 5 \rangle$ | 120198 |
| Layer 5 | $\langle 32, 15 \rangle$ | 80132 |
| Total | - | 963804 |
| Cross-Layer Optimization | $\langle 64, 7 \rangle$ | 1008246 |

In previous sections, we discussed how to find optimal implementation parameters for each convolutional layer. In a CNN application, these parameters may vary between different layers. Table 4 shows the optimal unroll factors ($Tm$ and $Tn$) for all layers of the example CNN application (see Figure 2).

Designing a hardware accelerator to support multiple convolutional layer with different unroll factors would be challenging. Complex hardware structures are required to reconfigure computation engines and interconnects.

An alternative approach is to design a hardware architecture with uniform unroll factors across different convolutional layers. We enumerate all legal solutions to select the optimal global design parameters. CNN accelerator with unified unroll factors is simple to design and implement, but may be sub-optimal for some layers. Table 4 shows that with unified unroll factors ($\langle 64, 7 \rangle$), the degradation is within 5% compared to the total execution cycles of each optimized convolutional layer. With this analysis, CNN accelerator with unified unroll factors across convolutional layers are selected in our experiments. The upper bound of the enumeration space size is 98 thousand legal designs, which can finish in 10 minutes at a common laptop.

## 4. IMPLEMENTATION DETAILS

This section describes the detailed implementation of our solution.

### 4.1 System Overview

Figure 10 shows an overview of our implementation. The whole system fits in one single FPGA chip and uses a DDR3 DRAM for external storage. MicroBlaze, a RISC soft processor core developed for Xilinx FPGAs, is used to assist with CNN accelerator startup, communication with host CPU and time measurement etc. AXI4lite bus is for command transfer and AXI4 bus is for data transfer. The CNN accelerator works as an IP on the AXI4 bus. It receives commands and configuration parameters from MicroBlaze through AXI4lite bus and communicate with customized data transfer engines through FIFO interfaces. This data

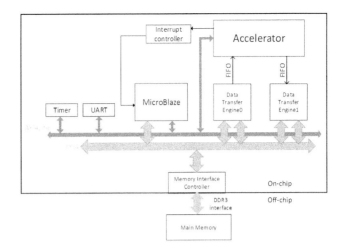

Figure 10: Implementation overview

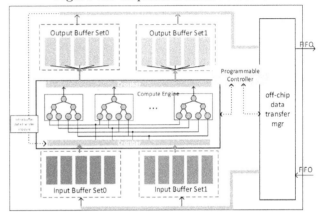

Figure 11: Block diagram of proposed accelerator

transfer engine can access external memory through AXI4 bus. Interruption mechanism is enabled between MicroBlaze and CNN accelerator to provide an accurate time measurement.

### 4.2 Computation Engines

The computation engine part in Figure 11 shows a block diagram of our implementation. They are designed according to our analysis in Section 3. The two-level unrolled loops ($T_m$, $T_n$ in Figure 2) are implemented as concurrently executing computation engines. A tree-shaped poly structure like that in Figure 7 is used. For the best cross-layer design ($\langle T_m, T_n \rangle = \langle 64, 7 \rangle$) case, the computation engine is implemented as a tree-shaped poly structure with 7 inputs from input feature maps and 7 inputs from weights and one input from bias, which is stored in the buffers of output feature maps. 64 poly structures are duplicated for unrolling loop $T_m$. An overview can be found in the compute engine part of Figure 11.

### 4.3 Memory Sub-System

On-chip buffers are built upon a basic idea of double-buffering, in which double buffers are operated in a ping-pong manner to overlap data transfer time with computation. Therefore, they are organized in four sets: two for input feature maps and weights and two for output feature

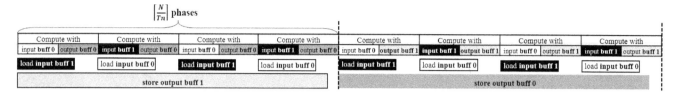

| Compute with | Compute with | Compute with | Compute with | Compute with | Compute with | Compute with | Compute with |
|---|---|---|---|---|---|---|---|
| input buff 0 · output buff 0 | input buff 1 · output buff 0 | input buff 0 · output buff 0 | input buff 1 · output buff 0 | input buff 0 · output buff 1 | input buff 1 · output buff 1 | input buff 0 · output buff 1 | input buff 1 · output buff 1 |
| load input buff 1 | load input buff 0 | load input buff 1 | load input buff 0 | load input buff 1 | load input buff 0 | load input buff 1 | load input buff 0 |

store output buff 1 · store output buff 0

**Figure 12: Timing graph**

maps. We first introduce each buffer set's organization and followed by the ping-pong data transfer mechanism.

Every buffer set contains several independent buffer banks. The number of buffer banks in each input buffer set is equal to $T_n$ (tile size of $input\_fm$). The number of buffer banks in each output buffer set is equal to $T_m$ (tile size of $output\_fm$).

Double buffer sets are used to realize ping-pong operations. To simplify discussion, we use a concrete case in Figure 9 to illustrate the mechanism of ping-pong operation. See the code in Figure 9. The "off-load" operation will occur only once after $\left\lceil \frac{N}{T_n} \right\rceil$ times of "load" operation. But the amount of data in every $output\_fm$ transfer are larger than that of $input\_fm$ in a ratio of $\approx \frac{T_m}{T_n} = \frac{64}{7}$. To increase the bandwidth utilization, we implement two independent channels, one for load operation and the other for off-load operation.

Figure 12 shows the timing of several compute and data transfer phases. For the first phase, computation engine is processing with input buffer set 0 while copying the next phase data to input buffer set 1. The next phase will do the opposite operation. This is the ping-pong operation of input feature maps and weights. When $\left\lceil \frac{N}{T_n} \right\rceil$ phases of computation and data copying are done, the resulting output feature maps are written down to DRAM. The "off-load" operation would off-load results in the output buffer set 0 in the period of $\left\lceil \frac{N}{T_n} \right\rceil$ phases till the reused temporary data in the output buffer set 1 generates the new results. This is the ping-pong operation of output feature maps. Note that those two independent channel for load and store operation mechanism work for any other data reuse situation in this framework.

## 4.4 External Data Transfer Engines

The purposes of using external data transfer engines are in two folds: 1) It can provide data transfer between accelerator and external memory; 2) It can isolate our accelerator from various platform and tool specific bandwidth features. Figure 13 shows an experiment with AXI4 bus bandwidth in Vivado 2013.4. In these two figures, we set two parameters, bitwidth of AXI bus to DRAM controller and DRAM controller's external bandwidth, at their highest configurations while changing the number of IP-AXI interfaces and the bitwidth of each IP. In Figure 13(a), the increase in IP-AXI interface bitwidth has no effect on bandwidth (400MB/s under 100MHz frequency). In Figure 13(b), with more IP interfaces added to AXI bus, its bandwidth increases almost linearly and the highest bandwidth is about 4.5 GB/s. In our CNN accelerator design, a minimal bandwidth of 1.55 GB/s is required. Therefore, 4 IP interfaces are sufficient for this design according to Figure 13. We use two AXI-IP interfaces in data transfer engine 0 and two in data transfer engine 1, as is shown in Figure 10.

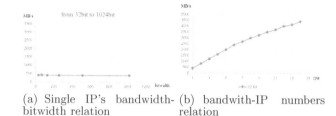

(a) Single IP's bandwidth-bitwidth relation  (b) bandwith-IP numbers relation

**Figure 13: IP-DRAM bandwidth(Vivado 2013.4)**

## 5. EVALUATION

In this section, we first introduce the environment setup of our experiments. Then, comprehensive experimental results are provided.

### 5.1 Experimental Setup

The accelerator design is implemented with Vivado HLS (v2013.4). This tool enables implementing the accelerator with C language and exporting the RTL as a Vivado's IP core. The C code of our CNN design is parallelized by adding HLS-defined pragma and the parallel version is validated with the timing analysis tool. Fast pre-synthesis simulation is completed with this tool's C simulation and C/RTL co-simulation. Pre-synthesis resource report are used for design space exploration and performance estimation. The exported RTL is synthesized and implemented in Vivado (v2013.4).

Our implementation is built on the VC707 board which has a Xilinx FPGA chip Virtex7 485t. Its working frequency is 100 MHz. Software implementation runs on an Intel Xeon CPU E5-2430 (@2.20GHz) with 15MB cache.

### 5.2 Experimental Results

In this subsection, we first report resource utilization. Then, we compare software implementation (on CPU) to our accelerator on FPGA. Finally, the comparison between our implementation and existing FPGA approaches is provided.

The placement and routing is completed with Vivado tool set. After that, the resource utilization of our implementation is reported out, as shown in Table 6. We can tell that our CNN accelerator has almost fully utilized FPGA's hardware resource.

**Table 6: FPGA Resource utilization**

| Resource | DSP | BRAM | LUT | FF |
|---|---|---|---|---|
| Used | 2240 | 1024 | 186251 | 205704 |
| Available | 2800 | 2060 | 303600 | 607200 |
| Utilization | 80% | 50% | 61.3% | 33.87% |

**Table 5: Comparison to previous implementations**

| | ICCD2013 [12] | ASAP2009 [14] | FPL2009 [6] | FPL2009 [6] | PACT2010 [2] | ISCA2010 [3] | Our Impl. |
|---|---|---|---|---|---|---|---|
| Precision | fixed point | 16bits fixed | 48bits fixed | 48bits fixed | fixed point | 48bits fixed | 32bits float |
| Frequency | 150 MHz | 115 MHz | 125 MHz | 125 MHz | 125 MHz | 200 MHz | 100 MHz |
| FPGA chip | Virtex6 VLX240T | Virtex5 LX330T | Spartan-3A DSP3400 | Virtex4 SX35 | Virtex5 SX240T | Virtex5 SX240T | Virtex7 VX485T |
| FPGA capacity | 37,680 slices 768 DSP | 51,840 slices 192 DSP | 23,872 slices 126 DSP | 15,360 slices 192 DSP | 37,440 slices 1056 DSP | 37,440 slices 1056 DSP | 75,900 slices 2800 DSP |
| LUT type | 6-input LUT | 6-input LUT | 4-input LUT | 4-input LUT | 6-input LUT | 6-input LUT | 6-input LUT |
| CNN Size | 2.74 GMAC | 0.53 GMAC | 0.26 GMAC | 0.26 GMAC | 0.53 GMAC | 0.26 GMAC | 1.33 GFLOP |
| Performance | 8.5 GMACS | 3.37 GMACS | 2.6 GMACS | 2.6 GMACS | 3.5 GMACS | 8 GMACS | 61.62 GFLOPS |
| | 17 GOPS | 6.74 GOPS | 5.25 GOPS | 5.25 GOPS | 7.0 GOPS | 16 GOPS | 61.62 GOPS |
| Performance Density | 4.5E-04 GOPs/Slice | 1.3E-04 GOPs/Slice | 2.2E-04 GOPs/Slice | 3.42E-04 GOPs/Slice | 1.9E-04 GOPs/Slice | 4.3E-04 GOPs/Slice | 8.12E-04 GOPS/Slice |

**Table 7: Performance comparison to CPU**

| float | CPU 2.20GHz (ms) | | FPGA | |
|---|---|---|---|---|
| 32 bit | 1thd -O3 | 16thd -O3 | (ms) | GFLOPS |
| layer 1 | 98.18 | 19.36 | 7.67 | 27.50 |
| layer 2 | 94.66 | 27.00 | 5.35 | 83.79 |
| layer 3 | 77.38 | 24.30 | 3.79 | 78.81 |
| layer 4 | 65.58 | 18.64 | 2.88 | 77.94 |
| layer 5 | 40.70 | 14.18 | 1.93 | 77.61 |
| Total | 376.50 | 103.48 | 21.61 | - |
| Overall GFLOPS | 3.54 | 12.87 | 61.62 | |
| Speedup | 1.00x | 3.64x | 17.42x | |

**Table 8: Power consumption and energy**

| | Intel Xeon 2.20GHz | | FPGA |
|---|---|---|---|
| | 1 thread -O3 | 16 threads -O3 | |
| Power (Watt) | 95.00 | 95.00 | 18.61 |
| Comparison | 5.1x | 5.1x | 1x |
| Energy (J) | 35.77 | 9.83 | 0.40 |
| Comparison | 89.4x | 24.6x | 1x |

**Figure 14: Power measurement of on-board execution**

**Table 9: Resource occupation comparison**

| 32-bit | DSP | LUT | FF |
|---|---|---|---|
| Fixed point(adder) | 2 | 0 | 0 |
| Fixed point(mul.) | 2 | 0 | 0 |
| Floating point(adder) | 2 | 214 | 227 |
| Floating point(mul.) | 3 | 135 | 128 |

The performance comparison between our accelerator and software based counterpart is shown in Table 7. We select our proposed cross-layer accelerator for comparison. The software implementations are realized in 1 thread and 16 threads using gcc with -O3 optimization options, respectively. **Overall**, our FPGA based implementation achieves up to a 17.42x speedup over software implementation of 1 thread. It also achieves a 4.8x speedup over software implementation of 16 threads. Our accelerator's overall performance achieves 61.62 GFLOPS.

Figure 14 shows a picture of our on-board implementation. A power meter is plugged in to measure its runtime power performance, which is 18.6 Watt. CPU's thermal design power is 95 Watt. Therefore, we can have a rough estimation of software and FPGA's implementations' power. Table 8 shows that the ratio of the consumed energy between software implementation and FPGA implementation is 24.6x at least. FPGA implementation uses much less energy than its software counterparts.

In Table 5, various existing FPGA based CNN accelerators are listed and compared to our implementation in this work. Since previous approaches use GMACS (giga multiplication and accumulation per second) and we use GFLOPS (giga floating point operations per second) as the performance metric, we first convert all result numbers to GOPS (giga operations per second) to employ the same metric. Note that each multiply-accumulate operation contains two integer operations. As shown in the 9th row of Table 5, our accelerator has a throughput of 61.62 GOPS, which outperforms other approaches by a speedup of at least 3.62x.

Since different work exploits different parallelism opportunities and use different FPGA platforms, it is hardly to have a straightforward comparison between them. In order to provide a fair comparison, we further present results of "performance density" in Table 5. It is defined as average GOPS per area unit (slice), which can represent the efficiency of a design independent of the FPGA platforms used for implementation. As shown in the last row of Table 5, our implementation achieves the highest performance density, which is 1.8x better than the second best. In addition, our method could achieve even better performance and performance density if using fixed point computation engines because fixed point processing elements uses much less resource (Table 9).

## 6. RELATED WORK

In this section, we discuss different design methods with reference to other previous work on FPGA-based CNN accelerator designs.

First, many CNN application accelerators are focused on optimizing computation engines. Implementations [6], [14] and [3] are three representatives. The earliest approach in work [6] was to build their CNN application mainly by software implementation while using one hardware systolic architecture accelerator to do the filtering convolution job. This design saves a lot of hardware resources and is used in embedded system for automotive robots. Implementations in work [14], [2] and [3] implement complete CNN applications on FPGA but exploits different parallelism opportunities. Work [14] and [2] mainly uses the parallelism within feature maps and convolution kernel. Work [3] uses "inter-output" and "intra-output" parallelism. Our parallelization method is similar to theirs, but they do not use on-chip buffers for data reuse; alternatively they use very high bandwidth and dynamical configurations to improve performance. Our implementation take advantage of data reuse, and balances limitations of bandwidth and FPGA computation power.

Second, work [12], considering CNN's communication issue, chooses to maximize date reuse and reduce bandwidth requirement to the minimum. But their approach do not consider maximizing computation performance. In addition, they need to take time (in order of 10 seconds) to program FPGA when shifting to next layers' computation while our solution only take no more than a microsecond to configure a few registers.

## 7. CONCLUSIONS

In this work, we propose a roofline-model-based method for convolutional neural network's FPGA acceleration. In this method we first optimize CNN's computation and memory access. We then model all possible designs in roofline model and find the best design for each layer. We also find the best cross-layer design by enumeration. Finally, we realize an implementation on Xilinx VC707 board which outperforms all previous work.

## 8. ACKNOWLEDGMENT

This work was supported in part by NSF China 61202072, RFDP 20110001110099, National High Technology Research and Development Program of China 2012AA010902 and C-FAR, one of six centers of STARnet, a Semiconductor Research Corporation program sponsored by MARCO and DARPA. We thank the UCLA/PKU Joint Research Institute for their support of our research.

## 9. REFERENCES

[1] D. Aysegul, J. Jonghoon, G. Vinayak, K. Bharadwaj, C. Alfredo, M. Berin, and C. Eugenio. Accelerating deep neural networks on mobile processor with embedded programmable logic. In *NIPS 2013*. IEEE, 2013.

[2] S. Cadambi, A. Majumdar, M. Becchi, S. Chakradhar, and H. P. Graf. A programmable parallel accelerator for learning and classification. In *Proceedings of the 19th international conference on Parallel architectures and compilation techniques*, pages 273–284. ACM, 2010.

[3] S. Chakradhar, M. Sankaradas, V. Jakkula, and S. Cadambi. A dynamically configurable coprocessor for convolutional neural networks. In *ACM SIGARCH Computer Architecture News*, volume 38, pages 247–257. ACM, 2010.

[4] T. Chen, Z. Du, N. Sun, J. Wang, C. Wu, Y. Chen, and O. Temam. Diannao: A small-footprint high-throughput accelerator for ubiquitous machine-learning. *SIGPLAN Not.*, 49(4):269–284, Feb. 2014.

[5] J. Cong and B. Xiao. Minimizing computation in convolutional neural networks. In *Artificial Neural Networks and Machine Learning–ICANN 2014*, pages 281–290. Springer, 2014.

[6] C. Farabet, C. Poulet, J. Y. Han, and Y. LeCun. Cnp: An fpga-based processor for convolutional networks. In *Field Programmable Logic and Applications, 2009. FPL 2009. International Conference on*, pages 32–37. IEEE, 2009.

[7] Google. Improving photo search: A step across the semantic gap. http://googleresearch.blogspot.com/2013/06/improving-photo-search-step-across.html.

[8] S. Ji, W. Xu, M. Yang, and K. Yu. 3d convolutional neural networks for human action recognition. *IEEE Trans. Pattern Anal. Mach. Intell.*, 35(1):221–231, Jan. 2013.

[9] A. Krizhevsky, I. Sutskever, and G. E. Hinton. Imagenet classification with deep convolutional neural networks. In F. Pereira, C. Burges, L. Bottou, and K. Weinberger, editors, *Advances in Neural Information Processing Systems 25*, pages 1097–1105. Curran Associates, Inc., 2012.

[10] H. Larochelle, D. Erhan, A. Courville, J. Bergstra, and Y. Bengio. An empirical evaluation of deep architectures on problems with many factors of variation. In *Proceedings of the 24th International Conference on Machine Learning*, ICML '07, pages 473–480, New York, NY, USA, 2007. ACM.

[11] Y. LeCun, L. Bottou, Y. Bengio, and P. Haffner. Gradient-based learning applied to document recognition. *Proceedings of the IEEE*, 86(11):2278–2324, 1998.

[12] M. Peemen, A. A. Setio, B. Mesman, and H. Corporaal. Memory-centric accelerator design for convolutional neural networks. In *Computer Design (ICCD), 2013 IEEE 31st International Conference on*, pages 13–19. IEEE, 2013.

[13] L.-N. Pouchet, P. Zhang, P. Sadayappan, and J. Cong. Polyhedral-based data reuse optimization for configurable computing. In *Proceedings of the ACM/SIGDA International Symposium on Field Programmable Gate Arrays*, FPGA '13, pages 29–38, New York, NY, USA, 2013. ACM.

[14] M. Sankaradas, V. Jakkula, S. Cadambi, S. Chakradhar, I. Durdanovic, E. Cosatto, and H. P. Graf. A massively parallel coprocessor for convolutional neural networks. In *Application-specific Systems, Architectures and Processors, 2009. ASAP 2009. 20th IEEE International Conference on*, pages 53–60. IEEE, 2009.

[15] S. Williams, A. Waterman, and D. Patterson. Roofline: An insightful visual performance model for multicore architectures. *Commun. ACM*, 52(4):65–76, Apr. 2009.

[16] W. Zuo, Y. Liang, P. Li, K. Rupnow, D. Chen, and J. Cong. Improving high level synthesis optimization opportunity through polyhedral transformations. In *Proceedings of the ACM/SIGDA International Symposium on Field Programmable Gate Arrays*, FPGA '13, pages 9–18, New York, NY, USA, 2013. ACM.

# Wavefront Skipping using BRAMs
# for Conditional Algorithms on Vector Processors

Aaron Severance
University of British Columbia
Vancouver, BC Canada
aaronsev@ece.ubc.ca

Joe Edwards
University of British Columbia
Vancouver, BC Canada
jedwards@ece.ubc.ca

Guy G.F. Lemieux
University of British Columbia
Vancouver, BC Canada
lemieux@ece.ubc.ca

VectorBlox Computing, Inc.
Vancouver, BC Canada
aseverance@vectorblox.com

VectorBlox Computing, Inc.
Vancouver, BC Canada
jedwards@vectorblox.com

VectorBlox Computing, Inc.
Vancouver, BC Canada
glemieux@vectorblox.com

## ABSTRACT

Soft vector processors can accelerate data parallel algorithms on FPGAs while retaining software programmability. To handle divergent control flow, vector processors typically use mask registers and predicated instructions. These work by executing all branches and finally selecting the correct one. Our work improves FPGA based vector processors by adding wavefront skipping, where wavefronts that are completely masked off are skipped. This accelerates conditional algorithms, particularly useful where elements terminate early if simple tests fail but require extensive processing in the worst case. The difference in logic speed and RAM area for FPGA based circuits versus ASICs led us to a different implementation than used in fixed vector processors, storing wavefront offsets in on-chip BRAM rather than computing wavefronts skipped dynamically. Additionally, we allow for partitioning the wavefronts so that partial wavefronts can skip independently of one another. We show that <5% extra area can give up to 3.2× better performance on conditional algorithms. Partial wavefront skipping may not be generally useful enough to be added to a fixed vector processor; it provides up to 65% more performance for up to 27% more area. In an FGPA, however, the designer can use it to make application specific tradeoffs between area and performance.

## 1. INTRODUCTION

Soft vector processors (SVPs) are a particular type of overlay that creates a vector processor inside of an FPGA. Having a software-programmable model reduces design cycle time and makes programming and debugging easier than writing at the RTL level. An SVP has one or more lanes (ALUs with their own local memory) that can process data in parallel; the data processed in a single cycle is called a

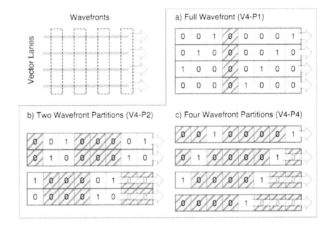

**Figure 1: Wavefront Skipping on a 4 Lane MXP**

wavefront. If the vector length is longer than the number of lanes the instruction will sequentially process one wavefront per cycle until the whole vector instruction has completed. For algorithms that use conditional execution, i.e. branching, the vector processor must execute both paths of the branch and mask off writes for elements not on the current branch. This can result in a large portion of execution unit results that are not used, especially for algorithms that can stop processing some data elements early depending on a conditional check.

In order to speed up these conditional algorithms, masked-off elements must not utilize execution slots. It is possible to compress vectors in order to remove masked-off elements, but this is costly for algorithms that use packed data such as stencil filters. Rather, we would like to skip over elements without rearranging data, which led us to implement wavefront skipping. A wavefront is one cycle of data within the parallel vector pipelines. In wavefront skipping, wavefronts where all the elements are masked off are skipped. We also implemented partial wavefront skipping, by which the wavefront is divided into partitions that can skip independently. This finer grained skipping can lead to performance increases, at the cost of requiring more resources.

Figure 1 helps illustrate how wavefront skipping works. The values shown are the mask bits corresponding to each data element; a zero indicates that element is masked off. In Figure 1a one of the eight wavefronts can be skipped since all elements are masked off. Normally this instruction would take eight cycles to process, but with wavefront skipping it can complete in seven. Figure 1b shows two wavefront partitions; the finer granularity means more partial wavefronts can be skipped, and so the instruction can run in only four cycles (the partition with only three cycles ends up being idle during the last cycle). And Figure 1c shows four wavefront partitions, at which point the partition size is a single element, and the instruction can execute in two cycles.

Our work gives the first implementation of wavefront skipping on SVPs. It uses a different approach than used on fixed vector processors, where the mask register is read out in parallel and the number of leading masked-off elements is computed each cycle. Instead, we took advantage of the relative cheapness of BRAMs on FPGAs by computing wavefront offsets beforehand in a setup instruction and storing them in BRAMs. Additionally, we implement partitioned wavefront skipping, where instead of entire wavefronts skipping together, partial wavefronts (down to individual bytes) can skip by different amounts. To our knowledge this is the first implementation of this idea in any vector processor. The full wavefront skipping implementation requires no more than 5% increase in area and a single BRAM and achieves speedups of up to 3.2× for early exit algorithms. The addition of partial wavefront skipping provides additional gains but requires up to 27% additonal area, so it might not make sense to implement in a hard vector processor. However, it may make sense to add in an SVP if the design has some unused BRAMs within the device or the algorithm is particularly sensitive to wavefront partitioning.

## 2. BACKGROUND

Vector processors have been used in supercomputers since the 1970's [3]. By performing the same operation on multiple elements, vector processors are able to achieve high throughput on data parallel problems using only a small amount of code. In particular, the inner loops of many scientific and signal processing algorithms can be converted to vector instructions. Vector processing is a form of SIMD (single instruction, multiple data) processing which is highly efficient for simple, regular algorithms such as dense linear algebra and stencil filters. In much of the supercomputer world, vector processors have given way to GPUs, which share many concepts and structures with vector processors but are more general purpose (at the cost of more area and power). Vector processing has a few niches still; for example the Convey HC-2ex [1] uses FPGAs as a vector coprocessor for memory-intensive applications, and IBM's ViVA (Virtual Vector Architecture) [5] allows programmers to treat multiple POWER processors as a single vector processor in supercomputer applications.

### 2.1 FPGA-based Soft Vector Processors

Given that vector processing is relatively inexpensive in terms of logic gates and can give high throughput for data parallel applications, it makes sense in hindsight for it to be used in FPGAs (where gates are much more expensive than ASICs). The history of the idea can be traced back to VIRAM [6], which was an ASIC vector processor that showed vector processing to be more efficient in both power and performance than superscalar or VLIW processors for

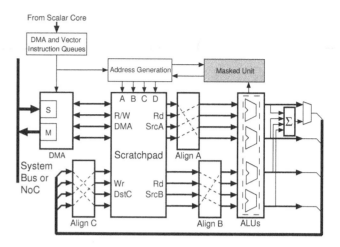

From Scalar Core

**Figure 2: VectorBlox MXP with four 32-bit lanes**

embedded media applications. Two parallel SVP implementations showed the feasibility of implementing a vector processor on an FPGA, VESPA from University of Toronto [13] and VIPERS from University of British Columbia [14]. Further work has been done to customize vector processors for FPGAs, with the most recent being the VectorBlox MXP [9] which has the ability to dispatch multi-operand custom instructions to the external FPGA fabric. Additional work on applications and programmability has been done at University of Cambridge [8] where a neural network simulation was implemented and a C++ library developed to encapsulate vectors as objects.

### 2.2 VectorBlox MXP

Our SVP, the VectorBlox MXP (MXP), is shown in Figure 2. It consists at a high level of a scalar core (Altera's Nios II/f) coupled to a vector core and DMA engine. The scalar core handles all control flow and I/O, and dispatches instructions to the vector core and DMA engine. All data processed by MXP is held in a flatly-addressable, multiple-bank scratchpad memory. Rather than have individual vector registers, a vector can start at any address in the scratchpad and be of any length. Data is initially read into the scratchpad using the DMA engine. Once it has been read into the scratchpad, a vector instruction can execute. If there are data hazards between the vector instruction and DMA transaction, hardware interlocks stall the vector core until the hazard is resolved.

When a new vector instruction is ready to issue, the address generation logic will generate the addresses for the vector operand wavefronts, then increment them appropriately each cycle until the end of the vector is reached. After the source operands are read from the scratchpad, they proceed through an alignment network. Alignment is required because vectors can start at any address within the scratchpad, hence be located in any bank of the scratchpad. The operands are then fed into the parallel ALUs to execute. An optional reduction-accumulate stage reduces the output to a single sum; a commonly needed operation in vector programs. Finally, the data is realigned to the destination bank before being written back to the scratchpad. The pipeline takes 8 stages from read to writeback, with extra stages added for alignment and reduction in wider vector processors.

We also support subword SIMD operations where two 16-bit operations or four 8-bit operations can execute in one lane. Additionally, we have a conditional move operation (discussed in Section 3) that will only overwrite the destination vector if a condition check is true. The conditional move uses byte enables to enable or disable writing to specific scratchpad banks.

## 2.3 Conditional Execution

Support for conditional execution in vector processors is well researched; a good summary is [11]. For short conditionals, implementations that use predicated operations or conditional moves can give good performance. These operations are performed on all data elements, with only the elements that pass some conditional test written back; the rest of the results are discarded. For longer conditional branches, though, this can lead to a large percentage of execution time spent on unused results. In these instances, it is desirable to skip elements that are not on the current branch. Three strategies can be employed (separately or together): compress/expand, scatter/gather, and wavefront skipping (also referred to as density-time masking).

Compress vector operations are a way to take a source vector and a mask and produce a new vector that only contains the valid (unmasked) elements without gaps. The expand vector operation is the opposite of a compress; it takes a compressed source vector and a mask and fills in the unmasked slots in the destination vector with the source data. VIRAM implemented VCOMPRESS and VEXPAND operators. During a long branch, the source operands can be compressed, followed by processing only the shorter (compressed) vector operations, and finally the result expanded. The main drawback to this approach is that all source operands must be compressed, and all destination operands must be expanded. In a MxN conditional stencil filter on an image, for instance, the MxN input pixels would all have to be separately compressed. Viola-Jones face detection operates in this manner, which is why compress/expand was not considered suitable for our implementation. This will be explained further in Section 3.4.

Scatter/gather is a method of performing indexed memory accesses (indexed store is a scatter, indexed load is a gather), either to the local memory store or external memory. Along with a compress operation or special index calculating instructions, scatter/gather can be used to speed up conditional execution. For the conditional stencil filter example, the indices of pixels to be processed could be compressed, and then the pixel data needed for each location could be loaded using gather operations. The main drawback of this approach is that parallelizing scatter and gather operations requires parallel memory accesses, which are nontrivial. VESPA could perform parallel scatter gather accesses within a single cache line. A special throughput cache [10] was developed for MXP to support scatter/gather operations, but even in the best case where all data could fit in a statically allocated multiple-bank on-chip memory, speedups were modest.

Wavefront skipping, by contrast, uses knowledge of the mask register to skip elements that do not need to be processed. An earlier implementation scans the mask register during instruction execution to determine if subsequent wavefronts can be skipped. This introduces enough latency that [7] gives a way to reduce the overhead by only skipping powers of 2 elements (at the cost of doing some extra work because the skipping is not exact). Given that an FPGA implementation is already slower than a hard processor and we are double-clocking our scratchpad to provide additional ports, we wished to avoid the additional latency in our design. Our implementation uses a special mask setup instruction to store the offsets of valid wavefronts in one or more BRAMs within the FPGA. Prior work [11] suggests the idea that each lane can skip forward individually rather than lockstep as entire wavefronts. We take this one step further by allowing the wavefront to be partitioned and separately implement wavefront skipping in each partition. The number of partitions can range from 1 (the entire wavefront) to four times the number of lanes (making each byte-lane in a separate partition). To our knowledge, we are the first to propose and implement partitioned wavefront skipping in a vector processor.

A similar concept exists in GPUs. GPUs divide up a kernel (consisting of hundreds of threads) into warps (analogous to our wavefronts, usually 16 or 32 threads). Inside a kernel, branch instructions allow different threads to diverge. If no threads inside a warp are on one of the branches, that warp is not scheduled to execute that branch; this is somewhat analogous to unpartitioned wavefront skipping in vector processors. Our method of wavefront skipping keeps more of the management of testing and skipping under software control; we consider this a good tradeoff for SVPs where logic gates and power are more precious than in custom chips. Additionally [4] gives simulation results for SIMT warp compaction. Their approach works within blocks of warps and moves elements between warps to reduce the amount of unnecessary work done. This achieves a similar result as our partitioned wavefront skipping where elements from different wavefronts are executed at the same time. To our knowledge no GPU has implemented this technique yet.

## 3. BRAM BASED WAVEFRONT SKIPPING

Prior to this work MXP supported predicated execution through conditional move, or CMOV, instructions only. This differs from wavefront skipping in that the CMOV operation does both a condition check and move in the same instruction, and it operates on the entire vector instead of just the valid wavefronts. The CMOV instruction checks conditions using a flag bit associated with each element; each 9-bit wide scratchpad BRAM stores 8-bits of data and one flag bit. The flag bit is set by earlier vector instructions; for instance an add instruction stores overflow while a shift right stores the bit shifted out. The flag bit is used along with whether the resulting byte is zero or non-zero to perform several different CMOV operations. The most common CMOV operations first perform a subtraction-based comparison; the result is predicated based on whether the result is less than zero (LTZ), less than or equal to zero (LTE), etc. The CMOV hardware is part of the ALUs shown in Figure 2.

## 3.1 Full Wavefront Skipping

Figure 3 gives an example of how to use wavefront skipping to perform strided operations, such as operating on every fifth element as in Figure 1. The first loop sets every

```
#define STRIDE 5

//Toy functition to double every fifth element
//in the vector v_a
void double_every_fifth_element( int *v_a,
                                 int *v_temp
                                 int vector_length )
{
  int i;

  //Initialize every fifth element of v_temp to zero
  for( i = 0; i < vector_length; i++ ) {
    v_temp[i] = i % STRIDE;
  }

  //Set the vector length which will be processed
  vbx_set_vl( vector_length );

  //Set mask for every element equal to zero
  vbx_setup_mask( CMOV_Z, v_temp );

  //Perform the wavefront skipping operation:
  //multiply all non-masked off elements of v_a by 2
  //and store the result back in v_a
  vbx_masked( SVW, MUL, v_a, 2, v_a );
}
```

**Figure 3: Code Example: Double Every Fifth Element of a Vector**

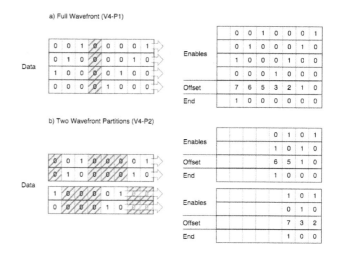

**Figure 4: Data Written to Mask BRAM (Every Fifth Element Valid)**

fifth element to be 0 (this could be done with vector divide or modulo instructions if the SVP supports them, but is shown in scalar code for clarity). The setup_mask instruction takes as input a comparison operation (CMOV_Z, or use the CMOV hardware to test for equal to zero) and a pointer to the vector operand (v_temp, which is a pointer to a vector of 32-bit data).

After the mask is set, the svp_masked instruction is executed. The 'SVW' type specifier indicates that it operates on a scalar (2) and vector (v_a) inputs and that the values are words (32-bit). The elements in the source and destination vector (both v_a) that are masked-off will be skipped, while the valid elements will be multiplied by 2. Although this is a trivial example and is not faster than using a conditional move, complex algorithms that reuse the mask several times and/or have sparse valid bytes can give significant speedup.

In order to support wavefront skipping, we need to alter the address generation logic of MXP. For normal vectors, the addresses of the operands are incremented by one wavefront every cycle. So, with a V2 MXP (meaning it has two 32-bit vector lanes), each address is incremented by 8 bytes (the width of one wavefront) each cycle. To support wavefront skipping, we want to add a variable number of wavefronts to the operand addresses depending on the value of a mask that has been set. We accomplish this by storing the offsets of wavefronts that have valid elements in a BRAM inside the 'masked unit'. Because not all elements in the wavefront may be valid, we also have to store a valid bit for each byte; during subsequent execution this becomes a byte enable upon writeback. Finally, the length of a wavefront skipped vector will (hopefully) be shorter than the length of the full vector, so we have to mark the last wavefront. We use an extra bit to mark the wavefront that is the end of the skipped vector. This is an implementation detail that was convenient in our design and could be replaced by storing the number of wavefronts in a register.

Block RAMs are limited in depth, however, and MXPs scratchpad can hold vectors of any length. To allow for wave-front skipping of vectors of the whole scratchpad length, the masked unit would need a BRAM as deep as the scratchpad itself. This would be wasteful for many applications, so we allow the user to configure a maximum masked vector length (MMVL). The minimum depth of BRAMs in the Stratix IV FPGAs we tested on is 256 words, so lower MMVL than 256 will result in underutilized BRAMs. The fact that wavefront skipping instructions have their own length restriction must be known by the programmer. In real applications data does not fit entirely in scratchpad memory and so is operated on in chunks (also known as strip-mining) even without an MMVL; the MMVL only affects the size of the chunks.

To generate the wavefront offsets, we added the mask setup instruction. This mask setup instruction uses the conditional move logic already in MXP to generate the valid bits set in the mask BRAM. Figure 4a shows the data written the mask BRAM during the mask setup instruction. For each wavefront processed, the offset and valid bytes are sent to the masked unit. If no valid bytes are set, as in wavefront 4 (data values 16-19), the masked unit does not write into the mask BRAM. If any of the valid bytes are set, the masked unit writes the current offset and the valid bytes to its current BRAM write address and increments the write address. The final wavefront (wavefront 7) causes the end bit to be written to the mask BRAM along with its offset and byte enables, provided there are any byte enables set. In this example the final wavefront has valid byte enables, but in instances where the final wavefront has no byte enables set we avoid writing an empty wavefront by redoing the last write to the mask BRAM with the end bit set.

In the case of algorithms with multiple early exit tests, it is often desirable to do a wavefront skipping 'setup_mask' instruction. This is a trivial extension of the normal mask setup instruction; instead of the wavefront numbers progressing linearly, they are taken from the output of the masked unit. In this way the number of valid elements can decrease until either the algorithm finishes or no more valid elements are left. When no valid elements are left, any wavefront skipping instructions will execute as NOPs. Alternatively, the scalar core can query a mask status register and exit the algorithm if it reports no valid elements are left.

```
for stage in classifier:
    for row in image:
        vector::init-mask

        for feat in stage:
            for rect in feat:
                vector::feat.sum += vector::image[rect]

            if vector::feat.sum > feat.threshold
                vector::stage.sum += feat.pass
            else:
                vector::stage.sum += feat.fail

        if vector::stage.sum < stage.threshold:
            vector::update-mask (exit early if possible)
```

**Figure 5: Pseduocode for Viola-Jones Face Detection**

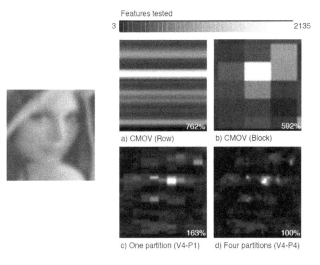

**Figure 6: Haar Features Calculated for Different Groupings (Relative to Minimum)**

## 3.2 Wavefront Partitioning

So far we have only discussed skipping whole wavefronts. When dealing with wide SVPs, it may be of little value to skip whole wavefronts, since it will be rare (i.e., improbable) that the *entire* wavefront is skippable. As a trivial example, the code from Figure 3 will skip 4/5 of wavefronts on a V1, 1/5 of wavefronts on a V4, and no wavefronts on wider MXPs (every wavefront will contain at least one valid word). To get a speedup on this code on a wide MXP, we need to support skipping at a narrower granularity than the wavefront. We support this by partitioning the wavefront into narrower units which each get their own BRAM in the masked unit; for instance, a V4's masked unit can have 1 BRAM (whole wavefront skipping), 2 BRAMs (pairs of lanes can skip together), or 4 BRAMs (each lane can skip individually). Each BRAM stores a separate offset and end bit, but the byte-enables are split across them.

Figure 4b shows the data written to the 2 mask partition BRAMs for the doubling every fifth element code from Figure 3. This mask will take 4 cycles to execute (the maximum of the depth written to all of the partitions), compared to the 7 cycles needed for the single partition shown in Figure 4a.

One complication with wavefront partitioning in our architecture is the mapping from partitions to scratchpad BRAMs. In an architecture with a simple register file or a scratchpad that did not allow unaligned accesses, each BRAM would get its offset from a fixed partition; in a V2 with two partitions lane 1 would get its offset from partition 1and lane 2 from partition 2. However, as mentioned in Section 2.2, our scratchpad supports unaligned addresses. This means that partitions are not directly associated with a scratchpad BRAM; instead, depending on the alignment of the vector operands a scratchpad BRAM address may come from any of the partitions. This means we had to implement an offset mapping network to map wavefront offsets to scratchpad BRAMs. With a single offset (full wavefront skipping) the same offset goes to all BRAMs, which is just a broadcast of the offset requiring no additional logic.

## 3.3 Application Example: Viola-Jones Face Detection

Figure 5 gives high level psuedocode for one of the benchmarks we've implemented, Viola-Jones face detection. Face detection attempts to detect a face at every (x,y) pixel location in an input image. To vectorize this, we will test several possible starting locations in parallel: a 2D vector of starting

locations characterized by $(x+i, y+j)$. In this way, we will be testing for $n^2$ face locations in the vector simultaneously.

The vector/SIMD algorithm must compute several thousand values, called Haar features, for each pixel location. Features are grouped into stages. The features in a stage must pass a threshold test if a face is to be detected at that location. If any stage fails this threshold test, there is no point in testing further features at that location.

Features are calculated in-order across a vector of locations. Utilizing predicated instructions, we require processing the maximum number of stages required by any location within the vector. Only if there is no face at any of the locations we are testing, can we exit early. In this model, parallelism due to vectorization runs against the ability to exit early; longer vectors are more likely to contain locations requiring computation of many features, leading to extensive processing for all elements in the vector. By using wavefront skipping, we can avoid processing elements that are already known not to contain a face. Further features are computed only for those locations still in question, effectively shortening the vector length to the relevant elements.

The only differences between the predicated/CMOV version (without wavefront skipping) and this code are the init-mask and update-mask instructions and the low level details of the early exit test. Were we not to exit early the code would continue to run correctly, but the vector instructions would skip all wavefronts and effectively become NOPs. Porting an existing predicated algorithm to wavefront skipping is therefore straightforward and requires minimal effort.

Figure 6 shows the amount of work done for different locations; at minimum 3 Haar features need to be calculated, and at maximum 2135. The three order of magnitude difference shows the need for some smarter form of predication than simply computing the worst case on all pixels. The input face is shown on the left, with the other subfigures showing the number of Haar features calculated at each location. In order to run the application on an SVP, groups of pixels must be operated on as parallel vectors. Larger groupings provide more parallelism, but without wavefront skipping (only using CMOV instructions) every pixel in a

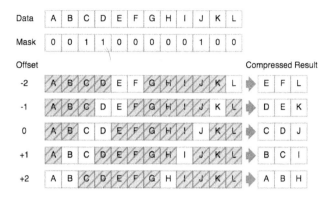

**Figure 7: Vector Compress Operations Needed for 5x1 Stencil Filter**

group must pass the maximum number of Haar feature tests of any pixels within the group. It can be difficult to balance the CMOV implementation; it is tempting to use the minimum vector length possible to reduce the amount of work done, but below a certain level the lack of parallelism means runtime actually increases. These results are from a 4 lane MXP implementation, and we found the runtime optimal vector length for CMOV implementations empirically.

A naive vector layout would be to have every row be a vector (6a), which does almost 8× as much work as the optimal. A slightly better method uses rectangular blocks to get better spatial locality (6b); getting sufficient parallelism still requires vectors long enough that almost 6× as much work as the minimum is done. In contrast, simply by changing the implementation to use wavefront skipping, the effective grouping is the wavefront partition width (6c). Wavefront skipping removes the need to profile an application to determine the best vector length to use; the wavefront skipping implementation can use the longest vector length possible and will always achieve at least the performance of the CMOV implementation. Finally, a fully partitioned design performs the minimal number of feature tests (6d), the same as a scalar implementation would.

### 3.4 Comparison with Vector Compress

An alternative method mentioned in Section 2.3 is a vector compress operation. The compress operation removes masked-off elements from a vector, creating a shorter vector as a result. Figure 7 demonstrates how this would work for a simple 5x1 stencil filter on our architecture. The stencil filter takes as inputs shifted versions of the input data, from an offset of -2 to +2. Before running the stencil filter, each of the inputs must be separately compressed. The 5 offseted versions of the data must be compressed into 5 scratchpad locations, each of which uses as much storage as the original in the worst case. After compressing the inputs, subsequent vector operations can operate on the shorter vectors at full speed.

The drawbacks of requiring a compress instruction and additional storage space for each input make it impractical in many stencil filter algorithms. For instance, on the Viola-Jones face detection application the amount of work and extra space needed would be prohibitive. The Haar feature tests operate on a sliding 20x20 window; each feature selects a subset of the window. Compressing the inputs

would require compressing each location, or 400 compress operations and 400 temporary vectors. The wavefront skipping method does not need to manipulate the input data, meaning MXP only needs one copy of the chunk of the image being scanned.

Compress operations also need the inverse vector expand operation to restore the output. This is less critical for algorithms like stencil filters where the number of outputs is fewer than the number of inputs. Note that the compress operation is only of use when the vector being compressed is used multiple times, because compressing the vector takes an extra instruction. Setting up a mask for wavefront skipping also takes an extra instruction, but the same mask can be used for multiple offsets in a stencil filter.

### 4. RESULTS

Our results were obtained using Altera Stratix IV GX230 FPGAs on the Terasic DE4-230 development board. FPGA builds were done using Quartus II 13.0sp1. We used one 64-bit DDR2 channel as our external memory.

### 4.1 Area Results

Table 1 shows the resources used and maximum frequency achieved for various configurations of MXP. In addition to the actual FPGA resources used we also report the area in equivalent ALMs (eALMs) [12]. By factoring the approximate silicon area of all of the resources used, eALMs are a convenient way to compare architectures that use different mixtures of logic, memory, and multipliers.

All MXP configurations shown have a maximum masked vector length (MMVL) of 256 wavefronts (the effect of MMVL on area and benchmark results will be investigated later). MXP configurations are listed as V$X$ P$Y$ where $X$ is the number of 32-bit vector lanes and $Y$ is the number of mask partitions. P0 means that masked instructions are disabled and only CMOV instructions can be used for conditionals. V1s are configured with 64kB of scratchpad, V4s 128kB, and V32s 256kB. The area numbers for MXP include the Nios scalar core used for control flow and vector instruction dispatch, as well as prefix sum and square root custom vector instructions that are only used in the face detection benchmark.

The eALM area penalty is 5.0% from no wavefront skipping to wavefront skipping with full wavefront skipping on a V1, mostly in ALMs. Since the number of ALMs for full wavefront skipping is roughly constant with respect to the number of lanes, the overhead drops to 3.6% on a V4 and <1% on a V32. For multiple partitions, the area overhead is much higher (up to 27.3% more eALMs in the V32-P32 case), because of the partition to scratchpad BRAM mapping needed (as explained in Section 3.2). We tried implementing this mapping using both a switching network and multiplexers; the area results were similar but the multiplexer implementation had lower latency and so was used for our results.

### 4.2 BRAM Usage

BRAM usage is minimal for the V1 and V4 as each mask partition uses just 1 BRAM. For the V32, a single partition uses 4 BRAMs since it has to store 128-bits worth of byte enables, 8 bits of offset, and 1 end bit, which fits in four 36-bit wide M9Ks. With more partitions, the number of byte enables per partition is reduced, so that the V32-P32 only

Table 1: Resource Usage

| MXP Configuration Vector Lanes - Wavefront Partitions | Logic ALMs | Memory M9Ks | DSP Blocks | Total Area eALMs | Area Increase % Over CMOV | fmax MHz |
|---|---|---|---|---|---|---|
| (CMOV) V1-P0 | 4,697 | 96 | 2 | 7,502 | | 206 |
| V1-P1 | 5,034 | 97 | 2 | 7,877 | 5.0% | 200 |
| (CMOV) V4-P0 | 9,732 | 152 | 5 | 14,243 | | 173 |
| V4-P1 | 10,210 | 153 | 5 | 14,750 | 3.6% | 176 |
| V4-P4 | 13,276 | 156 | 5 | 17,902 | 25.7% | 183 |
| (CMOV) V32-P0 | 63,334 | 414 | 33 | 76,198 | | 144 |
| V32-P1 | 63,027 | 418 | 33 | 76,005 | -0.3% | 144 |
| V32-P4 | 78,698 | 422 | 33 | 91,791 | 20.5% | 149 |
| V32-P32 | 83,220 | 446 | 33 | 97,002 | 27.3% | 146 |
| Nios II/f | 1,370 | 19 | 1 | 1,945 | | 283 |
| DE4230 Maximum | 91,200 | 1,235 | 161 | 131,434 | | – |

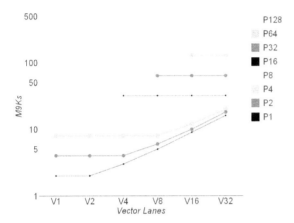

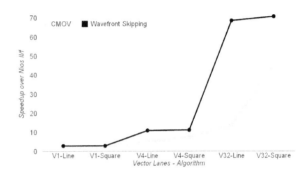

Figure 9: Mandelbrot Benchmark

## Figure 8: BRAM Usage vs Wavefront Partitions (MMVL = 1024)

uses 1 BRAM per partition. Although not shown, the V32 can use up to 128 partitions; this would require 128 more BRAMS than the 414 used in the P0 version. The masked unit has no critical timing paths; increasing the number of BRAMs used does make the placement job harder for the CAD tools, but the critical path always remains outside the masked unit. Since the contribution of this work is not affecting Fmax directly, we decided to remove this variability from our results by running all benchmarks shown here at 125MHz.

Figure 8 shows how many BRAMs are used in our partitioned wavefront skipping with a maximum masked vector length (MMVL) of 1024 wavefronts. With a small number of partitions, as the vector processor gets wider, multiple BRAMs per partition are required to store the byte enables. With a large number of partitions, the byte enables are divided up into small enough chunks that they always fit in a single BRAM per partition. This wide range in the number of BRAMs that can be used gives the designer freedom to allocate BRAMs on the FPGA device to achieve the needed performance for their algorithm.

## 4.3 Mandelbrot Benchmark

Figure 9 shows speedup results for computing the Mandelbrot set (geometric mean of 23 frames in a flyby demo). Results are shown compared to a scalar version run on the Nios II/f as a baseline. The Mandelbrot computation iterates a complex valued equation at each pixel until either the pixel reaches a set condition (the early exit) or else a maximum iteration count is reached. Without masked instructions (CMOV configurations) we can only exit early after all pixels in the group agree to exit early. We show two results, the 'line' implementation which naively computes pixels in raster order (row by row), and the 'square' implementation which computes a 2D block of pixels at a time. The 'line' implementation is more straightforward and is what we first used when writing this code. However, since the early exit pixels are correlated spatially, selecting a group of pixels closer together in a block results in less wasted computation and therefore higher performance.

For the CMOV configurations, the difference between the line and square implementations is vast; almost a 4× difference at V32. With the masked implementations, the difference between line and square are much less; 10% at most. The masked implementations always outperform the CMOV implementations. Partitioned wavefront skipping has little effect in Mandelbrot and so is not shown; the data is grouped together smoothly so that wavefronts exit at the same or nearly the same time. The CMOV implementation also uses a vector length determined by profiling; too long and early exits aren't helpful, too short and instruction dispatch rate and data hazards reduce performance. The masked implementation just uses the maximum vector length it can, which is either determined by the MMVL of the masked instructions or the size of the scratchpad and number of vectors needed. Between not having to profile to find the best vector length, and being able to use the naive 'line' implementation with little performance penalty, the masked implementation seems much easier for the programmer.

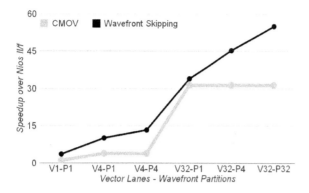

Figure 10: FAST9 Feature Detection

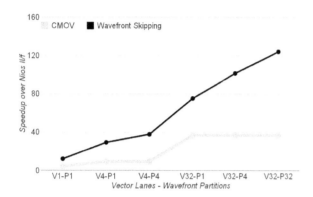

Figure 11: Viola-Jones Face Detection Speedup

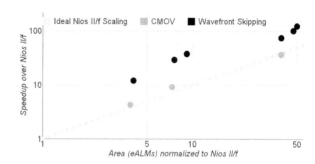

Figure 12: Viola-Jones Face Detection Speedup Vs Area

## 4.4 FAST9 Feature Detection

Figure 10 shows the results of FAST9 feature detection. FAST9 determines if a pixel is a feature by examinining a circle of pixels around the target location and looking for a consecutive series of pixels that are darker or lighter by a threshold. An early exit can happen if certain conditions hold, such as if neither of two pixels on opposite sides are above or below the threshold. All operations are byte-wide, taking advantage of MXPs subword-SIMD which executes byte operations 4× faster than word operations. While running FAST9 on simple input data with the CMOV code, we found checking early exit (as done in Mandelbrot) to be helpful. However, on a real image (Lenna again), the early exit code only helped on a V1. Thus, the CMOV code is doing the full calculation for all pixels on V4 and V32. In contrast, the masked code is able to achieve speedup by skipping at a more granular level. However, if the mask is too coarse, such as at V32-P1 which is 128 bytes wide, very little is gained. Only with 4 or 32 partitions is speedup achieved, and it may be possible to gain even more speed by using byte-wide partitions (our test configurations had a minimum partition size of one 32-bit lane wide).

## 4.5 Viola-Jones Face Detection

For Viola-Jones face detection, we used the settings of [2], a custom FPGA implementation using the same DE4 development board we are using. No reference image was specified in the publication, so we used the standard 'Lenna' image. Their hardware implementation with 32 PEs was able to achieve 30fps. Our SVP implementation has an inner loop of 9 or 13 instructions long (depending on the Haar classifier), instead of being fully pipelined as in a hardware implementation, so it is expected to be somewhat slower. Also, our implementation includes full data movement, from input image to framebuffers driving a DVI display.

Figure 11 shows the results for CMOV only and masked implementations including partial wavefront skipping. The masked implementations with a single partition are up to 3× faster than CMOV, and partitioning increases it to up to 4.1×. At V4, partitioning gives a 29% improvement from P1 to P4, and at V32 a 35% improvement from P1 to P4 and an additional 22% improvement from P4 to P32. While the impact of partitioning is not as dramatic as the impact of switching from CMOV instructions to wavefront skipping, it provides a performance increase without having to rewrite software.

Figure 12 presents the results as speedup versus area (eALMs). MXP without wavefront skipping is only able to achieve about the performance per area of a Nios II/f (which in practice can't scale ideally to achieve higher performance). Wavefront skipping provides significantly higher performance per area, since the area impact is minimal compared to the performance gained. The highest performance per area is 4.1× that of Nios II/f (37.8× faster with 9.2× more area for the V4-P4 configuration).

With our fastest configuration we achieve 3 frames per second, or about 1/10th that of the previous hardware result, on the Lenna input image. A blank image takes 60 frames per second; even though all locations exit early, the Viola-Jones algorithm requires multiple steps of resizing and calculating integral images.

## 4.6 Maximum Masked Vector Length (MMVL) Tradeoffs

So far we have examined tradeoffs in additional logic and BRAMs when using multiple partitions, but it's also possible to use more RAM to allow for longer masked vector instructions as mentioned in Section 3.1. Each BRAM needs to store an offset of width $log_2(MMVL)$ as well 4 byte enables per lane and an end bit; when partitioning, the byte enables are split between BRAMs but the other data is replicated. As explained in Section 3, we default to a MMVL of 256 wavefronts since that is the minimum depth of M9Ks. Figure 13 shows the BRAM usage for two configurations of MXP as the MMVL is varied. A MMVL of 128 or 256 wavefronts almost always has the same resource usage, except on a V16 with one partition where the width of the BRAM data

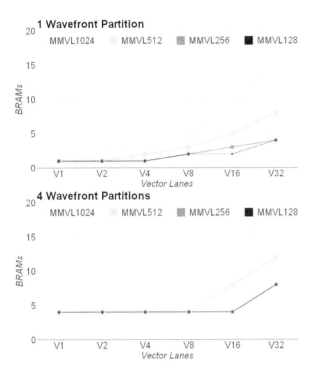

Figure 13: BRAM Usage for Masks When Varying Maximum Masked Vector Length (MMVL) for 1 (top) and 4 (bottom) Partitions

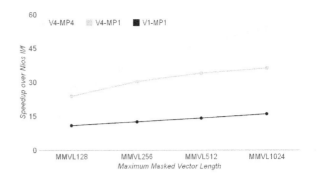

Figure 14: Effect of Changing MMVL on Viola-Jones Face Detection

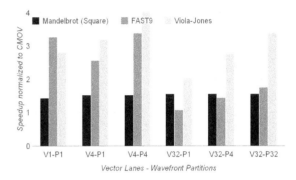

Figure 15: Speedup from Wavefront Skipping

goes from 72 and 73 bits and can no longer fit in two 36-bit wide M9Ks. Increasing MMVL to 512 does have a cost in BRAMs though once the width of the BRAM data gets past 18-bits, with an MMVL of 1024 requiring even more as BRAMs are only 9-bits wide at that depth.

Figure 14 shows the results of changing MMVL on the face detection benchmark. For V1, there is a reasonable gain to be had in increasing MMVL; 16% better performance from 128 wavefronts to 256, with an additional 13% improvement going from 256 wavefronts to 512. The results are even more dramatic on a V4: 100% faster from MMVL of 128 to 1024 with 4 mask partitions. The fact that a V4-P4 with MMVL 128 is actually slower than a V4-P1 with MMVL 256+ suggests that using BRAM for increased depth is better than using it for more partitions. The reason that increased MMVL makes such a large difference is that as masked instructions have fewer and fewer valid wavefronts, they start taking so few cycles that efficiency drops (either data hazards or instruction dispatch rates dominate). Longer MMVL means that fewer masked instructions are needed, and less time is spent in this low efficiency regime. However, by V32, masked vector length is no longer limited by MMVL but by the number of vectors needed and the size of the scratchpad. In this case, changing MMVL had no effect on the results so they are not shown. The trend for V1 and V4 does suggest that increased vector length (in this case by having a larger scratchpad) would provide higher performance on this application, though.

## 4.7 Results Summary

Figure 15 summarizes the speedup of wavefront skipping over the previous CMOV implementation on our three benchmarks, while Figure 16 shows the speedup per area (eALMs).

The maximum speedups for a single partition is 3.3× on FAST9 (V1-P1) and 3.2× on Viola-Jones (V4-P1). The biggest speedup from partitioning over full wavefront skipping is 65% on Viola-Jones (V32-P32 vs V32-P1). All of the benchmarks gain at least as much in speedup as the cost in area of the wavefront skipping implementation, with the minimum gain being 1.1× better performance per area for FAST9 on a V32 with one wavefront partition. Though increased partitions cause a large increase in the area of MXP, for FAST9 and Viola-Jones the performance per area continues to increase as the number of partitions increases. Wavefront skipping is therefore useful for all the benchmarks we tested, and partitioning useful for two of the three.

For a programmer implementing a conditional algorithm, the configuration of BRAM usage for scratchpad size, wavefront partitions, and maximum masked vector length will depend on the application. The designer will generally want to devote as much BRAM as possible to scratchpad data, as longer vectors will benefit all parts of an application. But, for heavily conditional applications like Viola-Jones, having long enough masked vectors to keep the vector core busy as the number of valid wavefronts shrink is also important. Few BRAMs are needed for just a single partition; using multiple partitions adds several BRAMs, but this may be justified when performance is absolutely necessary or the targetted FPGA has leftover BRAMs with a given design.

## 5. FUTURE WORK

We mentioned in Section 4.6 that it would be possible to support multiple masks at the same time. Multiple masks would allow for a greater degree of freedom in control flow

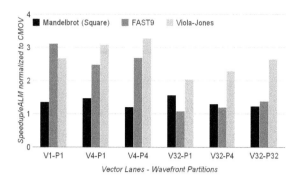

**Figure 16: Speedup per Area (eALMs) from Wavefront Skipping**

before having to save and restore the mask contents. With a short enough MMVL, multiple masks could share a BRAM.

We may also be able to repurpose our multiple partition addressing logic to increase the speed of transposed matrix accesses. Strided accesses already run at full speed provided they do not cause bank conflicts. We could similarly do transposed accesses for matrices of the correct dimensions ($2^N \pm 1$) or that were padded to the correct dimensions. However, in this case, we would want to write out the destination at different offsets than we read the input, requiring a different addressing mode or separate offsets for each operand.

## 6. CONCLUSIONS

This work has shown that integrating wavefront skipping into soft vector processors (SVPs) can be done efficiently in terms of logic and BRAM usage. Wavefront skipping not only allows for higher performance due to skipping masked off elements, it is much easier to use than checking early exit conditions on blocks of elements using predicated/CMOV instructions. Our implementation stores offsets in BRAMs, which are relatively cheaply available and high-performance in FPGAs. The alternative, which uses a count-leading-zeros operation, would have higher latency and also limit the number of wavefronts skipped in one cycle. Our approach keeps the mask logic simple and off the critical path, and can also skip an arbitrary number of wavefronts.

When not partitioned, our wavefront skipping implementation uses <5% extra area and can give up to 3.2× better performance on Viola-Jones face detection. Extra logic and BRAMs can be used to gain additional performance by partitioning, allowing parts of a wavefront to have different offsets. Though costly in terms of area, partitioning can give up to 65% extra performance. Partitioned wavefront skipping may not be a reasonable design tradeoff in a fixed vector processor. In an FPGA, partitioned wavefront skipping gives a designer an extra tool to tradeoff additional logic and BRAMs for application specific performance.

## 7. ACKNOWLEDGMENTS

The authors would like to thank Altera for donating hardware and software licenses used in this research, and MITACS and NSERC for providing funding.

## 8. REFERENCES

[1] The Convey HC-2 architectural overview. http://www.conveycomputer.com/index.php/download_file/view/143/142/.

[2] B. Brousseau and J. Rose. An energy-efficient, fast FPGA hardware architecture for OpenCV-compatible object detection. In *Field-Programmable Technology (FPT), 2012 International Conference on*, pages 166–173, Dec 2012.

[3] R. Espasa, M. Valero, and J. E. Smith. Vector architectures: Past, present and future. In *Proceedings of the 12th International Conference on Supercomputing*, pages 425–432, 1998.

[4] W. Fung and T. Aamodt. Thread block compaction for efficient SIMT control flow. In *High Performance Computer Architecture (HPCA), 2011 IEEE 17th International Symposium on*, pages 25–36, Feb 2011.

[5] J. Gebis, L. Oliker, J. Shalf, S. Williams, and K. Yelick. Improving memory subsystem performance using ViVA: Virtual vector architecture. In *Architecture of Computing Systems*, pages 146–158. 2009.

[6] C. Kozyrakis and D. Patterson. Vector vs. superscalar and VLIW architectures for embedded multimedia benchmarks. In *Microarchitecture*, pages 283–293, 2002.

[7] R. Lorie and H. Strong. Method for conditional branch execution in SIMD vector processors, Mar. 6 1984. US Patent 4,435,758.

[8] M. Naylor, P. Fox, A. Markettos, and S. Moore. Managing the FPGA memory wall: Custom computing or vector processing? In *Field Programmable Logic and Applications (FPL), 23rd International Conference on*, 2013.

[9] A. Severance, J. Edwards, H. Omidian, and G. Lemieux. Soft vector processors with streaming pipelines. In *The 2014 ACM/SIGDA International Symposium on Field-programmable Gate Arrays*, 2014.

[10] A. Severance and G. Lemieux. TputCache: High-frequency, multi-way cache for high-throughput FPGA applications. In *Field Programmable Logic and Applications (FPL), 2013 23rd International Conference on*, 2013.

[11] J. E. Smith, G. Faanes, and R. Sugumar. Vector instruction set support for conditional operations. *SIGARCH Comput. Archit. News*, pages 260–269, 2000.

[12] H. Wong, V. Betz, and J. Rose. Comparing FPGA vs. custom CMOS and the impact on processor microarchitecture. In *Proceedings of the 19th ACM/SIGDA international symposium on Field programmable gate arrays*, FPGA '11, pages 5–14, New York, NY, USA, 2011. ACM.

[13] P. Yiannacouras, J. G. Steffan, and J. Rose. VESPA: portable, scalable, and flexible FPGA-based vector processors. In *CASES*, 2008.

[14] J. Yu, C. Eagleston, C. H. Chou, M. Perreault, and G. Lemieux. Vector processing as a soft processor accelerator. *ACM TRETS*, 2(2):1–34, 2009.

# On Data Forwarding in Deeply Pipelined Soft Processors

Hui Yan Cheah, Suhaib A. Fahmy, Nachiket Kapre
School of Computer Engineering
Nanyang Technological University, Singapore
hycheah1@e.ntu.edu.sg

## ABSTRACT

We can design high-frequency soft-processors on FPGAs that exploit deep pipelining of DSP primitives, supported by selective data forwarding, to deliver up to 25% performance improvements across a range of benchmarks. Pipelined, in-order, scalar processors can be small and lightweight but suffer from a large number of idle cycles due to dependency chains in the instruction sequence. Data forwarding allows us to more deeply pipeline the processor stages while avoiding an associated increase in the NOP cycles between dependent instructions. Full forwarding can be prohibitively complex for a lean soft processor, so we explore two approaches: an external forwarding path around the DSP block execution unit in FPGA logic and using the intrinsic loopback path within the DSP block primitive. We show that internal loopback improves performance by 5% compared to external forwarding, and up to 25% over no data forwarding. The result is a processor that runs at a frequency close to the fabric limit of 500 MHz, but without the significant dependency overheads typical of such processors.

## Categories and Subject Descriptors

C.1.3 [**Processor Architectures**]: Other Architecture Styles—*Adaptable Architecture*

## Keywords

Field programmable gate arrays; soft processors; digital signal processing

## 1. INTRODUCTION

Processors find extensive use within FPGA systems, from management of system execution and interfacing, to implementation of iterative algorithms outside of the performance-critical datapath [13]. In recent work, soft processors have been demonstrated as a viable abstraction of hardware resources, allowing multi- processor systems to be built and programmed easily. To maximise the performance of such

Table 1: Assembly code comparison for $a \cdot x^2 + b \cdot x + c$ for a hypothetical 3-cycle processor. LOOPx operands indicate a loopback that does not need to be written back to the register file.

| (a) Original Assembly | (b) Assembly with Loopback |
|---|---|
| li $1, x | li $1, x |
| li $2, a | li $2, a |
| li $3, b | li $3, b |
| li $4, c | li $4, c |
| mul $5, $1, $2 | mul , $1, $2 |
| nop | mul $6, , $1 |
| nop | mul , $1, $3 |
| mul $6, $5, $1 | add , , $6 |
| mul $5, $1, $3 | add $8, , $4 |
| nop | nop |
| nop | nop |
| add $7, $5, $4 | sw $8, 0($y) |
| nop | |
| nop | |
| add $8, $7, $4 | |
| nop | |
| nop | |
| sw $8, 0($y) | |

soft processors, it is important to consider the architecture of the FPGA in the design, and to leverage unique architectural capabilities wherever possible. Architecture-agnostic designs, while widespread and somewhat portable, typically suffer from sub-par performance. Consider the LEON3 [1] soft processor: implemented on a Virtex 6 FPGA with a fabric that can support operation at over 400 MHz, it barely achieves a clock frequency of 100 MHz. Such designs, while useful for auxiliary tasks, cannot be used for core computation. Even when processors do not constitute the core computation, their sequential operation represents a hard limit on overall system performance, as per Amdahl's law [3].

Recent work on architecture-focused soft processor design has resulted in a number of more promising alternatives. These processors are designed considering the core capabilities of FPGA architecture, often benefiting from the performance and efficiency advantages of the hard macro blocks present in modern devices. Using such primitives also results in a power advantage over equivalent functions implemented in LUTs. Octavo [14] is one such architecture that builds around an Altera Block RAM to develop a soft processor that can run at close to the maximum Block RAM frequency. iDEA [8] is another example that makes use of the dynamic programmability of FPGA DSP blocks to build a lean soft

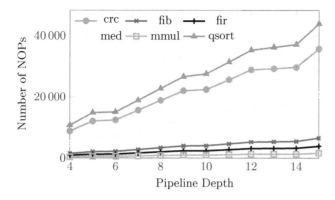

**Figure 1: NOP counts as pipeline depth increases with no data forwarding.**

processor which achieves a frequency close to the fabric limits of the DSP blocks found in Xilinx FPGAs. However, many hard blocks require deep pipelining to achieve maximum performance, and this results in long pipelines when they are used in a soft processor. Octavo and iDEA soft processor pipelines are 10 cycles deep to maximize operating frequency on the respective Altera and Xilinx devices. For a single-issue processor, deep execution pipelines result in significant penalties for dependent instructions, where NOPs have to be inserted to resolve dependencies, and can also increase jump penalties. In Figure 1, we show the rise in NOP counts for a deeply pipelined DSP block based soft processor, across a range of benchmark programs, as the pipeline depth is increased. These numbers are obtained as later described in Section 4.2, and demonstrate the significant penalty incurred at high pipeline depths.

In this paper, we explore how data forwarding can be added to the iDEA soft processor. Being based on the Xilinx DSP48E1, iDEA can be deployed across all Xilinx Artix-7, Kintex-7, Virtex-7, and Zynq device families. It is also easily portable to the DSP48E2 primitive found the next generation Xilinx UltraScale architecture. Since we do not have access to internal pipeline stages within the multi-stage DSP block, a standard approach to data forwarding, by adding a feedback path around the execution unit, would still require some NOP padding. We instead take advantage of a unique feature of the DSP48E1 primitive: the feedback path designed for multiply-accumulate operations when the DSP block is used to implement digital filters. This path allows the DSP-block output to be accessed at the input to the ALU stage one cycle later, potentially avoiding the need for this result to be written-back to the register file. We demonstrate that using this path for data forwarding results a significant impact on overall processor performance, while having minimal impact on area and frequency. We demonstrate a simple example of this phenomenon in Table 1 where the original code executes in 18 cycles while the optimized version with loopback requires only 12 cycles. The toolflow we develop automatically flags dependent operations for loopback in the instruction encoding.

The key contributions of this paper are:

- Parametric design of the iDEA soft processor to allow deep pipelining and loopback of operands.

- A detailed comparison between the proposed loopback forwarding and an external forwarding path.

- Development of a compiler flow and assembly backend that analyzes code for loopback potential and makes appropriate modifications to generated assembly.

- Preliminary results of IR-level analysis of the CHStone benchmark to identify opportunities for loopback in larger benchmarks.

## 2. RELATED WORK

**Processors on FPGAs**: Soft processors continue to be the method of choice for adding a level of software programmability to FPGA-based systems. They generally find use in the auxiliary functions of the system, such as managing non-critical data movement, providing an interface for configuration, or implementing the cognitive functions in an adaptive system. They provide a familiar interface for application programmers to work with the rest of the system, while supporting varied features based on need. Commercial soft processors include the Xilinx MicroBlaze [19], Altera Nios II [2], ARM Cortex-M1 [4], and LatticeMico32 [15], in addition to the open-source LEON3. All of these processors have been designed to be flexible, extensible, and general, but suffer from not being fundamentally built around the FPGA architecture. The more generalised a core is, the less closely it fits the low-level target architecture, and hence, the less efficient its implementation in terms of area and speed. This trade-off between portability and efficiency is clear when one considers that the performance of vendor-specific processors is much better than cross-platform designs.

Although a hard processors such as the PowerPC CPUs in Virtex-2 Pro and the ARM cores in the newer Zynq SoCs can offer better performance than an equivalent soft processor, they are inappropriate for situations where lightweight control and co-ordination [13] are required. Their fixed position in the FPGA fabric can also complicate design, and they demand supporting infrastructure for logic interfacing. When a hard processor is not used, or under-utilised, this represents a significant waste of silicon resources. In fact, the embedded PowerPCs from the Virtex-2 Pro series never gained significant traction and were dropped for subsequent high-density FPGA families.

**Octavo:** To maximise performance, it becomes necessary to reason about FPGA architecture capabilities, and there have been numerous efforts in this direction. Octavo [14] is a multi-threaded 10-cycle processor that can run at 550 MHz on a Stratix IV, representing the maximum frequency supported by Block RAMs in that device. A deep pipeline is necessary to support this high operating frequency. However, such a pipeline would suffer from the need to pad dependent instructions to overcome data hazards as a result of the long pipeline latency. The authors sidestep this issue by designing Octavo as a multi-issue processor, thus dependent instructions are always sufficiently far apart for such NOP padding not to be needed. However, this only works for highly-parallel code; when the soft processor is used in a sequential part of a computation, it will fail to deliver the high performance required to avoid the limits stated by Amdahl's law. Furthermore, no compiler tool flow has yet been developed for Octavo.

**iDEA:** We developed an alternative approach to such architecture-driven soft processor design in [8]. Here, we took advantage of the dynamic control signals of the Xilinx DSP block to build a soft processor that achieves a frequency of over 400 MHz on a Xilinx Virtex 6. In [6], we performed extensive benchmarking and highlighted the performance penalty of padding NOPs on total runtime, somewhat negating the benefits of high frequency.

**Managing Dependencies in Processor Pipelines:** A theoretical method for analysing the effect of data dependencies on the performance of in-order pipelines is presented in [9]. An optimal pipeline depth is derived based on balancing pipeline depth and achieved frequency, with the help of program trace statistics. A similar study for superscalar processors is presented in [11]. Data dependency of sequential instructions can be resolved statically in software or dynamically in hardware. Tomasulo's algorithm, allows instructions to be executed out of order, where those not waiting for any dependencies are executed earlier. For dynamic resolution in hardware, extra functional units are needed to handle the queueing of instructions and operands in reservation stations. Additionally, handling out-of-order execution in hardware requires intricate hazard detection and execution control. Synthesising a basic Tomasulo scheduler [5] on a Xilinx Virtex-6 yields an area consumption of 20× the size of a MicroBlaze, and a frequency of only 84 MHz. This represents a significant overhead for a small FPGA-based soft processor, and the overhead increases for deeper pipelines.

Data forwarding is a well-established technique in processor design, where results from one stage of the pipeline can be accessed at a later stage sooner than would normally be possible. This can increase performance by reducing the number of NOP instructions required between dependent instructions. It has been explored in the context of general soft processor design, VLIW embedded processors [17], as well as instruction set extensions in soft processors [12]. In each case, the principle is to allow the result of an ALU computation to be accessed sooner than would be possible in the case where write back must occur prior to execution of a subsequent dependent instruction.

**Our Approach**: In [7], we quantified the pipeline depth/performance trade-off in the design of iDEA and explored the possible benefits of a restricted forwarding approach. In this paper, we show that the feedback path typically used for multiply-accumulate operations allows us to implement a more efficient forwarding scheme that can significantly improve execution time in programs with dependencies, going beyond just multiply-add combinations. We compare this to the previously proposed external forwarding approach and the original design with no forwarding. Adding data forwarding to iDEA decreases runtime by up to 25% across range of small benchmarks, and we expect similar gains in large benchmarks.

## 3. SOFT PROCESSOR ARCHITECTURE

### 3.1 Overview

iDEA is based on a classic 32-bit, 5-stage load-store RISC architecture with instruction fetch, decode, execute, and memory stages, followed by a write- back to the register file. We tweak the pipeline by placing the memory stage in parallel with the execute stage to lower latency, effectively making this a 4-stage processor (see Figure 2). For this to be feasible, we use a dedicated adder to compute addresses rather than doing this through the ALU. We have used a MIPS-like ISA to enable existing open-source compilers to

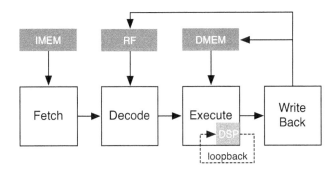

Figure 2: iDEA high-level pipeline overview.

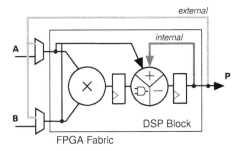

Figure 3: Execution unit datapath showing internal loopback and external forwarding paths.

target our processor. A more detailed description of the iDEA instruction set and architecture are presented in [6].

Each processor stage can support a configurable number of pipeline registers. The minimum pipeline depth for each stage is one. Fewer register stages results in a processor that achieves a lower clock frequency and fewer NOPs required between dependent instructions (See Figure 1). However, while deep pipelining of the core can result in a higher frequency, it also increases the dependency window for data hazards, hence requiring more NOPs for dependent instructions. We study this trade-off in Section 4.1.

The DSP block is utilized as the core execution unit in iDEA. All arithmetic and logical instructions use subsets of DSP block functionality. Program control instructions such as branch also use the DSP block to perform subtraction of two values in order to make a branch decision. The instruction and data memories are built using Block RAMs, while the register file is built using a quad-port RAM32M LUT-based memory primitive. The key novelty in this paper is our exploitation of the loopback path for data forwarding. The DSP block contains an internal loopback path that passes the DSP block output back into the final functional unit in its pipeline, without exiting the execute stage. This enables implementation of a fast multiply-accumulate operation in a digital filter. Through suitable selection of multiplexer controls we can use this loopback path to enable data forwarding, as described in the following section.

### 3.2 DSP Block Loopback Support

The DSP block is composed of a multiplier and ALU along with registers and multiplexers that control configuration options. More recent DSP blocks also contain a pre-adder allowing two inputs to be summed before entering the multi-

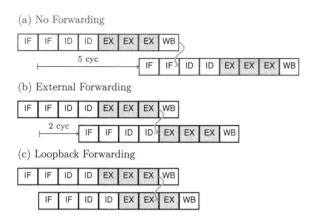

(a) No Forwarding

(b) External Forwarding

(c) Loopback Forwarding

**Figure 4: Instruction dependency with (a) no forwarding, (b) external forwarding, and (c) loopback forwarding.**

plier. The ALU supports addition/subtraction and logic operations on wide data. The required datapath configuration is set by a number of control inputs, and these are dynamically programmable, which is the unique feature allowing use of a DSP block as the execution unit in a processor [8].

When implementing digital filters using a DSP block, a multiply-accumulate operation is required, so the result of the final adder is fed back as one of its inputs in the next stage using a loopback path, as shown in Figure 3. This path is internal to the DSP block and cannot be accessed from the fabric, however the decision on whether to use it as an ALU operand is determined by the OPMODE control signal. The OPMODE control signal chooses the input to the ALU from several sources: inputs to the DSP block, output of multiplier, or output of the DSP block. When a loopback instruction is executed, the appropriate OPMODE instructs the DSP block to take one of its operands from the loopback path. We take advantage of this path to implement data forwarding with minimal area overhead.

### 3.3 Data Forwarding

In Figure 4 (a), we show the typical operation of an instruction pipeline without data forwarding. In this case, a dependent instruction must wait for the previous instruction to complete execution and the result to be written back to the register file before commencing its decode stage. In this example, 5 clock cycles are wasted to ensure the dependent instruction does not execute before its operand is ready. This penalty increases with the higher pipeline depths necessary for maximum frequency operation on FPGAs.

The naive approach to implementing data forwarding for such a processor would be to pass the execution unit output back to its inputs. Since we cannot access the internal stages of the DSP block from the fabric, we must pass the execution unit output all the way back to the DSP block inputs. This *external* approach is completely implemented in general purpose logic resources. In Figure 4 (b), this is shown as the last execution stage forwarding its output to the first execution stage of the next instruction, assuming the execute stage is 3 cycles long. This still requires insertion of up to 2 NOPs between dependent instructions, depending on how many pipeline stages are enabled for the DSP block (execution unit). This feedback path also consumes fabric resources, and may impact achievable frequency.

Using the loopback path that is internal to the DSP block enables the result of a previous ALU operation to be ready as an operand in the next cycle, eliminating the need to pad subsequent dependent instruction with NOPs. The proposed loopback method is not a complete forwarding implementation as it does not support all instruction dependencies and only supports one-hop dependencies. Instead, it still allows us to forward data when the immediate dependent instruction is any ALU operation except a multiplication. Figure 4 (c) shows the output of the execute stage being passed to the final cycle of the subsequent instruction's execute stage. In such a case, since the loopback path is built into the DSP block, it does not affect achievable frequency, and eliminates the need for any NOPs between such dependent instructions.

We can identify loopback opportunities in software and a loopback indication can be added to the encoded assembly instruction. We call these one-hop dependent instructions that use a combination of multiply or ALU operation followed by an ALU operation a loopback pair. For every arithmetic and logical instruction, we add an equivalent loopback counterpart. The loopback instruction performs the same operation as the original, except that it receives its operand from the loopback path (i.e. previous output of the DSP block) instead of the register file. The loopback opcode is differentiated from the original opcode by one bit difference for register arithmetic and two bit for immediate instructions.

Moving loopback detection to the compilation flow keeps our hardware simple and fast. In hardware loopback detection, circuitry is added at the end of execute, memory access, and write back stages to compare the address of the destination register in these stages and the address of source registers at the execute stage. If the register addresses are the same, then the result is forwarded to the execute stage. The cost of adding loopback detection for every pipeline stage after execute can be severe for deeply pipelined processors, unnecessarily increasing area consumption and delay.

### 3.4 NOP-Insertion Software Pass

Dependency analysis to identify loopback opportunities is done in the compiler's assembly. For dependencies that cannot be resolved with this forwarding path, sufficient NOPs are inserted to overcome hazards. When a subsequent dependent arithmetic operation follows its predecessor, it can be tagged as a loopback instruction, and no NOPs are required for this dependency. For the external forwarding approach, the number of NOPs inserted between two dependent instructions depends on the DSP block's pipeline depth (the depth of the execute stage). We call this the number of ALU NOPs. A summary of this analysis scheme is shown in Algorithm 1. We analyze the generated assembly for loopback opportunities with a simple linear-time heuristic. We scan the assembly line-by-line and mark dependent instructions within the pipeline window. These instructions are then converted by the assembler to include a loopback indication flag in the instruction encoding. We also insert an appropriate number of NOPs to take care of other dependencies.

### 4. EXPERIMENTS

**Hardware:** We implement the modified iDEA processor on a Xilinx Virtex-6 XC6VLX240T-2 FPGA (ML605

**Algorithm 1:** Loopback analysis algorithm.

---

**Data**: Assembly
**Result**: LoopbackAssembly<vector>
w ← Number of pipeline stages − number of IF stages;
**for** i ← 0 **to** size(Assembly) **do**
    window ← 0;
    DestInstr ← Assembly[i];
    **for** j ← 1 **to** w-1 **do**
        SrcInstr ← Assembly[i − j];
        **if** depends(SrcInstr,DestInstr) **then**
            loopback ← true;
            depth ← j;
            break;
        **end**
    **end**
    **for** j ← 0 **to** w-1 **do**
        **if** loopback **then**
            LoopbackAssembly.push_back(Assembly[i] |
            LOOPBACK_MASK) ;
        **end**
        **else**
            LoopbackAssembly.push_back(Assembly[i]);
            **for** k ← 0 **to** j-1 **do**
                LoopbackAssembly.push_back(NOP);
            **end**
        **end**
    **end**
**end**

---

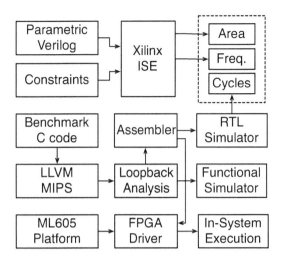

Figure 5: Experimental flow.

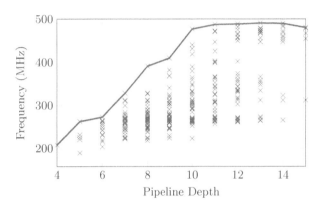

Figure 6: **Frequency of different pipeline combinations with internal loopback.**

platform) using the Xilinx ISE 14.5 tools. We use area constraints to help ensure high clock frequency and area-efficient implementation. We generate various processor combinations to support pipeline depths from 4–15. We evaluate performance using instruction counts for executing embedded C benchmarks. Input test vectors are contained in the source files and the computed output is checked against a hard- coded golden reference, thereby simplifying verification. For experimental purposes, the pipeline depth is made variable through a parameterizable shift register at the output of each processor stage. During automated implementation runs in ISE, a shift register parameter is incremented, increasing the pipeline depth beyond the default of one. We enable retiming and register balancing, which allows registers to be moved forwards or backwards to improve frequency. We also enable the shift register extraction option. In a design where the ratio of registers is high, and shift registers are abundant, this option helps balance LUT and register usage. ISE synthesis and implementation options are consistent throughout all experimental runs.

**Compiler**: We generate assembly code for the processor using the LLVM- MIPS backend. We use a post-assembly pass to identify opportunities for data forwarding and modify the assembly accordingly, as discussed in Section 3.4. We verify functional correctness of our modified assembly code using a customized simulator for internal and external loopback, and run RTL ModelSim simulations of actual hardware to validate different benchmarks. We repeat our validation experiments for all pipeline depth combinations. We show a high-level view of our experimental flow in Figure 5.

**In-System Verification**: Finally, we test our processor on the ML605 board for sample benchmarks to demonstrate functional correctness in silicon. The communication between the host and FPGA is managed using the open source

FPGA interface framework in [18]. We verify correctness by comparing the data memory contents at the end of functional and RTL simulation, and in-FPGA execution.

## 4.1 Area and Frequency Analysis

Since the broad goal of iDEA is to maximize soft processor frequency while keeping the processor small, we perform a design space exploration to help pick the optimal combination of pipeline depths for the different stages. We vary the number of pipeline stages from 1–5 for each stage: fetch, decode, and execute, and the resulting overall pipeline depth is 4–15 (the writeback stage is fixed at 1 cycle).

**Impact of Pipelining**: Figure 6 shows the frequency achieved for varying pipeline depths between 4–15 for a design with internal loopback enabled. Each depth configuration represents several processor combinations as we can distribute these registers in different parts of the 4-stage pipeline. The line traces points that achieve the maximum frequency for each pipeline depth. The optimal combination of stages, that results in the highest frequency for each depth, is presented in Table 2.

While frequency increases considerably up to 10 stages, beyond that, the increases are modest. This is expected

**Table 2: Optimal combination of stages and associated NOPs at each pipeline depth (WB = 1 in all cases)**

| Depth | IF | ID | EX | NOPs | ALUNOPs |
|-------|----|----|----|------|---------|
| 4 | 1 | 1 | 1 | 2 | 0 |
| 5 | 1 | 2 | 1 | 3 | 0 |
| 6 | 2 | 2 | 1 | 3 | 0 |
| 7 | 2 | 1 | 3 | 4 | 2 |
| 8 | 2 | 2 | 3 | 5 | 2 |
| 9 | 2 | 2 | 4 | 6 | 2 |
| 10 | 3 | 2 | 4 | 6 | 2 |
| 11 | 3 | 2 | 5 | 7 | 2 |
| 12 | 3 | 3 | 5 | 8 | 2 |
| 13 | 4 | 3 | 5 | 8 | 2 |
| 14 | 5 | 3 | 5 | 8 | 2 |
| 15 | 4 | 5 | 5 | 10 | 2 |

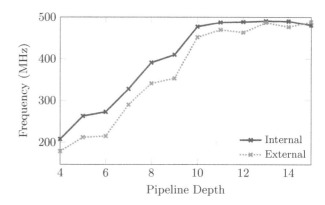

**Figure 9: Frequency with internal loopback and external forwarding.**

**Table 3: Static cycle counts with and without loopback for a 10 cycle pipeline with % savings.**

| Bench mark | Total Inst. | Loopback | |
|------------|-------------|----------|----|
| | | Inst. | % |
| crc | 32 | 3 | 9 |
| fib | 40 | 4 | 10 |
| fir | 121 | 1 | 0.8 |
| median | 132 | 11 | 8 |
| mmult | 332 | 3 | 0.9 |
| qsort | 144 | 10 | 7 |

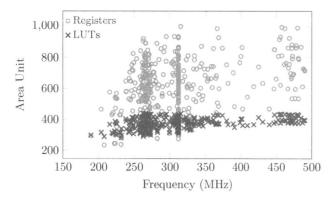

**Figure 7: Resource utilization of all pipeline combinations with internal loopback.**

as we approach the raw fabric limits around 500 MHz. For each overall pipeline depth, we have selected the combination of pipeline stages that yields the highest frequency for all experiments. With an increased pipeline depth, we must now pad dependent instructions with more NOPs, so these marginal frequency benefits can be meaningless in terms of wall clock time for an executed program. In Fig. 4, we illustrated how a dependent instruction must wait for the previous result to be written back before its instruction decode stage. This results in required insertion of 5 NOPs for that 8 stage pipeline configuration. For each configuration, we determine the required number of NOPs to pad dependent instructions, as detailed in Table 2.

Figure 7 shows the distribution of LUT and register consumption for all implemented combinations. Register consumption is generally higher than LUT consumption, and this becomes more pronounced in the higher frequency designs. Figure 8 shows a comparison of resource consumption between the designs with no forwarding, internal loopback, and external forwarding. External forwarding generally consumes the highest resources for both LUTs and registers. The shift register extraction option means some register chains are implemented instead using LUT-based SRL32 primitives, leading to an increase in LUTs as well as registers as the pipelines are made deeper.

**Impact of Loopback**: Implementing internal loopback forwarding proves to have a minimal impact on area, of under 5%. External forwarding generally uses slightly more resources, though the difference is not constant. External forwarding does lag internal forwarding in terms of frequency for all pipeline combinations, as shown in Figure 9, however, the difference diminishes as frequency saturates at the higher pipeline depths. Though we must also consider the NOP penalty of external forwarding over internal loopback.

## 4.2 Execution Analysis

**Static Analysis**: In Table 3, we show the percentage of occurrences of consecutive loopback instructions in each benchmark program. Programs that show high potential are those that have multiple independent occurrences of loopback pairs, or long chains of consecutive loopback pairs. Independent pairs of loopbacks are common in most programs, however for crc and fib, we can find a chain of up to 3 and 4 consecutive loopback pairs respectively.

**Dynamic Analysis**: In Table 4, we show the actual execution cycle counts without forwarding, with external forwarding, and with internal loopback, as well as the percentage of executed instructions that use the loopback capability. Although fib offers the highest percentage of loopback occurrences in static analysis, in actual execution, crc achieves the highest savings due to the longer loopback chain, and the fact that the loopback-friendly code is run more frequently.

**Internal Loopback**: In Figure 10, we show the Instructions per Cycle (IPC) savings for a loopback-enabled processor over the non-forwarding processor, as we increase pipeline depth. Most benchmarks have IPC improvements

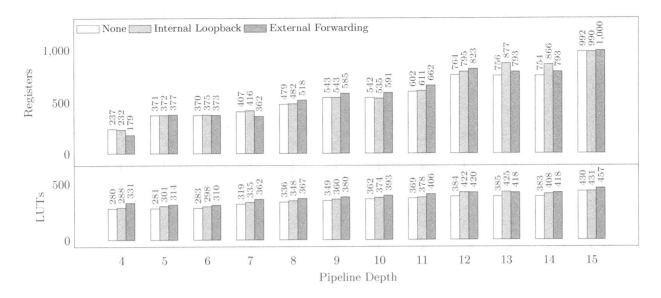

Figure 8: Resource utilization of highest frequency configuration for no forwarding, internal loopback, and external forwarding.

Table 4: Dynamic cycle counts with and without loopback for a 10 cycle pipeline with % savings.

| Bench mark | Loopback | | | | |
|---|---|---|---|---|---|
| | Without | External | % | Internal | % |
| crc | 28,426 | 22,426 | 21 | 20,026 | 29 |
| fib | 4,891 | 4,211 | 14 | 3,939 | 19 |
| fir | 2,983 | 2,733 | 8 | 2,633 | 11 |
| median | 1,5504 | 14,870 | 4 | 14,739 | 5 |
| mmult | 1,335 | 1,322 | 0.9 | 1,320 | 1 |
| qsort | 32,522 | 30,918 | 5 | 30,386 | 7 |

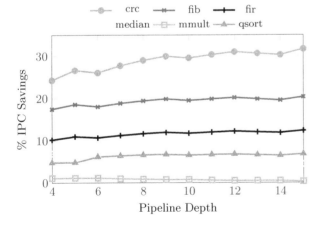

Figure 10: IPC improvement when using internal DSP loopback.

between between 5–30% except the `mmult` benchmark. For most benchmarks, we note resilient improvements across pipeline depths. From Table 4 we can clearly correlate the IPC improvements with the predicted savings.

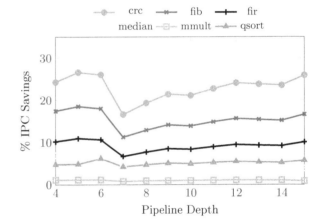

Figure 11: IPC improvement when using external loopback.

**External Loopback**: Figure 11 shows the same analysis for external forwarding. It is clear that external forwarding is not as improved as internal loopback, since we do not totally eliminate NOPs in chains of supported loopback instructions. For pipeline depths of 4–6, the IPC savings for internal and external loopback are equal, since the execute stage is 1 cycle (refer to Table 2), and hence neither forwarding method requires NOPs between dependent instructions. For external forwarding, when the execute stage is $K > 1$ cycles, we need $K - 1$ NOPs between dependent instructions, which we call ALU NOPs. Table 2 shows the number of NOPs for every pipeline combination and the corresponding ALU NOPs for external forwarding. As a result of the extra NOP instructions, the IPC savings decline marginally in Figure 11 and stay relatively low.

**Impact of Internal Loopback on Wall-Clock Time**
Figure 12 shows normalised wall-clock times for the different benchmarks. We expect wall-clock time to decrease as

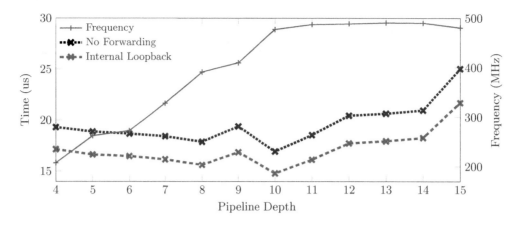

Figure 12: Frequency and geomean wall clock time with and without internal loopback enabled.

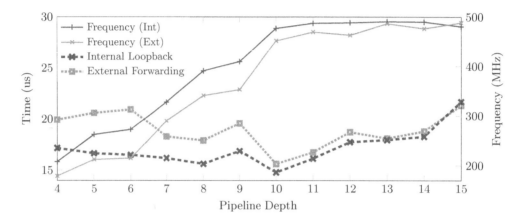

Figure 13: Frequency and geomean wall clock time on designs incorporating internal loopback and external forwarding.

we increase pipeline depth up to a certain limit. At sufficiently high pipeline depths, we expect the overhead of NOPs to cancel the diminishing improvements in operating frequency. There is an anomalous peak at 9 stages due to a more gradual frequency increase, visible in Figure 6, along with a configuration with a steeper ALU NOP count increase as shown in Table 2. The 10 cycle pipeline design gives the lowest execution time for both internal loopback and non-loopback. Such a long pipeline is only feasible when data forwarding is implemented, and our proposed loopback approach is ideal in such a case, as we can see from the average 25% improvement in runtime across these benchmarks.

**Comparing External Forwarding and Internal Loopback** Figure 13 shows the maximum frequency and normalised wall clock times for for internal loopback and external forwarding. As previously discussed, external forwarding results in higher resource utilisation and reduced frequency. At 4–6 cycle pipelines, the lower operating frequency of the design for external forwarding results in a much higher wall-clock time for the benchmarks. While the disparity between external and internal execution time is significant at shallower pipeline depths, the gap closes as depth increases. This is due to the saturation of frequency at pipeline depths greater than 10 cycles and an increase in the insertion of ALU NOPs. The 10 cycle pipeline configuration yields the lowest execution time for all three designs, with internal loopback achieving the lowest execution time.

# 5. FURTHER INVESTIGATION

We developed our soft processor for small compact loop bodies that execute control oriented code on the FPGA with a large number of complex instruction dependencies. Furthermore, in the long run, we expect to develop a parallel array of these lightweight soft processors to operate in tandem for compute-intensive parallel tasks. However, our processor is also capable of supporting larger programs from the CHstone benchmarks suite. Additionally, we have only considered loopback analysis at the post-assembly stage. This assumes that chains of dependent operations are always kept in close proximity by the compiler. In reality, this may not be the case, and a compiler pass (before backend code-generation) could increase the effectiveness of this approach by ensuring that compatible dependent instructions are kept in sequence.

**CHStone compatibility**: To explore the applicability of this approach in more complex applications supported with compiler-assisted analysis, we profiled LLVM [16] IR representations of 8 benchmarks from the CHStone benchmark suite [10]. Static analysis shows a significant number of compatible dependency chains. We also use the LLVM profiler

**Table 5: LLVM IR Profiling Results for CHStone**

| Bench mark | Static | | | Dynamic | | |
|---|---|---|---|---|---|---|
| | Instr. | Occur. | % | Instr. | Occur. | % |
| adpcm | 1367 | 184 | 13 | 71,105 | 8,300 | 11 |
| aes | 2259 | 51 | 2 | 30,596 | 3,716 | 12 |
| blowfish | 1184 | 314 | 26 | 711,718 | 180,396 | 25 |
| gsm | 1205 | 82 | 6 | 27,141 | 1,660 | 6 |
| jpeg | 2388 | 95 | 4 | 1,903,085 | 131,092 | 6 |
| mips | 378 | 15 | 3 | 31,919 | 123 | 0.3 |
| mpeg | 782 | 80 | 10 | 17,032 | 60 | 0.3 |
| sha | 405 | 64 | 15 | 990,907 | 238,424 | 24 |

and just-in-time (JIT) compiler to obtain dynamic counts of possible loopback occurrences. The results in Table 5 show a mean occurrence of over 10% within these benchmarks. We cannot currently support CHStone completely due to missing support for 32b instructions and other development issues.

**Program Size Sensitivity**: We also synthesized RTL for iDEA with increased instruction memory sizes to hold larger programs. We observed, that iDEA maintains its optimal frequency for up to 8 BRAMs. Beyond this, frequency degrades by 10–30% to support routing delays and placement effects of these larger memories. However, we envision tiling multiple smaller soft processors with fewer than 8 BRAMs to retain frequency advantages for a larger multiprocessor system, and to reflect more closely the resource ratio on modern FPGAs. Each processor in this system would hold only a small portion of the complete system binary.

# 6. CONCLUSIONS AND FUTURE WORK

We have shown an efficient way of incorporating data forwarding in DSP block based soft processors like iDEA. By taking advantage of the internal loopback path typically used for multiply accumulate operations, it is possible to allow dependent ALU instructions to immediately follow each other, eliminating the need for padding NOPs. The result is an increase in effective IPC, and 5– 30% (mean 25%) improvement in wall clock time for a series of benchmarks when compared to no forwarding and a 5% improvement when compared to external forwarding. We have also undertaken an initial study to explore the potential for such forwarding in more complex benchmarks by analysing LLVM intermediate representation, and found that such forwarding is supported in a significant proportion of dependent instructions. We aim to finalise full support for the CHStone benchmark suite as well as open-sourcing the updated version of iDEA and the toolchain we have described.

# 7. REFERENCES

[1] Aeroflex Gaisler. *GRLIB IP Library User's Manual*, 2012.

[2] Altera Corpration. *Nios II Processor Design*, 2011.

[3] G. M. Amdahl. Validity of the single processor approach to achieving large scale computing capabilities. In *Proceedings of the Spring Joint Computer Conference*, pages 483–485, 1967.

[4] ARM Ltd. *Cortex-M1 Processor*, 2011.

[5] S. Beyer, C. Jacobi, D. Kröning, D. Leinenbach, and W. J. Paul. Putting it all together - formal verification of the VAMP. *International Journal on Software Tools for Technology Transfer*, 8:411–430, 2006.

[6] H. Y. Cheah, F. Brosser, S. A. Fahmy, and D. L. Maskell. The iDEA DSP block based soft processor for FPGAs. *ACM Transactions on Reconfigurable Technology and Systems*, 7(3):19, 2014.

[7] H. Y. Cheah, S. A. Fahmy, and N. Kapre. Analysis and optimization of a deeply pipelined FPGA soft processor. In *Proceedings of the International Conference on Field Programmable Technology (FPT)*, pages 235–238, 2014.

[8] H. Y. Cheah, S. A. Fahmy, and D. L. Maskell. iDEA: A DSP block based FPGA soft processor. In *Proceedings of the International Conference on Field Programmable Technology (FPT)*, pages 151–158, Dec. 2012.

[9] P. G. Emma and E. S. Davidson. Characterization of branch and data dependencies in programs for evaluating pipeline performance. *IEEE Transactions on Computers*, 36:859–875, 1987.

[10] Y. Hara, H. Tomiyama, S. Honda, and H. Takada. Proposal and quantitative analysis of the CHStone benchmark program suite for practical C-based high-level synthesis. In *Journal of Information Processing*, 2009.

[11] A. Hartstein and T. R. Puzak. The optimum pipeline depth for a microprocessor. *ACM Sigarch Computer Architecture News*, 30:7–13, 2002.

[12] R. Jayaseelan, H. Liu, and T. Mitra. Exploiting forwarding to improve data bandwidth of instruction-set extensions. In *Proceedings of the Design Automation Conference*, pages 43–48, 2006.

[13] N. Kapre and A. DeHon. VLIW-SCORE: Beyond C for sequential control of SPICE FPGA acceleration. In *Proceedings of the International Conference on Field Programmable Technology (FPT)*, Dec. 2011.

[14] C. E. LaForest and J. G. Steffan. Octavo: an FPGA-centric processor family. In *Proceedings of the ACM/SIGDA International Symposium on Field Programmable Gate Arrays (FPGA)*, pages 219–228, Feb. 2012.

[15] Lattice Semiconductor Corp. *LatticeMico32 Processor Reference Manual*, 2009.

[16] C. Lattner and V. Adve. LLVM: A compilation framework for lifelong program analysis and transformation. In *International Symposium on Code Generation and Optimization*, pages 75–86, 2004.

[17] M. Sami, D. Sciuto, C. Silvano, V. Zaccaria, and R. Zafalom. Exploiting data forwarding to reduce the power budget of VLIW embedded processors. In *Proceedings of Design, Automation and Test in Europe, 2001*, pages 252–257, 2001.

[18] K. Vipin, S. Shreejith, D. Gunasekara, S. A. Fahmy, and N. Kapre. System-level FPGA device driver with high-level synthesis support. In *Proceedings of the International Conference on Field Programmable Technology (FPT)*, pages 128–135, Dec. 2013.

[19] Xilinx Inc. *UG081: MicroBlaze Processor Reference Guide*, 2011.

# Mapping-Aware Constrained Scheduling for LUT-Based FPGAs

Mingxing Tan, Steve Dai, Udit Gupta, Zhiru Zhang

School of Electrical and Computer Engineering, Cornell University, Ithaca, NY
{mingxing.tan, hd273, ug28, zhiruz}@cornell.edu

## ABSTRACT

Scheduling plays a central role in high-level synthesis, as it inserts clock boundaries into the untimed behavioral model and greatly impacts the performance, power, and area of the synthesized circuits. While current scheduling techniques can make use of pre-characterized delay values of individual operations, it is difficult to obtain accurate timing estimation on a cluster of operations without considering technology mapping. This limitation is particularly pronounced for FPGAs where a large logic network can be mapped to only a few levels of look-up tables (LUT).

In this paper, we propose MAPS, a mapping-aware constrained scheduling algorithm for LUT-based FPGAs. Instead of simply summing up the estimated delay values of individual operations, MAPS jointly performs technology mapping and scheduling, creating the opportunity for more aggressive operation chaining to minimize latency and reduce area. We show that MAPS can produce a latency-optimal solution, while supporting a variety of design timing requirements expressed in a system of difference constraints. We also present an efficient incremental scheduling technique for MAPS to effectively handle resource constraints. Experimental results with real-life benchmarks demonstrate that our proposed algorithm achieves very promising improvements in performance and resource usage when compared to a state-of-the-art commercial high-level synthesis tool targeting Xilinx FPGAs.

## 1. INTRODUCTION

As modern-day field-programmable gate arrays (FPGAs) integrate billions of transistors to meet the ever-increasing design complexity, high-level synthesis (HLS) is becoming a major player in improving design productivity and reducing the overall verification effort for large-scale FPGA-based designs [11]. HLS raises the level of design abstraction from register-transfer-level (RTL) modeling to high-level software programming by automatically transforming untimed behavioral descriptions into optimized cycle-accurate hardware

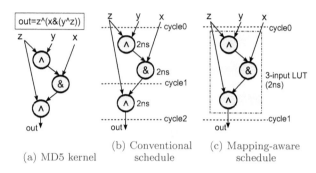

(a) MD5 kernel

(b) Conventional schedule

(c) Mapping-aware schedule

Figure 1: Reducing latency with mapping-aware scheduling for an MD5 kernel – Target clock period is $5ns$; each logic operation or LUT incurs a $2ns$ delay. Symbols $\wedge$ and & represent XOR and AND operations, respectively.

implementations. One of the most important steps in HLS is scheduling, which analyzes the parallelism in the input behavioral model and intelligently assigns time steps to operations based on the design constraints. As one would expect, scheduling dictates the clock frequency, latency, and throughput of the synthesized design; it also largely influences the area and power of the final hardware circuit.

When determining the clock boundaries (or placement of registers) given a target clock period, existing scheduling techniques typically rely on delay estimates from the pre-characterization of the RTL building blocks (e.g., logic gates, adders, multiplexers, etc.). The timing analysis on a cluster of operations is usually carried out by simply summing up the estimated delay values of the individual operations on the longest path. While such additive delay models are not unreasonable for FPGA designs dominated by arithmetic operations that use dedicated carry chains and DSP blocks, the estimated delay is often too pessimistic for logic-operation-intensive applications where a large logic network can be mapped to only a few levels of look-up tables (LUTs). Without considering the impact of technology mapping, the overestimation of logic delays during scheduling will easily result in suboptimal performance and resource usage for the synthesized circuit.

Figure 1(a) illustrates the data-flow graph (DFG) of a simple kernel from the MD5 message-digest algorithm, a widely used cryptographic hash function [27]. With a $5ns$ clock period constraint, conventional scheduling algorithms would simply compute the critical path delay of the DFG and insert registers as shown in Figure 1(b) to meet the target clock period constraint, assuming that each logic gate incurs a $2ns$

delay. As a result, the synthesized design requires a latency of two cycles and two LUTs. On the other hand, it is evident from the DFG that all operations can be scheduled combinationally and realized together with a single 3-input LUT, as illustrated in Figure 1(c). The importance of accounting for technology mapping during operation scheduling is obvious from this simple example. An accurate delay estimation of a cluster (or subgraph) of operations should not be a simple function that adds up operation delays on the critical path, but should instead factor in the level of LUTs needed to cover the subgraph. Otherwise, a suboptimal register placement from HLS would unnecessarily increase the latency of the synthesized design and in turn limit the scope of optimizations in the downstream CAD toolflow, including technology mapping.

In this paper, we propose **MAPS**, a **MAP**ping-aware constrained **S**cheduling algorithm for LUT-based FPGAs, to address the inherent inaccuracy of delay estimation in HLS due to the lack of information of LUT mapping. By employing a novel labeling approach that simultaneously produces the time steps of operations as well as their depths in LUT levels, MAPS generates a minimum-latency schedule in the perspective of both the scheduler and technology mapper. Our experiments with a collection of real-life benchmarks demonstrate that MAPS can significantly improve the performance and reduce the register and LUT usage compared to a state-of-the-art commercial high-level synthesis tool targeting Xilinx FPGAs. More specifically, our main contributions are as follows:

1. To our knowledge, we are the first to propose a truly integrated scheduling and mapping algorithm in HLS for FPGAs to fundamentally address and exploit the interdependence between scheduling and LUT mapping for optimizing the performance and area of the synthesized circuits.

2. We present a novel and scalable constrained scheduling algorithm using relaxation-based labeling that is able to achieve a latency-optimal schedule, while supporting a variety of design timing requirements expressed in a system of difference constraints.

3. We also propose an efficient incremental scheduling algorithm to optimize the schedule under resource constraints.

We emphasize that the proposed mapping-aware scheduling algorithm goes beyond a simple extension of traditional technology mapping techniques on a high-level dataflow graph [8, 9]. Technology mapping requires a pre-determined register placement, while scheduling determines such a register placement. We consider technology mapping during scheduling to address this interdependence between scheduling and mapping and optimally place registers such that the timing is met and the latency is minimized. In fact, our approach is analogous to a generalization of retiming-based technology mapping [23, 24]. However, unlike traditional or retiming-based technology mapping techniques, our algorithm starts with an untimed design and is able to handle a rich set of scheduling constraints. In addition, traditional and retiming-based technology mapping are not able to propagate registers into a cycle of a circuit, and do not solve the mapping-aware scheduling problem.

The rest of the paper is organized as follows: Section 2 reviews previous work on scheduling and mapping; Section 3 provides background on scheduling constraints and mapping techniques; Section 4 presents the MAPS algorithm; Section 5 reports experimental results, followed by additional discussions in Section 6; We conclude the paper in Section 7.

## 2. RELATED WORK

A large number of scheduling algorithms have been proposed to optimize for various design metrics related to performance, area, and power. Constrained scheduling is in general NP-hard and thus usually relies on heuristic algorithms. Examples of classical scheduling heuristics include force-directed scheduling [25] and list scheduling [1]. Recently, the application of system of difference constraints (SDC) [12, 15] has enabled an efficient and scalable linear programming approach to the constrained scheduling problem that encapsulates a rich set of realistic scheduling models including chained operations, multi-cycle operations, frequency constraints, and relative timing constraints in I/O protocols. SDC can be extended to handle loop pipelining [30, 4], an important scheduling optimization in the presence of loop-carried dependence. We note that our MAPS framework can also efficiently handle these SDC constraints.

In addition to optimizing HLS for classic design objectives such as performance [28, 16] and area [30], there is a growing trend in integrating upstream scheduling with downstream physical implementation. For example, Cong et al. [10] evaluate metrics for quantifying interconnect optimization opportunity during scheduling and envision a scheduling approach that generates layout-friendly RTL architecture. Most recently, Zheng et al. [31] propose an HLS flow that performs scheduling and place-and-route iteratively. By back-annotating more realistic post-place-and-route delay estimates after each iteration, the HLS tool is able to compute an improved schedule for timing closure. Obviously, an efficient back-annotation flow can also benefit our MAPS approach by providing more accurate delay estimates. In this work, we further address the limitation of the additive delay model assumed by the existing HLS tools.

In relation to scheduling, mapping is a downstream step in the design implementation flow and can affect the final quality of results (QoR) even with an optimized schedule [6]. There has been an extensive amount of research on mapping with optimization objectives ranging from LUT depth [8] and area [14, 5] traditionally to reliability [13] and even security [3] more recently. Prominent mapping techniques include FlowMap [8], CutMap [9], and DaoMap [5].

Apart from integrating mapping with upstream logic synthesis [7] and downstream placement [21], Pan et al. propose a retiming-based technology mapping technique that considers mapping for register repositioning to achieve the minimum clock period [23, 24]. While it is able to achieve the optimal clock period, the retiming-based mapping approach is limited to circuits with an initial register placement and cannot perform actual scheduling on an untimed circuit. In Section 6, we will show that MAPS is a generalization of the retiming-based mapping.

## 3. PRELIMINARIES

Scheduling is the problem of assigning time steps to operations from an untimed behavioral description to synthesize a cycle-accurate RTL model. Technology mapping (or mapping for short) is the process of transforming a graph of technology-independent logic elements into technology-dependent logic cells, such as LUTs, DSP blocks, and memories, on the target FPGA device. In this paper, we focus on the LUT mapping problem of logic operations. Operations that are not mapped to LUTs (e.g., memory operations) are referred to as *black-box operations*.

## 3.1 Scheduling Constraints

Constraints are an important ingredient of the scheduling formulation. Commonly encountered constraints in HLS include *dependence constraints* which arise from data and control dependences in the control-data flow graph (CDFG), *latency and relative timing constraints* which define the required maximum or minimum number of cycles between two operations (e.g., user-specified I/O protocols), and the *clock period constraint* which ensures that the critical path meets the target clock period.

It has been shown that all of the aforementioned constraints can be precisely represented and efficiently solved in the form of system of difference constraints, or SDC [15, 30]. Under the SDC formulation, dependence constraints can be represented in the form of $s_u - s_v \leq 0$, where $s_u$ and $s_v$ denote the control steps of operations $u$ and $v$. Latency and relative timing constraints are represented in the form $s_u - s_v \leq d$, where $d$ is the minimum schedule time difference between $u$ and $v$. SDC-based scheduling makes use of the *constraint graph* during feasibility checking and optimization. In the constraint graph, each edge $u \rightarrow v$ with a weight $d$ represents an SDC constraint $s_u - s_v \leq d$. The constraint graph can be easily constructed from the CDFG by keeping the same set of nodes on CDFG and adding edges for each SDC constraint [30].

It is important to note that although MAPS is designed to conveniently handle various SDC constraints, it purposely avoids clock period difference constraints. Such modeling of the clock period constraints assumes additive delay among chained operations as in conventional scheduling approaches and is a reason for sub-optimal QoR.

## 3.2 Technology Mapping

Mapping is typically performed on a directed acyclic graph (DAG) of logic gates, abstractly represented as nodes, for the combinational paths between register boundaries. Let $C_v$ denote a cone rooted at node $v$, defined as the sub-graph of $v$ and some of its predecessors such that there exists a path from any node in $C_v$ to $v$ that is entirely contained within $C_v$. The cone $C_v$ is $K$-feasible if there are no more than $K$ nodes outside $C_v$ with edges pointing to nodes in $C_v$. A cut of $C_v$, denoted as $CUT(C_v)$, is defined to be the set of input nodes of $C_v$. $CUT(C_v)$ is $K$-feasible if $C_v$ is a $K$-feasible cone. In Figure 1(c), for example, the three nodes form a 3-feasible cone rooted at the bottom node.

In LUT-based FPGAs, any $K$-feasible cones can be implemented with a $K$-input LUT (or $K$-LUT), so the mapping problem reduces to the problem of optimally covering the input graph with $K$-feasible cones [8, 23]. Such mapping framework generally consists of cut enumeration, cut ranking, cut selection, and final mapping generation. Cut enumeration explores all $K$-feasible cuts rooted at each node, while cut ranking evaluates these cuts based on the optimization objective. Cut selection typically follows a reverse

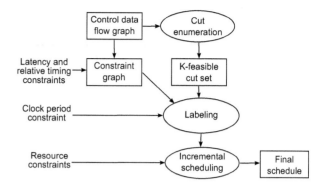

Figure 2: Overall design flow of MAPS.

topological order to select the most optimal cut for each node based on the previous ranking information to generate the final mapping solution. In Section 4.1, we will discuss our customized cut enumeration algorithm for MAPS.

## 3.3 MAPS Problem Formulation

We formulate the mapping-aware scheduling problem as an optimization problem formally stated as follows:

**Given:** (1) A CDFG $G$ that captures data and control dependence constraints; (2) A target clock period $T_{cp}$; (3) A set of additional scheduling constraints $C$, including latency and relative timing constraints expressed in the form of SDC, and resource constraints; (4) A target FPGA device using $K$-input LUTs.

**Goal:** Find a minimum-latency schedule for $G$ so that no constraints in $C$ are violated, and within each cycle, there exists a feasible $K$-LUT mapping that meets $T_{cp}$.

## 4. MAPS ALGORITHM

In this section we present MAPS, a mapping-aware constrained scheduling algorithm to address and exploit the interdependence between scheduling and LUT mapping to minimize the latency of the synthesized design. Figure 2 shows the overall flow for MAPS. MAPS takes the CDFG along with a variety of scheduling constraints as inputs, and generates a minimum-latency schedule. The algorithm consists of three major steps: (1) *Cut enumeration* generates all $K$-feasible cuts for each node in the CDFG using a work-list-based approach; (2) *Relaxation-based labeling* computes for each operation its minimum time step and minimum level (in terms of LUT depth) allowed by the design constraints; (3) *Incremental scheduling* legalizes the schedule for resource-constrained operations to avoid resource conflicts based on the results from labeling.

## 4.1 Cut Enumeration

MAPS generates all $K$-feasible cuts at each node as part of the process for determining the minimum schedule latency. Unlike traditional cut enumeration algorithms that typically operate on an acyclic DAG with logic operations, MAPS deals with both logic operations and *black-box operations* that cannot be mapped to LUTs, such as multiplications and memory reads/writes. In addition, MAPS needs to handle cycles that arise from loop-carried dependences on CDFG.

Typically, the $K$-feasible cut set for each node $v$ can be computed based on its inputs on the CDFG. Suppose $v$'s inputs are $u_1$, $u_2$, ..., $u_p$ and their own cut set are $CUTS_{u_1}$, $CUTS_{u_2}$, ..., $CUTS_{u_p}$, where $CUTS_{u_i}$ is a collection of cuts and each cut $c \in CUTS_{u_i}$ is a $K$-feasible cut. The K-feasible cut set for $v$ can be computed as follows:

- If $v$ is a black-box operation that does not map to LUTs, the only legal cut for $v$ is itself, which is a *trivial cut*, i.e., $CUTS_v = \{\{v\}\}$, as block boxes will never be packed together with any other operation.

- If $v$ is a logic operation, the $K$-feasible cuts for $v$ can be computed by merging the $K$-feasible cuts for all its inputs as follows:

$$CUTS_v = mergeCuts(u_1, ..., u_p) =$$
$$\{C' = C_1 \cup ... \cup C_p | C_i \in CUTS_{u_i}, |C'| < K\} \quad (1)$$

Without considering cycles, we can easily compute the cut set for each node by traversing the graph in topological order using conventional cut enumeration approaches [9]. However, a simple topological traversal is not enough when the graph contains cycles. To handle the cycles on CDFG, our cut enumeration algorithm iteratively applies Equation (1) to each node until convergence, when all $K$-feasible cuts are obtained. More specifically, we maintain a work list for nodes that need to be updated. Initially, the work list contains all operations, and the cut set for each node is the trivial cut. For each node in the work list, we apply Equation (1) to compute the new cut set. If a new cut is added for a node, we update its cut set and add all its successors to the work list. We remove a node from the work list each time it is visited. The algorithm terminates when the work list becomes empty. As suggested by previous studies [14], cut enumeration is an exponential algorithm with respect to $K$. Nevertheless, the actual runtime for cut enumeration is typically fast for $K \leq 6$.

Our cut enumeration algorithm can be applied on both word-level or bit-level dependence graphs. By decomposing the word-level CDFG into bit-level dependence graph [29], we are able to capture the exact bit-level inputs for each operation, but such graph decomposition would complicate our scheduling and mapping. To make our algorithm more scalable and efficient, we currently implement our cut enumeration algorithm on word-level CDFG. In this case, we cannot simply compute the inputs of each node based on word-level values, because each output bit may depend on multiple input bits of a single word-level value. For example, given an arithmetic operation $C[1:0] = A[1:0] + B[1:0]$, the highest output bit $C_1$ depends on four input bits $A_1$, $A_0$, $B_1$, and $B_0$, which come from only two word-level values $A$ and $B$ on CDFG.

To handle such bit-level dependence, our cut enumeration algorithm performs bit-level dependence analysis based on CDFG for different types of operations: (a) For bitwise logic operations such as AND, OR, and XOR, each bit is independent of the other bits, so we can compute the word-level dependence on the CDFG without considering the bits of each value; (b) For other bitwise operations such as SHIFT, ZEXT, SEXT, and TRUNC, each output bit depends on at most a single input bit, but not necessarily the one at the same position. In this case, we annotate each input value with bit positions to distinguish different bits of the same word-level value. (c) For arithmetic operations such as ADD and SUB, each output bit can be dependent on multiple input bits. The highest output bit is dependent on the largest number of input bits, and we always examine this bit to consider

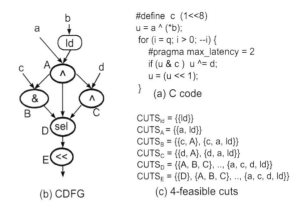

```
#define c (1<<8)
u = a ^ (*b);
   for (i = q; i > 0; --i) {
      #pragma max_latency = 2
      if (u & c)  u ^= d;
      u = (u << 1);
}          (a) C code
```

```
CUTS_ld = {{ld}}
CUTS_A = {{a, ld}}
CUTS_B = {{c, A}, {c, a, ld}}
CUTS_C = {{d, A}, {d, a, ld}}
CUTS_D = {{A, B, C}, .., {a, c, d, ld}}
CUTS_E = {{D}, {A, B, C}, .., {a, c, d, ld}}
```

(b) CDFG          (c) 4-feasible cuts

Figure 3: Cut enumeration for a CRC kernel – The memory read ld is a black-box operation, while A-E are logic operations; $\wedge$ = XOR; & = AND; $<<$ denotes a left shift; *sel* denotes a MUX operation.

the worst case. As with (b), we annotate each input value with the bit positions it depends on. For the given example $C[1:0] = A[1:0] + B[1:0]$, our analysis will determine that $C$ has four inputs $A_0$, $A_1$, $B_0$, and $B_1$.

Figure 3 demonstrates the cut enumeration for a cyclic redundancy check (CRC) kernel. Based on the source code (a) and the corresponding CDFG (b), the cut set for each node are listed in (c). For simplicity, we only consider one iteration of the loop. As shown in this figure, the black-box operation ld only has a trivial cut, but other operations can have multiple $K$-feasible cuts. Note that the AND between $u$ and a special constant $c = (1 << 8)$ is used to test the highest bit of $u$. For this special case, our bit-level dependence analysis will determine that the output value only depends on a single input bit.

## 4.2 Relaxation-Based Labeling

The labeling step aims to compute a minimum-latency schedule while considering mapping and respecting all SDC constraints for dependence, relative timing, latency, and clock period. Unlike conventional SDC scheduling algorithms, our technique considers LUT mapping and computes both the time step and the LUT level within the time step for each operation. Our technique also differs fundamentally from technology mapping algorithms, which operate on an acyclic DAG with pre-defined register boundaries; instead, it operates on an untimed CDFG along with user-specified timing constraints which may result in additional cycles. To this end, we introduce a relaxation-based labeling algorithm, which to our knowledge is the first to achieve a latency-optimal solution for both time step and LUT level under timing constraints captured in the SDC form.

To jointly represent the time step and LUT depths of each operation, we define the *L-value* of node $v$, $L_v = (s, l)$, where $s$ denotes the time step of $v$ in cycles, and $l$ denotes the arrival time of $v$ within a time step. Given a target clock period $T_{cp}$ in LUT levels, it follows that $s > 0$ and $1 \leq l < T_{cp}$. For simplicity we assume that the delay of each operation is quantized to LUT levels, and is less than $T_{cp}$ (that is, no combinational multi-cycle operations). However, the proposed approach can easily be generalized to handle real-valued delays and to multi-cycle operations.

We define the following operations for $L$-values below. Here $L_1 = (s_1, l_1)$, $L_2 = (s_2, l_2)$, *Delay* is a delay value

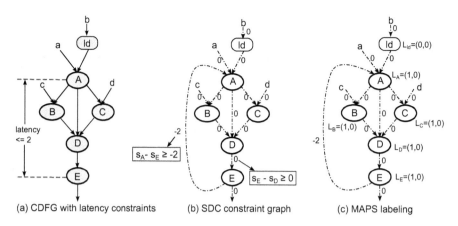

(a) CDFG with latency constraints     (b) SDC constraint graph     (c) MAPS labeling

Figure 4: MAPS labeling for CRC – (a) CDFG with a latency constraint for the loop body shown in Figure 3; (b) SDC constraint graph that captures dependence constraints (e.g., $s_E - s_D \geq 0$ where $s_D$ and $s_E$ denote the time step of $D$ and $E$, respectively.), and a latency constraint (i.e., $s_A - s_E \geq -2$); (c) MAPS labeling results for the constraint graph based on the cut information from Figure 3. Each label $L_v = (s, l)$ represents the $L$-value of node $v$, where $s$ denotes the time step of $v$ in cycles, and $l$ denotes the level of $v$ in LUT depth.

of a combinational operation quantized to LUT levels, and $Lat$ is a time step difference value imposed by user-defined relative timing and latency constraints. The first two operations are used to update the $L$-value for each node based on different constraints, while the following operations are used to facilitate the description of our labeling algorithm.

$$L_1 + (0, Delay) = \begin{cases} (s_1, l_1 + Delay) & \text{if } (l_1 + Delay) < T_{cp} \\ (s_1 + 1, Delay) & \text{otherwise} \end{cases}$$

$$L_1 + (Lat, 0) = (s_1 + Lat, 0)$$

$$L_1 < L_2 = \begin{cases} true & \text{if } (s_1 < s_2) \text{ or } (s_1 = s_2 \text{ and } l_1 < l_2) \\ false & \text{otherwise} \end{cases}$$

$$\min(L_1, L_2) = \begin{cases} L_1 & \text{if } L_1 < L_2 \\ L_2 & \text{otherwise} \end{cases}$$

$$\max(L_1, L_2) = \begin{cases} L_2 & \text{if } L_1 < L_2 \\ L_1 & \text{otherwise} \end{cases}$$

In order to obtain a minimum-latency schedule while considering a rich set of scheduling constraints, our labeling algorithm computes the *optimal L-values*, i.e. the minimum $L$-values among all legal schedules, based on the constraint graph of SDC [26] constructed from the CDFG. A straightforward idea for computing the optimal $L$-value of each node is to propagate the $L$-values from primary inputs of the CDFG to the primary outputs if the constraint graph is acyclic. However, additional constraints such as maximum relative timing constraints may result in cyclic dependences. To overcome this challenge, we introduce a relaxation-based labeling algorithm, which maintains a lower bound on the $L$-value of each node and successively relaxes this lower bound to meet each of the scheduling constraints for the node.

Algorithm 1 details the proposed relaxation-based labeling. Let $Delay_v$ denote the delay value of node $v$ quantized to the number of LUT levels, $Lat_{u \to v}$ denotes the weight of the edge from $u$ to $v$ on the SDC constraint graph, which also represents the minimum time step difference between $u$ and $v$. As shown in lines $1-2$, the $L$-value of each node $v$ is initialized to $(0, Delay_v)$, which is a trivial lower bound on $v$'s $L$-value without any constraints. The algorithm then iteratively updates the lower bound on each node's $L$-value (line 3-19) by propagating both mapping and scheduling

---

**Algorithm 1:** $Labeling(CG, CUTS)$

  **input** : $CG$ – constraint graph with nodes $V$ and edges $E$;
            $CUTS$ – cut set for all nodes on CDFG.
  **output**: $L$ – labels for each node.
1  **foreach** *node $v$ in $V$* **do**
2     $\lfloor$  $L_v \leftarrow (0, Delay_v)$
    // Tighten the labels by at most $B$ iterations
3  **for** $i \leftarrow 1$ to $B$ **do**
4     *updated* $\leftarrow$ *false*
5     **foreach** *node $v$ in $V$* **do**
        // Mapping constraints
6         $f_v \leftarrow (\infty, \infty)$
7         **foreach** *cut $C$ in $CUTS_v$* **do**
8             $L' \leftarrow (0, 0)$
9             **foreach** *node $u$ in cut $C$* **do**
10               $\lfloor$ $L' \leftarrow \max\{L', L_u + (0, Delay_v)\}$
11            $\lfloor$ $f_v \leftarrow \min(f_v, L')$
        // Latency & relative timing constraints
12         $g_v \leftarrow (0, 0)$
13         **foreach** *edge $u \to v$ in $E$* **do**
14             $\lfloor$ $g_v \leftarrow \max\{g_v, L_u + (Lat_{u \to v}, 0) + (0, Delay_v)\}$
15         **if** $L_v < \max\{f_v, g_v\}$ **then**
16            $L_v \leftarrow \max\{f_v, g_v\}$
17            *updated* $\leftarrow$ *true*
18     **if** *updated* = *false* **then**
19         $\lfloor$ **return** *SUCCESS*
20 **return** *FAILURE*

---

constraints according to Equations (2) and (3):

$$L_v \geq f_v = \min_{\forall C \in CUT_v} \max_{\forall u \in C} \{L_u + (0, Delay_v)\} \quad (2)$$

$$L_v \geq g_v = \max_{\forall u \to v \in E} \{L_u + (Lat_{u \to v}, 0) + (0, Delay_v)\} \quad (3)$$

Here $f_v$ and $g_v$ are two lower bounds of node $v$'s $L$-value required by mapping constraints and SDC scheduling constraints, respectively. Following Equation (2), lines $6 - 11$ in Algorithm 1 deal with mapping constraints, and calculate the the new $f_v$ of node $v$ by selecting the best cut for $v$. Similarly, lines $12 - 14$ calculate the new $g_v$ of node $v$ based on various SDC scheduling constraints on the constraint graph. If any of $f_v$ and $g_v$ is greater than the original $L_v$, we update $L_v = \max\{f_v, g_v\}$ via relaxation in lines $15 - 17$.

LEMMA 1. *For each iteration of Algorithm 1, $L_v$ is always a lower bound of node $v$'s $L$-value, i.e., $L_v$ is less than or equal to $v$'s $L$-value in any legal schedule that satisfies the mapping and scheduling constraints.*

PROOF. Let $S$ be a legal schedule, $\overline{L_v}$ be the $L$-value for each node $v$ in $S$, $\overline{f_v}$ and $\overline{g_v}$ be the lower bounds of $v$'s $L$-value computed according to Equations (2) and (3) for $S$:

$$\overline{f_v} = \min_{\forall C \in CUT_v} \max_{\forall u \in C} \{\overline{L_u} + (0, Delay_v)\}$$

$$\overline{g_v} = \max_{\forall u \to v \in E} \{\overline{L_u} + (Lat_{u \to v}, 0) + (0, Delay_v)\}$$

Because $S$ is a legal schedule, each node $v$ must satisfy both mapping and scheduling constraints, i.e., $\overline{L_v} \geq \max\{\overline{f_v}, \overline{g_v}\}$. Considering Algorithm 1, let $L_v^i$ denote node $v$'s $L$-value after iteration $i$ ($i \geq 0$). We prove by induction that for each iteration $i$:

$$L_v^i \leq \overline{L_v}, \quad \forall \text{ node } v \qquad (4)$$

**Base case**: When $i = 0$, our algorithm initializes $L_v^0 = (0, Delay_v)$, which is a trivial lower bound because every operation cannot finish before its own operation delay; therefore, it is evident that $L_v^0 \leq \overline{L_v}$.

**Induction step**: Suppose (4) is true for $i = k$, i.e., $L_u^k \leq \overline{L_u}$ for each node $u$. Considering $i = k + 1$, Algorithm 1 would update $L_v^{k+1}$ according to Equations (2) and (3):

$$f_v = \min_{\forall C \in CUT_v} \max_{\forall u \in C} \{L_u^k + (0, Delay_v)\} \leq \overline{f_v}$$

$$g_v = \max_{\forall u \to v \in E} \{L_u^k + (Lat_{u \to v}, 0) + (0, Delay_v)\} \leq \overline{g_v}$$

$$L_v^{k+1} = \max\{f_v, g_v\} \leq \max\{\overline{f_v}, \overline{g_v}\} \leq \overline{L_v}$$

It is clear for $f_v \leq \overline{f_v}$ and $g_v \leq \overline{g_v}$ by substitute every $L_u^k$ with $\overline{L_v}$ and applying the inductive assumption $L_u^k \leq \overline{L_u}$. Evidently, Equation (4) is also true for $i = k + 1$. □

Algorithm 1 iteratively relaxes $L$-values until convergence. SInce $L$-values are always lower bounds in each iteration, Algorithm 1 is guaranteed to converge to a legal schedule with optimal $L$-values if the problem is feasible.

LEMMA 2. *All nodes on the constraint graph would reach their optimal $L$-values within $B = D \cdot (|V| - 1) \cdot |V|$ iterations if the scheduling problem is feasible.*

Here $|V|$ denotes the total number of nodes on the constraint graph, while $D$ denotes the maximum delay in terms of LUT levels for any edge on the constraint graph. Lemma 2 is relatively obvious by considering the worst-case mapping. In the worst case, each node is mapped to a distinct LUT (i.e., only trivial cuts are chosen). Since any simple path on the constraint graph can include at most $|V| - 1$ nodes, the $L$-value of any node can be at most $D \cdot (|V| - 1)$. As shown in Algorithm 1, at least one of $L$-values is increased by at least one in each iteration; otherwise, all nodes would have obtained the optimal $L$-values and the algorithm would successfully exit. Therefore, after at most $B = D \cdot (|V| - 1) \cdot |V|$ iterations, all nodes should have settled at the optimal $L$-values if the scheduling problem is feasible.

THEOREM 1. *Algorithm 1 returns a legal schedule with optimal $L$-value for each node in pseudo-polynomial time, and thus is able to achieve a minimum-latency schedule with pseudo-polynomial complexity.*

---

**Algorithm 2:** $IncrementalScheduling(CG, C_r, L)$

> **input** : $CG$ – constraint graph; $C_r$ – resource constraints;
>        $L$ – initial labels from the labeling step.
> **output**: $S$ – final schedule.

1   $s \leftarrow 0$ // Time step
2   **while** *more resource-constrained nodes to schedule* **do**
3      **foreach** *unscheduled resource-constrained node $v$ with time step $s$, in ascending priority order* **do**
4          **if** *no resource conflict for $v$ at $s$* **then**
5             schedule $v$ at $s$
6             update resource scoreboard
7          **else**
8             $L_v \leftarrow (s + 1, 0)$
9             update the labels for $v$'s successors on $CG$
10             **if** *labeling is infeasible* **then**
11                report failure and exit
12      $s \leftarrow s + 1$;

---

If the scheduling problem is feasible, Algorithm 1 returns successfully after all nodes settle at their lower bounds while satisfying all dependence, relative timing, and clock period constraints (lines 17-18). Otherwise, it reports failure (line 19). As the $L$-value $L_v$ essentially represents the number of time steps plus the number of LUT levels from primary inputs to node $v$, we have shown that the $L$-values computed by Algorithm 1 are optimal $L$-values, and our schedule is thus minimum-latency.

Figure 4 illustrates the labeling process for the CRC kernel described in Figure 3. Given the CDFG and a user-specified latency constraint in Figure 3(a), our labeling algorithm first constructs the constraint graph as shown in Figure 4(b). The constraint graph contains the same set of nodes on the CDFG but includes a different set of weighted edges, with each edge representing an SDC constraint. For each edge on the CDFG, we add a zero-weighted edge accordingly to the constraint graph to represent a dependence constraint (e.g., $A \to ld$ captures $s_A - s_{ld} \geq 0$). For the latency constraint, we add an additional edge from $E$ to $A$ with a weight of $-2$, representing the latency constraint $s_A - s_E \geq -2$. As shown in Figure 4(b), the additional latency constraint can introduce a new cycle on the constraint graph. Based on the constraint graph, we compute the $L$-value for each node in topological order of the original data flow graph using Algorithm 1. Here we assume that the black-box operation $ld$ takes a full cycle. Therefore, node $A$ has a $L$-value of $(1,0)$, indicating that the earliest time step of $A$ is one and the minimum LUT depth is zero. Our algorithm computes the $L$-values for logic operations $A-E$ based on their cut information. For example, the best cut for node $E$ is $\{a,c,d,ld\}$, suggesting an optimal $L$-value of $(1,0)$. The final labeling results are shown in Figure 4 (c).

### 4.3 Incremental Scheduling

In this section we introduce an incremental scheduling algorithm to handle the resource constraints on black-box operations (e.g., memory port limits). Given that resource-constrained scheduling is NP-hard in general, MAPS employs a heuristic method which legalizes an initial schedule from the previous labeling step by incrementally rescheduling the operations that cause resource conflicts.

Algorithm 2 lists the pseudo-code for our incremental scheduling algorithm. We start from an initial schedule obtained from the labeling step where all nodes are labeled

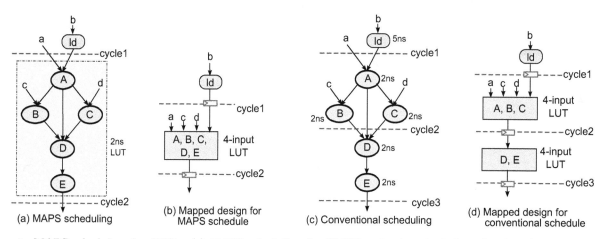

Figure 5: MAPS scheduling for CRC – (a) MAPS scheduling for CDFG nodes based on their $L$-values from Figure 4; (b) Mapped design for (a), which results in a 2-cycle latency with one LUT and two registers; (c) Conventional schedule for CRC based on pre-characterized delay values of individual operations; (d) Mapped design for (c), which results in a 3-cycle latency with two LUTs and three registers. Here we assume that the target clock period is $5ns$; each LUT or logic operation takes $2ns$; the black-box operation ld takes a full cycle.

with the optimal $L$-values, i.e., scheduled as-soon-as-possible (ASAP), and legalize the solution by gradually postponing resource-constrained nodes to later time steps based on a priority function. For each time step $s$, we check if a resource conflict exists for any resource-constrained nodes that are initially assigned to $s$. If so, we postpone the ones with the least priorities, which to some extent is similar to how list scheduling operates. The priority of each node is determined based on its ASAP label (i.e., the L-values obtained from Algorithm 1) and its as-late-as-possible (ALAP) label that can be computed in a similar manner using backward propagation. More specifically, we compute the ALAP label for each node by iteratively updating the upper bound of its $L$-value. Initially, the ALAP label of each node $v$ is set to the maximum $L$-value, the upper bound $L$-value without any constraints; afterwards, for each cone $C$ rooted at $r$ that contains $v$, we tighten the upper bound of $v$'s $L$-value by checking every successor of $r$; meanwhile, we also refine the upper bound of $v$'s $L$-value by checking each outgoing edge from $v$ on the constraint graph to ensure that all SDC timing constraints are satisfied. We repeatedly tighten the upper bound of $L$-value for each node until convergence. Otherwise, the problem is infeasible and we will stop after at most $B = D \cdot (|V| - 1) \cdot |V|$ iterations similar to the previous ASAP labeling process.

After obtaining both ASAP and ALAP labels, we can calculate the priority of each node based on its *mobility*, which is defined to be the difference between the ALAP and ASAP labels. Intuitively, nodes with a lower mobility are assigned with a higher priority. If we increase the label for a resource-constrained node $v$, we also incrementally update the labels for all the successors of $v$ using the relaxation-based labeling process introduced in the previous section.

Figure 5 illustrates the MAPS scheduling results for the CRC kernel. Since ld is the only black-box operation, there is no resource conflict for this example. The scheduled design will be further mapped to LUTs and registers as shown in Figure 5(b). For comparison, Figure 5 (c) and (d) illustrate the conventional schedule and the corresponding mapped design. Clearly, our MAPS algorithm is able to reduce the latency by mapping multiple operations into a single LUT,

and at the same time reduce the LUT and register usage by maximizing the utilization of each LUT.

**Overall Time Complexity** – It is important to notice that the $L$-values always increase monotonically during both relaxation labeling and incremental scheduling. According to Lemma 2, the upper bound of any $L$-value is $D \cdot (|V| - 1)$, so the maximum number of iterations involved during relaxation labeling and incremental scheduling will be bounded by $D \cdot (|V| - 1) \cdot |V|$. In each iteration, $L$-values are updated optimally according to each edge in the constraint graph, and the complexity for each iteration is bounded by $O(|E|)$. As a result, the total time complexity for the relaxation and incremental scheduling is $O(D \cdot |V|^2 \cdot |E|)$. Note that since the maximum latency value $D$ is usually a very small constant, our algorithm would converge in polynomial time $O(|V|^2 \cdot |E|)$.

## 5. EXPERIMENTAL RESULTS

Our experiments are conducted based on a widely used, state-of-the-art commercial HLS tool, which takes a behavioral C/C++ program as an input and outputs RTL code in VHDL or Verilog based on the LLVM compiler infrastructure [19]. To our knowledge, the commercial HLS tool makes use of pre-characterized delay values of individual operations to perform scheduling and relies on the underlying logic synthesis tool to perform technology mapping after the HLS stage (to which we refer as the baseline approach).

We have implemented the MAPS algorithm in C++ as an LLVM pass, which takes the LLVM IR from the original HLS tool as input, reorders instructions based on our proposed mapping-aware constrained scheduling algorithm, and generates tool-specific intrinsics (i.e., wait statements) to specify clock boundaries so that the HLS tool will preserve our scheduling results. We push the scheduling results through the same HLS engine and RTL back end to perform resource binding and RTL code generation. The generated Verilog RTL design is implemented by Xilinx Vivado 2013.4 targeting a Virtex-7 FPGA device. Notably, both the baseline approach and our MAPS approach rely on the same downstream CAD toolflow to perform technology mapping. Nevertheless, our MAPS approach can generate schedules

Table 1: Description for MAPS benchmarks.

| Design | Source | Application Domain | # of LLVM IR Operations | Description |
|--------|--------|-------------------|------------------------|-------------|
| XORR | Kernel | | 773 | XOR reduction on a bit vector |
| GFMUL | Kernel | | 85 | Galois field multiplication |
| CLZ | Kernel | | 450 | Couting the number of leading zeros in a 64-bit word |
| CRC | MiBench [17] | Communication | 58 | Cyclic redundancy check for error detection |
| MD5 | MiBench [17] | Cryptography | 996 | Message-digest algorithm |
| AES | CHStone [18] | Cryptography | 806 | Advanced encryption standard |
| SHA | CHStone [18] | Cryptography | 476 | Secure hash algorithm |
| DFADD | CHStone [18] | Scientific computing | 838 | Double-precision floating-point addition |
| MT | [22] | Scientific computing | 1171 | Mersenne twister 32-bit random number generator |
| RS | [2] | Communication | 840 | Reed-Solomon decoder |
| DR | [20] | Machine learning | 262 | Digit recognition based on K-nearest neighbors |

that are more friendly for LUT mapping, resulting in higher quality of results.

We have evaluated the proposed technique with a broad range of benchmarks used in a variety of application domains, such as cryptography, scientific computing, communication, and machine learning. Table 1 briefly describes these benchmarks. For each benchmark, we apply the same set of HLS front-end optimizations such as loop unrolling and array partition for both the baseline approach and our approach. Our proposed algorithm focuses on mapping optimization for logic operations (e.g. AND, OR, and XOR), bitwise operations (e.g. ZEXT, SEXT, SHIFT, and TRUNC), and narrow-bit-width arithmetic operations (e.g. ADD, SUB, and CMP), while all other operations are treated as black-box operations. We model the delay of each black-box operation using pre-characterized delay values parsed from the schedule report generated by the commercial HLS tool; the delay of non-black-box operations are modeled based on the delay of a single LUT.

## 5.1 Results for Representative Kernels

We first present the results for three representative application kernels, i.e. CLZ, XORR, GFMUL, which provide insights for the advantages of MAPS. In these kernels, most of the operations are logic operations, which can be aggressively chained and mapped to a few LUTs. Table 2 shows the detailed timing, latency, and resource usage for each kernel.

Figure 6 lists the C code snippets for all kernels. XORR applies a simple XOR operation over a bit vector and forms a balanced XOR reduction tree with tree-depth of 10. Given the $5ns$ target clock period, the original HLS tool can chain at most six levels of XOR operations into a single cycle based on the pre-characterized delay values, resulting in a two-cycle latency. By considering technology mapping, our maps algorithm is able to map all the XOR operations into five levels of 6-input LUTs, which can achieve a zero-latency combinational design while still meeting the target clock period constraint. Similarly, GFMUL applies a set of AND/XOR/SHIFT operations to a few inputs, while CLZ consists of a number of AND/OR operations to compute the number of leading zeros in a 64-bit word. Since all operations in these kernels are logic or bitwise operations, MAPS can effectively pack all operations of GFMUL to form a combinational circuit, and reduce the latency of CLZ to one.

By packing more logic operations together and enabling more aggressive operation chaining, our MAPS algorithm also provides added benefits by reducing register usage due to the shorter latency, and at the same time, reducing LUT

```
out = 0
for (i = 0; i < n; i++) {
    #prgma hls unroll
    out ^= in[i]
}

        (a) XORR
```

```
for (i = 0; i < n; i++) {
    #pragma hls unroll
    if (b & (1<<i))
        out ^= a << i;
}

        (b) GFMUL
```

```
zero = 1;  out = 0;
for (i = 0; i < 64; i++) {
    #pragma hls unroll
    if (x[i]) zero = 0;
    out += zero;
}

        (c) CLZ
```

Figure 6: C code snippets for three kernels.

usage by increasing the utilization of each individual LUT. For example, MAPS completely removes all registers (or FFs) for XORR and GFMUL. For the CLZ kernel, MAPS can reduce the number of FFs by 78% and LUTs by 40% with a $5ns$ target clock period.

## 5.2 Results for Real-Life Applications

We have also evaluated our approach on a number of real-life applications selected from a broad range of domains. Table 2 shows the latency and resource usage comparisons for these designs. We observe MAPS can significantly reduce the latency over the commercial HLS tool (up to 60%) while still meeting timing for all applications. These results provide further evidence that MAPS is able to generate more efficient solutions with shorter latency and hence higher performance by better utilizing the clock period through chaining more operations in each cycle.

From Table 2, we also observe that our approach can effectively reduce the usage of FFs and LUTs by eliminating unnecessary registers across clock boundaries and maximizing the utilization of each individual LUT. On average, MAPS reduces the number of FFs by 25% and the number of LUTs by 9% with the $5ns$ target clock period. However, it is worth noting that since our current approach mainly focuses on latency optimization, it may lead to LUT duplication and thus increase resource usage in a few cases (e.g. SHA and MD5).

## 5.3 Efficiency Analysis for MAPS

To understand the efficiency of MAPS, we have evaluated the execution time for the HLS process with different scheduling algorithms. Table 3 indicates that all benchmarks finish in several seconds, and the additional runtime overhead for MAPS is negligible. While the worst-case time complexity of MAPS is relatively high due to iterative labeling, our experimentation reports that the labeling algorithm converges within only a few iterations for all designs.

Table 3 also lists the number of operations per cycle for different scheduling algorithms. Compared to the baseline approach, MAPS can pack more operations together by con-

Table 2: Timing and resource usage comparison with target clock periods of 8ns and 5ns – CP = achieved clock period; LAT = latency in # of cycles; LUT = # of lookup-tables; FF = # of flip-flops; AVERAGE = the geometric mean of improvements for the eight real-life applications. Values in parentheses are percentage of increase (+) or decrease (-) over the baseline approach used in a state-of-the-art commercial HLS tool.

| Design | Approach | Target Clock Period = 5ns | | | | Target Clock Period = 8ns | | | |
|---|---|---|---|---|---|---|---|---|---|
| | | CP(ns) | LAT | LUT | FF | CP(ns) | LAT | LUT | FF |
| XORR | baseline | 2.88 | 1 | 133 | 17 | 4.38 | 1 | 124 | 3 |
| | MAPS | 2.28 | 0 (-100%) | 120 (-10%) | 0 (-100%) | 2.19 | 0 (-100%) | 120 (-3%) | 0 (-100%) |
| GFMUL | baseline | 2.93 | 2 | 50 | 27 | 4.38 | 1 | 50 | 18 |
| | MAPS | 1.68 | 0 (-100%) | 43 (-14%) | 0 (-100%) | 1.64 | 0 (-100%) | 43 (-14%) | 0 (-100%) |
| CLZ | baseline | 2.93 | 11 | 177 | 169 | 4.43 | 7 | 139 | 121 |
| | MAPS | 2.93 | 1 (-91%) | 107 (-40%) | 38 (-78%) | 4.38 | 1 (-86%) | 87 (-37%) | 17 (-86%) |
| CRC | baseline | 2.93 | 161 | 57 | 310 | 4.43 | 129 | 52 | 249 |
| | MAPS | 2.93 | 65 (-60%) | 41 (-28%) | 126 (-59%) | 4.43 | 65 (-50%) | 41 (-21%) | 126 (-49%) |
| MD5 | baseline | 4.39 | 126 | 9175 | 6747 | 5.83 | 67 | 9316 | 4952 |
| | MAPS | 4.24 | 95 (-25%) | 8812 (-4%) | 8417 (+25%) | 5.94 | 48 (-28%) | 8570 (-8%) | 6626 (+34%) |
| AES | baseline | 4.78 | 197 | 4895 | 5855 | 5.74 | 141 | 4322 | 4459 |
| | MAPS | 4.44 | 133 (-32%) | 3989 (-19%) | 3540 (-40%) | 5.90 | 109 (-23%) | 4007 (-7%) | 3369 (-24%) |
| SHA | baseline | 4.21 | 561 | 2916 | 3196 | 5.10 | 321 | 3720 | 2331 |
| | MAPS | 3.87 | 421 (-25%) | 3032 (+4%) | 3263 (+2%) | 5.97 | 241 (-25%) | 3146 (-15%) | 2466 (+6%) |
| DFADD | baseline | 4.81 | 11 | 5950 | 2735 | 6.44 | 8 | 5282 | 1671 |
| | MAPS | 4.80 | 10 (-9%) | 5528 (-7%) | 2106 (-23%) | 6.35 | 7 (-12%) | 4353 (-18%) | 1527 (-9%) |
| MT | baseline | 3.96 | 146 | 3617 | 4630 | 6.31 | 59 | 7652 | 2857 |
| | MAPS | 4.03 | 130 (-11%) | 3447 (-5%) | 2295 (-50%) | 6.37 | 57 (-3%) | 7850 (+3%) | 2060 (-28%) |
| RS | baseline | 4.23 | 124370 | 1710 | 974 | 4.95 | 105351 | 1502 | 875 |
| | MAPS | 4.30 | 79222 (-36%) | 1546 (-10%) | 828 (-15%) | 5.61 | 76040 (-28%) | 1598 (+6%) | 820 (-6%) |
| DR | baseline | 3.70 | 520021 | 625 | 432 | 5.06 | 340021 | 483 | 236 |
| | MAPS | 3.80 | 400021 (-23%) | 630 (+1%) | 427 (-1%) | 4.64 | 260021 (-24%) | 480 (-1%) | 214 (-9%) |
| AVERAGE | | | -29% | -9% | -25% | | -25% | -8% | -14% |

Table 3: Runtime and schedule statistics.

| | Runtime (seconds) | | Operations/cycle | |
|---|---|---|---|---|
| | baseline | MAPS | baseline | MAPS |
| XORR | 56.0 | 64.7 | 387 | 773 |
| GFMUL | 4.3 | 11.1 | 28 | 85 |
| CLZ | 24.0 | 29.7 | 38 | 225 |
| CRC | 3.9 | 11.8 | 10 | 19 |
| MD5 | 15.6 | 28.8 | 8 | 10 |
| AES | 20.5 | 61.9 | 16 | 24 |
| SHA | 8.9 | 19.6 | 16 | 22 |
| DFADD | 9.3 | 11.1 | 25 | 27 |
| MT | 36.5 | 193.5 | 8 | 11 |
| RS | 23.0 | 24.6 | 8 | 9 |
| DR | 44.5 | 50.5 | 9 | 11 |

sidering mapping, thus creating the opportunity for more aggressive operation chaining to minimize the schedule latency and area.

## 6. DISCUSSIONS

In this section, we will draw the distinction between MAPS and other integrated scheduling techniques and outline the relationship among MAPS, SDC scheduling, and retiming.

MAPS jointly performs scheduling and mapping to enable more aggressive operation chaining that is otherwise not possible with conventional scheduling approaches. The MD5 example in Figure 1(c) demonstrates that even the

most accurate delay estimates obtained using the post-place-and-route back-annotation approach proposed in Zheng et al. [31] fails to reveal that mapping all operations into a single LUT and scheduling them within the same cycle leads to the shortest latency. In fact, such an approach would quickly converge to a sub-optimal solution, like the one in Figure 1(b). The failure stems from the reliance on the additive delay model commonly assumed throughout HLS tools, which simply sums up the delay of the critical path to determine the necessary clock boundaries to meet timing. Such an additive delay model is inaccurate in the perspective of downstream physical implementation because it does not consider mapping optimizations that are able to cluster multiple operations into a single LUT. The fact that the flow proposed in [31] focuses on the accuracy of delay estimates, while MAPS emphasizes the fundamental property of LUT mapping, [31] serves as a complement to the MAPS framework.

Although MAPS is designed to efficiently handle various difference constraints, the problem it addresses cannot be easily solved by the SDC scheduling approach [30]. Specifically, the task of computing and using delay information in the presence of mapping is non-trivial. MAPS determines the minimum $L$-value of each node based on cut enumeration, which selects one of the possible cones rooted at the node. Such either-or constraints cannot be optimally handled by SDC without relying on a heuristic transformation.

On the other hand, MAPS bears similarity to the retiming-based mapping technique [24], but is in fact a generalization of the retiming-based mapping problem. Retiming-based mapping starts with a timed circuit with an initial register placement and aims to reposition these registers optimally such that the timing is met. MAPS instead takes in an untimed behavioral description and optimally add registers in between operations to achieve the minimum latency while meeting timing. An intuitive attempt to reduce the MAPS scheduling problem to the retiming-based mapping problem is to add different numbers of registers at the end of the input untimed circuit and allow the retiming-based algorithm to optimally propagate the registers into the circuit. While this approach simply requires a binary search on the number of registers, it is not optimal in the presence of cycles. The retiming-based mapping approach is unable to propagate the register into a cycle and will result in an infeasible mapping. It is possible to experiment with different initial register placements, but the complexity will be exponential, rendering the approach impractical.

# 7. CONCLUSIONS

In this paper, we propose a mapping-aware scheduling algorithm, which can efficiently incorporate mapping information into scheduling in order to generate much more efficient solutions for LUT-based FPGAs. Unlike conventional scheduling algorithms, our proposed algorithm jointly performs cut-based mapping and relaxation-based scheduling while respecting a variety of dependence, relative timing, latency, and resource constraints. We show that our algorithm can efficiently compute an optimized scheduling solution with reasonable execution time. Experimental results demonstrate that our proposed technique can achieve very promising improvements in performance and resource usage by enabling more aggressive operation chaining and maximizing the utilization of each LUT compared to the state-of-the-art commercial HLS tools.

# 8. ACKNOWLEDGMENTS

This work was supported in part by NSF Award CCF-1337240 and a research gift from Xilinx, Inc. We thank Dr. Peichen Pan at Xilinx for sharing his helpful insights on the problem of joint retiming and technology mapping.

# 9. REFERENCES

[1] T. L. Adam, K. M. Chandy, and J. R. Dickson. A Comparison of List Schedules for Parallel Processing Systems. *Communications of the ACM*, 17(12):685–690, Dec 1974.

[2] A. Agarwal, M. C. Ng, and Arvind. A Comparative Evaluation of High-Level Hardware Synthesis Using Reed–Solomon Decoder. *IEEE Embedded Systems Letters*, 2(3):72–76, 2010.

[3] T. Beyrouthy and L. Fesquet. An Asynchronous FPGA Block with its Tech-Mapping Algorithm Dedicated to Security Applications. *International Journal of Reconfigurable Computing*, 2013.

[4] A. Canis, S. Brown, and J. Anderson. Modulo SDC Scheduling with Recurrence Minimization in High-Level Synthesis. *Int'l Conf. on Field Programmable Logic and Applications (FPL)*, pages 1–8, 2014.

[5] D. Chen and J. Cong. DAOmap: A Depth-Optimal Area Optimization Mapping Algorithm for FPGA Designs. *Int'l Conf. on Computer-Aided Design (ICCAD)*, pages 752–759, 2004.

[6] D. Chen, J. Cong, and P. Pan. FPGA Design Automation: A Survey. *Foundations and Trends in Electronic Design Automation*, 1(3):139–169, 2006.

[7] G. Chen and J. Cong. Simultaneous Logic Decomposition with Technology Mapping in FPGA Designs. *Int'l Symp. on Field-Programmable Gate Arrays (FPGA)*, pages 48–55, 2001.

[8] J. Cong and Y. Ding. FlowMap: An Optimal Technology Mapping Algorithm for Delay Optimization in Lookup-Table Based FPGA Designs. *IEEE Trans. on Computer-Aided Design of Integrated Circuits and Systems (TCAD)*, 13(1):1–12, 1994.

[9] J. Cong and Y.-Y. Hwang. Simultaneous Depth and Area Minimization in LUT-based FPGA Mapping. *Int'l Symp. on Field-Programmable Gate Arrays (FPGA)*, pages 68–74, 1995.

[10] J. Cong, B. Liu, G. Luo, and R. Prabhakar. Towards Layout-Friendly High-Level Synthesis. *Int'l Symp. on Physical design (ISPD)*, pages 165–172, 2012.

[11] J. Cong, B. Liu, S. Neuendorffer, J. Noguera, K. Vissers, and Z. Zhang. High-Level Synthesis for FPGAs: From Prototyping to Deployment. *IEEE Trans. on Computer-Aided Design of Integrated Circuits and Systems (TCAD)*, 30(4):473–491, Apr 2011.

[12] J. Cong, B. Liu, and Z. Zhang. Scheduling with Soft Constraints. *Int'l Conf. on Computer-Aided Design (ICCAD)*, pages 47–54, 2009.

[13] J. Cong and K. Minkovich. LUT-based FPGA Technology Mapping for Reliability. *Design Automation Conf. (DAC)*, pages 517–522, 2010.

[14] J. Cong, C. Wu, and Y. Ding. Cut Ranking and Pruning: Enabling a General and Efficient FPGA Mapping Solution. *Int'l Symp. on Field-Programmable Gate Arrays (FPGA)*, pages 29–35, 1999.

[15] J. Cong and Z. Zhang. An Efficient and Versatile Scheduling Algorithm Based on SDC Formulation. *Design Automation Conf. (DAC)*, pages 433–438, Jul 2006.

[16] S. Dai, M. Tan, K. Hao, and Z. Zhang. Flushing-Enabled Loop Pipelining for High-Level Synthesis. pages 1–6, 2014.

[17] M. R. Guthaus, J. S. Ringenberg, D. Ernst, T. M. Austin, T. Mudge, and R. B. Brown. MiBench: A Free, Commercially Representative Embedded Benchmark Suite. *Int'l Symp. on Workload Characterization (IISWC)*, pages 3–14, 2001.

[18] Y. Hara, H. Tomiyama, S. Honda, H. Takada, and K. Ishii. CHStone: A Benchmark Program Suite for Practical C-Based High-Level Synthesis. *Int'l Symp. on Circuits and Systems (ISCAS)*, pages 1192–1195, 2008.

[19] C. Lattner and V. Adve. LLVM: a Compilation Framework for Lifelong Program Analysis & Transformation. *Int'l Symp. on Code Generation and Optimization (CGO)*, pages 75–86, 2004.

[20] Y. Lee. Handwritten Digit Recognition Using K Nearest-Neighbor, Radial-Basis Function, and Backpropagation Neural Networks. *Neural computation*, 3(3):440–449, 1991.

[21] J. Y. Lin, D. Chen, and J. Cong. Optimal Simultaneous Mapping and Clustering for FPGA Delay Optimization. *Design Automation Conf. (DAC)*, pages 472–477, 2006.

[22] M. Matsumoto and T. Nishimura. Mersenne twister: A 623-dimensionally equidistributed uniform pseudo-random number generator. *ACM Transactions on Modeling and Computer Simulation (TOMACS)*, 8(1):3–30, 1998.

[23] P. Pan, A. K. Karandikar, and C. Liu. Optimal Clock Period Clustering for Sequential Circuits with Retiming. *IEEE Trans. on Computer-Aided Design of Integrated Circuits and Systems (TCAD)*, 17(6):489–498, 1998.

[24] P. Pan and C.-C. Lin. A New Retiming-Based Technology Mapping Algorithm for LUT-based FPGAs. *Int'l Symp. on Field-Programmable Gate Arrays (FPGA)*, pages 35–42, 1998.

[25] P. G. Paulin and J. P. Knight. Force-Directed Scheduling for the Behavioral Synthesis of ASICs. *IEEE Trans. on Computer-Aided Design of Integrated Circuits and Systems (TCAD)*, 8(6):661–678, Jun 1989.

[26] V. Pratt. Two Easy Theories Whose Combination is Hard. Technical report, MIT, 1977.

[27] R. Rivest. The MD5 Message-Digest Algorithm. 1992.

[28] M. Tan, B. Liu, S. Dai, and Z. Zhang. Multithreaded Pipeline Synthesis for Data-parallel Kernels. *Int'l Conf. on Computer-Aided Design (ICCAD)*, pages 718–725, 2014.

[29] J. Zhang, Z. Zhang, S. Zhou, M. Tan, X. Liu, X. Cheng, and J. Cong. Bit-level optimization for high-level synthesis and FPGA-based acceleration. *Int'l Symp. on Field-Programmable Gate Arrays (FPGA)*, pages 59–68, 2010.

[30] Z. Zhang and B. Liu. SDC-Based Modulo Scheduling for Pipeline Synthesis. *Int'l Conf. on Computer-Aided Design (ICCAD)*, pages 211–218, 2013.

[31] H. Zheng, S. T. Gurumani, K. Rupnow, and D. Chen. Fast and Effective Placement and Routing Directed High-Level Synthesis for FPGAs. *Int'l Symp. on Field-Programmable Gate Arrays (FPGA)*, pages 1–10, 2014.

# Resource-Aware Throughput Optimization for High-Level Synthesis

Peng Li[1]   Peng Zhang[1]   Louis-Noël Pouchet[2,1]   Jason Cong[1]

{pengli, pengzh, pouchet, cong}@cs.ucla.edu
[1]Computer Science Department, University of California, Los Angeles
[2]Department of Computer Science and Engineering, The Ohio State University

## ABSTRACT

With the emergence of robust high-level synthesis tools to automatically transform codes written in high-level languages into RTL implementations, the programming productivity when synthesizing accelerators improves significantly. However, although the state-of-the-art high-level synthesis tools can offer high-quality designs for simple nested loop kernels, there is still a significant performance gap between the synthesized and the optimal design for real-world complex applications with multiple loops.

In this work we first demonstrate that maximizing the throughput of each individual loop is not always the most efficient approach to achieving the maximum system-level throughput. More area-efficient non-fully pipelined design variants may outperform the fully-pipelined version by enabling larger degrees of parallelism. We develop an algorithm to determine the optimal resource usage and initiation intervals for each loop in the applications to achieve maximum throughput within a given area budget. We report experimental results on eight applications, showing an average of 31% performance speedup over state-of-the-art HLS solutions.

## Keywords

High-level Synthesis; Throughput Optimization; Resource Sharing; Area Constraint

## 1. INTRODUCTION

The automatic transformation of algorithms written in high-level languages (e.g., C, C++, SystemC) to low-level implementations by high-level synthesis (HLS) can be the key enabling technology to address the programmability challenges of FPGA-based accelerator architectures. After three decades of research and development by academia and industry, HLS has become a promising productivity boost for the semiconductor industry [1]. For example, the Xilinx Vivado HLS tool [2] based on AutoPilot [3] is now part of the standard Xilinx Vivado Suite available to every Xilinx FPGA designer.

With effective operation scheduling and resource binding/sharing algorithms, the state-of-the-art HLS tools can generate highly

*FPGA'15*, February 22–24, 2015, Monterey, CA, USA.
Copyright 2015 ACM 978-1-4503-3315-3/15/02 ...$15.00.
http://dx.doi.org/10.1145/2684746.2689065 .

optimized RTL for a single module [4][1]. However, fully utilizing the impressive performance provided by FPGA devices often requires the designs to be implemented with massive parallelism. Traditional FPGA design flows follow a two-step approach. First, a single replica of the application is optimized intensively for best performance through efficient computation pipelines. Then the optimized replica is duplicated to fully utilize the overall capacity of the target FPGA device.

It is commonly believed that efficient loop pipelining can boost the performance of a single loop with acceptable area overhead. For example, [5] shows that with full loop pipelining enabled by using on-chip memory partitioning, the evaluated computation kernels can achieve an average speedup of 5.6X at the cost of only 45% area increase. While this is true for a single loop, for accelerators with multiple sequential loops, if the area increase to support loop pipelining is not shared efficiently across loops, the overall performance-area efficiency may be degraded.

In this paper, we first show a somewhat counter-intuitive example that maximizing the pipeline throughput of one replica will not always generate optimal designs with coarse-grained duplications. With less aggressive loop pipelining, logic components may be more efficiently shared among loops with better performance per area ratio. Duplicating such a design will achieve a higher global throughput. The optimize-then-duplicate approach fails to find such optimal solutions.

Then, we propose a resource-aware throughput optimization algorithm to identify the most efficient implementations by maximizing the resource sharing between different loops. The problem is different from traditional resource-constrained operator scheduling [6][7][8] or resource allocation and binding [9][10][11]. Instead of fine-grain control-data flow graphs (CDFGs), the inputs of our algorithm are loops with parameterized initiation interval ($II$). Different loop $II$ will generate loop implementations with a different number of shareable components, and the objective is to improve the throughput by maximizing area efficiency through resource sharing.

The work that is most relevant to this paper is [12], [13] and [14]. [12] focused on using module replication to meet the throughput target for streaming applications. [13] and [14] proposed a combination of module selection and replication algorithm based on a synchronous data flow (SDF) representation of streaming applications. All of these focus on streaming applications where all modules are executed in parallel and no resource can be shared among different modules. The techniques proposed in this paper can be applied to streaming applications as a special case, but also to more general applications where not all loops can be executed in parallel due to inter-loop dependence. For example, iterative stencil applications [15] are such examples with loop-carried dependence.

The contributions of the work include:

- We address the fact that high throughput replicas with efficient computation pipelines may not be good candidates for building massive parallel accelerators. Balanced replicas with efficient resource sharing between loops can be better building blocks.

- We formulate a resource-aware throughput optimization problem by simultaneously addressing the concept of loop pipelining, module selection, duplication and resource sharing within a unified framework. To the best of our knowledge, this the first attempt to co-optimize these problems within a single formulation.

- We make some initial attempts to solve the problem efficiently with branch-and-bound and ILP approaches.

This paper is organized as follows. Section 2 uses a motivational example to demonstrate the design trade-offs in resource-aware throughput optimization. Section 3 formulates the problem and Section 4 proposes several methods to solve the problem efficiently. Section 5 describes some implementations in more details. Section 6 presents the efficiency of the proposed throughput optimization algorithm over traditional approaches with experimental results and the conclusions are presented in Section 7.

## 2. A MOTIVATIONAL EXAMPLE

We now illustrate the resource-aware throughput optimization problem using a motivational example: Discrete Wavelet Transformation (DWT), an algorithm frequently used in various multimedia applications.

Fig. 1 illustrates a computation kernel in DWT. Array $tmp$ is a floating-point (FP) array and $a1, a2, a3, a4, k1, k2$ are floating-point variables. There are four loops in the code segment, namely L1 to L4. All the FP operations $(+, *)$ are emphasized in the code with $(\oplus, \otimes)$.

```
for i=0 to n−1 do
  L1:for j = 1 to m−3 step 2 do
     tmp[i][j]⊕=a1⊗(tmp[i][j−1]⊕tmp[i][j+1]);
  tmp[i][m−1]⊕=2⊗a1⊗tmp[i][m−2];
  L2:for j = 2 to m−1 step 2 do
     tmp[i][j]⊕=a2⊗(tmp[i][j−1]⊕tmp[i][j+1]);
  tmp[i][0]⊕=2⊗a2⊗tmp[i][1];
  L3:for j = 1 to m−3 step 2 do
     tmp[i][j]⊕=a3⊗(tmp[i][j−1]⊕tmp[i][j+1]);
     img[j/2 + m/2][i] = k2⊗tmp[i][j];
  tmp[i][m−1] = 2⊗a3⊗tmp[i][m−2];
  img[(m−1)/2 + m/2][i]=k2⊗tmp[i][m−1];
  L4:for j = 2 to m−1 step 2 do
     tmp[i][j]⊕=a4⊗(tmp[i][j−1]⊕tmp[i][j+1]);
     img[j/2][i] = k1⊗tmp[i][j];
  tmp[i][0] = 2⊗a4⊗tmp[i][1];
  img[0][i] = k1⊗tmp[i][0];
```

Figure 1: Discrete Wavelet Transformation (DWT)

Table 1 shows the FP operations performed in each loop and FP operators required if each loop will be fully pipelined. Due to the inter-loop data dependence, all loops must be executed sequentially. To save area, FP operators can be shared among loops. A total of two FP adders and two FP multipliers are needed for all the loops to be pipelined.

Table 1: FP Ops in DWT (Fully Pipelined)

|  | L1 | L2 | L3 | L4 |
|---|---|---|---|---|
| FP operations | $2\oplus, 1\otimes$ | $2\oplus, 1\otimes$ | $2\oplus, 2\otimes$ | $2\oplus, 2\otimes$ |
| Loop II | 1 | 1 | 1 | 1 |
| FP operators | 2+ , 1* | 2+ , 1* | 2+ , 2* | 2+ , 2* |

Fig. 2 illustrates the execution graph of all the FP operators. One FP multiplier is idle during the execution of loops L1 and L2. Considering replication to exploit coarse-grained parallelism, low area utilization will likely degrade the overall performance.

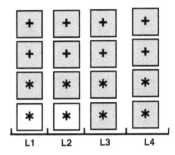

Figure 2: Fully Pipelined DWT Implementation

To improve the utilization of FP multipliers, we can have an alternative implementation that instantiate only one FP multiplier. Under such circumstances, loops L3 and L4 cannot be fully pipelined due to resource constraints. Table 2 shows the FP operations, loop II and FP operators under this configuration. A total of two FP adders and one FP multipliers are needed.

Table 2: FP Ops in DWT (Non-fully Pipelined)

|  | L1 | L2 | L3 | L4 |
|---|---|---|---|---|
| FP operations | $2\oplus, 1\otimes$ | $2\oplus, 1\otimes$ | $2\oplus, 2\otimes$ | $2\oplus, 2\otimes$ |
| Loop II | 1 | 1 | 2 | 2 |
| FP operators | 2+ , 1* | 2+ , 1* | 1+ , 1* | 1+ , 1* |

Fig. 3 illustrates the execution graph of all the FP operators in the non-fully pipelined scenario. The execution time L3 and L4 will be longer compared to the case of Fig. 2 due to the larger loop $II$. However, with $II = 2$, each fully-pipelined FP adder and multiplier can be virtualized to support two FP operations in each loop iteration. In this case, one FP adder is always idle during the execution of L3 and L4.

We use Xilinx Virtex-7 XC7V585T FPGA device as a test platform to evaluate the throughput of the two implementations. 512*512 image size is used in the experiments. Experimental results are shown in Table 3. Area and critical path data are reported by Vivado after place and route. Cycle data are reported by Vivado HLS RTL-level simulation. All performance numbers are normalized against the performance of the single replica performance of the fully-pipelined implementation. From the table, we observe that the single-replica performance of the fully-pipelined version is

Table 3: Experimental Results for DWT

| Implementation | LUT | FF | DSP | Cycles | CP(ns) | Replicas | Nomalized $\frac{Perf}{Replica}$ | Nomalized System Perf |
|---|---|---|---|---|---|---|---|---|
| Fully | 2855 | 1985 | 28 | 590337 | 8.800 | 45 | 1 | 45 |
| NonFully | 2716 | 1830 | 17 | 851457 | 8.821 | 74 | 0.71 | 50.7 |

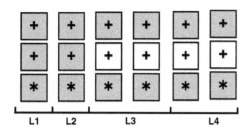

L1    L2         L3              L4

Figure 3: Non-fully Pipelined DWT Implementation

29% higher than the non-fully-pipelined version. However, with $74/45 - 1 = 64\%$ more replicas, the total performance of the non-fully-pipelined version is 13.7% higher than the fully-pipelined version after replication.

The relative efficiency comparison between the two DWT implementations will depend on many factors, including the area of both FP operators, the area of other components, trip counts of all loops and the available resource in the target device. In this paper we formulate the resource-aware throughput optimization problem with all these variables and propose some efficient solutions to solve the problem.

## 3. PROBLEM FORMULATION

From the motivational example, we can see that each loop in the accelerator can have different implementations with different resource usage and performance. Some resource can be shared among loop kernels. The challenge is to find the design with optimal performance under a given area constraint with resource sharing. In this section we will provide a formulation of the problem. The resource-aware throughput optimization problem can be formulated as:

| | | |
|---|---|---|
| Maximize | $D * Performance_{PerReplica}$ | (1) |
| Subject to | $D * Area_{PerReplica} \leq Area_{available}$ | (2) |

where $Performance_{PerReplica}$ and $Area_{PerReplica}$ represent the performance and area of single replica and $D$ are the number of replicas to be duplicated at coarse-grained level.

With resource sharing, the total area of the entire accelerator will probably be less than the sum of each loop kernels.

### 3.1 Shareable Component Candidate

Logic components (such as operators) can be shared among different statements/loops to save area. However, multiplexers introduced by component sharing is nontrivial on the FPGA platform. For example, the area, delay and power data of a 32-to-1 multiplexer are almost equivalent to an 18-bit multiplier in modern FPGA designs [16]. Therefore, not all components will benefit from resource sharing. The state-of-the-art HLS tools will only share the components with enough complexity compared to the I/O multiplexers, or *shareable component candidate*.

DEFINITION 1 (SHAREABLE COMPONENT CANDIDATE). *A Shareable Component Candidate is a component whose area is at least δ times larger than a 32-bit 8-to-1 multiplexer.*

$$\frac{Area_{Component}}{Area_{mux}} \geq \delta$$

On Xilinx Virtex-7 FPGAs, a 32-bit 8-to-1 multiplexer will take 96 LUTs and δ is set to 10 in our experiment. Table 4 shows the estimated area consumption of some shareable components on Virtex-7 FPGAs.

Table 4: Area of Example Shareable Component Candidates

| | LUT | FF | DSP |
|---|---|---|---|
| DP $\pm$ | 781 | 445 | 3 |
| DP $*$ | 203 | 299 | 11 |
| DP / | 3242 | 2230 | 0 |
| $\sqrt{x}$ | 1919 | 1303 | 0 |
| $\frac{1}{x}$ | 246 | 440 | 14 |
| $>$ | 113 | 130 | 0 |
| $sin$ | 9662 | 2597 | 17 |

Integer add/substract operations are not shareable component candidates.

DEFINITION 2 (LOOP SHAREABLE LOAD VECTOR). *Suppose that there are M types of shareable component candidates ($R_1$, $R_2$, ..., $R_M$) in an application, the shareable load vector of a loop $L_k$ is a vector $\langle s_{1,k}, s_{2,k}, ..., s_{j,k}, ..., s_{M,k} \rangle$ where $s_{j,k}$ is the number of shareable component candidate $R_j$ in loop $L_k$.*

EXAMPLE 1. *The shareable load vectors of loops L1 and L2 in Figure 1 are $\langle 2, 1 \rangle$. The shareable load vectors of loops L3 and L4 in Figure 1 are $\langle 2, 2 \rangle$.*

DEFINITION 3 (LOOP RESOURCE ALLOCATION VECTOR). *Suppose that there are M types of shareable component candidates ($R_1, R_2, ..., R_M$) in an application, the resource allocation vector of a loop $L_k$ is a vector $\langle a_{1,k}, a_{2,k}, ..., a_{j,k}, ..., a_{M,k} \rangle$ where $a_{j,k}$ is the number of shareable component candidates $R_j$ instantiated for loop $L_k$.*

EXAMPLE 2. *The resource allocation vectors of loops L1 and L2 in Figure 1 of the non-pipelined version are $\langle 1, 1 \rangle$. The resource allocation vectors of loops L3 and L4 in Figure 1 of the non-pipelined version are $\langle 2, 1 \rangle$.*

DEFINITION 4 (TOTAL RESOURCE ALLOCATION VECTOR). *Suppose that there are N Loops ($L_1, L_2, ..., L_N$) in an application, the resource allocation vector of the entire accelerator is a vector $\langle a_1, a_2, ..., a_j, ..., a_M \rangle$ where $a_j$ is the number of shareable component candidates $R_j$ instantiated for the entire accelerator.*

EXAMPLE 3. *The* resource allocation vector *of the fully-pipelined DWT accelerator is* $\langle 2, 2 \rangle$. *The* resource allocation vector *of the non-fully-pipelined DWT accelerator is* $\langle 2, 1 \rangle$.

PROPERTY 1. $\forall 1 \leq j \leq M, \max_{k=1}^{N} a_{j,k} \leq a_j \leq \sum_{k=1}^{N} a_{j,k}$.

The total number of shareable component candidates instantiated in the accelerator should be no more than the total number of components instantiated in each loop.

## 3.2 Performance and Area Estimation

In this section we describe the performance and area estimation methodology adopted in the paper.

Loop pipelining [17] is a key optimization technique in high-level synthesis. Using the technique, parallelism across loop iterations can be exploited by initiating the next iteration of the loop before the completion of the current iteration. Operations from several iterations are overlapped by loop pipelining to decrease the total execution cycles of the entire loop. The throughput achieved is limited both by resource constraints and data dependencies in the application.

$$Cycle_k = II_k * (TC_k - 1) + Dth_k \tag{3}$$

where $Cycle_k, II_k, TC_k, Dth_k$ are the total execution cycle, pipeline initiation interval, trip count and pipeline depth of loop $k$ respectively.

The total execution cycle of a pipelined loop can be estimated using Eq. (3). With given input data, the trip count of each loop ($TC_k$ in Eq. 3) is fixed. The minimum initiation interval $II_k$ is a function of the resource allocation vector $\langle a_{1,k}, a_{2,k}, ..., a_{M,k} \rangle$ defined by Eq. (4). Minimal $II_k$ is also constrained by loop-carried dependence or memory port conflict, as shown in Eq.(5). Loop depth $Dth_k$ is also affected by the resource allocation vector, but in this paper we made a simplification by treating it as a constant. When with non-trivial trip counts, the estimation could be high accurate, as shown in Sec. 6.

$$\forall 1 \leq j \leq M, II_k * a_{j,k} \geq s_{j,k} \tag{4}$$
$$\forall 1 \leq k \leq N, II_k \geq II_k^{Min} \tag{5}$$

The area consumption of a loop can be estimated by accumulating the areas of shareable and non-shareable component candidates. Multiplexers for resource sharing are non-shareable component candidates. However, since the area of shareable component candidates are significantly larger than the multiplexers by definition, in this paper, we made a simplification by assuming that the area of non-shareable component candidates is irrelevant to the resource allocation vectors. In Sec. 6 we will validate these assumptions by comparing the estimated results and synthesized results with real examples.

Suppose the resource allocation vector in the entire accelerator is $\langle a_1, a_2, ..., a_M \rangle$, the total area of the application can be estimated by:

$$Area = \sum_{k=1}^{N} Area_k^{NS} + \sum_{j=1}^{M} (Area_j^S * a_j) \tag{6}$$

where $Area_k^{NS}$ is the area of non-shareable component candidates in loop $k$ and $Area_j^S$ is the area of shareable component candidate $j$.

For FPGA devices, area consumption can be represented by a vector $\langle DSP, LUT, FF \rangle$, and Equation 6 can be formulated as:

$$DSP = \sum_{k=1}^{N} DSP_k^{NS} + \sum_{j=1}^{M} (DSP_j^S * a_j) \tag{7}$$

$$LUT = \sum_{k=1}^{N} LUT_k^{NS} + \sum_{j=1}^{M} (LUT_j^S * a_j) \tag{8}$$

$$FF = \sum_{k=1}^{N} FF_k^{NS} + \sum_{j=1}^{M} (FF_j^S * a_j) \tag{9}$$

## 3.3 Accelerators with Total Inter-Loop Dependency

If all loops in an accelerator have to be executed in sequence due to dependence, the total execution cycles can be estimated by accumulating the cycles of individual loops, as shown in Eq. (10). In such a case, all the shareable component candidates can be reused among loops, and the total shareable component candidates can be calculated by Eq. (11).

$$Cycle = \sum_{k=1}^{N} Cycle_k \tag{10}$$

$$a_j = max_{k=1}^{N} a_{j,k} \tag{11}$$

With Eq. (3) to Eq. (11), resource-constrained performance optimization with resource sharing among loops for an accelerator with sequential loops can be formulated as:

Maximize
$$Replica/Cycle \tag{12}$$

Subject to
$$DSP = \sum_{k=1}^{N} DSP_k^{NS} + \sum_{j=1}^{M} (DSP_j^S * a_j) \tag{13}$$
$$DSP * Replica \leq DSP_{Avail.} \tag{14}$$
$$LUT = \sum_{k=1}^{N} LUT_k^{NS} + \sum_{j=1}^{M} (LUT_j^S * a_j) \tag{15}$$
$$LUT * Replica \leq LUT_{Avail.} \tag{16}$$
$$FF = \sum_{k=1}^{N} FF_k^{NS} + \sum_{j=1}^{M} (FF_j^S * a_j) \tag{17}$$
$$FF * Replica \leq FF_{Avail.} \tag{18}$$
$$\forall 1 \leq j \leq M, \forall 1 \leq k \leq N, II_k * a_{j,k} \geq s_{j,k} \tag{19}$$
$$\forall 1 \leq k \leq N, Cycle_k = II_k * (TC_k - 1) + Dth_k \tag{20}$$
$$\forall Chain\{L_{t_1}, ..., L_{t_L}\} \subseteq \mathcal{P}, Cycle \geq \sum_{t=1}^{L} Cycle_{t_k} \tag{21}$$
$$\forall Antichain\{L_{t_1}, L_{t_2}, ..., L_{t_L}\} \subseteq \mathcal{P}, a_j \geq \sum_{t=1}^{L} a_{j,t_k} \tag{22}$$

where $D, Cycle, Cycle_k, a_j, a_{j,k}, II_k$ are integer variables, $Area$ is a rational variable, and $Area_k^{NS}, Area_j^S, Area_{Avail.}, s_{j,k}, II_k^{Min}, TC_k, Dth_k$ are constant values.

## 3.4 Accelerators with Partial Inter-Loop Dependency

Multiple loops without data dependence can be parallelized by HLS tools to improve performance. In this section, we will discuss the resource-constrained performance optimization for more general cases with arbitrary dependence between loops.

Since dependence relations between loops are reflexive, antisymmetric and transitive, they can be defined as a *partial order*. The *partially ordered set*, or *poset* for short, defined by loop dependence information is referred to the *loop dependence poset* $\mathcal{P}$.

DEFINITION 5 (COMPARABLE). *For any two elements a and b of a partially ordered set P, if $a \leq b$ or $b \leq a$, then a and b are* comparable. *Otherwise they are* incomparable.

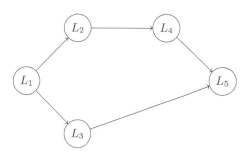

Figure 4: Example Loop Dependence Graph

In Fig. 4, $L_1$ are $L_2$ and comparable with $L_2 < L_1$; $L_2$ and $L_3$ are incomparable.

DEFINITION 6 (CHAIN). *A chain in a poset P is a subset $C \subseteq P$ such that any two elements in C are comparable.*

$\{L_1, L_2, L_4, L_5\}$ is a chain in Fig. 4.

DEFINITION 7 (ANTICHAIN). *An antichain in a poset P is a subset $A \subseteq P$ such that any two elements in A are incomparable.*

$\{L_2, L_3\}$ is an antichain in Fig. 4.

If loops in an accelerator can be parallel, the total execution cycles of the accelerator can be estimated by the maximum weighted chain of the dependence poset $\mathcal{P}$, as shown in Eq. (23).

$$\forall \text{Chain } \{L_{t_1}, L_{t_2}, ..., L_{t_P}\} \subseteq \mathcal{P}, Cycle \geq \sum_{t=1}^{P} Cycle_{t_k} \quad (23)$$

Under such circumstances, loops in an antichain may execute in parallel. Therefore, loops in an antichain will not share components with conservative scheduling. The total number of shareable component candidates can be calculated by the maximum weighted antichain of the dependence poset $\mathcal{P}$, as shown in Eq.(24).

$$\forall \text{Antichain } \{L_{t_1}, L_{t_2}, ..., L_{t_P}\} \subseteq \mathcal{P}, a_j \geq \sum_{t=1}^{P} a_{j,t_k} \quad (24)$$

Area-constrained performance optimization with resource sharing for an accelerator with arbitrary loop dependence can be formulated using Eq. (12) to (20), (23) and (24).

## 4. EFFICIENT SOLUTIONS

In Sec. 3, we formulated the problem of resource-constraint performance optimization with resource sharing. In the formulation, the objective and some constraints (12, 18 and 19) are not linear or posynomials (17, 20-24). Therefore, the problem cannot be directly solved by integer linear programming (ILP) or mixed integer geometric programming. In this section we will describe how to solve the problem with different approaches.

### 4.1 Enumeration-based Approach

The simplest approach to solving the problem is through enumeration. The initiation intervals of each loop $II_k$ can be bounded using Eq. (25). Given loop initiation interval $II_k$, the shareable component candidates allocated $a_{j,k}$ can be calculated using Eq.(26).

The total execution cycle and area can be estimated use Eq. (3), (6), (23) and (24).

$$\forall 1 \leq k \leq N,$$
$$II_k^{LB} \leq II_k \leq II_k^{UB} = max(II_k^{LB}, max_{j=1}^{M} s_{j,k}) \quad (25)$$

$$\forall 1 \leq j \leq M, \forall 1 \leq k \leq N, a_{j,k} = \lceil \frac{s_{j,k}}{II_k} \rceil \quad (26)$$

Note that not all $II$s in the range given by Eq. (25) will possibly generate solutions with Pareto-optimal performance under resource-constraint. Some values can be easily filtered out with local loop information.

If $II_k^{(1)} < II_k^{(2)}$ and $\forall 1 \leq j \leq M, \lceil \frac{s_{j,k}}{II_k^{(1)}} \rceil = \lceil \frac{s_{j,k}}{II_k^{(2)}} \rceil$ then $II_k^{(2)}$ is not a candidate II for Pareto-optimal solution.

EXAMPLE 4. *Given a loop with shareable load vector $s = \langle 16, 5 \rangle$ and $II_{LB} = 3$, the candidate IIs for Pareto-optimal solution and allocated component vector are listed as in the following table:*

| II | 3 | 4 | 5 | 6 | 8 | 16 |
|---|---|---|---|---|---|---|
| Resource | $\langle 6, 2 \rangle$ | $\langle 4, 2 \rangle$ | $\langle 4, 1 \rangle$ | $\langle 3, 1 \rangle$ | $\langle 2, 1 \rangle$ | $\langle 1, 1 \rangle$ |

*Only 6 different IIs out of 14 possible values can serve as candidates for Pareto-optimal solution, while other II variants can be filtered out with only local loop information.*

With the increase of loops and shareable component candidates, the simple brute-force enumeration approach may not scale well. Instead of enumerating all legal transformations in a brute-force approach, the features of resource-constrained performance optimization can be used to prune suboptimal partial results to greatly reduce the computation complexity of finding optimal solutions for large designs. In this section we propose an efficient branch-and-bound algorithm for the problem considering the weights of different loops and the interaction between partial loop $II$ selection results and maximum performance.

We observe that the execution cycle of a loop is proportional to its trip count. Therefore, design choices of loops with larger trip counts will have a larger impact on the overall resource-constrained performance. Based on this observation, we first sort the loops in the entire accelerator according to their trip counts and travel the enumeration tree branch by branch from the loop with the largest trip count to the loop with smallest trip count.

For each unenumerated loop $L_k$, we can estimate the lower bounds and upper bounds of area and execution cycle with Eq. (27) - (30), where $II_k^{UB}$ is defined in Eq. (25). The lower bound of the performance at branch B is calculated by $II$ and $a_j$ of the enumerated loops and $Cycle^{LB}$ and $a_j^{LB}$ of the unenumerated loops. The upper bound of the performance at branch B is calculated by $II$ and $a_j$ of the enumerated loops and $Cycle^{UB}$ and $a_j^{UB}$ of the unenumerated loops.

$$a_{j,k}^{LB} = (s_{j,k} \geq 1) \quad (27)$$
$$Cycle_k^{LB} = II_k^{LB} * (TC_k - 1) + Dth_k \quad (28)$$
$$a_{j,k}^{UB} = s_{j,k} \quad (29)$$
$$Cycle_k^{UB} = II_k^{UB} * (TC_k - 1) + Dth_k \quad (30)$$

We can prove that the performance range of a child branch is always covered by that of its parent branch: $LB_{Parent} \leq LB_{Child} \leq$

$UB_{Child} \leq UB_{Parent}$. If two branches have non-overlapped performance ranges, we can prune the branch with smaller performance and all its sub-branches without losing optimality.

## 4.2 Integer Linear Programming

Given an accelerator with $N$ loops and the number of candidate $II$s of each loop represented as $C_1, C_2, ..., C_N$, the total enumeration number is $\prod_{k=1}^{N} C_k$. The maximum enumeration number in all our experiments will not exceed $10^4$ and enumeration-based approach will finish within a second. Therefore, we just use the enumeration-based approach in our experiments. In this section, we show that the problem can be converted into an ILP optimization by parameterizing some variables and introducing extra binary variables, which could help on large scale problems.

The duplication factor $D$ can be bounded by Eq. (31).

$$D \leq \frac{Area_{Avail.}}{(\sum_{k=1}^{N} Area_k^{NS} + \sum_{j=1}^{M} Area_j^{S})} \quad (31)$$

For practical problem on the current platform, $D$ is typically less than 100. Under such an assumption, we can parameterize the duplication factor $D$ as a constant value and use an outer loop to enumerate $D$ for the global optimal solution.

Then we introduce a set of binary variables $\delta_{j,k,l,m}$, where $j$ is the type of the shareable component candidates ($1 \leq j \leq M$), $k$ is the loop index ($1 \leq k \leq N$), $l$ is the instance index of the shareable component candidate $j$ in loop $k$ ($1 \leq l \leq s_{j,k}$) and the component is scheduled to cycle $m$. With modulo scheduling used by loop pipelining, $1 \leq m \leq II_k^{UB}$, where $II_k^{UB}$ is bounded by Eq. (25). $\delta_{j,k,l,m} = 1$ indicates that the $l$-th type-$j$ shareable component candidate in loop $k$ is scheduled to cycle $m$ under modulo scheduling.

With these binary variables, we can replace the non-linear constraint Eq. (19) with a set of linear constraints, shown in Eq. (39) - (43). Eq. (40) describes a shareable component candidate is scheduled to one and only one cycle with modulo scheduling. Together with Eq. (40), Eq. (39) declares $\delta_{j,k,l,m}$ as binary variables. Eq. (41) converts resource constraint to an equivalent condition where at most $a_{j,k}$ type-$j$ shareable component candidates can be scheduled to the same cycle for loop $k$. $\gamma_{j,k,m}$ in Eq. (42) equals to 1 means that at least one shareable component candidate $j$ in loop $k$ is scheduled to cycle $m$. Therefor, $II_k$ will be at least the total number of cycles with $\gamma_{j,k,m} = 1$, as shown in Eq. (43).

---

Minimize

$$Cycle/D \quad (32)$$

Subject to

$$Area = \sum_{k=1}^{N} Area_k^{NS} + \sum_{j=1}^{M} (Area_j^{S} * a_j) \quad (33)$$

$$Area * D \leq Area_{Avail.} \quad (34)$$

$$\forall 1 \leq k \leq N, II_k \geq II_k^{Min} \quad (35)$$

$$\forall 1 \leq k \leq N, Cycle_k = II_k * (TC_k - 1) + Dth_k \quad (36)$$

$$\forall Chain \{L_{t_1}, ..., L_{t_P}\} \subseteq \mathcal{P}, Cycle \geq \sum_{t=1}^{P} Cycle_{t_k} \quad (37)$$

$$\forall Antichain \{L_{t_1}, ..., L_{t_P}\} \subseteq \mathcal{P}, a_j \geq \sum_{t=1}^{P} a_{j,t_k} \quad (38)$$

$$\forall j, k, l, m, \delta_{j,k,l,m} \geq 0 \quad (39)$$

$$\forall j, k, l, \sum_{m=1}^{II_k^{UB}} \delta_{j,k,l,m} = 1 \quad (40)$$

$$\forall j, k, m, \sum_{l=1}^{s_{j,k}} \delta_{j,k,l,m} \leq a_{j,k} \quad (41)$$

$$\forall j, k, l, m, \gamma_{j,k,m} \geq \delta_{j,k,l,m} \quad (42)$$

$$\forall j, k, \sum_{m=1}^{II_k^{UB}} \gamma_{j,k,m} \leq II_k \quad (43)$$

---

where $Cycle$, $Cycle_k$, $a_j$, $a_{j,k}$, $II_k$, $\delta_{j,k,l,m}$, $\gamma_{j,k,m}$ are integer variables, $Area$ is a rational variable, and $Area_k^{NS}$, $Area_j^{S}$, $Area_{Avail.}$, $s_{j,k}$, $II_k^{Min}$, $TC_k$, $Dth_k$ are constant values. $D$ is treated as a constant value and an outer loop is used to enumerate possible duplication factors for global optimal solution.

With such techniques, the problem formulation can be converted to a set of ILP optimizations. The number of binary variables introduced is less than the total number of shared components in the entire accelerator multiplied by the maximum loop $II$ defined by Eq. (25).

## 5. IMPLEMENTATION ISSUES

In this section, we will discuss some implementation related issues about performance optimization with resource constraint in HLS.

### 5.1 Computing Load Information Extraction

The first implementation issue is how to extract the shareable component information from the source code. It is relatively easy to detect whether there is a certain type of components in a certain loop, but to get the exact number is nontrivial. Direct syntactic extraction may be inaccurate due to the optimizations by HLS tools such as common subexpression elimination. Implementing a customized lightweight HLS tool [18] is one approach, but it is time-consuming and difficult to match perfectly to the result of a commercial HLS tool.

In this section, we will demonstrate how to extract the precise shareable component information by profiling the transformed/instrumented input code using HLS tools.

We first preprocess the input code by removing loop-carried dependence with HLS directives. Then we eliminate array port conflicts by replacing each distinct array reference with a temporal volatile scalar. The transformed code will have a different function with the original code, but the shareable component information remains unchanged.

Then, for each type of shareable component, we add HLS resource constraint directives to instantiate one instance of the component and perform HLS on the preprocessed code to obtain loop $II$ from the HLS report. In such cases, the number of shareable components in each loop is equal to the $II$ of the loop.

### 5.2 Trip Count Calculation

The second implementation issue is how to obtain the trip count of each loop. For simple loops with constant bounds, trip count of the loop can be calculated and reported by HLS tools. For loops with non-constant but affine loop bounds,[1] trip count of the loop can be calculated by integer point counting [19] of iterator polytopes. For a general HLS-synthesizable program, trip counts can be collected by executing the input code that has been instrumented with trip count calculation statements. Program slicing [20] can be used to reduce the profiled program to containing only statements that impact the control-flow.

### 5.3 Parallelization and Resource Sharing between Loops

In the Vivado HLS [2], coarse-grained parallelization is explored at function-level instead of loop-level. Loop-level parallelization is not directly supported but can be achieved by capsuling the parallel loops into functions. However, for scalability consideration,

---

[1]The set of iterations of these loop bodies can be exactly captured using inequalities on the values of the loop iterators and program constants.

resource sharing in Vivado HLS is performed within a function. Resource sharing between functions is disabled. These strategies are incompatible with our assumptions that paralleled loops can still share resources with their common preceding or succeeding loops.

Our current implementation is to first capsule the parallel loops into functions automatically and then modify the RTL generated by HLS for resource sharing between modules.

# 6. EXPERIMENTAL RESULTS

In this section we present our experimental results using a set of computation kernels and applications. We first use Segmentation as case study to illustrate details of the proposed algorithm. Then, we show the performance improvements of our proposed optimization technique with extensive benchmarks.

Although our algorithm is applicable to both ASIC and FPGA designs, we chose FPGA as the target device in this work because of the availability of downstream behavioral synthesis and implementation tools. The Xilinx Virtex-7 XC7V585T FPGA device is selected as the target hardware platform. The Xilinx Vivado HLS Suite 2013.4 is used to perform the HLS and physical implementation flow. Techniques proposed in the paper are also be applicable to other high-level synthesis tools e.g. LegUp [21].

## 6.1 Segmentation: A Case Study

Table 5: Program Information of Segmentation

|    | $\pm$ | $*$ | $/$ | $\sqrt{x}$ | $\frac{1}{x}$ | $>$ | $II_{LB}$ | TripCount |
|----|----|----|----|----|----|----|----|----|
| L1 | 3  | 1  | 1  | 0  | 0  | 0  | 1  | 32768 |
| L2 | 6  | 3  | 0  | 0  | 0  | 0  | 2  | 29791 |
| L3 | 5  | 7  | 1  | 1  | 1  | 1  | 1  | 32768 |
| L4 | 3  | 6  | 0  | 0  | 0  | 0  | 2  | 29791 |
| L5 | 16 | 2  | 1  | 0  | 1  | 2  | 5  | 32768 |

In this section, we use a more complicated benchmark Segmentation algorithm as a case study to demonstrate details in the proposed algorithm. Table 5 shows the basic information of the program. There are five loops and six types of shareable component candidates in the design. Some loops (L2, L4, L5) can not be fully pipelined because of loop-carried dependence or BRAM port constraint. The computation load vectors and trip count of each loop are specified in the table.

In Sec. 3, we assume that loop depths and the area of non-shareable component candidates will not change among different implementations. Table 6 is used to demonstrate the accuracy of the performance and area model against HLS results. From the table, we can observe that among the FPGA area tuple, DSP can always be precisely estimated. The error rate of lookup table (LUT) estimation is under 5%, while the error rate of flip-flop (FF) estimation can range up to 13.79%. The most possible reason is that pipeline registers will change significantly with loop $II$s. However, in all the implementations of Segmentation and all other benchmarks used in the paper, FF will never be the scarcest resource. Therefore, as shown in the table, we can always model the number of replicas $D$ with the proposed area model. The performance model is also very accurate, with a maximum error rate of 0.001% compared to RTL-level simulation by HLS tools.

Table 7 illustrates all the Pareto-optimal implementations of Segmentation with different $II$s and resource sharing vectors. Performance numbers are normalized against the performance of the first

Table 6: Error Analysis of Area and Performance Model

| #  | LUT (%) | FF (%) | DSP (%) | Cycle (%) | Dup (%) |
|----|----|----|----|----|----|
| 1  | 0    | 0     | 0 | 0       | 0 |
| 2  | 1.54 | 5.97  | 0 | 0       | 0 |
| 3  | 0.68 | 7.52  | 0 | 0       | 0 |
| 4  | 1.14 | 9.09  | 0 | 0.00042 | 0 |
| 5  | 1.14 | 7.78  | 0 | 0       | 0 |
| 6  | 2.27 | 6     | 0 | 0.00097 | 0 |
| 7  | 1.38 | 7.6   | 0 | 0.00089 | 0 |
| 8  | 1.87 | 9.26  | 0 | 0.00118 | 0 |
| 9  | 0.47 | 8.61  | 0 | 0.00055 | 0 |
| 10 | 4.02 | 8.53  | 0 | 0       | 0 |
| 11 | 2.69 | 10.3  | 0 | 0.00016 | 0 |
| 12 | 2.24 | 9.6   | 0 | 0.00048 | 0 |
| 13 | 0.41 | 13.79 | 0 | 0.00019 | 0 |
| 14 | 0.97 | 13.61 | 0 | 0       | 0 |

implementation. In the first implementation, single-replica performance is maximized by minimizing the $II$s of all loops. However, with the largest single-replica, the smallest number of replicas will be generated. With the increase of loop $II$s, less shareable component candidates will be allocated. Area consumption of a single replica is reduced at the cost of worse single-replica performance. Among all 14 implementations, implementation 4 achieves the optimal tradeoff between performance and area consumption. It has the highest performance/area ratio and the largest throughput under the area constraint of the FPGA device after module duplication.

## 6.2 Benchmark Description

In addition to DWT and Segmentation, we use six other real-world computation kernels and applications to evaluate the proposed throughput optimization algorithm. FDTD, MM and Syrk are selected from PolyBench/C 3.2[22]. Deno, IMin and EMin are extracted from X-Ray CT image pipeline algorithms. A description of each benchmark can be found in Table 8. The number of loops ($N$), types of shareable component candidates ($M$) and total number of shareable component candidates in the entire code ($\sum s_{j,k}$) of each benchmark are enumerated in the table. Some loops in IMin and FDTD can be executed in parallel. Loops in other benchmarks must be executed in sequence due to inter-loop dependence. Double precision floating point is used as the default data type in computations, as in the original code. Due to the relative small-size of the benchmarks, branch-and-bound solutions are used in the experiments.

## 6.3 Experimental Results

Table 9 compiles the experimental results for all benchmarks. In the Baseline implementation, the smallest loop $II$s are specified to achieve best performance for a single replica, then the replica is duplicated within the FPGA device capacity. We then enumerate all possible implementations with different $II$s and allocated shareable component candidates to find the optimal solution with the best overall performance under the area constraint of the FPGA device. HLS directives "#pragma HLS allocation instances = ComponentName limit=xx operation/ function" and "#pragma HLS pipeline II=yy" are inserted to the program to guide Vivado HLS tool to achieve optimal resource allocation and pipeline II generated by our proposed algorithm. Then Xilinx Vivado Design Suite is used to synthesize the transformed code to bitstream and perform RTL-level simulation to generate all the performance

Table 7: Design Space Exploration for Image Segmentation

| No. | Operators | | | | | | Initiation Intervals | | | | | Area | | | Cycles | #(Replica) | Performance |
|---|---|---|---|---|---|---|---|---|---|---|---|---|---|---|---|---|---|
| | $\pm$ | * | / | $\sqrt{x}$ | $\frac{1}{x}$ | > | L1 | L2 | L3 | L4 | L5 | LUTs | FFs | DSPs | | | |
| 1 | 5 | 7 | 1 | 1 | 1 | 1 | 1 | 2 | 1 | 2 | 5 | 16143 | 12801 | 106 | 348783 | 11 | 1 |
| 2 | 4 | 4 | 1 | 1 | 1 | 1 | 1 | 2 | 2 | 2 | 5 | 14983 | 11012 | 70 | 381551 | 18 | 1.496 |
| 3 | 4 | 3 | 1 | 1 | 1 | 1 | 1 | 2 | 3 | 2 | 5 | 14649 | 10640 | 59 | 414319 | 21 | 1.607 |
| 4 | 4 | 2 | 1 | 1 | 1 | 1 | 1 | 2 | 4 | 3 | 5 | 14512 | 10277 | 48 | 476876 | 25 | 1.662 |
| 5 | 4 | 1 | 1 | 1 | 1 | 1 | 1 | 3 | 7 | 6 | 5 | 14307 | 10189 | 37 | 694346 | 25 | 1.142 |
| 6 | 3 | 4 | 1 | 1 | 1 | 1 | 1 | 2 | 2 | 2 | 6 | 14296 | 10589 | 67 | 414315 | 18 | 1.378 |
| 7 | 3 | 3 | 1 | 1 | 1 | 1 | 1 | 2 | 3 | 2 | 6 | 13962 | 10218 | 56 | 447083 | 22 | 1.56 |
| 8 | 3 | 2 | 1 | 1 | 1 | 1 | 1 | 2 | 4 | 3 | 6 | 13825 | 9854 | 45 | 509640 | 26 | 1.618 |
| 9 | 3 | 1 | 1 | 1 | 1 | 1 | 1 | 3 | 7 | 6 | 6 | 13300 | 9702 | 34 | 727110 | 27 | 1.177 |
| 10 | 2 | 3 | 1 | 1 | 1 | 1 | 2 | 3 | 3 | 2 | 8 | 13532 | 9721 | 53 | 575182 | 23 | 1.268 |
| 11 | 2 | 2 | 1 | 1 | 1 | 1 | 2 | 3 | 4 | 3 | 8 | 13139 | 9357 | 42 | 637742 | 27 | 1.342 |
| 12 | 2 | 1 | 1 | 1 | 1 | 1 | 2 | 6 | 7 | 3 | 8 | 12870 | 9208 | 31 | 825422 | 28 | 1.076 |
| 13 | 1 | 2 | 1 | 1 | 1 | 1 | 3 | 6 | 5 | 3 | 16 | 11955 | 8679 | 39 | 1054796 | 30 | 0.902 |
| 14 | 1 | 1 | 1 | 1 | 1 | 1 | 3 | 6 | 7 | 6 | 16 | 11688 | 8491 | 28 | 1209703 | 31 | 0.813 |

Table 8: Benchmark Description

| Name | Description | $N$ | $M$ | $\sum s_{j,k}$ | Dep |
|---|---|---|---|---|---|
| Segmentation | Image Segmentation | 5 | 6 | 61 | Sequential |
| Denoise | Rician Noise Removal | 2 | 6 | 56 | Sequential |
| DWT | Discrete Wavelet Transform | 4 | 2 | 10 | Sequential |
| Image Minimization | X-Ray Image Minimization | 10 | 2 | 47 | Parallel |
| Edge Minimization | X-Ray Edge Minimization | 3 | 4 | 37 | Sequential |
| FDTD-2D | Finite Diff. Time Domain | 4 | 2 | 11 | Parallel |
| Matrix Multiplication | Matrix Multiplication | 3 | 2 | 6 | Sequential |
| Syrk | Symmetric Rank-k Operations | 2 | 2 | 6 | Sequential |

numbers. The entire experiment was implemented by a push-button flow shown in Figure 5.

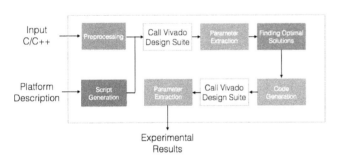

Figure 5: Experimental Flow

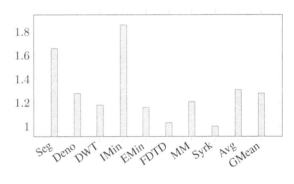

Figure 6: Performance Speedup

Compared to the base implementation, the speedup of optimal solution found by the proposed design space exploration algorithm ranges from 1X (Syrk) to 1.85X (IMin), with an average of 1.31X and the geometric mean as 1.28X, shown in Fig. 6. In Syrk, the traditional optimize-and-duplicate approach already achieves the optimal solution in terms of performance-area density.

The loop initiation intervals of the baseline and optimal implementations are shown in Table 10. From the table, we can see that except for Syrk, in all other benchmark designs, higher $II$s in some loops will better overall throughput after exploiting coarse-grained performance through duplication. Considering the moderate scale of the benchmark applications, branch-and-bound solution is se-

lected in the experiment. The runtime of the entire optimization algorithm is from 12.9s to 103s, as shown in Table 10.

For some benchmarks used in this paper, the outer-most loop is dependence-free. Another approach is to implement the designs with pipelined outer-most loop. The proposed inter-module sharing approach may not be beneficial when the task will be executed repeated in a pipeline fashion (which may not be always possible). For the DWT case where piplining outer-most loop is possible, the pipelined approach will outputform the proposed resource-sharing approach. This could be an interesting future work.

Table 9: Experimental Results

| Benchmark | Implemtation | LUT | FF | DSP | CP(ns) | Cycles | #(Replicas) | Performance |
|---|---|---|---|---|---|---|---|---|
| Seg | Baseline | 16143 | 12801 | 106 | 8.8 | 348783 | 11 | 1 |
| | Optimized | 14512 | 10277 | 48 | 8.821 | 476876 | 25 | 1.66 |
| | Comparison(%) | -10.1 | -19.7 | -54.7 | 0.2 | 36.7 | 127.3 | 66.2 |
| Deno | Baseline | 15330 | 11590 | 85 | 8.171 | 28849 | 14 | 1 |
| | Optimized | 12516 | 9514 | 54 | 8.194 | 37047 | 23 | 1.28 |
| | Comparison(%) | -18.4 | -17.9 | -36.5 | 0.3 | 28.4 | 64.3 | 27.9 |
| DWT | Baseline | 2855 | 1985 | 28 | 8.253 | 590337 | 45 | 1 |
| | Optimized | 2716 | 1830 | 17 | 8.091 | 851457 | 74 | 1.14 |
| | Comparison(%) | -4.9 | -7.8 | -39.3 | -2 | 44.2 | 64.4 | 14 |
| IMin | Baseline | 8969 | 6691 | 56 | 8.701 | 38196620 | 22 | 1 |
| | Optimized | 5437 | 4387 | 14 | 8.562 | 61789701 | 66 | 1.85 |
| | Comparison(%) | -39.4 | -34.4 | -75 | -1.6 | 61.8 | 200 | 85.5 |
| EMin | Baseline | 10496 | 8112 | 42 | 8.27 | 64882073 | 30 | 1 |
| | Optimized | 9452 | 7366 | 28 | 8.183 | 70780403 | 38 | 1.16 |
| | Comparison(%) | -9.9 | -9.2 | -33.3 | -1.1 | 9.1 | 26.7 | 16.1 |
| FDTD | Baseline | 4451 | 2737 | 23 | 8.125 | 7485620 | 54 | 1 |
| | Optimized | 2907 | 1852 | 17 | 8.214 | 9975630 | 74 | 1.03 |
| | Comparison(%) | -34.7 | -32.3 | -26.1 | 1.1 | 33.3 | 37 | 2.8 |
| MM | Baseline | 2276 | 1744 | 25 | 8.078 | 67620 | 50 | 1 |
| | Optimized | 2097 | 1471 | 14 | 7.982 | 100387 | 90 | 1.21 |
| | Comparison(%) | -7.9 | -15.7 | -44 | -1.2 | 48.5 | 80 | 21.2 |
| Syrk | Baseline | 1874 | 1553 | 25 | 8.171 | 2113560 | 50 | 1 |
| | Optimized | 1874 | 1553 | 25 | 8.171 | 2113560 | 50 | 1 |
| | Comparison(%) | 0 | 0 | 0 | 0 | 0 | 0 | 0 |

Table 10: Baseline and Optimal Loop $II$s

| Bmk. | Baseline | Optimal | Runtime |
|---|---|---|---|
| Seg | $\langle 1, 2, 1, 2, 5 \rangle$ | $\langle 1, 2, 4, 3, 5 \rangle$ | 103s |
| Deno | $\langle 4, 3 \rangle$ | $\langle 4, 5 \rangle$ | 15.5s |
| DWT | $\langle 1, 1, 1, 1 \rangle$ | $\langle 1, 1, 2, 2 \rangle$ | 12.9s |
| IMin | $\langle 3, 1, 5, 1, 1, 5, 5, 5, 1, 1, \rangle$ | $\langle 12, 1, 5, 1, 1, 5, 5, 5, 1, 1, \rangle$ | 23.7s |
| EMin | $\langle 5, 5, 1 \rangle$ | $\langle 6, 5, 1 \rangle$ | 14.0s |
| FDTD | $\langle 1, 1, 1, 1 \rangle$ | $\langle 1, 1, 1, 2 \rangle$ | 16.4s |
| MM | $\langle 1, 1, 1, 1 \rangle$ | $\langle 1, 2, 1, 1 \rangle$ | 16.7s |
| Syrk | $\langle 1, 1 \rangle$ | $\langle 1, 1 \rangle$ | 14.5s |

# 7. CONCLUSIONS

In this paper, we formulate an area-aware throughput optimization problem by simultaneously addressing the concept of loop pipelining, module selection, duplication and resource sharing within a unified framework. We propose some methods to solve the problem efficiently. Experimental results show that an average of 31% speedup can be achieved compared to previous results.

*Acknowledgment.* This work was supported in part by the National Science Foundation through awards 0926127 and 1321147; and C-FAR, one of six centers of STARnet, a Semiconductor Research Corporation program sponsored by MARCO and DARPA.

# 8. REFERENCES

[1] J. Cong, B. Liu, S. Neuendorffer, J. Noguera, K. Vissers, and Z. Zhang, "High-level synthesis for FPGAs: From prototyping to deployment," *Trans. Comp.-Aided Des. Integ. Cir. Sys.*, vol. 30, no. 4, pp. 473–491, Apr. 2011.

[2] "Vivado HLS," http://www.xilinx.com/products/design-tools/vivado/index.htm.

[3] Z. Zhang, Y. Fan, W. Jiang, G. han, and J. Cong, "AutoPilot: a platform-based esl synthesis system," in *High-Level Synthesis: From Algorithm to Digital Circuit.* Springer, 2008.

[4] B. D. T. Inc., "An independent evaluation of: High-level synthesis tools for xilinx FPGAs," http://www.bdti.com/MyBDTI/pubs/Xilinx_hlstcp.pdf, 2010.

[5] J. Cong, W. Jiang, B. Liu, and Y. Zou, "Automatic memory partitioning and scheduling for throughput and power optimization," *ACM Trans. Des. Autom. Electron. Syst.*, vol. 16, no. 2, pp. 15:1–15:25, Apr. 2011. [Online]. Available: http://doi.acm.org/10.1145/1929943.1929947

[6] P. G. Paulin and J. P. Knight, "Force-directed scheduling for the behavioral synthesis of ASICs," *Trans. Comp.-Aided Des. Integ. Cir. Sys.*, vol. 8, no. 6, pp. 661–679, Nov. 2006.

[7] K. Kuchcinski, "Constraints-driven scheduling and resource assignment," *ACM Trans. Des. Autom. Electron. Syst.*, vol. 8, no. 3, pp. 355–383, Jul. 2003.

[8] I. Ahmad, M. K. Dhodhi, and C.-Y. Chen, "Integrated scheduling, allocation and module selection for design-space exploration in high-level synthesis," in *Computers and Digital Techniques, IEE Proceedings-*, vol. 142, no. 1. IET, 1995, pp. 65–71.

[9] J. Cong and J. Xu, "Simultaneous FU and register binding based on network flow method," in *Proceedings of the Conference on Design, Automation and Test in Europe*, ser. DATE '08. New York, NY, USA: ACM, 2008, pp. 1057–1062.

[10] S. Hadjis, A. Canis, J. H. Anderson, J. Choi, K. Nam, S. Brown, and T. Czajkowski, "Impact of FPGA architecture on resource sharing in high-level synthesis," in *Proceedings of the ACM/SIGDA International Symposium on Field

*Programmable Gate Arrays*, ser. FPGA '12.   New York, NY, USA: ACM, 2012, pp. 111–114. [Online]. Available: http://doi.acm.org/10.1145/2145694.2145712

[11] D. Chen, J. Cong, Y. Fan, and J. Xu, "Optimality study of resource binding with multi-vdds," in *Proceedings of the 43rd Annual Design Automation Conference*, ser. DAC '06. New York, NY, USA: ACM, 2006, pp. 580–585.

[12] A. Hagiescu, W.-F. Wong, D. F. Bacon, and R. Rabbah, "A computing origami: Folding streams in FPGAs," in *Proceedings of the 46th Annual Design Automation Conference*, ser. DAC '09.   New York, NY, USA: ACM, 2009, pp. 282–287. [Online]. Available: http://doi.acm.org/10.1145/1629911.1629987

[13] J. Cong, M. Huang, B. Liu, P. Zhang, and Y. Zou, "Combining module selection and replication for throughput-driven streaming programs," in *DATE*, 2012, pp. 1018–1023.

[14] J. Cong, M. Huang, and P. Zhang, "Combining computation and communication optimizations in system synthesis for streaming applications," in *Proceedings of the 2014 ACM/SIGDA international symposium on Field-programmable gate arrays*.   ACM, 2014, pp. 213–222.

[15] Z. Li and Y. Song, "Automatic tiling of iterative stencil loops," *ACM Trans. Program. Lang. Syst.*, vol. 26, no. 6, pp. 975–1028, Nov. 2004.

[16] D. Chen, J. Cong, and Y. Fan, "Low-power high-level synthesis for FPGA architectures," in *Proceedings of the 2003 International Symposium on Low Power Electronics and Design*, ser. ISLPED '03.   New York, NY, USA: ACM, 2003, pp. 134–139.

[17] A. Aiken and A. Nicolau, "Perfect pipelining: A new loop parallelization technique." in *ESOP*, ser. Lecture Notes in Computer Science, H. Ganzinger, Ed., vol. 300.   Springer, 1988, pp. 221–235. [Online]. Available: http://dblp.uni-trier.de/db/conf/esop/esop88.html#AikenN88

[18] Y. S. Shao, B. Reagen, G.-Y. Wei, and D. Brooks, "Aladdin: A pre-rtl, power-performance accelerator simulator enabling large design space exploration of customized architectures," in *Proceedings of the International Symposium on Computer Architecture (ISCA)*, 2014.

[19] A. Barvinok, *Integer Points in Polyhedra*.   European Mathematical Society, 2008.

[20] M. Weiser, "Program slicing," in *Proceedings of the 5th International Conference on Software Engineering*, ser. ICSE '81.   Piscataway, NJ, USA: IEEE Press, 1981, pp. 439–449.

[21] A. Canis, J. Choi, M. Aldham, V. Zhang, A. Kammoona, T. Czajkowski, S. D. Brown, and J. H. Anderson, "Legup: An open-source high-level synthesis tool for fpga-based processor/accelerator systems," *ACM Trans. Embed. Comput. Syst.*, vol. 13, no. 2, pp. 24:1–24:27, Sep. 2013.

[22] Polybench3.2, http://polybench.sourceforge.net. [Online]. Available: http://polybench.sourceforge.net

# Numerical Program Optimization for High-Level Synthesis

Xitong Gao, George A. Constantinides
Department of Electrical and Electronic Engineering
Imperial College London
London SW7 2AZ, United Kingdom
{xi.gao08, g.constantinides}@imperial.ac.uk

## ABSTRACT

This paper introduces a new technique, and its associated open source tool, SOAP2, to automatically perform source-to-source optimization of numerical programs, specifically targeting the trade-off between numerical accuracy and resource usage as a high-level synthesis flow for FPGA implementations. We introduce a new intermediate representation, which we call metasemantic intermediate representation (MIR), to enable the abstraction and optimization of numerical programs. We efficiently discover equivalent structures in MIRs by exploiting the rules of real arithmetic, such as associativity and distributivity, and rules that allow control flow restructuring, and produce Pareto frontiers of equivalent programs that trades off LUTs, DSPs and accuracy. Additionally, we further broaden the Pareto frontier in our optimization flow to automatically explore the numerical implications of partial loop unrolling and loop splitting. In real applications, our tool discovers a wide range of Pareto optimal options, and the most accurate one improves the accuracy of numerical programs by up to 65%.

## Categories and Subject Descriptors

B.5.2 [**Hardware**]: Design Aids—Optimization

## General Terms

High-Level Synthesis, Numerical Accuracy, Round-off Error

## 1. INTRODUCTION

Floating-point numerical algorithms are essential to many applications. It is often desirable to compute their results as accurately as possible. Typically, computations are performed following the IEEE 754 standard [1]. Due to a finite number of values that can be represented in floating-point arithmetic, numerical algorithms generally always have round-off errors. Therefore, equivalence rules such as *associativity* $(a + b) + c \equiv a + (b + c)$, and *distributivity* $(a + b) \times c \equiv a \times c + b \times c$ for real arithmetic no longer hold under floating-point arithmetic. This allows us to exploit these equivalence

relations, to automatically generate different equivalent expressions from the same arithmetic expression. For the optimization of FPGA implementations, these equivalent expressions can then be selected for the optimal trade-off between resource usage when synthesized into circuits, that is, the number of look-up tables (LUTs) and digital signal processing (DSP) elements utilized, and accuracy when evaluated using floating-point computations. As an example, we optimize the program "if $(x < 1)$ then $(x := (x + y) + 0.1)$ else $(x := x + (y + 0.1))$" using our tool with single-precision floating-point format, given an input $x \in [0, 100]$ and $y \in [0, 2]$. On the one hand, we find that it is most accurate when the subexpression $(x + y) + 0.1$ is written as $(x + 0.1) + y$, because the subexpression is only evaluated when $x < 1$, our tool infers a tighter bound on $x$, $[0, 1]$, to optimize it. On the other hand, the original program uses fewest resources when subexpressions are shared and the if statement is eliminated, *i.e.* "$x := x + (y + 0.1)$". This kind of optimization generates a Pareto optimal set of implementations. A naïve strategy to search for the Pareto optimal implementations is to discover all possible equivalent expressions. However, this would result in combinatorial explosion and become intractable even for very small expressions [4, 6, 10]. To remedy this, Gao *et al.* [4] proposed a novel approach, known as SOAP, to significantly reduce the space and time complexity to produce a subset of the Pareto frontier.

In this paper, we propose a new general *program* optimization technique for numerical algorithms, which allows if statements as well as while loops, and developed its accompanied tool, SOAP2, to enable the joint optimization of accuracy and resource usage, as well as the trade-off between these performance metrics. The tool performs source-to-source optimization of numerical programs targeting FPGAs, and generate implementations that trade off resource usage and numerical accuracy.

Our main contributions in this paper are as follows:

1. A new intermediate representation (IR) of the behaviour of numerical programs, designed to be manipulated and analyzed with ease; a new framework of numerical program transformations to enable the back and forth translation between the program and the IR, which preserves the semantics of the original program.

2. Semantics-based analyses that reason about not only the resource utilization (number of LUTs and DSP elements), and safe ranges of values and errors for programs, but also potential errors such as overflows and non-termination.

3. A new tool, SOAP2, which trades off resource usage and accuracy by providing a safe, semantics-directed

and flexible optimization targeting numerical programs for high-level synthesis.

## 2. RELATED WORK

There are many existing techniques that trade off resource usage and numerical accuracy in circuits. Wordlength optimization is a classical method for trading off precision and performance by minimizing data path wordlengths [3]. In the high-level synthesis (HLS) community, a technique is developed in [2] to automatically trade-off the data path wordlengths of algorithms that contain loops. However, these methods changes datapath size by varying *precisions* of arithmetic operators, whereas there is currently little work on performing structural improvements to datapaths in HLS, except for SOAP's arithmetic expression optimization [4].

With regard to the structural optimization of only arithmetic expressions without control structures, currently there are only a handful of tools that could optimize by *truly restructuring*, *i.e.* they exploit any of the three equivalence relations in real arithmetic, namely associativity, commutativity and distributivity. Many target either numerical accuracy [6], or performance metrics such as resources, latency, or throughput [8, 11, 10, 5]. Currently, SOAP is the only tool that could trade off area and accuracy in this category.

For true numerical software transformation with control structures, a method has been developed in [9] to utilize abstract interpretation and natural semantics [7]. However, this technique can neither unroll loops partially, nor optimize across loop boundaries. Furthermore, they specifically optimize numerical accuracy, and found that frequently this technique produces much slower implementations, while we also consider performance, by improving both accuracy and the resource usage of programs.

As none of the above-mentioned looks at the multiple-objective optimization of numerical programs, we are the first to propose a tool that performs a semantics-directed and truly restructuring program transformation, which optimizes not only arithmetic expressions, but also numerical programs, for the trade-off between numerical accuracy and resource usage when synthesized to FPGAs.

## 3. LANGUAGE DEFINITION

Before we discuss program transform, we first introduce NumImp, a simple imperative language that supports arithmetic and Boolean expressions, `if` statements, as well as `while` loops. Our program transformation optimizes NumImp programs. Our language allows numerical data types `int` and `float`, respectively integer and floating-point types.

As a simple example, the program in (1) computes an approximate value of $\pi^2 a/6$. It has two inputs $a$, a floating point value between 0 and 1, and $n$, an integer value between 10 and 20, which determines the number of iterations for the loop, and a return variable $y$.

$$
\begin{aligned}
&\texttt{input } (a : [0.0, 1.0], n : [10, 20]); \texttt{output } (y); \\
&x := 0; y := 0.0; \\
&\texttt{while } (x < n) \texttt{ do } ( \\
&\quad x := x + 1; \\
&\quad y := y + a/(x \times x); \\
&);
\end{aligned}
\tag{1}
$$

Despite the simplicity of NumImp, it includes all the features of a full programming language rather than an expression language used in prior work [4]. Additional language features, for example, array and matrix types, and also power, exponentiation and logarithm operators, can be added with few changes to our method.

## 4. PROGRAM TO MIR

The first step of our approach is to analyze each program return value into a metasemantic intermediate representation (MIR), which is a mapping from program variables to expressions, with additional operators to represent control structures. We call these expressions *semantic expressions*. This procedure is called *metasemantic analysis* (MA). The MA abstracts away irrelevant information, and preserves the essence of program execution. Details such as temporary variables and the ordering of program statements are discarded, whereas the abstraction still retains dataflow dependencies and keeps only computations that contribute to the final results.

We work with the MIR as an abstraction of the program because the discovery of equivalent structures can be greatly simplified. For instance, the program "$x := 1; y := 2$" is the same as "$y := 2; x := 1$" because interleaving of non-dependent statements does not change program semantics. If we were to base our transformations on the program syntax, we will need to enable this kind of equivalent relation even though it has zero impact on our optimization with respect to resource usage and accuracy. A much simpler intermediate representation means that we can explore a much smaller search space.

In SOAP2, we have automated the above analysis. In this section we explain how it is performed in detail, by manually analyzing the simple example in (1) into an MIR.

Our analysis is compositional, which means that it starts by analyzing the individual statements in the program into MIRs, and these MIRs are then combined to form the program's MIR. We begin by analyzing the first statement, $s_1 = "x := 0"$. This assigns the value 0 to the variable $x$, and does not affect other program variables. The MIR of $s_1$ is trivially analyzed into $\mu_1 = [x \mapsto 0, y \mapsto y, a \mapsto a, n \mapsto n]$. This means that executing the statement changes the value of $x$ to 0, but not the values of other variables. We use the notation $x \mapsto e$, where $x$ is a variable and $e$ is an expression, to indicate $x$ is paired with $e$. Hence the variable $x$ is paired with the expression 0, while $y$ is paired with an expression that contains only the variable itself, $y$. Similarly $s_2 = "y := 0.0"$ can be analyzed into $\mu_2 = [x \mapsto x, y \mapsto 0.0, a \mapsto a, n \mapsto n]$. These two MIRs $\mu_1$ and $\mu_2$ can then combined to form the MIR of "$s_1; s_2$", which is the MIR of the two statements executed in sequence. It is constructed by substituting the variables in the expressions of $\mu_2$, with their corresponding expressions in $\mu_1$. For instance, the expression $x$ of $\mu_2$ has the variable $x$, which is substituted to become 0, the corresponding expression of $x$ in $\mu_1$. Therefore the MIR of "$s_1; s_2$" is $\mu_0 = [x \mapsto 0, y \mapsto 0.0, a \mapsto a, n \mapsto n]$.

The two statements in the loop body "$x := x + 1; y := y + a/(x \times x)$" can be analyzed in a similar fashion, which produces the MIR in Figure 1a. Because the resulting MIR shares common structures, for example, the subexpression $(x + 1) \times (x + 1)$ and the expression of $x$ share the same subexpression $x + 1$, a directed acyclic graph (DAG) is used to allow all common subexpressions to be shared among expressions in an MIR.

The next step is to analyze the `while` loop into an MIR. Because the output we care about is the value of $y$ after program termination, for simplicity, we derive the MIR for the variable $y$ only, and the expressions for other variables can be abbreviated as $\cdots$. The MIR for the loop is shown in Figure 1b. Syntactically, the fixpoint node "fix" is used to encode the necessary information about the `while` loop, where $b = x < n$ is the Boolean expression of the loop, $\mu_s$ is the MIR of the loop body (Figure 1a), and $y$ signifies that $y$ is the value at loop exit that we use as the evaluated value of the fixpoint expression. Mathematically, it is analogous to a recursive call in a functional programming language.

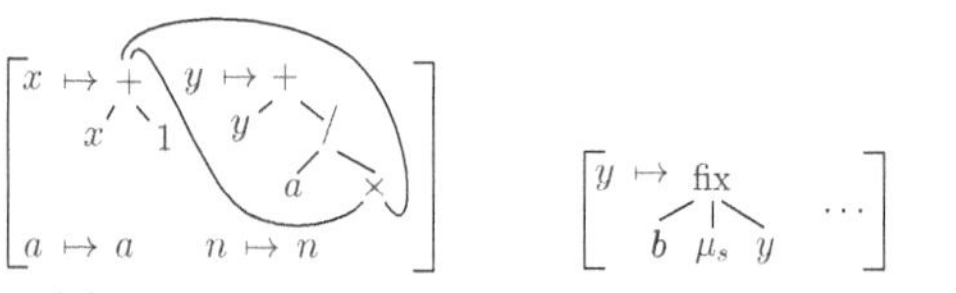

$$\begin{bmatrix} x \mapsto + & y \mapsto + \\ x' \quad 1 & y' \quad \\ & a \quad \times \\ a \mapsto a & n \mapsto n \end{bmatrix} \qquad \begin{bmatrix} y \mapsto \text{fix} \\ b \quad \mu_s \quad y \end{bmatrix}$$

(a) The loop body     (b) The `while` loop
Figure 1: The MIRs.

Finally, we combine Figure 1b and the MIR of the first two statements, $\mu_0$, to arrive at the full MIR of the program. Here, we use $e \star \mu$, where $e$ is an expression and $\mu$ is an MIR, to indicate that each variable $x$ in the expression $e$ are substituted with its corresponding expression in $\mu$.

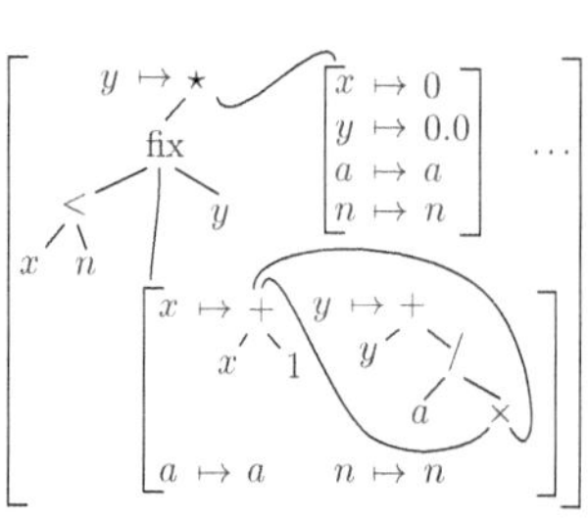

$$\begin{bmatrix} y \mapsto \star \\ \text{fix} \quad y \\ < \\ x \quad n \end{bmatrix} \begin{bmatrix} x \mapsto 0 \\ y \mapsto 0.0 \\ a \mapsto a \\ n \mapsto n \end{bmatrix} \quad \cdots \\ \begin{bmatrix} x \mapsto + & y \mapsto + \\ x' \quad 1 & y' \\ & a \quad \times \\ a \mapsto a & n \mapsto n \end{bmatrix} \qquad (2)$$

Although the example program (1) has no `if` statements, our analysis is capable of translating `if` statements into MIRs. As an example we consider the program "`if` $(x < 0)$ `then` $(y := x \times 2)$ `else skip`", where the set of program variables is $\{x, y\}$. The MIR of the program is shown in the left-hand side of (3). We introduce the conditional expression with the node "?", which is derived from C syntax, to signify conditional branches in expressions. The left-most, middle and right-most children of this node are respectively the Boolean expression, the true- and false-expressions. Because both true- and false-expressions of $x$ are the same, regardless of the truth value of $x < 0$, the two expressions will evaluated to the same value, we then further simplify it to become the one shown in the right-hand side.

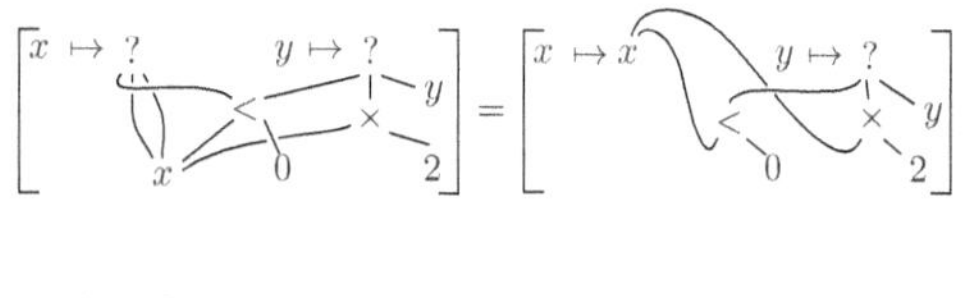

$$\begin{bmatrix} x \mapsto ? & y \mapsto ? \\ & \times \quad y \\ x \quad 0 \quad 2 \end{bmatrix} = \begin{bmatrix} x \mapsto x & y \mapsto ? \\ & < \quad \times \quad y \\ & 0 \quad 2 \end{bmatrix} \qquad (3)$$

# 5. TRANSFORMATIONS

The next step is to use the analyses of accuracy and resource usage of equivalent structures in MIRs to efficiently discover optimized equivalent MIRs. We start by explaining how the accuracy and the resource usage of programs encoded in MIRs are analyzed. After this, we explain how our analyses of accuracy and resource usage can guide the efficient discovery of equivalent structures in MIRs.

## 5.1 Performance Analyses

In a typical program execution, values of variables, typically integers and floating-point values, are modified according to the effect of the program statements, and they are propagated through arithmetic operators from the beginning to the end of the program. By comparison, not only do we propagate the values, but we use the static analysis approach of [4] to propagate the round-off errors associated with the numerical computations. For instance, if we know that floating point values $a$ and $b$ are respectively bounded by $[0, 1]$ and $[1, 2]$, and they have no round-off errors associated with them, then evaluating $a + b$ would result in a floating-point value that is bounded by $[1, 3]$, and we can compute the operation would result in a round-off error in the range of $[-1.19209304 \times 10^{-7}, 1.19209304 \times 10^{-7}]$. We use this method to propagate values and round-off errors starting from the leaves of a semantic expression, until we reach the root node, where we end up with the round-off error associated with the expression.

Expressions can have common subexpressions, we eliminate them when we construct DAGs from programs, which reduces resource usage. However, we can further merge multiple nodes into one to reduce resource usage. For example, the metasemantic analysis of the program "`if` $(x < 0)$ `then` $(x := 1; y := 2)$ `else` $(x := 3; y := 4)$" produces the following MIR in Figure 2a. Because we compute an abstraction of the program, the MIR does not keep the structure of the `if` statement to allow them to be optimized separately, as doing this would allow our optimization to produce more accurate implementations. The resulting MIR of the program consists of two conditional expressions as shown in Figure 2a. Because of this, after optimization, the MIR may has duplicate control paths. To resolve this, we introduce new kinds of nodes, as shown in Figure 2b, to "bundle up" more than one conditional expressions, when they share the same Boolean expression. Finally, resource statistics can be estimated by accumulating LUT and DSP counts of each operator in the DAG.

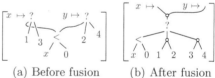

(a) Before fusion     (b) After fusion
Figure 2: The sharing of conditional expressions.

By combining both analyses, we can compare the accuracy and resource usage of each equivalent semantic expressions, and produce a Pareto frontier that trades off performance metrics including accuracy, and LUT and DSP counts.

## 5.2 Equivalent Structure Analysis

As we discussed earlier, discovering the full set of equivalent expressions by finding the transitive closure of the relations is infeasible because of combinatorial explosion. SOAP introduces a new method to drastically reduce the space and time complexity of discovering equivalent expressions, while achieving high quality optimizations [4]. We base our equivalent expression discovery on this method, but extend it to support additional program transform features. Our analysis starts by finding the set of equivalent expressions of the leaves of the DAG, which are the nodes themselves, for instance, a variable $x$ has a set of equivalent expressions $\{x\}$. After this, these equivalent expressions from the child nodes are propagated to the parent node, to form a set of equivalent parent expressions. We then discover equivalences of expressions in this set, using not only rules such as associativity, distributivity, constant propagation and many others that are derived from SOAP [4], but also additional rules to flexibly transform control structures. These rules enables partial loop unrolling and extends arithmetic rules to conditional expressions. Using these rules would often create a large number of equivalent structures, which requires us to analyze the accuracy and resource usage of each, and propagate only those that are Pareto optimal, to significantly reduce the amount of time required for our equivalent structure analysis. We keep propagating until the root of the DAG is reached, and we arrive at a set of equivalent expressions of the original expression under optimization.

## 6. CODE GENERATION

The final stage is to translate the optimized MIR back to a program in its original syntax. As discussed earlier, the MA produces an abstraction of the program, which means there are generally many ways of generating different programs from the same MIR. For this reason, certain heuristic optimizations are performed before or during code generation, such as branch and loop fusion transformations explained in our resource usage analysis to produce a unique and deterministic translation from the MIR. After this step, we perform a simple one-to-one mapping from MIRs to program code, using a breadth-first traversal of the MIR.

## 7. CONCLUSION

We use our tool, SOAP, to optimize the example program in (1), and produce the Pareto trade-off between the number of LUTs and the accuracy of the program in Figure 3a targeting an Altera Stratix IV device (EP4SGX530). Our tool automatically discovers that by partially unrolling the loop three times, although the program uses more resources, but it improves the accuracy by approximately 60%.

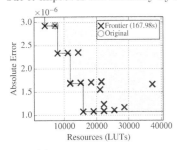
(a) Example program

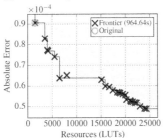
(b) `euler`

Figure 3: The Pareto frontiers.

Figure 3b shows the optimization of a program that uses Euler's method to solve the differential equation of a harmonic oscillator $\ddot{x} + \omega^2 x = 0$, with both an initial stationary position $x$ and $\omega^2$ bounded by $[0.0, 1.0]$, a step size of 0.1, and an iteration count $n \in [0, 20]$. It returns the position $x$ and velocity $\dot{x}$. In the optimization of `euler`, our optimization not only identifies that it is resource efficient when the two return variables are computed by the same loop, but also by individually optimizing the accuracy of the two variables, we produce a program with two loops, each with a different goal, that is to compute their respective return variables as accurately as possible, this generated a program that consists of two loops that have completely different structures.

With this, we further widen the trade-off curve with the most accurate option improving the accuracy by 65%.

With the foundation and framework that we developed, our tool can be extended in the following ways. First, it can be trivially extended to support additional numerical data structure such as arrays and matrices. Secondly, the Pareto optimization can be extended to optimize the latencies of equivalent programs, as restructuring programs and partially unrolling loops could have a notable impact on the ability to pipeline program loops, especially when arrays are incorporated. Finally, fixed point representations, along with the interaction between our structural optimization and multiple wordlength optimization [3] could also generate a lot of interest from the HLS community.

Our tool is open source and can be downloaded freely at: `https://github.com/admk/soap`.

## 8. REFERENCES

[1] ANSI/IEEE. IEEE standard for floating-point arithmetic. Technical report, Microprocessor Standards Committee of the IEEE Computer Society.

[2] D. P. Boland and G. A. Constantinides. Word-length Optimization Beyond Straight Line Code. In *Proceedings of the ACM/SIGDA International Symposium on Field Programmable Gate Arrays*, FPGA '13, pages 105–114, New York, NY, USA, 2013. ACM.

[3] G. Constantinides, P. Cheung, and W. Luk. The multiple wordlength paradigm. In *The 9th Annual IEEE Symposium on Field-Programmable Custom Computing Machines, 2001. FCCM '01.*, pages 51–60.

[4] X. Gao, S. Bayliss, and G. Constantinides. SOAP: Structural optimization of arithmetic expressions for high-level synthesis. In *2013 International Conference on Field-Programmable Technology (FPT)*, pages 112–119, Dec 2013.

[5] A. Hosangadi, F. Fallah, and R. Kastner. Factoring and eliminating common subexpressions in polynomial expressions. In *Proceedings of the 2004 IEEE/ACM International Conference on Computer-aided Design, ICCAD '04*, pages 169–174, 2004.

[6] A. Ioualalen and M. Martel. A new abstract domain for the representation of mathematically equivalent expressions. In *Proceedings of the 19th International Conference on Static Analysis, SAS '12*, pages 75–93.

[7] G. Kahn. Natural semantics. In *4th Annual Symposium on Theoretical Aspects of Computer Sciences on STACS 87*, pages 22–39, 1987.

[8] C. Lattner and V. Adve. LLVM: A Compilation Framework for Lifelong Program Analysis & Transformation. In *Proceedings of the International Symposium on Code Generation and Optimization*, CGO '04, page 75.

[9] M. Martel. Program transformation for numerical precision. In *Proceedings of the 2009 ACM SIGPLAN workshop on Partial evaluation and program manipulation, PEPM '09*, pages 101–110. ACM, 2009.

[10] C. Mouilleron. *Efficient Computation with Structured Matrices and Arithmetic Expressions*. PhD thesis, Ecole Normale Supérieure de Lyon-ENS LYON, 2011.

[11] Xilinx. Vivado Design Suite User Guide—High-Level Synthesis, 2014.

# System-level Linking of Synthesised Hardware and Compiled Software Using a Higher-order Type System

Shane Fleming, David Thomas, George Constantinides
Dept. of Electrical and Electronic Engineering
Imperial College London
{sf306,dt10,gac1}@ic.ac.uk

Dan Ghica
School of Computer Science
University of Birmingham
d.r.ghica@cs.bham.ac.uk

## ABSTRACT

Devices with tightly coupled CPUs and FPGA logic allow for the implementation of heterogeneous applications which combine multiple components written in hardware and software languages, including first-party source code and third-party IP. Flexibility in component relationships is important, so that the system designer can move components between software and hardware as the application design evolves. This paper presents a system-level type system and linker, which allows functions in software and hardware components to be directly linked at link time, without requiring any modification or recompilation of the components. The type system is designed to be language agnostic, and exhibits higher-order features, to enables design patterns such as notifications and callbacks to software from within hardware functions. We demonstrate the system through a number of case studies which link compiled software against synthesised hardware in the Xilinx Zynq platform.

## Categories and Subject Descriptors

C.0 [**Computer Systems Organization**]: General

## Keywords

Co-design, Heterogeneous Systems, HLS

## 1. INTRODUCTION

The introduction of devices containing tightly coupled CPUs and programmable logic within a single chip have made it possible to physically co-locate an application's software, hardware, and operating system, reducing board design and interconnect complexity. HLS tools allow creation of accelerated functions [2], and there exist reconfigurable operating systems to manage the functions [4], but usually the user must interface software with the accelerators. This process is largely manual, with developers using low-level platform-specific resources or platform independent stream abstractions to move data to and from the accelerator when

the function is called [1]. This encourages a client-server mentality, where the software is always in control, and hardware exists to service the software.

In this paper we present a system-level linker, which makes the process of linking together software and hardware components as simple as linking object files together in software. The user can move functions from software to hardware simply by swapping between two components, without modifying or recompiling any of those components. Our key contributions are:

- A minimal type system which captures functions defined in both software and high-level hardware languages, along with an abstract protocol for marshalling function calls.

- A practical system-level linker and tool flow for Zynq, which can combine, type-check, and link heterogeneous systems using a concrete protocol over AXI.

- Case studies demonstrating linking of C++ software and LangX Hardware components in a Zynq device, showing complex control flow including function callbacks, migration of functions between hardware to software by relinking, and inversion of control with the "main" function in hardware controlling software.

The system level linker described in this paper is fully working and automated, but has significant scope for improvement in terms of performance and extra functionality. We present this work to support our manifesto that a system design environment should have:

- **Type safety** - functions should be strongly typed, and checkable during linking.

- **Language independence** - allow functions written in one language to be called from many other languages.

- **Implementation independence** - functions do not rely on how or where other functions are implemented.

- **True peering** - function calls can freely cross from hardware to software and *vice versa*.

- **Higher order** - supports the callbacks and inversion of control found in contemporary software languages.

- **Automated** - user's only job is to specify which hardware and software modules should be linked together.

The system presented here demonstrates that by choosing a common type system, direct hardware to software linking is possible and these goals can be achieved.

Table 1: Mappings between type system and C.

| | Linker type | C type |
|---|---|---|
| 1 | val | int x |
| 2 | exp | int f() |
| 3 | com | void f() |
| 4 | val->com | void f(int a) |
| 5 | exp->com | void f(int (*a)() ) |
| 6 | com->com | void f(void (*a)() ) |
| 7 | val->val->exp | int f(int a, int b) |
| 8 | val->exp->exp | int f(int a, int (*b)() ) |
| 9 | (val->exp)->exp | int f(int (*b)(int a) ) |

## 2. A TYPE SYSTEM FOR SYSTEMS

Our type system is influenced by ML and Haskell, and is intended to be mapped to most language type systems supporting functions. There are three primitive types:

**Values** (val ) - Call-by-value; a fixed value passed to a function, such as integer parameters in C.

**Expressions** (exp ) - Call-by-name; a value which may change and cause side-effects each time it is evaluated.

**Command** (com ) - Call-by-name; returns no value, but can be evaluated to cause an execution with side-effects.

The three primitive types can be composed into functions using the arrow operator A->B, to describe a function with input type A and output type B. The input and output types can be either primitives, or other functions:

val->(exp->exp) : A function with argument of type val , producing a function of type exp->exp.

(val->exp)->exp : A function with argument of (function) type val->exp, producing a result of type exp .

The first form is a two input first-order function, while the second is a single input higher-order function. The first case is most common, so -> is defined to be right associative, meaning that val->(exp->exp)≡val->exp->exp.

The type system is derived from functional programming, but there is a direct mapping to languages such as C and C++, as well as many other common languages. Table 1 shows the mapping between linker types and C. To save space, we show unrefined val and exp types, which default to 32-bit int, but in the real system they are further refined to specify bit-width and how they should be interpreted, such as float or uint64_t.

Lines 1–3 show the primitive types, with a val representing a scope-level constant. The C types for exp and com show that they are call-by-name, so as functions they may have side-effects. Lines 4 & 5 take one integer argument, but differ in whether it is by value or name. Line 6 consumes a function without any arguments, so argument is executed as a callback purely for its side-effects. Lines 7 & 8 are both binary functions returning an integer, but in line 9 the brackets turn it into a unary function which takes another unary function as its argument.

Bindings for other software languages are similarly defined, and in all modern languages the syntax is both simpler and more natural. For example, in C++11 the approach maps naturally onto std::function to define arguments with function types, and lambdas/closures to define callback functions. Native support for higher-order func-

tions is present in scripting languages such as Python and Ruby, and modern systems languages such as Go and Rust.

The intrinsic and natural support for higher-order programming in almost all contemporary languages has led to software programmers adopting design patterns exploiting it. Modern standard libraries from C++ to Python make extensive use of functions as parameters to configure or modify the behaviour of library functions. Programmers have becomes used to the idea of defining lambda functions to represent tasks and callbacks, then using other functions to co-ordinate and schedule their execution.

We make the argument that higher-order functions are just as useful in a heterogeneous system, as they provide a simple and flexible way to dynamically configure and manage system behaviour. Higher-order programming in C++11 is often syntactic sugar with little overhead compared to C, and is directly supported by g++ in ARM. Similarly, Python and other languages run perfectly well in Zynq, so some system designers will eventually wish to use them.

## 3. ABSTRACT AND CONCRETE LINKING

At run-time we need a mechanism to allow function calls to be instigated from either hardware or software. The approach we take is adapted from the formal semantics of LangX , but is essentially a simple composable synchronisation protocol that maps well to both hardware and software.

Each primitive (com, exp, or val) is associated with three channels: question (Q), answer (A), and data (D). The Q and A channels carry events, while D transports values – for exp and val types D has the width of the value, while com produces no value, so can be elided. The Q event is written by the consumer (or client) of a value, while the A and D events are written by the producer (or server) of a value.

At an abstract level, the protocol only requires that: for exp and com , a Q request event must be answered by an A event before any any further Q request; for exp the D value must be valid when the A event occurs; for val the D value must be valid for the entire scope of a function call.

The exact mapping of these channels to device level constructs depends on where the consumer and producers are located. When both are in software and in the same thread, it becomes a function call: Q is a branch to a function address, D is a value returned in a register or stack, and A is a branch to return address. When both consumer and producer are synthesised together into hardware, Q and A are 1-bit wires, while the D channel is a multi-bit signal which must be valid in the same cycle as the A is signalled. This is how the existing LangX hardware compiler links functions, and can be cheaply translated to the ap_ack protocol from Vivado HLS.

To cross from hardware to software we need a concrete protocol to send events and data, and in the current linker, we take an approach supported by every language and compute domain in the system – memory mapping. At link time the primitives representing all function inputs and outputs are collected, then each primitive is mapped to a fixed address. Both producers and consumers share a known address for a particular channel, and memory writes in one compute domain can be eventually observed in all others.

An example of a linked system is shown in Figure 1, where a "main" function written in LangX is linked to two functions written in C. The hardware reads a stream of data from stdin, calculates the mean of the data, then prints it to

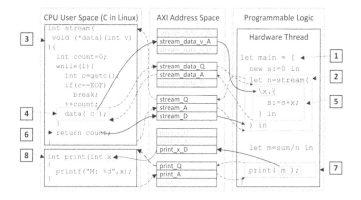

Figure 1: Example of hardware function calling functions in software

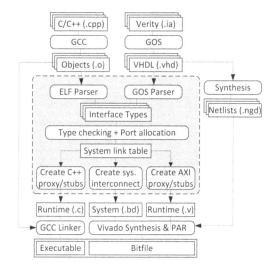

Figure 2: Design flow, with generic hardware and software toolchains at top, system linker in the middle in grey, and generic platform tools at the bottom.

stdout. The software `stream` with type `(exp->com)->exp`, using a callback function to push data back to the caller, rather than requiring the caller to pull data. The stages of execution are as follows:

1 - The LangX `main` function begins execution. There are no active user threads in software.

2 - The hardware calls `stream` with a lambda function (`\x.{...}`) as the parameter, by writing to `stream_Q`,

3 - The linker software run-time observes the event on `stream_Q`, and runs the software `stream` function on a worker thread.

4 - When `stream` calls the `data` callback, the runtime passes the argument by value by writing to `stream_data_v_D`, then executes the callback by writing to `stream_data_Q`.

5 - The event on `stream_data_Q` is observed, and routed it to the lambda function in LangX , which updates `sum` as a side-effect. Control is returned by writing to `stream_data_A`.

6 - Once the `stream` function consumes all data, it returns the number of values read by writing to `stream_D`, and signals completion via `stream_A`.

7 - The mean is calculated, then the `print` function is called.

8 - The value is printed in software and control then returns to hardware. At this point the LangX `main` function is finished, and the program halts.

Currently the linker supports software components written in plain C or C++, and hardware components written in LangX , with the design flow shown in Figure 2. The source and compilation flows at the top are pure C/C++ and LangX design flows – no special headers or platform need to be included for the code to work with the linker, and it is possible to link against third party compiled code for which the source is not available.

The system linker is shown in grey, and takes as input the software and hardware object files the user wishes to link. First the type information is parsed out of the binary files, either using the ELF information in the software binary, or LangX 's equivalent meta-data. All function names and types are then merged, performing the same checks that a software linker would: all symbols with the same name must have the same type, and any imported symbol must be exported by exactly one module. Violation of these rules results in a link error, just as in a software linker. All symbols are now resolved to one exporter and zero or more importers, and each function parameter and output is assigned

a unique location, that can be accessed from both hardware and software.

The final step is to generate linking code, which connects imported symbols in one module to exported symbols in another. Functions imported in software require a proxy with the same name, which translates calls to the proxy to writes on Q and reads on A addresses. Functions exported by software require a stub, which listens for requests on the Q channel, and routes the request to the target function. Proxies run on the thread of the user's code, while stubs inherit threads injected by the system linker at program startup. Stubs and proxies are also added on the hardware side, which sit between the AXI bus and the user's components. Write transactions at known Q addresses are translated to Q request events for the LangX module, while A and D responses from the module are routed to registers bound to the appropriate addresses.

The final stage is to combine all the components. The software side is linked together with the standard linker, bringing together the user's software and the system linker's proxies and stubs. For hardware, the system linker generates an IP block diagram, incorporating the processing system (CPU), user's hardware, and the AXI proxies and stubs. The result is a single executable, containing both software and hardware. When executed it will configure the hardware, start any stubs for software functions, then execute `main`, whether that is in hardware or software.

## 4. CASE STUDIES

The system linker currently supports the Zynq platform, and can link together ELF software modules with C++ type information against synthesised modules from LangX . Linking against Go and Vivado HLS is supported in a partially-manual alpha form, but here we concentrate on examples using the robust fully automated C++/LangX flow, and focus on qualitative examples of functionality and some limited quantitative results. The case studies used are:

**stream-avg.** : The example in Figure 1, with the main function in hardware, using IO exposed by software.

**Table 2: FPGA area usage and measured execution time in a Zynq ZedBoard running Linux.**

|            | Luts | FFs  | Exec. Time | control crossings |
|------------|------|------|------------|-------------------|
| stream-avg | 1992 | 3031 | 10.6ms     | 6                 |
| exp        | 690  | 849  | 1.29ms     | 1                 |
| exp-flip   | 1155 | 1188 | 2.06ms     | 1                 |
| filter     | 1453 | 2005 | 3.59ms     | 5                 |
| sort-cb    | 2151 | 519  | 3589ms     | 322k              |
| sort       | 2213 | 3529 | 163.8ms    | 1.6k              |
| sort-par2  | 3632 | 5388 | 20.5ms     | 1.6k              |

**Table 3: Comparison of system linker features against other approaches.**

|              | This | RPC | SWIG | LEAP | LegUp |
|--------------|------|-----|------|------|-------|
| Type-safe    | ✓    | ✓   | ✓    |      | ✓     |
| Lang. indep. | ✓    | ✓   | ✓    | ✓    |       |
| Impl. indep. | ✓    | ✓   | ✓    | ✓    | ✓     |
| True-peering | ✓    |     |      | ✓    |       |
| Higher order | ✓    |     |      |      |       |
| Automated    | ✓    |     |      |      | ✓     |

**exp & exp-flip** : a single `exp` exposed from hardware to software, or from software to hardware (flipped). This quantifies the underlying cost of the linker startup overhead.

**filter** : hardware exports a function of type `exp->(exp->exp)->(exp->com)->com`, where the first expression is a data source, the second is a filtering predicate, and the third is a data sink for data matching the predicated; overall there are five domain crossings required during execution to get from hardware back to software.

**sort-cb** : a single-threaded bubble sorter is exposed by hardware, with the comparison function supplied by the caller, similar to the C library function `qsort`. The software requests 800 elements to be sorted, stressing the AXI protocol due to the large number of comparisons needed.

**sort** : the same setup as *sort*, but now the hardware uses an internal comparison function, ignoring the one supplied by software (software remains the same).

**sort-par2** : the hardware exposes the same function type as sort, but now uses two parallel sorts then a merge.

The results in terms of area and performance are shown in Figure 2, measured on a ZedBoard running Linux. One main qualitative message is simply that it works – these examples utilise large numbers of cross domain calls, and the system is robust. Even on much larger and more complicated examples the system works, but becomes progressively slower.

Looking at the examples, *exp* and *exp-flip* give an idea of how long it takes to setup and tear-down the linker, which is mainly the cost of starting the stub threads. The marginal cost per call for *filter* and *stream-avg* is lower, as the setup cost is only needed once. The *sort-cb* example demonstrates one limitation of the current system, as while it is possible to use very fine-grain callbacks, the overhead is very high.

Overall *sort* and *sort-par2* demonstrate our claim that re-linking can be used to achieved an area-speed tradeoff. Introducing more parallelism in hardware means the function is faster, but this is a decision the system designer can make at link-time, without needing to modify the software.

## 5. RELATED WORK

The goals and features of the system linker can be broadly compared to two types of systems: software-oriented interface and Remote Procedure Call (RPC) generators for inter-language interoperability and distributed systems; and hardware-oriented frameworks for allowing software clients to access hardware accelerators over PCIe and other buses.

A software oriented interface generator with similar goals is SWIG (Simplified Wrapper and Interface Generator), which parses C++ headers and generates wrappers to expose the functions to languages such as Python, Tcl and Javascript [3]. SWIG focusses on in-process interfaces, but RPC systems can connect functions on different computers via networks, using a shared interface definition file to control marshalling of function parameters. RPC has some of the same aims as our system linker, but requires more manual effort to connect together nodes, and does not support hardware nodes.

One approach to manage hardware-software calls to provide a generic platform-independent abstraction, such as streams of data, with a platform-specific run-time providing the concrete implementations, such as LEAP [1]. Our approach is complementary to such systems, as while it currently uses its own AXI based transport, it can be layered over other channels. A more vertical approach is taken in systems such as LegUp, which takes a software application and identifies functions to accelerate through benchmarking [2]. Accelerators are compiled using HLS, and the original function call is re-routed to the accelerator. This involves many of the same processes as the system linker, such as the generation of software proxies, but only allows hardware to act as a server and is a single language approach.

## 6. CONCLUSION

This paper presents a system-level linker, which uses a language independent type system and abstract protocol to enable direct linking of hardware and software components. Components do not need to know whether they are talking to hardware or software, and can use higher-order functions to support modern programming practices. We demonstrate a fully functional and automated prototype in a Zynq platform, allowing hardware components to link directly to software components running in Linux. Future work will concentrate on increasing the scope of the linker in terms of languages and the optimality of the interconnect.

## 7. REFERENCES

[1] M. Adler, K. Fleming, A. Parashar, M. Pellauer, and J. S. Emer. Leap scratchpads: automatic memory and cache management for reconfigurable logic. In *Proc. FPGA*, pages 25–28, 2011.

[2] Andrew Canis et. al. Legup: An open-source high-level synthesis tool for fpga-based processor/accelerator systems. *ACM Trans. Embed. Comput. Syst.*, 13(2):24:1–24:27, Sept. 2013.

[3] D. M. Beazley. Swig: An easy to use tool for integrating scripting languages with C and C++. In *Proc. USENIX Tcl/Tk Workshop*, TCLTK'96, pages 15–15, Berkeley, CA, USA, 1996. USENIX Association.

[4] E. Lübbers and M. Platzner. Reconos: Multithreaded programming for reconfigurable computers. *ACM Trans. Embed. Comput. Syst.*, 9(1):8:1–8:33, Oct. 2009.

# Automatic Time-Redundancy Transformation for Fault-Tolerant Circuits

Dmitry Burlyaev
INRIA
Univ. Grenoble Alpes
dmitry.burlyaev@inria.fr

Pascal Fradet
INRIA
Univ. Grenoble Alpes
pascal.fradet@inria.fr

Alain Girault
INRIA
Univ. Grenoble Alpes
alain.girault@inria.fr

## ABSTRACT

We present a novel logic-level circuit transformation technique for automatic insertion of fault-tolerance properties. Our transformation uses double-time redundancy coupled with micro-checkpointing, rollback and a speedup mode. To the best of our knowledge, our solution is the only technologically independent scheme capable to correct the multiple bit-flips caused by a Single-Event Transient (SET) with double-time redundancy. The approach allows soft-error masking (within the considered fault-model) and keeps the same input/output behavior regardless error occurrences. Our technique trades-off the circuit throughput for a small hardware overhead. Experimental results on the ITC'99 benchmark suite indicate that the benefits of our methods grow with the combinational size of the circuit. The hardware overhead is 2.7 to 6.1 times smaller than full Triple-Modular Redundancy (TMR) with double loss in throughput. We do not consider configuration memory corruption and our approach is readily applicable to Flash-based FPGAs. Our method does not require any specific hardware support and is an interesting alternative to TMR for logic-intensive designs.

## Categories and Subject Descriptors

B.5.3 [**Hardware**]: Register-Transfer-Level Implementation-Reliability and Testing [Redundant design]; B.5.2 [**Hardware**]: Design Aids [Automatic synthesis, Verification]

## General Terms

Reliability; Verification

## Keywords

Time-Redundancy; Checkpointing; Single-Event Transient; Formal Methods

*FPGA'15*, February 22–24, 2015, Monterey, California, USA.
Copyright © ACM 978-1-4503-3315-3/15/02 ...$15.00.
http://dx.doi.org/10.1145/2684746.2689058.

## 1. INTRODUCTION

Circuit tolerance towards soft (non-destructive, non-permanent) errors has become a design characteristic as important as performance and power consumption [1]. Having been an object of attention in space and medical industries for many years [2], circuit fault-tolerance is nowadays a research topic for any application manufactured at modern technology nodes ($90nm$ and smaller) due to the increased risk of soft errors [1]. Such risk results from the continuous shrinking of transistor size that makes components more sensitive to perturbations induced by radiation [3].

The most common methods to make circuits fault-tolerant to soft errors rely on hardware redundancy, therefore incurring a significant area overhead. TMR [4] remains the most popular fault-tolerance technique and is widely supported by CAD tools for FPGAs [5] [6]. Time-redundant techniques for fault-tolerance require less hardware resources than spatial redundancy but decrease the circuit throughput. As in software, the standard implementation relies on a block-by-block processing and triple redundancy: an input data is processed three times to produce three outputs used by a majority voter which filters out a possible error. Consequently, latency and throughput are degraded three times.

In this paper, we propose a circuit transformation that is suitable for any type of processing (block or stream processing) and requires only double time redundancy. We target and evaluate our transformation for flash-based FPGA realization where the small hardware size is especially important and configuration memory upsets are nonexistent [7]. Since the approach does not require specific hardware support, it is applicable to ASICs as well. As any time-redundant scheme, our technique is not suited to applications that require high throughput. A particular target is FPGA-based designs of embedded systems such as controllers used in safety critical domains (space, nuclear, medical, ...).

There are two main types of soft errors caused by particle strikes: Single-Event Upsets (SEUs) (*i.e.*, bit-flips in flip-flops (FFs)) and Single-Event Transients (SETs) (i.e. pulses propagating in the combinational circuit). Since an SET may potentially lead to several bit-flips, SETs subsume SEUs. In this paper, we consider fault models of the form "at most one SET within $K$ clock cycles", denoted by $SET(1, K)$. Even in environments with high levels of ionizing radiations (e.g., space, particle accelerators), $K$ is considered to be larger than $10^{10}$ [8]. Our transformation masks SETs for any $K$ greater than $10$ cycles.

The main features of our Double-Time Redundant Transformation (DTR) transformation are illustrated in Fig. 1.

The primary input stream is upsampled twice and given to the combinational part to detect errors by comparison (written $C$). The line $\dots, s_1, s_2, t_1, t_2, \dots$ represents paired internal states and $\dots, a, a, b, b, \dots$ paired bits in the output stream. When an error is detected (e.g., $t_1 \neq t'_2$), a recovery process consisting of a rollback and a re-execution is triggered (resulting in the internal state $t_3$). The check-pointing mechanism is tolerant towards SETs and is performed every other cycle.

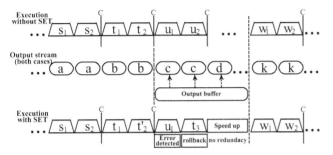

**Figure 1: Overview of the DTR transformation**

According to the fault-model $SET(1, K)$, no error occurs within $K$ clock cycles after the last error. This allows to switch off time-redundancy during the recovery phase and to "accelerate" the circuit twice (speed up phase in Fig. 1). Along with the use of specifically designed input and output buffers to produce delayed outputs (and record inputs) during that phase, this makes the recovery absolutely transparent to the surrounding circuit. The input/output behavior remains unchanged as if no SET had occurred. The output streams correctness and consistency ($\dots, a, a, b, b, \dots$) are guaranteed by the transformation. After an error, the check-pointing mechanism returns the circuit to a correct state (i.e., to the state that the circuit would have been if no error had occurred) within at most 10 clock cycles. Consequently, the allowed maximum fault rate is one every 10 clock cycles (i.e., $SET(1, 10)$).

To summarize, DTR is a new *automatic* logic-level transformation for fault-tolerance with the following benefits:

1. It is technologically independent, in particular it does not require specific hardware support nor control of clock lines. Therefore, it is applicable to Commercial Off-The-Shelf (COTS) FPGAs.

2. Its throughput loss for error-correcting is only double instead of the standard triple overhead.

3. It can be shown to mask all possible SETs, which is a more demanding fault-model than SEUs.

4. It is suitable for stream processing since the input/output streams are insensitive to SET occurrences.

Section 2 introduces notations and provides an overview of the transformation. It consists in replacing each memory cell by a *Memory Block* supporting redundancy and check-pointing, and adding a global *Control Block* providing control signals. Section 3 describes in details the DTR transformation. It ends with the proof that the transformed circuit is fault-tolerant for all possible errors according to the fault-model. Experimental results using the ITC'99 benchmark suite [9] are presented in Section 4. The hardware overheads and maximum throughputs of the original, TMR, and DTR circuits are compared. Section 5 presents related works that use time-redundancy or micro-level checkpointing for circuit fault-tolerance. Finally, we summarize our contributions and sketch possible extensions in Section 6.

## 2. NOTATIONS AND APPROACH

Any digital circuit can be represented in the most general way as in Figure 2. The circuit, which consists of combinational and sequential parts, takes a primary input bit vector $\vec{PI}$ and returns a primary output bit vector $\vec{PO}$ each clock cycle. The combinational part performs some memoryless boolean function $\varphi$.

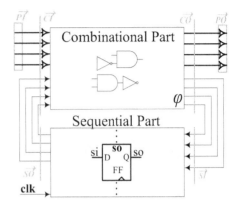

**Figure 2: Digital circuit before transformation.**

We denote the input (resp. output) bit vector of the combinational part by $\vec{CI}$ (resp. $\vec{CO}$) and the input (resp. output) bit vector of the sequential part by $\vec{SI}$ (resp. $\vec{SO}$). They satisfy the following equalities:

$$\vec{CO} = \varphi(\vec{CI}) \qquad \vec{CI} = \vec{PI} \oplus \vec{SO} \qquad \vec{CO} = \vec{PO} \oplus \vec{SI} \qquad (1)$$

where $\oplus$ denotes vector concatenation. We use lower case (e.g., $\vec{pi}, \vec{co}$, etc.) to denote the corresponding signals in the transformed circuits; they satisfy the same equalities.

Throughout the paper, we write $\vec{v}_i$ for the value of the bit vector $\vec{v}$ at the $i^{th}$ clock cycle (the numbering starts at $i = 1$). Values and outputs of memory cells are denoted by the same names. For instance, the memory cell in Figure 2 with output $so$ is itself denoted $so$.

An SET in a combinational circuit can lead to the non-deterministic corruption of any memory cell connected (by a purely combinational path) to the place where the SET occurred. A corrupted vector is written $\dagger\vec{v}$; it represents the vector $\vec{v}$ with an arbitrary number of bit-flips (corrupted bits). An SET in the combinational circuit of Figure 2 at some cycle $i$ can lead to the corruption of some outputs of the combinational circuit $\dagger\vec{CO}_i$. This leads to the corruption of the primary outputs $\dagger\vec{PO}_i$ and of inputs of the memory cells $\dagger\vec{SI}_i$, which, in turn, causes the corruption of the circuit's memory cells. This last corruption is visible at their outputs during the next clock cycle $\dagger\vec{SO}_{i+1}$. An SET can occur on any input/output wire. Note that SET subsumes the SEU fault-model since any SEU of a cell can be caused by a SET on its input line.

The DTR transformation consists of five steps (see Figure 3):

1. upsampling of the input stream;

2. substitution of each memory cell with a *memory block*;

3. addition of a *control block*;

4. addition of *input buffers* to all circuit primary inputs;

5. addition of *output buffers* to all circuit primary outputs.

Here, the combinational part of the circuit is kept unchanged but $\varphi(\vec{ci})$ is computed twice. The results are compared and, if an error is detected, $\varphi(\vec{ci})$ is recomputed the third time. The input stream is upsampled two times. If $\vec{pi}$ represents the upsampled primary input bit vector of the transformed circuit, it satisfied the following equalities:

$$\forall i \in \mathbb{N}^*.\ \vec{pi}_{2i-1} = \vec{pi}_{2i} = \vec{PI}_i \tag{2}$$

Each original memory cell is substituted with a memory block that implements the time-redundant mechanism. The memory blocks store the results of signal propagations but they also save recovery bits (or checkpoint bits). As an error-detection mechanism, a comparison takes place that, in case of an error, leads to the use of the recovery bits to rollback and re-execute. The control block takes the result of comparisons as an input and provides several control signals to schedule check-pointing and rollback. To prevent errors from corrupting the input/output behavior, additional input and output buffers are necessary. Input buffers store the last two input vectors to provide the necessary information for re-computation. During the re-computation, the control block speedups the circuit which, in a few cycles, catches up the state it should have had if no error had occurred. Output buffers emit the previously recorded correct outputs and filter out the corrupted data during the recovery process.

In the presented transformations, memory blocks, the control block, and the input/output buffers guarantee that the circuit is fault tolerant, *i.e.*, that an SET (within the fault-model) cannot corrupt the primary outputs. Even errors occurring directly at the primary outputs can be masked. Our output buffers provide three redundant output wires for each output of the original circuit, so the surrounding circuit can also vote to mask errors.

The following sections present the transformation in details.

## 3. DOUBLE-TIME REDUNDANT TRANSFORMATION

As we observed in Section 2, the circuit after DTR transformation can be represented as in Figure 3. We describe the new components of the DTR transformed circuit (marked with green) hereafter.

### 3.1 DTR Memory Blocks

The memory block is depicted in Figure 4. It consists of four memory cells:

- two cells $d$ and $d'$ (the data bits) to save redundant information for comparison; since the input stream is upsampled twice, $d$ and $d'$ contain the same value each *odd* cycle; *e.g.*, if the input stream leads to $si_1=u$, $si_2=u$, ... then the pair $(d, d')$ will contain successively the values $(0, 0)$, $(u, 0)$, $(u, u)$, ... where the initial values of the memory cells is supposed to be 0;

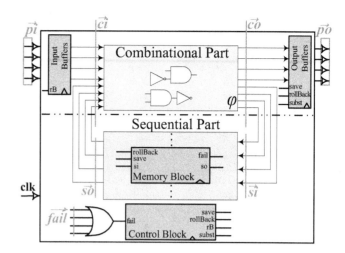

**Figure 3: Transformed circuit for DTR.**

- two cells $r$ and $r'$ (the recovery bits) with enable-input to keep the value of the $si$ input during four clock cycles and to allow the rollback after an error detection.

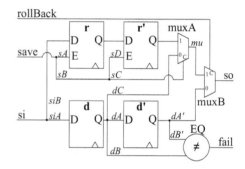

**Figure 4: DTR Memory Block.**

The DTR memory performs an error-detection comparison whose result is sent as a *fail* signal to the DTR control block. As noted above, the comparison of $d$ and $d'$ is meaningful only during the odd cycles and so is the *fail* signal which is read only at those cycles.

In addition to the data input signal ($si$ in Figure 4), each DTR memory block takes special global control signals *save* and *rollBack* produced by the control block and used to organize the circuit recovery after an error detection.

### 3.2 DTR Input Buffers

An input buffer is inserted at each primary input of the original circuit to keep the two last bits of the input stream. The buffer is implemented as a pipeline of two memory cells, $b$ and $b'$ as shown in Figure 5. The signal $rB$ is raised by the control block during the recovery process (Figure 7).

The cells $b$ and $b'$ are used only during the recovery process in order to re-execute the last two cycles. These bits are provided to the combinational part instead of the bits from the input streams. They also serve to store the inputs that keep coming during those two cycles. During the recovery, the vector $\vec{ci}$ consists of (i) the first part $\vec{pi}$ coming from the input buffers and (ii) the second part $\vec{so}$ coming from the rollbacked memory blocks. If the error is detected at cycle $i$, then the rollback is performed at cycle $i + 1$ and the vector

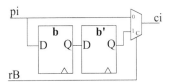

**Figure 5: DTR input buffer ($pi$ primary input)**

$\vec{pi}_{i-1} \oplus \vec{so}_{i-1}$ is provided to the combinational part (exactly the input vector already supplied 2 cycles before).

From Eq. (2), we see that $b$ and $b'$ represent two identical (resp. distinct) upsampled bits at each odd (resp. even) clock cycle: $\vec{b}_{2i-1} = \vec{b'}_{2i-1}$. Since the error detection occurs at odd cycles, the recovery, which starts a cycle after, will read two different inputs (i.e., not the same upsampled input) from $\vec{b}$ and $\vec{b'}$. This is consistent with the speedup of the circuit during recovery. The behavior of input buffers during recovery is illustrated in Section 3.6.

### 3.3 DTR Output Buffers

The error recovery procedure disturbs the vector stream $\vec{co}$ in comparison with the normal operating mode. To mask this effect at the primary outputs, we insert a DTR output buffer (Figure 6) before each primary output. They produce correct outputs but introduce in normal mode a latency loss of three clock cycles.

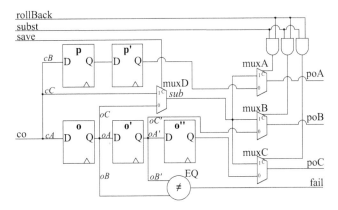

**Figure 6: DTR Output Buffer ($co$ output of the combinational part.**

The buffer is designed to be also fault-tolerant to any SET occurring inside or at its outputs. To achieve this property, the new primary outputs are triplicated ($poA$, $poB$, $poC$). The output buffers ensure that at least two out of them are correct at each *even* cycle. The surrounding circuit can thus read these outputs at even cycles and perform a vote to mask any SET that may have occurred at the outputs. This is just a possible implementation and a different design could be used, e.g., with a fault-model excluding/disregarding errors at the outputs or with different interface requirements.

Additional details about the behavior of output buffers are provided in Section 3.6.

### 3.4 DTR Control Block

The control block is shown in Figure 3. The control signals *save*, *rollBack* (for memory blocks), *rB* (for input buffers), and *subst* (for output buffers) are generated to support the transformed circuit functionality during *normal* and *recovery* modes.

Control block takes as an input the error detection signal *fail* (the disjunction of all memory blocks and output buffers individual *fail* signals). The functionality of the control block can be described as the Finite State Machine (FSM) of Figure 7. States *norm1* and *norm2* compose the *normal* mode which raises the *save* signal alternatively. When an error is detected (i.e., *fail* = 1), the FSM enters the recovery mode for 4 cycles and raises the corresponding signals.

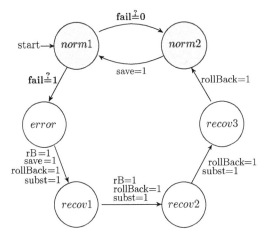

**Figure 7: FSM of the DTR control block: "$\overset{?}{=}$" denotes a guard, "=" an assignment and signals absent from an edge are set to 0.**

The control block itself is protected against SETs using TMR. Since its size (25 core cells) is negligible in comparison with the rest of the circuit, its triplication almost does not increase the hardware overhead (as confirmed by Figure 10). Therefore, the only way to corrupt the global control signals is by an SET outside the control block. This ensures that no two global control signals can be corrupted simultaneously.

It would be tedious to explain separately all the possible interactions of the control block with memory blocks and buffers. Instead, we present in Sections 3.5 and 3.6 the two operating modes of the DTR circuit: the *normal* mode (before a soft-error) and the *recovery* mode (after a soft-error). Section 3.7, which examines all possible SETs, also clarifies the mechanisms of the different components.

### 3.5 Normal Execution Mode

If no error is detected, the circuit is working in the normal operating mode. During this mode, the signal *rollBack* is always set to zero, while *save* is raised every even cycle:

$$save_{2i-1} = 0 \text{ and } save_{2i} = 1 \quad (3)$$

Since *save* is the enable signal of $r$ and $r'$, it organizes a four-cycle delay from $si$ to $r'$ in normal mode. The internal behavior of each DTR memory block in normal mode can be described by the following equations:

$$\begin{cases} rollBack_i = 0 \\ \vec{si}_i = \vec{d}_{i+1} = \vec{d}_{i+2} = \vec{so}_{i+2} \\ \vec{si}_{2i} = \vec{r}_{2i+1} = \vec{r}_{2i+2} = \vec{r'}_{2i+3} = \vec{r'}_{2i+4} \\ save_{2i-1} = 0, \; save_{2i} = 1 \end{cases} \quad (4)$$

It is easy to show that the DTR circuit verifies the same equalities as Eq. (1) for the original circuit:

$$\vec{co}_i = \varphi(\vec{ci}_i) \qquad \vec{ci}_i = \vec{pi}_i \oplus \vec{so}_i \qquad \vec{co}_i = \vec{po}_i \oplus \vec{si}_i \qquad (5)$$

From Eqs. (2), (4), and (5), we can derive two properties for the normal operating mode. First, the output bit stream $\vec{co}$ of the combinational part after the circuit transformation is a double-time upsampling of the corresponding bit stream $\vec{CO}$ of the original circuit. Formally:

PROPERTY 1. $\forall i \in \mathbb{N}^*. \; \vec{co}_{2i-1} = \vec{co}_{2i} = \vec{CO}_i$

PROOF. We assume that the two cells $d$ and $d'$ of each memory block are initialized as the original cell, and therefore $\vec{so}_1 = \vec{so}_2 = \vec{SO}_1$. By Eqs. (1) and (5), we have $\vec{co}_1 = \vec{co}_2 = \vec{CO}_1$. The proof is then a simple induction using Eqs. (1), (2), and (5). $\square$

Second, at each odd cycle, the outputs of the cells $d$ and $d'$ are equal.

PROPERTY 2. $\forall i \in \mathbb{N}^*. \; \vec{d}_{2i-1} = \vec{d'}_{2i-1}$

PROOF. At the first cycle ($i=1$), the property is true by the same initialization hypothesis as above. Property 2 and Eq. (5) entail that $\vec{si}_{2i-1} = \vec{si}_{2i}$. By Eq. (4), we have:

$$\begin{aligned}
\vec{si}_{2i} &= \vec{d}_{2i+1} &= \vec{d'}_{2i+2} \\
&\parallel \\
\vec{si}_{2i-1} &= \vec{d}_{2i} &= \vec{d'}_{2i+1}
\end{aligned}$$

and thus, $\forall i > 0, \vec{d}_{2i+1} = \vec{d'}_{2i+1}$, which is equivalent to $\forall i > 1, \vec{d}_{2i-1} = \vec{d'}_{2i-1}$. $\square$

For error detection, we check the violation of Property 2 which is performed by the $EQ$ comparator (Figure 4). If at some odd cycle $2j-1$ the $d$ and $d'$ cells of a memory block differ, an error is detected and the $fail$ signal will be raised ($fail_{2j-1} = 1$). The circuit has to rollback to the correct state stored in $\vec{r'}$ and to re-compute the previous step. The rollback is performed by propagating $\vec{r'}$ to $\vec{so}$. From Eq. (4), we can derive the following equation:

$$\vec{r'}_{2j-1} = \vec{r'}_{2j} = \vec{si}_{2j-4} \qquad (6)$$

Eq. (6) means that, at the moment of an error detection (and at the next clock cycle), the recovery bit $r'$ is set to the value of the input signal $si$ 3 cycles before. It will be shown in Section 3.7 that all recovery bits contain correct values when an error is detected (i.e., an error in the data bits never corrupts $\vec{r'}$).

## 3.6 Recovery Execution Mode

If an error has been detected, the circuit performs a rollback followed by three consecutive cycles during which the double time redundancy mechanism is switched-off. These steps are implemented by a sequence of signals ($save$, $rollBack$, $subst$, and $rB$) produced by the control block.

The left part of Table 3.5 (in white) shows the values of bit vectors in the transformed circuit cycle by cycle when an error is detected at clock cycle $i$. The behavior of the circuit in normal mode (when no error occurs) is shown in the right part (in gray). Recall that, in the normal mode, the vector $\vec{ci}$ at cycle $i$ is such that $\vec{ci}_i = \vec{pi}_i \oplus \vec{so}_i = \vec{pi}_i \oplus \vec{si}_{i-2}$. The principle of the rollback mechanism is that the DTR memory blocks re-inject the last correct saved state (the $\vec{si}$ vector)

while the DTR input buffers will re-inject the corresponding primary input (the $\vec{pi}$ component).

At the clock cycle $(i+1)$ following an error detection, the recovery starts and the correct state represented by $\vec{r'}$ is pushed through $\vec{so}$. Consequently, $\vec{so}_{i+1} = \vec{r'}_{i+1} = \vec{si}_{i-3}$ instead of the expected $\vec{si}_{i-1}$ in the normal mode. Thus, the second component of $\vec{ci}_{i+1}$ is $\vec{si}_{i-3}$. The primary input vector is also replaced by the vector kept in the input buffers; that is, at the $i+1$ cycle $\vec{pi}_{i+1}$ is replaced by $\vec{pi}_{i-1}$. Recall that, during recovery, the circuit is working with the throughput of the original circuit, which is twice higher than in the normal mode. In particular, during the cycles $i+2$, $i+3$, and $i+4$, $\vec{d}$ propagates directly through the $\vec{so}$ outputs of each memory block, bypassing the memory cells $\vec{d'}$. This is implemented by raising $rollBack$ and lowering $save$ which control the $muxA$ and $muxB$ multiplexers appropriately in each memory block. This is safe since the $SET(1, K)$ fault-model guarantees that no additional error can occur just after a SET.

Consider cycle $i+2$: the second component of $\vec{ci}_{i+2}$ is $\vec{si}_{i-1}$ ($\vec{si}_{i-2}$, which is identical to $\vec{si}_{i-1}$, has been skipped). Similarly, the primary input vector is replaced by $\vec{pi}_{i+1}$, since, in the input buffers, $\vec{b'}_{i+2} = \vec{pi}_i$ and $\vec{pi}_{i+1} = \vec{pi}_i$. It follows that $\vec{ci}_{i+1} = \vec{pi}_{i-1} \oplus \vec{si}_{i-3}$ and $\vec{ci}_{i+2} = \vec{pi}_{i+1} \oplus \vec{si}_{i-1}$.

Let us look more closely at how an error propagates and how it is masked. The error $\vec{d}_i \neq \vec{d'}_i$ detected at cycle $i$ does not indicate which of $\vec{d}$ or $\vec{d'}$ is corrupted. The fault-model only guarantees that their simultaneous corruption is not possible. We consider both of them as potentially corrupted and the † and ‡ marks indicate the two possible bit vector corruptions. We track the error propagation cycle by cycle based on data dependencies between vectors as shown in Table 3.5.

Case #1: If $\vec{d'}_i$ contains a corrupted value $\dagger\vec{si}_{i-2}$, it contaminates $\vec{ci}_i$. Since this input bit vector is corrupted, the outputs of the combinational circuit can be corrupted as well as $\vec{d}_{i+1}$ that latches $\dagger\vec{si}_i$. This corrupted value propagates to $\vec{d'}$, so $\vec{d'}_{i+2} = \dagger\vec{si}_i$. Since $\vec{d'}$ is bypassed and $\vec{d}$ propagates directly through the wires $\vec{so}$, the error at $\dagger\vec{si}_i$ is logically masked at $muxB$ by $rollBack$, which is raised during 4 cycles after the error detection.

Case #2: If $\vec{d}_i$ contains a corrupted value $\ddagger\vec{si}_{i-1}$, it will propagate to $\vec{d'}$ and $\vec{d'}_{i+1} = \ddagger\vec{si}_{i-1}$. Since $\ddagger\vec{si}_{i-1}$ has been latched by $\vec{d}$ and $\vec{r}$ at the same clock cycle, $\vec{r}_i$ is also corrupted: $\vec{r}_i = \ddagger\vec{si}_{i-1}$. When rollback happens at cycle $i+1$, $\vec{r}$ propagates to $\vec{r'}$ and remains in $\vec{r'}$ until the next raised $save$. The $save$ signal is raised only 5 cycles after the error-detection, when $rollBack$ is lowered again. As a result, any error in $\vec{r'}_{i+5}$ will be re-written with a new correct data and cannot propagate through signals $\vec{so}$ due to the logical masking by $rollBack = 0$ at $muxB$.

All corrupted signals disappear from the circuit state within 6 clock cycles after an error detection. The whole circuit returns to a correct state within 8 cycles. As it is shown in the next section, the error detection occurs at worst 2 cycles later after an SET.

Table 3.6 represents the behavior of output buffers in the same situation (i.e., the recovery procedure when an error is detected at cycle $i$). The signal names correspond to Figure 6.

We investigate all possible SETs in the next section.

| clk | $\vec{pi}$ | $\vec{b}$ | $\vec{b'}$ | $\vec{ci}$ | $\vec{d}$ | $\vec{d'}$ | $\vec{r}$ | $\vec{r'}$ | f | sa | ro | $\vec{ci}$ | $\vec{d}$ | $\vec{d'}$ | $\vec{r}$ | $\vec{r'}$ |
|---|---|---|---|---|---|---|---|---|---|---|---|---|---|---|---|---|
| $i-3$ | $\vec{pi}_{i-3}$ | $\vec{pi}_{i-4}$ | $\vec{pi}_{i-5}$ | $\vec{pi}_{i-3} \oplus \vec{si}_{i-5}$ | $\vec{si}_{i-4}$ | $\vec{si}_{i-5}$ | $\vec{si}_{i-5}$ | $\vec{si}_{i-7}$ | ? | 1 | 0 | $\vec{pi}_{i-3} \oplus \vec{si}_{i-5}$ | $\vec{si}_{i-4}$ | $\vec{si}_{i-5}$ | $\vec{si}_{i-5}$ | $\vec{si}_{i-7}$ |
| $i-2$ | $\vec{pi}_{i-2}$ | $\vec{pi}_{i-3}$ | $\vec{pi}_{i-4}$ | $\vec{pi}_{i-2} \oplus \vec{si}_{i-4}$ | $\vec{si}_{i-3}$ | $\vec{si}_{i-4}$ | $\vec{si}_{i-3}$ | $\vec{si}_{i-5}$ | 0 | 0 | 0 | $\vec{pi}_{i-2} \oplus \vec{si}_{i-4}$ | $\vec{si}_{i-3}$ | $\vec{si}_{i-4}$ | $\vec{si}_{i-3}$ | $\vec{si}_{i-5}$ |
| $i-1$ | $\vec{pi}_{i-1}$ | $\vec{pi}_{i-2}$ | $\vec{pi}_{i-3}$ | $\vec{pi}_{i-1} \oplus \vec{si}_{i-3}$ | $\vec{si}_{i-2}$ | $\vec{si}_{i-3}$ | $\vec{si}_{i-3}$ | $\vec{si}_{i-5}$ | ? | 1 | 0 | $\vec{pi}_{i-1} \oplus \vec{si}_{i-3}$ | $\vec{si}_{i-2}$ | $\vec{si}_{i-3}$ | $\vec{si}_{i-3}$ | $\vec{si}_{i-5}$ |
| $i$ | $\vec{pi}_i$ | $\vec{pi}_{i-1}$ | $\vec{pi}_{i-2}$ | $\vec{pi}_i \oplus \dagger\vec{si}_{i-2}$ | $\ddagger\vec{si}_{i-1}$ | $\dagger\vec{si}_{i-2}$ | $\ddagger\vec{si}_{i-1}$ | $\vec{si}_{i-3}$ | 1 | 0 | 0 | $\vec{pi}_i \oplus \vec{si}_{i-2}$ | $\vec{si}_{i-1}$ | $\vec{si}_{i-2}$ | $\vec{si}_{i-1}$ | $\vec{si}_{i-3}$ |
| $i+1$ | $\vec{pi}_{i+1}$ | $\vec{pi}_i$ | $\vec{pi}_{i-1}$ | $\vec{pi}_{i-1} \oplus \vec{si}_{i-3}$ | $\dagger\vec{si}_i$ | $\ddagger\vec{si}_{i-1}$ | $\ddagger\vec{si}_{i-1}$ | $\vec{si}_{i-3}$ | ? | 1 | 1 | $\vec{pi}_{i+1} \oplus \vec{si}_{i-1}$ | $\vec{si}_i$ | $\vec{si}_{i-1}$ | $\vec{si}_{i-1}$ | $\vec{si}_{i-3}$ |
| $i+2$ | $\vec{pi}_{i+2}$ | $\vec{pi}_{i+1}$ | $\vec{pi}_i$ | $\vec{pi}_{i+1} \oplus \vec{si}_{i-1}$ | $\vec{si}_{i-1}$ | $\dagger\vec{si}_i$ | $\vec{si}_{i-1}$ | $\ddagger\vec{si}_{i-1}$ | ? | 0 | 1 | $\vec{pi}_{i+2} \oplus \vec{si}_i$ | $\vec{si}_{i+1}$ | $\vec{si}_i$ | $\vec{si}_{i+1}$ | $\vec{si}_{i-1}$ |
| $i+3$ | $\vec{pi}_{i+3}$ | $\vec{pi}_{i+2}$ | $\vec{pi}_{i+1}$ | $\vec{pi}_{i+3} \oplus \vec{si}_{i+1}$ | $\vec{si}_{i+1}$ | $\vec{si}_{i-1}$ | $\vec{si}_{i-1}$ | $\ddagger\vec{si}_{i-1}$ | ? | 0 | 1 | $\vec{pi}_{i+3} \oplus \vec{si}_{i+1}$ | $\vec{si}_{i+2}$ | $\vec{si}_{i+1}$ | $\vec{si}_{i+1}$ | $\vec{si}_{i-1}$ |
| $i+4$ | $\vec{pi}_{i+4}$ | $\vec{pi}_{i+3}$ | $\vec{pi}_{i+2}$ | $\vec{pi}_{i+4} \oplus \vec{si}_{i+3}$ | $\vec{si}_{i+3}$ | $\vec{si}_{i+1}$ | $\vec{si}_{i-1}$ | $\ddagger\vec{si}_{i-1}$ | ? | 0 | 1 | $\vec{pi}_{i+4} \oplus \vec{si}_{i+2}$ | $\vec{si}_{i+3}$ | $\vec{si}_{i+2}$ | $\vec{si}_{i+3}$ | $\vec{si}_{i+1}$ |
| $i+5$ | $\vec{pi}_{i+5}$ | $\vec{pi}_{i+4}$ | $\vec{pi}_{i+3}$ | $\vec{pi}_{i+5} \oplus \vec{si}_{i+3}$ | $\vec{si}_{i+4}$ | $\vec{si}_{i+3}$ | $\vec{si}_{i-1}$ | $\ddagger\vec{si}_{i-1}$ | ? | 1 | 0 | $\vec{pi}_{i+5} \oplus \vec{si}_{i+3}$ | $\vec{si}_{i+4}$ | $\vec{si}_{i+3}$ | $\vec{si}_{i+3}$ | $\vec{si}_{i+1}$ |
| $i+6$ | $\vec{pi}_{i+6}$ | $\vec{pi}_{i+5}$ | $\vec{pi}_{i+4}$ | $\vec{pi}_{i+6} \oplus \vec{si}_{i+4}$ | $\vec{si}_{i+5}$ | $\vec{si}_{i+4}$ | $\vec{si}_{i+5}$ | $\vec{si}_{i-1}$ | 0 | 0 | 0 | $\vec{pi}_{i+6} \oplus \vec{si}_{i+4}$ | $\vec{si}_{i+5}$ | $\vec{si}_{i+4}$ | $\vec{si}_{i+5}$ | $\vec{si}_{i+3}$ |
| $i+7$ | $\vec{pi}_{i+7}$ | $\vec{pi}_{i+6}$ | $\vec{pi}_{i+5}$ | $\vec{pi}_{i+7} \oplus \vec{si}_{i+5}$ | $\vec{si}_{i+6}$ | $\vec{si}_{i+5}$ | $\vec{si}_{i+5}$ | $\vec{si}_{i-1}$ | ? | 1 | 0 | $\vec{pi}_{i+7} \oplus \vec{si}_{i+5}$ | $\vec{si}_{i+6}$ | $\vec{si}_{i+5}$ | $\vec{si}_{i+5}$ | $\vec{si}_{i+3}$ |
| $i+8$ | $\vec{pi}_{i+8}$ | $\vec{pi}_{i+7}$ | $\vec{pi}_{i+6}$ | $\vec{pi}_{i+8} \oplus \vec{si}_{i+6}$ | $\vec{si}_{i+7}$ | $\vec{si}_{i+6}$ | $\vec{si}_{i+7}$ | $\vec{si}_{i+5}$ | 0 | 0 | 0 | $\vec{pi}_{i+8} \oplus \vec{si}_{i+6}$ | $\vec{si}_{i+7}$ | $\vec{si}_{i+6}$ | $\vec{si}_{i+7}$ | $\vec{si}_{i+5}$ |

$\dagger = \ddagger$ but for two mutually-exclusive error propagation cases
*f*:fail; *sa*:save; *ro*:rollBack

**Table 3.6: Recovery Process: Input/Output Buffers Reaction for an Error Detection at Cycle $i$**

| clk | $\vec{pi}$ | $\vec{ci}$ | $\vec{o}$ | $\vec{o'}$ | $\vec{o''}$ | $\overrightarrow{poA}/B/C$ | $fail$ | sav | ro | rB | sub | $\vec{o}$ | $\vec{o'}$ | $\vec{o''}$ | $\overrightarrow{poA}/B/C$ |
|---|---|---|---|---|---|---|---|---|---|---|---|---|---|---|---|
| $i-3$ | $\vec{pi}_{i-3}$ | $\vec{pi}_{i-3} \oplus \vec{si}_{i-5}$ | $\vec{co}_{i-4}$ | $\vec{co}_{i-5}$ | $\vec{co}_{i-6}$ | $\vec{co}_{i-5}$ | ? | 1 | 0 | 0 | 0 | $\vec{co}_{i-4}$ | $\vec{co}_{i-5}$ | $\vec{co}_{i-6}$ | $\vec{co}_{i-5} = \vec{co}_{i-6}$ |
| $i-2$ | $\vec{pi}_{i-2}$ | $\vec{pi}_{i-2} \oplus \vec{si}_{i-4}$ | $\vec{co}_{i-3}$ | $\vec{co}_{i-4}$ | $\vec{co}_{i-5}$ | $ignore$ | 0 | 0 | 0 | 0 | 0 | $\vec{co}_{i-3}$ | $\vec{co}_{i-4}$ | $\vec{co}_{i-5}$ | $ignore$ |
| $i-1$ | $\vec{pi}_{i-1}$ | $\vec{pi}_{i-1} \oplus \vec{si}_{i-3}$ | $\vec{co}_{i-2}$ | $\vec{co}_{i-3}$ | $\vec{co}_{i-4}$ | $\vec{co}_{i-3}$ | ? | 1 | 0 | 0 | 0 | $\vec{co}_{i-2}$ | $\vec{co}_{i-3}$ | $\vec{co}_{i-4}$ | $\vec{co}_{i-3} = \vec{co}_{i-4}$ |
| $i$ | $\vec{pi}_i$ | $\vec{pi}_i \oplus \dagger\vec{si}_{i-2}$ | $\ddagger\vec{co}_{i-1}$ | $\ddagger\vec{co}_{i-2}$ | $\vec{co}_{i-3}$ | $ignore$ | 1 | 0 | 0 | 0 | 0 | $\vec{co}_{i-1}$ | $\vec{co}_{i-2}$ | $\vec{co}_{i-3}$ | $ignore$ |
| $i+1$ | $\vec{pi}_{i+1}$ | $\vec{pi}_{i-1} \oplus \vec{si}_{i-3}$ | $\dagger\vec{co}_i$ | $\ddagger\vec{co}_{i-1}$ | $\ddagger\vec{co}_{i-2}$ | $\vec{co}_{i-1}\ (\leftarrow)$ | ? | 1 | 1 | 1 | 1 | $\vec{co}_i$ | $\vec{co}_{i-1}$ | $\vec{co}_{i-2}$ | $\vec{co}_{i-1} = \vec{co}_{i-2}$ |
| $i+2$ | $\vec{pi}_{i+2}$ | $\vec{pi}_{i+1} \oplus \vec{si}_{i-1}$ | $\vec{co}_{i-1}$ | $\dagger\vec{co}_i$ | $\ddagger\vec{co}_{i-1}$ | $ignore$ | ? | 0 | 1 | 1 | 1 | $\vec{co}_{i+1}$ | $\vec{co}_i$ | $\vec{co}_{i-1}$ | $ignore$ |
| $i+3$ | $\vec{pi}_{i+3}$ | $\vec{pi}_{i+3} \oplus \vec{si}_{i+1}$ | $\vec{co}_{i+1}$ | $\vec{co}_{i-1}$ | $\dagger\vec{co}_i$ | $\vec{co}_{i+1}\ (\leftarrow)$ | ? | 0 | 1 | 0 | 1 | $\vec{co}_{i+2}$ | $\vec{co}_{i+1}$ | $\vec{co}_i$ | $\vec{co}_{i+1} = \vec{co}_i$ |
| $i+4$ | $\vec{pi}_{i+4}$ | $\vec{pi}_{i+4} \oplus \vec{si}_{i+3}$ | $\vec{co}_{i+3}$ | $\vec{co}_{i+1}$ | $\vec{co}_{i-1}$ | $ignore$ | ? | 0 | 1 | 0 | 0 | $\vec{co}_{i+3}$ | $\vec{co}_{i+2}$ | $\vec{co}_{i+1}$ | $ignore$ |
| $i+5$ | $\vec{pi}_{i+5}$ | $\vec{pi}_{i+5} \oplus \vec{si}_{i+3}$ | $\vec{co}_{i+4}$ | $\vec{co}_{i+3}$ | $\vec{co}_{i+1}$ | $\vec{co}_{i+3}$ | ? | 1 | 0 | 0 | 0 | $\vec{co}_{i+4}$ | $\vec{co}_{i+3}$ | $\vec{co}_{i+2}$ | $\vec{co}_{i+3} = \vec{co}_{i+2}$ |
| $i+6$ | $\vec{pi}_{i+6}$ | $\vec{pi}_{i+6} \oplus \vec{si}_{i+4}$ | $\vec{co}_{i+5}$ | $\vec{co}_{i+4}$ | $\vec{co}_{i+3}$ | $ignore$ | 0 | 0 | 0 | 0 | 0 | $\vec{co}_{i+5}$ | $\vec{co}_{i+4}$ | $\vec{co}_{i+3}$ | $ignore$ |
| $i+7$ | $\vec{pi}_{i+7}$ | $\vec{pi}_{i+7} \oplus \vec{si}_{i+5}$ | $\vec{co}_{i+6}$ | $\vec{co}_{i+5}$ | $\vec{co}_{i+4}$ | $\vec{co}_{i+5}$ | ? | 1 | 0 | 0 | 0 | $\vec{co}_{i+6}$ | $\vec{co}_{i+5}$ | $\vec{co}_{i+4}$ | $\vec{co}_{i+5} = \vec{co}_{i+4}$ |
| $i+8$ | $\vec{pi}_{i+8}$ | $\vec{pi}_{i+8} \oplus \vec{si}_{i+6}$ | $\vec{co}_{i+7}$ | $\vec{co}_{i+6}$ | $\vec{co}_{i+5}$ | $ignore$ | 0 | 0 | 0 | 0 | 0 | $\vec{co}_{i+7}$ | $\vec{co}_{i+6}$ | $\vec{co}_{i+5}$ | $ignore$ |

$\ddagger = \dagger$ but for two error-detection cases: $\ddagger$ - detection in Output Buffer; $\dagger$ - detection in a preceding Memory Block
$(\leftarrow)$ - data substitution performed by multiplixers $muxA$, $muxB$, $muxC$, $muxD$
$sav$ - save; $ro$ - rollBack; $sub$ - subst

## 3.7 Fault Tolerance Guarantees

Hereafter, we check all possible SET insertion cases. We write $j$ to denote the clock cycle where the SET occurs. The causal relationship is written as "$\rightarrow$".

① An SET in $\vec{ci}$, $\vec{si}$, the *rollBack* signal, the internal wire $dA'$, or the combinational part $\varphi$ may lead to $\dagger\vec{d}$ and $\dagger\vec{r}$. During odd cycles, the simultaneous corruption of $\vec{d}$ and $\vec{r}$ is not possible since the *save* signal logically masks SET propagation towards $r$ memory cell. As a result, there are two cases:

1. $\dagger\vec{d}_{j+1}$; *if* $j = 2i-1$. If $\vec{d}$ has been corrupted by an SET in the preceding combinational circuit, an error will be detected by the comparator within the next two cycles. $fail_{j+2} = 1$ since $\vec{d}_{j+2}$ is calculated correctly. Since $\vec{r'}$ is correct, the recovery will return the circuit to its correct state.

2. $\dagger\vec{d}_{j+1} \wedge \dagger\vec{r}_{j+1}$; *if* $j = 2i$. In this case, we must check that the error is detected before reaching $\vec{r'}$. Actually, the error will be detected at the next (odd) clock cycle after an error occurrence: $fail_{j+1} = 1$. But $\vec{r'}$ keeps its correct value because $save_{j+1} = 0$. The recovery process starts at cycle $j + 2$, re-writing the correct $\vec{r'}$ with a possible corrupted data, but in the same cycle $\vec{r'}_{j+2}$ outputs a correct value that rollbacks the circuit to a correct state.

② Consider the following SETs: $\dagger save_j$, $\dagger\vec{r}_j$, $\dagger\vec{r'}_j$, $\dagger\vec{mu}_j$, $\dagger siB_j$ and $\dagger\vec{dC}_j$, which may result in the corruption of the pipeline $r - r'$ (see Figure 4). Such corruption is not detected by the comparator and cannot propagate to the data bits. It disappears a few cycles later at $muxB$ by $rollBack = 0$. So, this failure is masked.

③ An SET during an odd clock cycle at the *fail* line possibly leads to spurious error detection followed by a recovery. But $\vec{r'}_{j+1}$ is valid and the recovery will be performed cor-

223

rectly. During even clock cycles, an SET at the *fail* line remains silent since, at these cycles, a *fail* is ignored by the control block.

④ An SET at the output signal of $d'$ may lead to three different cases:

1. $\dagger \vec{d'}_j \rightarrow \dagger \vec{so}_j \rightarrow \dagger \varphi_j$, which is equivalent to case ①;

2. $\dagger \vec{d'}_j \rightarrow \dagger \vec{fail}_j$, which is equivalent to case ③;

3. $\dagger \vec{d'}_j \rightarrow \dagger \varphi_j \wedge \dagger \vec{fail}_j$ *i.e.*, a simultaneous corruption of combinational circuit and a *fail* signal. The recovery process starts at the next clock cycle $j+1$ using the correct $\vec{r'}_{j+1}$.

⑤ An SET at the output signal of $d$ may lead to the corruption of $dA$, $dB$, and/or $dC$ (see Figure 4). First, a corruption of $dC$ will always be masked regardless of the possible common corruptions of $dA$ or $dB$. Indeed, if $dC$ is corrupted, then the propagation/corruption will be masked by $muxB$ since $rollBack = 0$ (a simultaneous corruption is impossible). Five other cases must be considered:

- If the error propagates to $dA$ (but not $dB$) and is latched by $d'$ during an *even* cycle, then an error will be detected at the next odd cycle $j+1$ and will be masked as in case ①;

- If the error propagates to $dA$ (but not $dB$) and is latched by $d'$ during an *odd* cycle, then it is equivalent to a corruption of the combinational circuit one clock cycle after the latch. It will be masked as in case ①;

- If the error propagates to $dA$ and $dB$ and corrupts $d'$ and *fail* at an even cycle, then we are back to the first case above; indeed, the control block reads *fail* only at odd cycles and the corruption of *fail* will not be considered;

- If the error propagates to $dA$ and $dB$ and corrupts $d'$ and *fail* at an odd cycle, then the recovery starts at the next clock cycle using the correct $\vec{r'}$ and disregarding the corrupted $\vec{d'}$;

- If the error propagates to $dB$ (but not $dA$), it may corrupt the *fail* signal and it is masked as in case ③.

An SET in the control block is fixed within one clock cycle since it is protected by TMR. The hardware overhead of TMR for this modest sub-circuit is small.

An SET may also occur in input buffers, in particular in the memory cells $b$ and $b'$ (see Figure 5). Such an error will be logically masked within two clock cycles by the signal $rB = 0$ at the multiplexer.

The most critical SET is the one that may occur at the primary input signals $\vec{pi}$ and is latched both by the memory blocks and the input buffers. Double-redundancy can detect the error but it has no way to replay the input signal. Such an SET can be masked only if a surrounding circuit can read the *fail* signal from the DTR circuit and provide a third copy of $\vec{pi}$. Here, we do not enforce such a requirement on the surrounding circuit and consider that the fault-model forbids the corruption of the primary inputs.

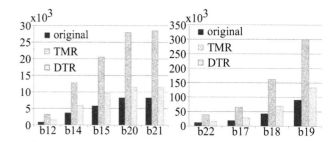

**Figure 8: Circuit size (in core cells) after transformation (large circuits).**

An SET occurring just before an output buffer at $\vec{co}$ (see Figure 6) will be detected by the comparator (like in memory blocks). The error will be masked at multiplexers $muxA$, $muxB$, or $muxC$. The structure of the output buffer provides an isolation for the pipelines $o - o' - o''$ and $p - p'$, which in turn guarantees that at least two memory cells among $o'$, $o''$, and $p'$ are correct during all even clock cycles. The new primary outputs, $poA$, $poB$, and $poC$, are identical during all even clock cycles if no SET occurs, and only one can differ from the others if an SET occurs. This fault-tolerance property still holds even if one of the control signals ($rollBack$, $subst$, or $save$) is corrupted by an SET. Furthermore, using three outputs, as in TMR, gives the surrounding circuit the capability to mask (by voting) any error occurring at the primary outputs.

## 4. EXPERIMENTAL RESULTS

The proposed DTR transformation has been applied to the *ITC*'99 benchmark suite [9]. We considered two transformations: full TMR (*i.e.*, with triplicated voters after each memory cell) and DTR as described before. Each transformed circuit was synthesized for FPGA using *Synplify Pro* without any optimization (resource sharing, FSM optimization, etc.). We have chosen flash-based ProASIC3 FPGA family as a synthesis target. Its configuration memory is immune to soft-errors [7] and data memory is protected with one of the above transformations.

The circuits are sorted according to the number of core cells of the original circuit after synthesis. Figures 8 shows the results for the largest circuits and 9 shows the results for the smallest ones.

The DTR circuits require significantly less hardware for almost all circuits of the suite. Since the technique reuses the combinational part, hardware benefits are growing with the size of the combinational part. The constant hardware cost of the supporting mechanisms (control block, input/output buffers) becomes negligible when the size of the original circuit is large enough.

Figure 8 shows that the DTR circuits are 1.39 to 2.1 times larger than the original ones. For comparison, TMR circuits are 3.3 to 3.9 larger than the original ones. The largest hardware overhead for all circuit transformations has been observed for $b12$ circuit, a game controller with 121 memory cells [9]. The TMR and DTR version of $b12$ are respectively 3.9 and 2.1 times larger than the original circuit.

Figure 9 shows that, for the majority of the smallest circuits ($< 100$ memory cells), DTR still have less hardware overhead than TMR. But this benefit is negated for the tiny circuits $b01$, $b02$, and $b06$ ($< 10$ memory cells) due to the

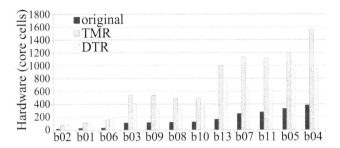

**Figure 9: Circuit size after transformation (small circuits).**

hardware overhead of the control block and input/output buffers. For such small circuits, TMR is clearly a better option.

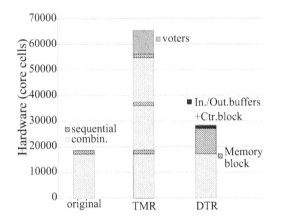

**Figure 10: Transformed circuits profiling (for *b17*).**

Figure 10 demonstrates why DTR transformation has significantly less hardware overhead compared to TMR. The synthesized circuit *b17* (first bar) consists of a large combinational part (bottom part: 17240 core cells) and a small sequential part (top part: 1415 core cells). In the TMR version of *b17* (second bar) the triplicated combinational part is dominant. The triplicated voters after each memory cell (for protection against SET) occupy 14.5% of the whole circuit. The DTR circuit (third bar) reuses the combinational part, so its size stays the same. The hardware cost of the DTR control block, input and output buffers is negligible (only 0.05% of all needed hardware resources). As a result, after DTR transformation, the circtuit occupies 153% of its original size (hardware overhead = 53%) whereas, after TMR, it takes 350% (harware overhead = 250%). The overhead of DTR is 4.7 times smaller than TMR for *b17* and between 2.7 to 6.1 times smaller for the whole *ITC*'99 benchmark suite.

Although DTR has a significantly smaller hardware overhead than TMR it decreases the circuit throughput. Indeed, since the technique requires the input streams to be upsampled, the throughput of the transformed circuit is at least divided by two. Figure 11 shows the ratio of the transformed circuit throughput *w.r.t.* the corresponding original throughput for the ITC'99 benchmark suite (sorted left to right *w.r.t.* the size of the original circuit). Throughput is defined as the number of significant bits (*i.e.*, those not created by the upsampling) processed per time unit. Besides the upsampling, the DTR transformation influences by itself

(as well as TMR) the circuit maximum frequency, which also changes the final throughput. In particular, the maximum synthesizable frequency after DTR transformation reaches ~75% of the original frequency for small circuits (for TMR it is ~77% ) and ~92% for large circuits (for TMR it is ~93%).

TMR voters clearly slow down the circuit: the decrease of throughput varies from 3–10% for large circuits (*e.g.*, *b17*, *b20 − b22*) to 25–35% for small ones (*e.g.*, *b02*, *b06*, *b03*). In the best case, the throughput of DTR circuits can reach 50% of the original circuit due to the double upsampling of inputs. The control block and the multiplexers in memory blocks also introduce a small extra overhead. For large circuits, the throughput is 40–50% of the original, while for small circuits it drops to 30–40%.

## 5. RELATED WORK

The principles of time-redundancy, check-pointing and roll-back have been implemented in various methods. However, the existing schemes are either ASIC-oriented requiring a strong control on the clock lines, or do not tolerate SETs.

An application-oriented use of time-redundancy can be found in fault-tolerant designs of arithmetic units [10, 11] and CPUs [12, 13]. In the former case, the regularity of an arithmetic operation is used to organize an optimized unit architecture with error-detection and error-masking characteristics. For ASICs, the hardware overhead (up to 72%) and the throughput overhead (up to 19%) depend on the number of bits of the operation. These techniques are limited to specific application domains. In the latter case, a CPU is reorganized so that it executes each instruction twice with a further comparison and a rollback upon an error detection in order to self-recover [12]. The hardware overhead for FPGAs is 50-60% with only 79% of fault coverage (the performance penalty is not indicated). Time-redundancy is used at a higher level in [13]: the thread level. Time overhead is stated to be 30% while fault-coverage is not given. In both cases, these techniques, dedicated to CPUs, require the knowledge of the macro-architecture and do not guaranty full error masking.

Some ASIC-oriented time-redundant techniques rely on latching-window masking when an SET glitch is not latched by memory cells, since it does not satisfy setup and hold time conditions. Nicolaidis *et al.* [14, 15] present such an approach with a hardware overhead of 20-50% and 97-100% error-detection efficiency. The performance overhead is comparable to the one of TMR. A similar technique has been presented in [16] for SRAM-based FPGAs. However, no indication is given about its throughput overhead and nor how to organize three independent clock lines shifted relatively to each other to guarantee SETs masking. The latching-window principle is commonly used in ASIC CPU pipelines [17–19]. A "shadow" latch with its own clock line is attached to each original memory cell to create an error detection mechanism through time properties tuning. Being developed to tolerate soft-errors to organize a safe voltage scaling, these techniques have a performance penalty as little as 3% providing near 100% fault-masking. However, all the mentioned restrictions (precise time properties tunings, additional clock lines, pipelined architecture) prevent the use of these approaches for FPGAs, where special circuitries to implement these techniques are not normally available.

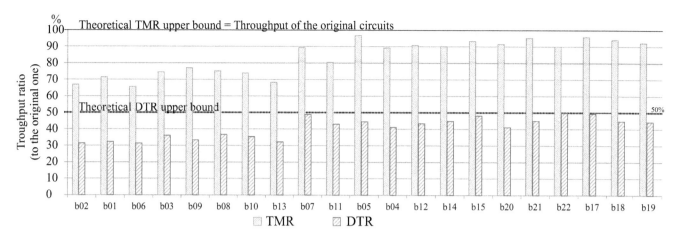

Figure 11: Throughput ratio of TMR, and DTR transformed circuits.

General check-pointing/rollback techniques have been proposed in [20, 21]. As in our technique, it is implemented using a micro-architectural transformation. However, the resulting circuit is tolerant to SEUs but not SETs, regardless of the error detection mechanism used. Indeed, an SET may corrupt both a cell (*i.e.*, the current state) and its copy (*i.e.*, its check-point). As a result, when an error is detected, the rollback may return the circuit to an incorrect state. Our implementation excludes such behavior, because an error is always detected before a potentially corrupted image (contained in $r$ cells, see Fig. 4) propagates to the checkpoints (represented by $r'$ cells).

A Synplicity Inc. patent [22] shows how time-redundancy can be implemented through a time-multiplexed combinatorial circuit. This technique is close to ours in that it replaces all memory cells by a circuit similar to our memory block. However, it does not mask all possible SETs and uses triple (or higher) time redundancy. Using micro-level checkpointing/rollback (as well as a speedup mode and IO buffers), we can implement stronger fault-tolerance guarantees using double-time redundancy only.

## 6. CONCLUSION

We proposed a novel and general logic-level circuit transformation to automatically introduce time-redundancy for fault-tolerance in digital circuits. Our DTR technique guarantees that the transformed circuits are tolerant towards any SET (*a fortiori* SEU) with no influence on output streams, provided that errors occur less frequently than one every 10 clock cycles. The DTR transformation is formally provable which is important for safety-critical systems. Our approach is technologically independent, does not require any specific hardware support, and is suitable for stream processing.

The technique is based on the time-redundancy principle where a combinational circuit is time-multiplexed. Our approach associates in a new way several techniques: double-time redundancy, error detection, micro-level checkpointing/rollback, a speedup mode, and input/output buffers. The transformations substitute the original memory cells with a small circuit (a memory block), which introduces a time-redundant masking mechanism in an automatic manner.

In order to verify the fault-tolerance of the transformed circuit, we exhaustively checked all possible occurrences of SETs. We have applied the proposed transformations to the *ITC'*99 benchmark suite. Experimental results for flash-based FPGA synthesis show that the hardware overhead of DTR is 2.7 to 6.1 times smaller compared to TMR. It makes the overall size of DTR circuits 1.9 to 2.5 times smaller than TMR for circuits with more than 100 memory cells. DTR is less beneficial for small circuits (less than 100 memory cells and small combinational logic).

Such significant hardware reduction has been achieved with a trade-off on the transformed circuit's throughput. The throughput of a DTR circuit is 50–55% of the corresponding TMR circuit throughput. However, other existing time-redundant error-correcting techniques implementable in COTS FPGAs have higher throughput loss. However, the proposed technique is harder to apply selectively to subcircuit as it can be done with TMR. The input/output streams upsampling may lead to adjustments of surrounding circuits.

Our transformation is an alternative to TMR for any logic intensive circuits where hardware overhead takes precedence over throughput. As in software, hardware time redundancy is only suited to applications that do not require high throughput. A particular target is flash-based FPGA designs (where hardware size is crucial) for embedded systems used in safety critical domains (*e.g.*, physical-device controllers, power supply sequencers, crypto cores). Existing FPGA synthesis tools can easily be enriched with our DTR technique.

An easy extension to DTR allows the surrounding circuit to switch off time redundancy (as the control block does in the recovery phase). This feature permits to dynamically and temporarily give up fault-tolerance and speed up the circuit. The motivations for such changes can be based on the observed change in radiation environment or the processing of (non)critical data.

In addition, DTR introduces new pipelined cells which may allow optimizations using retiming. In particular, memory cells $r$ and $d$ might be moved into the combinatorial circuit to break its critical path.

In this paper, we did not consider SETs on the clock line. DTR could be made tolerant to this kind of faults by using two independent and synchronous clocks. They would be used to prevent the simultaneous corruption of particular memory cells and guarantee error detection and proper recovery. For instance, memory cells $(d, d')$ should use two different clocks to avoid their simultaneous corruption that would prohibit error-detection.

Finally, even if we have manually checked all possible occurrences of SETs and performed fault-insertions on a few transformed circuits with the *ModelSim* simulator, a mechanically checked proof is necessary for a complete assurance. We have started the formal certification of such transformations using the Coq proof assistant [23]. We describe program transformations on a simple gate-level hardware description language and the fault-model is described in the operational semantics of the language. The main theorem states that, for any circuit, for any input stream and for any SET allowed by the fault-model, its transformed version produces a correct output. We have already used this approach to prove the correctness of transformations implementing TMR and triple time redundancy. At the time of writing, the proof of the DTR transformation is in progress.

# 7. REFERENCES

[1] S. Mitra, N. Seifert, M. Zhang, Q. Shi, and K. S. Kim, "Robust system design with built-in soft-error resilience," *IEEE Computer*, vol. 38, no. 2, pp. 43–52, Feb. 2005.

[2] P. D. Bradley and E. Normand, "Single event upsets in implantable cardioverter defibrillators," *IEEE Transactions on Nuclear Science*, vol. 45, no. 6, pp. 2929–2940, 1998.

[3] P. Shivakumar, M. Kistler, S. Keckler, D. Burger, and L. Alvisi, "Modeling the effect of technology trends on the soft error rate of combinational logic," in *Int. Conference on Dependable Systems and Networks*, 2002, pp. 389–398.

[4] J. von Neumann, "Probabilistic logic and the synthesis of reliable organisms from unreliable components," *Automata Studies, Princeton Univ. Press*, pp. 43–98, 1956.

[5] B. Bridgford, C. Carmichael, and C. W. Tseng, "Single-event upset mitigation selection guide," *Xilinx Application Note XAPP987*, vol. 1, 2008.

[6] A. Sutton, "Creating highly reliable FPGA designs," *Military&Aerospace Technical Bullentin*, vol. 1, pp. 5–7, 2013.

[7] "Neutron-induced single event upset SEU," *Microsemi Corporation*, no. 55800021-0/8.11, August 2011.

[8] A. Bogorad *et al.*, "On-orbit error rates of RHBD SRAMs: Comparison of calculation techniques and space environmental models with observed performance," *IEEE Trans. on Nuclear Science*, vol. 58, no. 6, pp. 2804–2806, 2011.

[9] F. Corno, M. Reorda, and G. Squillero, "RT-level ITC'99 benchmarks and first ATPG results," *Design Test of Computers, IEEE*, vol. 17, no. 3, pp. 44–53, 2000.

[10] Y.-M. Hsu, V. Piuri, and E. Swartzlander, "Efficient time redundancy for error correcting units and convolvers," in *Int. Workshop on Defect and Fault Tolerance in VLSI Systems*, 1995, pp. 198–206.

[11] W. Townsend, J. Abraham, and E. Swartzlander, "Quadruple time redundancy adders [error correcting adder]," in *Defect and Fault Tolerance in VLSI Systems, 2003. Proceedings. 18th IEEE International Symposium on*, Nov 2003, pp. 250–256.

[12] K. Makoto, A. Masayuki, F. Satoshi, and I. Kazuhiko, "Time redundancy processor with a tolerance to transient faults caused by electromagnetic waves," *DSN*, 2007.

[13] E. Rotenberg, "Ar-smt: a microarchitectural approach to fault tolerance in microprocessors," in *Twenty-Ninth Annual International Symposium on Fault-Tolerant Computing.*, June 1999, pp. 84–91.

[14] M. Nicolaidis, "Time redundancy based soft-error tolerance to rescue nanometer technologies," in *17th IEEE VLSI Test Symposium*, 1999, pp. 86–94.

[15] L. Anghel, D. Alexandrescu, and M. Nicolaidis, "Evaluation of a soft error tolerance technique based on time and/or space redundancy," in *13th Symp. on Integrated Circuits and Syst. Design*, 2000, pp. 237–242.

[16] F. L. Kastensmidt, C. Luigi, and R. Reis, "Fault-Tolerance Techniques for SRAM-based FPGAs," *Frontiers in Electronic Testing*, 2006.

[17] D. Ernst *et al.*, "Razor: a low-power pipeline based on circuit-level timing speculation," in *Int. Symp. on Microarchitecture, MICRO-36.*, Dec 2003, pp. 7–18.

[18] N. Avirneni, V. Subramanian, and A. Somani, "Low overhead soft error mitigation techniques for high-performance and aggressive systems," in *Int. Conf. on Dependable Systems Networks*, June 2009, pp. 185–194.

[19] G. Sohi, M. Franklin, and K. Saluja, "A study of time-redundant fault tolerance techniques for high-performance pipelined computers," in *FTCS-19*, June 1989, pp. 436–443.

[20] C. Chan, D. Schwartz-Narbonne, D. Sethi, and S. Malik, "Specification and synthesis of hardware checkpointing and rollback mechanisms," in *Design Automation Conference*, 2012, pp. 1222–1228.

[21] D. Koch, C. Haubelt, and J. Teich, "Efficient hardware checkpointing: Concepts, overhead analysis, and implementation," ser. FPGA '07, 2007, pp. 188–196.

[22] K. S. McElvain, "Circuits with modular redundancy and methods and apparatuses for their automated synthesis," *Synplicity, Inc. Patent No.US007200822B1*, April 2007.

[23] Coq development team. The coq proof assistant, software and documentation available at http://coq.inria.fr/, 1989-2014.

# 200 MS/s ADC implemented in a FPGA employing TDCs

## Harald Homulle
Delft University of Technology
Delft, The Netherlands
h.a.r.homulle@tudelft.nl

## Francesco Regazzoni
USI - ALaRI
Lugano, Switzerland
regazzoni@alari.ch

## Edoardo Charbon
Delft University of Technology
Delft, The Netherlands
e.charbon@tudelft.nl

## ABSTRACT

Analog signals are used in many applications and systems, such as cyber physical systems, sensor networks and automotive applications. These are also applications where the use of FPGAs is continuously growing. To date, however there is no direct integration between FPGAs, which are digital, and the analog world (except for the newest generation of FPGAs). Currently, an external analog-to-digital converter (ADC) has to be added to the system, thus limiting its overall compactness and flexibility.

To address this issue we propose a novel architecture implementing a high speed ADC in reconfigurable devices. The system exploits picosecond resolution time-to-digital converters (TDCs) to reach a conversion as fast as its clock speed. The resulting analog-through-time-to-digital converter (ATDC) can achieve a sampling rate of 200 MS/s with a 7 bit resolution for signals ranging from 0 to 2.5 V. Except for the external resistor needed for the analog reference ramp, the system is fully integrated inside the target FPGA. Moreover, our design can be easily scaled for multichannel ADCs, proving the suitability of reconfigurable devices for applications requiring a deep integration between analog and digital world.

## Keywords

ADC; TDC; FPGA; analog-to-digital; time-to-digital

## 1. INTRODUCTION

Analog-to-digital Conversion is needed in a large number of applications, ranging from sensor nodes, industrial control systems to (high energy) physics experiments. Devices used in these applications typically consist of an analog component which senses one or more parameters (for instance temperature, position, ECG or EEG), that is connected to a digital world, often a system-on-chip, composed of DSPs, processors and coprocessors. The analog part of the system is used to collect the data, while the digital part, often a reconfigurable circuit, e.g. a FPGA, analyses the data and reacts accordingly.

The conventional approach is to use an external device to carry out the conversion between analog and digital. This approach is not optimal, because it has a limited scalability, limited flexibility, and cannot achieve the compactness needed for several applications. When an external ADC is used, the interface with the FPGA is fixed at design time, and cannot be easily changed. As an additional component is needed, the overall size of the system increases, usually requiring extra connectors and PCBs. Finally, the use of an external ADC increases the overall system power consumption.

A better approach would be to completely integrate an ADC in the FPGA, either an ASIC ADC on-chip or a reconfigurable ADC.

This need has been recognised by FPGA manufacturers. E.g. Xilinx now includes an on-chip ADC (XADC) in the new 7 Family generation of FPGAs, ranging from the low-cost Artix 7 to the high-end Virtex 7. Advantages over external ADCs are the smaller size, lower power and easier interfacability. The main drawback of this solution is that it is fixed in terms of conversion rate, voltage range and number of input channels. Secondly this ASIC takes die area that one cannot use for anything else, whether one plans to use the XADC or not.

Another solution is an ADC implemented directly into reconfigurable hardware, that eventually can be used as any other IP. This would guarantee the advantage of having the digital information directly available inside the FPGAs, allowing faster processing of the digitized data. Furthermore, such an ADC could be interfaced easily and in a flexible way, allowing, for instance, to adjust the number of ADCs to the needs of the target application. Finally, the overall size of the system would be smaller allowing for an easy integration also in compact devices.

In this paper, we tackle this problem and we propose an ADC architecture which can be implemented into reconfigurable devices. Except for a small single resistor needed to create the analog reference ramp (to date, the creation of analog signals inside the FPGA is not possible), the whole ADC is completely implemented in the FPGA. The design comprises two TDCs and a $LVDS$ transceiver, and it is synthesized, placed, routed, and tested on a Spartan 6 FPGA.

Similarly to soft-core processors, which are used even in FPGAs with integrated hard-core processors, our soft-core

ADC architecture complements and extends the possibilities offered by hard-core ADCs.

The remainder of this paper is organized as follows. In Section 2 we review the state-of-the-art of low cost ADCs and TDCs implemented using reconfigurable devices. In Section 3 we present our architecture for implementing ADCs using FPGAs. Finally Section 4 reports the area occupation and the performance of our design and compares them with results reported in literature.

## 2. RELATED WORKS

In the past several works addressed the problem of creating low cost, highly precise and high speed digital converters using reconfigurable hardware. Most of them address the problem of time-to-digital conversion, but few attempts of implementing ADCs were also undertaken.

Favi and Charbon [1] proposed the first picosecond resolution TDC implemented using a FPGA. The main problem which designers have to face, while implementing a TDC using reconfigurable hardware, is how to reach a time resolution greater than the clock frequency. This is usually obtained with a so called thermometer. A number of registers is connected to build a chain. Each of the registers has a specific and small propagation delay towards the next register.

At the beginning of the measurement, a '1' is written to the first register and, till the stop signal is high, it is propagated into the next registers. At the end of the measurement, the chain is read out, and the number of ones gives the time stamp of the thermometer. The registers are formed by a chain of Carry4 elements: the elements in the FPGA with the smallest propagation delay, as it is a single chain with a dedicated path. The same base architecture was improved in a number of follow-up works [2, 3, 4].

Previous works implementing ADCs on FPGAs are usually based on delta sigma modulators [5, 6]. In this approach, a stream of pulses is generated and compared with the analog input signal using a feedback loop. This approach however is capable of detecting changes which occurred in the analog signal rather than attempting to read its absolute value.

Attempts to implement ADCs with a TDC using single or double slope schemes were also proposed in the past. Among them, the design of Wu *et al.* [7] is probably the most relevant for our work. The ADC is implemented using a reduced number of external components (3 resistors and 1 capacitor) and the reference ramp is generated using this passive *RC* network. The comparators are built using the differential inputs of the FPGA, and the signals are digitized using TDCs based on different phases of the clock. However, the performance of this design was still very limited, and the level of integration and compactness was limited by the amount of components, which were not integrated into the FPGA.

## 3. SYSTEMS ARCHITECTURE

The proposed architecture is depicted in Figure 1. The internal structure includes a *LVDS* transceiver, acting as comparator, two carrychain TDCs for the time measurement (indicated as TDC 1 and TDC 2), and the logic needed for controlling the clock (Digital Clock Management Tiles or *DCM*) and readout. Furthermore two inverters are added

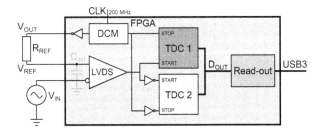

Figure 1: High level block diagram of the proposed analog-through-time-to-digital converter. The architecture comprises two TDCs, one *LVDS*, a *DCM* and a resistor $R_{REF}$. The analog signal $V_{IN}$ is digitized into the digital signal $D_{OUT}$.

to measure both the rising and falling edge of the comparator.

Additionally, an external resistor $R_{REF}$ is needed to generate the reference voltage. The system has three inputs (the input analog signal $V_{IN}$, the reference voltage generated by the $RC$ circuit $V_{REF}$, and a clock signal $CLK$ operating at 200 MHz) and two outputs (the digital conversion of the input analog signal ($D_{OUT}$), and the output voltage ($V_{OUT}$) used to generate the reference voltage for the $LVDS$ comparator).

The waveforms representing the timing diagram of the whole systems are depicted in Figure 2; the clock signal controls the overall operation of the circuit. It is used as stop signal for TDC 1 and, inverted, as stop signal for the TDC 2. Additionally, again inverted, it drives the output signal $V_{OUT}$ connected to the $RC$ network, generating a semi-exponential ramp. The output voltage is set to 3.3 V, whereas the maximum voltage reached on the input is 2.5 V. This ensures that the ramp operates on the most linear possible regime on the $RC$ curve.

The input voltage and reference voltage are compared with the $LVDS$ transceiver. A '1' is generated when the reference ramp $V_{REF}$ becomes higher than the input voltage $V_{IN}$. The time interval between a '0'→'1' transition caused by the $LVDS$ and the next rising edge of the clock

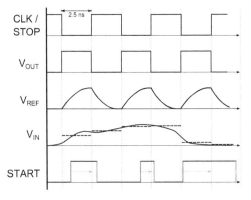

Figure 2: Timing diagram of the proposed ATDC. The reference clock signal is on top. The clock signal, inverted, is also used to drive $V_{OUT}$, and to generate $V_{REF}$. The analog input signal $V_{IN}$ is sampled two times per clock period by comparing with $V_{REF}$.

is measured by TDC 1 and stored in a register. The time interval between the '1'→'0' transition caused by the $LVDS$ and the next rising edge of the inverted clock is measured in TDC 2 and again stored in a register.

The two timing intervals measured by TDC 1 and TDC 2 are then added. This addition guarantees that our design produces a single digital word corresponding to each analog input voltage with a 200 MS/s rate. It also allows to achieve one additional bit of resolution and to filter noise. The converted signals are finally transferred to the external world, in this case a standard personal computer, using the USB protocol implemented using an FX3 controller [8].

## 3.1 Implementation

A more detailed block representation of our ADC is depicted in Figure 3. From the figure, we can see the carrychains, the flip-flops, the thermometer decoder, and the read-out. In each clock period the $LVDS$ generates a '1'. This signal is delayed through the carrychain, implemented using Carry4 blocks. The carry value in each Carry4 block is latched on the next clock edge. The time stamp measured with this thermometer is converted into a binary time stamp. The decoder for the thermometer is a decoder implemented using multiplexers that select to forward the upper or the lower part of the thermometer depending on the value stored in the middle bit of the thermometer, as will be detailed in the rest of this section.

The main reason to use the carrychains is the fact they are the fastest elements available in FPGAs. The carry-to-carry delay is approximately 20 ps (the exact value is obviously dependent on the specific FPGA platform).

To reach this performance, it is for optimal performance best to manually place the TDCs carrychains. Manual placement avoids (many) clock domain crossings and ensures the best possible linearity. The rest of the whole design is automatically placed and routed using standard FPGA design tools.

To measure the analog input voltage with a TDC, the analog signal has to be converted into the time domain. This step requires a small external circuit. By using the parasitic capacitance of the system, we can achieve a high sample rate for our ADC. The internal pin capacitance is dominated by the PCB, therefore it is different from board to board. In

our setup, the $C_{INT}$ was measured to be in the order of 50 pF. By combining $C_{INT}$ with an external resistor $R_{REF}$ of 100 Ω we can achieve a ramp with a rise time $\tau$ of approximately 5 ns. This is indeed larger than the half of the clock period and it ensures the maximum linearity of the input ramp.

## 3.2 Resources

Considering the target application of foreseen for our ADC, we synthesized our design using a low cost FPGA (Spartan 6 [9]). The reported results were obtained using a XC6SLX100-3FGG676 FPGA on a custom PCB, augmented with an onboard clock crystal which generates the system clock signal at a frequency of 200 MHz. The design occupies 366 FPGA slices, roughly 2% of what is available in the target platform. The power consumption, estimated with the Xilinx XPower Analyzer, is 410 mW (not considering, however, the power dissipated by the data transfer). The onboard clock jitter ($\sigma$), measured with a LeCroy WaveMaster 8600A, was measured to 30 ps after going through the FPGA's DCM tiles.

The reference ramp created through the resistor is driven by the same clock, thus the same jitter applies. However since the measurement is started from one clock period and finishes at the next one, the measurement jitter will be in the order of 40 ps. This jitter does not meet the ADC's jitter requirement:

$$\text{Jitter} < \frac{1}{2^q \pi f_s}, \qquad (1)$$

which states that the jitter should be < 22 ps (for a 7 bit ADC). Therefore for a higher performance a clock with lower jitter is needed, although for our application this precision is not required.

The noise introduced into the system by the 100 Ω resistor follows Boltzmann's law $V_{noise\ RMS} = \sqrt{4kTRB} < 20\,\mu V$, at $40°C$ and a 200 MHz bandwidth. This is significantly less than the quantization error, therefore it can be ignored. The resistor does not require a strict tolerance as this is a one time calibration problem. Therefore a simple and cheap resistor will fulfil our needs.

## 3.3 Calibration

Measuring the transfer curve of the ADC, the input - output relation will produce the uncalibrated result as shown in Figure 4. Each measurement has a standard deviation error $\sigma$ of 1.9 LSB, see Subsection 4.1. The resolution of the ADC, found by fitting through the transfer curve, is 17 mV = 1 LSB. The digital range spans 7.2 bits. The performance of the system is bound by the quantization error, where the signal-to-quantization noise ratio is

$$SQNR = 20 \cdot \log_{10}(2^q) \qquad (2)$$

For a system with 7.2 bits, the $SQNR = 43$ dB. This will be reduced by jitter and non linearities. The result can be eventually improved by applying a number of calibration steps to the system.

### 3.3.1 Bubbles

A problem to address is that of the so-called bubbles. Bubbles are unwanted 'gaps' in the thermometer code. For instance, a consistent thermometer code is

··· 0000111111 ···

the carry propagates right to left.

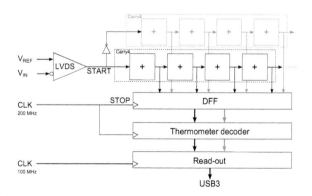

Figure 3: More detailed block diagram of our ATDC. It is possible to see the thermometer implemented using Carry4 elements, the LVDS, the flip-flops, the thermometer decoder, and the interface for the readout.

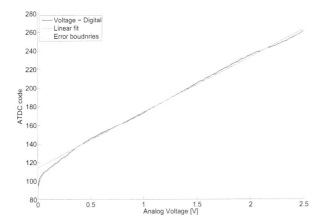

Figure 4: Analog voltage vs. digital output (before calibration). The figure shows the measured transfer function (blue), the ideal transfer function (red) and the error on the measurement (dashed). It is possible to notice the non perfect linearity of the deviation between the measured and the ideal transfer functions.

On the contrary, a bubble is present in the following code:
⋯0001011111⋯
Bubbles are caused by different phenomena: fast carry look ahead, clock slew, slack, and setup and hold time violations are the most common ones. The most common approach to correct a bubble is to fill the gap by adding the missing '1', as for instance in the following code:
⋯0001111111⋯
This however causes an overestimation of the original value which had to be stored in the thermometer. As a result, if the bubbles always occur in the same way at a delay, i.e. they are consistent with respect to time, the bubble should not be corrected at all, as it is intended behaviour of the carry structure.

For this reason, the last stages of our thermometer to binary decoder are not based on the same structure based on multiplexers, but on a simple bit counter. The bits that are high are counted to give the exact amount of all bits that were '1' in the thermometer code without filling any of the potential gaps caused by bubbles.

### 3.3.2 Dithering

From a density test, we can estimate the frequency of the ADC bins, where frequency refers to the rate at which a given event occurs in a particular bin. This frequency is estimated assuming that the non linearities of the system are the ones discussed in Subsection 4.2. When the bins are uniform, namely when all the bins have size equivalent to the same time interval, all bins would have the same frequency. However some carry blocks are faster than others, as can be noticed also from the simulation reported in Table 1. This is the case, for instance of bin 31 with a delay difference of 36 ps. Those large bins cause large non linearities in the TDC output. Dithering is a way to pseudo compensate the bin frequency. Dithering is a random non linear mapping, in which each bin is randomly divided over multiple bins dependent on the bin delay. The operating principle is shown in Figure 5.

Using this approach, bin 31 can be divided into three bins,

Table 1: Delay of the carrychain simulated with Xilinx Spartan 6 post place and route model. For each bin, we report the exact delay in ns and the difference from the previous bin in ps. It is possible to notice the large difference between the delays of the different bins (bin 31 in particular has an exceptionally large delay).

| Bin | Delay [ns] | Delay difference [ps] |
|---|---|---|
| ⋮ | ⋮ | ⋮ |
| 28 | 1.243 | 18 |
| 29 | 1.256 | 13 |
| 30 | 1.266 | 10 |
| 31 | 1.302 | **36** |
| 32 | 1.319 | 17 |
| 33 | 1.333 | 14 |
| ⋮ | ⋮ | ⋮ |

Figure 5: Dithering applied to the carrychain output. The mapping between the actual value and the dithered one is obtained by estimating the delay of each bin with the ADC density test of Subsection 4.2. Dithering allows to correct the delay of the carrychain by applying a Gaussian map between the estimated bin delay and a fixed bin width.

where the side bins partially overlap with the original bins 30 and 32 to equalize the delays. The probability that bin 31 corresponds to a specific time is a Gaussian probability function. It must be noted that, although dithering introduces random noise, it increases the linearity of the system as the bins are more equally spaced in time.

The transfer function after adding dithering and offset correction is given in Figure 6. There is no downsampling or any other technique applied to improve linearities. Comparing Figure 6 with Figure 4, a more linear characteristic can be immediately noticed. This comes at the expense of a slightly larger deviation on the measurements (due to dithering) of 0.1 LSB and a slight increase in random noise.

### 3.4 Design alterations

The design presented can be tailored to the specific needs of the target application. The most important parameters which a designer can trade are:

- **Sample rate**: Reducing the sample rate to 100 MS/s increases the resolution of 1 bit. A sample rate of 50 MS/s adds an additional bit.

- **Resources**: Reducing the required resources by using only one TDC (instead of two) decreases the resolution by 1 bit. By decreasing also the sample rate to 100 MS/s the resolution is unchanged.

- **Voltage range**: The input voltage range (0-2.5 V) can be adjusted by increasing or decreasing the output drive strength. The same result can be achieved by changing the resistor value.

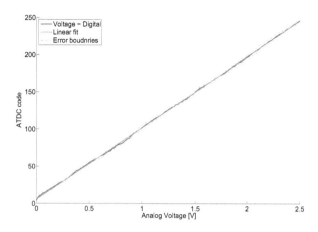

Figure 6: Analog voltage vs. digital output (after calibration). Comparing this plot with Figure 4, it is possible to notice that the calibration increases the linearity of the transfer function.

# 4. RESULTS

In this section we report and discuss the results of the full characterization of our architecture, implemented using a configuration consisting of a single channel ATDC.

## 4.1 DC measurement

The first experiment consisted in a single shot measurement. A DC voltage is applied to the input of the ADC. This measurement shows the fluctuation of measuring a single voltage; i.e. the measurement error or jitter.

After accumulating single shot statistics, we estimate the error by applying a Gaussian distribution. The result is shown in Figure 7. Over the entire measurement campaign, the average error was $\leq 2$ LSB ($1 \cdot \sigma$).

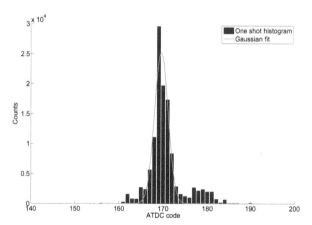

Figure 7: Single shot measurement obtained by applying a DC voltage to the ATDCs input. The measurement error over the entire measurement range, calculated using a Gaussian fit, is $\leq 2$ LSB ($1 \cdot \sigma$).

## 4.2 Non linearities: density test

The non linearities can be identified in different ways. One possible way is to compare the ideal and the measured transfer curves. Another is to generate measurement points over the entire input range. As a result, a ramp that exceeds

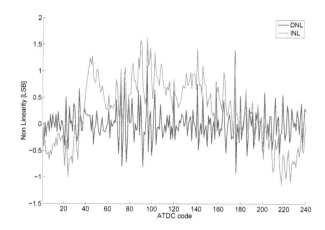

Figure 8: Non linearities (DNL and INL) extracted from ADC density test. The ADCs density is produced by applying a ramp that exceeds both negative and positive input range to the input of the ADC.

both the positive and the negative ADC input range is generated. In case of a perfect linear system, the points are equally spread over the entire ADC range. In presence of a non linear transfer function, some bins have more counts than others. The results in each bin are summed to compute the ADC density. Each code $n$ has a total counts $C(n)$. In an ideal system, the counts in each bin would be equal to the average $\overline{C} = \frac{\sum_{i=1}^{N} C(n)}{N}$.

From the ADC density the differential and integral non linearities (DNL and INL) can be found using the following formulas:

$$\mathrm{DNL}(n) = \frac{C(n)}{\overline{C}} \qquad (3a)$$

$$\mathrm{INL}(n) = \sum_{i=1}^{n} \mathrm{DNL}(i) \qquad (3b)$$

The DNL and INL for the system are in the range [-0.9 1.4] LSB and [-1.1 1.6] LSB, respectively.

The main contributors to DNL and INL in the system are the intrinsic non linear transfer function of the reference ramp, the clock distribution in the FPGA and the unevenly spaced delays of the carry blocks. The last two factors are intrinsic FPGA problems and occur everywhere in the device. They can be partially overcome by applying dithering, as discussed. However in the placement of the delayline it is essential to avoid so-called bad spots: particular carrychains that exhibit higher non linearities and have lower resolution.

## 4.3 AC measurement

The AC measurement allows to estimate the signal-to-noise-and-distortion-ratio ($SNDR$) and the effective number of bits ($ENOB$). To do so, we applied a 2.2 $V_{pk-pk}$ sine wave with a 1 MHz oscillation frequency.

The external AC signal of 1 MHz is generated with a Rohde & Schwarz HMF2550 function generator. The signal has a jitter of 4 ns (implying a 0.25 MHz deviation). All harmonics are suppressed $> 40$ dB, as measured with a LeCroy WaveMaster 8600A oscilloscope.

The signal in time domain, as measured with the implemented ATDCs is plotted in Figure 10. This is a result

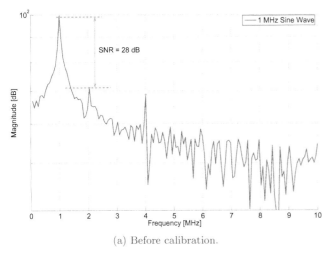

(a) Before calibration.

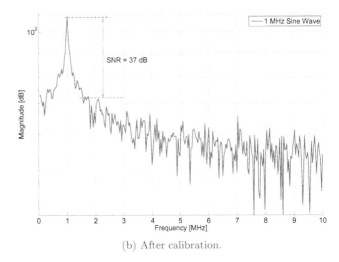

(b) After calibration.

Figure 9: FFT of the 1 MHz 2.2 $V_{pk-pk}$ sinewave for $SNDR$ estimation.

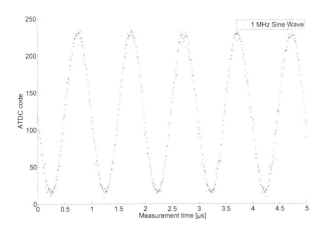

Figure 10: 1 MHz 2.2 $V_{pk-pk}$ sinewave digitized at 200 MS/s.

after calibration.

Using the FFT, the frequency domain plots of Figure 9 are derived. They show the frequency components in the input signal, respectively before and after calibration.

The peak at 1 MHz is approximately 37 dB above the noise threshold (this result is obtained after calibration). From this $SNDR$, the $ENOB$ can be calculated with Equation 4 to be approximately 6 bits.

$$ENOB = \frac{SNDR - 1.76}{6.02} \qquad (4)$$

All the harmonics of the 1 MHz sinewave are below the noise threshold. This result is compared with the measurement obtained before calibration. The harmonics are above the noise threshold and the $SNDR$ is only 28 dB. Therefore calibration significantly enhances the result with an increase in $ENOB$ of over 1.5 bit.

Although both $SNDR$ and $ENOB$ are improved by calibration (and thus dithering), the noise floor is increased due to the random noise added in the dithering process.

For higher frequencies, up to the Nyquist sampling rate, the $SNDR$ drops to roughly 34 dB.

## 4.4 Comparison

Our design is compared with existing implementations of reconfigurable ADCs on FPGAs and the built-in XADC. Other implementations are based on Clock phase TDC [7] and delta sigma modulation [5, 6]. The XADC is a dual-channel ADC integrated in the 7 Family of Xilinx FPGAs [10]. A comparison is given in Table 2. The details in the two works on reconfigurable ADCs we used for comparison, are generally not sufficient to carry out an exhaustive comparison. Nevertheless, the comparison of several parameters, such as sampling rate and resolution, can still be carried out in a meaningful way.

A first comparison between the implementation based on Clock phase TDC and our work, shows that our design is capable of reaching both a higher resolution and a much higher sampling rate. An immediate fair comparison with the implementation based on delta sigma modulation is not possible. Nevertheless we can extrapolate the performance of our design assuming that it is running at a lower sampling rate. As described in Subsection 3.4 by halving the sampling rate, an additional bit in digital resolution is gained. Extrapolating this trend, an $ENOB$ of 9 bits can be achieved by $2^3$ divisions of the sampling rate to 25 MS/s, outperforming the design based on delta sigma modulation in speed by a factor of 20, even assuming an additional 2× division of our sampling rate.

As a result, to the best of our knowledge, the ADC design proposed in this paper outperforms the sampling rate of all previously reported ADCs implemented using reconfigurable logic.

For completeness, we compared our design with ASIC implementations, with the FPGA built-in XADC as reference. As also shown in Table 2 the XADC has an $ENOB$ of 10 bits with a maximum sampling rate of 1 MS/s. The XADC is limited to two channels, whereas our implementation can scale to a number of channels limited only by the slice utilization. In contrast to reconfigurable FPGA ADCs, this built-in ADC doesn't require any additional external com-

Table 2: Comparison between our architecture and previous ADCs implemented in reconfigurable hardware. Additionally we compare with the XADC available in Xilinx 7 series FPGAs. We use *n.a.* to indicate that the corresponding data is not available.

| ADC based on: | | Carrychain TDC [this work] | Clock phase TDC [7] | Delta Sigma Modulator [5, 6] | XADC [10] |
|---|---|---|---|---|---|
| Clock speed | [MHz] | 200 | 360 | 100 | |
| Conversion rate | [MS/s] | 200 | 22.5 | 0.5 to 0.05 | 1 |
| Voltage range | [V] | 0 - 2.5 | 0 - 3.3 | 0 - 3.3 | 0 - 1.0 |
| Digital range | | 7.2 bit | 6 bit | 10 to 16 bit | 12 bit |
| ENOB | | 6 bit | n.a. | 9 bit | 10 bit |
| Resolution (LSB) | [mV] | 17 | 52 | 3 | 0.25 |
| DNL | [LSB] | [-0.9 1.4] | n.a. | n.a. | $\pm 1$ |
| INL | [LSB] | [-1.1 1.6] | n.a. | n.a. | $\pm 2$ |
| Error $\sigma$ | [LSB] | 2 | n.a. | n.a. | 1 |
| Power consumption | [mW] | 410 | n.a. | n.a. | n.a. |
| FPGA slices | | < 400 | n.a. | < 80 | dedicated |
| External components | n.a. | 1 | 4 | 2 - 3 | 0 |

ponents nor any FPGA slices. This of course is comes at a cost of an additional space requirement on the FPGA die.

Moreover, our design has the possibility to reach both a higher resolution and conversion rate, whereas XADC is fixed in all ways.

For the comparison with other ASIC ADCs, we referred in particular to the tables collected by Murmann [11], who keeps a yearly updated ranking of ADCs published in major design conferences such as the International VLSI symposium [12] and ISSCC [13]. The results of our comparison are reported in Figure 11. The figures show an immediate visual positioning of a particular design for ranking different Figure of Merits commonly used for ADCs, such as speed, resolution and power consumption.

Obviously, the comparisons of our design, implemented using reconfigurable logic, with ASIC implementations is unfair, as it is well known that even state of the art FPGAs cannot reach the performance achieved by the more recent ASIC designs reported. However, we can see that our design is already comparable to ASIC implementations of ADCs realized with somewhat older technologies.

Another interesting information from these graphs is the trend for ASICs: we are moving towards smaller feature sizes, with the direct consequences that the designs will achieve lower power consumption and higher speeds. A similar trend can be expected for FPGAs: the next generations will be based on smaller geometries. Because of this, we also expect for our design a reduction in power consumption as well as an increase of the speed.

## 5. CONCLUSIONS

A novel architecture for a high speed ADC was presented, using low cost Spartan 6 FPGA families, and fully characterized. Our design can convert up to 200 MS/s with a 7 bit resolution. Additionally, our system shows a high linearity (DNL [-0.9 1.4] LSB and INL [-1.1 1.6] LSB), an *ENOB* of 6 bit (37 dB *SNDR*) and can be implemented using only 366 FPGA slices (2% of what is available). To the best of our knowledge, this is the fastest ADC fully implemented in a FPGA reported. Our system enables an easy integration between the analog world and FPGAs, without the need of external ADCs, paving the way to a large number of low cost industrial, medical, and sensing applications where analog signals have to be converted in a cheap and reliable way.

## 6. SUPPLEMENT

The VHDL code and accompanying documentation is available on: http://cas.tudelft.nl/fpga_tdc/.

## 7. ACKNOWLEDGEMENTS

The authors are grateful to Xlinix Inc. for hardware donations.

## 8. REFERENCES

[1] C. Favi and E. Charbon, "A 17 ps Time to Digital Converter implemented in 65 nm FPGA technology," in *Proceedings of the ACM/SIGDA International Symposium on Field Programmable Gate Arrays*, ser. FPGA '09. New York, USA: ACM, 2009, pp. 113–120.

[2] H. Menninga, C. Favi, M. Fishburn, and E. Charbon, "A multi-channel, 10 ps resolution, FPGA-based TDC with 300ms/s throughput for open-source PET applications," in *Nuclear Science Symposium and Medical Imaging Conference (NSS/MIC), 2011 IEEE*, Oct. 2011, pp. 1515–1522.

[3] S. Bourdeauducq, "Time to Digital Converter core for Spartan 6 FPGAs," Nov. 2011. [Online]. Available: http://www.ohwr.org/attachments/855/tdc_v3.pdf

[4] J. Wu and Z. Shi, "The 10 ps wave union TDC: Improving FPGA TDC resolution beyond its cell delay," in *Nuclear Science Symposium Conference Record, 2008. NSS '08. IEEE*, Oct. 2008, pp. 3440–3446.

[5] "Leveraging FPGA and CPLD digital logic to implement analog to digital converters," Lattice Semiconductor, Mar. 2010. [Online]. Available: http://www.latticesemi.com/~/media/Documents/WhitePapers/AG/CreatingAnADCUsingFPGAResources.PDF?document_id=36525

[6] "Integrated ADC for Altera Cyclone-IV devices," Missing Link Electronics, Apr. 2011. [Online]. Available: http://www.missinglinkelectronics.com/devzone/files/papers/MLE-TB20110419.pdf

[7] J. Wu, S. Hansen, and Z. Shi, "ADC and TDC implemented using FPGA," in *Nuclear Science Symposium Conference Record, 2007. NSS '07. IEEE*, Oct. 2007, pp. 281–286.

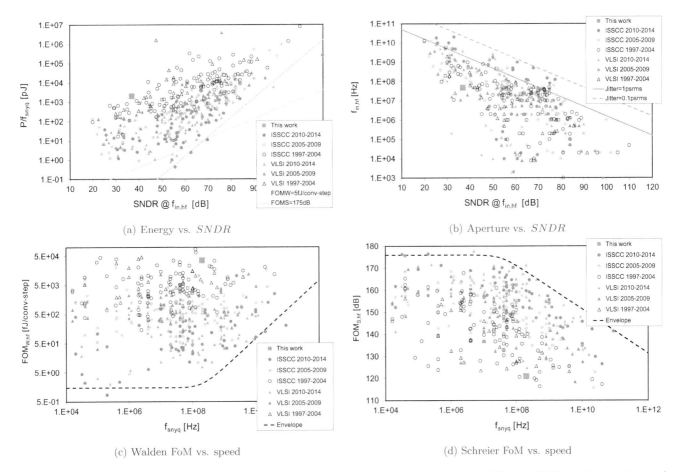

(a) Energy vs. $SNDR$

(b) Aperture vs. $SNDR$

(c) Walden FoM vs. speed

(d) Schreier FoM vs. speed

Figure 11: Graphical comparison of the ADC presented in this work (red square) with different ASIC implementations of ADCs, using the following Figures of Merit: (a) energy per conversion versus $SNDR$ (b) frequency of the measured signal versus $SNDR$. (c) energy per conversion versus sampling rate. (d) Schreier FoM $= SNDR + 10 \cdot \log(f_{sample/2}/Power)$ versus sampling rate. It is possible to notice that our design, despite the use of a FPGA, compares with other ASIC designs. The comparison is based on the survey maintained by [11].

[8] "EZ-USB FX3 SuperSpeed USB 3.0 peripheral controller," Cypress. [Online]. Available: http://www.cypress.com/fx3/

[9] "Spartan 6 FPGA family," Xilinx. [Online]. Available: http://www.xilinx.com/products/silicon-devices/fpga/spartan-6/

[10] "7 series FPGAs and Zynq-7000 all programmable SoC XADC," Xilinx. [Online]. Available: http://www.xilinx.com/support/documentation/user_guides/ug480_7Series_XADC.pdf

[11] B. Murmann, "ADC performance survey 1997-2014," June 2014. [Online]. Available: http://web.stanford.edu/~murmann/adcsurvey.html

[12] "VLSI Symposia on VLSI technology and circuits." [Online]. Available: http://www.vlsisymposium.org/

[13] "IEEE international solid-state circuits conference." [Online]. Available: http://isscc.org/

# 0.5-V Highly Power-Efficient Programmable Logic using Nonvolatile Configuration Switch in BEOL

Makoto Miyamura, Toshitsugu Sakamoto, Yukihide Tsuji,

Munehiro Tada, Naoki Banno, Koichiro Okamoto, Noriyuki Iguchi, and Hiromitsu Hada

Low-power Electronics Association & Project (LEAP)

West 7, 16-1 Onogawa, Tsukuba, Ibaraki 305-8569 Japan

miyamura@leap.or.jp

## ABSTRACT

A low-power nonvolatile programmable-logic cell array is proposed for energy-constrained applications such as wireless sensor nodes and mobile apparatuses. A 64x64 programmable-logic cell array includes a 9.2-Mbit nonvolatile switch, namely atom switch, as the routing switch and configuration memory. A 16-bit arithmetic logic unit, which is a building block of the micro-controller unit, was implemented to compare the speed and power consumption with a state-of-the-art low power field-programmable gate array. The proposed programmable-logic array exhibited 30% dynamic power saving and x2.5 faster operation in the low-voltage region. Zero sleep power was also demonstrated.

**Categories and Subject Descriptors:** B.7.1
[**Integrated Circuits**]: Types and Design Style—*gate arrays*

**General Terms:** Measurement; Performance; Design

**Keywords:** Programmable logic, atom switch, nonvolatile, low power

## 1. INTRODUCTION

Field-programmable gate arrays (FPGAs) are attractive for applications in power-constrained environments. High-performance computation in FPGAs with hardware parallelism, for example, enables wireless sensor nodes (WSNs) to immediately process various signals from sensors and compress the data locally, reducing communication activity and associated energy consumption. Data processing is completed much faster compared to that done by a low-power micro-controller unit that processes data in a sequential manner [1]. However, FPGAs require loading configuration data from an external memory when powering on, because static random-access memory (SRAM) loses data after powering down. This in turn requires significant energy dissipation during wake-up due to higher dynamic power associated with restoring the configuration due to large parasitic capacitance. A nonvolatile FPGA with embedded Flash or one-time programming memory allows avoidance of the external ROM and power efficient wakeup. However, this has the drawback of a high programming voltage of more than 5 V, resulting in relatively lower scaling capability and higher operating power. A few works have also been reported to integrate novel bake-end-of-line (BEOL) device such as resistive random access memory (RRAM) or phase change memory (PCM) into FPGA circuits in [2]-[4]. In this paper, nonvolatile programmable logic based on atom switch, which can be configured around 3 V, is discussed. Low-power and nonvolatile programmable logic results in higher computational capability for battery-powered WSNs.

## 2. 3-DIMENSIONAL PROGRAMMABLE LOGIC BASED ON ATOM SWITCH

Atom switch formed in BEOL, i.e., copper (Cu) interconnect, is a promising candidate for programmable switches replacing SRAM and pass transistors [5]. Stacking the configuration memory and switch over the core programmable logic significantly improves functional-block density and reduces interconnect lengths (Fig. 1) [6]. The non-volatility also conserves stand-by power, while an SRAM-based FPGA is suffering from gate tunneling current and source-drain leakage. We previously proposed the complementary atom switch (CAS), which consists of two two-terminal atom switches connected in series with opposite direction (Fig. 1) [7].

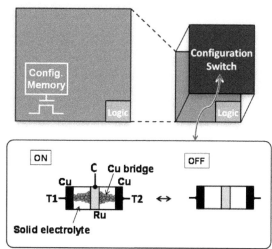

**Figure 1. Conventional 2D and 3D FPGAs with complementary atom switch (CAS).**

*FPGA '15*, February 22-24 2015, Monterey, CA, USA.
Copyright is held by the owner/author(s). Publication rights licensed to ACM.
ACM 978-1-4503-3315-3/15/02...$15.00
http://dx.doi.org/10.1145/2684746.2689088

For the ON state of the CAS, both atom switches are set to ON, and for the OFF state both are programmed to OFF. The signal transfers between terminals T1 and T2 of the ON-state CAS. A program voltage as small as 3 V is applied via the select transistor connected to terminal C. A Cu bridge is formed in the solid electrolyte sandwiched between the Cu and ruthenium (Ru) electrodes when a positive voltage is applied to the Cu electrode, relative to the Ru electrode. The ON and OFF resistances of the CAS at a supply voltage (VDD) of 1 V are about 2 k and 800 M$\Omega$, respectively. The OFF resistance slightly decreases with increasing ambient temperature. Below 85°C, the change in the OFF resistance is less than 20%, which does not significantly increase the static power in the programmable logic. The cycling endurance is up to 10k cycles [7]. The OFF state persists for 10 years even when a DC voltage of 1 V and ambient temperature of 85°C are applied. The ON state is also reliable for more than 3000 hours at 150°C [8].

Use of atom switch in signal routing decreases delay, not only due to the reduced wire length but also the reduced switch level structure and input capacitance. Figure 2 shows an example of an 8-to-1 multiplexer (MUX). A conventional MUX is composed of dozens of SRAMs and pass transistors. Since the area occupied by the SRAM is larger than that by a pass transistor, the use of the SRAM is limited. For the tradeoff between area and delay, a typical 8-input routing MUX implemented as a two-level structure composed of 12 pass transistors sharing 6 SRAMs. When atom switch in the BEOL is applied, the layout footprint is negligible and a single-level structure is possible. The delay is also improved due to the small capacitance of the OFF-state two-terminal atom switch ($C_{SW} < 0.20$ fF), even though the fan-in of the crossbar switch is large (= 8).

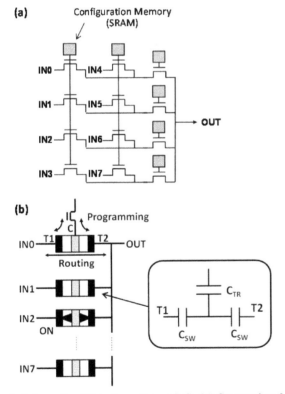

**Figure 2. Schematic of 8-to-1 routing switch. (a) Conventional MUX with SRAMs and (b) CAS-based MUX. Equivalent circuit for OFF state CAS is also shown.**

For the OFF-state CAS, the parasitic capacitance of the cell transistor ($C_{TR}$) does not affect the input capacitance. The capacitance of the ON-state CAS transferring a selected input signal is attributed to $C_{TR}$. Thus, the input capacitance of a CAS-based 8-to-1 MUX is ~ $7C_{SW} + C_{TR}$, when $C_{SW} < C_{TR}$. This is much smaller than that in an SRAM-based MUX ($4C_{TR}$).

## 3. PHYSICAL IMPLEMENTATION

The CAS is integrated on a 65-nm-node CMOS with 1-Poly-7-Metal (1P7M) process (Fig. 3(a)). The embedded process of the CAS is fully compatible with CMOS, since no degradation in the CMOS transistor and interconnects have been confirmed. The CAS is implemented on 4th Metal (M4) interconnect. We use a polymer-solid electrolyte, which enables low programming voltage of lower than 3V [7].

The logic block consists of two pairs of 4-input look up tables (LUTs) and D flip-flops (DFFs) [10] (Fig. 3(b)). A pair of CASs connected in series is used for the data memory in an LUT and several configuration bits. Each CAS is connected to VDD and ground (GND), respectively. The two CASs then form a resistive divider. The voltage at the middle node represents the LUT data and configuration bit. When one of CASs is set to ON state and the other is set to OFF state alternately, the middle node provides output logic "1" or "0". A 100-bit CAS is used for the data memory of an LUT and configuration bits in the configurable logic block (CLB). The function block is connected by the input multiplexers (IMUX) with directional segment wires. The IMUX is composed of 8 instances of a 51-to-1 MUX, which is implemented with the 8x51 crossbar switch of the CAS. Fifty-one inputs are from 48 segment wires, 2 feedback lines, and a fixed-low line, which is assigned for unused MUXs to avoid floating nodes. In the same way, a 12x51 crossbar outputs the signal to segment wires functioning as the switch multiplexers (SMUX). The output of the SMUX is buffered to prevent signal delay. Totally, these routing MUXs use 20x51 CASs, resulting in a single-level structure. Moreover, due to the elimination of the configuration memory required for SRAM-based CLBs, the CAS-based MUXs consume less area. Figure 3(c) shows the routing diagram. The cells are connected with directional segment wires of length 4. Each cell has 12 outputs, which are connected to 3 lanes each in 4 directions. The segment length and the lane number are chosen to have the capability of routing all of the MCNC "golden 20" circuits. The segment wires are buffered by an AND gate at the section between the second and third CLB. The AND gate also terminates unused wires to reduce the parasitic capacitance of segment wires.

## 4. EVALUATION

The operational speed and power consumption were evaluated on 64x64 programmable logic cell arrays and compared with those of a commercial low-power oriented FPGA device. For the comparison, the same resistor transfer level (RTL) code, a 16-bit arithmetic logic unit (ALU) circuit, was used.

The 16-bit ALU circuit with a 1k-gate scale includes an instruction decoder and input signal generator (Fig. 4). 332 LUTs and 73 flip-flops are used in the test design. A count-up signal generated by a mapped 16-bit counter is assigned for the input as the operand of ALU. All 28 instructions are cyclically asserted using a one-hot signal generator. The configuration data were generated using an in-house tool-chain [2]. Each logic cell has

2,240 atom switches (or 1,120 CAS) for signal routing and configuration memory. The configuration was done by setting the designated 140 atom switches (or 70 CASs) to the ON state in each cell. Devices were evaluated using a logic tester with the verification pattern, which was generated from the Verilog test bench.

Figure 5 (a) shows 2-dimensional shmoo plots in terms of clock period and VDD. The circuit mapped on the CAS-based programmable logic cell arrays operated at 2.5 times faster clock frequency when VDD = 0.8 V, compared to that on the state-of-the-art low power FPGA [10] shown in Fig. 5(b). The novel programmable logic also operated down to VDD as low as 0.5 V.

The power consumption was compared at the minimum VDD for 15-MHz operation. The CAS-based programmable logic operated at 0.73 V and 15 MHz with the active power of 550 μW. Contrarily, the VDDmin of the reference chip was 0.94 V, and the active power 630 μW. The dynamic power of the programmable logic cell arrays (= 28.0 μW/MHz) was also lower than that of the reference (= 39.5 μW/MHz). These improvements are mainly originated from the small capacitance of the CAS and a single level structure in the MUX. High ON/OFF conductance ratio contributes to suppress static power.

(a)

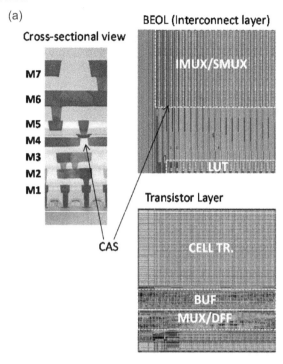

(b)

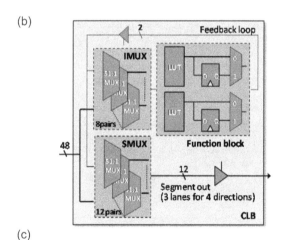

(c)

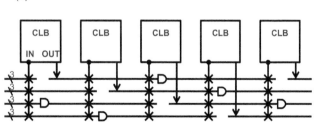

Figure 3. (a) Cross-sectional view of CAS integrated in 65-nm-node 7-metal process. Layout of programmable logic cell: BEOL and transistor layer. Cell area is 74.33x74.92 μm². Block diagram of (b) programmable logic cell and (C) segment wires.

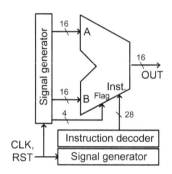

Figure 4. Diagram of mapped 16-bit ALU.

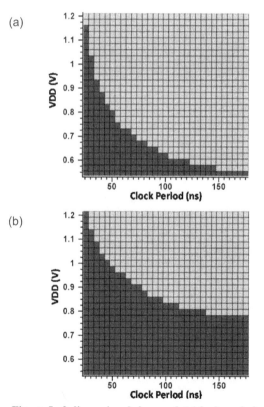

Figure 5. 2 dimensional shmoo plot (clock period vs. VDD) in (a) CAS-based programmable logic cell arrays, and (b) conventional low-power FPGA [10].

The intermittent operation of the novel nonvolatile programmable logic was investigated. For the sleep mode, the VDD was set to 0 V to reduce power consumption. In this mode, states in flip-flops in CLB may be swept out because of its volatility. Figure 6 shows a transient waveform demonstrating intermittent operation of 16-bit ALU circuits mapped on nonvolatile programmable logic cell arrays. Input signal "CLK", output signal "OUT[0]", and supply current are shown. After the sleep mode, the correct output signal was confirmed without resuming operation. The zero sleep energy was achieved, which was different from the low-power FPGA, the power of which was around 40 µW. During the sleep mode, configuration data were retained by the non-volatility of atom switch, resulting in the instant-on at a wake-up operation. A tiny rush current was needed to activate the programmable logic cell arrays. The zero sleep power overcomes the power issue in the intermittent operation of FPGA.

A die photo is shown in Fig. 7. The programming decoders, drivers, and IO buffers are placed at outside of cell arrays. The chip has 128 IOs for the user's application. Performance is summarized in Table 1. Nevertheless the test chip is fabricated in the previous process generation compared with the reference one, the power consumption and the signal delay are improved by atom switch.

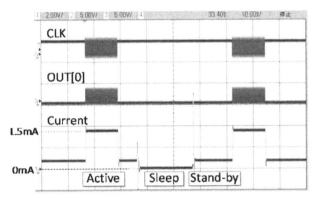

**Figure 6. Transient waveform in active, stand-by, and sleep mode. In active mode, VDD is 0.9 V and clock frequency is 15 MHz. Surge current accompanied with sleep-in and wake-up sequence comes from stray capacitance of performance board.**

**Figure 7. Die photograph of 64x64 programmable logic cell arrays. Programming decoders and drives for CAS are placed outside of cell array.**

**Table 1. Summary of performance comparison.**

| Features | This work | Ref.[10] |
|---|---|---|
| Switch | Atom switch | Pass Tr. |
| Process node | 65 nm | 40 nm |
| Number of LUTs | 8192 | 1280 |
| Max. speed at 0.8 V | 18.2 MHz | 7.1 MHz |
| VDDmin at 15 MHz | 0.73 V | 0.94 V |
| Dynamic power at VDDmin | 28.0 µW/MHz | 39.5 µW/MHz |
| Active power at VDDmin | 550 µW | 630 µW |

## 5. CONCLUSIONS

We proposed an ultra-low-power nonvolatile programmable logic using a CAS, which ensured 0.73-V operation and 28-µW/MHz dynamic power with higher performance than a conventional FPGA. Non-volatility enabled intermittent operation with zero standby power, which is suitable for WSN applications.

## 6. ACKNOWLEDGEMENT

This work was performed as "Ultra-Low Voltage Device Project" funded and supported by the Ministry of Economy, Trade and Industry (METI) and the New Energy and Industrial Technology Development Organization (NEDO).

## 7. REFERENCES

[1] S. Nakaya, et al., "A non-volatile reconfigurable offloader for wireless sensor nodes," *ACM SIGARCH Computer Architecture News*, 40, 5, pp.87-92 (2012). DOI=http://dx.doi.org/10.1145/2460216.2460232

[2] C. Wen, et al., "A non-volatile look-up table design using PCM (phase-change memory) cells," In *proc. VLSIC*, pp. 302-303 (2011).

[3] Y. Y. Liauw, et al., "Nonvolatile 3D-FPGA with monolithically stacked RRAM-based configuration memory," In *proc. ISSCC*, pp.406-408 (2012). DOI= http://dx.doi.org/10.1109/ISSCC.2012.6177067

[4] K. Huang, et al., "A Low Active Leakage and High Reliability Phase Change Memory (PCM) based on Non-Volatile FPGA Storage Element," *Circuits and Systems, IEEE Trans.*, 61, 9, pp.2605-2613 (2014). DOI= http://dx.doi.org/10.1109/TCSI.2014.2312499

[5] M. Miyamura, et al., "Programmable cell array using rewritable solid-electrolyte switch integrated in 90nm CMOS," In *proc. ISSCC*, pp.228-229 (2011). DOI= ttp://dx.doi.org/10.1109/ISSCC.2011.5746296

[6] M. Lin, et al., "Performance benefits of monolithically stacked 3D-FPGA", *Int. Symposium on FPGA Dig. of Tech. Paper*, pp. 113-122 (2006). DOI=http://dx.doi.org/10.1109/TCAD.2006.887920

[7] M. Tada, et al., "Improved ON-State Reliability of Atom Switch Using Alloy Electrodes," *Electron Devices, IEEE Trans.*, 60, 10, pp.3534-3540 (2013). DOI=http://dx.doi.org/10.1109/TED.2013.2275188

[8] T. Sakamoto, et al., "Electronic Conduction Mechanism in Atom Switch Using Polymer Solid Electrolyte," *Electron Devices, IEEE Transactions*, 59, 12, pp.3574-3577 (2012). DOI= http://dx.doi.org/10.1109/TED.2012.2219051

[9] M. Miyamura, et al., "Low-power programmable-logic cell arrays using nonvolatile complementary atom switch," In *proc. ISQED*, pp.330-334 (2014). DOI=http://dx.doi.org/10.1109/ISQED.2014.6783344

[10]http://www.latticesemi.com/Products/FPGAandCPLD/iCE40.aspx

# Energy and Memory Efficient Mapping of Bitonic Sorting on FPGA[*]

Ren Chen, Sruja Siriyal, Viktor Prasanna
Ming Hsieh Department of Electrical Engineering
University of Southern California, Los Angeles, USA 90089
{renchen, siriyal, prasanna}@usc.edu

## ABSTRACT

Parallel sorting networks are widely employed in hardware implementations for sorting due to their high data parallelism and low control overhead. In this paper, we propose an energy and memory efficient mapping methodology for implementing bitonic sorting network on FPGA. Using this methodology, the proposed sorting architecture can be built for a given data parallelism while supporting continuous data streams. We propose a streaming permutation network (*SPN*) by "folding" the classic Clos network. We prove that the *SPN* is programmable to realize all the interconnection patterns in the bitonic sorting network. A low cost design for sorting with minimal resource usage is obtained by reusing one *SPN*. We also demonstrate a high throughput design by trading off area for performance. With a data parallelism of $p$ ($2 \leq p \leq N/\log^2 N$), the high throughput design sorts an $N$-key sequence with latency $O(N/p)$, throughput (# of keys sorted per cycle) $O(p)$ and uses $O(N)$ memory. This achieves optimal memory efficiency (defined as the ratio of throughput to the amount of on-chip memory used by the design) of $O(p/N)$. Another noteworthy feature of the high throughput design is that only single-port memory rather than dual-port memory is required for processing continuous data streams. This results in 50% reduction in memory consumption. Post place-and-route results show that our architecture demonstrates 1.3x~1.6x improvment in energy efficiency and 1.5x~5.3x better memory efficiency compared with the state-of-the-art designs.

## Categories and Subject Descriptors

B.0 [**Hardware**]: GENERAL

---

[*]This work was partially supported by the US NSF under grant CCF-1018801 and by the DARPA PERFECT program. Equipment grant from Xilinx, Inc. is gratefully acknowledged.

## General Terms

Parallel algorithm, Energy, Performance, Memory

## Keywords

Sorting, Bitonic sorting network, Clos network, FPGA acceleration, energy efficiency, memory efficiency

## 1. INTRODUCTION

Sorting is one of the most fundamental computing problems. It has been widely used in many applications including digital signal processing, biological computing and large-scale scientific computing [4, 6, 15, 19, 24]. With the advent of Big Data, there is tremendous interest in speeding up solutions for sorting either using software or hardware. Parallel comparison-based sorting networks have been widely utilized in practice for hardware implementation. Benefiting from their straight-forward data flow graphs and simple control schemes, these networks are highly desirable for realizing high speed and parallel sorting architectures.

Bitonic sorting is a parallel comparison-based sorting network [6]. Using $O(N \log^2 N)$ comparators it sorts an arbitrary sequence of $N$ inputs in $O(\log^2 N)$ time. This network has been widely employed in hardware implementations for sorting [17, 26, 28]. Although many other parallel sorting networks with $O(\log N)$ depth have been introduced [4, 19], the bitonic sorting network is still one of the most practical solutions. Many parallel software implementations for sorting have been proposed based on bitonic sorting network [13, 21, 22]. These works either improve the sorting algorithms in terms of throughput and latency, or adapt the algorithms to a variety of general purpose parallel architectures such as SIMD or MIMD machines. However, when considering both energy and performance as the key metrics, hardware-based sorting solutions are preferred. A number of VLSI implementations of sorters have been proposed or implemented in hardware [13, 26]. These VLSI sorters are usually evaluated using area×time$^2$ performance as one of the key metrics. High performance with low I/O bandwidth requirement can be achieved by these designs, while throughput was not considered. Recently, as a trade-off solution between energy and performance, FPGA-based systems with re-programmability have become popular for realizing sorting [15, 16, 17, 20, 25, 28]. Latency, area, and throughput have been used as the key metrics for performance evaluation. High performance implementations have been realized by exploiting the key features of FPGAs.

In this paper, our focus is to map bitonic sorting network onto FPGA, considering performance, energy and memory efficiency (defined as the ratio of throughput to the amount of on-chip memory used by the design). We develop a mapping methodology utilizing the classic Clos network [14] to perform data movement between the adjacent sorting stages. It is straight forward to map bitonic sorting network onto hardware using cascaded comparators if all the input data are available concurrently. However, for large data sets, this simple approach is not technically feasible due to high routing complexity, area consumption, as well as limited I/O bandwidth. For large data sets, we show how to "fold" the bitonic sorting network as well as the Clos network to construct a sorting architecture with available data parallelism and I/O bandwidth. Our contributions in this work are:

- We propose a mapping approach to obtain a parallel sorting architecture by utilizing Clos network for inter-stage communication. The sorting architecture is parameterizable with respect to data parallelism, problem size, and data width.

- We prove that the constructed sorting architecture can process continuous data streams without any memory conflicts (concurrent read or write access to more than one word in a single-port memory).

- We propose a fully pipelined streaming permutation network (*SPN*) by mapping the Clos network with a data parallelism smaller than the input problem size. We develop an in-place permutation in time algorithm for *SPN* to process continuous data streams. This algorithm enables the use of single-port memory rather than dual-port (a read port and a write port) memory and reduces the memory consumption by 50%.

- We show that for a given data parallelism of $p$ (a divisor of $N$), the *SPN* is programmable to realize all the interconnection patterns in the bitonic sorting network, with a low logic overhead.

- We demonstrate the trade-off among throughput, latency and area using two illustrative designs including a high throughput design and a low cost design. Both designs are parameterizable.

- We perform detailed performance analysis, showing that for the high throughput design, assuming the available data parallelism is $p$ ($2 \leq p \leq N/\log^2 N$), the latency for sorting $N$-key sequence is $O(N/p)$, the throughput (# of keys sorted per cycle) is $O(p)$, and the memory consumption is $O(N)$.

- We conduct detailed experiments on a state-of-the-art FPGA device. Post place-and-route results show that our architecture demonstrates 1.3x~1.6x improvement in energy efficiency and 1.5x~5.3x better memory efficiency compared with the state-of-the-art designs.

## 2. BACKGROUND AND RELATED WORK

### 2.1 Bitonic Sorting Algorithm

Hardware implementation of bitonic sorting has been extensively studied in the literature, especially in the VLSI area [13, 21, 26]. The key building blocks of a bitonic sorting network are the bitonic merge (BM) networks which rearrange bitonic sequences to be ordered. A bitonic sequence is a sequence with $n_0 \leq ... \leq n_k \geq ... \geq n_{N-1}$ for some $k$ ($0 \leq k \leq N-1$), or a circular shift of such a sequence [6]. Throughout this paper, we use $N$ to denote the size of a

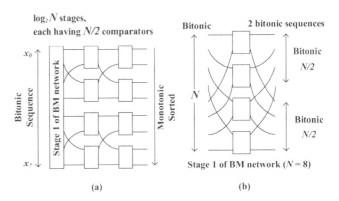

Figure 1: Constructing a bitonic merge network: a) Bitonic merge network for $N = 8$, b) Splitting a bitonic sequence into two bitonic sequences

data sequence to be sorted. Without losing generality, we assume $N$ is a power of two. For any given bitonic sequence of $N$ keys, we can use a column of $N/2$ comparators to split it into two bitonic sequences of $N/2$ keys each [6]. Fig. 1b shows the first stage of BM network for splitting a 8-key bitonic sequence. By iteratively splitting the sequence to be sorted, a BM network can sort an $N$-key bitonic sequence into sorted order in $\log N$ stages[1], where each stage consists of $N/2$ comparators. Fig. 1a shows the BM network for sorting a 8-key bitonic sequence. A bitonic sorting network for $N$-key sequence can be built using two bitonic sorting networks for $\frac{N}{2}$-key sequences and a BM network for $N$-key bitonic sequence. After recursively applying this rule, a bitonic sorting network built using BM networks needs $(\log N)(\log N + 1)/2$ stages of comparators.

### 2.2 Clos Network

Clos network is a multi-stage interconnection network first developed in the 1950s for telephone switching systems [14]. Now Clos network is still widely used in the design of switching systems such as IP routers, data center network, and VLSI interconnection network [14]. Fig. 2a shows the basic structure of a Clos network. $r$ is the number of crossbars in the first and third stages. The number of crossbars in the middle stage is denoted as $d$. The number of inputs (outputs) of the first (third) stage crossbars is $s$. $N = sr$ is the network input size. A network is *rearrangeably non-blocking* if an unused input can always be connected to an unused output with the need to rearrange the existing connections [14]. The Clos network is *rearrangeably non-blocking* so long as $d \geq s$ [14]. We will use this result in Section 4.2 to prove the correctness of our proposed mapping approach. Fig. 2b shows a routing example of using the Clos network to perform the permutation $i \rightarrow (i + 3)$ mod 9.

### 2.3 Hardware-Based Sorting Architectures

A hardware algorithm for sorting $N$ elements with a fixed number of I/O ports is presented in [22]. They extend the column sort algorithm to sort data elements in row-major order. They also develop a multi-way merge algorithm to obtain the sorted sequence. It sorts $N$ elements in $\Theta(\frac{N \log N}{p \log p})$ time using a sorting network of fixed I/O size $p$ and depth $O(\log^2 p)$. In [18], algorithms to reduce communication cost

---

[1]In this paper, all logarithms are to the base 2.

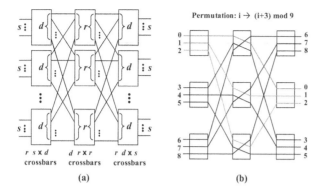

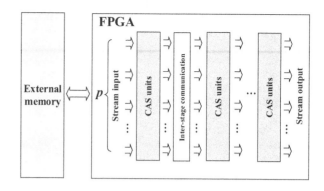

Figure 2: a) Clos network, b) A routing example

Figure 3: Architectural framework

for bitonic sorting on SIMD and MIMD processors are introduced. They reduce the communication between processors and shared-memory by almost one half when compared with the straight-forward bitonic sorting algorithms.

The area× time$^2$ performance of various designs for VLSI sorters is investigated in [26]. Three bitonic sort based VLSI designs are discussed. These designs use $\log N$, $\log^2 N$, and $\sqrt{N \log N}$ processors, and achieve time performance of $O(N \log^2 N)$, $O(N \log N)$ and $O(N/\log N)$, respectively. In [15], the authors present a modular design technique to obtain a high throughput and low latency sorting unit using 65-nm TSMC technology. The proposed sorter is applicable for cases when $m$ largest numbers need to be selected from $N$-key sequences. In [28], the SPIRAL project develop DSL (Domain Specific Language) to enable mapping sorting algorithms with flexible design choices. Their design supports processing continuous data streams, while energy and memory efficiency are not considered. Several existing sorting architectures on FPGAs are implemented and evaluated in [16]. FIFO or tree based merge sorter as well as bucket sorter are selected as target designs for implementation. They also discuss how to use partial run-time reconfiguration to obtain minimal resource consumption. In [17], a parameterized sorting architecture using bitonic merge network is presented. Their key idea is to build a recurrent architecture of bitonic sorting network to achieve throughput area trade-offs. Hardware designs to perform primitive database operations including selection, merge join and sorting are presented in [9]. High memory bandwidth utilization is achieved by implementing their proposed design on an FPGA-based system. Performance comparison between our design and some of the related work is detailed in Section 6. Some other high performance sorting architectures are developed for platforms other than FPGA [5, 24]. However, it is not clear how to apply their techniques on FPGAs.

## 3. ARCHITECTURE FRAMEWORK

**Problem definition:** The sorting problem consists of re-ordering an $N$-key sequence. The input sequences are stored in the external memory. With an available data parallelism of $p$ ($2 \le p \le N$), $p$ keys are fed into the design in each clock cycle. After a certain amount of time $T$, the first batch of sorted keys are output, $p$ keys in each clock cycle. With continuous data streams, the throughput is $p$ keys per clock cycle and the latency is $T$.

Fig. 3 shows the architectural framework within which we propose our mapping approach using FPGA as the target platform. The details of our architectural framework are:

- Data memory: We assume the input consists of several data sequences, each has length of $N$. External memory is employed to store the inputs.
- Input/output: The input data sequences are fed into the FPGA continuously in a streaming manner. The input data sequences enter the on-chip design at a fixed rate. After a specific delay, the sorted data sequences are output at the same rate.
- CAS units: Compare-and-swap (CAS) units are used for executing the basic operations required by the sorting algorithm. Each CAS unit can be implemented using LUTs and can be pipelined using flip-flops. Fig. 3 shows several stages of CAS units. Each stage consists of $p/2$ CAS units.
- Inter-stage communication: A sorting architecture is composed of cascaded comparison stages. The communication between adjacent stages (inter-stage communication) is performed by permuting data using interconnections and on-chip memories.
- Data parallelism: It is the number of keys processed in parallel each clock cycle in a comparison stage. $p$ (a divisor of $N$) is used to denote the data parallelism.

## 4. MEMORY EFFICIENT MAPPING

### 4.1 Interconnection Patterns

The interconnection patterns in a bitonic sorting network can be represented using stride permutations. A stride permutation can be defined using matrix representation. Given an $m$-element data vector $x$ and a stride $t$ ($1 \le t \le m-1$), the data vector $y$ produced by the stride-by-$t$ permutation over $x$ is given as $y = P_{m,t}x$, where $P_{m,t}$ is a permutation matrix. $P_{m,t}$ is an invertible $m \times m$ bit matrix such that

$$P_{m,t}[i][j] = \begin{cases} 1 & \text{if } j = (t \times i) \bmod m + (\lfloor t \times i/m \rfloor) \\ 0 & \text{otherwise} \end{cases} \quad (1)$$

where mod is the modulus operation and $\lfloor \ \rfloor$ is the floor function. For example, $P_{4,2}$ performs $x_0, x_1, x_2, x_3 \rightarrow x_0, x_2, x_1, x_3$; $P_{4,3}$ performs $x_0, x_1, x_2, x_3 \rightarrow x_0, x_3, x_1, x_4$.

Fig. 1a shows that at the first stage of the BM network, to sort $N$-key sequences, $P_{N,\frac{N}{2}}$ and $P_{N,2}$ are performed at the input and the output respectively. At the output, two bitonic sequences are generated and then permuted using $P_{\frac{N}{2},\frac{N}{4}}$. Therefore, the interconnection pattern at the output can be represented as $(I_2 \otimes P_{\frac{N}{2},\frac{N}{4}}) \cdot P_{N,2} = Q_N$, where

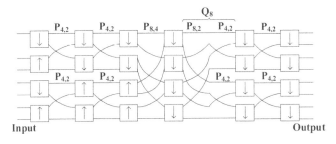

Figure 4: Interconnection patterns in 8-input bitonic sorting network (arrows show the sorting order)

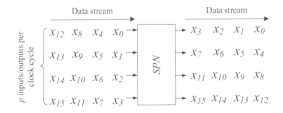

Figure 5: Example: data permutation on streaming data ($N = 16, t = 4, p = 4$)

$I_2$ is the identity matrix and $\otimes$ is the tensor (or Kronecker) product. By using the divide-and-conquer method discussed in Section 2.1, we therefore obtain a total of $(\log N)(\log N + 1)/2$ interconnection patterns. Note that there are $2\log N$ unique patterns. All the interconnection patterns can be realized using Clos network. Fig. 4 shows the interconnection patterns in an 8-input bitonic sorting network.

## 4.2 Mapping the Clos Network

In this section, we will introduce how to map the Clos network into a streaming permutation network ($SPN$) to perform the *permutation on streaming data*, which is defined as: given a hardware block with a data parallelism of $p$, the $N$-key input flows into the hardware block over $N/p$ consecutive cycles, after a certain amount of delay, the input is reordered as specified by the required permutation and flows out over $N/p$ consecutive cycles. The object of our mapping approach is to obtain such a hardware block, where multiple single-port memories rather than a $p$-port memory are employed. Fig. 5 illustrates a streaming version of the stride permutation $P_{16,4}$.

A well known hardware solution to perform stride permutation in bitonic sorting is the delay feedback or delay commutator module widely used in FFT designs [10, 11]. However, using the delay feedback or delay commutator for sorting needs the inputs to be fed in with some particular temporal order. This requirement is easily met for FFT applications as input data is sampled in time. But for sorting this constraint is not necessarily to be met. With limited data parallelism, using the delay feedback or commutator modules cannot fully utilize the high bandwidth provided by the state-of-the-art memory devices [1]. Also the interconnection pattern $Q_N$ composed of three stride permutations makes delay feedback or commutator inefficient.

As shown in Fig. 6, we propose an $SPN$ by "folding" the Clos network to perform the data permutations in bitonic sorting. Data permutation on streaming input has been recently studied [23]. Compared with this work, not only we

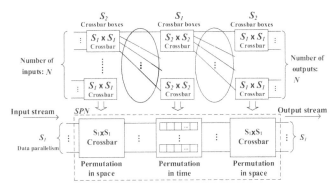

Figure 6: Folding the Clos network into an $SPN$

build the connection between the classic permutation network and the $SPN$, but also our hardware design is memory efficient and uses only single-port memory blocks. Fig. 6 shows the key idea for mapping the Clos network where $d = s = S_1$, $r = S_2$. Assuming the input size is $N$, and $N = S_1 \times S_2$, a Clos network can be built to be *rearrangeably non-blocking* if $S_2 \geq S_1$ [14]. We can map the Clos network onto an $SPN$ with a data parallelism of $S_1$. We use permutation in space to represent data permutation performed by the crossbar interconnections while permutation in time is defined as permuting temporal order of data elements in a given data sequence. As shown in Fig. 6, in the proposed $SPN$, permutation in space is performed in the first and third stage by two $S_1 \times S_1$ crossbars, and permutation in time is executed in the second stage by $S_1$ independent single-port memory blocks, each having a memory size of $S_2$. In the $SPN$, a *memory conflict* is said to occur if concurrent read or write access to more than one word in a single-port memory block is performed in a clock cycle.

THEOREM 4.1. *With a data parallelism of $S_1$, the proposed $SPN$ can realize any given permutation on streaming input of an $N$-key data sequence without any memory conflicts using $S_1$ single-port memory blocks, each of size $S_2$, where $S_2 \geq S_1$ and $N = S_1 \times S_2$.*

**Proof:** In the Clos network shown in Fig. 6, where $N = S_1 \times S_2$, each $S_1 \times S_1$ crossbar in the first or third stage has exactly one connection to each of the $S_1$ $S_2 \times S_2$ crossbars in the second stage. Similarly, there is exactly one connection between each middle stage crossbar and each first or third stage crossbar. This network is *rearrangeably non-blocking* and thus can realize arbitrary data permutation on an $N$-key data sequence [14]. Clearly, a routing on this network can also be realized by the proposed $SPN$ shown in Fig. 6. By reusing the $S_1 \times S_1$ crossbar in the first stage of $SPN$ $S_2$ times, the routing of the first stage in the Clos network can be realized. Likewise, the crossbar in the third stage of $SPN$ can also be used to implement the routing of the third stage of the Clos network. Each memory block in the second stage of $SPN$ has a memory size of $S_2$ and can be written by an output of the $S_1 \times S_1$ crossbar in the first stage. In $S_2$ steps, the $S_1$ memory blocks in the second stage of $SPN$ realize the routing of the second stage of the Clos network. Therefore, the proposed $SPN$ simulates the Clos network in Fig. 6, hence proving the theorem. ∎

With a data parallelism $p = S_1$, an $SPN$ having the control information to perform all the interconnection patterns in bitonic sort is programmable with respect to $m$, $t$, and $v$. $m$

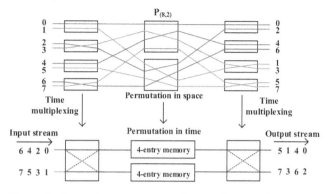

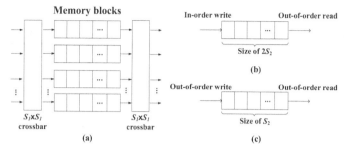

Figure 7: Example: 3-stage mapping for $P_{(8,2)}$ and $p = 2$

Figure 8: a) $SPN$ unit, b) Permutation in time on dual-port (a read port and a write port) memory before data remapping, c) Permutation in time on single-port memory after data remapping

and $t$ represent length of data sequence to be permuted and stride value, respectively. $v$ is used to differentiate $P_{m,t}$ and $Q_m$. Here programming refers to switching the context of control information to configure $m$, $t$, and $v$ during run-time. We denote programmable $SPN$ as $SPN(p, m, t, v)$. It can be programmed to perform either $P_{m,t}(v = 0)$ or $Q_m(v = 1)$ arising in the bitonic sorting network. Theorem 4.1 states that $SPN(p, m, t, v)$ is programmable with respect to $m$, $t$ and $v$ if $S_1 \times S_2 \geq m$ and $m/S_1 \geq S_1$. Also the latency is $m/S_1$. In Section 5.3, we will show how we achieve a low cost design for sorting, by programming the $SPN(p, m, t, v)$. Fig. 7 shows a mapping example where the Clos network is configured to perform stride permutation $P_{8,2}$. In this example, $N = 8$, $S_1 = 2$ and $S_2 = 4$. To execute $P_{8,2}$, the $SPN$ needs two $2 \times 2$ crossbars and two 4-entry memories. The control information for the $SPN$ can be easily obtained using a routing algorithm for Clos network [14]. This observation is non-trivial as any of the previous optimizations on routing algorithms for Clos network can be reused for realizing $SPN$. In this paper, we adopt a well known routing algorithm for Clos network to obtain all the control information for $SPN$ [7]. In the second stage of $SPN$, each memory block can be implemented with single-port memory to permute a single data sequence. However, when processing continuous data streams, dual-port memory is required as concurrent read and write access to different memory locations need to be performed. An algorithm which enables the use of single-port memory for processing continuous data streams is introduced next.

### 4.3 In-Place Permutation in Time

In this section, we develop an algorithm to perform the permutation in time in the second stage of $SPN$. This algorithm enables the use of single-port memory to process continuous data streams, i.e., processing of $p$ keys from a new data sequence starts immediately after the final set of the previous data sequence enters the sorter. A single-port memory needs to support simultaneous read-write operation (read first) to the same memory location [3]. In the state-of-the-art [23], dual-port memory is required to perform permutation in time on continuous data streams.

#### 4.3.1 In-place algorithm

Fig. 8a shows the overall design of the $SPN$ network which consists of two $S_1 \times S_1$ crossbars and $S_1$ memory blocks (each having $S_2$ locations). Fig. 8b shows how permutation in time is realized in [23]. A data sequence of length $S_2$ is written into a memory block over $S_2$ memory access cycles. To per-

form in-order write, the data sequence is written with an address sequence $e = (0, 1, ..., S_2 - 1)$, address $e[i]$ is used in the $i$th $(0 \leq i \leq S_2 - 1)$ clock cycle. Similarly, out-of-order write can be performed using an address sequence resulting from permuting the address sequence $e$. In-order or out-of-order read operation can be defined likewise. Using this approach, when processing continuous data streams, each memory block is read from and written into simultaneously possibly at different memory locations in each memory access cycle. An $S_2$-key sequence can be permuted in time either using a dual-port memory of size $2S_2$ or two single-port memories, each of size $S_2$.

---

**Algorithm 1** In-place permutation in time in the $SPN$

**Input:** $data_{i,k}$, $addr_{i,j}$
**Constants:** $n_1$, $n_2$

1: {Initialization}
2: **for** $i = 0$ to $S_1 - 1$ **do**
3:     Initialize $addr_{i,j}$
4: **end for**
5: {Permutation in time}
6: $j = 0$
7: **for** $k = 0$ to $n_2 - 1$ **do**
8:     **for** $i = 0$ to $S_1 - 1$, in parallel **do**
9:         **for** $h = 0$ to $S_2 - 1$ **do**
10:             Simultaneous read-write operation:
11:             Read $data_{i,k-1,h}$ from the memory block $i$
12:             with address $addr_{i,j,h}$;
13:             Write $data_{i,k,h}$ into the memory block $i$ with
14:             address $addr_{i,j,h}$.
15:         **end for**
16:         **if** $(j == n_1 - 1)$ **then**
17:             $j = 0$
18:         **else**
19:             $j = j + 1$
20:         **end if**
21:     **end for**
22: **end for**
23: {End of the algorithm}

---

To reduce the memory consumption, we remap the data when writing to each memory block so that the read and write operations can be always performed at the same memory location, and the input data sequence is reordered correctly as specified by the permutation in time. Fig. 8c shows the key idea of our proposed *in-place algorithm* for permutation in time. Each memory block is written out-of-order (with a dynamically updated address sequence) rather than in-order. In this way, each memory location is written with a new value once the old value is read out, thus the proposed permutation in time algorithm is an *in-place algorithm*.

Algorithm 1 shows the details of the proposed *in-place algorithm* in the second stage of *SPN*. We use index $i$ ($0 \leq i \leq S_1 - 1$) to represent the $S_1$ single-port memory blocks. $P_i$ denotes the permutation (in time) to be performed on the input stream to memory block $i$. $addr_{i,j,h}$ and $data_{i,k,h}$ represent the addresses and data for accessing the memory block $i$ respectively. $j$ ($0 \leq j \leq n_1 - 1$) is the index of the address sequences, $k$ ($0 \leq k \leq n_2 - 1$) is the index of the data sequences, and $h$ ($0 \leq h \leq S_2 - 1$) is the index of an element in a data/address sequence. $addr_{i,j}$ is calculated based on $P_i$. $n_1$ is the number of address sequences required for data remapping. $n_2$ is the number of data sequences to be permuted. Both $n_1$ and $n_2$ are constants (the range of values are discussed next). The above analysis leads to:

THEOREM 4.2. *Any permutation in time on continuous data streams consisting of $S_2$-key data sequences can be realized using a single-port memory block of size $S_2$.*

### 4.3.2 *Data remapping overhead*

To implement the proposed *in-place algorithm*, address sequences need to be pre-computed for data remapping. Algorithm 1 requires $addr_{i,j}$ to be computed in advance. In hardware implementation, we can either use LUTs on FPGA to store $addr_{i,j}$ or dynamically update the memory address using a customized logic unit. To estimate the data remapping cost, we need to evaluate the range of $n_1$. Again let $P_i$ represent the permutation to be performed on the memory block $i$. Assuming $addr_{i,0} = [0, 1, 2, ..., S_2 - 1]^T$, to implement the *in-place algorithm*, we need to iteratively compute $addr_{i,j}$ ($0 \leq j \leq n_1 - 1$) using the following equation:

$$addr_{i,j+1} = P_i \cdot addr_{i,j}, \ 0 \leq j \leq n_1 - 2 \qquad (2)$$

such that finally $addr_{i,0} = P_i \cdot addr_{i,n_1-1}$. Our key observation is that $n_1$ always exsits to be a constant determined by $P_i$. This leads to:

THEOREM 4.3. *For any given permutation in time, the proposed in-place algorithm requires a constant number of address sequences for data remapping.*

**Proof:** Consider permutation $P_i$ to be performed on memory block $i$ ($0 \leq i \leq S_1 - 1$). Based on Equation 2, $P_i \cdot addr_{i,n_1-1} = P_i^2 \cdot addr_{i,n_1-2} = ... = P_i^{n_1} \cdot addr_{i,0}$. Thus, we have $P_i \cdot addr_{i,n_1-1} = addr_{i,0}$ when $P_i^{n_1} = I$. Note that some power (a constant) of a permutation matrix is the identity matrix [8]. Therefore, we can always find a constant $n_1$ such that $P_i^{n_1} = I$. The value of $n_1$ depends on $P_i$. The address sequences $addr_{i,0}, addr_{i,1}, ..., addr_{i,n_1-1}$ are the required address sequences for accessing memory block $i$. ∎

As each memory block has a size of $S_2$, the memory address width is $\log S_2$. According to [8], stride permutation is periodic, i.e., $P_{S_2,t}^{\log S_2} = I$. Thus, when $P_i$ is a stride permutation, the number of address sequences $n_1$ for memory block $i$ is $\log S_2$. The routing results show that $P_i$ is a stride permutation, a cyclic shift, or a combination of both for all the *SPN*s. For all the above cases, $n_1$ is $O(\log S_2)$. Based on the analysis above, for $N = 1024$, using $S_1 = 8$ and $S_2 = 128$ in *SPN*, the number of bits required for storing all the address sequences is $\leq \log S_2 \times \log S_2 \times S_2 \times S_1 = 49 \ kbits$. In actual implementation, it is not required to store the entire address sequence as we can update the addresses dynamically using

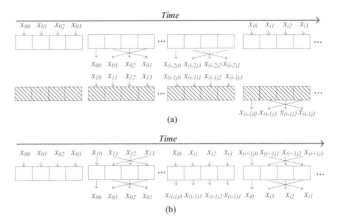

Figure 9: Permutation in time on 4-key sequences: a) using two single-port memories b) using one single-port memory

an initial address. Using this approach, the memory needed for storing all the address sequences in an *SPN* for bitonic sort is $\leq \log S_2 \times \log S_2 \times S_1 = 0.38 \ kbits$. Note that, on the state-of-the-art FPGA, each block RAM (BRAM) has a memory capacity of 18 *kbits* [3]. In our implementations, we decide whether to apply the in-place algorithm or not based on the value of $S_2$ of an *SPN*.

Fig. 9 illustrates how permutation on continuous data streams is performed. Continuous input data sequences including $x_0, x_1, ..., x_i, ...$ (each of length four) are successively permuted temporally. For each data sequence $x_j$ ($j \geq 0$), a permutation of $[x_{j0}, x_{j1}, x_{j2}, x_{j3}] \rightarrow [x_{j0}, x_{j3}, x_{j2}, x_{j1}]$ is performed. Fig. 9a shows the permutation process using two single port memories. As shown in this figure, the two single port memories are alternately read and written during consecutive time periods. For each data element $x_{jk}$, $k$ represents the index of its time sequence when $x_j$ is written into a memory block. We can see that the data elements in each data sequence are reordered in time. In each cycle, read and write operations are executed concurrently using different memory addresses. Fig. 9b shows performing the permutation using one single port memory using our proposed in-place algorithm. Read and write operations are performed simultaneously using one address in each cycle. When permuting a data sequence, if address sequence $\{0, 1, 2, 3\}$ is used for memory access, then for the next data sequence, address sequence $\{0, 3, 2, 1\}$ will be used. These two address sequences are used alternately for permuting continuous data streams. To dynamically generate the two address sequences, each of size 4, we can employ a 2-bit up counter and a 2-bit down counter. Note that the single-port memory should support concurrent read-write operation (read first) in a memory access cycle.

## 5. ARCHITECTURE IMPLEMENTATION

In this section, we develop a high throughput design and a low cost design to realize bitonic sorting on FPGA. The high throughput design is fully pipelined and takes advantage of the on-chip distributed (dist.) RAM or BRAM to achieve high performance. With a high data parallelism, it supports processing continuous input data streams without constraints on input temporal order. The low cost design consumes minimal hardware resources by reusing the architectural components. It achieves high resource efficiency by

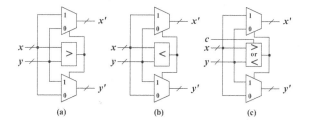

Figure 10: CAS units: for generating a) ascending order, b) for descending order, c) either order

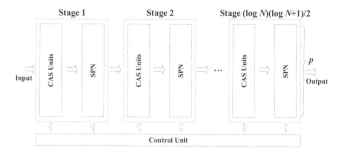

Figure 11: Overall architecture of high throughput design

dynamically reusing one *SPN* to perform all the inter-stage communication. In our designs, we use two basic building blocks: compare-and-swap (CAS) unit and *SPN* unit.

## 5.1 Architectural Components

### 5.1.1 CAS unit

A CAS unit is used to compare two input values and swap the values either in ascending or descending order. Three different designs of CAS unit are shown in Fig. 10. Fig. 10a shows the CAS unit used to swap the input values to output in ascending order. Similarly, the design in Fig. 10b is used to produce output values in descending order. Besides, we also design a configurable CAS unit shown in Fig. 10c for resource sharing purpose.

### 5.1.2 SPN unit

An *SPN* unit is composed of memory blocks and crossbars. As introduced in Section 4.2, data parallelism needs to be fixed before implementing an *SPN* unit. For a given $p$, we use $SPN(p, m, t, v)$ to denote an *SPN* supporting permutations including $P_{m,t}(v = 0)$ and $Q_m(v = 1)$. In the *SPN*, each memory block can be bound to dist. RAM or BRAM on FPGA. According to [3], BRAM is more power and area efficient than dist. RAM when used for implementing large size memories. However, for a small size memory, it is more power efficient to implement the memory with dist. RAM. Therefore, we empirically perform the memory binding to optimize the memory power consumption based on related experimental results in [10, 12]. Besides, using the proposed in-place permutation in time algorithm, each memory block is implemented using a single-port BRAM which is configured to be in the read-before-write mode [3]; thus data previously stored at the write address appears at the outputs while input data is being stored in the same memory location. Dist. RAM inherently supports this feature. Several LUT-based multiplexers are used to realize a crossbar switch. A logic unit for address generation is designed to dynamically update the memory address for accessing each memory block.

## 5.2 High Throughput Design

The high throughput design consists of a series of SPN units and CAS units. This design supports sorting of continuous data streams. During sorting, each *SPN* unit or CAS unit keeps on processing continually incoming data streams without interrupts. To build a high throughput design, after the data parallelism ($p = S_1$) is fixed, we need at most $(\log N)(\log N + 1)/2$ stages of *SPN*s, each *SPN* is responsible for executing a specific permutation at that stage. When $m \leq p$, *SPN* is replaced with an $m$-to-$m$ crossbar. For ex-

ample, a high throughput design ($p=2$) for sorting an 8-key sequence needs five *SPN*s and three of them are designed for realizing $P_{4,2}$, other two perform $P_{8,4}$ and $Q_8$ respectively. Similarly, $(\log N)(\log N + 1)/2$ stages of comparators are required, and each stage needs $p/2$ comparators. Fig. 11 shows the overall architecture of high throughput design.

In the high throughput design, there are $(\log N)(\log N + 1)/2$ stages of *SPN*. Each *SPN* denoted as $SPN(p, m, t, v)$ has its own parameter values for $m$, $t$ and $v$. The latency introduced by all the *SPN*s denoted as $T_{SPNs}(N, p)$ can be calculated by

$$T_{SPNs}(N,p) = \sum_{i=\log p}^{\log N - 1} \left( \sum_{j=\log p}^{i} \frac{2^{j+1}}{p} + \frac{2^{i+1}}{p} \right) \qquad (3)$$

which is $(6(N - p) - 2\log(N/p))/p$. As the latency introduced by CAS units is $O((\log p)\log^2 N)$, the entire latency of the high throughput design is $O(N/p)$ ($2 \leq p \leq N/\log^2 N$). Similarly, we can show that the memory consumed by all the *SPN*s is $O(N)$. Furthermore, the high throughput design can be pipelined to process continuous data streams, resulting in a throughput of $p$. To achieve a high throughput, a pipeline stage can be inserted after each of the $(\log N)(\log N + 1)/2$ comparison stages. The area consumption is $O(p \log^2 N)$ and the interconnect complexity is $O(p)$. When using external memory as data memory, the required number of I/Os is $O(p)$. Each stage consists of $p/2$ CAS units. No control bits are needed for CAS units shown in Fig. 10a and Fig. 10b. Each CAS unit shown in Fig. 10c requires only one control bit. The total number of control bits for all the CAS units is $O(\log^2 N)$. In $SPN(p, m, t, v)$, two $p$-to-$p$ crossbars require $O(p \log p)$ control bits.

## 5.3 Low Cost Design

Fig. 12 shows the architecture of the low cost design. The low cost design cannot support processing continuous data streams, thus the proposed in-place permutation in time algorithm is not applicable. For a given data parallelism $p$, the low cost design requires an $SPN(p, m, t, v)$ and $p/2$ CAS units. During sorting, $SPN(p, m, t, v)$ is reused by programming $m$, $t$ and $v$ so that all the permutations $P_{m,t}$ and $Q_m$ for the sorting problem can be realized. In this way, this design achieves the highest resource efficiency at the expense of throughput. Based on the introduction in Section 4.1, only $2 \log N$ different interconnection patterns exist between the $\log^2 N$ comparison stages in the bitonic sorting network. Thus $2 \log N$ states are introduced for control.

To complete execution of one comparison stage in the bitonic sorting network, $p/2$ CAS units are reused $N/p$ times. Since the total number of comparison stages is $(\log N)(\log N+$

Table 1: Performance comparison of sorting architectures

| Design | Latency | Logic | Memory | Memory type | Throughput[1] | Memory throughput ratio[4] | Support for continuous data streams |
|---|---|---|---|---|---|---|---|
| [9] | $o((N\log p)/p)$ | $o(p\log N)$ | $o(Np)$ | Dual-port and p-port | $o(p)$ | $2N + o(N)$ | No |
| [22] | $o(\frac{N\log N}{p\log p})$ | $o(p\log^2 p)$ | $o(N)$ | Dual-port | $o(\frac{p\log p}{\log N})$ | $o(\frac{N\log N}{p\log p})$ | No |
| [16] | $o(N)$ | $o(\log N)$ | $2N + o(N)$ | Dual-port | $o(1)$ | $2N + o(N)$ | Yes |
| SPIRAL [28][2] | $6N/p + o(N/p)$ | $o(p\log^2 N)$ | $12N + o(N)$ | Dual-port | $o(p)$ | $12N/p + o(N)$ | Yes |
| [26][3] | $3N + o(N)$ | $o(\log^2 N)$ | $6N + o(N)$ | Dual-port | $o(1)$ | $6N + o(N)$ | Yes |
| High throughput design | $6N/p + o(N/p)$ | $o(p\log^2 N)$ | $6N + o(N)$ | Single-port | $o(p)$ | $6N/p + o(N)$ | Yes |
| Low cost design | $o(N\log^2 N/p)$ | $o(p)$ | $o(N)$ | Dual-port | $o(p/\log^2 N)$ | $o(N\log^2 N/p)$ | No |

[1] Throughput $\neq$ 1/Latency as all $N$ data elements are sorted concurrently or when processing continuous data streams
[2] The highest throughput design in their work. [3] $O(\log^2 N)$-processor bitonic sort. [4] The reciprocal of the memory efficiency (used for asymptotic analysis)

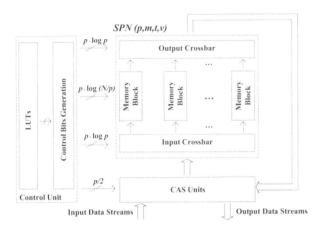

Figure 12: Overall architecture of low cost design

$1)/2$, the low cost design has a latency of $O((\log^2 N)N/p)$ for sorting. Before the execution of next stage, the intermediate results of the current stage needs to be stored. Thus, the required on-chip memory size is exactly $N$. The CAS units are programmed to generate an ascending order or a descending order of the inputs based on the comparison results. To complete each comparison stage, the CAS units needs to be programmed $N/p$ times. Benefiting from the symmetric property of bitonic sorting network, only one state machine with $\log N$ states for updating $p/2$ bits is required to program all the CAS units. Therefore, the programming overhead with respect to memory bits for CAS units is $O((p/2)\log N)$. Similarly, $SPN(p, m, t, v)$ needs to be reused $(\log N)(\log N + 1)/2$ times to perform all the comparison stages. For accessing each memory block in the $SPN(p, m, t, v)$, a $\log(N/p)$-bit counter is required for read, and $p$ state machines (each having $2\log N$ states) for updating $p\log(N/p)$ control bits are realized for write. Similarly, to program the crossbars in the $SPN$, two state machines (each having $2\log N$ states) for updating $p\log p$ control bits are required. As a result, the programming overhead of the $SPN(p, m, t, v)$ is $O((p\log N)\log(N/p))$.

# 6. EXPERIMENTS

## 6.1 Experimental Setup

Both the high throughput design and the low cost design were implemented on Virtex-7 FPGA (XC7VX690T, speed grade -2L). This device has 2940 BRAMs (each 18 *kbits*) and 108300 slices. The designs were synthesized and place-

and-routed by Vivado 2014.2 [2]. Post place-and-route simulations were conducted for behavior and timing verification. We created input test vectors having an average toggle rate of 50% for simulation. We used SAIF (switching activity interchange format) files as inputs to Vivado power analysis tool to produce accurate power dissipation estimation [3].

## 6.2 Performance Metrics

We consider the following metrics:
- Throughput: is defined as the number of bits sorted per second (Gbits/s). The *throughput* is computed as the product of number of keys sorted per second and data width per key.
- Energy efficiency (or power efficiency): is defined as the number of bits sorted per unit energy dissipated (Gbits/Joule) by the design and is calculated as the throughput divided by the average power consumed by the design.
- Memory efficiency: measured as the throughput achieved divided by the amount of on-chip memory used by the design (in bits).

## 6.3 Performance Evaluation

In this section, we use HT Design to denote the high throughput design. LUT-L and LUT-M represent LUTs in logic and LUTs in memory, respectively. We configure the data parallelism $p$ as four in all our implementations.

### 6.3.1 Asymptotic analysis

Table 1 presents an asymptotic analysis of the performance of various sorting architectures. The details of some of the prior designs are introduced in Section 2.3. The proposed HT Design is one of the designs achieving a linear time complexity (latency) which decreases with the available data parallelism $p$. We also show the constants with little $o$ notation in the asymptotic expressions for the sake of comparison [27]. The table shows that the memory throughput ratio (the reciprocal of memory efficiency) of the HT Design is $6N/p + o(N)$. When $p \geq 4$ and $N \geq 128$, the HT Design outperforms all the other designs with respect to memory efficiency. Moreover, benefiting from the proposed in-place permutation in time algorithm, the HT Design uses only single-port memory to process continuous data streams.

### 6.3.2 Results of design points

We employ a baseline architecture implemented using the HT Design without applying the proposed in-place permutation in time algorithm discussed in Section 4.3. We fix

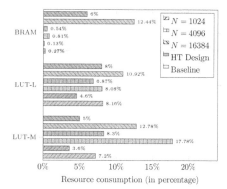

Figure 13: Memory and logic resource used by the HT Design and the baseline

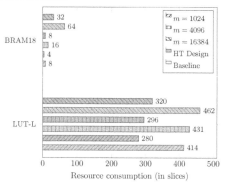

Figure 14: Memory and logic resource used by *SPN*

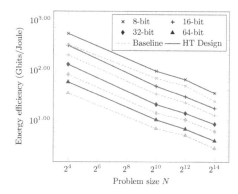

Figure 15: Energy efficiency for various problem sizes

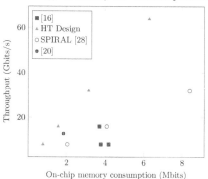

Figure 16: Memory efficiency comparison of various designs

the data width as 32-bit for the HT Design and the baseline architecture. For both of them, we evaluate the amount of BRAM, LUT-L, LUT-M consumed for problem sizes $N = 1024, 4096$, and $16384$. The results are shown in Fig. 13. In this plot, the available amount of BRAMs or LUTs is normalized to one on the $x$-axis. The red bars and blue bars show the resource consumption of the HT Design and the baseline, respectively. The problem size is differentiated by the bar fill pattern. The figure shows that the consumption of both BRAM and LUT-M nearly doubles for the baseline for all the problem sizes. The reduction in memory usage is especially significant for $N = 16K$. Moreover, the figure shows that the utilization of LUT-L is also reduced in the HT Design for the selected problem sizes. This shows that as dual-port memory is eliminated and the total memory size is halved, LUT-L needed for implementing memories is reduced significantly. Thus, it implies that the logic overhead for implementing the proposed *in-place algorithm* is almost negligible, and it demonstrates the superiority of our proposed in-place algorithm. The figure shows that the LUT-M consumption for $N = 4096$ is more than that for $N = 16384$. The reason is that most of the memory blocks are implemented using BRAMs when $N = 16384$.

We also evaluate resource consumption of $SPN(p, m, t, v)$ alone, for both the HT Design and the baseline. The results are presented in Fig. 14. $p, t, v$ are fixed as 4, 2, and 0 respectively. We selected $m$ as 1024, 4096, and 16384 in the experiments for illustration. The number of BRAM18 (18kb BRAM) and LUT-L are shown using bars on $y$-axis. Considering the selected values of $m$, the memory blocks in $SPN$ are all implemented using BRAMs, thus there is no LUT-M used. Clearly it shows that the the number of

BRAM18 is exactly halved for all the selected problem sizes. Besides, the elimination of dual-port memory also results in reduction in the amount of LUT-L used; up to 32% logic reduction is achieved. The above results show that using our proposed mapping methodology, the data permutations in bitonic sorting network can be performed efficiently with respect to memory and logic consumption.

We further evaluate the energy efficiency of HT Design and the baseline for $N = 16, 1024, 4096$, and $16384$. The operating frequency is fixed at 250 MHz for the sake of power evaluation. All our designs were pipelined to achieve this clock rate. The data width is varied from 8-bit to 64-bit. The experimental results are presented to demonstrate the benefit of the proposed in-place permutation in time algorithm for sorting from a power point of view. Fig. 15 shows that the energy efficiency of both designs are sensitive to data width. This is because we create testbench with 50% toggle rate for each design. When the data width increases, the switching activity of the designs increases significantly. The results also show that as the data width and problem size are varied, the HT design achieves 33%∼67% improvement in energy efficiency. In the experiments, we aggressively optimized speed for both designs by inserting pipeline stages after each comparison stage. We believe more energy efficiency can be gained by trading off the speed.

### 6.3.3 Performance comparison

Fig. 16 presents a scatter plot comparing the design points of our work with several prior work. The design points labeled [16] are developed for sorting $43K$-key or $21.5K$-key data sequence. The design points labeled HT Design and SPIRAL [28] are realized for sorting $16K$-element data sequence. The design in [20] can process up to 250 MB data

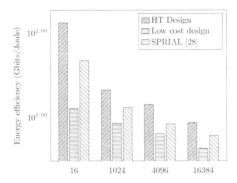

Figure 17: Energy efficiency comparison

sets consisting of 8-key data sequences. An embedded system based sorting solution is presented in [20]. The $x$-axis represents the on-chip memory consumption (in Mbits) of a design point, and the $y$-axis represents the throughput achieved by the design. Design points closer to the upper left corner of the plot achieve higher throughput with less on-chip memory. In Fig. 16, all our designs are dominating designs: for every design in the literature considered in this evaluation, one of our designs offers superior throughput or memory efficiency or both. Our designs achieve 2.3x~5.3x better memory efficiency compared with [16]. Our best design provides 2.6x and 1.5x better memory efficiency compared with SPIRAL and [20], respectively.

We also compare both the HT Design and the low cost design with the designs developed by the SPIRAL project [28] with respect to energy efficiency. Their tool automatically generates customized sorting soft IP cores in synthesizable RTL Verilog with user specified parameters, including problem size, data parallelism, data precision, etc. For the sake of illustration, the operating frequency is set to 250 MHz for power evaluation and the data parallelism was set to four. Energy efficiency of our design is compared against that of the soft IP cores having the same data parallelism. The problem size is chosen to be 16, 1024, 4096 and 16384. As shown in Fig. 17, for various $N$, the HT Design improves energy efficiency by up to 1.6x. The results also show that the low cost architecture consumes the most amount of energy. The reason is that a considerable amount of energy is consumed by the path connecting the design and I/O ports. We believe the low cost design can achieve a much higher energy efficiency if implemented using VLSI technologies.

## 7. CONCLUSIONS

In this work, we presented an energy and memory efficient mapping of bitonic sorting on FPGA. We proposed a streaming permutation network which is programmable to perform all the data permutations in the bitonic sorting network. We constructed two illustrative designs: a high throughput design and a low cost design. We developed an in-place permutation in time algorithm so that the high throughput design is able to employ single-port memory to process continuous data streams. Experimental results show that our design dominates all other designs in the literature with regard to memory efficiency. The proposed mapping approach can be used to generate high performance designs to optimize latency, throughput and energy efficiency. In the future, we plan to work on an accurate performance model for energy-efficiency estimation, which can be used for de-

sign space exploration to obtain power optimized sorting architectures with various constraints.

## 8. REFERENCES

[1] DDR4 SDRAM.
http://www.micron.com/products/dram/ddr4-sdram.

[2] Vivado design suite user guide: design flows overview.
http://www.xilinx.com/support/documentation/.

[3] XST user guide for Virtex-6, Spartan-6, and 7 series devices.
http://www.xilinx.com/support/documentation.

[4] M. Ajtai, J. Komlós, and E. Szemerédi. An $O(n \log n)$ sorting network. In *Proc. of ACM STOC*, pages 1–9. ACM, 1983.

[5] K. Andryc, M. Merchant, and R. Tessier. FlexGrip: A soft GPGPU for FPGAs. In *Proc. of IEEE FPT*, pages 230–237, Dec 2013.

[6] K. E. Batcher. Sorting networks and their applications. In *Proc. of AFIPS*, pages 307–314. ACM, 1968.

[7] V. E. Benes. Permutation groups, complexes, and rearrangeable connecting networks. *Bell System Technical Journal*, 43(4):1619–1640, 1964.

[8] R. A. Brualdi. *Combinatorial matrix classes*, volume 13. Cambridge University Press, 2006.

[9] J. Casper and K. Olukotun. Hardware acceleration of database operations. In *Proc. of ACM/SIGDA FPGA*, 2014.

[10] R. Chen, H. Le, and V. K. Prasanna. Energy efficient parameterized FFT architecture. In *Proc. of IEEE International Conference on FPL*, 2013.

[11] R. Chen, N. Park, and V. K. Prasanna. High throughput energy efficient parallel FFT architecture on FPGAs. In *Proc. of IEEE International Conference on HPEC*, pages 1–6, 2013.

[12] R. Chen and V. K. Prasanna. Energy-efficient architecture for stride permutation on streaming data. In *Proc. of IEEE International Conference on ReConFig*, pages 1–7, Dec 2013.

[13] M. V. Chien and A. Y. Oruc. Adaptive binary sorting schemes and associated interconnection networks. *IEEE TPDS*, 5(6):561–572, 1994.

[14] C. Clos. A study of non-blocking switching networks. *Bell System Technical Journal*, 32(2):406–424, 1953.

[15] A. Farmahini-Farahani, H. Duwe, M. Schulte, and K. Compton. Modular design of high-throughput, low-latency sorting units. *IEEE TC*, 62(7):1389–1402, July 2013.

[16] D. Koch and J. Torresen. FPGASort: A high performance sorting architecture exploiting run-time reconfiguration on FPGAs for large problem sorting. In *Proc. of ACM/SIGDA FPGA*, pages 45–54, 2011.

[17] C. Layer, D. Schaupp, and H.-J. Pfleiderer. Area and throughput aware comparator networks optimization for parallel data processing on FPGA. In *Proc. of IEEE ISCAS*, pages 405–408, May 2007.

[18] J.-D. Lee and K. Batcher. Minimizing communication in the bitonic sort. *IEEE TPDS*, 11(5):459–474, May 2000.

[19] T. Leighton. Tight bounds on the complexity of parallel sorting. In *Proc. of ACM STOC*, pages 71–80, 1984.

[20] R. Mueller, J. Teubner, and G. Alonso. Sorting networks on FPGAs. *International Journal on VLDB*, 21(1):1–23, 2012.

[21] D. Nassimi and S. Sahni. Bitonic sort on a mesh-connected parallel computer. *IEEE TC*, 100(1):2–7, 1979.

[22] S. Olarlu, M. C. Pinotti, and S. Q. Zheng. An optimal hardware-algorithm for sorting using a fixed-size parallel sorting device. *IEEE TC*, 49(12):1310–1324, 2000.

[23] M. Püschel, P. A. Milder, and J. C. Hoe. Permuting streaming data using rams. *Journal of the ACM*, 56(2):10:1–10:34, 2009.

[24] A. Rasmussen, G. Porter, M. Conley, H. V. Madhyastha, R. N. Mysore, A. Pucher, and A. Vahdat. Tritonsort: A balanced and energy-efficient large-scale sorting system. *ACM TOCS*, 31(1):3, 2013.

[25] V. Sklyarov, I. Skliarova, D. Mihhailov, and A. Sudnitson. Implementation in FPGA of address-based data sorting. In *Proc. of IEEE FPL*, pages 405–410. IEEE, 2011.

[26] C. Thompson. The VLSI complexity of sorting. *IEEE TC*, C-32(12):1171–1184, Dec 1983.

[27] J. D. Ullman, A. V. Aho, and J. E. Hopcroft. The design and analysis of computer algorithms. *Addison-Wesley, Reading*, 4:1–2, 1974.

[28] M. Zuluaga, P. Milder, and M. Puschel. Computer generation of streaming sorting networks. In *Proc. of ACM/EDAC/IEEE DAC*, pages 1241–1249, June 2012.

# Ramethy: Reconfigurable Acceleration of Bisulfite Sequence Alignment

James Arram
Department of Computing
Imperial College
jma11@imperial.ac.uk

Wayne Luk
Department of Computing
Imperial College
wl@imperial.ac.uk

Peiyong Jiang
Department of Chemical
Pathology
The Chinese University of
Hong Kong
jiangpeiyong@cuhk.edu.hk

## ABSTRACT

This paper proposes a novel reconfigurable architecture for accelerating DNA sequence alignment. This architecture is applied to bisulfite sequence alignment, a stage in recently developed bioinformatics pipelines for cancer and non-invasive prenatal diagnosis. Alignment is currently the bottleneck in such pipelines, accounting for over 50% of the total analysis time. Our design, Ramethy (Reconfigurable Acceleration of METHYlation data analysis), performs alignment of short reads with up to two mismatches. Ramethy is based on the FM-index, which we optimise to reduce the number of search steps and improve approximate matching performance. We implement Ramethy on a 1U Maxeler MPC-X1000 dataflow node consisting of 8 Altera Stratix-V FPGAs. Measured results show a 14.9 times speedup compared to soap2 running with 16 threads on dual Intel Xeon E5-2650 CPUs, and 3.8 times speedup compared to soap3-dp running on an NVIDIA GTX 580 GPU. Upper-bound performance estimates for the MPC-X1000 indicate a maximum speedup of 88.4 times and 22.6 times compared to soap2 and soap3-dp respectively. In addition to runtime, Ramethy consumes over an order of magnitude lower energy while having accuracy identical to soap2 and soap3-dp, making it a strong candidate for integration into bioinformatics pipelines.

## Categories and Subject Descriptors

J.3 [**LIFE AND MEDICAL SCIENCES**]: Biology and genetics

## General Terms

Design, Performance, Experimentation

## Keywords

bioinformatics, alignment, reconfigurable hardware, next-generation-sequencing

## 1. INTRODUCTION

DNA methylation is a biochemical process which involves the addition of a methyl group to cytosine or adenine nucleotides. It commonly occurs on cytosines belonging to a CG pair (cytosine followed by guanine), which serves as a mechanism for gene regulation by turning certain genes off. Studies have shown that methylation is vital to healthy growth and development, and aberrant methylation has been associated with the development of cancer. With the advent of next-generation sequencing (NGS), it is now possible to conduct whole-genome methylation analysis at single base resolution. This has recently been used in developing methods for cancer [6] and non-invasive prenatal diagnosis [16]. However, a major challenge impeding such methods is the data analysis, which can take an inordinate amount of time, and is performed by a multitude of dissociated programs.

Methy-Pipe [10] is a recently developed integrated pipeline for whole-genome methylation analysis. It not only fulfils the core data analysis requirements such as sequence alignment and differential methylation analysis, but also provides useful tools for methylation data annotation and visualisation. When compared to previous related efforts, Methy-Pipe has greater functionality and user-friendliness, making it an invaluable tool for researchers and clinical scientists. However, its usefulness is limited by the time it takes to transform raw sequenced data into appropriate information to enable diagnosis.

The bottleneck of Methy-Pipe is sequence alignment, in which short sequences of DNA letters (called reads) are mapped to locations in a known reference genome. Alignment of 300M short reads to the Human genome takes roughly 5 hours when running on a system with dual 12-core Intel Xeon processors and 100GB of RAM. Consequently, Methy-Pipe is still yet to meet the requirements for large-scale clin-

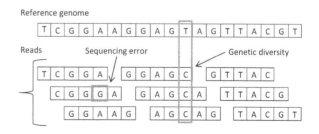

**Figure 1: Alignment of reads to a reference genome.**

ical adoption, in which patient turnaround time is critical. Accelerating alignment would shorten the diagnosis time, thereby allowing faster responses and increasing the number of patient samples that can be analysed per day. This achievement would facilitate bridging the gap between research and practice, enabling the diagnosis techniques developed to become part of routine clinical procedures.

There currently exist multiple freely available software tools for alignment, including Soap [14], BWA [13], and Bowtie [12]. These tools utilise the latest pattern matching algorithms and hardware technologies to perform the alignment process quickly. However, there is reliance on extensive computing resources to deliver this performance. For example, the 1000 genome project uses a 1192-processor cluster to align reads, while the BGI Bio-cloud computing platform has a current total of 14774 processors delivering 157T flops of performance. Such approaches are short-sighted, as simply scaling across more machines cannot keep up with the projected growth of sequenced data which far exceeds Moore's Law.

Reconfigurable hardware, such as the field programmable gate array (FPGA), is a promising candidate for accelerating alignment. The multiple levels of exploitable parallelism can provide substantial speed-up, whilst the low operational clock frequencies allow reduced energy consumption and high rack unit densities. Several papers have been published which report the use of FPGAs to accelerate the alignment process [7, 19, 8]. Whilst these designs outperform most of the software tools, the speed comes at the cost of accuracy, functionality, and platform independence. As a result, few hardware-based alignment tools have been fully integrated into a bioinformatics pipeline.

In this paper we present a novel reconfigurable architecture for accelerating alignment, which is applied to bisulfite sequencing alignment – the specific type of alignment used in methylation data analysis. Our aim is to show how reconfigurable hardware can be used to deliver substantial improvements in runtime, energy consumption and form factor, making it an ideal candidate for integration into bioinformatics pipelines. The contributions of this work include:

- A novel architecture for accelerating alignment consisting of a multi-configuration alignment pipeline. This architecture exploits the reconfigurability of FPGAs to allow for highly efficient, yet flexible alignment designs.
- An application of this architecture to accelerate bisulfite sequence alignment, which is the bottleneck in whole-genome methylation analysis. Our design, referred to as Ramethy, is based on accelerating the FM-index, a pattern matching algorithm.
- A novel optimisation to the FM-index which improves the pattern matching performance. We propose a new index structure which reduces the number of search steps and computational complexity compared to previous efforts.
- An implementation of Ramethy on a Maxeler MPC-X1000 dataflow node. The runtime, energy consumption and alignment accuracy is evaluated and compared to the fastest CPU, GPU and FPGA-based alignment programs currently available.

The rest of this paper is organised as follows: Section 2 provides background information on the ideas and algorithms used throughout the paper. Section 3 gives an overview of related efforts in this field. Section 4 presents the reconfigurable architecture for accelerating alignment. Section 5 covers the algorithm optimisation developed to improve the pattern matching performance of the FM-index. Section 6 gives an overview of the design of Ramethy. Section 7 evaluates the performance of Ramethy and provides comparison with the fastest CPU, GPU and FPGA-based alignment programs currently available. Finally, Section 8 concludes the paper.

## 2. BACKGROUND

In this section, background information on the algorithms used to perform alignment is presented. Particular attention is paid to the FM-index, the chosen algorithm for acceleration in this work. This information will help clarify the proposed architecture and algorithm optimisations presented later in this work.

### 2.1 Alignment Algorithms Overview

The algorithms used by currently available alignment software tools can be categorised into two groups: 1) suffix-trie algorithms, such as the FM-index [9], in which reads are aligned using an index generated from the suffixes of the reference genome, and 2) seed-and-extend algorithms, such as the Smith-Waterman algorithm [20], in which subsequences (seeds) of the read are aligned to the reference genome, and any candidate locations are extended using a scoring matrix. The alignment parameters of an experiment typically dictate which group is chosen. For reads with less than 150 bases and small edit distances, suffix-trie algorithms provide the best performance. Conversely, for reads with hundreds to thousands of bases and large edit distances, seed-and-extend algorithms provide the best performance. The objective of this work is to speedup Methy-Pipe, a bisulfite sequencing data analysis pipeline, in which reads of 75 bases are aligned to the Human genome with up to two mismatches. As a result, suffix-trie algorithms, specifically the FM-index, are chosen for hardware acceleration.

### 2.2 FM-index

Indexing a reference sequence is a well established method for accelerating pattern matching. For the Human genome, the time spent on creating an index can take several hours. However, this time is amortised given that the Human genome version changes infrequently, so the index only needs to be created once for a large number of alignment jobs to be performed. The FM-index is the most common indexing method used by currently available alignment software tools due to its small memory footprint and efficient substring searching. The design of the FM-index is based on the Burrows-Wheeler compression algorithm (BWT) [4] and the suffix-array (SA) data structure [18].

The SA of a text $R$ is the permutation of the lexicographically sorted suffixes of $R$, where each suffix is represented by its starting position. To simplify the substring searching operation, the symbol '\$', which is lexicographically smaller than all other symbols in the alphabet $\Sigma$, is appended to the text. The SA for a text $R = $ ACGTTAAA\$ is shown in Table 1(a).

An interval in an SA represents a sequence of lexicographically consecutive suffixes of $R$. The interval (*low*, *high*) corresponds to the smallest and largest indexes in SA which have the same prefix. The result of searching for a pattern $Q$

in $R$ can be represented as an SA interval. If $low \leq high$, the query can be located in the text. Conversely if $low > high$, the query cannot be located in the text. For a query $Q = $ AA, the SA interval equals $(2, 3)$. This solution interval can be converted from SA to text coordinates using the relationship $R_1 = SA[low]$, $R_2 = SA[low + 1]$, ... , $R_n = SA[high]$. For the interval $(2, 3)$, the corresponding positions in $R$ which have $Q$ as prefix are 6 and 5.

The FM-index is built upon the BWT, a data compression technique which generates a permutation of the symbols in a text $R$. The BWT of a text (denoted by $B$) is a *self index*, which refers to the property that it does not require $R$ and SA to perform a search operation. Each position in $B$ is computed from $R$ and SA using the relationship $B[i] = R[(SA[i] - 1) \bmod |R|]$. For a text $R = $ ACGTTAAA\$, the corresponding $B = $ AAAT\$ACTG. The FM-index supports searching operations through two counting functions derived from $B$. $C(c)$ is a function that returns the number of symbols in $B$ that are lexicographically smaller than $c$, and $Occ(c, i)$ is a function that returns the number of occurrences in $B$ of character $c$, from positions 0 to $i$. These functions are typically precomputed and stored as arrays to improve performance. As a trade-off between memory space and time, only the $Occ()$ values for positions that are a multiple of some integer distance $d$ are stored. This technique (referred to as bucketing) allows compression of Occ(), but requires counting some of the occurrence directly from $B$. Table 1(b) displays the functions $C()$ and $Occ()$ for a text $R = $ ACGTTAAA\$.

**(a)**

R = ACGTTAAA\$

| $i$ | sorted suffixes | SA[$i$] |
|---|---|---|
| 0 | \$ | 8 |
| 1 | A\$ | 7 |
| 2 | AA\$ | 6 |
| 3 | AAA\$ | 5 |
| 4 | ACGTTAAA\$ | 0 |
| 5 | CGTTAAA\$ | 1 |
| 6 | GTTAAA\$ | 2 |
| 7 | TAAA\$ | 4 |
| 8 | TTAAA\$ | 3 |

**(b)**

$Occ()$

| $i$ | $B[i]$ | A | C | G | T |
|---|---|---|---|---|---|
| 0 | A | 1 | 0 | 0 | 0 |
| 1 | A | 2 | 0 | 0 | 0 |
| 2 | A | 3 | 0 | 0 | 0 |
| 3 | T | 3 | 0 | 0 | 1 |
| 4 | \$ | 3 | 0 | 0 | 1 |
| 5 | A | 4 | 0 | 0 | 1 |
| 6 | C | 4 | 1 | 0 | 1 |
| 7 | T | 4 | 1 | 0 | 2 |
| 8 | G | 4 | 1 | 1 | 2 |

$C()$

| A | C | G | T |
|---|---|---|---|
| 1 | 5 | 6 | 7 |

Table 1: (a) SA for a text $R = $ACGTTAAA\$, and (b) the corresponding function tables $Occ()$ and $C()$.

Algorithm 1 shows the procedure for searching for a query $Q$ in a text $R$. Concisely written, the SA interval is first initialised to $(1, |R|)$. Then moving from the last symbol of $Q$ to the first, the SA interval is iteratively updated using $C()$ and $Occ()$ (a backward search). After the final iteration, the SA interval gives all the consecutive indexes in the SA which have $Q$ as prefix, which are subsequently converted into text coordinates. Currently available alignment software tools typically augment this algorithm with backtracking to support approximate matching between the query and text. In this approach edit operations (substitutions, insertions or deletions) are performed to the query. A stack is used to store the state at each edit position. If the modified query cannot be located in the text, the state is restored from the edit position and a new edit operation is performed. Heuris-

tics for improving the approximate matching performance have been developed, such as the 2-way BWT algorithm [11].

---

**Algorithm 1:** Algorithm for substring searching using the FM-index.

**Input** : Query $Q$, $C()$, $Occ()$ and SA, corresponding to the text $R$

**Output**: Locations in $R$ where $Q$ is a prefix

**begin**
  $(low, high) \leftarrow (1, |R|)$
  **for** $i \leftarrow |Q| - 1$ **to** 0 **do**
    $low \leftarrow C(Q[i]) + Occ(Q[i], low - 1)$
    $high \leftarrow C(Q[i]) + Occ(Q[i], high) - 1$
  **end**
  **for** $i \leftarrow 0$ **to** $high - low$ **do**
    $Locations[i] \leftarrow$ SA$[low + i]$
  **end**
  **return** $Locations$
**end**

---

## 3. RELATED WORK

Currently, there are multiple software tools available for alignment. Some of the freely available programs include Soap2, BWA, and Bowtie. In the case of whole-genome alignment, extensive computational resources are required to run these tools with a reasonable runtime. For example a mid-size cluster with high-end multicore processors and a large amount of RAM in each node would be adequate for small-scale processing.

As a response to the rapidly increasing sequencing machine throughput, GPU-based tools have been developed to improve the alignment performance. Notable GPU-based tools include soap3-dp [17] and CUSHAW [15], which perform up to 10 times faster than CPU-based tools.

There are various efforts related to accelerating alignment with FPGAs, among which accelerating the Smith-Waterman algorithm is the most popular approach. These designs typically target a single hardware platform with a specific number of FPGA devices and memory architecture. Olson et al. [19] propose an FPGA-based alignment design based on the Smith-Waterman algorithm. In their work, both the seed location and score table computation are performed in hardware. The design is partitioned into 8 Pico M-503 boards, each with one Xilinx Virtex-6 FPGA. This 8-FPGA system can align 50 million reads in 34 seconds. Fernandez et al. [7, 8], propose FPGA-based alignment design based on the FM-index. In the first work, the index of a small reference genome is stored in on-chip BRAM. The design is implemented on a single Xilinx Virtex-6 FPGA and can exactly align 1000 reads in 60.2us. In the second work, their previous design is extended to allow for approximate alignment. For every $n$ mismatches allowed, $n + 1$ exact string matchers statically populate an FPGA device in a pipeline. If a mismatch is detected, multiple copies of the read are generated in which the mismatched symbol is replaced with other symbols from the reference genome alphabet. The copies are sent to the next exact string matcher in the pipeline for further processing. The design is implemented on the Convey HC-1 platform and can align 18M reads in 138 seconds.

Arram et al. [1, 2, 3] propose FPGA-based alignment design based on the FM-index. In the first work, the FM-index is extended with depth-first backtracking to support approximate alignment. The design is implemented on a single Xilinx Virtex-6 FPGA and can align reads up to 8 times faster than soap2. In the second work, a two-stage architecture for accelerating alignment is proposed. The reads are first aligned using exact string matchers based on the FM-index and reads which are unable to be aligned are subsequently processed by approximate string matchers based on the Smith-Waterman algorithm. Performance estimates of the interesting design regions indicate that a dynamically reconfigurable design achieves the highest performance. In the third work, an overview of a reconfigurable architecture for accelerating suffix-trie alignment algorithms is presented. An application of this architecture based on the FM-index is implemented on a single Xilinx Virtex-6 FPGA and can align reads 3 times faster than soap2. In contrast to that work, Section 4 of this paper formalises a reconfigurable architecture which is not confined to suffix-trie alignment algorithms; Section 6 illustrates how this architecture is applied to bisulfite sequence alignment.

# 4. RECONFIGURABLE ARCHITECTURE

In this section we present a reconfigurable architecture for accelerating alignment. Our approach generalises the work in [3] to all alignment algorithms, and provides analytical methods for estimating design performance.

## 4.1 Rationale

In the various efforts related to accelerating alignment using FPGAs, the target device is statically configured with a circuit functionally equivalent to an alignment algorithm. These circuits consist of several interlinked modules corresponding to the different stages of the alignment algorithm. For example, in [19] the Smith-Waterman circuit consists of modules for seed extraction, seed location and score computation. Similarly in [8], the FM-index circuit consists of modules for exact match, one mismatch and two mismatches alignment. With a static configuration these modules are able to process data concurrently, however there exist a number of limitations for this approach which can reduce both the performance and usefulness of a design.

**Data Hazards.** Alignment algorithms feature numerous data hazards in which execution of the next stage depends on the result from the previous stage. For example, in an FM-index circuit, a read will only be processed by the one mismatch module if it cannot be aligned by the exact match module. For a statically configured design all modules in the circuit are mapped to the target device. Data hazards result in some modules being left idle from time to time which reduces the hardware efficiency.

**Distinct Module Latencies.** Each module in a circuit takes a particular number of cycles to process an item of data. To create a balanced pipeline, certain modules are replicated more than others in an attempt to match their latencies. For a statically configured design this approach can be challenging given the limited resources available on the target device fabric. For example, in a Smith-Waterman circuit the score computation module must be replicated a large number of times to match the throughput of the seed location module. It is often impossible to replicate this

module a sufficient number of times given the large amount of resources consumed by the other modules.

**Extensive Resource Usage.** For large static circuits comprising many modules, the resources required to map the circuit may exceed that available on the target device fabric. In this case, a subset of the modules are implemented in software to reduce the resources required to map the circuit. This solution comes at the cost of potential speedup, which is reduced according to Amdahl's Law. For example, in a Smith-Waterman circuit the seed location module often requires more off-chip memory than most hardware platforms have available. As a result, this module is often implemented in software which reduces the overall speedup.

**Inflexible Alignment Parameters.** Alignment parameters, such as the maximum number of mismatches, gap size and hit reporting method, will change depending on the sequenced data quality and experiment being performed. For a statically configured design there is limited control over these parameters as the circuit is fixed. Any substantial changes will often require several modules to be redesigned, and the circuit to be re-placed and re-routed. This process can take days to complete, which reduces the usefulness of a design.

## 4.2 Architecture Description

This section proposes a general architecture for accelerating alignment which exploits the reconfigurability of FPGAs. In this architecture distinct FPGA configurations are created for each stage of an alignment algorithm. The configurations comprise a homogeneous array of modules which are functionally equivalent to the corresponding algorithm stage. Runtime reconfiguration is used to load each configuration onto the target device consecutively, where the data are processed concurrently by the modules. Figure 2 illustrates how the proposed architecture is applied to an alignment algorithm with 3 stages. In step 1 modules are designed which are functionally equivalent to a stage in the alignment algorithm. In step 2 the modules are replicated to form an FPGA configuration. The number of times a given module can be replicated is given by Equation 1, in which $P_i$ is the module population, $A$ is the total available resources on the target device, and $r_i$ is the amount of resources required for the module.

$$P_i = \frac{A}{r_i} \qquad (1)$$

In Step 3, the computational workflow shown in Algorithm 2 is performed. For each stage in the alignment algorithm the corresponding configuration is loaded onto the target device. Data from the previous stage (or initial data) are streamed to the target device, where they are processed concurrently by the modules. The output data from the modules are stored in off-chip memory attached to the target device, or in host memory.

The performance of this architecture can be modelled using Equation 2, in which $T$ is the alignment time, $N_i$ is the number of data items processed by a given alignment stage, $t_i$ is the time for the corresponding module to process a single item of data, and $P_i$ is the population of modules in the configuration. The overhead of this architecture is the reconfiguration time $t_r$, and the data communication overhead $t_o$. For typical alignment workloads these overheads

---
**Algorithm 2:** Multi-configuration alignment pipeline algorithm.

---
**Data**: Reads
**Result**: Alignment locations

**for** $i \leftarrow 1$ **to** *number of stages in algorithm* **do**

    load configuration $i$ onto target device

    **if** $i = 1$ **then**
    | stream initial data from host mem.
    **else if** *intermediate data in off-chip mem.* **then**
    | stream data from off-chip mem.
    **else**
    | stream data from host mem.

    process data on target device

    **if** $i = $ *last stage in algorithm* **then**
    | stream alignment locations to host mem.
    **else if** *intermediate data fits in off-chip mem.* **then**
    | stream output data to off-chip mem.
    **else**
    | stream data to host mem.

**end**

---

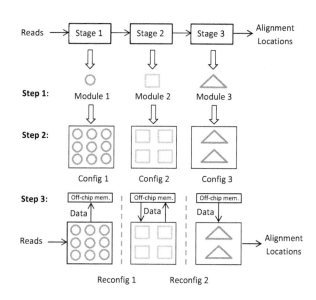

**Figure 2: Multi-configuration alignment pipeline.**

are negligible compared to the total runtime.

$$T = \sum_i \left( t_r + t_o + \frac{N_i t_i}{P_i} \right) \quad (2)$$

The reconfigurable property of this architecture addresses the limitations of a statically configured design. First, each configuration consists of a homogeneous array of independent modules, therefore there are no data hazards or unbalanced pipeline stages. This feature comes at the cost of concurrent processing of the algorithm stages. However, the number of modules in each algorithm stage is maximised according to the available resources on the target device fabric, which increases the intra-stage parallelism. Second, distinct configurations are created for each algorithm stage, therefore it is easier to fully map large alignment algorithms to hardware. Finally, runtime reconfiguration of the target device allows the user greater control over the alignment parameters. Configurations can be re-ordered, added, or removed at runtime, making this architecture completely modular. For example, the computational workflow can be dynamically modified based on whether certain runtime conditions are met. This feature allows highly flexible designs to be created which can address a large number of experiments.

## 5. FM-INDEX OPTIMISATION

In this work, the architecture in Section 4 is applied to bisulfite sequence alignment. Given the parameters for this type of alignment, our choice of alignment algorithm is the FM-index. In this section we present an algorithm optimisation to improve the performance of the FM-index.

### 5.1 n-step FM-index

In Algorithm 1, each step of the for-loop matches a single symbol in query $Q$. After $|Q|$ steps, the final interval gives all the consecutive indexes in the SA, which have $Q$ as a prefix. Chacón et al. [5] propose the n-step FM-index, an algorithmic variation of the FM-index which reduces the number

of steps required, in order to improve execution time. In essence this variation reduces the number of steps by a factor of $n$ by allowing $n$ symbols in $Q$ to be matched per step. This reduction of search steps comes at the cost of increased computational complexity per step and a larger index size. We extend this work to allow for improved execution time, but with identical computational complexity to the standard FM-index search operation. The novel feature of our modification is a compression and merging step when generating the n-step FM-index, which reduces the complexity of search operations compared to previous efforts.

To generate the index, first the reference genome is compressed into a reduced bitmap. For a reference genome $R$ = AGT\$ the corresponding reduced bitmap is $R_r = [00, 01, 10, 11]$. The number of bits required for each symbol is $log_2|\Sigma|$. Note that the appended \$ symbol is included in the alphabet size. To allow for $n$ symbols to be matched per step, $n$ BWTs are generated from $R_r$ and the SA of $R$, as shown in Algorithm 3. These BWTs are merged together to form a single BWT, denoted by $B$, in which each element is $n \times log_2|\Sigma|$ bits.

Next, $B$ is divided into buckets of $d$ elements, such that the $i^{th}$ bucket contains the sequence of elements from $B[i \cdot d]$ to $B[((i+1) \cdot d) - 1]$. For each bucket a set of $|(\Sigma - 1)^n|$ counters are computed using Equation 3, in which $str$ is the reduced bitmap for each $n$ symbol permutation of $\Sigma$ (excluding the \$ symbol which does not appear in the query), $i$ is the bucket index, and $Occ()$ and $C()$ are the two counting functions defined in Section 2. For the alphabet $\Sigma = \{A, G, T, \$\}$ and $n = 2$, $str = [0000 (AA), 0001 (AG), \ldots, 1010 (TT)]$.

$$Counters(str) = C(str) + Occ(str, (i \cdot d) - 1) \quad (3)$$

Finally, the index denoted by $F$ is formed by interleaving the buckets of $B$ with their corresponding counters. The index structure is illustrated in Figure 3.

Algorithm 4 shows the new procedure for searching for a query $Q$ in a text $R$. It is worth noting that if $|Q|$ is not exactly divisible by $n$, the interval is first updated for

**Algorithm 3:** Algorithm to generate the merged BWT $B$. Note: The concatBits function concatenates the bits in the argument (left to right) from high to low order bits.

> **Input** : SA corresponding to the text $R$, and reduced bitmap of text $R_r$
> **Output:** $B$
> **begin**
>     /* generate $n$ BWTs: $b_1, b_2, \ldots, b_n$ */
>     **for** $i \leftarrow 1$ **to** $n$ **do**
>         **for** $j \leftarrow 0$ **to** $|R_r|$ **do**
>           | $b_i[j] = R_r[(\mathrm{SA}[j] - i) \bmod |R_r|]$
>         **end**
>     **end**
>     /* merge BWTs to form $B$ */
>     **for** $i \leftarrow 0$ **to** $|R_r|$ **do**
>         | $B[i] = \mathrm{concatBits}(b_n[i], b_{n-1}[i], \ldots, b_1[i])$
>     **end**
>     **return** $B$
> **end**

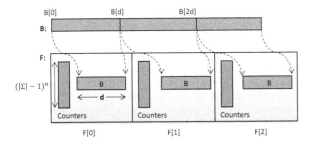

Figure 3: n-step FM-index structure.

**Algorithm 4:** Algorithm for substring searching using the n-step FM-index.

> **Input** : reduced bitmap of $Q$ ($Q_r$), $F$, and SA corresponding to the text $R$
> **Output:** Locations in $R$ where $Q$ is a prefix
>
> **begin**
>     $(low, high) \leftarrow (1, |R|)$
>     **for** $i \leftarrow |Q| - 1$ **to** $n$ **step** $-n$ **do**
>         $str \leftarrow \mathrm{concatBits}(Q_r[i-(n-1)], \ldots, Q_r[i-1], Q_r[i])$
>         $low \leftarrow F[low-1/d].Counters(str) + Count(str, F[low-1/d].B, low-1 \bmod d)$
>         $high \leftarrow F[high/d].Counters(str) + Count(str, F[high/d].B, high \bmod d)$
>     **end**
>     **for** $i \leftarrow 0$ **to** $high - low$ **do**
>         | $Locations[i] \leftarrow \mathrm{SA}[low+i]$
>     **end**
>     **return** $Locations$
> **end**
>
> **function** $Count(str, B, pos)$:
>     $cnt \leftarrow 0$
>     **for** $i \leftarrow 0$ **to** $pos$ **do**
>         **if** $str = B[i]$ **then**
>           | $cnt \leftarrow cnt + 1$
>     **end**
>     **return** $cnt$
> **end**

the excess symbols using precomputed values, after which Algorithm 4 is applied.

Our modification reduces the number of steps in a search operation by a factor of $n$, but contains the same computational complexity as the standard FM-index (in which the index is bucketed). Consequently, the performance for search operations increases by a factor of $n$. This increase in performance comes at the cost of increased index size, however the cost can be alleviated by increasing the bucket size $d$. The total memory required for $F$ can be calculated using Equation 4. For example, with $n = 3$ and $d = 128$, an index of the Human genome can fit in 10GB of memory.

$$M = \frac{4 \cdot |R| \cdot (|\Sigma| - 1)^n}{d} + \frac{|R| \cdot n \cdot \log_2 |\Sigma|}{8} \quad \text{Bytes} \quad (4)$$

## 6. RAMETHY: BISULFITE SEQUENCE ALIGNMENT DESIGN

In this section we present Ramethy, our bisulfite sequence alignment design. First, the alignment parameters specific to this type of alignment are described. Second, an overview of Ramethy, including the module designs and workflow is provided.

### 6.1 Bisulfite Sequencing Alignment

Whole-genome bisulfite sequencing involves treating the DNA with sodium bisulfite to convert all cytosines (Cs) into uracils (Us), whilst the methylated cytosines remain unchanged. In the sequencing process, all Us are identified as thymines (Ts), therefore the methylation state of the DNA can be inferred by counting the number of Cs and Ts in the treated DNA at each genomic cytosine site in the original DNA. Our work targets Methy-Pipe [10], a recently developed integrated bioinformatics pipeline for whole-genome bisulfite sequencing data analysis. Methy-Pipe uses two consecutive software modules to perform methylation data analysis. The first module is the aligner, which performs the bisulfite sequence alignment, and the second module is the data analysis module which provides various functions to facilitate downstream methylation data analysis.

Bisulfite sequencing alignment differs from the standard alignment procedure as all the Cs in the reads and reference genome are converted to Ts, reducing their alphabet to $\Sigma = \{A, G, T\}$. For seed-and-extend algorithms, this feature increases the computational workload as the average number of candidate locations which must be extended increases by a factor of $4^n/3^n$, in which $n$ is the seed length. The alignment parameters used in Methy-Pipe are: 1) reads must be aligned to the reference genome with a maximum of two mismatches, and 2) only reads which are uniquely aligned are reported.

### 6.2 Module Designs

To support the first alignment parameter, modules based on the n-step FM-index are designed for exact match, one mismatch and two mismatches alignment. For the proposed reconfigurable architecture there are two techniques for improving the design performance: 1) pipeline the module operations to increase the throughput, and 2) replicate the modules on the target device to increase the parallelism.

For the exact match module, Algorithm 4 is mapped to hardware. The index is too large to fit in on-chip BRAM, and is therefore stored in off-chip DRAM directly attached to the FPGA device. Accessing the off-chip DRAM adds latency to the module, which coupled with the step interdependence results in a non-full pipeline. To address this issue the processing of multiple reads are interleaved such that in each pipeline stage a different read is being processed. Consequently, the pipeline can be completely filled, which allows a throughput of one SA interval update per clock cycle. This feature is implemented using a circular buffer that can store a batch of reads with a size equal to the total module latency. The cost of this throughput improvement is the additional resources required to store the batch of reads and their corresponding alignment states. In order to reduce the impact of this cost on the number of times the module can be replicated, techniques are developed to minimise the module latency. For example, the computation with the largest latency is the $Count()$ function. A binary adder tree is developed to count the occurrences in parallel so that the latency for this computation can be reduced by a factor of $(\log_2 d)/d$ in comparison to the sequential version.

Figure 4 illustrates the high level design for the exact match module. In each cycle the index elements $F[low-1/d]$ and $F[high/d]$ for a given read are accessed from off-chip DRAM via an intermediate data buffer. The index data, along with the corresponding read symbols and the current interval are used to compute the new interval. The new values of $low$ and $high$ are stored in the circular buffer (overwriting the previous values), and $low-1/d$ and $high/d$ are streamed as addresses to the off-chip memory command generator. If the required number of alignment steps have been performed, the final interval is transferred to host memory.

The one and two mismatches modules are based on the exact match module with additional logic incorporated to control the backtracking. To support the second alignment parameter, all possible mismatch positions in the read must be tested to ensure it is uniquely aligned. This specification is covered for by a breadth-first backtracking strategy. A challenge with using backtracking for approximate match-

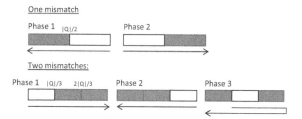

**Figure 5: Computational phases for the one and two mismatches modules. In this diagram, a read $Q$ is represented by a rectangle. The non-shaded segments are exact match regions, whilst the shaded segments are regions where mismatch/s are tested for. The arrows indicate the search direction.**

ing is that the number of steps required to align a read increases exponentially with the number of mismatches permitted. To address this challenge we incorporate features from the 2-way BWT algorithm into our design. The basis of this algorithm comes from the property that in each step of the for-loop of Algorithm 4, the interval can only decrease or remain the same size. By constraining the mismatch position in the read, long segments of the read can be initially exactly matched to the reference genome, reducing the search space size. As a result, the number of steps spent on aligning read permutations which do not occur in the reference genome is substantially reduced. Each mismatch module has a number of computational phases according to where the mismatch position is constrained. These positions are chosen in order to maximise the segment of the read which can be exactly matched. Figure 5 illustrates the different computational phases for the one and two mismatches modules. To permit forward searching, the index of the reversed reference genome is used.

## 6.3 Ramethy Workflow

In accordance with the reconfigurable architecture presented in Section 4, each module is replicated as many times as possible to create distinct FPGA configurations. Prior to alignment, the reads are loaded onto the host machine memory and are compressed into a reduced bitmap. For reads whose length is not exactly divisible by the index parameter $n$, the initial interval is updated for the excess symbols using precomputed values, otherwise it is set to $(1, |R|)$. Once this processing is complete, the FPGA device is configured with the exact match configuration. The compressed reads along with their initial interval are streamed to the FPGA device where they are processed concurrently by the modules. The final interval for each read is streamed back to the host, which determines if it is aligned ($low \leq high$) or unaligned ($low > high$). Next, the FPGA device is reconfigured with the one mismatch configuration. The unaligned reads are streamed to the FPGA device where they are processed concurrently by the modules according to the computational phases in Figure 5. If a read can be aligned, a single interval is streamed back to the host, as well as the total number of alignment hits detected (in order to determine if the read is uniquely aligned). This step is then repeated again for the two mismatches configuration. After alignment, the host converts the intervals for the aligned reads into reference genome coordinates using the SA. It is

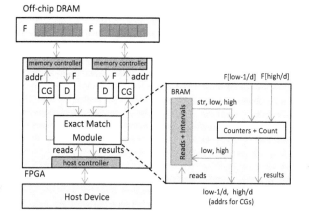

**Figure 4: Exact match module design. In this Figure, data buffers are denoted by D, and memory command generators are denoted by CG.**

worth noting that most of the software processing time can be hidden by the hardware processing.

# 7. EVALUATION

In this section we evaluate the performance of Ramethy on the Maxeler MPC-X1000 dataflow node. The runtime, energy consumption and alignment accuracy are compared to the fastest CPU, GPU and FPGA-based alignment programs currently available.

## 7.1 Maxeler Platform

The MPC-X1000 provides up to 8 dataflow engines (DFEs) in a 1U form factor with power consumption comparable to a single high-end server. Each DFE comprises a single Altera Stratix V FPGA connected to 48GB of DRAM. The DRAM consists of six 8GB memory modules, which are coupled together to give a word length of 384 Bytes. A single memory controller is used to manage the read and write operations. The DFEs are a shared resource on a network and are connected to a CPU host machine via Infiniband. To implement a design on the Maxeler Platform, first the software code is expressed as a dataflow design using the MaxJ language, based on the Java language. The MaxCompiler then maps the design into an FPGA configuration and enables its use from a host application.

The memory architecture of the MPC-X1000 coupled with the random access pattern of the FM-index are the limiting factors of performance. Our implementation of Ramethy is restricted to just a single module per configuration running with an off-chip memory bandwidth of approximately 4.2 GB/s (11% of the theoretical peak 38.5 GB/s). To improve the performance, the memory modules can be decoupled to allow up to six memory controllers per DFE. This modification permits multiple modules in each configuration by allowing parallel read operations to the index. Although this solution has not been implemented, we use it to provide an upper bound performance estimate for the MPC-X1000.

## 7.2 Experimental Parameters

Ramethy is implemented on a MPC-X1000 with 8 DFEs. The index is constructed with the parameter values $n = 3$, $d = 368$ and $|\Sigma| = 4$. Consequently, an index of the Human genome can fit in 3.3GB of memory. Our experimental results include two performance measurements for Ramethy. The first (denoted by v1) is based on actual measurements obtained from our system, in which Ramethy is mapped onto 8 DFEs with a population of one module per configuration. The second (denoted by v2) is an upper bound estimate for the MPC-X1000 in which the memory modules attached to each DFE are decoupled, allowing for 3 modules per configuration. Note that each module requires two memory controllers to access the index elements $F[low - 1/d]$ and $F[high/d]$ in parallel, and there are six memory controllers per DFE.

The runtime, energy consumption and accuracy of Ramethy is compared to those of soap2 running on a 1U rack server with dual Intel Xeon E5-2650 CPUs and soap3-dp running on an NVIDIA GTX-580 GPU. These programs are used in our comparison as: a) they are widely regarded as the fastest CPU and GPU-based alignment tools currently available, and b) the bisulfite sequence alignment program developed for Methy-Pipe is based on soap2, with future releases utilising soap3-dp. It is worth noting that in all

runtime measurements reported, only the alignment time is considered.

```
$ ./soap -a reads.fastq -D index -v 2
  -p 16 -o output

$ ./soap3-dp single index reads -s 2 -h 3
  -o output
```

In the following experiments Chromosome 22 of the Human genome is used as the reference genome. Sherman, a bisulfite sequencing read simulator, is used to generate single-end reads. The following command is used to simulate reads with similar properties to experimental data:

```
$ ./Sherman -q 40 -l 75 -CG 20 -CH 98 -e 0
```

Given the relatively small workload used (3% of a full alignment workload), the reconfiguration time (3-4 seconds per configuration) for the MPC-X1000 is not included in the runtime measurements of Ramethy, as it would introduce a large negative bias to the results. With a full alignment workload of 300M reads the reconfiguration time would amount to approximately 3.5% of the alignment time.

## 7.3 Experimental Results

In the first experiment, the alignment performance of Ramethy is measured for exact match, one mismatch and two mismatches. Three data sets are generated in which 10M reads of 75 bases are directly sampled from the reference genome. Mismatches are inserted at random positions in the reads according to the number being tested. The graph in Figure 6 indicates that the exact match, one mismatch and two mismatches configurations are all faster at aligning reads than both soap2 and soap3-dp. The largest performance improvement is with the exact match configuration, which is 45.1 times and 10.1 times faster than soap2 and soap3-dp respectively. The mismatch configurations show less substantial improvements as additional time is spent processing the reads with each alignment phase and the previous configuration(s). The upper bound performance estimates indicate that a high population of modules in each configuration yield significant performance improvements over soap2 and soap3-dp. For example, Ramethy can be up to 270.6 times and 60.5 times faster at exactly aligning reads than soap2 and soap3-dp respectively.

In the next experiment the resource usage of each module is analysed. The final resource usage for look-up tables

**Figure 6: Configuration performance compared to soap2 and soap3-dp.**

(LUTs), flip-flops (FFs), and BRAMs, as well as the achievable clock frequency are recorded from the build report of Ramethy. Table 2 indicates that all three modules utilise approximately 24–27% of the available resources on the device fabric. If each module is replicated on the device fabric as many times as possible given the available resources, there could be up to 3 modules per configuration, which is identical to the populations for the upper bound estimate. Aside from the number of memory controllers supported, the critical resource for each module is BRAMs. An explanation for this result is that the circular buffer used to store the batch of reads and the corresponding alignment states is implemented using BRAMs. Future implementations could benefit from FPGA devices with increased BRAM and logic resources at the cost of DSP blocks (which are entirely unused), which would allow a higher population of modules per configuration.

Next, the performance of Ramethy is measured for realistic bisulfite sequenced data. The Sherman read simulator is used to generate 10M reads of 75 bases from the reference genome. To make the data as realistic as possible, the bisulfite conversion rate of the reads is adjusted to values typically seen in real experiments. For completeness, the alignment time of Ramethy is also compared to notable hardware-based designs, including the Smith-Waterman design in [19] and the FM-index design in [8]. Since different data sets and alignment parameters are used in these efforts, we define a normalised performance merit, bases aligned per second (bps), to allow for a fairer comparison.

$$bps = \frac{read\ length \times read\ count}{alignment\ time} \quad (5)$$

Table 3 indicates that Ramethy is approximately 14.9 times faster than soap2 running on dual Intel Xeon E5-2650 CPUs and 3.8 times faster than soap3-dp running on a NVIDIA GTX-580 GPU. The upper bound performance estimate for the MPC-X1000 indicates that Ramethy can achieve a maximum speedup of 88.4 times and 22.6 times compared to soap2 and soap3-dp respectively. All of these systems are housed in a 1U rack unit, suggesting that Ramethy offers the highest performance per unit volume.

To evaluate the proposed reconfigurable architecture, the performance of Ramethy is compared to a statically configured design. Given the available resources on the MPC-X1000, and the process time for each configuration, the optimal static design would appear as illustrated in Figure 7. Assuming there is zero communication overhead between modules and the modules are never stalled, the maximum performance for a static design is given by Equation 6, in which $N_i$ is the number of reads processed by the $i$ mismatch module, $t_i$ is the time for the corresponding module

to process a read and $P_i$ is the module population.

$$T = max\left(\frac{N_0 t_0}{P_0}, \frac{N_1 t_1}{P_1}, \frac{N_2 t_2}{P_2}\right) \quad (6)$$

Table 3 indicates that Ramethy exceeds the maximum performance for a static design. When accounting for the reconfiguration time in a full alignment workload, Ramethy is 11% faster than the static design.

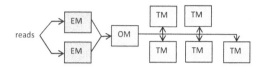

**Figure 7: Optimal statically configured design. Note: EM, OM, and TM denote exact match, one mismatch and two mismatches respectively, and each module is mapped to a single DFE.**

Given that the alignment time scales linearly with the read count, the runtime of Ramethy can be linearly extrapolated to that of a typical alignment workload. Experiments typically sequence DNA using a single flow cell lane, which produces approximately 300M reads with 75 bases. Ramethy can align this volume of reads in 6 minutes, whilst the upper bound estimate gives a minimum time of just over a minute. Considering that an alignment workload this size can take hours for a high-end server to complete, Ramethy can significantly shorten the diagnosis time, which would allow faster responses and increase the number of patient samples that can be analysed per day.

The bps values in Table 3 indicate that Ramethy is approximately 5.0 times faster than the design in [8], yet 1.8 times slower than the design in [19]. The upper bound performance estimate for the MPC-X1000 indicates that if the platform-specific limitations are addressed, Ramethy can achieve 3.3 times speedup compared to the design in [19]. Whilst it is difficult to directly compare these hardware-based designs fairly, it can be noted that Ramethy has three distinct advantages over the FM-index based designs in previous efforts. First, the n-step FM-index modification reduces the required number of steps in each alignment with no increase in the computational complexity of each step. Second, the incorporation of the 2-way BWT into the one and two mismatches modules greatly increases the approximate matching performance. Third, the breadth-first backtracking strategy improves the alignment accuracy, which is identical to that of soap2 and soap3-dp.

In the final experiment the energy consumption of Ramethy is measured. Power values are taken from the vendors product information for the CPU and GPU devices, and directly from the operating system in the case of the MPC-X1000 dataflow node. Table 4 indicates that Ramethy consumes approximately an order of magnitude less energy than

| Module | Clock (MHz) | LUT | FF | BRAM |
|---|---|---|---|---|
| EM | 150 | 70676 (27%) | 124224 (24%) | 690 (27%) |
| OM | 150 | 70267 (27%) | 124001 (24%) | 621 (24%) |
| TM | 150 | 70858 (27%) | 125624 (24%) | 633 (25%) |

**Table 2: Module resource usage on a Altera Stratix V FPGA. Note: EM, OM, and TM denote exact match, one mismatch and two mismatches respectively.**

| Program | Total Power (W) | Energy Consumption (kJ) |
|---|---|---|
| soap2 | 190 | 31.9 |
| soap3-dp | 244 | 10.5 |
| Ramethy v1 | 72 | 1.5 |

**Table 4: Energy consumption.**

**Table 3: Performance comparison.**

| program | read length | read count (M) | platform | clock freq. (MHz) | devices | runtime (s) | bps (million) | speedup |
|---|---|---|---|---|---|---|---|---|
| soap2 | 75 | 10 | Intel E5-2650 | 2000 | 2 | 168 | 4.5 | 1.0x |
| soap3-dp | 75 | 10 | NVIDIA GTX-580 | 772 | 1 | 43 | 17.4 | 3.9x |
| [8] | 101 | 18 | Convey HC-1 | 150 | 4 | 138 | 13.2 | 3.0x |
| [19] | 76 | 54 | Pico M-503 | 250 | 8 | 34 | 120 | 26.8x |
| static design | 75 | 10 | MPC-X1000 | 150 | 8 | 12.8 | 58.5 | 13.1x |
| Ramethy v1 | 75 | 10 | MPC-X1000 | 150 | 8 | 11.3 | 66.4 | 14.9x |
| Ramethy v2 | 75 | 10 | MPC-X1000 | 150 | 8 | 1.9 | 395 | 88.4x |

soap2 and soap3-dp. This result can be explained by the low operational clock frequencies which the FPGAs are run at, coupled with the shorter runtime. This result suggests that the relatively high initial cost of the MPC-X1000 can be amortised given the much lower operational energy costs.

# 8. CONCLUSION

This paper presents a novel reconfigurable architecture for accelerating sequence alignment. This architecture is applied to bisulfite sequence alignment, a bottleneck in recently developed bioinformatics pipelines for cancer and non-invasive prenatal diagnostics. Our design, referred to as Ramethy, is based on the FM-index which we optimise to reduce the amount of search steps and improve approximate matching performance. Ramethy is implemented on the Maxeler MPCX-1000 dataflow node and measured results show a 14.9 times speedup compared to soap2, and 3.8 times speedup compared to soap3-dp. In addition to runtime, Ramethy consumes over an order of magnitude lower energy, and has an accuracy identical to soap2 and soap3-dp, making it a strong candidate for integration into bioinformatics pipelines. Future work involves accelerating the other stages of the Methy-Pipe application, exploring how the proposed reconfigurable architecture can be applied to other bioinformatics pipelines, and automating the implementation of such pipelines from a high-level description.

## Acknowledgement

We thank Dennis Lo, Rossa Chiu and Alex Ross for their advice and encouragement. This work was supported in part by Maxeler University Programme, Xilinx, UK EPSRC, the European Union Seventh Framework Programme under grant agreement number 257906, 287804 and 318521, and the HiPEAC NoE.

# 9. REFERENCES

[1] J. Arram et al. Hardware acceleration of genetic sequence alignment. In *ARC*, pages 13–24, 2013.

[2] J. Arram et al. Reconfigurable acceleration of short read mapping. In *FCCM*, pages 210–217, 2013.

[3] J. Arram et al. Reconfigurable filtered acceleration of short read alignment. In *FPT*, pages 438–441, 2013.

[4] M. Burrows and D. Wheeler. A block-sorting lossless data compression algorithm. Technical report, Digital Equipment Corporation, 1994.

[5] A. Chacón et al. n-step fm-index for faster pattern matching. *Procedia Computer Science*, 18(0):70 – 79, 2013.

[6] K. C. Chan et al. Noninvasive detection of cancer-associated genome-wide hypomethylation and copy number aberrations by plasma DNA bisulfite sequencing. *Proc. Natl. Acad. Sci. U.S.A.*, 110(47):18761–18768, Nov 2013.

[7] E. Fernandez et al. String matching in hardware using the FM-index. In *FCCM*, pages 218–225, May 2011.

[8] E. Fernandez et al. Multithreaded FPGA acceleration of DNA sequence mapping. In *HPEC*, pages 1–6, Sept 2012.

[9] P. Ferragina and G. Manzini. An experimental study of an opportunistic index. In *Proc. SODA*, pages 269–278, 2001.

[10] P. Jiang et al. Methy-pipe: An integrated bioinformatics pipeline for whole genome bisulfite sequencing data analysis. *PLoS ONE*, 9(6):e100360, 06 2014.

[11] T. W. Lam et al. High throughput short read alignment via bi-directional BWT. In *BIBM*, pages 31–36, November 2009.

[12] B. Langmead and S. L. Salzberg. Fast gapped-read alignment with Bowtie 2. *Nat. Methods*, 9(4):357–359, Apr 2012.

[13] H. Li and R. Durbin. Fast and accurate short read alignment with Burrows-Wheeler transform. *Bioinformatics*, 25(14):1754–1760, Jul 2009.

[14] R. Li et al. Soap2: an improved ultrafast tool for short read alignment. *Bioinformatics*, 25(15):1966–1967, 2009.

[15] Y. Liu et al. CUSHAW: a CUDA compatible short read aligner to large genomes based on the Burrows-Wheeler transform. *Bioinformatics*, 28(14):1830–1837, Jul 2012.

[16] F. M. Lun et al. Noninvasive prenatal methylomic analysis by genomewide bisulfite sequencing of maternal plasma DNA. *Clin. Chem.*, 59(11):1583–1594, Nov 2013.

[17] R. Luo et al. SOAP3-dp: fast, accurate and sensitive GPU-based short read aligner. *PLoS ONE*, 8(5):e65632, 2013.

[18] U. Manber and G. Myers. Suffix arrays: A new method for on-line string searches. In *Proceedings of the First Annual ACM-SIAM Symposium on Discrete Algorithms*, SODA '90, pages 319–327, 1990.

[19] C. Olson et al. Hardware acceleration of short read mapping. In *FCCM*, pages 161–168, April 2012.

[20] T. F. Smith and M. S. Waterman. Identification of common molecular subsequences. *J. Mol. Biol.*, 147(1):195–197, Mar 1981.

# POSTER SESSION 1

## An Efficient and Flexible FPGA Implementation of a Face Detection System

Hichem Ben Fakih, *Technical University of Berlin*
Ahmed Elhossini, *Technical University of Berlin*
Ben Juurlink, *Technical University of Berlin*
Contact: ahmed.elhossini@tu-berlin.de

Robust and rapid face detection systems are constantly gaining more interest, since they represent the first stone for many challenging tasks in the field of computer vision. In this paper a software-hardware co-design approach is presented, that enables the detection of frontal faces in real time. A complete hardware implementation of all components taking part of the face detection is introduced. This work is based on the object detection framework of Viola and Jones, which makes use of a cascade of classifiers to reduce the computation time. The proposed architecture is flexible, as it allows the use of multiple instances of the face detector. This makes developers free to choose the speed range and reserved resources for this task. The current implementation runs on the Zynq SoC and receives images over IP network, which allows exposing the face detection system as a remote service that can be consumed from any device connected to the network. We performed several measurements for the final detector and the software equivalent. Using three Evaluator cores, the ZedBoard system achieves a maximal average frame rate of 13.4 FPS when analysing an image containing 640x480 pixels. This stands for an improvement of 5.25 times compared to the software solution and represents acceptable results for most real-time systems. On the ZC706 system, a higher frame rate of 16.58 FPS is achieved. The proposed hardware solution achieved 92% accuracy, which is low compared to the software solution (97%) due to different scaling algorithm. The proposed solution achieved higher frame rate compared to other solutions found in the literature.

**ACM Categories & Descriptors:** B.0 Hardware, General

**Keywords:** FPGA, Computer Vision, Face Detection, Viola and Jones

**DOI:** http://dx.doi.org/10.1145/2684746.2689095

## A Novel Method for Enabling FPGA Context-Switch

Alban Bourge, *University Grenoble Alpes*
Olivier Muller, *University Grenoble Alpes*
Frédéric Rousseau, *University Grenoble Alpes*
Contact: alban.bourge@imag.fr

Modern FPGAs provide great computational power, flexible resources and a versatile environment. Managing to obtain the best of these three worlds is rather complicated given the actual design flows. Our work focuses on enabling task multiplexing, as part of a more flexible FPGA usage. Task multiplexing in FPGAs raises indeed a lot of questions. Multiplexing the usage of a reconfigurable fabric is leading to a better utilization of its surface because it offers to share its resources not only in space (number of slices allocated to a task) but also in time (tasks are allowed in time slots). The base mechanism known as context-switch consists in removing a task after its allowed time slot has passed. The first step toward efficiently multiplex tasks in a reconfigurable fabric is to decide when this removal will have the least possible impact on the system. This poster presents our preliminary results concerning what we consider as necessary in order to enable such a feature. Our work focus on finding automatically the best instants of the task execution in order to effectively remove a running task from the FPGA, taking into account the time needed to extract a relevant context necessary to restart it later. This instant selection is performed at a high level of abstraction, enabling us to make choices with an accurate knowledge of the task nature and specificities. The second part of this poster presents the entire mechanism which makes use of the previously selected slots in order to switch between tasks.

**ACM Categories & Descriptors:** B.6.3 Design Aids

**Keywords:** Design flow; Multiplexing; Context-Switch; Optimization; FPGA

**DOI:** http://dx.doi.org/10.1145/2684746.2689096

## FPGA Acceleration for Simultaneous Image Reconstruction and Segmentation based on the Mumford-Shah Regularization

Wentai Zhang, *Peking University*
Li Shen, *Peking University*
Thomas Page, *University of Bremen*
Guojie Luo, *Peking University*
Peng Li, *University of California, Los Angeles*
Peter Maaß, *University of Bremen*
Ming Jiang, *Peking University*
Jason Cong, *University of California, Los Angeles*
Contact: gluo@pku.edu.cn

X-ray computed tomography is an important technique for clinical diagnose and nondestructive testing. In many applications a number of image processing steps are needed before the image information becomes useful. Image segmentation is one of such processing steps and has important applications. The conventional flow is to first reconstruct the image and then obtain image segmentation afterwards. In contrast, an iterative method for simultaneous reconstruction and segmentation (SRS) with Mumford-Shah model has been proposed, which not only regularizes the ill-posedness of the tomographic reconstruction problem, but also produces the image segmentation at the same time. The Mumford-Shah model is both mathematically and computationally difficult. In this paper, we propose a data-decomposed algorithm of the SRS method, accelerate it using FPGA devices. The proposed algorithm has a structure that invokes a single kernel many times without involving other computational tasks. Though this structure seems best fit on GPU-like devices, experimental results show that a 73X, 11X, and 1.4X speedup can be achieved by the FPGA acceleration over the CPU implementation of the original SRS algorithm and ray-parallel SRS algorithm, and the GPU implementation of the ray-parallel SRS.

**ACM Categories & Descriptors:** B.7.1 [Types and Design Styles]: Algorithms implemented in hardware; J.3 [Life and Medical Sciences]: Medical information systems

**Keywords:** FPGA Acceleration; High-Level Synthesis; Image Reconstruction; X-ray Computed Tomography

**DOI:** http://dx.doi.org/10.1145/2684746.2689097

## Logic Gates in the Routing Network of FPGAs

Elias Vansteenkiste, *Ghent University*
Berg Severens, *Ghent University*
Dirk Stroobandt, *Ghent University*
Contact: Elias.Vansteenkiste@gmail.com

We propose a new kind of FPGA architecture with a routing network that not only provides interconnections between the functional blocks but also performs some logic operation. More specifically we replaced the routing multiplexer node in the conventional architecture with an element that can be used as both AND gate and multiplexer. A conventional routing multiplexer node consists of a multiplexer and a two stage buffer. In our new architecture a NAND gate replaces the first inverter stage of the buffer and two multiplexers half the size of the original multiplexer replace the original multiplexer. The aim of this study is to determine if this kind of architecture is feasible and if it is worth to implement pack, placement and routing tools in the future. We developed a new technology-mapping algorithm and sized the transistors in this new architecture to evaluate the area and delay. Preliminary results indicate that the gain in logic depth and area achieved by mapping to not only LUTs but also to AND gates outweighs the overhead of introducing AND gates in the routing network with a net reduction in area-delay product of 5.6. Designs implemented on the proposed architecture would require 11.2 % more area, but they will have a 14 % decreased logic depth and the architecture has a slightly faster representative critical path. These results are preliminary because the pack, place and route routines are not implemented yet.

**ACM Categories & Descriptors:** B.7.2 [Integrated circuits]: Design Aids

**Keywords:** Programmable interconnection architecture. Technology Mapping, Transistor sizing, Logic gates

**DOI:** http://dx.doi.org/10.1145/2684746.2689098

## Real-Time Obstacle Avoidance for Mobile Robots via Stereoscopic Vision Using Reconfigurable Hardware

Martinianos Papadopoulos, *University of Cyprus*
Christos Ttofis, *University of Cyprus*
Christos Kyrkou, *University of Cyprus*
Theocharis Theocharides, *University of Cyprus*
Contact: mp727@cam.ac.uk

An embedded, real-time, and low power obstacle avoidance system is a critical component towards fully autonomous robots that can be used in safety missions, space exploration, and transportation systems among others. In this paper a complete prototyping platform for the evaluation of obstacle avoidance systems and autonomous robots is realized on reconfigurable hardware. An efficient stereo vision algorithm for producing the necessary 3D and an obstacle avoidance subsystem were both implemented on an ATLYS Spartan-6 FPGA board equipped with a *VmodCam* stereo camera module. A modified *FDX Vantage 1/10* electric car platform was used for testing the proposed architecture in indoor and outdoor real-world scenes. The system receives stereo image data from the *VmodCam* module and a decision-making algorithm is applied on a specified *Region of Interest* (RoI) on the produced disparity map. The algorithm outputs the direction that the robot should move to in order to avoid any obstacles present. Experimental evaluation results indicate that the FPGA-based robotic platform can avoid obstacles in real-time (i.e. can process and identify obstacles within a $1/30^{th}$ of a second that a stereo image takes to be processed) in both indoor and outdoor environments, with 91.7% accuracy, equivalent to software implementations. The overall power consumption of the proposed architecture, excluding the electronic car platform, is 6 W, making it ideal for use on mobile robots, without becoming a significant drain on its battery life.

**ACM Categories & Descriptors:** I.2.9 Robotics; I.2.10 Vision and Scene Understanding

**Keywords:** Hardware Based Autonomous Navigation; Stereoscopic Vision; FPGA Obstacle Avoidance

**DOI:** http://dx.doi.org/10.1145/2684746.2689099

## Towards More Efficient Logic Blocks by Exploiting Biconditional Expansion

Pierre-Emmanuel Gaillardon, *EPFL*
Gain Kim, *EPFL*
Xifan Tang, *EPFL*
Luca Amarù, *EPFL*
Giovanni De Micheli, *EPFL*
Contact: pierre-emmanuel.gaillardon@epfl.ch

Nowadays, *Field Programmable Gate Arrays* (FPGA) exploit *Look-Up Tables* (LUTs) to generate logic functions. A *K*-input LUT can implement any Boolean functions with *K* inputs. Thanks to this flexibility, LUTs remained conceptually unchanged in FPGAs, only the number of inputs increased in time.

Unfortunately, the flexibility does not come for free and LUTs have non-negligible costs in both circuit-level performances (large number of memories, area or delay penalties) and logic-level capabilities (limited fan-out). Here, we propose an FPGA fabric based on two novel logic blocks. First, we introduce a new LUT design showing reduced power consumption with no sacrifice in the logic flexibility. Then, we present a block suited to arithmetic functions but preserving enough versatility to implement general logic functions. The two blocks are supported by a recently introduced logic representation called *Biconditional Binary Decision Diagrams* (BBDDs). Using architectural-level benchmarking, we showed that an FPGA architecture exploiting the novel blocks performs significantly better than current state-of-the-art FPGA architectures at 40nm technological node over a large set of test circuits. While reducing the power consumption of MCNC big20 benchmarks by 29%, the proposed architecture is able to efficiently implement arithmetic circuits as compared to its traditional LUT-based FPGA counterpart. For instance, a 256-bit adder can be realized with a 43% gain in area×delay product. While considering large general and arithmetic logic benchmarks, we observe, on average, 4%, 3% and 10% improvements in area, delay and power respectively.

ACM Categories & Descriptors: H.3.6 Programmable logic elements

Keywords: FPGA; Arithmetic functions; BBDD; Logic Element

DOI: http://dx.doi.org/10.1145/2684746.2689100

# An Automated Design Framework for Floating Point Scientific Algorithms using Field Programmable Gate Arrays (FPGAs)

Michaela E. Amoo, *Howard University*
Youngsoo Kim, *North Carolina A&T State University*
Vance Alford, *North Carolina A&T State University*
Shrikant Jadhav, *North Carolina A&T State University*
Naser I. El-Bathy, *North Carolina A&T State University*
Clay S. Gloster, *North Carolina A&T State University*
Contact: ykim12@ncat.edu

This paper presents a reconfigurable computing environment while addressing the problem of porting High Performance Computing (HPC) applications directly to Field Programmable Gate Arrays (FPGAs)-based architectures. The objectives of this research are developing a comprehensive floating point library of essential functions for scientific applications; demonstrate order of magnitude speedup of reconfigurable computing applications, demonstrating the effectiveness of automated design framework for both development and test of scientific algorithms. The developed framework can be reused in various scientific applications which shares kernel functions. The study of this research has identified an exponential function as a kernel for cellular ophthalmoscopy camera processing, traffic monitoring and light wave simulation. The paper demonstrates 30x speedup

of these kernels in three algorithms using its novel architecture and its automated toolset. Exponential kernel generation case study and its flexible hardware implementation on an FPGA has been validated onto a Xilinx LX-100 device and the Nallatech H101-PCIXM FPGA board.

ACM Categories & Descriptors: C.3 [SPECIAL-PURPOSE AND APPLICATION-BASED SYSTEMS] - Signal processing systems

Keywords: FPGA; HPC; Exponential; Floating point

DOI: http://dx.doi.org/10.1145/2684746.2689101

# Sequence-based In-Circuit Breakpoints for Post-Silicon Debug

Yutaka Tamiya, *Fujitsu Laboratories, Ltd.*
Yoshinori Tomita, *Fujitsu Laboratories, Ltd.*
Toshiyuki Ichiba, *Fujitsu Laboratories, Ltd.*
Kaoru Kawamura, *Fujitsu Laboratories, Ltd.*
Contact: tamiya.yutaka@jp.fujitsu.com

Recently, simulation and/or formal verification in pre-silicon verification cannot accomplish the whole system-level verification with exhaustive input data and run-time because of lack of sufficient speed and logic capacities. Consequently, post-silicon validation, such as in-circuit debugging, becomes increasingly important.

In this paper we propose a novel breakpoint mechanism, which improves controllability of in-circuit debugging. Our contributions are summarized as follows: (1) A basic concept of a new breakpoint method is proposed, which stops the target hardware by detecting a data sequence of arbitrary length, (2) The breakpoint is shown to be implemented in an efficient pipelined hardware, which works "at-speed", in realtime and with small area overheads using CRC (Cyclic Redundancy Check), and (3) Our experimental results of detecting a data sequence in a pseudo random stream data shows that false positives can be suppressed by the CRC width and the number of sub-sequences. Since changing breakpoint conditions does not require re-implementation of the hardware, it is expected to reduce much debugging effort in post-silicon validation.

ACM Categories & Descriptors: B.6.3 [LOGIC DESIGN]: Design Aids – *Verification*

Keywords: Post-Silicon Debug, In-Circuit Breakpoint, CRC, FPGA

DOI: http://dx.doi.org/10.1145/2684746.2689102

# Cost-Effective Memory Architecture to Achieve Flexible Configuration and Efficient Data Transmission for Coarse-Grained Reconfigurable Array

Chen Yang, *Tsinghua University*
Leibo Liu, *Tsinghua University*
Shouyi Yin, *Tsinghua University*
Shaojun Wei, *Tsinghua University*
Contact: liulb@tsinghua.edu.cn

The memory architecture has a significant effect on the flexibility and performance of a coarse-grained reconfigurable array (CGRA), which can be restrained due to configuration overhead and large latency of data transmission. Multi-context structure and data preloading method are widely used in popular CGRAs as a solution to bandwidth bottlenecks of context and data. However, these two schemes cannot balance the computing performance, area overhead, and flexibility. This paper proposed group-based context cache and multi-level data memory architectures to alleviate the bottleneck problems. The group-based context cache was designed to dynamically transfer and buffer context inside CGRA in order to relieve the off-chip memory access for contexts at runtime. The multi-level data memory was designed to add data memories to different CGRA hierarchies, which were used as data buffers for reused input data and intermediate data. The proposed memory architectures are efficient and cost-effective so that performance improvement can be achieved at the cost of minor area overhead. Experiments of H.264 video decoding program and scale invariant feature transform algorithm achieved performance improvements of 19% and 23%, respectively. Further, the complexity of the applications running on CGRA is no longer restricted by the capacity of the on-chip context memory, thereby achieving flexible configuration for CGRA. The memory architectures proposed in this paper were based on a generic CGRA architecture derived from the characteristics found in the majority of existing popular CGRAs. As such, they can be applied to universal CGRAs.

**ACM Categories & Descriptors:** B.7.1 [**Integrated Circuits**]: Types and Design Styles

**Keywords:** memory architecture; CGRA; context cache; cache prefetch; data memory

**DOI:** http://dx.doi.org/10.1145/2684746.2689103

# Exploring Efficiency of Ring Oscillator-Based Temperature Sensor Networks on FPGAs

Navid Rahmanikia, *Ferdowsi University of Mashhad*
Amirali Amiri, *Technical University of Munich*
Hamid Noori, *Ferdowsi University of Mashhad*
Farhad Mehdipour, *Kyushu University*
Contact: rahmanikia.navid@gmail.com

Due to technology advances and complexity of designs, thermal issue is a bottleneck in electronics designs. Various dynamic thermal management techniques have been proposed to address this issue. To effectively apply thermal management techniques, providing an accurate thermal map of chips is highly required. For this goal, a network of temperature sensors ought to be provided. There are various implementations for temperature sensors and network of sensors on Field Programmable Gate Arrays (FPGAs). This work defines and formulates four metrics and criteria, in terms of area, thermal, and power overheads and thermal map accuracy for exploring and evaluating efficiency of different implementations

of Ring Oscillator-based Temperature Sensor (ROTS) networks on FPGAs and reports the comparison results for 12 networks with various sensor configurations. According to our metrics and experiments, the sensor that it is composed of NOT gates with open latches and RNS ring counter has lower thermal and power overheads compared to other configurations. Moreover, in this work, a new ROTS is presented that occupies 25% less resources than the most compact temperature sensor. Also, it provides 1.72 times higher sensitivity than the best sensitive ROTS design.

**ACM Categories & Descriptors:** C.4 [**Performance of Systems**]: *Design studies, Measurement techniques, Performance attributes*; B.8.2 [**Performance and Reliability**]: Performance Analysis and Design Aids

**Keywords:** FPGA; Temperature; Soft-Sensor; Ring Oscillator; Network of Temperature Sensor; Exploration; Efficiency; Area Overhead; Thermal Overhead; Power Overhead; Thermal Map Accuracy

**DOI:** http://dx.doi.org/10.1145/2684746.2689104

# Formal Verification ATPG Search Engine Emulator

Gregory Ford, *IBM Microelectronics*
Aswin Krishna, *CWRU*
Jacob A. Abraham, *University of Texas Austin*
Daniel G. Saab, *CWRU*
Contact: ark70@cwru.edu

Bounded Model Checking (BMC), as a formal method of verifying VLSI circuits, shows violation of a given circuit property by finding a counter-example to the property along bounded state paths of the circuit. In this paper, we present an emulation framework for Automatic Test Pattern Generation (ATPG)-BMC model capable of checking properties on gate-level design. In our approach, counterpart to a property is mapped into a structural monitor with one output. A target fault is then injected at the monitor output, and a modified ATPG-based state justification algorithm is used to find a test for this fault which corresponds to formally establishing the property. In this paper, emulating the process of ATPG-based BMC on reconfigurable hardware is presented. The ATPG-BMC emulator achieves a speed-up over software based methods, due to the fine-grain massive parallelism inherent to hardware. As circuit sizes approach limits of even ATPG-based method feasibility, further solutions are required. In this presentation, we propose an ATPG-based algorithm for formal verification implementation on reconfigurable hardware (FPGA). This implementation is shown to have a linear relationship between the size of the circuit being verified and FPGA resource utilization. This implies a reasonable bound on the size of the implementation, as opposed to an exponential utilization explosion as circuit size increases.

This method has also been shown to be 3 orders of magnitude faster than a similar software-based approach, based on the time for solving a given ATPG problem. At the same time, though, total runtime for the FPGA emulation based implementation is significantly limited by the parts of its process still in software. Further enhancement is proposed to reduce this overhead and increase the benefit over software solvers.

**ACM Categories & Descriptors:** B.6.3 [LOGIC DESIGN]:

Design Aids - *Verification, VHDL, Verilog*

**Keywords:** Emulation; Verification; ATPG; VLSI; Test

**DOI:** http://dx.doi.org/10.1145/2684746.2689105

# Platform-Independent Gigabit Communication for Low-Cost FPGAs

Ralf Salomon, *University of Rostock*
Ralf Joost, *University of Rostock*
Matthias Hinkfoth, *University of Rostock*
Contact: matthias.hinkfoth2@uni-rostock.de

Among other things, field-programmable gate arrays (FPGAs) available today contain numerous bit-serial transceivers for communication purposes. Unlike analog modulation schemes, such as quadrature amplitude modulation, bit-serial communication is relatively easy to implement in digital hardware, and is thus usually used for inter FPGA communication. In this view, only the data rate and frequency limit the bandwidth of the circuit. In order to overcome the bandwidth limit, this research proposes a pulse-width modulation (PWM) scheme for data transmission. The information is coded by modulating the length of the high and low voltage parts of the pulse. Although this approach is not new, existing PWM modulators have unsatisfactorial data rates due to their synchronous implementation nature. Therefore, this research implements both the modulator and demodulator by using asynchronous logic. The result is a proof-of-concept comprising two Terasic DE2-70 development boards and a 1 m coaxial cable. Both the PWM modulator and demodulator run at 333 MHz, and pulses are transmitted every 3 ns. Each pulse carries 3 to 4 bits of data. The experimental results indicate an achievable data rate of one gigabit per second, which is about 50 % larger than the FPGA's handbook states.

**ACM Categories & Descriptors:** B.7.1 [Types and Design Styles] Algorithms implemented in hardware

**Keywords:** Experimentation

**DOI:** http://dx.doi.org/10.1145/2684746.2689150

# POSTER SESSION 2

## An FPGA-Based Accelerator for the 2D Implicit FDM and Its Application to Heat Conduction Simulations

Yutaro Ishigaki, *Tokyo University of Agriculture and Technology*
Ning Li, *Tokyo University of Agriculture and Technology*
Yoichi Tomioka, *Tokyo University of Agriculture and Technology*
Akihiko Miyazaki, *NTT Device Technology Laboratories*
Hitoshi, Kitazawa, *Tokyo University of Agriculture and Technology*
Contact: 50014645202@st.tuat.ac.jp

Field-programmable gate arrays (FPGAs) are extremely advanced with regard to high performance; they are becoming one of the primary device choices to realize high-performance computing (HPC). In this work, we propose an FPGA-based accelerator for the two-dimensional (2D) finite difference method (FDM) with the implicit scheme and implement a 2D unsteady-state heat conduction simulation using red/black successive over-relaxation (SOR). The accelerator consists of a 2D single-instruction multiple-data (SIMD) array processor, which has pipelined processing elements (PEs) including 32-bit floating point calculation units. This processor can avoid the memory-access bottleneck and perform with high operating efficiency and low waiting time for data transfer by applying the proposed control method with *synchronous shift data transfer*. We demonstrate that the experimental hardware implemented on an Altera Stratix V FPGA (5SGSMD5K2F40C2N) reaches a 99.83% operating rate of the calculation units for the computation of red/black SOR. In addition, it is approximately six times faster than GPU computing on an NVIDIA GeForce GTX 770 for a 32-bit floating-point calculation of a printed circuit board (PCB) heat conduction simulation, and it is about eight times faster than an NVIDIA Tesla C2075 for the same calculation.

**ACM Categories & Descriptors:** C.1.2 [Multiple Data Stream Architecture (Multiprocessors)]: Single-instruction-stream, multiple-data-stream processors (SIMD); J.2 [Physical Sciences and Engineering]: Physics

**Keywords:** FPGA; Parallel Processing; 2D SIMD Array Processor; Finite Difference Method; Red/black SOR; 2D Unsteady-State Heat Conduction

**DOI:** http://dx.doi.org/10.1145/2684746.2689112

## An FPGA Implementation of a Timing-Error Tolerant Discrete Cosine Transform

Yaoqiang Li, *University of Waterloo*
Pierce I-Jen Chuang, *University of Waterloo*
Andrew Kennings, *University of Waterloo*
Manoj Sachdev, *University of Waterloo*
Contact: lyaoqian@uwaterloo.ca

We present a Discrete Cosine Transform (DCT) unit embedded with Error Detection Sequential (EDS) and Dynamic Voltage Scaling (DVS) circuits to speculatively monitor its noncritical datapaths. This monitoring strategy requires no buffer insertions with only minimal modifications to the existing digital design methodology and is therefore applicable for Field-Programmable Gate Array (FPGA) implementations. The proposed design is implemented in an FPGA. The duty cycles of the constraint clock and the actual clock are differentiated to guide the synthesizer to place the EDS circuits with specific timing margin. The proposed design is tested with two classic images and is able to detect timing errors in the noncritical datapaths due to dynamic process, voltage and temperature (PVT) variations. The DVS circuit correspondingly controls a linear voltage regulator to adjust the supply voltage to the Point of First Failure (PoFF). No actual timing errors are generated, primarily because of the unique speculative characteristic of the proposed monitoring strategy. Our proposed design incurs a 0.3% logic element overhead and 3.5% maximum frequency degradation. By lowering the supply voltage by 8.3%, the proposed design saves up to 16.5% energy when operating at the same frequency as a highly optimized baseline DCT implementation.

**ACM Categories & Descriptors:** B.5.3 Reliability and Testing

**Keywords:** Dynamic variations; EDS; DVS; FPGA; DCT

**DOI:** http://dx.doi.org/10.1145/2684746.2689113

## A Parallel and Scalable Multi-FPGA based Architecture for High Performance Applications

Venkatasubramanian Viswanathan, *Nolam Embedded Systems*
Rabie Ben Atitallah, University of Valenciennes
Jean-Luc Dekeyser, *University of Lille1*
Benjamin Nakache, Nolam Embedded Systems
Maurice Nakache, Nolam Embedded Systems
Contact: venkat.viswanathan@inria.fr

Several industrial applications are becoming highly sophisticated and distributed as they capture and process real-time data from several sources at the same time. Furthermore, availability of acquisition channels such as I/O interfaces per FPGA, also dictates how applications are partitioned over several devices. Thus computationally intensive, resource consuming functions are implemented on multiple hardware accelerators, making low-latency communication to be a crucial factor. In such applications, communication between multiple devices means using high-speed point-to-point protocols with little flexibility in terms of communication scalability. The problem with the current systems is that, they are usually built to meet the needs of a specific application, i.e., lacks flexibility to change the communication topology or upgrade hardware resources. This leads to obsolescence, hardware redesign cost, and also wastes computing power. Taking this into consideration, we propose a scalable, modular and customizable computing platform, with a parallel full-duplex communication network, that redefines the computation and communication paradigm in such applications. We have implemented a scalable distributed secure H.264 encoding application with 3 channels over 3 customizable FPGA modules. In a distributed architecture, the inter-FPGA communication time is almost completely overshadowed by the overall execution time for bigger data-sets, and is comparable to the overall execution time of a non-distributed architecture, for the same implementation scaled down to 1 channel for 1 FPGA. This makes our architecture highly scalable and suitable for high-performance streaming applications. With 3 detachable FPGA modules, each sending and receive data simultaneously at 3 GB/s each, we measured the total net unidirectional traffic at any given time in the system is 9 GB/s, making the total net bidirectional bandwidth for 6 modules to be 36 GB/s.

**ACM Categories & Descriptors:** Architecture; Applications; Measurement;

**Keywords:** Scalable system; Parallel Reconfigurable Architecture; Distributed intensive signal processing;

**DOI:** http://dx.doi.org/10.1145/2684746.2689115

## A Mixed-Grained Reconfigurable Computing Platform for Multiple-Standard Video Decoding

Leibo Liu, *Tsinghua University*
Yingjie Chen, *Tsinghua University*
Dong Wang, *Beijing Jiaotong University*
Min Zhu, *Tsinghua University*
Shouyi Yin, *Tsinghua University*
Shaojun Wei, *Tsinghua University*
Contact: wangdong@bjtu.edu.cn

A mixed-grained reconfigurable computing platform targeting multiple-standard video decoding is proposed in this paper. The platform integrates eight coarse-grained Reconfigurable Processing Units (RPUs), each of which consists of 16×16 multi-functional Processing Elements (PEs) and are implemented in TSMC 65 nm technology and two Altera Stratix IV EP4SE820 FPGAs. By exploiting dynamic reconfiguration of the RPUs and static reconfiguration of the FPGAs, the proposed platform achieves scalable performances and cost trade-offs to support a variety of video coding standards, including H.264, MPEG-2, AVS and HEVC. Two types of platform configuration are tested in this work. One configuration utilizes two RPUs and targets multiple-standard high-definition (HD) video decoding, while the

*FPGA'15*, February 22–24, 2015, Monterey, California, USA.
ACM 978-1-4503-3315-3/15/02.

other utilizes only one RPU, which works under a lower frequency and targets at standard resolution (SD) decoding. The HD configuration can decode 1920×1080 H.264 video streams at 30 frames per second (fps) under 200 MHz and 1920×1080 HEVC video streams at 30 fps under 236 MHz. It achieves a 25% performance gain over an industrial coarse-grained reconfigurable processor for H.264 decoding, and a 3.85× performance boosts over the Intel i5 general-purpose CPU for HEVC decoding.

**ACM Categories & Descriptors:** B.7.1 [**Hardware**]: Types and Design Styles – *advanced technologies, algorithms implemented in hardware, gate arrays*

**Keywords:** Coarse-grained reconfigurable array; reconfigurable computing; field-programmable gate array; video decoding

**DOI:** http://dx.doi.org/10.1145/2684746.2689116

## FiT - An Automated Toolkit for Matching Processor Architecture to Applications

Charles Mutigwe, *NxCORES Research*
Johnson Kinyua, *Virginia International University*
Farhad Aghdasi, *University of Fort Hare*
Contact: cmutigwe@ieee.org

As the complexity of designing electronic systems continues to grow, the most commonly used solution has been to move the design process to higher levels of abstraction via software tools. In this work we present one such tool that can be used to automatically generate custom processors and systems-on-chip (SoC) from C source code or application binary files, with no requirement for the user to understand any of the underlying hardware systems. This tool also does not call for the application to be profiled for any 'hot spots' as a prerequisite for generating the custom processor. We use the toolkit to generate two types of custom processors; the area-optimized processors and the performance-optimized processors. We study the resource utilization of the custom processors and compare them with those predicted by the core density model. We find that the performance-optimized processor results are as predicted by the core density model.

**ACM Categories & Descriptors:** B.5.2 [REGISTER-TRANSFER-LEVEL IMPLEMENTATION]: Design Aids - Automatic synthesis, Hardware description languages; C.0 [Computer Systems Organization]: GENERAL - Modeling of computer architecture

**Keywords:** Application-specific soft processor; C-to-silicon compiler; electronic system level (ESL) design; reconfigurable computing

**DOI:** http://dx.doi.org/10.1145/2684746.2689117

## FPGA-based BLOB Detection Using Dual-pipelining

Naoto Nojiri, *Ritsumeikan University*
Lin Meng, *Ritsumeikan University*
Katsuhiro Yamazaki, *Ritsumeikan University*
Contact: menglin@fc.ritsumei.ac.jp

Binary Large OBject (BLOB) detection is utilized in various fields such as car cameras, traffic sign recognition and surveillance systems. Although labeling is an important component in BLOB detection, it is difficult to be parallelized using a look-up table (LUT) in terms of data dependency. Since BLOB detection takes a long time, recognition speed and accuracy need to be improved. This research aims to detect BLOBs as fast as possible by using dual-pipelining image processing on the FPGA. Dual-pipelining is to perform pipeline processing in parallel to the upper and lower portions of an original image after dividing it into two portions. We have to consider the timing of each module around the borderline because of the data dependency in label generation. The image processing consists of Gaussian filtering, binarization, labeling, and BLOB analysis. Generally, labeling uses a LUT to combine multiple numbers for one object into the smallest number of temporary labels. In order to simplify the labeling, the connected components of each BLOB are stored and revised just in the LUT. In our approach, a BLOB can be detected when multiple temporary labels are stored in a same entry of the LUT, thus enabling us to detect BLOBs by dual-pipelining. Although our labeling method does not revise temporary labels into a unified label, BLOBs can be detected and their numbers, areas, and centroids are correctly computed. We compared our approach with a related work, which consists of three steps: identifying the connected pixels in each row, labeling the counted pixels in different rows, computing the area and centroid. Experimental results show that the dual-pipelining system using FPGA can detect BLOBs in 0.06 ms, which is 3.92 times faster than the related work and 1.83 times faster than a single-pipelining system. The dual-pipelining system utilized 1.5% of Registers, 8.4% of LUT, 24.3% of LUT-FF pairs, 91.9% of BRAM in Virtex V. The dual-pipelining system is about twice as large as the single-pipelining system. Our approach can be applied for the other areas such as traffic sign recognition and vehicle detection.

**ACM Categories & Descriptors:** B.2.1 [ARITHMETIC AND LOGIC STRUCTURES]: Design Styles - *Pipeline; Parallel* ; C.3 [SPECIAL-PURPOSE AND APPLICATION-BASED SYSTEMS]: GENERAL - *Real-time and embedded systems*

**Keywords:** BLOB detection; dual-pipelining; labeling; FPGA

**DOI:** http://dx.doi.org/10.1145/2684746.2689118

## An FPGA Implementation of Multi-stream Tracking Hardware using 2D SIMD Array

Ryota Takasu, *Tokyo University of Agriculture and Technology*
Yoichi Tomioka, *Tokyo University of Agriculture and Technology*
Takashi Aoki, *NTT Device Technology Laboratories*
Hitoshi Kitazawa, *Tokyo University of Agriculture and Technology*
Contact: 50013645214@st.tuat.ac.jp

Worldwide, many surveillance systems are in operation for crime deterrence purposes. An effective system should be characterized by requiring low-power consumption, a small storage capacity, and little human effort. Multi-stream tracking on field programmable gate array (FPGA) is important for such surveillance systems. In this paper, we propose multi-stream tracking hardware that can extract moving objects and their motion vectors from a multi-stream received from 64 cameras in real time. The key technology for multi-stream processing is as follows. (1) In order to avoid maintaining the background, we apply a frame difference method.

Moreover, the flows of object are calculated by block matching. The flows are effective for analyzing human motion. (2) In order to avoid a bus bottleneck and memory contention in the communication between processing elements (PEs), synchronous shift data transfer (SSDT), which transfers data in the same direction for all PEs, is applied. In this paper, an extended SSDT is proposed for communication between PEs when multi-blocks are processed in one PE. (3) C++ based integrated control code development tool is shown. Control code written in C++ language can easily be assembled and verified by the tool. We implemented the proposed hardware on a Stratix V 5SGXEA7K2F40C2N device. The operating frequency is 50 MHz and the average number of clocks for processing a set of four frames of QVGA images is 394k clocks. The proposed hardware achieved 520 fps, and can process multi-stream video from 64 cameras. The execution time on 3.4 GHz Core i7-3770 CPU was 8.4 fps. Therefore, the proposed hardware was about 62 times faster than that CPU.

**ACM Categories & Descriptors:** C.1.2 Multiple Data Stream Architectures (Multiprocessors) I.4.8 Scene Analysis

**Keywords:** FPGA; 2D SIMD array processor; synchronous shift data transfer; multi-stream tracking

**DOI:** http://dx.doi.org/10.1145/2684746.2689119

## 300 Thousand Gates Single Event Effect Hardened SRAM-based FPGA for Space Application

Chen Lei, *Beijing Microelectronics Technology Institute*
Zhao Yuanfu, *Beijing Microelectronics Technology Institute*
Wen Zhiping, *Beijing Microelectronics Technology Institute*
Zhou Jing, *Beijing Microelectronics Technology Institute*
Li Xuewu, *Beijing Microelectronics Technology Institute*
Zhang Yanlong, *Beijing Microelectronics Technology Institute*
Sun Huabo, *Beijing Microelectronics Technology Institute*
Contact: plbabygirl@126.com

SRAM-based FPGAs have been widely used in space engineering. However, the configuration memory in SRAM-based FPGA is susceptible to the single event effects (SEE). It can disrupt the communication or control functions of the spacecraft. To mitigate SEE effects of the SRAM-based FPGAs used in space radiation environment, Beijing Microelectronics Technology Institute (BMTI) developed a 300 thousand gates Single Event Effect hardened SRAM-based FPGA -- BQVR300RH. The BQVR300RH employs Radiation Harden by Design (RHBD) technique. Hardened standard cell library based on Adaptive SRAM (ASRAM) structure is established. For especially sensitive and important resource, other assistant techniques are also adopted. The experiment results show that the BQVR300RH improved the anti-SEU characteristic a lot, compared with Xilinx 300 thousand gates space-grade SRAM-based FPGA (XQVR300). The SEU threshold of BQVR300RH is 19.06 MeV·cm$^2$/mg. The anti-SEU characteristic improves three orders of magnitude than XQVR300. The improvement of anti-SEU behavior expands the usage of SRAM-based FPGA in aerospace applications. Currently, BQVR300RH has been used in space field in China.

**ACM Categories & Descriptors:** B.7.1 [**Hardware**]: Integrated Circuits – *Type and Design Styles*

**Keywords:** SRAM-based FPGA; Single Event Upset; Radiation Harden by Design

**DOI:** http://dx.doi.org/10.1145/2684746.2689120

# REPROC: A Dynamically Reconfigurable Architecture for Symmetric Cryptography

Bo Wang, *Tsinghua University*
Leibo Liu, *Tsinghua University*
Contact: liulb@tsinghua.edu.cn

The paper presents a VLSI architecture of a reconfigurable processor. The proposed architecture can efficiently implement symmetric ciphers, while maintaining flexibility through reconfiguration. A series of optimization methods are introduced during this process. The InterConnection Tree between Rows (ICTR) decreases the area overhead through reducing the complexity of interconnection. The use of the Hierarchical Context Organization (HCO) scheme reduces the total size of contexts and increases the speed of dynamic configuration. The proposed architecture has the ability of implementing most symmetric ciphers, such as AES, DES, SHACAL-1, SMS4 and ZUC, etc. The performance, area efficiency (throughput/area) and energy efficiency (throughput/power) of the proposed architecture have obvious advantages over the state-of-the-art architectures in literatures.

**ACM Categories & Descriptors:** B.7.1 [**Integrated Circuits**]: Types and Design Styles—*VLSI, Algorithms implemented in hardware*; E.3 [**Data**]: Data Encryption

**Keywords:** Reconfigurable crypto architecture; symmetric cryptography; flexibility; performance; area efficiency; energy efficiency.

**DOI:** http://dx.doi.org/10.1145/2684746.2689121

# Architecture of Reconfigurable-Logic Cell Array with Atom Switch: Cluster Size & Routing Fabrics

Xu Bai, *Low-power Electronics Association & Project*
Yukihide Tsuji, *Low-power Electronics Association & Project*
Ayuka Morioka, *Low-power Electronics Association & Project*
Makoto Miyamura, *Low-power Electronics Association & Project*
Toshi Sakamoto, *Low-power Electronics Association &*

*Project*
Munehiro Tada, *Low-power Electronics Association & Project*
Naoki Banno, *Low-power Electronics Association & Project*
Koichiro Okamoto, *Low-power Electronics Association & Project*
Noriyuki Iguchi, *Low-power Electronics Association & Project*
Hiromitsu Hada, *Low-power Electronics Association & Project*
Contact: x-bai@bc.jp.nec.com

Emerging nonvolatile memories (NVMs) have a potential to overcome the issues in the conventional static random-access memory (SRAM) based reconfigurable logic cell arrays (RLCAs). Replacing a CMOS switch element composed of a SRAM and a pass transistor by a NVM reduces chip size. And non-volatility reduces the stand-by power. More importantly, the compactness of NVM allows fine-grain logic cells (small cluster size), which advantageously enables a highly efficient cell usage, resulting in compact circuit for applications. In this paper, we investigate the fine-grain cell architecture using atom switch which is one of the NVMs. We evaluate the effect of the cluster size and the segment length on the atom-switch-based RLCA to confirm the optimal point considering area-delay product. Cluster size is optimized to be 4, which is smaller than that in the conventional SRAM- and multiplexer-based RLCA. This optimization is originated from the fact that the inter-delay among clusters is only twice of the intra-delay in cluster for atom-switch-based RLCA with routing block formed by crossbar switches because of very small capacitance and resistance of atom switches. On the other hand, the segment length is optimized to be 4, which is the same as that in the conventional SRAM- and multiplexer-based RLCA.

**ACM Categories & Descriptors:** B.6.1 [Logic Design]: Design Styles – logic arrays; B.7.2 [Integrated Circuits]: Design Aids – Placement and Routing, Simulation

**Keywords:** Programmable logic; Cross bar switch; Atom switch; Nonvolatile; Cluster; Routing fabrics

**DOI:** http://dx.doi.org/10.1145/2684746.2689122

# A Novel Method for FPGA Test Based on Partial Reconfiguration and Sorting Algorithm

Xianjian Zheng, *Beijing Microelectronics Technology Institute*
Fan Zhang, *Beijing Microelectronics Technology Institute*
Lei Chen, *Beijing Microelectronics Technology Institute*
Zhiping Wen, *Beijing Microelectronics Technology Institute*
Yuanfu Zhao, *Beijing Microelectronics Technology Institute*
Xuewu Li, *Beijing Microelectronics Technology Institute*
Contact: fantaxy1990@gmail.com

The programmability of an FPGA poses a number of challenges when it comes to complete and comprehensive testing of the FPGA itself. A large number of configurations must be downloaded into the FPGA to test the programmable sources. A great many methods were proposed to reduce the number of configurations to minimize the test time, but few of papers were focus on reducing single configuration time. This paper proposes a novel method to reduce more than 30% of the total configuration time based on partial reconfiguration technology and sorting algorithm. This method is implemented on a series of SRAM-based FPGAs. The experimental result shows that this method reduces 30%-45% of the total configuration time and can be generally applied to all SRAM-based FPGAs currently.

ACM Categories & Descriptors: B.7.3 [Integrated Circuits]: Reliability and Testing – *test generation*

Keywords: FPGA Test; Partial Reconfiguration; Sorting Algorithm

DOI: http://dx.doi.org/10.1145/2684746.2689123

# A Novel Composite Method to Accelerate Control Flow on Reconfigurable Architecture

Junbin Wang, *Tsinghua University*
Leibo Liu, *Tsinghua University*
Jianfeng Zhu, *Tsinghua University*
Shouyi Yin, *Tsinghua University*
Shaojun Wei, *Tsinghua University*
Contact: liulb@tsinghua.edu.cn

Reconfigurable Architecture provides a promising solution for embedded systems for high performance, low power and flexibility. Control dependence and control divergence are critical problems that impact the performance. Many methods were proposed to handle control flows efficiently, such as predicated execution and speculative execution. However, they exhibit different performances for different types of control flows, so composite methods are required to provide overall optimal performance. In this paper, a novel architecture is proposed which combines Triggered Instruction and parallel condition. It is designed on the basis of triggered instruction architecture (TIA) while each PE incorporates multiple arithmetic logic units with fast mutual control as in the technique of parallel condition. It can remove branch instructions as well as parallelize control and compute instructions without reconciliation operation, so it explores parallelism in branch level while avoids over-serialization execution in program-counter-based PE. The experiment was conducted on a model in C language and the result shows that the proposed architecture can achieve 80.0% higher performance on average than TIA.

ACM Categories & Descriptors: C.1.3 Other Architectual Styles

Keywords: Reconfigurable computing; triggered instruction; predicate execution; control-intensive

DOI: http://dx.doi.org/10.1145/2684746.2689124

# POSTER SESSION 3

## Acceleration of Synthetic Aperture Radar (SAR) Algorithms using Field Programmable Gate Arrays (FPGAs)

Youngsoo Kim, *North Carolina A&T State University*
William Harding, *North Carolina A&T State University*
Clay S. Gloster, *North Carolina A&T State University*
Winser E. Alexander, *North Carolina State University*
Contact: ykim12@ncat.edu

Algorithms for radar signal processing, such as Synthetic Aperture Radar (SAR) are computationally intensive and require considerable execution time on a general purpose processor. Reconfigurable logic can be used to off-load the primary computational kernel onto a custom computing machine in order to reduce execution time by an order of magnitude as compared to kernel execution on a general purpose processor. Specifically, Field Programmable Gate Arrays (FPGAs) can be used to house hardware-based custom implementations of these kernels to speed up these applications. In this paper, we demonstrate a methodology for algorithm acceleration. We used SAR as a case study to illustrate the tremendous potential for algorithm acceleration offered by FPGAs. Initially, we profiled the SAR algorithm and implemented a homomorphic filter using a hardware implementation of the natural logarithm. Experimental results show an average speed-up of 188 when using the FPGA-based hardware accelerator as opposed to using a software implementation running on a typical general purpose processor.

**ACM Categories & Descriptors:** **C.3** [SPECIAL-PURPOSE AND APPLICATION-BASED SYSTEMS] - Signal processing systems

**Keywords:** FPGA; Synthetic Aperture Radar; Logarithmic; Homomorphic; Floating point

**DOI:** http://dx.doi.org/10.1145/2684746.2689125

## An Embedded FPGA Operating System Optimized for Vision Computing

Zhilei Chai, *Jiangnan University*
Jin Yu, *Jiangnan University*
Zhibin Wang, *Jiangnan University*
Jie Zhang, *Jiangnan University*
Zhilei Chai, *State Key Laboratory of Mathematical Engineering and Advanced Computing*
Haojie Zhou, *State Key Laboratory of Mathematical Engineering and Advanced Computing*
Contact: zlchai@jiangnan.edu.cn

Although FPGA's power and performance advantages were recognized widely, designing applications on FPGA-based systems is traditionally a task undertaken by hardware experts. It is significant to allow application-level programmers with less system-level but more algorithm knowledge to realize their applications conveniently on FPGAs. In this paper, an embedded FPGA operating system is proposed to facilitate application-level programmers to use FPGAs. Firstly, it builds specific I/Os and optimizes bus interconnection among I/Os, DDR memory, user IPs etc within the FPGA for vision computing. Secondly, it manages resources of the FPGA such as I/Os, DDR memory, communication etc, frees users from low-level details. Thirdly, it schedules tasks (IPs) executed on the FPGA dynamically in runtime, which makes the FPGA multiplexed when necessary. After porting the FPGA operating system to different FPGA platforms and implementing vision algorithms based on that, it shows the FPGA operating system is able to simplify algorithm development on FPGA platforms and improve portability of user applications. Furthermore, implementation results of several popular vision algorithms show the FPGA operating system is efficient and effective for vision computing. Finally, experimental results shows that for multiple algorithms requiring more FPGA resources, runtime task scheduling of multiple IPs is more efficient than a fixed IP when the SoC of FPGA is considered.

**ACM Categories & Descriptors:** C.0.3 [System architectures]: Systems Application Architecture

**Keywords:** FPGAs; Operating systems; Vision computing; Application programmers; Portability of applications

**DOI:** http://dx.doi.org/10.1145/2684746.2689127

## FPGA Implementation of Trained Coarse Carrier Frequency Offset Estimation and Correction for OFDM Signals

Marko Jacovic, *Drexel University*
James Chacko, *Drexel University*
Doug Pfiel, *Drexel University*
Nagarajan Kandasamy, *Drexel University*
Kapil R. Dandekar, *Drexel University*
Contact: mj355@drexel.edu

This paper develops an FPGA implementation of a trained coarse Carrier Frequency Offset estimation and correction scheme using MATLAB System Generator. The designed system is capable of supporting variable FFT sizes for Orthogonal Frequency Division Multiplexing signals and different pilot symbol structures making it compatible with a large number of wireless communication standards, unlike other work that is protocol specific. This design stands out from its more common implementations as it requires only one pilot symbol to be considered for synchronization by using a data-aided modified correlation scheme, allowing for an increase in throughput. The Bit Error Rate of the corrected signal received over an Additive White Gaussian Noise channel is compared to the case without correction. This scheme demonstrated increased performance throughput since only a single pilot symbol was used.

**ACM Categories & Descriptors:** B.2.4 [Hardware]:
ARITHMETIC AND LOGIC STRUCTURES – High-speed
Arithmetic, Cost/performance; Algorithms

**Keywords:** Carrier Frequency Offset, Data-aided Synchronization,
OFDM, Pilot Symbol Design

**DOI:** http://dx.doi.org/10.1145/2684746.2689128

# Energy-Efficient High-Order FIR Filtering through Reconfigurable Stochastic Processing

Mohammed Alawad, *University of Central Florida*
Mingjie Lin, *University of Central Florida*
Contact: mingjie@eecs.ucf.edu

High-order FIR filtering is widely used in many important DSP applications in order to achieve filtering stability and linear-phase property. This paper presents a hardware- and energy-efficient approach to implementing energy-efficient high-order FIR filtering through reconfigurable stochastic processing. We exploit a basic probabilistic principle of summing independent random variables to achieve approximate FIR filtering without costly multiplications. Our new multiplierless approach has two distinctive advantages when compared with the conventional multiplier-based or DA-based FIR filtering methods. First, our new probabilistic architecture is especially effective for high-order FIR filtering because it bypasses costly multiplications and does not rely on large size of memory to store store pre-computed coefficient products. Second, this new probabilistic convolver is significantly more robust or fault tolerant than the conventional architecture because all signal values will be represented and computed probabilistically, and local signal corruption cannot easily destroy the overall probabilistic patterns, therefore achieving much higher error tolerance. For example, our proposed approach allows our proposed FIR architecture, for a standard 128-tap FIR filter, to achieve about 9 times and 4 times less power consumption than the conventional multiplier-based and DA-based design, respectively. Additionally, when compared with the state-of-the-art systolic DA-based design, our design can achieve about 3 times reduction in hardware usage.

**ACM Categories & Descriptors:** B. Hardware; B.2
ARITHMETIC AND LOGIC STRUCTURES; B.2.4 High-Speed
Arithmetic

**Keywords:** High-order FIR; Reconfigurable; Stochastic Processing

**DOI:** http://dx.doi.org/10.1145/2684746.2689129

# Silicon Verification using High-Level Design Tools

Tomsz S. Czajkowski, *Altera Corporation*
Contact: tczajkow@altera.com

Modern FPGAs comprise ever more complex blocks to enable a wide variety of customer applications. Verification of the complex blocks can be a time consuming process, especially at the late stages of the release cycle. A key challenge is the time it takes to create circuits that can run on a target device to test a given block. This paper demonstrates how High-Level Design tools, such as Altera SDK for OpenCL, can be utilized to aid in this work to verify the operation of complex hardened blocks.

As a proof of concept, we present the methodology used to verify the correctness of hardened single-precision floating point adder, subtractor and multiplier units on Altera Arria 10 FPGA in a single day. Each design comprised an instance of a hardened floating point unit, either an adder, subtractor or a multiplier, and a functional equivalent there of implemented purely using Lookup Tables (LUTs). Both the hardened module instance and the LUT implementation were generated from OpenCL description using Altera SDK for OpenCL. The results for each computation were compared between the two implementations and any single discrepancy constituted a test failure. To simplify the test, the I/O for each design comprised LEDs (for pass/fail/running/done status) and two switches – start and reset.

The test design for adder, subtractor and a multiplier were all written in OpenCL, the compilation of each design took approximately 30 minutes for each test design. Each design tested 4 billion test vectors, generated on-chip using a Mersenne Twister, and each test completed within 30 seconds. All tests passed verification in hardware.

**ACM Categories & Descriptors:** B.6.2 [Reliability and Testing]
Test Generation

**Keywords:** FPGA; DSP Blocks; Floating Point.

**DOI:** http://dx.doi.org/10.1145/2684746.2689131

# A Hardware Implementation of a Unit for Geometric Algebra Operations With Parallel Memory Arrays

Gerardo Soria García, CINVESTAV UGdl
Adrian Pedroza de la Crúz, CINVESTAV UGdl
Susana Ortega Cisneros, CINVESTAV UGdl
Juan José Raygoza Panduro, CUCEI UdeG
Eduardo Bayro Corrochano, CINVESTAV UGdl
Contact:{sortega, jgsoria}@gdl.cinvestav.mx

Geometric algebra (GA) is a powerful and versatile mathematical tool which helps to intuitively express and manipulate complex geometric relationships. It has recently been used in engineering problems such computer graphics, machine vision, robotics, among others. The problem with GA in its numeric version is that it requires many arithmetic operations, and the length of the input vectors is unknown until runtime in a generic architecture operating over homogeneous elements. Few works in hardware architectures for GA were developed to improve the performance in GA applications. In this work, a hardware architecture of a unit for GA operations (geometric product) for FPGA is presented. The main contribution of this work is the use of parallel memory arrays with access conflict avoidance for dealing with the issue of unknown length of input/output vectors, the intention is to reduce memory wasted when storing the input and output vectors. In this first stage of the project, we have implemented only a single access function (fixed-length) in the memory array in order to test the core of geometric product. In future works we will implement a full set of access functions with different lengths and shapes. In this work, only the simulations are presented; in the future, we will also present the experimental results.

**ACM Categories & Descriptors:** B.5.1 [Register-transfer-level implementation]: [design] – Arithmetic and logic units

**Keywords:** Geometric algebra; FPGA; memory arrays; address generator; geometric product

**DOI:** http://dx.doi.org/10.1145/2684746.2689132

# Efficient Generation of Energy and Performance Pareto Front for FPGA Designs

Sanmukh R. Kuppannagari, *University of Southern California*
Viktor K. Prasanna, *University of Southern California*
Contact: kuppanna@usc.edu

Analysis of trade-offs between energy efficiency and latency is essential to generate designs complying with a given set of constraints. Improvements in FPGA technologies offer a myriad of choices for power and performance optimizations. Various algorithm intrinsic parameters also affect these objectives. The design space is compounded by the available choices. This requires efficient techniques to quickly explore the design space. Current techniques perform Gate/RTL level or functional level power modeling which are slow and hence not scalable. In this work we perform efficient design space exploration using a high level performance model. We develop a semi-automatic design framework to generate energy efficiency and latency trade-offs. The framework develops a performance model given a high level specification of a design with minimal user assistance. It then explores the entire design space to generate the dominating designs with respect to energy efficiency and latency metrics. We illustrate the framework using convolutional neural network which gained significance due to its application in deep learning. We simulate a few designs from the dominating set and show that the performance estimation for the dominating designs are close to the simulated results. We also show that our framework explores 6000 design points per minute on a commodity platform such as Dell workstation as opposed to state-of-the-art techniques which explore at 50 to 60 design points per minute.

**ACM Categories & Descriptors:** C.1.3 [Other Architecture Styles]: Adaptable architectures----Design Space Exploration, Performance Modeling

**Keywords:** High Level Performance Model; Design Space Exploration; Energy Efficiency; Design Framework; Convolutional Neural Networks;

**DOI:** http://dx.doi.org/10.1145/2684746.2689133

# A Novel Coefficient Address Generation Algorithm for Split-Radix FFT

Zhuo Qian, *University of Massachusetts Lowell*
Martin Margala, *University of Massachusetts Lowell*
Contact: Zhuo_Qian@student.uml.edu

Split-Radix Fast Fourier Transform (SRFFT) has the lowest number of arithmetic operations among all the FFT algorithms. Since arithmetic operations dramatically contribute to the dynamic power consumption, SRFFT is an ideal candidate for the implementation of a low power FFT processor. In the design of such processors, an efficient addressing scheme for FFT data as well as coefficients is required. The signal flow graph of split-radix algorithm is the same as radix-2 FFT except for the location and value of coefficients, therefore conventional radix-2 FFT data address generation scheme could also be applied to SRFFT. However, the mixed radix property of SRFFT algorithm leads to irregular locations of coefficients and forbids any conventional address generation algorithm. This paper presents a novel coefficient address generation algorithm for shared-memory based SRFFT processor. The core part of the proposed algorithm is to use two control variables to track trivial and non-trivial multiplications. We found the relationship between the value of the control variables and the butterfly and pass counter. The corresponding hardware implementation is simple consisting of a shift register and a dual port RAM bank. Compared to look-up table approach, which pre-computes the addresses of all coefficients and stores the addresses in memory units, the proposed algorithm is scalable and only requires small amount of memory to find the correct addresses of coefficients.

**ACM Categories & Descriptors:** B.7.1 [Integrated Circuits]: Algorithms Implemented in Hardware

**Keywords:** Split-Radix FFT; Address Generation; Low Power

**DOI:** http://dx.doi.org/10.1145/2684746.2689134

# RapidPath: Accelerating Constrained Shortest Path Finding in Graphs on FPGA

Chao Wang, *University of Science and Technology of China*
Xi Li, *University of Science and Technology of China*
Qi Guo, *University of Science and Technology of China*
Xuehai Zhou, *University of Science and Technology of China*
Contact: cswang@ustc.edu.cn

Emerging applications, such as Software Defined Network (SDN), Social Media, and Location Based System (LBS), are typical big graph based applications. Due to the explosive network flood, it is essential to speed-up the computation process in the big graph application, such as Constrained Shortest Path Finding (CSPF) algorithm is one of the most challenging part. Meanwhile, FPGA has been an effective and efficient platform in novel big data architectures and systems, due to its computing power and low power consumption. It enables the researchers to deploy massive accelerators within one single chip. In this paper, we present RapidPath, an acceleration method for CSPF algorithm in software defined networks, which decomposes a large and complex system of programs into small single-purpose source code libraries that perform specialized tasks in parallel. Only the CSPF step is implemented in hardware and the rest steps run on the processor. We have built a prototyping system on Zynq with CSPF case studies. The ARM processor uses a shared memory with the FPGA based accelerator using DMA based channels. Control signals are transferred via AXI bus interfaces. Experimental results depict that RapidPath is able to achieve up to 43.75X speedup at 128 nodes, comparing to the software execution (without cache) on Xilinx Zynq board. Furthermore, hardware cost and overheads reveal that the RapidPath architecture can achieve high speed-up with insignificant cost.

This work was supported by the National Science Foundation of China under grants No. 61379040, No. 61272131 and No. 61202053.

ACM Categories & Descriptors: B.5.1 Hardware Register-Transfer-Level Implementation Arithmetic and logic units

Keywords: Constrained Shortest Path Finding; Software Defined Networks; FPGA

DOI: http://dx.doi.org/10.1145/2684746.2689135

# High Level Programming of Document Classification Systems for Heterogeneous Environments using OpenCL

Nasibeh Nasiri, *University of Massachusetts Lowell*
Oren Segal, *University of Massachusetts Lowell*
Martin Margala, *University of Massachusetts Lowell*
Wim Vanderbauwhede, *University of Glasgow*
Sai Rahul Chalamalasetti, *HP Servers*
Contact: Nasibeh_Nasiri@student.uml.edu

Document classification is at the heart of several of the applications that have been driving the proliferation of the internet in our daily lives. The ever growing amounts of data and the need for higher throughput, more energy efficient document classification solutions motivated us to investigate alternatives to the traditional homogenous CPU based implementations. We investigate a heterogeneous system where CPUs are combined with FPGAs as system accelerators. Incorporating FPGAs as accelerators in a heterogeneous computing environment allows for the creation of flexible custom hardware solutions that can potentially offer increased power efficiency and performance gains. One of the main issues delaying wide spread adoption of FPGAs as standard heterogeneous system accelerators is the difficulty in programming them. The OpenCL standard offers a unified C programming model for any device that adheres to its standards. An Altera OpenCL FPGA based implementation of a document classification system is

investigated in which a stream of HTML documents is scored according to a profile on a document-by-document basis. The results show that the throughput of the document classification application with and without Bloom Filters is 312MB/s and 343MB/s respectively, when running on CPU, and 354MB/s and 452MB/s respectively, when running on an FPGA. Our results also show up to 32% power efficiency improvement for the FPGA implementation over the CPU implementation. We would like to thank Davor Capalija from Altera for his invaluable advice during our work on the FPGA version of the algorithm.

ACM Categories & Descriptors: D.1.3 [Programming Techniques]: Parallel programming

Keywords: FPGA; Bloom Filter; OpenCL; heterogeneous computing; document classification

DOI: http://dx.doi.org/10.1145/2684746.2689136

# Low-Resource Bluespec Design of a Modular Acquisition and Stimulation System for Neuroscience

Paulo Matias, *University of São Paulo*
Rafael T. Guariento, *University of São Paulo*
Lirio O. B. de Almeida, *University of São Paulo*
Jan F. W. Slaets, *University of São Paulo*
Contact: matias@ifsc.usp.br

We have compared two different resource arbitration architectures in our developed data acquisition and stimuli generator system for neuroscience research, entirely specified in a high-level Hardware Description Language (HDL). One of them was designed with a decoupled and latency insensitive modular approach, allowing for easier code reuse, while the other adopted a centralized scheme, constructed specifically for our application. The usage of a high-level HDL allowed straightforward and stepwise code modifications to transform one architecture into the other. Despite the logic complexity penalty of synthesizing our hardware from a highly abstract language, both architectures were implemented in a very small programmable logic device without even consuming all the hardware resources. While the decoupled design has shown more resilience to input activity bursts, the centralized one gave an economy of about 10-15% in the device logic element usage. This system is not only useful for neuroscience protocols that require timing determinism and synchronous stimuli generation, but has also demonstrated that high-level languages can be effectively used for synthesizing hardware in small programmable devices.

ACM Categories & Descriptors: C.3 [Special-purpose and Application-based Systems]: Real-time and embedded systems; F.3.1 [Logics and Meanings of Programs]: Specification techniques; B.4.5 [Reliability, Testing, and Fault-Tolerance]: Hardware reliability; J.3 [Life and Medical Sciences]: Biology and genetics

Keywords: Spiking Neurons; Data Acquisition; Resource Arbitration; Latency Insensitive

DOI: http://dx.doi.org/10.1145/2684746.2689137

# POSTER SESSION 4

## Bridging Architecture and Programming for Throughput-Oriented Vision Processing

Amir Momeni, Hamed Tabkhi, Gunar Schirner, David Kaeli, *Northeastern University*
Contact: momeni@ece.neu.edu

With the expansion of OpenCL support across many heterogeneous devices (including FPGAs, GPUs and CPUs), the programmability of these systems has been significantly increased. At the same time, new questions arise about which device should be targeted for each OpenCL software kernel. Once we select a device, then we are left to customize the application, selecting the right granularity of parallelism and frequency of host-to-device communication. In this paper, we study the impact of source-level decisions on the overall execution time when developing OpenCL program across different heterogeneous devices. We focus on two mainstream architecture classes (GPUs and FPGAs), and consider throughput-oriented advanced vision processing. To guide this exploration, we propose a new vertical classification for selecting the grain of parallelism for advanced vision processing applications. To carry out this study we have selected the Mean-shift object tracking algorithm as a representative candidate of advanced vision algorithms. Overall, our evaluation demonstrates that fine-grained parallelism can greatly benefit FPGA execution (up to a 4X speed-up), while a combination of coarse-grained and fine-grained parallelism achieves the best performance on a GPU (up to a 6X speed-up). Also, there can be a large benefit if we can execute both the parallel and serial parts of the program on a FPGA (up to a 21X speed-up).

**ACM Categories & Descriptors:** C.1.3 [Other Architecture Styles]: Heterogeneous (hybrid) systems

**Keywords:** OpenCL; Parallelism granularity; FPGA; GPU; Object tracking

**DOI:** http://dx.doi.org/10.1145/2684746.2689140

## An Automatic Design Flow for Hybrid Parallel Computing on MPSoCs

Hongyuan Ding, *University of Arkansas*
Miaoqing Huang, *University of Arkansas*
Contact: mqhuang@uark.edu

State-of-the-art high-level synthesis (HLS) tools are able to lower the threshold for designers to exploit performance benefits of hardware accelerators. However, it is still a challenge to achieve parallelism on a hybrid multiprocessor system-on-chip (MPSoC). In this work, we present an automatic hybrid design flow. The hybrid hardware platform as well as both the hardware and software

kernels can be generated through this flow. In addition, a hybrid OpenCL-like programming model is proposed to combine software and hardware kernels running on the unified hardware platform. Our results show that our automatic design flow can not only significantly minimize the development time, but also gain about 11 times speedup compared with pure software parallel implementation for a matrix multiplication benchmark.

**ACM Categories & Descriptors:** [Computer systems organization]: Architectures–Other architectures[Reconfigurable computing]

**Keywords:** FPGA; automatic design flow; hybrid and parallel computing

**DOI:** http://dx.doi.org/10.1145/2684746.2689141

## MedianPipes: An FPGA based Highly Pipelined and Scalable Technique for Median Filtering

Umer I. Cheema, *University of Illinois at Chicago*
Gregory Nash, *Altera Corporation*
Rashid Ansari, *University of Illinois at Chicago*
Ashfaq A. Khokhar, *Illinois Institute of Technology*
Contact: ucheem2@uic.edu

We propose *MedianPipes*, a novel, FPGA based, highly pipelined and scalable architecture for median filtering. Median filters and its variants are widely used for noise suppression in image processing. All variants of median filter depend on the computation of median values. *MedianPipe* is a highly pipelined architecture and hence an ideal fit for FPGAs. It does not make any assumptions about the image to fit on the on-chip memory. Instead, the image is assumed to be streamed-in in the form of image slices. Multiple *MedianPipe* modules are used depending on the size of image slice and hence the overall hardware complexity of proposed technique scales linearly with image-slice size. The architecture for *MedianPipe* is based on the principle of merge sort and uses a median window of size *3 x 3*. It consists of two stepped sorting process: The first step is to sort the pixels within each row of median window to get sorted rows. This sorting is done using a single comparator over multiple clock cycles. The sorted rows are saved in block memory based First-In-First-Out (FIFO) memory and reused to calculate the medians corresponding to three median windows. The second step is to merge these sorted rows to find the median using a merger block. The merger block consists of three comparators and read out a single value every cycle once the pipeline is filled. Without loss of generality, the pixels of an image slice are assumed to be read in a column major format. All the median values within the column of the image slice can be computed in parallel using multiple *MedianPipes*. The computation of median values in the following column is delayed by a clock cycle. Hardware resources scale linearly by varying the pixel sizes and number of *MedianPipes*. The pixel rate achieved for various pixel sizes is well above 124 MHz which is the standard for 1080p High-Definition.

**ACM Categories & Descriptors:** B.5.1 Design

Keywords: Design; Median Filter; Merge Sort; Scalable; Pipeline; FPGA

DOI: http://dx.doi.org/10.1145/2684746.2689142

## Toward Wave Digital Filter based Analog Circuit Emulation on FPGA

Wei Wu, *University of California, Los Angeles*
Peng Gu, *Tsinghua University*
Yen-Lung Chen, *National Central University*
Chien-Nan Liu, *National Central University*
Sudhakar Pamarti, *University of California, Los Angeles*
Chang Wu, *Fudan University*
Lei He, *University of California, Los Angeles*
Contact: weiw@seas.ucla.edu

Software simulation of analog and mixed-signal circuits often takes a long computing time. Unlike digital circuits that can be validated by FPGA emulation, there is no winning emulation solution for analog circuits. As the first step to applying wave digital filter (WDF) to emulate post-layout analog circuits, we present how to map linear and nonlinear components in an original circuit to WDFs with exactly same behaviors. To validate, we implement the emulation circuit (i.e., WDFs) in FPGA. To be more specific, each emulation time step is executed as a finite state machine, while all the computing resource, e.g. floating point units (FPU), are shared as a resource pool and used only when it is necessary, which result in a very small resource consumption on FPGA. Virtually perfect match is obtained between the Verilog and SPICE simulations for a number of primitive analog circuits, indicating the high accuracy of the proposed emulation. In terms of runtime, the WDF implementation is about 3-4x faster than HSPICE on a small two-stage differential amplifier circuit. And better speedup can be anticipated when it scales to larger circuits because of the underlying binary tree structure of the WDF implementation.

ACM Categories & Descriptors: B.7.2 [Hardware]: INTEGRATED CIRCUTIS – Design Aids

Keywords: Analog Circuits; Wave Digital Filter; FPGA; Emulation; Circuit Simulation

DOI: http://dx.doi.org/10.1145/2684746.2689143

## Optimized Fixed-Point FPGA Implementation of SVPWM for a Two-Level Inverter

Danyal Mohammadi, *Boise State University*
Said Ahmed-Zaid, *Boise State University*
Nader Rafla, *Boise State University*
Contact: danyalmohammadi@boisestate.edu

This paper presents an optimized fixed-point implementation of

space-vector pulse-width modulation (SVPWM) for a two-level inverter. Bit-width fixed-point signals as well as circuit area are minimized by meeting the desired design accuracy. Most of the designs currently available are specified in floating-point precision to speed the process of simulating their functionality. However, area-optimized hardware implementation of these algorithms requires fixed-point precision. A generic function is used to formulate the precision required for each signal to get the proper accuracy. A non-convex optimization problem is solved for the number of required bit-widths for the signals. This solution has been implemented to verify the resulting accuracy.

ACM Categories & Descriptors: G.1.0 [Numerical Analysis]: General-*error analysis*; G.1.6 [Numerical Analysis]: Optimization-*simulated annealing*; C.3.2 [Special Purpose and Application-Based Systems]: Process control systems, Industrial control

Keywords: Fixed-Point; FPGA; SVPWM; Simulated Annealing

DOI: http://dx.doi.org/10.1145/2684746.2689144

## Area Optimization of Arithmetic Units by Component Sharing for FPGAs

Shao Lin Tang, *University of British Columbia*
Guy Lemieux, *University of British Columbia*
Contact: sltang@ece.ubc.ca

Floating point implementation has been a hot topic in recent FPGA research. This paper describes a method to optimize area of combined floating point and integer arithmetic unit through sharing the largest component in each operation on an FPGA. Specifically, the operations included are: addition, subtraction, multiplication, division, shift left/right, rotate left/right, as well as integer-to-floating-point and floating-point-to-integer conversion. The resource usage for the fused unit is compared with the segregated units that are multiplexed. Result shows a significant area reduction achieved using this technique with minimal performance penalty.

ACM Categories & Descriptors: B.2.0 Arithmetic and Logic Structures

Keywords: Arithmetic Logic Unit Integration; Area Optimization; Goldschmidt Division; Component Sharing; FPGA Circuit Design

DOI: http://dx.doi.org/10.1145/2684746.2689146

## Customizable and High Performance Matrix Multiplication Kernel on FPGA

Jie Wang, *Tsinghua University*
Jason Cong, *UCLA*
Contact: wangjie11@mails.tsinghua.edu.cn

This work presents a customizable FPGA accelerator of matrix multiplication. We use our systolic modules as building blocks to compose the overall architecture. The size and the number of blocks are parameterized to enable full design space exploration. Several optimization strategies are used here, including the data and controller sharing among MM blocks. These mechanisms help increase the frequency while saving the area occupied. In addition, we present a CAD flow to automate the design space exploration and generate a complete FPGA accelerator design of the target MM for users. We parameterize our architecture and optimize the architecture configuration for the highest GFLOPs on a target FPGA platform. This kernel can be integrated into HLS tools as a library component. Experiments show that for 512×512 single precision MM, we can achieve as high as 358 GFLOPs on the Xilinx Virtex-7 XC7VX485T-2, which outperforms the state-of-the-art FPGA accelerator design by at least 28.3%.

**Acknowledgement:** The authors wish to thank Bingjun Xiao and Peng Zhang in UCLA for helpful discussions and comments on the earlier draft of this work.

**ACM Categories & Descriptors:** B.7.1 [Integrated Circuits]: Types and Design Styles – Algorithms implemented in hardware

**Keywords:** Matrix Multiplication; Customizable

**DOI:** http://dx.doi.org/10.1145/2684746.2689147

# Accelerating Complete Decision Support Queries Through High-Level Synthesis Technology

Gorker Alp Malazgirt, *Bogazici University*
Nehir Sonmez, *Barcelona Supercomputing Center*
Arda Yurdakul, *Bogazici University*
Osman Unsal, *Barcelona Supercomputing Center*
Adrian Cristal, *Barcelona Supercomputing Center*
Contact: gorkeralp@gmail.com

Recently, with the rise of Internet of Things and Big Data, acceleration of database analytics in order to have faster query processing capabilities has gained significant attention. At the same time, High-Level Synthesis (HLS) technology has matured and is now a promising approach to design such hardware accelerators. In this work, we use a modern HLS, Vivado to design high-performance database accelerators for filtering, aggregation, sorting, merging and join operations. Later, we use these as building blocks to implement an acceleration system for in-memory databases on a Virtex-7 FPGA, detailed enough to run full TPC-H benchmarks completely in hardware. Presenting performance, area and memory requirements, we show up to 140x speedup compared to a software DBMS, and demonstrate that HLS technology is indeed a very appropriate match for database acceleration.

**ACM Categories & Descriptors:** C.1.3 Other Architecture Styles

**Keywords:** Hardware acceleration, High level synthesis, Decision support queries, Database, Join, Sort

**DOI:** http://dx.doi.org/10.1145/2684746.2689151

# FPGA Acceleration of Irregular Iterative Computations using Criticality-Aware Dataflow Optimizations

Siddhartha, *Nanyang Technological University*
Nachiket Kapre, *Nanyang Technological University*
Contact: nachiket@ieee.org

FPGA acceleration of large irregular dataflow graphs is often limited by the long tail distribution of parallelism on fine-grained overlay dataflow architectures. In this paper, we show how to overcome these limitations by exploiting criticality information along compute paths; both statically during graph pre-processing and dynamically at runtime. We statically reassociate the high-fanin dataflow chains by providing faster routes for late arriving inputs. We also perform a fanout decomposition and selective node replication in order to distribute serialization costs across multiple PEs. Additionally, we modify the dataflow firing rule in hardware to prefer critical nodes when multiple nodes are ready for dataflow evaluation. Effectively these transformations reduce the length of the tail in the parallelism profile for these large-scale graphs. Across a range of dataflow benchmarks extracted from Sparse LU factorization, we demonstrate up to 2.5× (mean 1.21×) improvement when using the static pre-processing alone, a 2.4× (mean 1.17×) improvement when using only dynamic optimizations and an overall 2.9× (mean 1.39×) improvement when both static and dynamic optimizations are enabled. These improvements are on top of 3–10× speedups over CPU implementations without our transformation enabled.

**ACM Categories & Descriptors:** C.1.3 Dataflow Architectures; B.7.1 Algorithms implemented in hardware

**Keywords:** Dataflow, Sparse Graph, Criticality, Scheduling

**DOI**: http://dx.doi.org/10.1145/2684746.2689110

# On Implementation of LUT with Large Numbers of Inputs

Masahiro Fujita, *University of Tokyo*
Contact: fujita@ee.t.u-tokyo.ac.jp

A LUT is implemented with a set of flipflops which are connected to a series of multiplexers, or alternatively with a small memory, and needs exponentially many storage elements with respect to the numbers of inputs. Due to this FPGA uses LUTs having around 6 inputs, but LUTs with larger numbers of inputs may be better from various performance viewpoints as well as its applications to flexible logic debugging and Engineering Change Order (ECO) as there are less interconnects among LUTs. Such LUTs may accommodate changes of designs including logic debugging and ECO. We discuss implementations for LUTs having relatively large numbers of inputs, such as 12-inputs. If we implement a single LUT with 12-inputs, we need $2^{12} = 4,096$ storage elements. On the other hand, we can construct 12-input subcircuits of fixed topologies only with sets of LUTs having small numbers of inputs, such as 4-inputs. Although such subcircuits can only realize very small subsets of all possible logic functions with 12-inputs, if they can realize most of the logic functions we need for actual designs by only reprogramming the sets of 4-input LUTs, they are practically worthwhile to be used. We present several such fixed-topology subcircuits as well as automatic compilation methods from given logic functions. Experimental results show almost all functions (more than 99%) which appear benchmark circuits with partially disjoint decomposability can be implemented by the proposed topologies. Sophisticated circuit portioning methods can always generate networks of subcircuits with partially disjoint decomposability.

**ACM Categories & Descriptors:** B.6.1 [Design Styles] Logic arrays

**Keywords:** Look Up Table (LUT), Logic synthesis with pre-layout, Circuit partitioning, Engineering Change Order, Logic debugging and rectification

**DOI:** http://dx.doi.org/10.1145/2684746.2689107

# Design of a Loeffler DCT using Xilinx Vivado HLS

Seung Yeol Baik, *Korea University*
Seokjin Jeong, *Korea University*
Hyeong-Cheol Oh, *Korea University at SeJong*
Contact: ohyeong@korea.ac.kr

Loeffler discrete cosine transform (DCT) algorithm is recognized as the most efficient one because it requires the theoretically least number of multiplications. However, many applications still encounter difficulty in performing the 11 multiplications required by the algorithm to calculate a 1D eight-point DCT. To avoid expensive multipliers in the hardware, we used two design methods, namely, distributed arithmetic (DA) and shift-and-add (SAA) methods, to design the DCT accelerator. The memory bandwidth is 60 bits: 24 bits for reads of the R(red), G(green), and B(blue) data of a pixel and 36 bits for writes of three corresponding 12-bit DCT coefficients. Thus, the 1D eight-point DCT accelerator for each of R, G, and B can have one 12-bit input port and one 12-bit output port so that it can calculate a 2D DCT by row-column decomposition method. The designs are adjusted to produce the same latency and interval. DA seems promising because Loeffler DCT requires only three small tables with four input bits. However, our experiments using Xilinx Vivado HLS show that the SAA design is better than the DA design for the considered applications. Furthermore, simulation results suggest that the optimal accelerator design can be obtained by adjusting the SAA design to the considered applications. The resultant SAA design requires only 13 adders (per color component) and can calculate one DCT coefficient per clock cycle. The precision of the internal hardware has been adjusted, such that the reconstructed images have PSNR values of at least 39.1 dB for all test images (Lenna, Pepper, House, and Cameraman). If a precision of 13bits is allowed, PSNR becomes at least 44.8 dB. Our presentation describes the architecture and operation of the optimized SAA design.

**ACM Categories & Descriptors:** C.3 Special-purpose and application-based systems; G.1.0 General

**Keywords:** Loeffler DCT; Accelerator; Shift-and-add method

**DOI:** http://dx.doi.org/10.1145/2684746.2694735

*FPGA'15*, February 22–24, 2015, Monterey, California, USA.
ACM 978-1-4503-3315-3/15/02.

# Author Index